DATA ANALYSIS
USING SAS®

DATA ANALYSIS
USING SAS®

C. Y. Joanne Peng

Indiana University

Los Angeles • London • New Delhi • Singapore • Washington DC

For information:

 SAGE Publications, Inc.
2455 Teller Road
Thousand Oaks,
    California 91320
E-mail: order@sagepub.com

SAGE Publications Ltd.
1 Oliver's Yard
55 City Road
London EC1Y 1SP
United Kingdom

SAGE Publications India Pvt. Ltd.
B 1/I 1 Mohan Cooperative
    Industrial Area
Mathura Road, New Delhi 110 044
India

SAGE Publications
    Asia-Pacific Pte. Ltd.
33 Pekin Street #02-01
Far East Square
Singapore 048763

Printed in the United States of America

Library of Congress Cataloging-in-Publication Data

Peng, C. Y. Joanne.
Data analysis using SAS/C.Y. Joanne Peng.
    p. cm.
Includes bibliographical references and index.
ISBN 978-1-4129-5674-1 (pbk.)
    1. Mathematical statistics—Data processing. 2. SAS (Computer file) I. Title.

QA276.4.P46 2009
519.50285—dc22   2008008497

Printed on acid-free paper

08   09   10   11   12   10   9   8   7   6   5   4   3   2   1

Acquiring Editor:	Vicki Knight
Associate Editor:	Sean Connelly
Editorial Assistant:	Lauren Habib
Production Editor:	Sarah K. Quesenberry
Copy Editor:	QuADS Prepress (P) Ltd.
Typesetter:	C&M Digitals (P) Ltd.
Proofreader:	Scott Oney
Indexer:	Wendy Allex
Cover Designer:	Gail Buschman
Marketing Manager:	Stephanie Adams

Contents_____

Part II. Statistical Procedures

Preface

In this era of information explosion, understanding data and their implications has become a marker of every learned scholar and student. And mastering the powerful statistical software—SAS®—to reach this goal is an inevitable and valid learning experience for many enrolled in statistics and research methodology courses. This book presents step-by-step demonstrations of using SAS for data processing, statistical analysis, and file management. Ample examples from business, the health sciences, education, psychology, and other disciplines are included in each chapter along with problem-based exercises. Each output is clearly and comprehensively interpreted. Statistical assumptions are discussed and emphasized. Power analysis and sample size estimation are introduced, as well as the SAS output delivery system. All examples, output results, and data are accessible from the Web site www.sagepub.com/pengstudy. This book is suitable as a textbook or supplementary workbook for introductory courses on statistics, research methods, and data analysis using SAS. It can also be used as a self-paced tutorial for researchers and data analysts in the social, health, and behavioral sciences.

I have used and taught the SAS system for more than 30 years to undergraduates, graduates, and professionals in diverse fields. I must say that I have had only one regret in all those years: I wish I had learned SAS sooner! This book is my way of urging you not to have the same regret as I had; get on with learning this great software now!

Many reviewers and former students of mine contributed to the much improved finished product that you now hold in your hands. In particular, I owe much gratitude to Dr. Tak-Shing Harry So, Dr. John Samuel of Indiana University, Professor Jon E. Grahe of Pacific Lutheran University, Professor Julia F. Klausli of the University of Texas at Dallas, Professor Nicole M. Traxel of the University of Wisconsin–Milwaukee, Professor Han S. Kim of the University of Utah, Professor Lantry L. Brockmeier of Florida A&M University, Professor Xiaofeng Steven Liu of the University of South Carolina, Professor Carole Bernett of DePaul University, Professor Vivian Lew of the UCLA Department of Statistics, Professor Patti Costello of Eastern Kentucky University, and Professor D. F. Duncan III of the University of North Carolina at Chapel Hill for their insightful and careful reviews of various drafts of this book. I also extend a heartfelt appreciation to my Indiana University graduate students, Yuhao Cen, Li-Ting Chen, Andrew Cornett, Lijang Guo, Jocelyn Holden, Hui-Chun Hsieh, Yu-Chih Huang, Kaigang Li, Haiying Long,

John V. Moore III, and Meihua Qian, for reading and rereading many drafts of each chapter and for suggesting changes. Their suggestions and corrections greatly enhanced the quality of this book. The dedication and expertise of the SAGE editorial staff (Vicki Knight, Sean Connelly, Lauren Habib, and Sarah Quesenberry) and former staff (Lisa Cuevas Shaw and Margo Crouppen) kept me on task throughout the writing process. It was truly a pleasure and privilege to work with each of them. All errors remaining are solely my responsibility. Send your suggestions and corrections to me at peng.cyj@gmail.com.

Above all, I thank my parents for their encouragement to pursue education and to indulge in the joy of learning all my life. To them, Mr. and Mrs. Shou-Chih Peng 彭守智先生,彭賈懷貞女士, I dedicate this book with love.

—C. Y. Joanne Peng

PART I

Introduction to SAS and Basic Data Analysis

1

Why Do You Need to Learn SAS for Data Analysis?

---- **OBJECTIVE** ----

This chapter presents convincing reasons why readers need the knowledge and skills of SAS for data analysis and file management and how this book can help them acquire these skills.

1.1 Seven Reasons to Learn SAS for Data Analysis
  ❶ Knowledge of SAS is an asset in many job markets
  ❷ SAS can read data files created by other statistical software packages
  ❸ Various data formats can be imported into SAS with ease
  ❹ The versatility and power of SAS is sufficient to meet many data analysis needs
  ❺ The worldwide electronic network of SAS users is accessible at your fingertips
  ❻ The SAS users' annual conferences are great places to exchange ideas with other users and view demos of the SAS Institute's latest developments
  ❼ Several helpful phone/fax numbers from the SAS Institute are available to assist you

1.2 What Is the History of the SAS Institute and Its Current Clientele?

1.3 What Is the SAS System and What Can It Do? A Quick Walk-Through of SAS Products

1.4 What Is the Scope and Style of This Book?

1.5 Summary

1.6 Exercises

_____ 1.1 Seven Reasons to Learn SAS for Data Analysis

There are at least seven reasons why you should learn SAS. If you don't find any of these reasons convincing, you can stop right here and return this book for a refund—but I doubt this will happen!

First, *knowing SAS is an asset in many job markets*. Many ads ask for SAS experience. The following Web addresses, retrieved in December 2007, represent a handful of Web sites devoted specifically to SAS jobs. Many of these sites include a salary analysis and claim to be one of the fastest growing sites for SAS professionals.

www.sas-jobs.com

http://sas-jobs.dice.com

www.jobster.com/find/US/jobs/for/sas

www.sconsig.com

www.statisticsjobs.com

www.newtyne.com/sas_resources/index.html

www.itjobswatch.co.uk/jobs/uk/sas.do

www.globalstatements.com/sas/jobs/index.html

www.icrunchdata.com

As a matter of fact, a Google® search with the keyword "SAS jobs" will turn up many more Web sites with current job listings that require a variety of SAS expertise. Try it and you will be impressed.

Second, *SAS can read data files created by other statistical packages*. SAS allows data files created by SPSS®, Excel®, Minitab®, Stata®, Systat®, and others to be incorporated into a SAS program directly or through file conversion software. Thus, to experienced users of these statistical packages, SAS presents no threat at all because it is possible to convert data files created by these packages into a SAS file format.

Third, *various data formats can be imported into SAS with relative ease*. In other words, learning SAS will not make you abandon data formats you previously mastered or managed. These formats include those generated and supported by database software such as Oracle®.

Fourth, *SAS is versatile and powerful enough to meet your needs in data analyses*. SAS is flexible, with a variety of input and output formats and numerous procedures for descriptive, inferential, and forecasting types of statistical analyses. Because the SAS System is an integrated system with similar architecture shared by modules or products, once you master one module, you can easily transfer the knowledge to other modules.

Fifth, *there is a worldwide electronic network of SAS users accessible at your fingertips*. This network consists of SAS users who subscribe to a Listserv. Subscribers to this list can converse with each other on the Internet. For details, refer to Appendix A.

Sixth, *the SAS users' conference is a professional gathering held annually at a pleasant location for all "SASaholics."* SAS users with diverse expertise and varying degrees of sophistication gather once a year at this conference to exchange ideas and view demonstrations of the latest products developed by the SAS Institute. If you cannot attend this annual event, there are many regional or local SAS users groups to be involved with. Tips on connecting to a users group at the local or international level are found in Appendix A.

Seventh, the *SAS Institute will not forsake you when you are in trouble.* There are many helpful phone numbers, fax numbers, and subsidiaries or distributors located around the world to enable you to overcome obstacles. This information is found in Appendix A.

Last, but not the least, SAS is not as hard as you think. It is straightforward to enter data and set up data files in SAS. If you can type, you can learn SAS. So why not start the learning process now with this book?

1.2 What Is the History of the SAS Institute and Its Current Clientele?

SAS began in 1966 with the work of a computer scientist, A. J. Barr, at North Carolina State University. A year later, a colleague of his, Dr. J. H. Goodnight, contributed the regression analysis program to SAS. Thus, the basis for initial SAS releases was the general linear model. Since then, SAS has had eight major releases with additional products added to each release. In August of 2002, SAS acquired the powerful file transfer family of products (DBMS/COPY) from Conceptual Software Inc. (retrieved April 20, 2007, from www.conceptual.com), thus further strengthening its position as the leading software for general data analysis and information delivery. For detailed information about the company and its products, visit the company's Web site at www.sas.com.

Since its incorporation in July of 1976, the company has grown tremendously, with an unbroken trend of revenue increases each year of the Institute's history. The number of clients around the globe is more than 3.5 million. SAS products have been installed at more than 43,000 sites in more than 110 countries, including the dismantled U.S.S.R. and Eastern European regions. Approximately 75% of SAS installations have been for businesses including more than 90% of the 2007 *Fortune* 100 companies, 5% have been for educational institutions, and 20% for government agencies.

1.3 What Is the SAS System and What Can It Do? A Quick Walk-Through of SAS Products

SAS software is best described as an information delivery system suitable for an entire organization. As software, SAS represents a modular, integrated, and hardware-independent computing package. As an information delivery system, SAS is capable of building a well-rounded, self-sufficient environment that is based on an organization's databases. Any trained data analyst can transform these data sets into useful information that is subsequently delivered to decision makers at the right moment to maximize the utility of the information. All these steps can be accomplished within SAS!

To attain the goal of efficient and timely information delivery, SAS is designed to (a) provide universal data access, (b) maximize the capabilities and breadth of applications in the software, (c) provide user interfaces, and (d) support and exploit the advantages of computer hardware platforms.

In simple words, SAS is a high-level programming language with flexible input/output styles and file management capabilities. It includes a wide range of analysis procedures to help users navigate through data so that the most succinct features in data may be readily transparent and subsequently analyzed. When faced with the challenge of dealing with multiple data formats or computing environments, you will find SAS capable of meeting such a challenge. This book, written with ample examples drawn from the social and behavioral sciences, will help you appreciate and master many useful features of SAS and their applications.

Behind the power of SAS is an array of versatile SAS products that are available for social and behavioral scientists. These products are called modules. SAS modules are capable of spreadsheet analysis, graphics, descriptive and inferential statistical analysis, report generation, database access, decision support, applications development, project management, client/server computing, executive information systems (i.e., EIS), and much more. These modules are sold separately or in a set. As far as computing environments are concerned, SAS integrates well with mainframes as well as with personal computers, including Macintoshes. Furthermore, a variety of UNIX operating systems are compatible with SAS. The following is a list of SAS products, commonly used by researchers and data analysts, along with their purposes and applications:

Purpose	Module	Contents
Connectivity to the SAS System	SAS/ASSIST	A menu-driven interface to the SAS System
Basic data processing and research tools	SAS/BASE	This is the core of the SAS System; it performs data management, analysis, and report writing
	SAS/FSP	Tool software for full-screen data entry, editing, querying, and letter writing

Purpose	Module	Contents
Statistical analysis	SAS/STAT	A collection of descriptive and inferential statistical procedures
	SAS/QC	Software for statistical quality improvement
	SAS/OR	Software for project management, operations research, scheduling, and linear programming
	SAS/LAB	A fully menu-driven module of guided data analysis in an experimental study
	SAS/ETS	Module for econometrics and time series analysis
	SAS/PH-Clinical	Software for reviewing and assimilating clinical trials data
Graphical representation of data or information	SAS/GRAPH	Software for information and representation of color graphics
	SAS/INSIGHT	Software for graphical data analysis
User-defined calculations	SAS/IML	An interactive matrix language for advanced numerical analysis
	SAS/CALC	Electronic spreadsheets
Linking the SAS system with other hardware environments, databases, or software	SAS/SHARE	A multiuser access tool for concurrent updating of SAS data libraries and data sets on mainframe systems
	SAS/ACCESS	Interfaces for linking the SAS System with various databases, such as ORACLE, CA-DATACOM, CA-IDMS, INGRES, INFORMATION, ADABAS, SYSTEM 2000 Data Management software, OS/2 Database Manager, etc.
	SAS/CONNECT	Facility for cooperative processing
Holistic systemwide application of SAS	SAS/EIS	Facility for building and maintaining executive information systems
	SAS/AF	An interactive facility with menus and screens for applications development, computer-based training, and online help systems
	SAS/TOOLKIT	Facility for extending the SAS System's capabilities

1.4 What Is the Scope and Style of This Book?

Topics covered in this book range from "Why should you learn SAS?" and "Where do you start?" to descriptive and inferential statistical analyses such as analysis of variance and regression. These topics are included to prepare you to deal with data frequently encountered in school projects, psychological experiments, social surveys, public polling, health research, clinical trials, marketing research, environmental studies, and many other contexts.

Specifically, the book is divided into three parts. Part I introduces SAS and basic data processing techniques (Chapters 1 through 7). Part II presents statistical procedures covered by most introductory statistics or research methods courses (Chapters 8 through 17). Part III deals with advanced data and file management (Chapters 18 through 20).

Chapters 1 and 2 are "starter" chapters that lay the groundwork for starting to learn more about data analysis and SAS. Chapters 3 to 5 address input and output formatting issues in data analysis. These issues include how you prepare your data for SAS to process, reading data stored in different formats by SAS, reading missing data in SAS, and displaying analysis results in SAS. Chapters 6 and 7 cover details of data processing such as recoding or transforming data, documenting SAS programs and output, registering variable types, verifying data, and debugging SAS programs.

Chapters 8 to 17 present SAS procedures (or commands in SPSS language) for descriptive and inferential statistical analyses. These procedures are for summarizing data, visually displaying data, analyzing categorical or continuous data, conducting average comparisons, and making predictions for individual observations. Conceptual explanations of statistical terms or equations are offered throughout these chapters, yet rigorous mathematical theories or proofs will not be presented.

Questions such as how to selectively and repetitively process data/ variables/observations and how to manage data sets are dealt with in Chapters 18 to 20 (Part III).

Following these 20 chapters are three appendixes (A, B, and C). Appendix A contains information on reference books, hotlines, and a wealth of Internet resources that will help you continue to develop analytical and research skills with the power of SAS. Data sets used in this book are described in Appendix B; they are available from the SAGE Web site at www.sagepub .com/pengstudy, along with solutions (SAS programs and output) to all exercise questions at the end of each chapter. You may further develop your analytical competence by exploring different aspects of these data or raising different questions concerning the same data. Appendix C presents information on reading SPSS, Stata, Excel, Minitab, and SYSTAT data set files in the SAS System.

The writing style of this book is informal and conversational. Each data analysis technique is illustrated with at least one example that in turn can serve as a template for your own data analysis. The explanation of SAS output is succinct and contextualized. Exercises provided at the end of each chapter will further develop your ability to reason with statistics and quantitative information. Solutions to these exercises are posted at the above Web site.

1.5 Summary

In this chapter, seven reasons were given for learning and mastering SAS. I hope that these reasons were convincing! Furthermore, a brief history of the SAS Institute (the brain behind the software!) and the dazzling array of its products were introduced. The products offer everything from data entry, data analysis, data reporting, data warehousing, and database management to natural language processing, specially designed to fully utilize the strengths of SAS.

This chapter ends with a description of the coverage of topics and the style of presentation adopted for this book. I hope that this chapter has aroused your interest in learning SAS for data analysis. Tricks published in this book will not only "convert" you to SAS but also hone your skills in making informed decisions and interpretations based on empirical data. Remember that SAS and computers have infinite patience. If you don't give up along the way, the mastery is ultimately yours!

So go for it!

1.6 Exercises

1. Look for additional resources at www.sagepub.com/pengstudy and bookmark this site.

2. Download the 10 data sets that accompany this book from www.sagepub.com/pengstudy and save these data sets on your computer hard drive or on a flash drive so that you may use them later when you begin to follow examples in this book.

3. Bookmark the SAS company site at www.sas.com and explore its various departments, especially the following:

   SAS Knowledge Base at http://support.sas.com/resources
   Technical Support at http://support.sas.com/techsup
   Training at http://support.sas.com/training/index.html
   SAS Discussion Forums at http://support.sas.com/forums/index.jspa
   Overall help at http://support.sas.com

4. Check out a local or the international SAS users group at http://support.sas.com/usergroups/intro.html

   Bookmark this site for future references.

5. Bookmark the online documentation for SAS version 9.1.3 at http://support.sas.com/documentation/onlinedoc/91pdf/index_913.html

   The two documents that are particularly relevant to this book are

   SAS/STAT 9.1 User's Guide (SAS Institute Inc., 2004d)

   Base SAS 9.1.3 Procedures Guide, 2nd ed. (SAS Institute Inc., 2006a)

6. Join the SAS-L Listserv by following the instructions given in Appendix A of this book.

7. Use an Internet search engine to search for sites that advertise jobs for SAS data analysts in your discipline.

2

Where Do You Start?

O B J E C T I V E

This chapter teaches you how to read raw data into a SAS program and analyze them in the Windows environment. Concepts such as a SAS program file, the Program Editor window, the log file, the Log window, the output file, the Output window, and error messages are explained and illustrated. A framework for writing additional SAS programs is introduced. Notations used throughout this book are also introduced.

This chapter teaches you how to read raw data into a SAS program and analyze them in the Windows environment. Concepts such as a SAS program file, the Program Editor window, the log file, the Log window, the output file, the Output window, and error messages are explained and illustrated. A framework for writing additional SAS programs is introduced. Notations used throughout this book are also explained.

2.1 General Appearance of a SAS Program: The DATA Step and the PROC Step

To analyze data in SAS, you need to learn to write a SAS program. A SAS program generally consists of a DATA step and a PROC step. Each step is a block of SAS statements with the leading keyword DATA or PROC. A SAS statement is a command executable by SAS. Statements in the DATA step are commands that establish or modify a SAS data set. Statements in the PROC step are commands that process or analyze a SAS data set.

Example 2.1 contains a single DATA step and a single PROC step. The DATA step starts with the keyword DATA and ends with the first RUN; statement. The PROC step starts with the keyword PROC and ends with the second RUN; statement. These RUN statements are to issue a go-ahead to the SAS compiler (the central processing unit in SAS) so that it may begin executing all commands written up to this point. SAS will not execute commands stored in the compiler until it encounters a RUN statement in both the DATA and the PROC steps. The first RUN statement is necessary in this program. It is also needed if a SAS program contains only the DATA step and no PROC step. It is a good habit to end either the DATA or the PROC step with a RUN statement.

Sentences enclosed by /* and */ are for commentaries only; they are not executable by SAS and do not interfere with the rest of the SAS program.

Example 2.1 A Simple SAS Program

```
DATA new;                    /* Defines a data set called 'new' */
      INPUT id score;
DATALINES;
1  200
2  100
RUN;                         /* Executes the above DATA step statements */

PROC PRINT DATA=new;         /* Prints the data set 'new' */
RUN;                         /* Executes the above PROC PRINT statement */
```

Take a look at another SAS program in Example 2.2 and see if you can distinguish those SAS statements that belong to the DATA step from those that belong to the PROC step.

Example 2.2 DATA and PROC in a SAS Program

```
DATA trans;
    INPUT test1 test2 test3;
    final=(test1+test2+test3)/3;
    LABEL test1='first test'
          test2='second test'
          test3='third test'
          final='overall score';
DATALINES;
60   80 99
50   87 65
100  99 98
RUN;

PROC PRINT DATA=trans;
RUN;
PROC MEANS;
RUN;
```

All SAS programs illustrated in this book are more complicated than the two shown above. Yet if you look carefully for the two keywords, DATA and PROC, you will nonetheless recognize them to be the building blocks in every program. In fact, the DATA step and the PROC step alternate and interweave throughout SAS programs. The flow from one step to the next is organized by a SAS compiler. The diagram in Figure 2.1 explains the alternation between a DATA step and a PROC step.

All SAS statements

- end with a semicolon (;),
- can start in any column of a line,
- are written in either upper- or lowercase, and
- may have any number of blank lines before or after.

More than one SAS statement may appear on a line. Likewise, a SAS statement may continue into the next line or two. Any indentation or spacing shown in a SAS program is for visual clarity only.

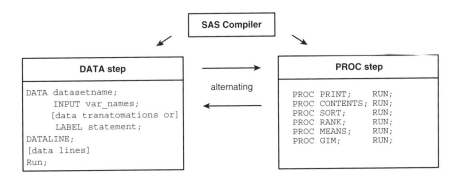

Figure 2.1   The Relationship Between a DATA Step and a PROC Step

2.2 Notations Used Throughout This Book

Before proceeding any further, let us introduce the notations used in this book. Some are used in the text and others are for SAS statements. They are summarized in Table 2.1.

Thus, when UPPERCASE lines appear in an example or exercise question, they imply that you are to type the text exactly according to the way it is shown. At the end of each line, you are to press the <Return> key. The <Return> key is generally located in the middle section of the keyboard to the right. A <Return> key may alternatively be labeled as <Enter> or < ↵ >.

Each SAS program shown in this book will be written in a mixture of upper- and lowercase type. The use of both upper- and lowercase is intended to help you distinguish SAS keywords from characters that can be changed by you.

Table 2.1   Notations Used in This Book

Notations Used in This Book	For What?
Sabon	The standard font used in the text.
Bold	For normal names such as **McNemar**'s test. It is also used to highlight keywords in SAS programs or output, such as **MODEL Y = .**
underscored lowercase	For character variable values, variable names, file names, or data set names that can be replaced by readers with a different name.
Courier	For SAS statements, SAS logs, and SAS output.
Notations Used in SAS Programs	For What?
UPPERCASE	For SAS syntax; they must be typed exactly as shown.
lowercase	For user-specified variable name, title, data set name, etc., in SAS programs; these can be substituted by reader's specification.
lowercase, Italic	For generic portions of SAS syntax.
Courier	For SAS statements, SAS logs, and SAS output.

2.3 Steps for Preparing and Executing a SAS Program in the Windows Environment

In the Windows environment, the following five steps are needed to analyze data by SAS:

1. Initialize SAS

2. Prepare a SAS program

3. Submit the SAS program

4. Diagnose possible error(s)

5. Examine the output

Each step is illustrated and explained in greater detail below.

Step 1   Initialize SAS by double clicking on the SAS icon or finding it
              under Start → Programs → SAS

Before SAS is initialized, you may first see a computer screen such as
Figure 2.2.

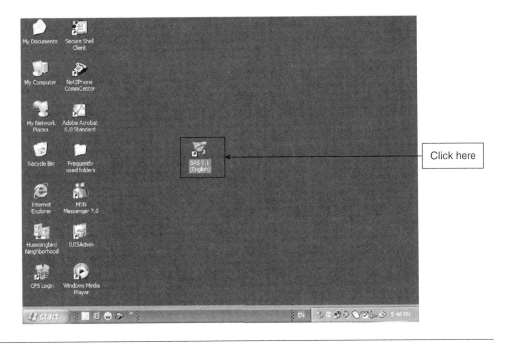

Figure 2.2   A Computer Screen Before SAS-Windows Is Initialized

On this screen, move the cursor to the SAS icon, namely, the object
labeled "SAS 9 1 (English)" and click on it. Immediately after the click, the
computer screen shows the SAS software logo and then changes to the display shown in Figure 2.3.

The computer screen in Figure 2.3 displays three windows. The two windows on the right are most relevant now: The top right is the Log window
and the bottom right is the Program Editor window. Click on the ☐ button
(located in the upper-right corner) of the Program Editor window to enlarge
the window till it fills the entire screen. Now, you are ready to type your first
SAS program.

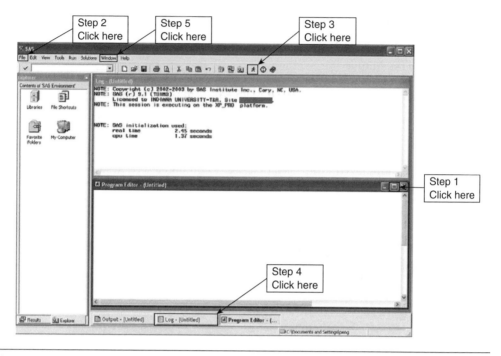

Figure 2.3   The Computer Screen After SAS-Windows Is Initialized

Step 2 Prepare a SAS program in the Program Editor window

In the Windows environment, you either write a SAS program from scratch or call up an existing program. Assuming that you want to write a SAS program exactly like Example 2.1, simply type those lines in the Program Editor window. At the end of each line, press the <Return> key to move the cursor to the next line. Remember that a SAS statement can start and end anywhere on a line as long as you remember to end each statement with a semicolon (;).

Later, you may wish to bring up an existing SAS program for modification. To do this, move the cursor up to the menu bar and click on the word **File.** On the **File** pull-down menu, click on the option **Open.** Follow the path to locate a SAS program that is already prepared and stored either on the hard drive (say, the C: drive) or on a USB drive (say, the E: drive). A SAS program should have the file extension .sas.

Step 3 Submit the SAS program for compilation

When a SAS program is ready to be submitted, move the cursor to the menu bar and click on the word **Run.** On the **Run** pull-down menu, click the option **Submit** to submit the program. After submitting the program, the cursor turns into an "hourglass" while the screen may be frozen for a few seconds or minutes, depending on the length of time taken by SAS to process your program. When compilation finishes and the cursor returns to the "arrow" shape, you are ready for the next step. The sequence of

Run+**Submit** commands can also be executed by clicking the running person icon () that appears on the toolbar.

Step 4   Diagnose error message(s) in the Log window

Before you can assert that the output is accurate, you need to examine the log (or journal) of the compilation process. The log is displayed in the Log window. To get there, click on the word **Window** on the menu bar, then click on the option **Log**. Or, click on the **Log** window on the **Window** bar. For Example 2.1, the Log window looks like Figure 2.4.

Fortunately, the log in Figure 2.4 does not issue any errors or warnings that you need to worry about. So you wrote a perfect program! Having examined the content of the Log window and determined that there is no alarming error message to worry about, you may now proceed to the next step.

Figure 2.4   The Log Window of Example 2.1

Step 5   Examine the output in the Output window

The results obtained from Step 3 are displayed in the Output window. This window may be opened by clicking **Window** → **Output** on the menu bar or by pressing the <Alt/Tab> keys simultaneously. Based on the program submitted in Step 3, the Output window should look like Figure 2.5.

Results shown in the Output window can be saved as a permanent file with the extension **.lst** (which stands for listing), or it can be printed as hard copy. Both options are available from the **File** pull-down menu. Use the point-and-click approach to choose either option. To save the output results into a file, go to the Output window, click on the **Save** or the **Save as** option. To print the results, click on the **Print** option.

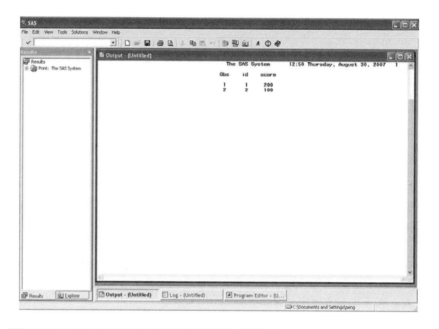

Figure 2.5   The Output Window of Example 2.1

Tips

• If you need to cycle through Steps 3 through 5 a few times in order to obtain a satisfactory result, make sure you always click on **Clear_All** (an option on the **Edit** pull-down menu) in both the Log and the Output windows before the next SAS program is submitted.

• To retrieve a SAS program after its execution, open up the Program Editor window. On the **Run** pull-down menu, click on **Recall Last Submit**; the SAS program just submitted reappears on the screen. Some installations of SAS will automatically recall the last SAS program submitted in the Program Editor window. In this case, you may skip this step.

• The content of the Log window can be saved as a permanent file with the extension **.log** or it can be printed as hard copy. Both options are available from the **File** pull-down menu. To save the log, click on the **Save** or the **Save as** option. To print the log, click on the **Print** option. The Log window displays useful information about the processing of a SAS program including error messages. As you learn SAS, you will also learn to dissect error messages and the content of the Log window.

• As you begin to learn to write your own programs, you may encounter errors on the log. These errors are usually noted by a different color. Some errors, such as syntax errors, will cause the program to be terminated, while others, such as logical errors (e.g., dividing a number by zero), are acknowledged by a warning or a note in the log. Most error messages are self-explanatory. More practice with diagnosing error messages is provided at the end of this chapter.

2.4 Summary

This chapter should get you started on the versatile SAS system. Steps were outlined for executing a SAS program and retrieving results in the Windows environment. SAS-related concepts such as the Program Editor window, the Log window, the Output window, and error messages were explained. If you are presently computing in an environment other than Windows, such as one that uses a mainframe, please consult with your local expert on how to start up the SAS system and how to prepare and execute a SAS program in your environment.

2.5 Exercises

1. Practice the five steps outlined in **Section 2.3** with the SAS program in Example 2.2. After running the program and checking any warning or error message in the Log window, save the program, the log, and the output as 2-2.sas, 2-2.log, and 2-2.lst respectively.

2. Here's another SAS program (roster.sas) to give you practice with the five steps. You may type out this entire program or download the roster.sas program from www.sagepub.com/pengstudy.

```
DATA roster;                                        /* Creates a data set 'roster' */

     INPUT name $ sex $ id $ stand pretest first second final; /* $ declares 'name' and 'id' */
                                                    /* as character variables     */
     composite = pretest + first + second + final;

     LABEL stand = 'academic standing in college';

DATALINES;
JOHN   m    1   1    9   31      45     .           /* A period (.) means a missing score */
DAN    m    2   4   18   46      53    54
LYNN   f    3   1    7   38      33    43
CATHY  f    4   2   12   34      50    32
JAMES  m    5   2   14   31      47    43
TIM    m    6   4   20   45      51    57
HOPE   f    7   4   17   34      46    50
TED    m    8   2   12   44      52    47
SASSY  f    9   4   18   50      57    56
NANCY  f   10   3   15   29      39    42
PAUL   m   11   3   15   24      48    49
LIN    m   12   4   18   48      54    54
TOM    m   13   4   21   48      52    42
BOB    m   14   1   11   32      41    40
RUN;

PROC PRINT; RUN;                                    /* Prints the raw data in 'roster' */

PROC MEANS DATA=roster; RUN;                        /* Computes averages */

PROC RANK DESCENDING OUT=temp;                      /* Ranks students by their 'composite' */
     VAR composite;
     RANKS rank;
RUN;

PROC SORT;                                          /* Sorts students by their 'rank' */
     BY rank;
RUN;

PROC PRINT DATA=temp;                               /* Prints the ranked students */
RUN;
```

 a. What steps did you follow in writing and submitting this program?
 b. What does the output look like? What is the average score of the _final_ variable?
 c. Who is Number **1** in the class according to the ranked data?
 d. What special note or warning is there in the Log window?

3. The following program is modified from the <u>roster.sas</u> program used in Exercise 2 above. Execute this program and diagnose errors in it based on messages printed in the Log window.

```
Line
Number     SAS Program modified from roster.sas

1          DATA ro ster;
2               INPUT name id $ pretest first second final;
3               composite = pretest + first + second + final;
4          DATALINES
5          JOHN   1    9 31 45  .
6          DAN    2   18 46 53 54
7          LYNN   3    7 38 33 43
8          CATHY  4   12 34 50 32
9          JAMES  5   14 31 47 43
10         TIM    6   20 45 51 57
11         HOPE   7   17 34 46 50
12         TED    8   12 44 52 47
13         SASSY  9   18 50 57 56
14         NANCY 10 15 29 39 42
15         PAUL   11 15 24 48 49
16         LIN    12 18 48 54 54
17         TOM    13 21 48 52 42
18         BOB    14 11 32 41 40
19         RUN;
20         PROC PRINT; RUN;
21         PROC MEANS DATA=roster; RUN;
22         PROC RANK DESCENDING OUT=temp;
23         VAR  composite;
24         RANK rank;
25         RUN;
26         PROC SORT;
27         BY rank;
28         RUN;
29         PROC PRINT DATA=temp;
30         RUN;
```

2.6 Answers to Exercises

1. Here is the content of the Log window, and also 2-2.log:

```
1          DATA trans;
2               INPUT test1 test2 test3;
3               final=(test1+test2+test3)/3;
4               LABEL test1='first test'
5                    test2='second test'
```

```
6                              test3='third test'
7                              final='overall score';
8               DATALINES;

NOTE: The data set WORK.TRANS has 3 observations and 4 variables.
NOTE: DATA statement used (Total process time):
      real time            0.09 seconds
      cpu time             0.07 seconds


12              RUN;
13
14              PROC PRINT DATA=trans;
15              RUN;

NOTE: There were 3 observations read from the data set WORK.TRANS.
NOTE: The PROCEDURE PRINT printed page 1.
NOTE: PROCEDURE PRINT used (Total process time):
      real time            0.17 seconds
      cpu time             0.12 seconds


16              PROC MEANS;
17              RUN;

NOTE: There were 3 observations read from the data set WORK.TRANS.
NOTE: The PROCEDURE MEANS printed page 2.
NOTE: PROCEDURE MEANS used (Total process time):
      real time            0.44 seconds
      cpu time             0.08 seconds
```

Here is the content of the Output window, and also 2-2.lst:

```
                The SAS System                                                    1

Obs     test1     test2     test3      final
1        60        80        99      79.6667
2        50        87        65      67.3333
3       100        99        98      99.0000
```

```
                              The SAS System                                      2

                            The MEANS Procedure

Variable   Label           N       Mean        Std Dev       Minimum       Maximum
----------------------------------------------------------------------------------
test1      first test      3    70.0000000    26.4575131    50.0000000   100.0000000
test2      second test     3    88.6666667     9.6090235    80.0000000    99.0000000
test3      third test      3    87.3333333    19.3476958    65.0000000    99.0000000
final      overall score   3    82.0000000    15.9617599    67.3333333    99.0000000
----------------------------------------------------------------------------------
```

2. a. You should have written the program in the Program Editor window and submitted
   the program according to steps outlined in **Section 2.3**.
   b. The output should look as follows; the average score of <u>final</u> is <u>46.8461538</u>.

```
                                    The SAS System                                      1

   Obs    name     sex    id    stand    pretest    first    second    final    composite

    1     JOHN      m      1      1         9         31       45        .          .
    2     DAN       m      2      4        18         46       53       54        171
    3     LYNN      f      3      1         7         38       33       43        121
    4     CATHY     f      4      2        12         34       50       32        128
    5     JAMES     m      5      2        14         31       47       43        135
    6     TIM       m      6      4        20         45       51       57        173
    7     HOPE      f      7      4        17         34       46       50        147
    8     TED       m      8      2        12         44       52       47        155
    9     SASSY     f      9      4        18         50       57       56        181
   10     NANCY     f     10      3        15         29       39       42        125
   11     PAUL      m     11      3        15         24       48       49        136
   12     LIN       m     12      4        18         48       54       54        174
   13     TOM       m     13      4        21         48       52       42        163
   14     BOB       m     14      1        11         32       41       40        124
```

```
                                    The SAS System                                      2

                                  The MEANS Procedure

   Variable     Label                              N        Mean        Std Dev       Minimum
   -----------------------------------------------------------------------------------------
   stand        academic standing in college      14     2.7857143     1.2513729     1.0000000
   pretest                                         14    14.7857143     4.1727794     7.0000000
   first                                           14    38.1428571     8.4839862    24.0000000
   second                                          14    47.7142857     6.5330941    33.0000000
   final                                           13    46.8461538     7.3467244    32.0000000
   composite                                       13   148.6923077    21.8608654   121.0000000
   -----------------------------------------------------------------------------------------

                    Variable     Label                           Maximum
                    -------------------------------------------------------
                    stand        academic standing in college    4.0000000
                    pretest                                      21.0000000
                    first                                        50.0000000
                    second                                       57.0000000
                    final                                        57.0000000
                    composite                                   181.0000000
                    -------------------------------------------------------
```

```
                                    The SAS System                                      3

   Obs    name     sex    id    stand    pretest    first    second    final    composite    rank

    1     JOHN      m      1      1         9         31       45        .          .           .
    2     SASSY     f      9      4        18         50       57       58        101          1
    3     LIN       m     12      4        18         48       54       54        174          2
    4     TIM       m      6      4        20         45       51       57        173          3
    5     DAN       m      2      4        18         46       53       54        171          4
    6     TOM       m     13      4        21         48       52       42        163          5
    7     TED       m      8      2        12         44       52       47        155          6
    8     HOPE      f      7      4        17         34       46       50        147          7
    9     PAUL      m     11      3        15         24       48       49        136          8
   10     JAMES     m      5      2        14         31       47       43        135          9
   11     CATHY     f      4      2        12         34       50       32        128         10
   12     NANCY     f     10      3        15         29       39       42        125         11
   13     BOB       m     14      1        11         32       41       40        124         12
   14     LYNN      f      3      1         7         38       33       43        121         13
```

c. SASSY! It was located on the second line (or Obs = 2) of Page 3 of the output. I will explain why JOHN preceded SASSY in my answer to the next question.

d. The Log window displayed a special note, which caused a temporary scare in me; did it scare you too?

```
NOTE: Missing values were generated as a result of performing an operation on
missing values.
      Each place is given by: (Number of times) at (Line):(column).
      1 at 6:43
```

This note was the result of SAS attempting to compute a <u>composite</u> score for JOHN, but it couldn't due to JOHN's missing score on <u>final</u>. Consequently, JOHN's <u>composite</u> score was missing and so was his rank. By default, observations with missing ranks are listed first, preceding the first-ranked person. This is the reason why SASSY (the true No. 1) was listed below JOHN on Page 3 of the output.

3. There are four errors in the SAS program:
   i. In Line 1, "DATA ro ster;" should be typed as "DATA roster;".
   ii. In Line 2, a dollar sign ($) should be typed after "name".
   iii. In Line 4, a ";" should be inserted after "DATALINES".
   iv. In Line 24, "RANK rank" should be typed as "RANKS rank" because RANKS is a SAS keyword, whereas <u>rank</u> is a variable name specified by the user/ programmer.

Now that you have perfected the program, run it and compare its output with the one below:

```
                              The SAS System                               1

 Obs    name     id    pretest    first    second    final    composite

   1    JOHN     1         9       31        45         .          .
   2    DAN      2        18       46        53        54        171
   3    LYNN     3         7       38        33        43        121
   4    CATHY    4        12       34        50        32        128
   5    JAMES    5        14       31        47        43        135
   6    TIM      6        20       45        51        57        173
   7    HOPE     7        17       34        46        50        147
   8    TED      8        12       44        52        47        155
   9    SASSY    9        18       50        57        56        181
  10    NANCY   10        15       29        39        42        125
  11    PAUL    11        15       24        48        49        136
  12    LIN     12        18       48        54        54        174
  13    TOM     13        21       48        52        42        163
  14    BOB     14        11       32        41        40        124
```

```
                              The SAS System                                    2

                             The MEANS Procedure

Variable      N          Mean         Std Dev        Minimum         Maximum
-----------------------------------------------------------------------------
pretest       14     14.7857143       4.1727794      7.0000000      21.0000000
first         14     38.1428571       8.4839862     24.0000000      50.0000000
second        14     47.7142857       6.5330941     33.0000000      57.0000000
final         13     46.8461538       7.3467244     32.0000000      57.0000000
composite     13    148.6923077      21.8608654    121.0000000     181.0000000
-----------------------------------------------------------------------------
```

```
                              The SAS System                                    3

Obs     name      id    pretest    first    second    final    composite    rank

  1     JOHN       1        9        31        45        .           .         .
  2     SASSY      9       18        50        57       56         181         1
  3     LIN       12       18        48        54       54         174         2
  4     TIM        6       20        45        51       57         173         3
  5     DAN        2       18        46        53       54         171         4
  6     TOM       13       21        48        52       42         163         5
  7     TED        8       12        44        52       47         155         6
  8     HOPE       7       17        34        46       50         147         7
  9     PAUL      11       15        24        48       49         136         8
 10     JAMES      5       14        31        47       43         135         9
 11     CATHY      4       12        34        50       32         128        10
 12     NANCY     10       15        29        39       42         125        11
 13     BOB       14       11        32        41       40         124        12
 14     LYNN       3        7        38        33       43         121        13
```

3 How to Prepare Data for SAS Processing

OBJECTIVE

This chapter demonstrates how to code data into SAS for data analysis. Fundamental concepts such as observation, variable, data matrix, coding schemes, and missing values are introduced. In addition, variables are differentiated according to their types: character or numeric. Values of a numeric variable are treated differently than those of a character variable by SAS. By the same token, missing values are handled separately for these two types of variables.

In this era of information explosion, one inevitably has taken a survey or been involved in designing one. The importance of survey methods for gathering information is best summarized in the book *What Is a Survey?* (retrieved August 7, 2007, from www.whatisasurvey.info):

> It has been said the United States is no longer an "industrial society" but an "information society." That is, our major problems and tasks no longer mainly center on the production of the goods and services necessary for survival and comfort.
>
> Our "society," thus, requires a prompt and accurate flow of information on preferences, needs, and behavior. It is in response to this critical need for information on the part of the government, business, and social institutions that so much reliance is placed on surveys. (Scheuren, 2004)

It is true that the survey method is the one most commonly employed by pollsters, policymakers, government agencies, market analysts, health researchers, and social scientists to gather information from a targeted population through a selection of a group of individuals (a sample) so that certain aspects of the targeted population, such as purchasing behavior, lifestyle, eating habits, and so on, may be understood in a composite way. In this chapter and the next, you will learn the nuts and bolts of designing a survey instrument and analyzing survey data in SAS. Fundamental concepts such as observation, variable, variable value, data matrix, coding schemes, and missing data treatments are introduced. Along the way, you will learn practical skills such as developing coding schemes suitable for the type of data collected and properly treating missing information from respondents. One particular survey, a course evaluation, is used throughout this chapter to illustrate these concepts. This course evaluation survey has been used for many years in a research design course of a Research I university to gather information about the instructor's teaching effectiveness.

3.1 What Are Data?

Data consist of quantifiable information collected for specific purposes or to answer specific questions. To illustrate this definition, let's suppose that you fill out a course evaluation form called the Course Evaluation Survey for a research design course (Y777) at the end of a semester. The form consists of three parts: Topics, Instructor/Course, and Self-Evaluation. The first two sections include Likert-scaled items, and the last section is mostly open-ended. The Topics section asks students to indicate their ability or knowledge about each topic covered before and after taking this course. The Instructor/Course section asks for students' feedback on the instructors' teaching effectiveness and course organization, and the Self-Evaluation section instructs students to describe their study habits, career aspirations, and suggestions for improving the course. A student's response to each question is a datum. Two or more datum is "data."

Course Evaluation Survey

The purpose of this survey is to help the instructor understand your perception of how well this course was taught. Specifically, your assessment of (1) the coverage of topics, (2) the instructor/course, and (3) your study habits and goals is sought by the following items. Your response to each item should be as truthful as possible and according to the direction given for each part. Mark your responses directly on the sheet. Leave the question BLANK if the item DOES NOT APPLY or asks for information UNKNOWN to you. Thank you.

Part I: Topics

Directions: Indicate your ability or knowledge about the following topics obtained prior to enrolling in Y777 by a check mark ($\checkmark$). Show your current ability or knowledge by a circle (O). The scale is interpreted as follows:

1 = Very poor   2 = Poor   3 = Average   4 = Good   5 = Very good

1. Sampling methods and sampling distributions such as χ^2 and F.

   1 2 3 4 5

2. Ability to apply ANOVA–fixed effects model.

   1 2 3 4 5

3. Ability to apply multiple comparison procedures within the ANOVA framework.

   1 2 3 4 5

4. Application of randomized block designs.

   1 2 3 4 5

5. Knowledge of Latin squares design and its efficiency.

   1 2 3 4 5

6. Ability to apply the split-plot factorial designs and knowledge of underlying assumptions.

   1 2 3 4 5

7. Knowledge of analysis of covariance design and its applications.

   1 2 3 4 5

8. Knowledge of the ANOVA's general approach and its assumptions (e.g., normality, equal variance, and independent errors).

   1 2 3 4 5

Part II: Instructor/Course

Directions: Circle your response in an appropriate place on the scale, which is interpreted as follows:

1 = Strongly Disagree   2 = Disagree   3 = Neutral   4 = Agree   5 = Strongly Agree

9. The instructor was prepared for each lecture.   1   2   3   4   5

10. The instructor was available to help students.   1   2   3   4   5

11. Practical application was provided on each   1   2   3   4   5
    research design.

12. The instructor demonstrated overall knowledge   1   2   3   4   5
    of the course material, and incorporated
    up-to-date information into lectures
    and discussions.

13. The instructor treated her students with respect.   1   2   3   4   5

14. The handouts were useful for clarifying   1   2   3   4   5
    confusion and difficult concepts.

15. The textbook was a good supplement to   1   2   3   4   5
    lectures and handouts.

Part III: Self-Evaluation

16. On the average, I studied Y777 _____ hours per week.

17. Circle a number that best describes your aptitude in statistics:

    Beginner   Expert
    1   2   3   4   5

18. Circle a number that best describes your attitude toward learning statistics:

    Unfavorable   Favorable
    1   2   3   4   5

19. Circle a number that best describes your anxiety about learning statistics:

    Low   High
    1   2   3   4   5

20. Do you hope to become a _____? Check all that apply:

    _____ faculty at a university   _____ researcher at a research institute

    _____ administrator   _____ public policy consultant

    _____ data analyst   _____ others; please specify:_____

21. How can this course be improved?

_____

_____

_____

   If this survey is well designed, every response should provide a piece of information sought by the instructor. For example, if a student circled "5" on Question 14 and a "1" on Question 15, these two responses might convey one message to the instructor, that is, that the textbook adopted for the course was lousy and this student turned to handouts for clarification. If a majority of students in this course respond similarly, that is, "4" or "5" to Question 14 and "1" or "2" to Question 15, the instructor needs to do something about the textbook. Perhaps she could replace the required text by a different book, use a text that is simpler and less mathematical as a supplemental guide, or completely do away with the textbook and rely on lectures and handouts instead.

   Even no response to a question constitutes a datum. For example, a student might have chosen not to respond to Question 21 because he or she ran out of time or was not sure what to write down. In this case, a blank response is regarded as "missing data." The term "missing data" refers to all missing information shown on a survey. Depending on reasons for missing data and the nature of missing information, missing data can be treated differently by SAS. These different treatments are discussed in **Section 3.5** on how to handle missing values.

3.2 Designing a Survey Instrument

There are basic design principles that can make a survey instrument useful and, therefore, the resulting data relevant. Some simple tips are given below:

1. The purpose of the survey should be stated clearly on the cover sheet of the instrument.

2. Instructions on how to answer the questions should precede the questions.

3. Make sure there is sufficient space for written responses, especially for open-ended questions.

4. If a scale is used to solicit responses, its categories, such as 1, 2, . . . , 5, should be defined clearly in the directions.

5. An odd-numbered response scale is preferred over an even-numbered scale because the former scale provides a central point, such as 3 on a 5-point scale, which is also defined on the scale.

6. No more than seven categories should be used on a response scale (e.g., the Likert-type scale).

7. Similar questions should be grouped together, such as questions in Parts I, II, and III.

8. Assessment of changes in knowledge, ability, attitude, and so forth can be measured by using different response types to the same question, such as a check mark (✓) for before and a circle (O) for after taking a course or receiving an intervention.

9. Open-ended questions are placed at the end (e.g., Question 21).

10. Questions that solicit multiple responses, such as Question 20, are treated as multiple questions for the purpose of data analysis. Thus, Question 20 will be treated as a series of Yes/No subquestions in a SAS program, such as

   20a. Do you hope to become a faculty member   Yes No
        at a university?

   20b. Do you hope to become a researcher at a   Yes No
        research institute?

   20c. Do you hope to become an administrator?   Yes No

   20d. Do you hope to become a public policy   Yes No
        consultant?

   20e. Do you hope to become a data analyst?   Yes No

   20f. Do you hope to become a counselor
        (written in by a student)?   Yes No

   and more if other responses besides counselor are given.

   Each of these subquestions leads to a unique column in a data matrix, explained in the next section.

11. Put an identification (ID) number somewhere on the survey, for example, on the back. This allows you to locate the form quickly when you want to verify a response or check for errors. Even if a survey is confidential and no personal identity is to be revealed, an ID number helps you keep

a record of surveys completed, not-yet-returned, damaged, or incomplete. This information is needed for tracking and data analysis purposes.

Additional tips on survey designs and data analysis can be found from the following links:

www.amstat.org/sections/srms (the Web site of the Survey Research Methods Section of the American Statistical Association) or www.amstat .org (the home page of the American Statistical Association).

3.3 Coding the Data

Once students fill out the course evaluation form, the instructor is interested in analyzing the feedback collected from the entire class. How can one organize the massive amount of information and still maintain the uniqueness of each individual's responses? The answer lies in a structure called the data matrix. The data matrix is a useful format for recording raw data, namely, information provided by respondents without interpretation or manipulation. Before going further, let's distinguish three terms: *observation*, *variable*, and *variable value*.

An **observation** is a collection of information about an individual, such as his or her responses to the course evaluation survey, height, weight, or grade point average (GPA). Such information focuses on an individual who is identified either by name, ID number, social security number, or other personal identity. An observation can also mean the individual himself or herself who responded to the survey. By this definition, an observation may also be a city, school, clinic, company, community, etc., depending on the sampling unit of the survey or study.

A **variable** is a piece of information about an observation (say, an individual) such as his or her response to Question 18 on the course evaluation survey, height, weight, GPA, etc. Each variable is identified by a name, such as q18. Other names, such as height, weight, or gpa, therefore, refer to other variables.

A **variable value** is the specific information provided by an observation for a variable, such as a "4" to Question 18 on the course evaluation survey, or "data analyst" for Question 20. Obviously, a variable can take on different values depending on respondents' responses. Likewise, different variables can solicit different types of information, such as numerical information on Questions 1 through 19, yet nonnumerical or qualitative information on Question 21.

Data Matrix

A data matrix is a data recording structure with rows and columns, much like a spreadsheet or a simple matrix. Rows are arranged horizontally and columns vertically. Rows are used for observations and columns for variables (see the sample data matrix below). Each observation in the sample data matrix is identified by an ID number. This ID number is used to distinguish between respondents, and also between instruments or booklets. Alternatively, observations may be identified by a name as long as respondents are guaranteed the confidentiality of their individual responses. Let's suppose that you and 19 other students completed the course evaluation; your responses are summarized in the following sample data matrix (the last column is left blank because of the open-ended nature of the question):

<u>Sample Data Matrix</u>

ID	q1 before (✔)	q1 after (O)	q2 before (✔)	q2 after (O)	. . .	q16	q17	q18	q19	q20a	. . .	q20f	q21
1	3	4	2	5	. . .	24	5	1	3	yes		no	
2	1	3	2	4	. . .	5	1	3	5	no		yes	
.	.	.	.	.	.	.	.	.	.	.		.	
.	.	.	.	.	.	.	.	.	.	.		.	
.	.	.	.	.	.	.	.	.	.	.		.	
20	2	5	3	5	. . .	35	5	2	4	no		no	

Developing Coding Schemes

Recording data from a survey instrument into the data matrix requires the correct reading of responses and, in some instances, the best interpretation of the responses as well. The process is referred to as "coding the data," which needs to be guided by "coding schemes." A coding scheme is a system of interpretations and decision making that help the coder, or you, be consistent in interpreting all responses. For example, on the 5-point scale used for Questions 1 to 15, someone may respond midway between 3 and 4. In this case, what should a coder do? Discard such a response or record it as 3.5? Or, on Question 17 regarding aptitude in statistics, a respondent might write down 9 and circle it as his or her response. Also, what do we do with open-ended questions such as Question 21? How about Question 20, which can solicit multiple responses? To deal with these possible scenarios, the following coding schemes may be adopted:

- For Questions 1 to 15 and 17 to 19, the number checked or circled is the number entered into the data matrix.
- For Questions 1 to 15 and 17 to 19, a response marked between two points on the scale is coded as an average of the two adjacent numbers.
- For Questions 1 to 15 and 17 to 19, a response outside the range of 1 to 5 is considered invalid; therefore, it is interpreted as a missing response.
- For Question 16, a valid response is the number of hours actually written in the blank space. All other responses are considered invalid and, therefore, missing.
- Question 20's responses are recoded as data to six (or more) subquestions; the first (q20a) is recoded to faculty at a university, the second (q20b) to researcher, and so on (refer back to Tip 10 in **Section 3.2: Designing a Survey Instrument**). Each of these coded responses is in the form of "yes" or "no". Thus, you can assign a value of 1 to the "yes" response (or originally, a checked category that applies) and 0 to the "no" response (or originally, a blank, unchecked category).

The last column, q21, is left blank in the data matrix because original questions were constructed as open ended. An open-ended question undoubtedly elicits a variety of responses that seem unquantifiable at first glance. Yet the responses can still be categorized and coded. Some suggestions are offered next.

How to Code Responses to an Open-Ended Question

Take, for example, Question 21 from the Course Evaluation Survey; it asks for ideas to improve the course. Of all responses collected, you may identify only five distinct response categories such as the following:

1. Assign more problems to practice with.

2. Dismiss each class on time.

3. Make the take-home exams easier and shorter.

4. Teach SAS to analyze data.

5. Change the textbook.

Other responses are merely variations of these five response categories, such as "Don't run over the class time!," "Include fewer questions on the take-home exams," or "Use the textbook by Dr. Dolittle instead." Thus, you may classify each response into one of these five categories and code each response as a yes or a no to each of these five categories, much like the coding schemes developed for Question 20. This treatment of open-ended questions ensures that multiple responses from the same respondents are accepted into the final data matrix.

Alternatively, you may want to pilot test your instrument on one class of students, collect their responses, and classify them. Based on feedback from the pilot testing, you may subsequently include all likely answers to Question 21. On the final form, respondents need only to check those that apply to them. Even with this procedure, you should still anticipate receiving responses not listed or not collected from pilot testing. Thus, blank spaces should be provided for respondents to write in their own answers.

If responses to Question 21 are unclear or illegible, the best way to handle them is to go back to the source—interview students orally or by phone or e-mail to fully understand what they meant. Maybe they had very specific ideas but ran out of time in writing them down. In this case, the instructor may wish to track down these students to learn about their specific ideas and the best way or ways to implement these ideas in the next course offering. A good reference on the topic of coding data from surveys is found in Newton and Rudestam's (1999) book *Your Statistical Consultant: Answers to Your Data Analysis Questions.*

3.4 Types of Variables

Once data are recorded into a data matrix, you are set to analyze them with SAS. The first and foremost task in analyzing the data is to recognize the nature of each variable and register that information into SAS. According to the SAS terminology, there are two types of variables: character and numeric. Accordingly, variable values are either character or numeric. Character variables are qualitative or nominal in nature. Character variables convey textual information or information about distinctiveness of responses. Examples of character variables are gender (male vs. female), social security number, phone number, and region of a country (northwest, west, southwest, midwest, etc.). Although social security numbers, phone numbers, and the like, appear to be numeric, these numbers convey information of distinctness, not degree of quantity. Therefore, they should be declared character variables. To code a character data value, you may use letters, numbers, or special characters such as underscores (_), pound signs (#), or ampersands (&).

Numeric variables, on the other hand, convey numerical information about an observation, such as his or her height, weight, family size, number of e-mail accounts owned, and so on. Data values for a numerical variable are simply numbers, including those expressed in the scientific E-notation, decimal points, and signs (+ or −). Numeric information can be either continuous (e.g., hours studying for an exam) or discrete (e.g., number of credit cards owned). The measurement of numeric information can be either at the ordinal level, the interval level, or the ratio level, according to Stevens' (1946) theory of measurement scales.

Indeed the variable's type, its measurement level, and its declaration in SAS directly determine the kind of analyses SAS applies to that variable. For example, numeric variable values can be averaged, whereas character variable values cannot; they are tabulated instead. Even so, both types of variables can be sorted, in an ascending or descending order, according to the rules established by the SAS compiler.

It is important to note that variables of the character nature may be recoded into numbers, such as 1 for cured and 0 for not cured, or 1 for public schools and 2 for private schools. The numerical recoding of character variables is for data analysis purposes, especially, in regression. Yet the character nature of these qualitative variables or nominal-level measures remains the same. In other words, it is meaningless to compute descriptive statistics, such as the mean or the standard deviation, for character variables even after they have been recoded in numbers. Furthermore, if a statistical test is applied to data, the data should meet the test's statistical assumptions (e.g., normality), or at least not exhibit evidence of violating them. The robustness of statistical assumptions is discussed in Chapters 9 through 17, along with each statistical test.

For data collected by the course evaluation survey, I'd regard those on Questions 1 to 19 as numeric, the rest as character.

Check Your Understanding

What is the type of the following variables, character or numeric?

(1) PIN number for bank accounts	(2) Monthly income	(3) Mileage of your car
(4) Daily usage of Internet phone	(5) Password for e-mail	(6) Attitude toward immigrants
(7) Your favorite sport	(8) Religious beliefs	

[The answers appear in **Section 3.6: Summary**]

3.5 How to Handle Missing Values

There is a saying among data analysts: "There are no bad data, only uninterpretable data." This saying is particularly true when you deal with missing data. Missing data can provide valuable information, if interpreted correctly and analyzed properly. The mechanism designed by SAS for handling missing values makes this software a powerful tool for properly analyzing and reporting data. Before going further, let's first define "missing data." Missing data refer to incomplete, invalid, or unusable information from respondents. They abound in health and social science data sets. Often, missing data are the rule rather than the exception in research. In this book, three reasons for missing data are distinguished. Data can be missing because of

1. an absence of information,

2. invalid responses, or

3. unusable responses.

If a survey is timed and a respondent does not have sufficient time to complete the entire survey, say, because he missed the last three questions, then his responses to the last three questions are "missing data." This is the first kind of missing—absence of information.

The second kind of missing data is due to invalid responses. For example, in a questionnaire asking social workers for their years of experience in the profession; one person might give a response of "I don't care." Such a response may well mean something, but as far as the question is concerned, the person has provided no answer. Hence, a missing value of the second type is recorded. Other instances of invalid responses include the following: (1) out-of-range responses, such as "9" on a Likert scale of 1 to 5; (2) nonsense responses, such as "I am a nerd" to the question of occupations; and (3) compound responses, such as "all of the above" on the question of current marital status, implying the respondent is simultaneously single, married, divorced, and separated from his or her spouse!

The third kind of missing data is unusable data. For example, a respondent might write down only "September 1," without the year, for her birth date.

These three (and additional) kinds of missing data can be recorded differently, and therefore distinguished, within the SAS system. Numeric missing values can be differentiated by a period (.), letters A through Z (or a through z, not case sensitive), or the underscore (_). If you do not specify different types of missing data, SAS uses a period (.) to denote numeric missing data. Special codes for missing data are declared by the "MISSING;" statement, usually at the beginning of a SAS program. The following program makes a distinction among three kinds of missing data on the variable income: a, b, and a period (.).

Example 3.1 Three Kinds of Missing Data

```
DATA miss1;
    MISSING a b;              /* Declares codes for missing data */
    INPUT name $ income;
    IF income=. OR income=.a OR income=.b THEN OUTPUT;
        /* If 'income' is missing, then output this observation to data set 'miss1' */
DATALINES;
Alice   .
Alfred  10000
Bob     a
```

```
Dan       50000
Penny     b
RUN;

PROC PRINT DATA=miss1;
RUN;
```

Output 3.1 Three Kinds of Missing Data

```
      The SAS System                                                      1

 Obs      name        income

   1      Alice           .
   2      Bob             A
   3      Penny           B
```

As for character missing values, a period (.) or a blank space can denote a missing value. The following program shows how the missing character values are denoted by either a period (.) or a blank space:

Example 3.2 Missing Character Values

```
DATA miss2;
     INPUT name $ 1-10 sex $;
     IF name=' ' THEN DELETE;     /* If 'name' is missing, then delete this observation */
DATALINES;
Alice      f
Bob        m
.          m                      /* Missing is coded by a period (.)                   */
Brenda     f
           f                      /* Missing is coded by a blank space                  */
RUN;
PROC PRINT DATA=miss2;
RUN;
```

When referring to missing values of a character variable in a conditional statement, single quotes with a blank space in between are needed, as in the statement "IF name =' ' THEN DELETE; ". Therefore, the output of Example 3.2 contains only three observations, those based on Alice, Bob, and Brenda.

Output 3.2 Missing Character Values

```
     The SAS System                                              1

   Obs     name      sex

    1       Alice      f
    2       Bob        m
    3       Brenda     f
```

If you do not specify different types of missing data, SAS uses a period (.) to denote missing data.

3.6 Summary

In this chapter, you were introduced to fundamental concepts in data analysis. These included observations, character variables and character data, numeric variables and numeric data, the data matrix, coding schemes, and missing data. Topics not covered in this chapter are survey theories including sampling methods, desirable sample sizes, and various forms of surveys (e.g., mailing, telephone interviews, e-mail, and Web-based surveys). These topics are left to readers to explore with resources such as Scheuren's (2004) free book *What Is a Survey?*, available from www.whatisasurvey.info. In the next chapter, you will learn how to enter data including missing values into a data matrix, and then to establish a SAS data set and perform simple analyses.

Answers to questions posted in **Section 3.4: Types of Variables**, are as follows:

Numeric variables are (2) monthly income, (3) mileage of your car, and (4) daily usage of Internet phone (measured either by time or by the number of calls made).

(1) PIN number for bank accounts, (5) password for e-mail, and (7) most favorite sports are character variables.

Data collected from (6) attitude toward immigrants and (8) religious beliefs need clarification. In terms of attitude toward immigrants, the surveyor may employ a Likert-type scale of 1 to 5, where 1 means "strongly positive," 2 means "positive," 3 "neutral," 4 "negative," and 5 "strongly negative" to measure a general affective component of the attitude. The use of such a scale makes this variable numeric, as far as SAS analysis is concerned. As far as

Stevens' theory of measurement scales is concerned, Likert-scaled scores are typically treated as ordinal measures.

Alternatively, the survey may present several statements and then ask respondents to indicate if they agree or disagree with each statement. See the following sample statements:

a. Immigrants are contributing members of this country.   Agree   Disagree

b. The economy of this country is weighed down by immigrants.   Agree   Disagree

c. Immigrants have strange lifestyles.   Agree   Disagree

d. I believe our culture is enhanced by the diversity of its people.   Agree   Disagree

By phrasing the response scale as either "Agree" or "Disagree," the surveyor has essentially made each statement a character variable. However, for the purpose of quantifying the underlying attitude toward immigrants, "Agree" responses may be coded as 1 and "Disagree" as 0. Thus, the sum of all responses to statements (a) through (d) above is numeric, indicating the degree to which a respondent agreed with these four statements, and thus, the attitude toward immigrants.

"Religious belief," likewise, can be either numeric or character. If it is measured by types of religious belief, such as "Catholic," "Jewish," "Protestant," or "Other," then its data are character. If it is assessed by the degree of a person's religiosity, then data so defined may be treated as numeric.

So the way you designed an instrument determines the type and quality of information you gather. In turn, the type and quality of information determine the type of analyses and interpretation(s) you may apply to the data. This chain of impacts should be carefully considered when designing a survey instrument.

3.7 Exercises

1. Identify the nature of the following variables as either numeric (N) or character (C):
   a. Paper-and-pencil test of altruism
   b. Top 10 country music songs
   c. Grading in a pass/fail course
   d. Language proficiency in Russian
   e. Daily usage of iPod
   f. School violence
   g. Traffic in downtown LA

    h. Birthplace in the United States or elsewhere
    i. Lottery ticket number
    j. Income tax
    k. Rank in a harp contest
    l. Square footage in a house
    m. Favorite Saturday night TV program

2. If a 5-point scale is to be used to gather information about the following variables, how do you define these five points?
    a. Attitude toward violence and sex on TV
    b. Rating of the current president's performance on the job
    c. NATO's expansion
    d. Legislation limiting political contributions made by political action committees (PAC)
    e. Confidentiality of Web users

3. Based on the scale and scale points defined in Exercise 2 above, develop a coding scheme for data collected on these variables.

4. The following four questions were from a General Social Survey. Ask these questions among 20 of your friends or family members and develop coding schemes for the data you collected:
    a. Were you living at home while you attended the college?
    b. How often do you participate in religious services per month?
    c. Do you think this country should adopt a policy of compulsive military service for young men and women?
    d. Should public elected officers be held accountable for their personal integrity in their personal lives?

5. What improvements can you make to the following short survey that was constructed to measure pain experienced by cancer patients during chemotherapy?

    Age _____   Name _____   Sex _____   Race _____

    a. How well did you sleep last night?_____
    b. How much pain did you usually experience during chemotherapy?
        i.   None
        ii. A little
        iii. More than usual
        iv. A lot

    c. Are you troubled by pain? _____
    d. Are you more susceptible to flu now than before the chemotherapy?

e. How do you deal with pain?
   i. Not much
   ii. Very well
   iii. Not too well
   iv. None of your business

3.8 Answers to Exercises

1. a. Paper-and-pencil test of altruism (N)
   b. Top 10 country music songs (N, if ranks are of interest, or C, if the song titles are of interest)
   c. Grading in a pass/fail course (C)
   d. Language proficiency in Russian (N in terms of score, or C in terms of levels or types of proficiency in Russian)
   e. Daily usage of iPod (N in terms of time and frequency)
   f. School violence (N in terms of degree of violence, C in terms of type of violence)
   g. Traffic in downtown LA (N in terms of traffic flow)
   h. Birthplace in the United States or elsewhere (C)
   i. Lottery ticket number (C)
   j. Income tax (N)
   k. Rank in a harp contest (N)
   l. Square footage in a house (N)
   m. Favorite Saturday night TV program (C, N in terms of Nelson rankings)

2. a. (1 = "Strongly Negative," 2 = "Negative," 3 = "Neutral," 4 = "Positive," 5 = "Strongly Positive")
   b. (1 = "Fail," 2 = "D," 3 = "C," 4 = "B," 5 = "A")
   c. (1 = "Strongly Disagree," 2 = "Disagree," 3 = "Neutral," 4 = "Agree," 5 = "Strongly Agree")
   d. (1 = "Strongly Unsupportive," 2 = "Unsupportive," 3 = "Neutral," 4 = "Supportive," 5 = "Strongly Supportive")
   e. (1 = "Not Guaranteed," 2 = "Rarely Guaranteed," 3 = "Sometimes Guaranteed," 4 = "Frequently Guaranteed," 5 – "Always Guaranteed")

3. a. For questions (a) to (e), the number checked or circled is the number entered into the data matrix.
   b. For questions (a) to (e), a response marked between two points on the scale is coded as an average of the two adjacent numbers.
   c. For questions (a) to (e), a response outside the range of 1 to 5 is considered invalid; therefore, it is interpreted as a missing response.

4. a. Use "Yes" or "No" answer
   b. Use open-ended answer for a numeric value
   c. Use a 5-point scale from "Strongly Not Support" to "Neutral" to "Strongly Support"
   d. Use "Should" or "Should Not" answer

5. a. Use a 5-point scale from "Not Very Well" to "Average" to "Very Well"
   b. Use a 5-point scale from "None" to "Usual" to "A Lot"
   c. Use "Yes" or "No" format
   d. Use "Yes" or "No" format
   e. Use a 5-point scale from "Not Very Well" to "Average" to "Very Well"
   f. State the purpose of this survey in the beginning of the survey.

4

From Data to a SAS Data Set

OBJECTIVE

This chapter demonstrates how to create a SAS data set from raw data. The raw data are either embedded within a SAS program or stored in a location external to the SAS program. Once raw data are read into a SAS program, they become part of a SAS data set. A SAS data set can be subsequently analyzed by SAS statistical procedures or further processed within the DATA step.

4.1 Preparing a Raw Data File

In Chapter 3, you were shown a survey instrument that was constructed to evaluate a research design course, Y777. Say 20 students responded to that instrument; their responses to the first five questions, both *before* and *after* taking the course, and to Questions 16 through 20a (faculty at a university) are used here to illustrate the preparation of a raw data file. Coding schemes were developed in **Section 3.3**, along with their rationales, to help you or the coder to code the raw data into a data matrix. Based on those coding schemes, let's suppose that the 20 students gave the following responses, with blank spaces indicating no response. The gray top row in the data matrix lists variable names; they are not part of the data.

The first column of the data matrix contains <u>id</u> numbers assigned to these 20 students' booklets. Each student's information is represented by a row in the matrix. Each row is an observation. Beyond the <u>id</u> column, the remaining

15 columns represent 15 variables. Thus, <u>a1</u>, <u>a2</u>, ... , <u>a5</u> are five variable names that measure students' ability or knowledge on the first five topics *after* taking the course, whereas <u>b1</u>, <u>b2</u>, ... , <u>b5</u> measure ability or knowledge acquired *before* taking the course. The next four variables, <u>q16</u> to <u>q19</u>, are responses to Questions 16 through 19, respectively; <u>q20a</u> is students' yes or no response to their aspiration to become a faculty member at a university. Blank spaces, as noted before, indicate missing data.

Data matrix for 20 students on the Y777 Course Evaluation Survey

id	a1	a2	a3	a4	a5	b1	b2	b3	b4	b5	q16	q17	q18	q19	q20a
1	4	5	3	5	3	1	2	3	1	1	24	5	1	3	yes
2	4	5	4	5	2	1	2	2	1	1	5	5	1	3	yes
3	5	5	3	4	2	1	3	2	1	1	10	5	1	3	yes
4	3	5	4	4	3	1	4	2	1	2	20	5	1	3	yes
5	5	4	5	4	4	1	4	2	1	1		5	2	3	yes
6	5	5	4	3	5	2	3	3	1	1	30	3	5	3	yes
7	4	5	4	4	4	1	3	3	1	1	17	3	5	3	no
8	3	4	5	4	3	2	3	2	1	1	15	3	5	3	yes
9	4	4	3	5	2	1	3	3	1	1	10	3	5		
10	3	5	4	4	3	1	3	1	2	1		3	2		yes
11	3	4	5	4	3	1	3	2	1	1	25	4	2		no
12	2	5	4	5	4	1	4	2	1	1	20	4	2		yes
13	4	3	4	4	4	1	2	1	3	2	8	4	2	1	yes
14	5	4	3	3	3	2	2	2	1	1	60	4	2	1	yes
15	3	5	4	3	4	3	3	3	1	1	23	4	3	1	
16	3	5	5	4	3	1	3	3	2	2	15	5	1	1	yes
17	4	4	4	4	3	1	3	2	1	1	9	5	1	1	yes
18	4	5	4	5	3	1	4	2	1	1	14	5	1	1	yes
19	3	5	4	3	4	1	3	1	1	1	22	5	1	1	yes
20	2	4	4	3	5						35	5	1	1	no

At this point, you are ready to analyze these data by SAS. There are two ways to bring data into a SAS program: One is by embedding data directly into the SAS program; the other is by preparing a raw data file first and then

referring to this data file in the SAS program. In this chapter, we will demonstrate both approaches. Other data formats, such as Excel® and SPSS®, are
dealt with in Appendix C.

Extracting data from the data matrix into a file creates a raw data file, say
Y777.dat. This data file looks like the following, without the border:

1	4	5	3	5	3	1	2	3	1	1	24	5	1	3	yes
2	4	5	4	5	2	1	2	2	1	1	5	5	1	3	yes
3	5	5	3	4	2	1	3	2	1	1	10	5	1	3	yes
4	3	5	4	4	3	1	4	2	1	2	20	5	1	3	yes
5	5	4	5	4	4	1	4	2	1	1	.	5	2	3	yes
6	5	5	4	3	5	2	3	3	1	1	30	3	5	3	yes
7	4	5	4	4	4	1	3	3	1	1	17	3	5	3	no
8	3	4	5	4	3	2	3	2	1	1	15	3	5	3	yes
9	4	4	3	5	2	1	3	3	1	1	10	3	5	.	.
10	3	5	4	4	3	1	3	1	2	1	.	3	2	.	yes
11	3	4	5	4	3	1	3	2	1	1	25	4	2	.	no
12	2	5	4	5	4	1	4	2	1	1	20	4	2	.	yes
13	4	3	4	4	4	1	2	1	3	2	8	4	2	1	yes
14	5	4	3	3	3	2	2	2	1	1	60	4	2	1	yes
15	3	5	4	3	4	3	3	3	1	1	23	4	3	1	.
16	3	5	5	4	3	1	3	3	2	2	15	5	1	1	yes
17	4	4	4	4	3	1	3	2	1	1	9	5	1	1	yes
18	4	5	4	5	3	1	4	2	1	1	14	5	1	1	yes
19	3	5	4	3	4	1	3	1	1	1	22	5	1	1	yes
20	2	4	4	3	5	.	.	.	.	.	35	5	1	1	no

Adjacent data values are separated by at least one space. Furthermore, the
blank spaces in the original data matrix are now replaced by a period (.).
Periods, as explained in Chapter 3, indicate missing data in SAS. The file,
Y777.dat, contains nothing else but the raw data. It is an ASCII, or text-only,
file. Such a raw data file can be named by a different extension, such as .txt,
or a file name such as Y777.txt. As long as the data file is in an ASCII format, it is a raw data file. Be very careful not to accidentally stick in an empty
line at the bottom of the file due to your habit of hitting the <Return> or

<Enter> key. A data file should not contain variable names. Nor should it contain any word processing keystrokes such as centering or underscore. Next, you will learn how to read Y777.dat into a SAS data set so that data can be analyzed by SAS.

4.2 How to Analyze a Raw Data File in SAS

A raw data file must be read into a SAS data set before it can be analyzed by SAS. In other words, SAS data sets are units of analysis for SAS. To establish a SAS data set from Y777.dat, you need an INFILE statement that refers to the physical location of the file, such as "d:\data\y777.dat". This INFILE statement is followed by the INPUT statement that names variables (also columns) in the data file. Below is a simple SAS program (called Y777.sas) that illustrates both INFILE and INPUT statements and analyzes data by three procedures: PRINT, MEANS, and FREQ.

Example 4.1 Reading Data With INFILE

```
DATA eval;                            /* Establishes a SAS data set called 'eval' */
     INFILE 'd:\data\y777.dat';
     INPUT id $ a1-a5 b1-b5 q16 q17 q18 q19 q20a $;
RUN;
PROC PRINT DATA=eval;                 /* Prints the raw data on the output */
RUN;
PROC MEANS DATA=eval;                 /* Computes descriptive stat for numeric variables */
RUN;
PROC FREQ DATA=eval;                  /* Tabulates frequency for character variable */
     TABLES q20a;
RUN;
```

In Example 4.1, three statements, DATA, INFILE, and INPUT, define a SAS data set called eval. This name, not Y777.dat, is the name you should use when referring to a data set within a SAS program. Multiple SAS data sets can be defined and analyzed within a program. Each is created by specifying a data set name, such as eval, followed by a definition of variables in that data set. The name of a SAS data set is given in the statement "DATA eval;". When naming a SAS data set, you should

- start the name with a letter, from A through Z, or a through z, or an underscore (_); the rest can be letters, numbers, or underscores;
- not use any blanks in a name;
- use no more than 32 characters if your SAS version is 7 or newer;
- not use _NULL_, _DATA_, or _LAST_ as data set names as these are SAS internal data set names;

- choose a name that helps you readily recognize the content or purpose of the data; and
- give every data set a different name.

These same rules apply to naming variables on the INPUT statement. Remember that a SAS program can be written in both upper- and lowercase, including SAS data sets and variable names (refer back to Step 2 of **Section 2.3** in Chapter 2). This book follows certain typographical rules that use uppercase for SAS syntax and lowercase for reader-specified variable names, titles, data set names, and so on, that you can change (refer back to Table 2.1).

The second keyword, INFILE, points to an address where the data file Y777.dat is located. The address is in single quotes followed by a semicolon. The third keyword, INPUT, links raw data values from Y777.dat to variable names. The dollar sign ($) indicates that the preceding variable is a character variable. Thus, both id and q20a are declared as character variables while the rest are numeric. The INFILE statement must precede the INPUT statement.

Once the SAS data set eval is established, the program applies three analysis procedures—PRINT, MEANS, and FREQ—to the data. The PRINT procedure is intended to reproduce all data in the eval data set; the MEANS procedure calculates descriptive statistics, for example, average, standard deviations, minimum, and maximum, of all numeric variables, and the FREQ procedure tabulates the frequency of responses ("Yes" or "No") in categories of q20a—a character variable. In applying PROC MEANS to Likert-scaled data (a1 to a5, b1 to b5, q17 to q19), we are making the assumption that measured responses can be treated as interval-level data. Below is the output (Y777.lst) obtained from the program:

Output 4.1 Reading Data With INFILE

```
                                    The SAS System                                    1

Obs   id   a1   a2   a3   a4   a5   b1   b2   b3   b4   b5   q16   q17   q18   q19   q20a

  1    1    4    5    3    5    3    1    2    3    1    1    24    5     1     3    yes
  2    2    4    5    4    5    2    1    2    2    1    1     5    5     1     3    yes
  3    3    5    5    3    4    2    1    3    2    1    1    10    5     1     3    yes
  4    4    3    5    4    4    3    1    4    2    1    2    20    5     1     3    yes
  5    5    5    4    5    4    4    1    4    2    1    1     .    5     2     3    yes
  6    6    5    5    4    3    5    2    3    3    1    1    30    3     5     3    yes
  7    7    4    5    4    4    4    1    3    3    1    1    17    3     5     3    no
  8    8    3    4    5    4    3    2    3    2    1    1    15    3     5     3    yes
  9    9    4    4    3    5    2    1    3    3    1    1    10    3     5     .
 10   10    3    5    4    4    3    1    3    1    2    1     .    3     2     .    yes
 11   11    3    4    5    4    3    1    3    2    1    1    25    4     2     .    no
 12   12    2    5    4    5    4    1    4    2    1    1    20    4     2     .    yes
 13   13    4    3    4    4    4    1    2    1    3    2     8    4     2     1    yes
 14   14    5    4    3    3    3    2    2    2    1    1    60    4     2     1    yes
```

15	15	3	5	4	3	4	3	3	3	1	1	23	4	3	1	
16	16	3	5	5	4	3	1	3	3	2	2	15	5	1	1	yes
17	17	4	4	4	4	3	1	3	2	1	1	9	5	1	1	yes
18	18	4	5	4	5	3	1	4	2	1	1	14	5	1	1	yes
19	19	3	5	4	3	4	1	3	1	1	1	22	5	1	1	yes
20	20	2	4	4	3	5	.	.	.	.	.	35	5	1	1	no

The SAS System   2⁻

The MEANS Procedure

Variable	N	Mean	Std Dev	Minimum	Maximum
a1	20	3.6500000	0.9333020	2.0000000	5.0000000
a2	20	4.5500000	0.6048053	3.0000000	5.0000000
a3	20	4.0000000	0.6488857	3.0000000	5.0000000
a4	20	4.0000000	0.7254763	3.0000000	5.0000000
a5	20	3.3500000	0.8750940	2.0000000	5.0000000
b1	19	1.2631579	0.5619515	1.0000000	3.0000000
b2	19	3.0000000	0.6666667	2.0000000	4.0000000
b3	19	2.1578947	0.6882472	1.0000000	3.0000000
b4	19	1.2105263	0.5353034	1.0000000	3.0000000
b5	19	1.1578947	0.3746343	1.0000000	2.0000000
q16	18	20.1111111	12.7504966	5.0000000	60.0000000
q17	20	4.2500000	0.8506963	3.0000000	5.0000000
q18	20	2.2000000	1.5423837	1.0000000	5.0000000
q19	16	2.0000000	1.0327956	1.0000000	3.0000000

The SAS System   3

The FREQ Procedure

q20a	Frequency	Percent	Cumulative Frequency	Cumulative Percent
no	3	16.67	3	16.67
yes	15	83.33	18	100.00

Frequency Missing = 2

Page 1 output results from PROC PRINT, page 2 shows the results from PROC MEANS and page 3 shows the results from PROC FREQ. Since PROC PRINT merely reproduces what is already in Y777.dat, you don't find too many surprises here, except for the first column. The first column is headed by the name **Obs**. This column is added by the SAS compiler for keeping track of observation numbers.

Page 2 output shows a summary of numeric data in the eval data set, because PROC MEANS is applicable to numeric variables only. The heading **N** stands for valid (or nonmissing) data points, **Mean** is the arithmetic average, **Std Dev** is the standard deviation, **Minimum** is the smallest value, and **Maximum** is the largest value. By examining this summary table, you can quickly form ideas about general trends in the data. For example, the class as a whole improved in terms of their knowledge about and ability to apply various ANOVA models and designs because a1 through a5 means are higher than their corresponding b1 through b5 means. Furthermore, on average, students studied approximately 20.11 hours per week on class materials (q16). The class as a whole described their aptitude in statistics to be almost at an expert level (mean of 4.25 on q17), better than their average attitude toward learning statistics (mean of 2.20 on q18), and higher than their self-disclosed anxiety about learning statistics (mean of 2.00 on q19). Finally, the majority of students aspired to become a faculty member at a university (number of yes = 15, or 83.33% out of 18 students who responded to q20a). Two students missed this question.

You can also detect coding errors by noticing (a) an out-of-range minimum or maximum, (b) unusually large or small standard deviations, (c) an extremely low response rate, (d) an odd relationship between mean and standard deviation, (e) a situation in which variables that you thought were character variables, such as id, show up in the table as numeric variables, and so on. Before you conduct any analysis of the data, I'd recommend that PRINT, MEANS, and FREQ procedures be applied once to data so that you may catch and correct all coding errors. The FREQ procedure is particularly well suited for character variables and ordinal-level data. Now, let's see what the Log window has for you!

Log 4.1 Reading Data With INFILE

```
Part (A)

1          DATA eval;
2              INFILE 'd:\data\y777.dat';
3              INPUT id $ a1-a5 b1-b5 q16 q17 q18 q19 q20a $;
4          RUN;

NOTE: The infile 'd:\data\y777.dat' is:
      File Name=d:\data\y777.dat,
      RECFM=V,LRECL=256

NOTE: 20 records were read from the infile 'd:\data\y777.dat'.
      The minimum record length was 35.
      The maximum record length was 35.
NOTE: The data set WORK.EVAL has 20 observations and 16 variables.
NOTE: DATA statement used (Total process time):
      real time          0.08 seconds
      cpu time           0.01 seconds

Part (B)

5          PROC PRINT DATA=eval;      /* Prints the raw data on the output */
6          RUN;
```

```
NOTE: There were 20 observations read from the data set WORK.EVAL.
NOTE: The PROCEDURE PRINT printed page 1.
NOTE: PROCEDURE PRINT used (Total process time):
      real time            0.16 seconds
      cpu time             0.01 seconds

Part (C)

7            PROC MEANS DATA=eval;     /* Computes descriptive stat for numeric variables */
8            RUN;

NOTE: There were 20 observations read from the data set WORK.EVAL.
NOTE: The PROCEDURE MEANS printed page 2.
NOTE: PROCEDURE MEANS used (Total process time):
      real time            0.52 seconds
      cpu time             0.09 seconds

Part (D)

9            PROC FREQ DATA=eval;      /* Tabulates frequency for character variable */
10               TABLES q20a;
11           RUN;

NOTE: There were 20 observations read from the data set WORK.EVAL.
NOTE: The PROCEDURE FREQ printed page 3.
NOTE: PROCEDURE FREQ used (Total process time):
      real time            0.01 seconds
      cpu time             0.02 seconds
```

Log 4.1 displays the processing history of the SAS program, starting from Line 1 through Line 11—those SAS statements from Example 4.1. For the purpose of explanation, the log is divided into four parts: (A), (B), (C), and (D).

Part (A) identifies the external location of the raw data file, Y777.dat, reads its content (20 observations, 16 variables, the minimum record length is 33 and the maximum is 35), and establishes a SAS data set based on Y777.dat. This SAS data set is internally recognized by the SAS compiler as WORK.EVAL, though you can refer to it simply as eval, as in Example 4.1. This step took 0.08 seconds real time or 0.01 seconds CPU time.

Part (B) presents information on the application of PROC PRINT to the SAS data set WORK.EVAL, or simply eval. The PRINT procedure recognizes 20 observations in the data set, and the result is printed on page 1 of Output 4.1 (also the Output window). The processing took 0.16 seconds real time or 0.01 seconds CPU time.

Part (C) presents information of the processing of the same SAS data set by PROC MEANS. Again, the MEANS procedure recognizes 20 observations in the data set and sends the result to page 2 of Output 4.1. The processing of the MEANS procedure took 0.52 seconds real time or 0.09 seconds CPU time. Last, Part (D) presents information of PROC FREQ's processing that took 0.01 seconds real time or 0.02 seconds CPU time. Results of PROC FREQ are shown on page 3 of Output 4.1.

4.3 How to Analyze Data That Are Embedded in a SAS Program

Sometimes you may wish to embed raw data into a SAS program. To accomplish this, rewrite the Y777.sas program into the following (Y777a.sas):

Example 4.2 Reading Data in a SAS Program

```
DATA eval;
     INPUT id $ a1-a5 b1-b5 q16 q17 q18 q19 q20a $;
DATALINES;
1   4 5 3 5 3 1 2 3 1 1 24 5 1 3 yes
2   4 5 4 5 2 1 2 2 1 1  5 5 1 3 yes
3   5 5 3 4 2 1 3 2 1 1 10 5 1 3 yes
4   3 5 4 4 3 1 4 2 1 2 20 5 1 3 yes
5   5 4 5 4 4 1 4 2 1 1  . 5 2 3 yes
6   5 5 4 3 5 2 3 3 1 1 30 3 5 3 yes
7   4 5 4 4 4 1 3 3 1 1 17 3 5 3 no
8   3 4 5 4 3 2 3 2 1 1 15 3 5 3 yes
9   4 4 3 5 2 1 3 3 1 1 10 3 5 . .
10  3 5 4 4 3 1 3 1 2 1  . 3 2 . yes
11  3 4 5 4 3 1 3 2 1 1 25 4 2 . no
12  2 5 4 5 4 1 4 2 1 1 20 4 2 . yes
13  4 3 4 4 4 1 2 1 3 2  8 4 2 1 yes
14  5 4 3 3 3 2 2 2 1 1 60 4 2 1 yes
15  3 5 4 3 4 3 3 3 1 1 23 4 3 1 .
16  3 5 5 4 3 1 3 3 2 2 15 5 1 1 yes
17  4 4 4 4 3 1 3 2 1 1  9 5 1 1 yes
18  4 5 4 5 3 1 4 2 1 1 14 5 1 1 yes
19  3 5 4 3 4 1 3 1 1 1 22 5 1 1 yes
20  2 4 4 3 5 . . . . . 35 5 1 1 no
RUN;
PROC PRINT DATA=eval;                    /* Prints the raw data on the output */
RUN;
PROC MEANS DATA=eval;                    /* Computes descriptive stat for numeric variables */
RUN;
PROC FREQ DATA=eval;                     /* Tabulates frequency for character variable */
     TABLES q20a;
RUN;
```

Note that the INFILE statement is now replaced by the DATALINES statement, placed after the INPUT statement and before the raw data. The first RUN; statement concludes the DATA step and issues the go-ahead to the SAS compiler to establish the SAS data set called eval. As before, PROC PRINT, MEANS, and FREQ follow the establishment of the eval data set. The Output 4.2 is identical to Output 4.1; hence, it is not repeated here. Now, let's examine Log 4.2 to find out how it is different from Log 4.1.

Log 4.2 Reading Data in a SAS Program

```
Part (A)

1          DATA eval;
2              INPUT id $ a1-a5 b1-b5 q16 q17 q18 q19 q20a $;
3          DATALINES;
```

```
NOTE: The data set WORK.EVAL has 20 observations and 16 variables.
NOTE: DATA statement used (Total process time):
      real time              0.09 seconds
      cpu time               0.08 seconds
```

Part (B)

```
24           RUN;
25
26           PROC PRINT DATA=eval;     /* Prints the raw data on the output */

27           RUN;

NOTE: There were 20 observations read from the data set WORK.EVAL.
NOTE: The PROCEDURE PRINT printed page 1.
NOTE: PROCEDURE PRINT used (Total process time):
      real time              0.13 seconds
      cpu time               0.10 seconds
```

Part (C)

```
28           PROC MEANS DATA=eval;     /* Computes descriptive stat for numeric variables */
29           RUN;

NOTE: There were 20 observations read from the data set WORK.EVAL.
NOTE: The PROCEDURE MEANS printed page 2.
NOTE: PROCEDURE MEANS used (Total process time):
      real time              0.14 seconds
      cpu time               0.08 seconds
```

Part (D)

```
30           PROC FREQ DATA=eval;      /* Tabulates frequency for character variable */
31               TABLES q20a;
32           RUN;

NOTE: There were 20 observations read from the data set WORK.EVAL.
NOTE: The PROCEDURE FREQ printed page 3.
NOTE: PROCEDURE FREQ used (Total process time):
      real time              0.11 seconds
      cpu time               0.02 seconds
```

For the purpose of explanation, the log is again divided into four parts: (A), (B), (C), and (D). If you look closely, you will note that these four parts are quite similar to their corresponding parts in Log 4.1. Two differences still remain: In **Part (A)**, Log 4.2 does not identify an external location for the raw data file (because there is none existing) or record lengths, and in **Part (B)**, the line starts as 24 because data records take up the preceding 20 lines from 4 to 23—one line per record.

Embedding raw data into a SAS program has both pros and cons. The advantage is that data are right there for you to inspect and verify. The disadvantage is that processing raw data in a SAS program can be time-consuming, especially with large data sets. So my advice for you is to use the embedded data approach once to verify data carefully to ensure 100% data accuracy. Afterward, you may save raw data into a data file and retrieve the file with the INFILE statement in subsequent analyses. When you process a large data set or data previously verified in a SAS program, it is more efficient to use the INFILE approach than the DATALINES approach. Ensuring the accuracy of data is the first, and also the most important, step in data analysis. Chapter 6 includes additional strategies for verifying data and debugging SAS programs; stay tuned.

4.4 The INPUT Statement

Regardless of which approach you take to bring raw data into a SAS data set, the key lies in the INPUT statement. The INPUT statement interprets data as variable values. In this section, you will learn three styles of the INPUT statement; each is suitable for certain data matrix structures.

(1) The List Input Style

The list input style reads data sequentially according to the order of variable names listed on the INPUT statement. Specifically,

- variable names are listed in the same order as variable values in the data matrix;
- the dollar sign ($) is used to indicate that the preceding variable is a character variable;
- values of a character variable cannot exceed 8 characters (this default can be overriden by the LENGTH statement; see the example below);
- sequential variable names are represented by the first and the last names with a hyphen (-) in between, such as INPUT name $ test1-test10; and
- missing values must be recorded by a period (.).

Example 4.3 List Input Style

```
LENGTH name $ 9;                    /* Declaring the length of 'name' values */
INPUT name $ sex $ age $ height $ weight;
```

When the list input style is interpreted according to Example 4.3,

- data values must be separated by at least one blank space. Hence, the first data record below is correct, the second is incorrect:

Columns	1	2	3	4	5	6	7	8	9	10	11	12	13	14	15	16	17	18	19	20	21	22
Correct	A	l	i	c	e						f		1	4		6	8		1	0	0	
Incorrect	A	l	i	c	e						f		1	4	6	8			1	0	0	

- missing character or numeric values must be represented by a period (.), not blanks. Hence, the first data record below is correct, the second is incorrect:

Columns	1	2	3	4	5	6	7	8	9	10	11	12	13	14	15	16	17	18	19	20	21	22
Correct	A	l	i	c	e						f				.		6	8		1	0	0	
Incorrect	A	l	i	c	e						f						6	8		1	0	0	

- the sequence of variable values in the data matrix must be the same as the variables listed on the INPUT statement. Hence, the first data record below is correct, the second is incorrect:

Columns	1	2	3	4	5	6	7	8	9	10	11	12	13	14	15	16	17	18	19	20	21	22
Correct	A	l	i	c	e						f		1	4		6	8		1	0	0	
Incorrect	f						A	l	i	c	e		1	4		6	8		1	0	0	

- character values should not contain embedded blanks. Hence, the first data record below is correct, the second is incorrect:

Columns	1	2	3	4	5	6	7	8	9	10	11	12	13	14	15	16	17	18	19	20	21	22
Correct	O	.	J	.							m		1	4		6	8		1	0	0	
Incorrect	O		J								m		1	4		6	8		1	0	0	

Example 4.3a List Input Style With Single Embedded Blanks

If the modifier "&" is added after "$", such as name $ & ;, in the example below, character values containing single embedded blanks can be read in the list input style.

```
LENGTH name $ 9;                    /* Declaring the length of 'name' values */
INPUT name $ & ;
```

In this case, embedded blanks in character variable values must be limited to one blank. Hence, the first four data records below are correct, but the fifth record is incorrect in reading the name "O.J.Doe", "O J Doe", "O JDoe", or "OJ Doe" into the SAS data set because it contains two blank spaces between "O" and "J".

Columns	1	2	3	4	5	6	7	8	9	10	11	12	13	14	15	16	17	18	19	20	21	22
Correct	O	.	J	.	D	o	e															
Correct	O		J		D	o	e															
Correct	O		J	D	o	e																
Correct	O	J		D	o	e																
Incorrect	O			J	D	o	e															

The list input style is the easiest way to write an INPUT statement. It has limitations though, because it requires that adjacent data values be separated by blank spaces and that embedded blanks be single in character values with the & modifier. Fortunately, these limitations are overcome by the column input style.

(2) The Column Input Style

The column input style reads data according to their locations in a data matrix. That is, each variable on the INPUT statement is followed by the column or columns in which its values are located. Specifically,

- variable names are followed by column numbers in which data values are located in each data record (or observation defined in **Section 3.3: Coding the Data**);
- the dollar sign ($) is used to indicate that the preceding variable is a character variable;
- variable names can be listed in any order;
- data values, or parts of data values, can be reread; and
- missing values are best handled by a period (.), though they can be left blank.

All three INPUT statements below read data identically, namely, six variables—initial, name, sex, age, height, and weight—each according to its own location specified by the column number on data records.

Example 4.4a Column Input Style

```
INPUT initial $ 1 name $ 1-10 sex $ 11 age 13-14 height 16-17 weight 19-21;
```

Example 4.4b Column Input Style

```
INPUT sex $ 11 initial $ 1 name $ 1-10 age 13-14 height 16-17 weight 19-21;
```

Example 4.4c Column Input Style

```
INPUT name $ 1-10 initial $ 1 sex $ 11 age 13-14 height 16-17 weight 19-21;
```

When the column input style is used,

- data values must be located in the columns specified on the INPUT statement. Thus, according to Example 4.4, the first data record is correct while the second is incorrect:

Columns	1	2	3	4	5	6	7	8	9	10	11	12	13	14	15	16	17	18	19	20	21	22
Correct	A	l	i	c	e						f		1	4		6	8		1	0	0	
Incorrect	A	l	i	c	e		f		1	4		6	8		1	0	0					

- missing character or numeric values can be left as blanks. Thus, according to Examples 4.4a to 4.4c, both data records below are correct:

Columns	1	2	3	4	5	6	7	8	9	10	11	12	13	14	15	16	17	18	19	20	21	22
Correct	A	l	i	c	e						f					6	8		1	0	0	
Correct	A	l	i	c	e						f			.		6	8		1	0	0	

- embedded blanks are allowed in character data. Thus, according to Examples 4.4a to 4.4c, both data records below are correct:

Columns	1	2	3	4	5	6	7	8	9	10	11	12	13	14	15	16	17	18	19	20	21	22
Correct	A	l	i	c	e		M	a	u		f					6	8		1	0	0	
Correct	A	l	i	c	e	_	M	a	u		f			.		6	8		1	0	0	

- the length of character values can range from 1 to 32,767 bytes, including blanks. Thus, both data records below are correct for the INPUT statement, INPUT address $ 1-100;.

Correct	My address–Apartment #28, Woodbridge Building, 100 Main Street, USA town, IN 47406-4356
Correct	P.O. Box 12345, Springfield, Illinois, 60612 U.S.A.

The column input style works well with data already in a structured format. Unlike the list input style, it does not require that adjacent data values be separated by at least one blank space. Character values can have blanks embedded in them; the length of character values can be up to 32,767 bytes. Missing values need not be recorded by a period (.). The only drawback with this style is its rigidity. If data values are off by one or more columns, the entire observation will be misread by SAS. For this reason, it is essential that data be read correctly into a SAS data set before they are further analyzed or interpreted.

(3) The Formatted Input Style

This input style reads data to data formats prespecified by SAS. Specifically, the following apply:

- Variable values are read according to pointer controls and informats.
- Pointer controls move to a specific column or line in data to find the variable value (see Table 4.1).
- Informats define a format for reading variable values (see Table 4.1).
- Sequential variables sharing the same informat are grouped in parentheses.
- The dollar sign ($) is used to indicate that the preceding variable is a character variable.
- Character values can be as long as 32,767 bytes, and embedded blanks are allowed.
- Sequential variable names are represented by the first and the last names with a hyphen (-) in between.
- Missing values are best handled by the period (.), though they can be left blank.

Table 4.1   Summary of Commonly Used Pointer Controls and Informats

	Symbol	Meaning	Example
Pointer controls	@n	Go to the *n*th column.	`INPUT @1 name $ @11 sex $ @13 age @16 height @19 weight;`
	+n	Skip the next *n* columns.	`INPUT name $ +3 sex $ +1 age +1 height +1 weight;`
	#n	Go to the *n*th record or line.	`INPUT name $ #2 sex $ #3 age height weight;`
	/	Skip to the next record.	`INPUT name $ / sex $ / age height weight;`
Informats	w.	Specifies width of a numeric variable.	`INPUT age 2. height 2. weight 3.;`
	w.d	Specifies width of a numeric variable with *d* decimal places.	`INPUT height 3.1 weight 4.1;`
	$ w.	Specifies width of a character variable.	`INPUT name $ 20. sex $ 1.;`
	Ew.d	Specifies width of a numeric variable value stored in the scientific notation with *d* decimal places.	`INPUT @1 income E10.;`
	BZw.d	Converts blanks in numeric values to zeros.	`INPUT @1 income BZ10.2;`
	COMMAw.d	Removes all embedded characters in a numeric value and converts left parenthesis to a minus sign (–). Numeric values are read in *w* width with *d* decimal places, if there is no decimal point present.	`INPUT @1 income COMMA10.2;`
	DATEw.	Number of days since January 1, 1960. Data expressed in *ddmmyy* or *ddmmyyyy*.	`INPUT @10 days DATE9.;` `[31DEC2007 will return a value of 17531]`
	MMDDYYw.	Number of days since January 1, 1960. Data expressed in *mmddyy* or *mmddyyyy*.	`INPUT @10 days MMDDYY10.;` `[12/31/2007 will return a value of 17531]`
	DDMMYYw.	Number of days since January 1, 1960. Data expressed in *ddmmyy* or *ddmmyyyy*.	`INPUT @10 days DDMMYY10.;` `[31/12/2007 will return a value of 17531]`
	TIMEw.	Number of seconds past midnight. Data expressed in *hours:minutes:seconds*.	`INPUT @20 seconds TIME8.;` `[13:05:00 will return a value of 47100]`
	DATETIMEw.	Number of seconds past midnight of January 1, 1960. Data expressed in *ddmmyy hours:minutes:seconds*.	`INPUT @20 seconds DATATIME18.;` `[01JAN2008/00:00:00 will return a value of 1514764800]`

Additional informats and pointer controls for the INPUT statement are found in *SAS Help and Documentation* or in Chapters 5 and 7, respectively, of *SAS 9.1.3 Language Reference: Dictionary* (SAS Institute Inc., 2006b). When numeric data contain a decimal point, the data value overrides the informat used, such as w.d, Ew.d, BZw.d, or COMMAw.d. Below are examples of the formatted input style.

Example 4.5a Formatted Input Style

```
INPUT name $ 10. @12 sex $ 1. +5 age 2. +3 height;
```

This reads the following data records and saves data values as shown in Output 4.5a:

1	2	3	4	5	6	7	8	9	10	11	12	13	14	15	16	17	18	19	20	21	22	23	24	25	26	27	28	29	30
A	l	i	c	e							f						1	4				6	8						
						B	o	b			m							.				3	0						
A	n	n	a		M	a	r	i	e								1	0				5	5						

Output 4.5a Formatted Input Style

```
                    The SAS System                                      1

        Obs     name            sex     age     height

          1     Alice            f       14       68
          2     Bob              m        .       30
          3     Anna Marie               10       55
```

Example 4.5b Formatted Input Style

```
INPUT #1 name $ 10. / @1 price E7. #3 profit 6.2;
```

This reads the following data records, three records per observation, and saves data values as shown in Output 4.5b:

1	2	3	4	5	6	7	8	9	10	11	12	13	14	15	16	17	18	19	20	21	22	23	24	25	26	27	28	29	30
A	l	i	c	e																									
	1	2	3	E	2																								
5	0	0	7	8																									
						B	o	b																					
	9	.	9	9	E	5																							
-	3	0	0	0	0																								
A	n	n	a		M	a	r	i	e																				
-	1	0	0	0	0																								

Output 4.5b Formatted Input Style

```
            The SAS System                                        1

    Obs    name            price      profit

     1     Alice           12300      500.78
     2     Bob            999000     -300.00
     3     Anna Marie          .     -100.00
```

Example 4.5c Formatted Input Style

```
INPUT name $ 10. @12 sex $ 1. address $ 13-22 +3 age 2.
      @30 income COMMA7.;
```

This reads the following data records and saves data values as shown in Output 4.5c:

1	2	3	4	5	6	7	8	9	10	11	12	13	14	15	16	17	18	19	20	21	22	23	24	25	26	27	28	29	30	31	32	33	34	35	36
A	l	i	c	e							f	P	.	O	.		B	o	x	#	5				1	4			5						
						B	o	b			m																		$		0	.	0	0	
A	n	n	a		M	a	r	i	e			1	3		M	a	i	n		S	t				1	9			1	0	0	,	0	0	0

Output 4.5c Formatted Input Style

```
                    The SAS System                                1

    Obs    name          sex     address      age    income

     1     Alice          f      P.O. Box#5    14        5
     2     Bob            m                     .        0
     3     Anna Marie            13 Main St    19   100000
```

Example 4.5d Formatted Input Style

```
INPUT address $ 13-22 @1 name $ 10. @12 sex $ 1. age 26-27 income 30-36;
```

This reads the following data records and saves data values as shown in Output 4.5d:

1	2	3	4	5	6	7	8	9	10	11	12	13	14	15	16	17	18	19	20	21	22	23	24	25	26	27	28	29	30	31	32	33	34	35	36
A	l	i	c	e							f	P	.	O	.		B	o	x	#	5				1	4			5						
					B	o	b				m																		0	.	0	0			
A	n	n	a		M	a	r	i	e			1	3		M	a	i	n		S	t				1	9			1	0	0	0	0	0	0

Output 4.5d Formatted Input Style

```
                         The SAS System                                    1

   Obs        address       name          sex     age      income

    1       P.O. Box#5     Alice           f       14          5
    2                      Bob             m       .           0
    3       13 Main St     Anna Marie              19     100000
```

Example 4.5e Formatted Input Style

```
INPUT name $ 1-10 (item1-item4)(1.);
```

This reads the following data records and saves data values as shown in Output 4.5e:

1	2	3	4	5	6	7	8	9	10	11	12	13	14	15	16	17	18	19	20	21	22	23	24	25	26	27	28	29	30
A	l	i	c	e							3	4	5																
					B	o	b				1																		
A	n	n	a		M	a	r	i	e	1	.	3																	

Output 4.5e Formatted Input Style

```
                        The SAS System                                    1

      Obs      name         item1     item2     item3     item4

       1       Alice           .          3         4         5
       2       Bob             .          .         .         1
       3       Anna Marie      1          .         3         .
```

Each input style has its advantages and disadvantages. The list input style is the easiest to write; it imposes no column restrictions on data layout. However, it is restrictive regarding the length of a character value or blanks embedded in character values. The formatted input style is more flexible than either the list or the column style in reading nonstandard data. Yet it requires the specification of pointer controls and informats. So why not mix up styles, as shown in Examples 4.5c through 4.5e?

4.5 Practical Considerations

• Reading multiple records into a single observation

A record is a line in your data file. It usually corresponds to a row in the data matrix. Records are typically separated by a hard <Return>. If a massive amount of information was gathered from individuals, as in the census survey, it is necessary to store all data on two or more records. In this case, you have several methods of reading multiple records into a single observation. Each method assumes that equal numbers of records are used for all individuals. Examples 4.6 to 4.8 below read values for four variables, from three records.

Example 4.6 Using a Slash (/) to Advance to the Next Record

```
INPUT name $ 10. / address $ 1-10 / price E7. profit 6.2;
```

This reads the following data records, three records per observation, and saves data values as shown in Output 4.6:

1	2	3	4	5	6	7	8	9	10	11	12	13	14	15	16	17	18	19	20	21	22	23	24	25	26	27	28	29	30
A	l	i	c	e																									
P	.	O	.		B	o	x	#	5																				
1	2	3	E	2			5	0	0	7	8																		
					B	o	b																						
9	.	9	9	E	5		-	3	0	0	0	0																	
A	n	n	a		M	a	r	i	e																				
1	3		M	a	i	n		S	t																				
							-	1	0	0	0	0																	

Output 4.6 Using a Slash (/) to Advance to the Next Record

```
                        The SAS System                                    1

    Obs     name             address         price      profit

     1      Alice          P.O. Box#5        12300      500.78
     2      Bob                              999000    -300.00
     3      Anna Marie     13 Main St           .      -100.00
```

Example 4.7 Using the Pointer Control (#n) to Advance

Use the pointer control (#n) to advance to the first column of the nth record; the highest n is the total number of records:

```
INPUT #3 price E7. profit 6.2 #2 address $ 1-10 #1 name $ 10.;
```

This reads the data records in Example 4.6 and saves data values as shown in Output 4.6.

Example 4.8 Using INPUT Statements to Advance

Use as many INPUT statements as there are records; the order of INPUT statements matches the order of data records in the raw data file. Thus, the following three input statements read <u>name</u> as a character variable from the first record from Columns 1 through 10, <u>address</u> as a character variable from the second record in Columns 1 through 10, <u>price</u> as a numeric variable from the third record in scientific notation, in Columns 1 through 7 and finally <u>profit</u> also as a numeric variable from the third record, in six columns width with 2 decimal places, from Columns 8 through 13.

```
INPUT name $ 10.;
INPUT address $ 1-10;
INPUT price E7. profit 6.2;
```

These read the data records in Example 4.6 and save data values as shown in Output 4.6.

- Reading multiple observations from a single record

In certain instances, data are sparse for each individual. It is therefore practical to read several observations onto a single record in order to save time in typing. How can you still separate one observation from another in this case? The answer lies in the double trailing at sign (or @@). The @@ symbol holds an input data line till the pointer moves past the end of the line. In the example below, each observation is formed from one <u>group</u> value and one <u>score</u> value. There are altogether 12 observations, four on each data record, and also four from each group (see Output 4.9).

Example 4.9 Using @@ to Read Multiple Observations

```
DATA double;
     INPUT group $ score @@;
DATALINES;
1   67  1   87  1   98  1   50
2   44  2   67  2   49  2   82
3   99  3   98  3   88  3   69
RUN;
PROC PRINT DATA=double; RUN;
```

Output 4.9 Using @@ to Read Multiple Observations

```
                                                            1
 Obs     group     score

   1       1         67
   2       1         87
```

```
        3         1         98
        4         1         50
        5         2         44
        6         2         67
        7         2         49
        8         2         82
        9         3         99
       10         3         98
       11         3         88
       12         3         69
```

- Separating data records by levels or types

When data records are mixed, for example, when some are about a county while others are about its residents, you need a single trailing at sign (@ symbol) and several INPUT statements to sort data according to their levels or types. In the example below, the variable type indicates whether the record is about a county (type='c') or about its residents (type='r'). If the record is about a county, that is, type='c', then the second INPUT statement is executed. If, however, type='r', then the third INPUT statement is executed.

Example 4.10 Separating Data Records

```
DATA single;
     INPUT type $ 1. @;
        IF type='c' THEN INPUT name $ pop COMMA10.;
        ELSE IF type='r' THEN INPUT income 10. tax 8.;
DATALINES;
c  Monroe      8,000
c  Green      15,340
r  19000       3520
r  65000      20000
RUN;
PROC PRINT DATA=single; RUN;
```

Output 4.10 Separating Data Records

```
                     The SAS System                              1

   Obs    type     name      pop     income     tax

    1      c      Monroe    8000        .         .
    2      c      Green    15340        .         .
    3      r                   .      19000     3520
    4      r                   .      65000    20000
```

The use of a single trailing @ is to hold each data record in an input buffer till the next INPUT statement is processed. The record put on hold is released by the INPUT statement that does not have the @ symbol. An input buffer is a memory area into which each record of raw data is stored immediately after each INPUT statement is executed.

- Sharing identical informat by several variables

At times, it is convenient to "recycle" the same informat with several variables. For example, the first 10 items on the <u>Course Evaluation Survey</u> always yield responses between 1 and 5. For these responses, the same informat, say "1.", may be applied to all these items. Hence, you may choose any of the following three INPUT statements to read these responses into a SAS data set.

Example 4.11 Sharing Identical Informat by Several Variables

```
(a)  INPUT (a1-a10)(1.)  (b1-b10)(1.);
(b)  INPUT (a1-a10 b1-b10)  (20*1.) ;
(c)  INPUT (a1-a10 b1-b10)  (1.) ;
```

The three INPUT statements (a) through (c) read <u>a1</u> to <u>a10</u> and <u>b1</u> to <u>b10</u> variables by the informat of one column per variable (see the data record layout below).

1	2	3	4	5	6	7	8	9	10	11	12	13	14	15	16	17	18	19	20	21	22	23	24	25	26	27	28	29	30	31	32	33	34	35	36	37	38	39
a1	a2	a3	a4	a5	a6	a7	a8	a9	a10	b1	b2	b3	b4	b5	b6	b7	b8	b9	b10																			

A more complex example using informats repetitively is as follows:

Example 4.12 Using Informats Repeatedly

```
INPUT (x1-x4)  (+2 3. +3 $5.)  (x5-x10)  (2. +1);
```

According to the INPUT statement above, two spaces are skipped before <u>x1</u> and <u>x3</u> are read by the "3." informat, whereas <u>x2</u> and <u>x4</u> are read by the "$5." informat. Between <u>x1</u> and <u>x2</u> there are three spaces. Between <u>x2</u> and <u>x3</u> there are two spaces. By the same logic, <u>x5</u>, <u>x6</u>, <u>x7</u>, . . . , <u>x10</u> are all read by the "2." informat with a single space between adjacent variables (see the data record layout on the next page).

1	2	3	4	5	6	7	8	9	10	11	12	13	14	15	16	17	18	19	20	21	22	23	24	25	26	27	28	29	30	31	32	33	34	35	36	37	38	39	40	41	42	43	44	45
			x1					x2 (character)				x3				x4 (character)			x5			x6			x7			x8			x9			x10		

When using the same informat repeatedly to read several variables, you need to enclose the variables and the informat in parentheses. The INPUT statement is applied in a cyclic manner to all variables in parentheses till all are read into a SAS data set.

- Reading blanks as missing

The MISSOVER option in Example 4.13 is used with the list input style to prevent SAS from going to a new data record, even when it does not find values in the current record for all variables listed on the INPUT statement.

Example 4.13 Using MISSOVER to Read Blanks as Missing

```
DATA miss;
    INFILE DATALINES MISSOVER;
    INPUT name $ item1-item5;
DATALINES;
Alice  1 2 3
Bob      5 5 5 5
Cindy  1 1 1 1
RUN;
PROC PRINT DATA=miss; RUN;
```

Output 4.13 Using MISSOVER to Read Blanks as Missing

```
            The SAS System                                        1

    Obs    name     item1    item2    item3    item4    item5

     1     Alice      1        2        3        .        .
     2     Bob        5        5        5        5        5
     3     Cindy      1        1        1        1        1
```

Because MISSOVER is specified, Alice now has data on item1, item2, and item3; her scores on item4 and item5 are missing, shown in Output 4.13 as a period (.). Bob and Cindy are shown to have complete information on all five items, as expected. The MISSOVER option is part of an INFILE statement, used in conjunction with the list input style. The keyword DATALINES on the INFILE statement is to direct the SAS compiler to read data lines that begin immediately following the DATALINES statement.

If Alice, Bob, and Cindy's data have been stored externally, say, at "d:\data\miss.dat", Example 4.13 needs to be modified into Example 4.13a. Try executing this program on your own and make sure the results are identical to Output 4.13.

Example 4.13a Using MISSOVER in INFILE to Read Blanks as Missing

```
DATA miss;
     INFILE 'd:\data\miss.dat' MISSOVER;
     INPUT name $ item1-item5;
RUN;
PROC PRINT DATA=miss; RUN;
```

Example 4.14 Using TRUNCOVER to Read Blanks as Missing

Similar to MISSOVER, the TRUNCOVER option in Example 4.14 is used
with the column or the formatted input style to prevent SAS from going to
a new data record, even when it does not find values in the current record
for all variables listed on the INPUT statement.

```
DATA miss;
     INFILE DATALINES TRUNCOVER;
     INPUT name $ 1-7 @8 (item1-item5)(2.0);
DATALINES;
Alice  1 2 3
Bob    5 5 5 5 5
Cindy  1 1 1 1 1
RUN;
PROC PRINT DATA=miss; RUN;
```

Output 4.14 Using TRUNCOVER to Read Blanks as Missing

```
                    The SAS System                                      1

Obs     name      item1    item2    item3    item4    item5

 1      Alice       1        2        3        .        .
 2      Bob         5        5        5        5        5
 3      Cindy       1        1        1        1        1
```

Again, if Alice's, Bob's, and Cindy's data have been stored according to the
column style specified in Example 4.14 externally, say, at "d:\data\miss.dat",
Example 4.14 needs to be modified into Example 4.14a. Try executing this program on your own and make sure the results are identical to Output 4.14.

Example 4.14a Using TRUNCOVER in INFILE to Read Blanks as Missing

```
DATA miss;
     INFILE 'd:\data\miss.dat' TRUNCOVER;
     INPUT name $ 1-7 @8 (item1-item5)(2.0);
RUN;
PROC PRINT DATA=miss; RUN;
```

So far in this chapter, you have created four SAS data sets, namely, <u>single</u>, <u>double</u>, <u>eval</u>, and <u>miss</u>. If these four SAS data sets have been created in one SAS session, then they are stored in SAS libraries under the folder "Work". You can locate these four SAS data sets by first clicking on **Explorer,** to reveal **Contents of SAS Environment,** and then clicking on **Libraries,** followed by the **Work** folder (see the three screen displays below).

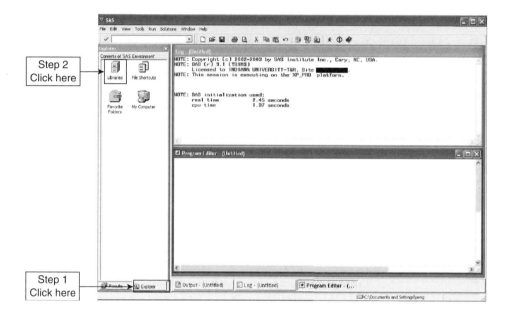

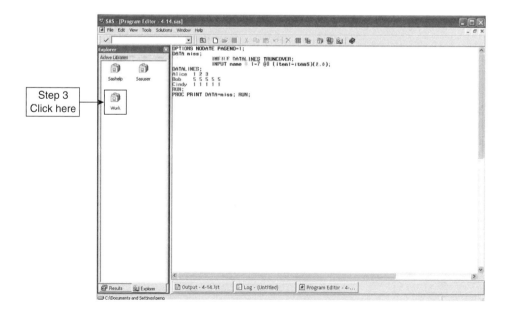

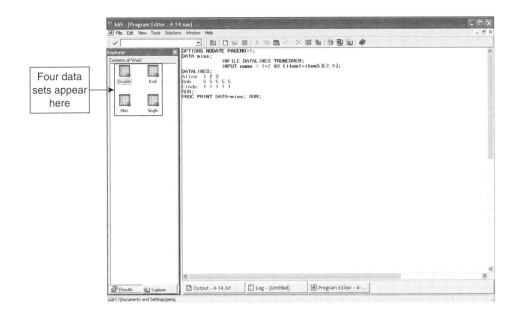

4.6 Storing and Retrieving SAS Data Sets as Permanent Data Files

The examples you have explored so far have been creating SAS data sets in the working memory of your computer. These data sets will be erased once you exit out of SAS. Thus, SAS data sets created in the working memory of a computer are temporary. Yet you may need to permanently store SAS data sets on a computer or in another storage medium and retrieve them later. Here is how to do it:

Example 4.15 Creating a Permanent SAS Data Set File

In this example, the path "d:\data\" is first linked to a folder called <u>research</u> by the LIBNAME statement. This folder is created in **Libraries** in the **SAS Environment**. Next, a SAS data set with the two-stage name <u>research.eval</u> is created with raw data embedded in the program. At the end of the SAS processing, a permanent SAS data set file is created at "d:\data\eval.sas7bdat". Now, try this program and check out this new file at the designated location!

The extension, <u>sas7bdat</u>, stands for a SAS data set created with SAS versions 7, 8, and 9. The <u>sas7bdat</u> file extension is automatically inserted under Windows, UNIX, or Open VMS systems. For other systems, please consult your local SAS experts.

```
LIBNAME research 'd:\data\';        /* Links 'research' library to folder 'data' on d: drive */

DATA research.eval;                 /* Links 'research' to SAS data set 'eval' */
     INPUT id $ a1-a5 b1-b5 q16 q17 q18 q19 q20a $;

DATALINES;
1    4 5 3 5 3 1 2 3 1 1 24 5 1 3 yes
2    4 5 4 5 2 1 2 2 1 1  5 5 1 3 yes
3    5 5 3 4 2 1 3 2 1 1 10 5 1 3 yes
4    3 5 4 4 3 1 4 2 1 2 20 5 1 3 yes
5    5 4 5 4 4 1 4 2 1 1  . 5 2 3 yes
6    5 5 4 3 5 2 3 3 1 1 30 3 5 3 yes
7    4 5 4 4 4 1 3 3 1 1 17 3 5 3 no
8    3 4 5 4 3 2 3 2 1 1 15 3 5 3 yes
9    4 4 3 5 2 1 3 3 1 1 10 3 5 . .
10   3 5 4 4 3 1 3 1 2 1  . 3 2 . yes
11   3 4 5 4 3 1 3 2 1 1 25 4 2 . no
12   2 5 4 5 4 1 4 2 1 1 20 4 2 . yes
13   4 3 4 4 4 1 2 1 3 2  8 4 2 1 yes
14   5 4 3 3 3 2 2 2 1 1 60 4 2 1 yes
15   3 5 4 3 4 3 3 3 1 1 23 4 3 1 .
16   3 5 5 4 3 1 3 3 2 2 15 5 1 1 yes
17   4 4 4 4 3 1 3 2 1 1  9 5 1 1 yes
18   4 5 4 5 3 1 4 2 1 1 14 5 1 1 yes
19   3 5 4 3 4 1 3 1 1 1 22 5 1 1 yes
20   2 4 4 3 5 . . . . . . 35 5 1 1 no
RUN;
```

The library, research, is a temporary holding place for the SAS data set, eval. The name, research, is specified by users. Any name that is suitable for a SAS data set name is also suitable for the library folder. As an exercise, you may change research to something else, such as goodyear, and rerun Example 4.15. The outcome should be the same as before, namely, that a permanent SAS data set is established at "d:\data\eval.sas7bdat". Now, let's confirm the establishment of this permanent SAS data set file with Log 4.15.

Log 4.15 Creating a Permanent SAS Data Set File

```
1    LIBNAME goodyear 'd:\data\';
NOTE: Libref RESEARCH was successfully assigned as follows:
      Engine:        V9
      Physical Name: d:\data
1    !                                          /* Identifies the path to an external
1    ! location */
2
3    DATA goodyear.eval;                        /* Links 'goodyear' to SAS data set 'eval' */
4        INPUT id $ a1-a5 b1-b5 q16 q17 q18 q19 q20a $;
5
6    DATALINES;

NOTE: The data set GOODYEAR.EVAL has 20 observations and 16 variables.
NOTE: DATA statement used (Total process time):
      real time          0.80 seconds
      cpu time           0.00 seconds

27   RUN;
```

The following example illustrates how to retrieve an external SAS data set file from "d:\data\eval.sas7bdat" and then print the content out using PROC PRINT.

Example 4.16 Retrieving a Permanent SAS Data Set File

```
LIBNAME research 'd:\data\';      /* Links 'research' library to folder 'data' on d: drive   */

PROC PRINT DATA=research.eval;    /* Uses SAS data set file 'eval.sas7bdat' from 'research', */
RUN;                              /* also 'data' folder on d: drive                          */
```

If two SAS data set files are stored externally at "d:\data\eval.sas7bdat" and "d:\data\miss.sas7bdat", respectively, both can be retrieved in the same program in two statistical procedures as follows.

Example 4.17 Retrieving Two Permanent SAS Data Set Files

```
LIBNAME research 'd:\data\';      /* Links 'research' library to folder 'data' on d: drive   */

PROC PRINT DATA=research.eval;    /* Uses SAS data set file 'eval.sas7bdat' from 'research', */
RUN;                              /* also 'data' folder on d: drive                          */

PROC PRINT DATA=research.miss;    /* Uses SAS data set file 'miss.sas7bdat' from 'research', */
RUN;                              /* also 'data' folder on d: drive                          */
```

4.7 Using SAS Data Sets in Statistical Analyses

Statistical analyses are carried out in the PROC step. All statistical procedures use SAS data sets, not data matrices or raw data files. A SAS data set is specified by the DATA= option, as shown in Example 4.18. Each DATA= option invokes one SAS data set, and each PROC uses one SAS data set. By default, SAS will use the most recently created data set if the DATA= option is not specified.

Example 4.18 Using SAS Data Sets in Statistical Procedures

```
DATA eval;
     INPUT id $ a1-a5 b1-b5 q16 q17 q18 q19 q20a $;
DATALINES;
1  4 5 3 5 3 1 2 3 1 1 24 5 1 3 yes
2  4 5 4 5 2 1 2 2 1 1  5 5 1 3 yes
3  5 5 3 4 2 1 3 2 1 1 10 5 1 3 yes
4  3 5 4 4 3 1 4 2 1 2 20 5 1 3 yes
5  5 4 5 4 4 1 4 2 1 1  . 5 2 3 yes
6  5 5 4 3 5 2 3 3 1 1 30 3 5 3 yes
7  4 5 4 4 4 1 3 3 1 1 17 3 5 3 no
8  3 4 5 4 3 2 3 2 1 1 15 3 5 3 yes
9  4 4 3 5 2 1 3 3 1 1 10 3 5 . .
10 3 5 4 4 3 1 3 1 2 1  . 3 2 . yes
11 3 4 5 4 3 1 3 2 1 1 25 4 2 . no
12 2 5 4 5 4 1 4 2 1 1 20 4 2 . yes
13 4 3 4 4 4 1 2 1 3 2  8 4 2 1 yes
14 5 4 3 3 3 2 2 2 1 1 60 4 2 1 yes
15 3 5 4 3 4 3 3 3 1 1 23 4 3 1 .
16 3 5 5 4 3 1 3 3 2 2 15 5 1 1 yes
```

```
17 4 4 4 3 1 3 2 1 1  9 5 1 1 yes
18 4 5 4 5 3 1 4 2 1 1 14 5 1 1 yes
19 3 5 4 3 4 1 3 1 1 1 22 5 1 1 yes
20 2 4 4 3 5 . . . . . 35 5 1 1 no
RUN;
PROC PRINT DATA=eval;
RUN;
PROC MEANS DATA=eval;
RUN;
```

The use of permanent SAS data set files stored externally is demonstrated in Example 4.16 for one SAS data set file, and in Example 4.17 for two SAS data set files. Alternatively, you may input the full path name to a permanent SAS data set file in statistical procedures, assuming again a permanent SAS data set file is already located at "d:\data\eval.sas7bdat". Note that this specification of a SAS data set file requires you to write out the full path name for each PROC, as demonstrated in Example 4.19. As long as the data set file is of the type ".sas7 bdat", you can simplify the path name in the DATA= option as, DATA='d: \data\eval'. Try this simplified path reference in Example 4.19 on your own.

Example 4.19 Referencing Permanent
SAS Data Set Files in Statistical Procedures

```
PROC PRINT DATA=' d:\data\eval.sas7bdat' ;
RUN;
PROC MEANS DATA=' d:\data\eval.sas7bdat' ;
RUN;
```

4.8 Summary

This chapter presented important information on how to bring a raw data file into a SAS System. Raw data are either embedded within a SAS program or stored in a location external to the SAS program. Three styles of the INPUT statement were introduced and illustrated for linking variable names to data values. Pros and cons of using each input style were presented, along with practical considerations such as how to read multiple records into a single observation, how to read multiple observations from a single record, and so on. Once raw data are read into a SAS program, they become part of a SAS data set. A SAS data set can be subsequently analyzed by SAS statistical procedures or further processed within the DATA step.

SAS data sets are units of analysis in SAS. Each SAS data set is identified by a unique name. Its content includes observations and variables, such as variables' names, their values, the character or numeric nature of each variable, missing data, the length of data records, and the nature of the entire data set: raw data, correlation, covariance, and so forth. Once a SAS data set has been created in a SAS program, it is saved in the SAS data library, called **Work**, during the processing of a SAS program. All SAS data sets disappear once the SAS session is terminated; thus, they are temporary. You can make SAS data sets permanent by storing them on a computer hard drive, a server, a disk, or an external drive.

In the weeks and months ahead, as you become proficient with SAS and its versatility, you will no doubt refer back to this chapter to refresh your memory and also to help diagnose error messages that have appeared in your Log Window! Don't be discouraged or stressed over errors; they are valuable—each error teaches you a lesson. Isn't that true in life also?

4.9 Exercises

1. Missing values in a list input style are coded by a (an) _____.

2. What does the $ mean in an INPUT statement? _____.

3. According to the following INPUT statement, what are the values for v1, v2, v3, and v4?

```
DATA example;
    INPUT v1 $ 8. @ 9 v2 $ #2 v3 $ v4 $;
DATALINES;
ABCDEFGHIJK
LMNOP QRST UV WXYZ
ABCDEF HIJKL
MN OP QRST UVWXYZ
RUN;
PROC PRINT;  RUN;
```

4. Which of the following gives the correct order of SAS statements?
   a. DATA target; INPUT x y; DATALINES; PROC PRINT;
   b. INPUT x y; DATALINES; PROC PRINT;
   c. PROC PRINT; INPUT x y; DATALINES; DATA target;
   d. DATALINES; DATA target; PROC PRINT; INPUT x y;

5. What input style is used in the following INPUT statement?

```
INPUT name $ 1-20  course_no  22-45  score  47-48;
```

   a. The list input style
   b. The column input style
   c. The formatted input style

6. When you write INPUT statements, which rule below is **not** applicable?
   a. All variable names must be 8 characters or fewer.
   b. For the list input style, missing values should be left as blanks.
   c. For the column input style, blanks are allowed as character values.
   d. Numerical values can be declared as characters for a character variable.

7. For the following data lines, which input statement does **not** produce the same data set as the others?

```
123 456
789 012
```

   a. INPUT   x y;
   b. INPUT   x 1-3 y 5-7;
   c. INPUT   x $ y $;
   d. INPUT   x 3. +4 y 5-7;
   e. INPUT   x 3. @5 Y 3.;

8. Run the following program to determine the values for x:

```
DATA  a;
      INPUT  x 5.2;
DATALINES;
1120
112.0
112
RUN;
PROC PRINT;
RUN;
```

a. 1120.0	b. 1120.00	c. 11.20	d. 1120	e. 1120.00
112.00	112.00	112.00	11.20	112.0
1.12	112.00	1.12	11.20	11.20

9. Which of the following INPUT statements is **wrong** given the raw data file below?

```
Columns:
                      1 1 1 1 1 1 1 1 1 1 2 2 2 2 2 2 2 2 2
1 2 3 4 5 6 7 8 9 0 1 2 3 4 5 6 7 8 9 0 1 2 3 4 5 6 7 8
s m i t h                       f   3 4   1 2 5 . 7
h I t c h c o c k - t y l e r   m   2 6     9 8 . 2
```

   a. INPUT name $ 15. +1 sex $ 1. +1 age 2. @22 score 5.;
   b. INPUT name $ 1-15 sex $ 17 age 19-20 score 22-26;
   c. INPUT name $ 15. sex 1. age 2. score 5.;
   d. INPUT name $ 15. +1 sex $ age 19-20 @22 score 5.;
   e. INPUT name $ 15. +1 sex $ age 19-20 @22 score;

10. Which `INPUT` statement will yield data set <u>b</u> from data set <u>a</u>?

   a. `INPUT x y z @@;`
   b. `INPUT x y x  @@;`
   c. `INPUT x @ y @ z @;`
   d. `INPUT x y z;`

11. What will the SAS data set <u>example</u> contain, given the following SAS statements?

```
DATA example;
     INPUT x y z @@;
DATALINES;
10 20 30 40 50 60
RUN;
```

   a. <u>x</u>   <u>y</u>   <u>z</u>   b. <u>x</u>   <u>y</u>   <u>z</u>   c. <u>x</u>   <u>y</u>   <u>z</u>   <u>x</u>   <u>y</u>   <u>z</u>
      10 20 30   10 20 30   10 20 30 40 50 60
                       40 50 60

   d. No data set is created because of an error in the INPUT statement.

12. Given the following INPUT statement, how many character variables are specified?

```
INPUT name $ @10 sex $ 1. / @ 10 ss_no $ +1 @20 age 2.;
```

   a. 3
   b. 4
   c. 5

13. Given the INPUT statement in Question 12 above, how many records are read for each observation?
   a. 1
   b. 2
   c. 3

14. What is the input style of the INPUT statement in Question 12 above?
    a. List
    b. Column
    c. Formatted
    d. A mixture of all three above

15. Which interpretation of the following INPUT statement is **incorrect**?

```
INPUT #1 aa $ 1-8 bb $ 11 #2 cc 30-31 #3 dd 1-7 ee 8-14 #4;
```

    a. It reads variables <u>aa</u> and <u>bb</u> from Record 1, <u>cc</u> from Record 2, <u>dd</u> from Record
       3, and then <u>ee</u> from Record 4.
    b. You don't need "#1" immediately after INPUT since SAS automatically begins
       with the first record.
    c. #4 tells SAS that there is a 4th record for each observation.
    d. The above program has the same result as the following statement:

```
INPUT #3 dd 1-7 ee 8-14 #1 aa $ 1-8 bb $ 11 #2 cc 30-31 #4;
```

16. On the INPUT statement, a character variable is denoted by
    a. putting the variable in parenthesis.
    b. a $ sign written after the variable name.
    c. an @ symbol inserted after the variable name.
    d. its variable values.

17. Which of the following statements is **not** true in reading character data into a SAS
    data set?
    a. Blanks cannot be embedded in character values.
    b. Uppercase characters are different from lowercase characters as data values.
    c. The SAS System determines the length of the character variable from its first
       occurrence on the INPUT statement.
    d. Missing character values may be represented by a period (.).

18. Mark in the appropriate columns and record number for all variables listed on the
    INPUT statement below:

```
INPUT (x1-x5)(+1 2. +2 $ 4.)/ (x6-x8)(3. +1);
```

Record	1	2	3	4	5	6	7	8	9	10	11	12	13	14	15	16	17	18	19	20	21	22	23	24	25	26	27	28	29	30
#1																														
#2																														

19. Write at least two INPUT statements to read <u>name</u>, <u>gender</u>, <u>age</u>, and <u>state</u> of the following data records into a SAS data set called <u>sample</u> correctly:

1	2	3	4	5	6	7	8	9	10	11	12	13	14	15	16	17	18	19	20
J	I	M					M		2	7		I	N	D	I	A	N	A	
S	A	R	A	H			F		3	2		G	E	O	R	G	I	A	

4.10 Answers to Exercises

1. A period (.)

2. The preceding variable is a character variable.

3.

v1	v2	v3	v4
ABCDEFGH	IJK	LMNOP	QRST
ABCDEF H	IJKL	MN	OP

4. a

5. b

6. a, b

7. c

8. c

9. c

10. a

11. b

12. a

13. b

14. d

15. a

16. b

17. a, c

18.

Record	1	2	3	4	5	6	7	8	9	10	11	12	13	14	15	16	17	18	19	20	21	22	23	24	25	26	27	28	29	30
#1		x1				x2 (character)					x3				x4 (character)					x5										
#2		x6			x7			x8																						

19.

```
DATA sample;
     INPUT name $ 7. gender $ 1. +1 age 2. +1 state $ 8.;
DATALINES;
```

```
DATA sample;
     INPUT name $ 1-7 @8 gender $ 1. @10 age 2. @13 state $ 8.;
DATALINES;
```

5

Enhancing the Readability of SAS Programs and Output

OBJECTIVE

This chapter covers an array of strategies that enhance the readability of SAS programs and SAS output. These strategies help document the nature of the data set, the purpose of data analysis, how and when data were collected, details of coding schemes, and other relevant background information. These skills groom you to be a responsible and forward-thinking data analyst too.

The need for clarity is obvious for both SAS programs and output. One way to enhance clarity in a SAS program is to document the purpose and the logic of data analysis as part of a program. A documented SAS program takes you less time to figure out its logic than a program without documentation. It is also easier for another data analyst to modify or update such a program.

Similarly, a well-documented SAS output leads to a clear understanding and comprehensive interpretation of the result. This is particularly important because SAS output is not accompanied by its SAS program or log. Consequently, information about the purpose or logic of the corresponding SAS program is lost when you are reading only the output. For this reason, the output needs to be documented as well.

This chapter teaches you how to enhance the readability of a SAS program and its output. All tricks illustrated are SAS programming statements. Once you master these tricks, you will find them invaluable and indispensable, particularly when the SAS program and its output are long and complex.

5.1 Documenting a SAS Program

For each SAS program, a responsible and forward-thinking data analyst should surely document its purpose. The documentation of a program's purpose is a minimum. More desirable is to include information on the numeric or character nature of the data, how and when data were collected, some details about coding schemes, logic in analysis, and any other relevant background information. There are five ways to accomplish this: (1) matching /* and */ marks, (2) comment statements, (3) blank lines, (4) indentations, and (5) TITLE statements. The raw data file roster.dat is used throughout this chapter. It consists of 14 students' scores on four tests along with their name, gender, identification number, and academic standing. This data file is downloadable from the SAGE Web site at www.sagepub.com/pengstudy.

Example 5.1 Matching /* and */ Marks

```
DATA roster;                          /* A SAS data set 'roster' is created */
    INFILE 'd:\data\roster.dat';
    INPUT name $ sex $ id $ stand pretest first second final;
                                      /* 3 character and 5 numeric variables are read */
    composite = SUM(pretest,first,second,final);
                                      /* A new variable 'composite' is the total of 4 tests */
RUN;
```

Example 5.1 demonstrates that the matching /* and */ marks enclose material that explains or elaborates on the preceding SAS statement. They can occur anywhere in blank spaces of the program, as many times as needed. They should not, however, appear in the middle of another SAS statement, a variable name, a variable value, or SAS keywords. The semicolon mark ($;$) is allowed within the matching $/*$ and $*/$.

In certain computing environments, the symbols $/$ and $*$ cannot be placed in Columns 1 and 2. Check out this restriction with your local SAS consultant if you are not using SAS in the Windows environment.

Example 5.2 Comment Statements

```
*This is an illustration of a comment statement;
*-------------------------------------------------------*
|                      Example 5.2 in                    |
|           Data Analysis Using SAS by Joanne Peng       |
*-------------------------------------------------------;
DATA roster;
    INFILE 'd:\data\roster.dat';
    INPUT name $ sex $ id $ stand pretest first second final;
*
*    A new variable 'composite' is the total of four variables.
*;
    composite = SUM(pretest,first,second,final);
RUN;
PROC PRINT DATA=roster;
RUN;
```

A comment statement is a SAS statement that begins with an asterisk ($*$) and ends with a semicolon ($;$). If used wisely and artfully as illustrated in Example 5.2, comment statements add commentaries and aesthetic appeal to a SAS program without interfering with the actual analysis of data. A second semicolon cannot be inserted within a comment statement because a semicolon means the end of a SAS statement. Hence, only one is allowed for each comment statement. There can be other symbols inserted, such as -----, " | ", or "   " (blank spaces), to create the desired visual effect—a box in this case.

Example 5.3 The Use of Blank Lines

Technically speaking, blank lines do not contain any commentary or information. As such, they are not counted as comments by SAS— contrast this example with Example 5.2. Yet if inserted at proper places, they help to break up the drudgery of a program, making the program more readable. Example 5.3 easily shows that two procedures (CONTENTS and MEANS) are applied to the SAS data set roster, whereas without the blank lines, the program will appear more complicated and loaded than it really is. In your own programming, you may freely use as many, or as few, blank lines as needed to highlight statements clustered by their similar purposes.

```
DATA roster;
    INFILE 'd:\data\roster.dat';
    INPUT name $ sex $ id $ stand pretest first second final;
RUN;

PROC CONTENTS DATA=roster;
RUN;

ROC MEANS DATA=roster;
    VAR pretest first second final;
RUN;
```

Example 5.4 Proper Indentation

In this example, the variable <u>average</u> is used as the basis for assigning course grades to students in <u>roster.dat</u>. Note how the four grades ("A", "B", "C", and "failed") are progressively defined, one after the other. The conditions under which a grade is assigned are clearly presented because of the indentation of four programming lines starting with "IF...THEN...;" and ending with "ELSE....;". As a result, anyone reading this program can easily conclude that the cutoff for "A" is 40, for "B" is 35, and for "C" is 30; an <u>average</u> below 30 is a "failed" grade.

```
DATA roster;
    INFILE 'd:\data\roster.dat';
    INPUT name $ sex $ id $ stand pretest first second final;
    LENGTH grade $10.;              /* The length of 'grade' values is 10 characters or less */
    average = MEAN(pretest,first,second,final);
    IF average >= 40 THEN grade = 'A';
        ELSE IF average >= 35 THEN grade = 'B';
            ELSE IF average >= 30 THEN grade = 'C';
                ELSE grade = 'failed';
RUN;

PROC MEANS DATA=roster;
    VAR pretest first second final average;
RUN;
```

Example 5.5 TITLE Statements

```
TITLE 'This is an illustration of the TITLE statement';

DATA roster;
    INFILE 'd:\data\roster.dat';
    INPUT name $ sex $ id $ stand pretest first second final;
    composite = SUM(pretest,first,second,final);
RUN;

TITLE2 'Results of PROC MEANS';

PROC MEANS DATA=roster;
    VAR pretest first second final composite;
RUN;
```

The use of a TITLE statement is similar to that of a comment statement; it helps to highlight the purpose of the entire program or a cluster of SAS statements. A major difference between a TITLE and a comment is that the text on the TITLE statement is processed and subsequently displayed in the SAS Output window, whereas a comment statement is not (refer to Example 5.2). The difference is also shown in Output 5.5 in the next section. A few rules are in place regarding TITLE statements:

- All TITLE texts are enclosed by either single quotes, double quotes, or no quotes, although no quotes are not recommended.
- All TITLE statements end with a semicolon (;).
- The expression of possessive forms is either

```
TITLE 'Professor Dolittle"s research';        or

TITLE "Professor Dolittle's research";
```

- Though the length of the text depends on your computing environment and the width of the SAS output file, it is safe to restrict the length to 60 characters, including blank spaces.
- The first TITLE statement is written either as TITLE or TITLE1. It appears on all pages of the output, unless another subsequent TITLE statement overrides it.
- Subtitles or subheadings are written as TITLE2, TITLE3, and so on, up to TITLE10.
- A TITLE statement is executed when the DATA or PROC step, of which it is a part, is processed.

5.2 Titling the Entire Output or Its Parts by the TITLE Statement

As Example 5.5 previously explained, TITLE statements serve two purposes: (1) documenting a SAS program and (2) documenting the output. Let's take a look at the output produced by Example 5.5.

Output 5.5 TITLE Statements

```
              This is an illustration of the TITLE statement          1
                        Results of PROC MEANS

                        The MEANS Procedure

Variable     N          Mean        Std Dev       Minimum        Maximum
-----------------------------------------------------------------------
pretest     14     14.7857143      4.1727794     7.0000000      21.0000000
first       14     38.1428571      8.4839862    24.0000000      50.0000000
second      14     47.7142857      6.5330941    33.0000000      57.0000000
final       13     46.8461538      7.3467244    32.0000000      57.0000000
composite   14    144.1428571     27.0351826    85.0000000     181.0000000
-----------------------------------------------------------------------
```

Notice how this page is titled with the text string programmed into the TITLE statement. According to the rule, the text strings of a higher-ordered TITLE, such as the TITLE2 statement, appear after TITLE statement(s) of a lower order, that is, TITLE1. For this reason, this page has two titles: the first derived from the TITLE statement and the second or secondary title from the TITLE2 statement.

The use of TITLE statements is an effective way to document both the output and sections of the program. You are encouraged to always use one TITLE statement for the entire SAS program. For sections of the program, it is preferable to write one TITLE statement for each DATA or PROC step.

5.3 Labeling Variables by the LABEL Statement _____

The LABEL statement is used to describe variables, beyond their names. Whenever these variables appear in the output, so will their labels. Labels are usually necessary because a variable's meaning often cannot be fully described by its name. For example, how do you describe a teenager's attitude to 10 "conservative values," such as altruism, loyalty to friends, commitment to marriage, fear of God, patriotism, and so forth? It is difficult to abbreviate these values collectively into a name. Furthermore, some variable names may imply multiple meanings, such as the name party. Does this name mean "political party," "social party," or "party date"? For these reasons, it is helpful to describe variables in depth with the LABEL statement.

Each variable label is placed in single or double quotes up to 256 characters, including blank spaces. Between the keyword LABEL and the semi-colon (;) mark, there can be multiple variable labels, written in the style of variable_name = 'variable label'. Below is an example modified from Example 5.5 with an additional LABEL statement.

Example 5.6 The Use of the LABEL Statement

```
TITLE 'This is an illustration of the LABEL statement';

DATA roster;
    INFILE 'd:\data\roster.dat';
    INPUT name $ sex $ id $ stand pretest first second final;
    composite = SUM(pretest,first,second,final),
    LABEL name = 'student''s name'
          id = 'student id number'
          stand = 'academic standing'
          pretest = 'pretest score'
          first = 'first midterm score'
          second = 'second midterm score'
          final = 'final score'
          composite = 'composite score';
RUN;

TITLE2 'Results of PROC MEANS';

PROC MEANS DATA=roster;
    VAR pretest first second final composite;
RUN;
```

Output 5.6 The Use of the LABEL Statement

```
                    This is an illustration of the LABEL statement              1
                              Results of PROC MEANS

                             The MEANS Procedure


Variable    Label                    N        Mean      Std Dev       Minimum       Maximum
-----------------------------------------------------------------------------------------
pretest     pretest score           14   14.7857143    4.1727794     7.0000000    21.0000000
first       first midterm score     14   38.1428571    8.4839862    24.0000000    50.0000000
second      second midterm score    14   47.7142857    6.5330941    33.0000000    57.0000000
final       final score             13   46.8461538    7.3467244    32.0000000    57.0000000
composite   composite score         14  144.1428571   27.0351826    85.0000000   181.0000000
-----------------------------------------------------------------------------------------
```

Notice that next to each variable name (the first column), labels of variables are printed. With variable labels in the second column, it is easier to interpret what each variable represents and whether the mean, the standard deviation (**Std Dev**), the minimum, and the maximum make sense. Variable labels also help readers who are unfamiliar with the data or variable names to read the results with understanding and insight.

When labeling a variable with the LABEL statement, you should observe the following:

- Enclose all labels in single or double quotes, or neither (no quotes is not recommended).
- End the LABEL statement with a semicolon (;).
- Write possessive forms as part of a label as follows:

```
LABEL name = 'student"s name';          or
LABEL name = "student's name";
```

- Use no more than 256 characters, including blank spaces, for each label.

5.4 Labeling Variable Values by PROC FORMAT and FORMAT Statements _____

The previous section taught you to label variables. This section will teach you how to label values of variables. Labeling variable values preserves the coding scheme used in coding the data. For example, if the variable school is coded as 1 for public schools and 2 for private schools, do you suppose you or others will remember this coding scheme next year when looking at the printout or the program again? Probably not! For this reason, it is often helpful to document a variable's values, especially if they represent categories. This is where PROC FORMAT and FORMAT statements enter the picture. Value labeling takes two steps: The first step is to define formats with PROC FORMAT, and the second step is to apply formats to variables. Let's demonstrate these two steps in Example 5.7, which is interested in tabulating frequency counts of <u>sex</u> and academic <u>stand</u>ing with PROC FREQ (described in Chapter 11).

Step 1: Define Formats With PROC FORMAT

PROC FORMAT is used to define meanings of various values, such as "female" for <u>f</u> and "male" for <u>m</u>, in a generic format name, such as <u>$gender</u>. Subsequently, the <u>$gender</u> format is applied to the variable <u>sex</u> as a character format, in <u>$gender.</u>, with a period. In Example 5.7, two formats are defined: <u>$gender.</u> and <u>status.</u>. The <u>$gender.</u> format interprets two values, whereas the <u>status.</u> format interprets four values, 1 for "freshman", 2 for "sophomore", 3 for "junior", and 4 for "senior". A character format must be prefixed with the dollar sign ($) as in <u>$gender</u>. The character format is suitable for labeling character values. In contrast, the <u>status.</u> format is numeric, suitable for labeling numeric values.

Step 2: Apply Formats to Variables

The permanent link between a format and a variable takes place in the DATA step. Note that the FORMAT statement is placed immediately after the INPUT statement. On the FORMAT statement, a variable name comes before the format name. That is the reason why <u>sex</u> is followed by <u>$gender.</u> with a period after the format. By the same token, the variable <u>stand</u> is followed by the <u>status.</u> format.

Example 5.7 Labeling Variable Values

```
TITLE 'This is an illustration of PROC FORMAT and FORMAT statements';

PROC FORMAT;
    VALUE $gender 'f'='female' 'm'='male';
    VALUE status 1='freshman' 2='sophomore' 3='junior' 4='senior';
RUN;

DATA roster;
    INFILE 'd:\data\roster.dat';
    INPUT name $ sex $ id $ stand pretest first second final;
    FORMAT sex $gender.
           stand status.;
RUN;

TITLE2 'Results of PROC FREQ';

PROC FREQ DATA=roster;
    TABLES sex*stand;              /* Creates a 2-way frequency table with 'sex' & 'stand' */
RUN;
```

Output 5.7 Labeling Variable Values

```
This is an illustration of PROC FORMAT and FORMAT statements          1
                        Results of PROC FREQ

                        The FREQ Procedure

                      Table of sex by stand

      sex           stand

      Frequency|
      Percent  |
      Row Pct  |
      Col Pct  |freshman|sophomor| junior | senior |  Total
               |        |e       |        |        |
      ---------+--------+--------+--------+--------+
      female   |      1 |      1 |      1 |      2 |      5
               |   7.14 |   7.14 |   7.14 |  14.29 |  35.71
               |  20.00 |  20.00 |  20.00 |  40.00 |
               |  33.33 |  33.33 |  50.00 |  33.33 |
      ---------+--------+--------+--------+--------+
      male     |      2 |      2 |      1 |      4 |      9
               |  14.29 |  14.29 |   7.14 |  28.57 |  64.29
               |  22.22 |  22.22 |  11.11 |  44.44 |
               |  66.67 |  66.67 |  50.00 |  66.67 |
      ---------+--------+--------+--------+--------+
      Total           3        3        2        6       14
                  21.43    21.43    14.29    42.86   100.00
```

The output displays a 2 by 4 table that shows the breakdown of frequencies according to sex and academic standing. Had the values of these two variables not been labeled, you would have read a table with f, m for the two rows and 1, 2, 3, and 4 for the four columns—how uninformative that would be!

The heading of the second column lists "sophomore" on two lines instead of one. This is because the default width for displaying the cell's information in PROC FREQ is 7 characters. If you want to display the entire word "sophomore" on the same line, simply rewrite the TABLES statement into TABLES sex*stand / FORMAT=10.;. Now, try this trick and find out what happens to Output 5.7!

The FORMAT statement is sometimes applied in a PROC step for the duration of the PROC processing. Example 5.8 modifies the previous example by linking the two formats, $gender. and status., to variables sex and stand, respectively, in PROC FREQ. Consequently, the variable values are labeled only during the processing of FREQ, and hence, not permanently. Output 5.8 is identical to Output 5.7; therefore, it is not shown here.

Example 5.8 Labeling Variable Values in the PROC Step

```
TITLE 'This is an illustration of PROC FORMAT and FORMAT statements';

PROC FORMAT;
    VALUE $gender 'f'='female' 'm'='male';
    VALUE status 1='freshman' 2='sophomore' 3='junior' 4='senior';
RUN;

DATA roster;
    INFILE 'd:\data\roster.dat';
    INPUT name $ sex $ id $ stand pretest first second final;
RUN;

TITLE2 'Results of PROC FREQ with two formats';

PROC FREQ DATA=roster;
    TABLES sex*stand;
    FORMAT sex $gender.
           stand status.;
RUN;
```

5.5 Other Controls of SAS Output by the OPTIONS Statement

The OPTIONS statement affects processing aspects of a SAS program. Here, only those options that manipulate SAS log and SAS output are presented. The general syntax of the OPTIONS statement is

OPTIONS *options*;

The options listed here are system options that remain in effect for the entire execution of the program unless they are redefined. For your own work, you may use one or more of the following options to affect SAS log and SAS output:

CENTER	centers the output produced by SAS procedures.
NOCENTER	left justifies the output produced by SAS procedures.
DATE	requests that the date and time when the SAS job began be included in the log or any output produced by the SAS System. Hence, the next option means the opposite.
NODATE	requests that the date and time information be excluded from the log or any output produced by the SAS System.
LABEL	requests that variable labels be used in lieu of variable names by SAS procedures.

NOLABEL	requests that variable labels not be used by SAS procedures.
LINESIZE (or LS)=	specifies the width of SAS log and output produced by the DATA step and procedures. The LS values range from 64 to 256.
PAGENO=	pecifies the beginning page number for the next printed output. Usually it is set to 1.
PAGESIZE (or PS)=	specifies the length (or printed lines) of each print page on the output. PS values range from 15 to 32,767.

Example 5.9 Options That Affect the SAS Output

```
OPTIONS LS=80 PS=60 DATE PAGENO=1 NOCENTER;
```

Try these options on the program in Example 5.7 and compare your output with Output 5.7.

5.6 Summary

This chapter presents numerous ways for enhancing the readability of a SAS program and its output. Specifically, you learned to write labels for variables and values, place headings on output pages, and change the appearance of the output. Five strategies were suggested and illustrated, including (a) documenting a SAS program, (b) titling the output, (c) labeling variables, (d) labeling values of categorical variables, and (e) customizing the appearance of an output. These strategies can make a SAS program comprehensible, its logic easy to follow, and its output interpretable. Though these strategies are nonessential to the purpose and success of a SAS program, they will surely make you (and those who come after you on the same project) happier in the long run!

5.7 Exercises

1. The following four questions are taken from the General Social Survey at http://gss.norc.org. Write appropriate INPUT and LABEL statements to define four variables corresponding to these questions:
   a. Were you living at home while you attended college?
   b. How often do you attend religious services per month?

    c. Do you think compulsive military service should be extended to women?

    d. Should our president be held accountable for his personal integrity, even in his private life?

2. Out of the four questions in Exercise 1 above, Questions (a), (c), and (d) can be answered by "yes" or "no" and Question (b) can be answered by a Likert-type scale such as 1 = never, 2 = rarely, 3 = sometimes, 4 = frequently, and 5 = always. Write two formats to apply proper labels to responses collected from these questions.

3. How many TITLE statements do you think you need to describe the General Social Survey data concerning those four questions? How do you write these TITLE statements?

4. Insert appropriate TITLE, LABEL, and FORMAT statements into Example 4.1 so that variables and their values are clearly identified and the purpose of that example as well as each analysis procedure is captured in the TITLE statement.

5. Execute the enhanced Example 4.1 from Exercise 4 above and compare the output of Exercise 4 with Output 4.1, and the log from Exercise 4 with Log 4.1.

5.8 Answers to Exercises

```
1. INPUT     q1-q4;
   LABEL     q1='living at home in college'
             q2='attending religious services a month'
             q3='women required in compulsive military service'
             q4='President accountable for personal integrity';


2. PROC      FORMAT;
             VALUE two 1='yes' 2=no';
             VALUE five 1='never' 2='rarely' 3='sometimes'
             4='frequently' 5='always';
   DATA exercise2;
   INPUT     q1-q4;
   FORMAT    q1 two.;
   FORMAT    q2 five.;
   FORMAT    q3-q4 two.;


3. TITLE     'General Social Survey';
   TITLE2    'Conducted in 2006';
   TITLE3    'Question 1 (or 2,3,4)';
```

4. Enhancing the readability of Example 4.1

```
TITLE  'Example 4.1 Reading data with INFILE';
TITLE2 'Data came from Y777 course evaluation';
PROC FORMAT;
     VALUE learn 1 = 'Very poor' 2 = 'Poor' 3 = 'Average' 4 = 'Good' 5 = 'Very good';
     VALUE aptitude 1 = 'Beginner' 5 = 'Expert';
     VALUE attitude 1 = 'unfavorable' 5 = 'favorable';
     VALUE anxiety  1 = 'low' 5 = 'high';

DATA eval;                              /* Establishes a SAS data set called 'eval'  */
     INFILE 'd:\data\y777.dat';
     INPUT id $ a1-a5 b1-b5 q16 q17 q18 q19 q20a $;
     LABEL id = 'Identification number of students'
           a1 = 'Current knowledge about sampling methods & distributions'
           a2 = 'Current ability to apply ANOVA-fixed effects model'
           a3 = 'Current ability to apply multiple comparison procedures'
           a4 = 'Current knowledge of randomized block designs'
           a5 = 'Current knowledge of Latin squares designs'
           b1 = 'Prior knowledge about sampling methods & distributions'
           b2 = 'Prior ability to apply ANOVA-fixed effects model'
           b3 = 'Prior ability to apply multiple comparison procedures'
           b4 = 'Prior knowledge of randomized block designs'
           b5 = 'Prior knowledge of Latin squares designs'
           q16 = 'Hours studying per week'
           q17 = 'Aptitude in statistics'
           q18 = 'Attitude toward statistics'
           q19 = 'Anxiety about statistics'
           q20a = 'To become a faculty at a university';

     FORMAT a1 a2 a3 a4 a5 b1 b2 b3 b4 b5 learn.
            q17 aptitude.
            q18 attitude.
            q19 anxiety.;
RUN;

TITLE3 'Disclosing the data';
PROC PRINT DATA=eval;                        /* Prints the data on the output */
RUN;

TITLE3 'Descriptive statistics for numeric variables';
PROC MEANS DATA=eval;                        /* Computes descriptive stat for numeric variables */
RUN;

TITLE3 'Tabulating frequency for character variables';
PROC FREQ DATA=eval;                         /* Tabulates frequency for character variable */
     TABLES q20a;
RUN;
```

5. Output for the enhanced program of Example 4.1

```
                       Example 4.1 Reading data with INFILE                          1
                          Data came from Y777 course evaluation
                                Disclosing the data

Obs   id   a1            a2            a3            a4            a5            b1           b2

  1    1   Good          Very good     Average       Very good     Average       Very poor    Poor
  2    2   Good          Very good     Good          Very good     Poor          Very poor    Poor
  3    3   Very good     Very good     Average       Good          Poor          Very poor    Average
  4    4   Average       Very good     Good          Good          Average       Very poor    Good
  5    5   Very good     Good          Very good     Good          Good          Very poor    Good
  6    6   Very good     Very good     Good          Average       Very good     Poor         Average
  7    7   Average       Very good     Good          Good          Good          Very poor    Average
  8    8   Average       Good          Very good     Good          Average       Poor         Average
  9    9   Good          Good          Average       Very good     Poor          Very poor    Average
 10   10   Average       Very good     Good          Good          Average       Very poor    Average
 11   11   Average       Good          Very good     Good          Average       Very poor    Average
```

12	12	Poor	Very good	Good	Very good	Good	Very poor	Good
13	13	Good	Average	Good	Good	Good	Very poor	Poor
14	14	Very good	Good	Average	Average	Average	Poor	Poor
15	15	Average	Very good	Good	Average	Good	Average	Average
16	16	Average	Very good	Very good	Good	Average	Very poor	Average
17	17	Good	Good	Good	Good	Average	Very poor	Average
18	18	Good	Very good	Good	Very good	Average	Very poor	Good
19	19	Average	Very good	Good	Average	Good	Very poor	Average
20	20	Poor	Good	Good	Average	Very good	.	.

Obs	b3	b4	b5	q16	q17	q18	q19	q20a
1	Average	Very poor	Very poor	24	Expert	unfavorable	3	yes
2	Poor	Very poor	Very poor	5	Expert	unfavorable	3	yes
3	Poor	Very poor	Very poor	10	Expert	unfavorable	3	yes
4	Poor	Very poor	Poor	20	Expert	unfavorable	3	yes
5	Poor	Very poor	Very poor	.	Expert	2	3	yes
6	Average	Very poor	Very poor	30	3	favorable	3	yes
7	Average	Very poor	Very poor	17	3	favorable	3	no
8	Poor	Very poor	Very poor	15	3	favorable	3	yes
9	Average	Very poor	Very poor	10	3	favorable	.	
10	Very poor	Poor	Very poor	.	3	2	.	yes
11	Poor	Very poor	Very poor	25	4	2	.	no
12	Poor	Very poor	Very poor	20	4	2		yes
13	Very poor	Average	Poor	8	4	2	low	yes
14	Poor	Very poor	Very poor	60	4	2	low	yes
15	Average	Very poor	Very poor	23	4	3	low	
16	Average	Poor	Poor	15	Expert	unfavorable	low	yes
17	Poor	Very poor	Very poor	9	Expert	unfavorable	low	yes
18	Poor	Very poor	Very poor	14	Expert	unfavorable	low	yes
19	Very poor	Very poor	Very poor	22	Expert	unfavorable	low	yes
20	.	.	.	35	Expert	unfavorable	low	no

```
                    Example 4.1 Reading data with INFILE                     2
                     Data came from Y777 course evaluation
                    Descriptive statistics for numeric variables
                          The MEANS Procedure
```

Variable	Label	N	Mean
a1	Current knowledge about sampling methods & distributions	20	3.6500000
a2	Current ability to apply ANOVA-fixed effects model	20	4.5500000
a3	Current ability to apply multiple comparison procedures	20	4.0000000
a4	Current knowledge of randomized block designs	20	4.0000000
a5	Current knowledge of Latin squares designs	20	3.3500000
b1	Prior knowledge about sampling methods & distributions	19	1.2631579
b2	Prior ability to apply ANOVA-fixed effects model	19	3.0000000
b3	Prior ability to apply multiple comparison procedures	19	2.1578947
b4	Prior knowledge of randomized block designs	19	1.2105263
b5	Prior knowledge of Latin squares designs	19	1.1578947
q16	Hours studying per week	18	20.1111111
q17	Aptitude in statistics	20	4.2500000
q18	Attitude toward statistics	20	2.2000000
q19	Anxiety about statistics	16	3.0000000

Variable	Label	Std Dev	Minimum
a1	Current knowledge about sampling methods & distributions	0.9333020	2.0000000
a2	Current ability to apply ANOVA-fixed effects model	0.6048053	3.0000000
a3	Current ability to apply multiple comparison procedures	0.6488857	3.0000000
a4	Current knowledge of randomized block designs	0.7254763	3.0000000
a5	Current knowledge of Latin squares designs	0.8750940	2.0000000
b1	Prior knowledge about sampling methods & distributions	0.5619515	1.0000000
b2	Prior ability to apply ANOVA-fixed effects model	0.6666667	2.0000000
b3	Prior ability to apply multiple comparison procedures	0.6882472	1.0000000
b4	Prior knowledge of randomized block designs	0.5353034	1.0000000
b5	Prior knowledge of Latin squares designs	0.3746343	1.0000000
q16	Hours studying per week	12.7504966	5.0000000
q17	Aptitude in statistics	0.8506963	3.0000000
q18	Attitude toward statistics	1.5423837	1.0000000
q19	Anxiety about statistics	1.0327956	1.0000000

```
Variable  Label                                                          Maximum
--------------------------------------------------------------------------------
   a1       Current knowledge about sampling methods & distributions     5.0000000
   a2       Current ability to apply ANOVA-fixed effects model           5.0000000
   a3       Current ability to apply multiple comparison procedures      5.0000000
   a4       Current knowledge of randomized block designs                5.0000000
   a5       Current knowledge of Latin squares designs                   5.0000000
   b1       Prior knowledge about sampling methods & distributions       3.0000000
   b2       Prior ability to apply ANOVA-fixed effects model             4.0000000
   b3       Prior ability to apply multiple comparison procedures        3.0000000
   b4       Prior knowledge of randomized block designs                  3.0000000
   b5       Prior knowledge of Latin squares designs                     2.0000000
   q16      Hours studying per week                                     60.0000000
   q17      Aptitude in statistics                                       5.0000000
   q18      Attitude toward statistics                                   5.0000000
   q19      Anxiety about statistics                                     3.0000000
--------------------------------------------------------------------------------
```

```
        Example 4.1 Reading data with INFILE                              3
          Data came from Y777 course evaluation
       Tabulating frequency for character variables


                 The FREQ Procedure


          To become a faculty at a university
                              Cumulative    Cumulative
   q20a    Frequency     Percent    Frequency     Percent
   ------------------------------------------------------------
   no            3       16.67          3       16.67
   yes          15       83.33         18      100.00


                 Frequency Missing = 2
```

Log for the enhanced program of Example 4.1

```
3           TITLE  'Example 4.1 Reading data with INFILE';
4           TITLE2 'Data came from Y777 course evaluation';
5           PROC FORMAT;
6               VALUE learn 1 = 'Very poor' 2 = 'Poor' 3 = 'Average' 4 = 'Good' 5 = 'Very good'
6       ! ;
NOTE: Format LEARN has been output.
7               VALUE aptitude 1 = 'Beginner' 5 = 'Expert';
NOTE: Format APTITUDE has been output.
8               VALUE attitude 1 = 'unfavorable' 5 = 'favorable';
NOTE: Format ATTITUDE has been output.
9               VALUE anxiety  1 = 'low' 5 = 'high';
NOTE: Format ANXIETY has been output.
10
NOTE: PROCEDURE FORMAT used (Total process time):
      real time             0.08 seconds
      cpu time              0.02 seconds

11          DATA eval;                           /* Establishes a SAS data set called 'eval'
11      ! */
12              INFILE 'd:\data\Y777.dat';
13              INPUT id $ a1-a5 b1-b5 q16 q17 q18 q19 q20a $;
14              LABEL id = 'Identification number of students'
15                    a1 = 'Current knowledge about sampling methods & distributions'
16                    a2 = 'Current ability to apply ANOVA-fixed effects model'
17                    a3 = 'Current ability to apply multiple comparison procedures'
18                    a4 = 'Current knowledge of randomized block designs'
```

```
19                a5 = 'Current knowledge of Latin squares designs'
20                b1 = 'Prior knowledge about sampling methods & distributions'
21                b2 = 'Prior ability to apply ANOVA-fixed effects model'
22                b3 = 'Prior ability to apply multiple comparison procedures'
23                b4 = 'Prior knowledge of randomized block designs'
24                b5 = 'Prior knowledge of Latin squares designs'
25               q16 = 'Hours studying per week'
26               q17 = 'Aptitude in statistics'
27               q18 = 'Attitude toward statistics'
28               q19 = 'Anxiety about statistics'
29              q20a = 'To become a faculty at a university';
30
31          FORMAT a1 a2 a3 a4 a5 b1 b2 b3 b4 b5 learn.
32                 q17 aptitude.
33                 q18 attitude.
34                 q19 anxiety.;
35       RUN;

NOTE: The infile 'd:\data\Y777.dat' is:
      File Name=d:\data\Y777.dat,
      RECFM=V,LRECL=256

NOTE: 20 records were read from the infile 'd:\data\Y777.dat'.
      The minimum record length was 33.
      The maximum record length was 35.
NOTE: The data set WORK.EVAL has 20 observations and 16 variables.
NOTE: DATA statement used (Total process time):
      real time              0.12 seconds
      cpu time               0.09 seconds


36
37       TITLE3 'Disclosing the data';
38       PROC PRINT DATA=eval;                    /* Prints the data on the output */
39       RUN;

NOTE: There were 20 observations read from the data set WORK.EVAL.
NOTE: The PROCEDURE PRINT printed page 1.
NOTE: PROCEDURE PRINT used (Total process time):
      real time              0.14 seconds
      cpu time               0.11 seconds


40
41       TITLE3 'Descriptive statistics for numeric variables';
42       PROC MEANS DATA=eval;                    /* Computes descriptive stat for numeric
42       ! variables */
43       RUN;

NOTE: There were 20 observations read from the data set WORK.EVAL.
NOTE: The PROCEDURE MEANS printed page 2.
NOTE: PROCEDURE MEANS used (Total process time):
      real time              0.44 seconds
      cpu time               0.08 seconds


44
45       TITLE3 'Tabulating frequency for character variables';
46       PROC FREQ DATA=eval;                     /* Tabulates frequency for character
46       ! variable */
47          TABLES q20a;
48       RUN;

NOTE: There were 20 observations read from the data set WORK.EVAL.
NOTE: The PROCEDURE FREQ printed page 3.
```

6

Verifying Data

OBJECTIVE

Once a SAS data set is created, chores remain to ensure that data values are correctly and completely read. Furthermore, variable names, variable types, and missing values should be checked to make sure that each piece of information registered in a SAS data set is error free. Only when no error is contained in a SAS data set can you trust the results derived from it. In this chapter, you will learn how to verify data by

- listing data with the PRINT procedure,
- displaying data characteristics with the CONTENTS procedure,
- rearranging data by the SORT procedure, and
- ordering data by the RANK procedure.

In Chapters 4 and 5, you have learned how to read raw data into a SAS data set. Each SAS data set has a name and contains information about variable names, their types, data values of these variables, missing values, and a few other features about the data. Because SAS data sets are directly analyzed by a SAS procedure, it is absolutely important that data in a SAS data set be 100% error free. For this reason, this chapter teaches you four useful procedures to verify the accuracy of data stored in a SAS data set. These four procedures are PRINT, CONTENTS, SORT, and RANK. The PRINT and CONTENTS procedures reveal information stored in a SAS data set, whereas the SORT and RANK procedures examine data accuracy by rearranging the data in an ascending or descending order so that you may detect irrational or irregular patterns in data quickly. PROC SORT can be used in conjunction with other procedures to perform subgroup analyses, such as with PROC MEANS to compute average blood pressures for men and women separately.

6.1 Listing Data With the PRINT Procedure _____

The PRINT procedure is designed to list data in a SAS data set. It has been used in previous chapters to verify data. Its syntax is shown below:

PROC	PRINT	DATA= *sas_dataset_name <options>*;
	VAR	*variable(s)*;
	BY	*classification_variable(s)*;
	PAGEBY	*names_of_ BY_ variable(s)*;
	SUM	*variable(s)*;
	SUMBY	*names_of_ BY_ variable(s)*;

On the first statement, that is, **PROC PRINT**, the **DATA=** option names a SAS data set. If the DATA= option is omitted, the PRINT procedure uses the most recently created SAS data set. This convention applies to all PROCs in SAS. Other options that are commonly used on PROC PRINT include the following:

N	prints the number of observations in the data set on the output.
DOUBLE (or D)	uses double space for printing.
UNIFORM	controls the appearance of print pages to make them uniform.
ROUND	rounds up unformatted numeric data values to two decimal points before totaling.
LABEL	prints variable labels on the output.

The second statement, **VAR**, is used to name variables from the SAS data set whose values are to be printed. If VAR is not used, all variables in the SAS data set will be shown.

The third statement, **BY**, divides the data set into subgroups according to diverse values of the BY variable(s). As a result, printed data values are separated by subsets. Each subset is defined by a value of the BY variable, such as F and M of gender. If more than one BY variable is specified, such as gender and grade (1, 2, and 3), all possible combinations of values of BY variables are used in dividing up the entire data set into subsets. In this case, six subsets result: F and M for each of the three grades. To invoke the BY statement, you need to make sure that the SAS data set is structured in the ascending order of the BY variable(s). If it is not, you can presort the data set with the SORT procedure, which is introduced later, in **Section 6.3**.

The fourth statement, **PAGEBY**, is used to list subset results on a new page. This statement must be used concurrently with the BY statement.

The fifth statement, **SUM**, is used to compute the total of all observations for variables named in this statement.

The sixth statement, **SUMBY**, is used to compute the subtotal of each subset of observations for variables named in the SUM statement. If the SUM statement is omitted, the subtotals for the variables listed in the VAR statement are calculated. The SUMBY statement must be used concurrently with the BY statement.

The following example demonstrates the DOUBLE option and the VAR statement. Data are read into a SAS data set, called roster, from the d drive and the folder data. The raw data file, roster.dat, was previously used in Chapter 2, **Section 2.5**. It consists of 14 students' scores on four tests, along with their names, gender, identification numbers, and academic standings. Data are downloadable from the SAGE Web site at www.sagepub.com/pengstudy. The VAR statement is written in such a way that all variables between first and final are to be included. Hence, the output contains data values for the first, second, and final variables.

Example 6.1 PRINT Procedure With
DOUBLE Option and VAR Statement

```
/* The following bolded SAS statements establish the SAS data set 'roster' */

DATA roster;
    INFILE 'd:\data\roster.dat';
    INPUT name $ sex $ id $ stand pretest first second final;
    LABEL first = 'first midterm score'
          second = 'second midterm score'
          final = 'final exam score';
RUN;

TITLE 'Example 6.1 PROC PRINT with options';

PROC PRINT DATA=roster DOUBLE;
    VAR name first--final;     /* Double hyphen (--) means all variables between    */
                               /* 'first' and 'final' are included in the VAR statement */
RUN;
```

Output 6.1 PRINT Procedure With
DOUBLE Option and VAR Statement

```
      Example 6.1 PROC PRINT with options                                      1

    Obs     name      first     second     final

      1     JOHN        31         45         .

      2     DAN         46         53        54

      3     LYNN        38         33        43

      4     CATHY       34         50        32

      5     JAMES       31         47        43

      6     TIM         45         51        57

      7     HOPE        34         46        50

      8     TED         44         52        47

      9     SASSY       50         57        56

     10     NANCY       29         39        42

     11     PAUL        24         48        49

     12     LIN         48         54        54

     13     TOM         48         52        42

     14     BOB         32         41        40
```

Example 6.1a PRINT Procedure
With DOUBLE and LABEL Options

```
/* See Example 6.1 for the DATA step in creating the SAS data set 'roster' */

TITLE 'Example 6.1a PROC PRINT with options';

PROC PRINT DATA=roster DOUBLE LABEL;
    VAR name first--final;    /* Double hyphen (--) means all variables between      */
                              /* 'first' and 'final' are included in the VAR statement */
RUN;
```

When the option LABEL is used in the PROC PRINT statement, the output will print variable labels as headings, instead of variable names specified on the VAR statement. Try executing Example 6.1a and see what you find. Sometimes if the data set is large and it is time-consuming to display all observations, you can list only the first 10 observations, for instance. To specify the first 10 observations, modify the first statement in Example 6.1 as PROC PRINT DATA=roster(OBS=10) DOUBLE;. On the output, you will see only the first 10 observations printed, that is, from JOHN (Obs=1) through NANCY (Obs=10). Verify this on your own.

If you'd like to specify the third observation, namely, LYNN, or Obs=3, to be the first printed, you need to insert an additional option, FIRSTOBS=3, before the OBS=10 option, in parentheses. Try executing Example 6.2 below to find out if your output looks like Output 6.2.

Example 6.2 PRINT Procedure With Selected Observations

```
/* See Example 6.1 for the DATA step in creating the SAS data set 'roster' */

TITLE 'Example 6.2 PROC PRINT with selected observations';

PROC PRINT DATA=roster(FIRSTOBS=3 OBS=10) DOUBLE; /*Prints observations 3 to 10 */
    VAR name first--final;
RUN;
```

Output 6.2 PRINT Procedure With Selected Observations

```
Example 6.2 PROC PRINT with selected observations                            1

    Obs     name      first     second      final

     3      LYNN       38        33          43

     4      CATHY      34        50          32
```

5	JAMES	31	47	43
6	TIM	45	51	57
7	HOPE	34	46	50
8	TED	44	52	47
9	SASSY	50	57	56
10	NANCY	29	39	42

Are you a little surprised by Output 6.2? It does present the third observation, LYNN, as the first one, preceding the other 7 observations ending with NANCY (Obs=10). So you learn that the specification of OBS=10 instructs SAS to continue processing the data set up to and including the 10th observation, namely, the last observation. The FIRSTOBS= option instructs SAS to start the data processing from the observation specified. If the FIRSTOBS= option is not specified, SAS begins processing the data from the first observation of the data set. In other words, the default value for the option FIRSTOBS= is 1.

Example 6.3 PRINT Procedure for Totals

This example illustrates simple computing capabilities available in the PRINT procedure. Specifically, the roster data set is first sorted by the SORT procedure according to the two values of the variable sex. Then, first and final values are totaled for the entire data set as well as for the f (female) and m (male) subgroups.

```
/* See Example 6.1 for the DATA step in creating the SAS data set 'roster' */

PROC SORT DATA=roster;
     BY sex;
RUN;

TITLE 'Example 6.3 PROC PRINT for totals';
PROC PRINT DATA=roster;
     BY sex;
     SUM first final;
     SUMBY sex;
RUN;
```

Output 6.3 PRINT Procedure for Totals

```
                                                                           1
                        Example 6.3 PROC PRINT for totals

---------------------------------- sex=f ----------------------------------------

    Obs    name     id    stand    pretest    first    second    final

     1     LYNN      4      1          7        38        33       43
     2     CATHY     6      2         12        34        50       32
     3     HOPE      9      4         17        34        46       50
     4     SASSY    12      4         18        50        57       56
     5     NANCY    13      3         15        29        39       42
    ---                                        -----              -----
    sex                                         185                223


---------------------------------- sex=m ----------------------------------------

    Obs    name     id    stand    pretest    first    second    final

     6     JOHN      1      1          9        31        45        .
     7     DAN       3      4         18        46        53       54
     8     JAMES     7      2         14        31        47       43
     9     TIM       8      4         20        45        51       57
    10     TED      10      2         12        44        52       47
    11     PAUL     14      3         15        24        48       49
    12     LIN      15      4         18        48        54       54
    13     TOM      16      4         21        48        52       42
    14     BOB      17      1         11        32        41       40
    ---                                        -----              -----
    sex                                         349                386
                                               =====              =====
                                                534                609
```

The output is divided into two subgroups: one based on "sex=f" and the other based on "sex=m". Subtotals of first and final are calculated for each subgroup. So for the five girls, their first total is 185 and final total is 223. For the nine boys, first total = 349 and final total = 386. The grand total for both girls and boys is given beneath the ===== line at the end of the output: 534 (= 185 + 349) for the first and 609 (= 223 + 386) for the final. Thus, this example demonstrates a simple additive capability provided by the PRINT procedure for numeric variables.

6.2 Displaying Data Characteristics With the CONTENTS Procedure

The CONTENTS procedure is written simply as

    PROC   CONTENTS   DATA= sas_dataset_name <options>;

The CONTENTS procedure reveals descriptions of a SAS data set: its name, creation date, the number of observations and of variables, indices, observation length, variables' type, length, position on a data record, format, informat, and label, and so forth. In Example 6.1, the LABEL statement labels three variables, first, second, and final. These labels are disclosed in the output by the CONTENTS procedure. Let's apply the CONTENTS procedure to the roster data set.

Example 6.4 PROC CONTENTS Illustrated

```
/* See Example 6.1 for the DATA step in creating the SAS data set 'roster' */

TITLE 'Example 6.4 PROC CONTENTS illustrated';

PROC CONTENTS DATA=roster;
RUN;
```

Output 6.4 PROC CONTENTS Illustrated

```
                        Example 6.4 PROC CONTENTS illustrated                    1
                             The CONTENTS Procedure

        Data Set Name       WORK.ROSTER                 Observations         14
        Member Type         DATA                        Variables            8
        Engine              V9                          Indexes              0
        Created             Thu, Sep 06, 2007 05:51:39 PM  Observation Length   64
        Last Modified       Thu, Sep 06, 2007 05:51:39 PM  Deleted Observations 0
        Protection                                      Compressed           NO
        Data Set Type                                   Sorted               NO
        Label
        Data Representation WINDOWS_32
        Encoding            wlatin1  Western (Windows)


                        Engine/Host Dependent Information

    Data Set Page Size       8192
    Number of Data Set Pages 1
    First Data Page          1
    Max Obs per Page         127
    Obs in First Data Page   14
    Number of Data Set Repairs 0
    File Name                C:\DOCUME~1\peng\LOCALS~1\Temp\SAS Temporary
                             Files\_TD1064\roster.sas7bdat
    Release Created          9.0101M3
    Host Created             WIN_PRO


                        Alphabetic List of Variables and Attributes

            #   Variable   Type   Len   Label

            8   final      Num    8     final exam score
            6   first      Num    8     first midterm score
            3   id         Char   8
            1   name       Char   8
            5   pretest    Num    8
            7   second     Num    8     second midterm score
            2   sex        Char   8
            4   stand      Num    8
```

It is evident from Output 6.4 that PROC CONTENTS provides a quick way for you to check the description of a SAS data set; the description in turn can alert you to errors, if there are any. By default, variables and their attributes are listed in alphabetic order. If you wish to list variables in the order of the INPUT statement, you may add the option VARNUM to the PROC CONTENTS statement, as shown in Example 6.4a. Try executing this program and find out what the output looks like.

Example 6.4a PROC CONTENTS With VARNUM Option

```
/* See Example 6.1 for the DATA step in creating the SAS data set 'roster' */

TITLE 'Example 6.4a PROC CONTENTS with VARNUM option';

PROC CONTENTS DATA=roster VARNUM;
RUN;
```

6.3 Rearranging Data by the SORT Procedure

The SORT procedure is used primarily to rearrange observations in an ascending or descending sequence within a SAS data set. The sequence is determined by observations' values on one or more variables. For example, a professor can use this procedure to post his or her students' test scores from the highest to the lowest. Or a credit card company can keep track of customers who owe the most to the least on a monthly basis with the SORT procedure. By the same token, a telemarketing firm can use a list of alphabetized last names of consumers for direct marketing. In this last case, PROC SORT can be used to sort observations in ascending order of the first character of last names. It is also possible to base sorting on two variables, such as the last name (character) and annual income (numeric). Below is the simple syntax of the SORT procedure:

```
PROC   SORT        DATA= sas_dataset_name OUT= sas_dataset_name;

       BY          classification_variable(s);
```

Only two statements are needed: **PROC SORT** and **BY**. Two essential options are available with the PROC SORT statement: **DATA=** and **OUT=**. The DATA= option names a SAS data set that is to be sorted. The other option, OUT=, is used to store the sorted data set by a different name so that you may have two data sets after the sorting: one is the presorted data set (specified by DATA=) and the other is the postsorted, or simply sorted, data set (specified by OUT=). If you wish to save the sorted data set by the original name, skip the OUT= option. The default is to save the sorted data set by the original data set name.

The BY statement specifies variables on which the sorting is based, such as name, annual income, and so on. By default, PROC SORT sorts observations in ascending order from a to z, from A to Z, or from the lowest to the highest values. To reverse this default order, the keyword DESCENDING is inserted before the variable name, such as income, on the BY statement. Thus, the statement below will sort observations first by name in ascending order from A to Z, then by income in descending order from the highest to the lowest value.

```
BY name DESCENDING income;
```

Using the same data set, roster.dat, the next four examples demonstrate the versatile applications of PROC SORT. Example 6.5 sorts data by one numeric variable (average), Example 6.6 sorts data by two numeric variables (pretest and average), Example 6.7 by one character variable (name), and Example 6.8 by two character variables (sex and name). Let's examine each output and differences among them.

Example 6.5 Sorting by One Numeric Variable

```
* The following bolded SAS statements establish the SAS data set 'rostera' */

DATA rostera;
    INFILE 'd:\data\roster.dat';
    INPUT name $ sex $ id $ stand pretest first second final;
    average = MEAN(pretest,first,second,final);              /* compute the average */
RUN;

TITLE 'Example 6.5 Sorting by one numeric variable';

PROC SORT DATA-rostera;
    BY DESCENDING average;
RUN;

PROC PRINT DATA=rostera;
RUN;
```

Output 6.5 Sorting by One Numeric Variable

```
                Example 6.5 Sorting by one numeric variable                    1

 Obs    name    sex    id    stand    pretest    first    second    final    average
  1     SASSY    f     12      4        18         50       57        56     45.2500
  2     LIN      m     15      4        18         48       54        54     43.5000
  3     TIM      m      8      4        20         45       51        57     43.2500
  4     DAN      m      3      4        18         46       53        54     42.7500
```

5	TOM	m	16	4	21	48	52	42	40.7500
6	TED	m	10	2	12	44	52	47	38.7500
7	HOPE	f	9	4	17	34	46	50	36.7500
8	PAUL	m	14	3	15	24	48	49	34.0000
9	JAMES	m	7	2	14	31	47	43	33.7500
10	CATHY	f	6	2	12	34	50	32	32.0000
11	NANCY	f	13	3	15	29	39	42	31.2500
12	BOB	m	17	1	11	32	41	40	31.0000
13	LYNN	f	4	1	7	38	33	43	30.2500
14	JOHN	m	1	1	9	31	45	.	28.3333

SASSY's name is on the top with the highest <u>average</u> (45.2500). The next example demonstrates how the same data set is sorted according to two variables, <u>pretest</u> and <u>average</u>.

Example 6.6 Sorting by Two Numeric Variables

```
/* See Example 6.5 for the DATA step in creating the SAS data set 'rostera' */

TITLE 'Example 6.6 Sorting by two numeric variables';

PROC SORT DATA=rostera;
    BY DESCENDING pretest DESCENDING average;
RUN;

PROC PRINT DATA=rostera;
RUN;
```

Output 6.6 Sorting by Two Numeric Variables

```
                    Example 6.6 Sorting by two numeric variables                      1

Obs    name    sex    id    stand    pretest    first    second    final    average

  1     TOM     m     16      4        21        48        52       42      40.7500
  2     TIM     m      8      4        20        45        51       57      43.2500
  3     SASSY   f     12      4        18        50        57       56      45.2500
  4     LIN     m     15      4        18        48        54       54      43.5000
  5     DAN     m      3      4        18        46        53       54      42.7500
  6     HOPE    f      9      4        17        34        46       50      36.7500
  7     PAUL    m     14      3        15        24        48       49      34.0000
  8     NANCY   f     13      3        15        29        39       42      31.2500
  9     JAMES   m      7      2        14        31        47       43      33.7500
 10     TED     m     10      2        12        44        52       47      38.7500
 11     CATHY   f      6      2        12        34        50       32      32.0000
 12     BOB     m     17      1        11        32        41       40      31.0000
 13     JOHN    m      1      1         9        31        45        .      28.3333
 14     LYNN    f      4      1         7        38        33       43      30.2500
```

Output 6.6 looks different from Output 6.5 in that TOM is now on the top because he scored the highest on <u>pretest</u>. Since no one else has achieved TOM's level on the <u>pretest</u>, no sorting was necessary on the second variable, average. This is also the case with TIM. Below TOM and TIM, three students (SASSY, LIN, and DAN) are tied on the pretest (= 18). Because SASSY's average is the highest (= 45.25), she is listed as the highest among these three. She is followed by LIN with an average of 43.5 and DAN with an average of 42.75. Thus, when two variables are used for sorting, observations are sorted first by values of the first variable (pretest in this example), then by values of the second variable (average). If the keyword DESCENDING had been omitted from the variable average, SAS would have sorted SASSY, LIN, and DAN conversely from the lowest to the highest on average. So be aware that the default setting is ascending.

Next, let's learn sorting by character variables—first, by one character variable (Example 6.7), then by two (Example 6.8).

Example 6.7 Sorting by One Character Variable

```
/* See Example 6.5 for the DATA step in creating the SAS data set 'rostera' */

TITLE 'Example 6.7 Sorting by one character variable';

PROC SORT DATA=rostera;
     BY name;
RUN;

PROC PRINT DATA=rostera;
RUN;
```

Since the keyword DESCENDING is omitted from the program, the output will show names arranged in an alphabetical sequence, that is, in ascending order.

Output 6.7 Sorting by One Character Variable

```
                    Example 6.7 Sorting by one character variable                    1

Obs    name     sex    id    stand    pretest    first    second    final    average

  1    BOB       m     17      1        11        32       41       40       31.0000
  2    CATHY     f      6      2        12        34       50       32       32.0000
  3    DAN       m      3      4        18        46       53       54       42.7500
  4    HOPE      f      9      4        17        34       46       50       36.7500
  5    JAMES     m      7      2        14        31       47       43       33.7500
  6    JOHN      m      1      1         9        31       45        .       28.3333
  7    LIN       m     15      4        18        48       54       54       43.5000
  8    LYNN      f      4      1         7        38       33       43       30.2500
  9    NANCY     f     13      3        15        29       39       42       31.2500
 10    PAUL      m     14      3        15        24       48       49       34.0000
 11    SASSY     f     12      4        18        50       57       56       45.2500
 12    TED       m     10      2        12        44       52       47       38.7500
 13    TIM       m      8      4        20        45       51       57       43.2500
 14    TOM       m     16      4        21        48       52       42       40.7500
```

The output shows that when a character variable (name) is used as the basis for sorting, the sorting is performed by the first character of name, unless the first character of two names are identical. This is the reason why BOB is followed by CATHY and JOHN comes after JAMES. Next, we will look at an example that employs two character variables in sorting.

Example 6.8 Sorting by Two Character Variables

```
/* See Example 6.5 for the DATA step in creating the SAS data set 'rostera' */

TITLE 'Example 6.8 Sorting by two character variables';

PROC SORT DATA=rostera;
    BY sex name;
RUN;

PROC PRINT DATA=rostera;
RUN;
```

In the example above, the first sorting variable (sex) is used to divide the data set into two subsets: f for females and m for males. Within each subset, name is used to further sort observations alphabetically. Output 6.8 shows how 14 observations were sorted by the SORT procedure.

Output 6.8 Sorting by Two Character Variables

```
                    Example 6.8 Sorting by two character variables                    1

 Obs    name     sex    id    stand    pretest    first    second    final    average

  1     CATHY     f      6      2         12        34       50        32      32.0000
  2     HOPE      f      9      4         17        34       46        50      36.7500
  3     LYNN      f      4      1          7        38       33        43      30.2500
  4     NANCY     f     13      3         15        29       39        42      31.2500
  5     SASSY     f     12      4         18        50       57        56      45.2500
  6     BOB       m     17      1         11        32       41        40      31.0000
  7     DAN       m      3      4         18        46       53        54      42.7500
  8     JAMES     m      7      2         14        31       47        43      33.7500
  9     JOHN      m      1      1          9        31       45         .      28.3333
 10     LIN       m     15      4         18        48       54        54      43.5000
 11     PAUL      m     14      3         15        24       48        49      34.0000
 12     TED       m     10      2         12        44       52        47      38.7500
 13     TIM       m      8      4         20        45       51        57      43.2500
 14     TOM       m     16      4         21        48       52        42      40.7500
```

In general, numeric and character sorting can be carried out for any characters found on the keyboard. Below are three lists of ascending priorities used by the SORT procedure in sorting. The first two lists are used for character sorting and the third for numeric sorting.

List A. Sorting Character Variables (in ASCII code used by UNIX and its derivatives, VMS, and Windows operating systems)

```
===================================================================
blank ! " # $ % & ' ( ) * + , - . / 0 1 2 3 4 5 6 7 8 9 : ; < = > ? @
A B C D E F G J I J K L M N O P Q R S T U V W X Y Z [ \ ] ^ _
a b c d e f g h i j k l m n o p q r s t u v w x y z { } ~
===================================================================
```

List B. Sorting Character Variables (in EBCDIC code used by the z/OS operating system)

```
=============================================================
blank . < ( + | & ! $ * ) ; ¬   / , % _ > ? : # @ ' = "
a b c d e f g h i j k l m n o p q r ~ s t u v w x y z
{ A B C D E F G J I } J K L M N O P Q R \ S T U V W X Y Z
0 1 2 3 4 5 6 7 8 9
=============================================================
```

List C. Sorting Numeric Variables

```
=========================================================
missing values ( ._ )    ( . )    ( .A to .Z ),
numeric values (negative values, zero, positive values)
=========================================================
```

In addition, the option ASCII can be specified in the PROC SORT statement when you sort a character variable by ASCII codes in a system where EBCDIC is the native collating sequence. Similarly, the option EBCDIC needs to be specified when you sort by EBCDIC codes in systems where ASCII is the native collating sequence.

6.4 Ordering Data by the RANK Procedure _____

Yet another way for you to verify data in a SAS data set is to rank the order of observations according to one or more numeric variables. The ranked data may be subsequently examined to determine if they meet your expectations. Ranking is carried out by the RANK procedure. The RANK procedure assigns ranks from high to low, or low to high, much like the SORT procedure. However, ranking is based on only one variable. Multiple independent rankings can be accomplished by simultaneously specifying two or more variables on the VAR and RANKS statements. If several observations are tied on the criterion variable, the RANK procedure assigns the average rank to all tied observations. Examples 6.9 to 6.11 illustrate the application of the RANK procedure.

Example 6.9 Ranking by One Numeric Variable

```
/* The following bolded SAS statements establish the SAS data set 'roster1' */

DATA roster1;
    INFILE 'd:\data\roster.dat';
    INPUT name $ sex $ id $ stand pretest first second final;
    average = MEAN(pretest,first,second,final);    /* Computes the average */
RUN;

TITLE 'Example 6.9 Ranking by one numeric variable';

PROC RANK DATA=roster1 OUT=roster2;
    VAR average;
    RANKS rankave;
RUN;

PROC PRINT DATA=roster2;
RUN;
```

Example 6.9 assigns ranks to observations based on their average scores. These ranks become values of a new variable called rankave. This new variable, along with all other variables, is saved into a new SAS data set called roster2; it is subsequently displayed in the output by the PRINT procedure.

Output 6.9 Ranking by One Numeric Variable

```
                    Example 6.9 Ranking by one numeric variable              1

Obs    name    sex    id    stand    pretest    first    second    final    average    rankave

 1     JOHN     m      1      1          9        31       45         .      28.3333       1
 2     DAN      m      3      4         18        46       53        54      42.7500      11
 3     LYNN     f      4      1          7        38       33        43      30.2500       2
 4     CATHY    f      6      2         12        34       50        32      32.0000       5
 5     JAMES    m      7      2         14        31       47        43      33.7500       6
 6     TIM      m      8      4         20        45       51        57      43.2500      12
 7     HOPE     f      9      4         17        34       46        50      36.7500       8
 8     TED      m     10      2         12        44       52        47      38.7500       9
 9     SASSY    f     12      4         18        50       57        56      45.2500      14
10     NANCY    f     13      3         15        29       39        42      31.2500       4
11     PAUL     m     14      3         15        24       48        49      34.0000       7
12     LIN      m     15      4         18        48       54        54      43.5000      13
13     TOM      m     16      4         21        48       52        42      40.7500      10
14     BOB      m     17      1         11        32       41        40      31.0000       3
```

Note that rankave contains information about ranks of observations according to average ascending scores. Therefore, JOHN received the first rank, LYNN the second rank, and SASSY the highest rank (14, also the size of the sample). If an observation has a missing value on average, then he or she is automatically ranked the lowest, or 1.

Sometimes, you may want to assign the first rank to the observation with the highest score. This is done with the keyword DESCENDING, as illustrated in Example 6.10.

Example 6.10 Ranking From High to Low

```
/* See Example 6.9 for the DATA step in creating the SAS data set 'roster1' */

TITLE 'Example 6.10 Ranking from high to low';

PROC RANK DATA=roster1 OUT=roster2 DESCENDING;
    VAR average;
    RANKS rankave;
RUN;

PROC PRINT DATA=roster2;
RUN;
```

Output 6.10 Ranking From High to Low

```
                      Example 6.10 Ranking from high to low                        1

 Obs   name    sex   id   stand   pretest   first   second   final   average   rankave

   1   JOHN     m     1     1        9        31      45        .     28.3333     14
   2   DAN      m     3     4       18        46      53       54     42.7500      4
   3   LYNN     f     4     1        7        38      33       43     30.2500     13
   4   CATHY    f     6     2       12        34      50       32     32.0000     10
   5   JAMES    m     7     2       14        31      47       43     33.7500      9
   6   TIM      m     8     4       20        45      51       57     43.2500      3
   7   HOPE     f     9     4       17        34      46       50     36.7500      7
   8   TED      m    10     2       12        44      52       47     38.7500      6
   9   SASSY    f    12     4       18        50      57       56     45.2500      1
  10   NANCY    f    13     3       15        29      39       42     31.2500     11
  11   PAUL     m    14     3       15        24      48       49     34.0000      8
  12   LIN      m    15     4       18        48      54       54     43.5000      2
  13   TOM      m    16     4       21        48      52       42     40.7500      5
  14   BOB      m    17     1       11        32      41       40     31.0000     12
```

If you compare Output 6.10 with Output 6.9, you will notice that the two ranks assigned to the same observation are complementary to each other. In other words, each observation's two rankaves, obtained from both outputs, add to 15, which equals the total number of observations (14) plus 1.

Example 6.11 Ranking by Two Numeric Variables

```
/* See Example 6.9 for the DATA step in creating the SAS data set 'roster1' */

TITLE 'Example 6.11 Ranking by two numeric variables';

PROC RANK DATA=roster1 OUT=roster2;
    VAR pretest average;
    RANKS rankpre rankave;
RUN;

PROC PRINT DATA=roster2;
RUN;
```

Output 6.11 Ranking by Two Numeric Variables

```
              Example 6.11 Ranking by two numeric variables                    1

Obs   name   sex   id   stand   pretest   first   second   final   average   rankpre   rankave

  1   JOHN    m     1     1         9        31      45       .     28.3333     2.0        1
  2   DAN     m     3     4        18        46      53      54     42.7500    11.0       11
  3   LYNN    f     4     1         7        38      33      43     30.2500     1.0        2
  4   CATHY   f     6     2        12        34      50      32     32.0000     4.5        5
  5   JAMES   m     7     2        14        31      47      43     33.7500     6.0        6
  6   TIM     m     8     4        20        45      51      57     43.2500    13.0       12
  7   HOPE    f     9     4        17        34      46      50     36.7500     9.0        8
  8   TED     m    10     2        12        44      52      47     38.7500     4.5        9
  9   SASSY   f    12     4        18        50      57      56     45.2500    11.0       14
 10   NANCY   f    13     3        15        29      39      42     31.2500     7.5        4
 11   PAUL    m    14     3        15        24      48      49     34.0000     7.5        7
 12   LIN     m    15     4        18        48      54      54     43.5000    11.0       13
 13   TOM     m    16     4        21        48      52      42     40.7500    14.0       10
 14   BOB     m    17     1        11        32      41      40     31.0000     3.0        3
```

Output 6.11 displays two additional variables, rankpre and rankave, that are ranks of pretest and average scores, respectively, from low to high.

The syntax of the RANK procedure is easy to write:

PROC RANK	DATA= *SAS_data_set* OUT= *SAS_data_set* DESCENDING;
VAR	*numeric_variable(s)*;
RANKS	*new_variable_name(s)*;
BY	*classification_variable(s)*;

In the **PROC RANK** statement, the **DATA=** option specifies a SAS data set that contains the unranked observations, whereas **OUT=** names a SAS data set that stores the ranked data. The default to ranking is from the lowest to the highest. To reverse this, you specify the option **DESCENDING** that assigns the rank of 1 to the highest score, 2 to the second highest, and so on.

Observations tied on the same numeric value are assigned the average rank, which is the default. The **BY** statement is used to perform ranking within subsets of data. The subsets are created according to diverse values of the BY variable(s). To specify the BY statement, the SAS data set must be presorted by the SORT procedure, either in ascending or descending order. Additional applications of the RANK procedure are found in nonparametric statistical techniques that use ranks in analyses, instead of the raw data. For details, consult with PROC RANK in *Base SAS 9.1.3 Procedures Guide* (SAS Institute Inc., 2006a).

6.5 Summary

Four procedures were introduced in this chapter for verifying data in a SAS data set. The PRINT procedure is used to list variable names and data values, including missing values. It provides the simplest and quickest way to verify information stored in a SAS data set. The PRINT procedure can also be used for simple descriptive analysis, such as summing values of numeric variables for the entire SAS data set or for its subsets. The CONTENTS procedure is used to retrieve summative information about a data set's creation date, number of observations, and variables—their names, types, formats, column locations, labels, and so on. The information disclosed by PROC CONTENTS is useful for quick reference and for verification. The SORT procedure rearranges observations based on one or more variables so that you may grasp a general trend in the data. Last, the RANK procedure assigns ranks to observations according to numeric variable values. The ranks can then be used to identify miscoded values or observations.

Until you are fully confident that all information stored in a SAS data set is complete and 100% error free, the energy and time invested in further analyses of the data are in vain.

6.6 Exercises

1. Which of the following SAS statements is correct?
   a. ```
      PROC SORT DATA=class;
      PROC PRINT DATA=class; BY sex;
      SUM height weight;
      SUMBY sex;
      ```

   b. ```
      PROC SORT DATA=class; BY sex;
      PROC PRINT DATA=class; BY sex;
      SUM height weight; BY sex;
      ```

   c. ```
      PROC SORT DATA=class; BY sex;
      PROC PRINT DATA=class; BY sex;
      SUM height weight;
      SUMBY sex;
      ```

   d. ```
      PROC SORT DATA=class; BY sex;
      SUM height weight; VAR sex;
      ```

2. What is the output result of the SAS program below?

```
DATA a; INPUT x y $ z;
DATALINES;
    1    1    1
    .    *    2
    2    a    3
    2    A    4
    3    a    5
    .    A    6
RUN;
PROC SORT;  BY x y; RUN;
PROC PRINT; RUN;
```

a. Obs	x	y	z		b. Obs	x	y	z
1	1	1	1		1	.	A	6
2	2	A	2		2	.	*	2
3	2	a	3		3	1	1	1
4	3	a	5		4	2	A	2
5	.	A	6		5	2	a	3
6	.	*	2		6	3	a	5

c. Obs	x	y	z		d. Obs	x	y	z
1	.	*	2		1	.	*	2
2	.	A	6		2	.	A	6
3	1	1	1		3	1	1	1
4	2	a	3		4	2	A	4
5	2	A	2		5	2	a	3
6	3	a	5		6	3	a	5

3. Cynthia wants to compare income (salary plus commission) of male and female salespersons in a company. Here is the SAS program she wrote. Will she get the information she wants?

```
DATA sales;
    INPUT name $ sex $ salary commission;
DATALINES;
[data lines]
PROC PRINT DATA=sales;
    BY sex;
    SUM salary commission;
    SUMBY sex;
RUN;
```

   a. No, because she did not create a new variable, income, that adds salary to commission.
   b. Yes, she would.
   c. No, because the SUM statement is not written correctly.
   d. No, because the SUMBY statement is unnecessary after the BY and SUM statements.
   e. No, because the data set sales needs to be presorted by PROC SORT before being analyzed by PROC PRINT.

4. Given the following program, identify statements or keywords that should immediately precede PROC MEANS.

```
PROC MEANS DATA=ht_wt;
    BY age;
    VAR height weight;
PROC PRINT;
RUN;
```

a. DATA ht_wt; INPUT age height weight; DATALINES;
b. PROC SORT; BY age; RUN;
c. PROC SORT; BY height weight; RUN.

5. Given the following information in data set a below,

VARIABLES:	name	sex	age	room	s.e.s	income (in $1000)
	ANDY	M	28	122	H	9.6
	SOPHIA	F	42	412	M	7.4
	LOUIS	M	34	213	L	2.3
	LANDERS	M	40	216	M	5.8
	TED	M	68	101	H	8.8
	DICKENS	M	37	135	M	6.3
	RUTH	F	39	430	L	1.3
	CHARLIE	M	54	222	M	4.7
	MICHAEL	M	25	118	M	6.0
	WOLF	M	51	104	H	8.4
	ANNE	F	58	404	H	10.2
	REBECCA	F	43	423	M	7.1
	DAVID	M	47	117	M	5.2
	RICHARD	M	28	240	H	9.2
	SAM	M	36	231	M	6.4
	TINA	F	31	302	M	4.3
	PETER	M	65	108	L	3.3
	SHEILA	F	24	336	M	5.7
	TIM	M	27	115	H	8.2
	LINDA	F	20	425	M	5.5

a. Sort data set a alphabetically by name.
b. Assume that the room numbers represent floor levels. For example, Room 404 is a room on the fourth floor and Room 117 is on the first floor. Sort the data set first by floor level, then by sex. Find the relationship, if there is any, between sex and floor level of rooms.
c. Define five age groups according to the following age ranges:
   Group 1 = 20 to 29 years old
   Group 2 = 30 to 39 years old
   Group 3 = 40 to 49 years old
   Group 4 = 50 to 59 years old
   Group 5 = 60 to 69 years old
   What is the total income earned in each age group and by the entire data set?
d. What is the total income earned in each ses group?

6. Rewrite Example 6.6 so that the variable pretest is sorted in ascending order and the variable average is in descending order. Compare your output with Output 6.6.

7. Rewrite Example 6.8 so that the variable name is sorted in ascending order and the variable sex is in descending order. Compare your output with Output 6.8.

6.7 Answers to Exercises

1. c

2. d

3. a, c

4. d

5. a. Data set <u>a</u> sorted by <u>name</u>:

```
                 Exercise 6.5a Sorting data by name            1

      Obs      name      sex      age      room      ses      income

        1      ANDY       M        28       122       H         9.6
        2      ANNE       F        58       404       H        10.2
        3      CHARLIE    M        54       222       M         4.7
        4      DAVID      M        47       117       M         5.2
        5      DICKENS    M        37       135       M         6.3
        6      LANDERS    M        40       216       M         5.8
        7      LINDA      F        20       425       M         5.5
        8      LOUIS      M        34       213       L         2.3
        9      MICHAEL    M        25       118       M         6.0
       10      PETER      M        65       108       L         3.3
       11      REBECCA    F        43       423       M         7.1
       12      RICHARD    M        28       240       H         9.2
       13      RUTH       F        39       430       L         1.3
       14      SAM        M        36       231       M         6.4
       15      SHEILA     F        24       336       M         5.7
       16      SOPHIA     F        42       412       M         7.4
       17      TED        M        68       101       H         8.8
       18      TIM        M        27       115       H         8.2
       19      TINA       F        31       302       M         4.3
       20      WOLF       M        51       104       H         8.4
```

b. From the sorted data below, it appears that all men lived on the first and the second floors while women lived on the third and the fourth floors.

```
        Exercise 6.5b Sorting data by floor and sex              2

 Obs    name       sex     age     room     ses     income     level

   1    ANDY        M       28      122       H       9.6         1
   2    DAVID       M       47      117       M       5.2         1
   3    DICKENS     M       37      135       M       6.3         1
   4    MICHAEL     M       25      118       M       6.0         1
   5    PETER       M       65      108       L       3.3         1
   6    TED         M       68      101       H       8.8         1
   7    TIM         M       27      115       H       8.2         1
   8    WOLF        M       51      104       H       8.4         1
   9    CHARLIE     M       54      222       M       4.7         2
  10    LANDERS     M       40      216       M       5.8         2
```

11	LOUIS	M	34	213	L	2.3	2
12	RICHARD	M	28	240	H	9.2	2
13	SAM	M	36	231	M	6.4	2
14	SHEILA	F	24	336	M	5.7	3
15	TINA	F	31	302	M	4.3	3
16	ANNE	F	58	404	H	10.2	4
17	LINDA	F	20	425	M	5.5	4
18	REBECCA	F	43	423	M	7.1	4
19	RUTH	F	39	430	L	1.3	4
20	SOPHIA	F	42	412	M	7.4	4

   c. Total income for the entire data set = 125.7 (in thousands of dollars)
   Total income for the first age-group = 44.2
   Total income for the second age-group = 20.6.
   Total income for the third age-group = 25.5.
   Total income for the fourth age-group = 23.3.
   Total income for the fifth age-group = 12.1.

   d. Total income for the H ses group = 54.4, for the M group = 64.4, and for the L group = 6.9 in thousands of dollars.

6.

Exercise 6.6 Sorting by two numeric variables   1

Obs	name	sex	id	stand	pretest	first	second	final	average
1	LYNN	f	4	1	7	38	33	43	30.2500
2	JOHN	m	1	1	9	31	45	.	28.3333
3	BOB	m	17	1	11	32	41	40	31.0000
4	TED	m	10	2	12	44	52	47	38.7500
5	CATHY	f	6	2	12	34	50	32	32.0000
6	JAMES	m	7	2	14	31	47	43	33.7500
7	PAUL	m	14	3	15	24	48	49	34.0000
8	NANCY	f	13	3	15	29	39	42	31.2500
9	HOPE	f	9	4	17	34	46	50	36.7500
10	SASSY	f	12	4	18	50	57	56	45.2500
11	LIN	m	15	4	18	48	54	54	43.5000
12	DAN	m	3	4	18	46	53	54	42.7500
13	TIM	m	8	4	20	45	51	57	43.2500
14	TOM	m	16	4	21	48	52	42	40.7500

7.

Exercise 6.7 Sorting by two character variables   1

Obs	name	sex	id	stand	pretest	first	second	final	average
1	BOB	m	17	1	11	32	41	40	31.0000
2	DAN	m	3	4	18	46	53	54	42.7500
3	JAMES	m	7	2	14	31	47	43	33.7500
4	JOHN	m	1	1	9	31	45	.	28.3333
5	LIN	m	15	4	18	48	54	54	43.5000
6	PAUL	m	14	3	15	24	48	49	34.0000
7	TED	m	10	2	12	44	52	47	38.7500
8	TIM	m	8	4	20	45	51	57	43.2500
9	TOM	m	16	4	21	48	52	42	40.7500
10	CATHY	f	6	2	12	34	50	32	32.0000
11	HOPE	f	9	4	17	34	46	50	36.7500
12	LYNN	f	4	1	7	38	33	43	30.2500
13	NANCY	f	13	3	15	29	39	42	31.2500
14	SASSY	f	12	4	18	50	57	56	45.2500

7

Data Transformation

OBJECTIVE

Data in a SAS data set are not always in an appropriate form or structure to yield helpful information. Therefore, they need to be shaped up. This chapter demonstrates general steps and several useful functions for transforming data. Specifically, simple arithmetic operations, arithmetic and mathematical functions, trigonometric functions, descriptive statistics functions, probability functions, character functions, and functions that generate pseudorandom numbers are introduced and illustrated. Cautions are issued when readers mix character variables with numeric variables and when missing data are present in a data set.

7.1 Why Do You Need to Transform Data?

In Chapters 2 through 6, the focus has been on establishing a SAS data set from raw data and verifying its content. However, data in a SAS data set are not always in an ideal form. Hence, recoding or transforming data is necessary before further data analyses can be applied. For example, you designed a Likert-type questionnaire with five response categories:

A—Strongly Agree   B—Agree   C—Disagree   D—Strongly Disagree
E—Not Applicable

After data were collected and coded from "A" to "E" or "1" to "5", you realized that the fifth response category, "E", does not imply a stronger degree of disagreement than category "D—Strongly Disagree". This "E" category is in fact a conceptually different category from the other four. Thus, "E" or "5" responses need to be recoded, perhaps to missing values.

Also, new variables may be needed for statistical modeling, such as in regression. These new variables are intended to improve the fit of a regression model to data. They may be a transformation such as a square root of an existing variable or a sum of two variables.

Sometimes new information is needed for each observation; hence, existing information is compiled into new information. For example, after recording students' midterm and final scores, you wish to compute their overall score (= midterm + final) in a course. The overall score is created using either a SAS function or an algebraic equation applied to the midterm and final scores. This new overall score is technically a transformation of existing variables (i.e., midterm plus final scores).

Another reason for transformation is theoretical in the sense that for certain studies, random numbers are needed in order to investigate the robustness of a statistical assumption or to randomly select observations from a data set. Random numbers are those numbers generated randomly from a known theoretical distribution, such as the normal or the uniform distribution. These numbers can be obtained in SAS from pseudorandom number–generating functions that generate numbers as randomly as possible.

There are other reasons for modifying data to suit your purposes. Whatever the reason may be, this step is inevitable in almost all data analyses. Data modification is sometimes referred to as "data preprocessing" or "data recoding" by data analysts. In this book, it will be called "data transformation." This chapter focuses on a variety of data transformation techniques that enable you to modify data values, create new variables, summarize information on the basis of observations, and generate pseudorandom numbers.

7.2 How to Transform Data

All data transformations covered in this chapter occur within the DATA step. It is generally a good idea to follow the steps outlined below in data transformation:

Step 1 Read original data into a SAS data set

Step 2 Transform data with SAS functions or symbols

Step 3 Name the original and new variables with the LABEL statement

Step 4 Verify all transformations with the PRINT procedure

Transcribing these steps into SAS syntax results in one of the following two templates depending on the way raw data were read into the SAS program (see Table 7.1).

Table 7.1   Two Templates for Data Transformations in SAS

Raw Data Stored in a Location External to the SAS Program	Raw Data Embedded Within a SAS Program
| ```
DATA data_set_name;
    INFILE 'd:\data_file.dat';
    INPUT variable_list;
    new_var=transformation of
        original-variable(s);
    LABEL 1st_var='1st variable label'
         2nd_var='2nd variable label'
                .
                .
         last_var='last variable
                  label';
RUN;
PROC PRINT;
RUN;
``` | ```
DATA data_set_name;
    INPUT variable_list;
    new_var=tranformation of original-
        variable(s);
    LABEL 1st_var='1st variable label'
         2nd_var='2nd variable label'
                .
                .
         last_var='last variable label';
DATALINES;
[ data lines]
RUN;
PROC PRINT;
RUN;
``` |

The LABEL statement allows you to elaborate on each variable name with 256 or fewer characters in quotes (refer back to Chapter 5). Here is a short program that illustrates the four steps and the LABEL statement. This program first reads 10 item scores of an attitudinal scale into the SAS data set <u>trans</u>, and then creates a new variable, <u>meanatt</u>, as the average of these item scores. Finally, a second new variable, <u>attitude</u>, character in nature, converts the score of <u>meanatt</u> into either "positive" or "negative" using a cutoff of 3.5. All variables, old and new, are labeled in the LABEL statement.

```
DATA trans;
    INPUT (att1-att10) (1.);
    meanatt = MEAN (OF att1-att10);
    IF meanatt > 3.5 THEN attitude = 'positive';
       ELSE attitude = 'negative';
    LABEL att1 = 'Attitude item 1 on scale 1-5'
          att2 = 'Attitude item 2 on scale 1-5'
          att3 = 'Attitude item 3 on scale 1-5'
          att4 = 'Attitude item 4 on scale 1-5'
          att5 = 'Attitude item 5 on scale 1-5'
          att6 = 'Attitude item 6 on scale 1-5'
          att7 = 'Attitude item 7 on scale 1-5'
          att8 = 'Attitude item 8 on scale 1-5'
          att9 = 'Attitude item 9 on scale 1-5'
          att10 = 'Attitude item 10 on scale 1-5'
          meanatt = 'Average attitude'
          attitude = 'Attitude toward legal abortion';
DATALINES;
1212121212
5555544444
.123455432
RUN;

PROC PRINT DATA=trans;
RUN;
```

7.3 Overview of SAS Data Transformations

As the general syntax demonstrates, data transformations begin with original (or existing) variables. Any new variable or a new meaning assigned to existing variables is created in the style of an assignment statement. An assignment statement assigns the result of the operation on the right-hand side of the equal sign (=) to the variable on the left-hand side. Various assignment statements can be used to perform data transformations. For example,

Numeric variable <u>n</u> is assigned a constant value: `n = 1;`

Character variable <u>season</u> is assigned a constant value:
`season = 'autumn';`

Variable <u>income</u> is defined: `income = revenue - expenses;`

Variable <u>year</u> is replaced by <u>year</u> + 1900: `year = year + 1900;`

Variable <u>c</u> is derived from a SAS function: `c = SQRT(x);`

Note that the equal sign (=) in all the assignment statements above does not mean "equal" in a mathematical sense. It means substituting the value found on the right for the variable named on the left. Because of this definition for the equal sign, it is permissible to write "`year = year + 1900;`". This statement means that, for each observation, the current value of <u>year</u> is increased by 1900; the increased value is re-stored in the variable <u>year</u>.

7.4 Simple Arithmetic Operations

Simple arithmetic operations are the addition, subtraction, multiplication, and division of numbers. These operations are carried out by notations such as + (for addition), – (for subtraction), * (for multiplication), / (for division), and ** for exponential functions, such as square (**2) and cube (**3). Examples of these operations are presented in Table 7.2.

Table 7.2   Examples of Simple Arithmetic Operations

Example	SAS Code	Explanation
7.1	sum = x + y;	<u>sum</u> is the total of <u>x</u> and <u>y</u>.
7.2	diff = x - y;	<u>diff</u> is the difference between <u>x</u> and <u>y</u>.
7.3	twice = x * 2;	<u>twice</u> is <u>x</u> multiplied by 2.
7.4	half = x / 2;	<u>half</u> is <u>x</u> divided by 2.
7.5	cubic = x ** 3;	<u>cubic</u> is <u>x</u> raised to the power of 3, hence, <u>cubic</u> = x^3.
7.6	sign = - x;	<u>sign</u> is <u>x</u> in opposite sign. Hence, <u>sign</u> and x are opposite in signs and equal in absolute values.

Recall from your elementary math books that arithmetic operations are inherently hierarchical. The lowest priorities are addition (+) and subtraction (–). The highest priorities are given to exponential function (**), sign (+ or –), or those operations grouped in parentheses. In between are multiplication (*) and division (/), as shown below:

<u>Highest priority</u>	---------------->	<u>Lowest priority</u>
( ), or sign (+ or –), or **	* or /	+ or –

Missing values of any variable in an arithmetic operation will result in missing values of the new variable on the left-hand side of the operation. This is because SAS is unable to perform the operation on missing values. In this case, missing values will be denoted as a period (.).

7.5 Arithmetic and Mathematical Functions

A number of arithmetic and mathematical functions are available in SAS. They are invoked by a specific name. For example, ABS stands for absolute value, MOD stands for modular, or remainder function, and so on. Each function is written with its argument(s) enclosed in parentheses. Table 7.3 presents several commonly used functions and their illustrations.

Table 7.3   Examples of Arithmetic and Mathematical Functions

Example	SAS Code	Explanation
7.7	y = ABS(x);	y is the absolute value of x.
7.8	y = MOD(10,3);	y is the remainder of 10/3; hence, y = 1.
7.9	y = SIGN(-7);	y is the sign of −7; hence, y = −1.
7.10	y = SQRT(4);	y is the square root of 4; hence, y = 2.
7.11	y = EXP(2);	y is e raised to the power of 2; hence, $y = e^2 = 7.38906$, where e is the base of the system of natural logarithms; it equals to 2.718 approximately.
7.12	y = LOG(1);	y is the natural logarithm of 1; hence, y = 0.
7.13	y = LOG2(2);	y is the logarithm to the base 2 of 2; hence, y = 1.
7.14	y = LOG10(100);	y is the logarithm to the base 10 of 100; hence, y = 2.
7.15	y = ROUND(x, 0.1);	y is the rounded-off value of x with round-off unit of 0.1. If x = 6.1936, then y = 6.2.
7.16	y = LAG1(x);	y is one lag behind x. If x = 1, 2, 3, 4, consecutively, then y = . [missing], 1, 2, 3. If y = LAG2(x);, then y = . [missing], . [missing], 1, 2. The LAG function can be up to 100 lags.

If an argument in any of these functions is either missing or illogical, such as −3 as an argument for the LOG or LOG10 function, the resulting y will be missing, denoted by a period (.) in the data set.

7.6 Trigonometric and Hyperbolic Functions

All trigonometric and hyperbolic functions are referred to by the same name in SAS as in mathematics. For example, SIN stands for the sine function, COS means cosine, TAN means tangent, ARSIN means arc sine, ARCOS means arc cosine, ARTAN means arc tangent, SINH means hyperbolic sine function, and so on. The argument for these trigonometric functions is in radians, or in units of π. Table 7.4 presents several commonly used trigonometric and hyperbolic functions and their illustrations.

Table 7.4   Examples of Trigonometric and Hyperbolic Functions

Example	SAS Code	Explanation
7.17	y = SIN(0);	y is the sine function of a zero degree angle; hence, y = 0.
7.18	y = COS(0);	y is the cosine of a zero degree angle; hence, y = 1.
7.19	y = TAN(3.1416/3);	y is the tangent of a $\pi/3$ angle; hence, y = 1.732047.
7.20	y = ARSIN(0);	y is the arc sine function of 0; hence, y = 0.
7.21	y = ARCOS(1);	y is the arc cosine function of 1; hence, y = 0.
7.22	y = SINH(0);	y is the hyperbolic sine function of 0; hence, y = 0.

7.7 Descriptive Statistics Functions

Simple descriptive statistics can be obtained for each observation by invoking those function names in Table 7.5.

Table 7.5   Examples of Selected Functions That Calculate Simple Statistics

Example	SAS Code	Explanation
7.23	y = MIN(OF x1-x7);	y is the minimum among variables x1 through x7.
7.24	y = MAX(OF x1-x7);	y is the maximum among variables x1 through x7.
7.25	y = MEAN(OF x1-x3);	y is the average of three variables x1 through x3.
7.26	y = SUM(OF x1-x3);	y is the total of three variables x1 through x3.

(Continued)

(Continued)

Example	SAS Code	Explanation
7.27	`y = N(OF x1-x7);`	y is the number of valid data on x1 through x7.
7.28	`y = NMISS(OF x1-x7);`	y is the number of missing data on x1 through x7.
7.29	`y = RANGE(OF x1-x7);`	y is the range between variables x1 and x7.
7.30	`y = SKEWNESS(0,1,1);`	y is the skewness among 0, 1, and 1; hence, $y = -1.73$.
7.31	`y = KURTOSIS(0,1,0,1);`	y is the kurtosis among 0, 1, 0, and 1; hence, $y = -6$.
7.32	`y = STD(1,2,3);`	y is the standard deviation of 1, 2, and 3, using $k - 1$ as the denominator, where k = number of values in the argument. Hence, $y = 1$.
7.33	`y = STDERR(2,6,3,4);`	y is the mean's standard error; hence, $y = 0.8539$.
7.34	`y = VAR(1,1,1,1);`	y is the variance of four 1's; hence, $y = 0$. Variance is defined with $k-1$ as the denominator, where k = number of values in the argument.

NOTE: The keyword **OF** is required if a variable list is specified within the parentheses, as in Examples 7.23 to 7.29.

These statistical values, denoted by y above, are constants with regard to each observation. When executed, these functions bypass missing values and use valid scores only. In contrast, the arithmetic operations (+, −, *, /, and **) cannot be applied to missing scores. For example, if t1 = 5, t2 = 4, t3 = 4, t4 = . (missing) , and t5 = 3, then the statement

```
avrg = MEAN(OF t1-t5);
```

yields the result of avrg = 4, or (5 + 4 + 4 + 3)/4. However, if this statement is rewritten as

```
avrg = (t1 + t2 + t3 + t4 + t5)/5;
```

then avrg will equal missing (.) due to the missing value of t4.

7.8 Probability Functions

Probability functions are useful for finding cumulative probabilities or percentiles (or critical values) from a theoretical distribution, such as normal, t, F, or chi-square. These functions are particularly needed when published tables of these distributions do not contain values you need. Fortunately, any cumulative probability can be obtained from built-in probability functions in SAS. Likewise, any percentile or critical value can be derived from the inverse functions of probabilities through SAS functions. Table 7.6 presents examples of probability functions and their inverse functions most commonly used in social science research.

Table 7.6   Examples of Probability Functions

Example	SAS Code	Explanation
7.35	y = PROBNORM(1.96);	y is the cumulative standard normal probability at 1.96; hence, y = 0.975.
7.36	y = PROBIT(0.975);	y is the 97.5th percentile on the standard normal distribution; hence, y = 1.96. 1.96 is also the upper critical value for a one-tailed z test conducted at $\alpha = 0.025$ or a two-tailed z test at $\alpha = 0.05$.
7.37	y = PROBT(2.086,20);	y is the cumulative Student t probability at 2.086 with df = 20; hence, y = 0.975.
7.38	y = TINV(0.975,20);	y is the 97.5th percentile on the Student t distribution with df = 20; hence, y = 2.086. 2.086 is also the upper critical value for a one-tailed t test conducted with df = 20 at $\alpha = 0.025$ or a two-tailed t test at $\alpha = 0.05$, also with df = 20.
7.39	y = PROBCHI(31.264,11);	y is the cumulative chi-square probability at 31.264 with df = 11; hence, y = 0.999.
7.40	y = CINV(0.999,11);	y is the 99.9th percentile on the chi square distribution with df = 11; hence, y = 31.264. 31.264 is also the upper critical value for a one-tailed chi-square test conducted with df = 11 at $\alpha = 0.001$ or a two-tailed chi-square test at $\alpha = 0.002$, also with df = 11.
7.41	y = PROBF(3.32,2,30);	y is the cumulative F probability at 3.32 with df = 2,30; hence, y = 0.95.

(Continued)

(Continued)

Example	SAS Code	Explanation
7.42	`y = FINV(0.95,2,30);`	y is the 95th percentile on the F distribution with df = 2, 30; hence, y = 3.32. 3.32 is also the upper critical value for a one-tailed F test conducted with df = 2, 30 at α = 0.05 or a two-tailed F test at α = 0.10, also with df = 2, 30.
7.43	`y = PROBBNML(0.5,10,4);`	y is the cumulative binomial probability of 4 with N = 10 and p = 0.5; hence, y = 0.37695.
7.44	`y = POISSON(1,2);`	y is the cumulative Poisson probability of 2 with the parameter = 1; hence, y = 0.9197.

Note that for the continuous distributions (Examples 7.37 through 7.42), parameters (i.e., degrees of freedom) follow either the random variable value or the cumulative probability from the distribution. However, for discrete cumulative probability distributions (Examples 7.43 and 7.44), parameters in parentheses precede the random variable value, such as 4 and 2 in PROBBNML and POISSON functions, respectively. Probabilities for discrete values of the binomial and Poisson random variables are derived by subtraction. For instance, to obtain the binomial probability for $X = 4$ successes with $N = 10$ trials and $p = 0.5$, you modify Example 7.43 into the following statement:

```
binomial4 = PROBBNML(0.5,10,4) - PROBBNML(0.5,10,3);
```

Likewise, to obtain the Poisson probability for $X = 2$ with the parameter = 1, you modify Example 7.44 into the following statement:

```
poisson2 = POISSON(1,2) - POISSON(1,1);
```

7.9 Functions That Generate Pseudorandom Numbers

Random numbers are frequently employed in simulation studies to test the robustness of a statistical assumption, such as the normality assumption. Truly random numbers are impossible to obtain from computing software due to the finite memory of software and confined physical setting of computers. Consequently, pseudorandom numbers are generated instead. These pseudorandom numbers are as random as is computationally feasible. Two functions in SAS are particularly useful for generating pseudorandom numbers. One generates pseudorandom numbers from a uniform distribution and the other from a normal distribution (see Table 7.7).

Table 7.7   Examples of Functions That Generate Pseudorandom Numbers

Example	SAS Code	Explanation
7.45	`y = RANNOR(123);` `tscore = 50 + 10 * y;`	y is a pseudorandom variable from the standard normal distribution. tscore is a derived score based on the standard normal y score with a mean of 50 and standard deviation of 10.
7.46	`y = RANUNI(456);`	y is a pseudorandom variable from the uniform distribution on the scale of 0 to 1.

Both functions call for a seed number as an argument. The specification of a seed number ensures that identical random numbers are generated each time when the same seed number is used. As a result, analyses of random numbers can be replicated and further expanded. The seed number is any number less than or equal to $2^{31} - 1$. If a positive number is used, the random number generator is initialized directly. If zero or a negative number is used, the random number generator is initialized by reading the time of the day from the computer clock. In this case, the random number generated cannot be replicated because it is different each time.

7.10 Character Functions: COMPRESS, INDEX, LEFT, LENGTH, REPEAT, REVERSE, RIGHT, SUBSTR, TRIM, UPCASE, and VERIFY

A variety of functions are capable of handling character variable values. Only 11 are illustrated in Table 7.8. Others can be found in the user's manual—*SAS® 9.1.3 Language Reference: Dictionary* (SAS Institute Inc., 2006b).

Table 7.8   Examples of Character Functions

Example	SAS Code	Explanation
7.47	`x = 'a b c d';` `y = COMPRESS(x);`	y is the compressed value of x; hence, y = 'abcd'.

7.48	`x = 'abcdefghijklmn';`
	`i = 'jkl';`
	`y = INDEX(x,i);`
		y is the position of the first character of the character string 'jkl' in x; hence, y = 10.

(Continued)

(Continued)

Example	SAS Code	Explanation
7.49	x = ' Hello, there!'; y = LEFT(x);	y is the left-justified value of x; hence, y = 'Hello, there!'.
7.50	y = LENGTH('dear');	y is the length of the character string in the argument; hence, y = 4.
7.51	y = REPEAT('me',2);	y is the character string repeated twice plus the original string; hence, y = 'mememe'.
7.52	y = REVERSE(' DOG');	y is the reversed spelling of the text in ' '; hence, y = 'GOD '.
7.53	y = RIGHT('True Love ');	y is the right-justified spelling of the text in ' '; hence, y = 'True Love'.

7.54	x = 'Dr. Nofuss';
	y = SUBSTR (x, 1, 2);
	name = SUBSTR(x, 5, 6);
		y is the text string in x that begins in column 1 and stretches for 2 columns; hence, y = 'Dr'. name is the text string in x that begins in column 5 and stretches for 6 columns; hence, name = 'Nofuss'.

7.55	first = 'Dear '; last = ' me'; y = TRIM(first)||' '||TRIM(last);	y = 'Dear me' which is the concatenation of trimmed values in first and last. The symbol || means concatenation. Between || and ||, a blank space is inserted by y's definition. Hence, there is a space between 'Dear' and 'me'.
7.56	x = 'Dr. Nofuss'; y = UPCASE(x);	y is the uppercase of x. Hence, y = 'DR. NOFUSS'.

7.57	DATA survey;
	    INPUT ses $1.;
	    check = 'hml';
	    y = VERIFY(ses,check);
	    IF y GT 0 THEN
	    PUT 'Invalid SES
	coding=' ses;
		y is the result of verifying ses values against check values. If ses values match with one of the characters in check, then y = 0. If no match is found, then y = the position of the first character in ses that does not match with any of the check characters. When this happens, the PUT statement sends the text string "Invalid SES coding=" to the Log window plus the value of ses for which no match is found.

7.11 Conversions Between Numeric and Character Variables

One problem frequently encountered by inexperienced SAS programmers is that they fail to distinguish between numeric and character variables in an assignment statement. For example, in the following two statements,

```
id = '10';

z = RANNOR(id);
```

id is first declared as a character variable, because its value is enclosed by single quotes. In the second statement, however, id is used as a seed number—which must be numeric—for the RANNOR function. When this happens, SAS attempts to convert the variable type from character to numeric or from numeric to character so that variable values match with the variable type that is called for by an assignment statement. In doing so, SAS follows these rules:

Rule 1: If you specify a numeric variable on the left side of an assignment statement and a character variable on the right, the character variable is converted to numeric.

Rule 2: If you specify a character variable on the left side of an assignment statement and a numeric variable on the right, SAS converts the numeric variable to character. The numeric variable will first be reformatted with the BESTn. format, where n is the length of the character variable on the left. Then, the reformatted numeric values will be transformed into character strings literally. The BESTn. is a numeric format that allows SAS to select the most suitable format for presenting the value with the available field width. The maximum for n is 32.

Rule 3: If you specify a character variable with an operator, such as +, that requires a numeric variable, SAS converts the character variable to numeric.

Rule 4: If you compare a character variable with a numeric variable with an operator, such as EQ or =, SAS automatically converts the character variable to numeric.

Rule 5: If a numeric variable is used in an operator, such as || (concatenation), that requires a character variable, the numeric variable is converted to character using the BEST12. format.

Whenever an automatic conversion takes place, SAS flags a message to this effect in the Log window. If a conversion from character to numeric leads to an invalid numeric value, SAS assigns a missing value (.) to the outcome. It also flags an error message in the Log window. So be aware of the implications of mixing character variables with numeric variables and the consequences of conversion performed by SAS. See Exercises 10a to 10e in this chapter to further practice with these rules.

7.12 Summary

Once data are successfully read into a SAS data set, there may still be practical as well as theoretical reasons that require data transformations. This chapter illustrates a variety of data transformations that are possible within

SAS. Most of the syntaxes are not complicated, but you may still run into error messages due to missing values, the mismatch of variable types, illogical arguments, misunderstanding of parameters, and so on. When this occurs, carefully review the error message in the Log window and the definition of each function before trying to correct the error. Additional help with these functions can be found in online documents available from www.sas.com.

7.13 Exercises

1. Which statement will produce a random integer between 1 and 10?
   a. x = ROUND(RANUNI(0), 1);
   b. x = RANUNI(0) * 10;
   c. x = ROUND(RANUNI(10), 10);
   d. x = ROUND(RANUNI(0) * 10, 1);

2. Which statement(s) will generate pseudorandom variables?
   a. y = RANUNI(0);
   b. y = RANUNI(12469);
   c. y = RANUNI(123579);
   d. y = RANUNI(1234568);

3. For the following SAS program, determine the correct output:

```
DATA  example;
      INPUT x;
      aa = ROUND (x,  1);
      bb = ROUND (x,  .1);
      cc = ROUND (x,  100);
DATALINES;
5487.529
1992.46
RUN;
PROC PRINT;
RUN;
```

a.

x	aa	bb	cc
5487.529	5488	5487.5	5500
1992.46	1992	1992.5	2000

b.

x	aa	bb	cc
5487.529	5487	5487.5	5400
1992.46	1992	1992.4	1900

c.

x	aa	bb	cc
5487.529	5488	5487.6	5500
1992.46	1993	1992.5	2000

4. Which statement is **incorrect** regarding the following SAS program?

```
DATA a;
    INPUT apt $ 1-10;
    building = SUBSTR(apt, 1,4);
    floor = SUBSTR(apt, 5,1);
    room = SUBSTR(apt, 6,2);
DATALINES;
ROSE123
AQUA247
GOLD395
BLUE453
RUN;
```

   a. "`floor = SUBSTR(apt, 5,1);`" tells SAS to read one column width starting from the fifth column.

   b. The `SUBSTR` function extracts subtext from any variable.

   c. If there are no errors in the program, the values stored in the data set <u>a</u> are

apt	building	floor	room
ROSE123	ROSE	1	23
AQUA247	AQUA	2	47
GOLD395	GOLD	3	95
BLUE453	BLUE	4	53

   d. To successfully execute this program, a dollar sign ($) is needed after the variable <u>apt</u> since the SUBSTR function only works for character variables.

5. What happens when SAS encounters a division by zero, such as the z variable below?

```
DATA a; INPUT x y @@; z=x/y;
DATALINES;
1 2 2 1 3 2 1 0 1 3 4 2 2 3 5 4 3 1 1 5
;
PROC PRINT DATA=a;
RUN;
```

   a. A missing value (.) is noted for <u>z</u>.

   b. Only 3 observations are stored in the data set <u>a</u>.

   c. There is no observation stored in the data set <u>a</u>.

   d. It depends on which version of SAS is being used.

6. If a data set contains missing values on certain variables, what is best to use when one computes the total or average of these variables?

   a. arithmetic operations + and /

   b. statistical functions SUM or MEAN

   c. constant assignment

7. What function should be used to extract subtext from the character variable <u>location</u>?
   a. TRUNCATE(location, 1, 1);
   b. SUBSTR(location, 1, 1);
   c. PARTIAL(location, 1, 1);
   d. TRUNC(location, 1, 1);
   e. INDEX(location, 1, 1);

```
DATA demo;
     INPUT x @@; y = LAG2(x);
     total = total+x+y;
DATALINES;
1 2 3 4
RUN;
PROC PRINT;
RUN;
```

8. What are the values of <u>total</u> in data set <u>demo</u>?
   a. 1, 3, 7, 13
   b. 0, 0, 4, 10
   c. ., ., ., . (missing)
   d. ., ., 4, 6

9. Reshape the following state population data and compute statistics from different points of view:

state	pop1940	pop1950	pop1960	pop1970
NY	13470	14830	16782	18237
NJ	4160	4835	9987	10005
PA	9900	10433	12569	15000
OH	6908	7956	8831	9234
IN	1234	2345	3456	4567

   a. Read data into a SAS data set <u>a</u>.
   b. Compute population gains across the decades:
      gain40   gain50   gain60
   c. Print data set <u>a</u>.
   d. Compute the mean population gain across states for each decade.

10. **Section 7.11** discusses five rules used by SAS to resolve the mixture of numeric and character variables in an assignment statement. Try executing the following programs and check into the Log and/or the Output window to find out how each of the five rules is applied:

a. The application of Rule 1

```
DATA temp;
  INPUT x $ y;
  y=x;
DATALINES;
12345678  1
RUN;
PROC PRINT; RUN;
PROC CONTENTS; RUN;
```

b. The application of Rule 2

```
DATA temp;
  INPUT x y $ 5.;
  y=x;
DATALINES;
12345678     y
RUN;
PROC PRINT; RUN;
PROC CONTENTS; RUN;
```

c. The application of Rule 3

```
DATA temp;
  INPUT x y $ 5.;
  z=x+y;
DATALINES;
12345678     1
RUN;
PROC PRINT; RUN;
```

d. The application of Rule 4

```
DATA temp;
  INPUT x y $;
  IF x <= y THEN z = 1;
    ELSE z = 0;
DATALINES;
12345678 12345678
12345678          1
RUN;
PROC PRINT; RUN;
```

e. The application of Rule 5

```
DATA temp;
  INPUT x y;
  z=x||y;
DATALINES;
12345678     1
RUN;
PROC PRINT; RUN;
PROC CONTENTS; RUN;
```

7.14 Answers to Exercises

1. d

2. a, b, c, d

3. a

4. b

5. a

6. b

7. b

8. c

9. a, b, and c

SAS Programming

```
DATA a;
    INPUT state $ pop1940 pop1950 pop1960 pop1970;  } (a)
    gain40 = pop1950 - pop1940;
    gain50 = pop1960 - pop1950;                      } (b)
    gain60 = pop1970 - pop1960;
DATALINES;
NY 13470 14830 16782 18237
NJ  4160  4835  9987 10005
PA  9900 10433 12569 15000
OH  6908  7956  8831  9234
IN  1234  2345  3456  4567
RUN;

PROC PRINT DATA=a; RUN;                              } (c)
PROC MEANS;
    VAR gain40 gain50 gain60;                        } (d)
RUN;
```

Note that in SAS data set a, three new variables appear, in addition to the initial five: gain40, gain50, and gain60, which correspond to population gains from 1940 to 1950, 1950 to 1960, and 1960 to 1970, respectively.

Obs	state	pop1940	pop1950	pop1960	pop1970	gain40	gain50	gain60
1	NY	13470	14830	16782	18237	1360	1952	1455
2	NJ	4160	4835	9987	10005	675	5152	18
3	PA	9900	0433	12569	15000	533	2136	2431
4	OH	6908	7956	8831	9234	1048	875	403
5	IN	1234	2345	3456	4567	1111	1111	1111

d. the mean population gain across the states for each decade

```
Variable      N        Mean     Std Dev      Minimum      Maximum
-----------------------------------------------------------------
gain40        5  945.4000000  336.5387051  533.0000000    1360.00
gain50        5     2245.20      1711.08  875.0000000    5152.00
gain60        5     1083.60  942.4562589   18.0000000    2431.00
-----------------------------------------------------------------
```

10. a.

```
2           TITLE 'Exercise 7-10a';
3           DATA temp;
4             INPUT x $ y;
5             y=x;
6           DATALINES;

NOTE: Character values have been converted to numeric values at the places given by:
      (Line):(Column).
      5:5
NOTE: The data set WORK.TEMP has 1 observations and 2 variables.
NOTE: DATA statement used (Total process time):
      real time            0.21 seconds
      cpu time             0.07 seconds
```

The Log file indicates that the character value has been converted to a numeric value. The output is shown below:

```
      Exercise 7-10a                                              1

Obs      x          y

 1    12345678    12345678
```

The PROC PRINT output shows that the value of variable x was copied to y. The format of variable y is numeric, as shown in the PROC CONTENTS output:

```
                        Exercise 7-10a                            2

                     The CONTENTS Procedure

[Part of the PROC CONTENTS output is not shown here]

            Alphabetic List of Variables and Attributes

              #    Variable    Type    Len

              1    x           Char     8
              2    y           Num      8
```

b.

```
2            TITLE 'Exercise 7-10b';
3            DATA temp;
4              INPUT x y $ 5.;
5              y=x;
6            DATALINES;

NOTE: Numeric values have been converted to character values at the places given by:
      (Line):(Column).
      5:5
NOTE: The data set WORK.TEMP has 1 observations and 2 variables.
NOTE: DATA statement used (Total process time):
      real time           0.10 seconds
      cpu time            0.06 seconds
```

The Log file indicates that the numeric value has been converted to a character value. The output is shown below:

```
      Exercise 7-10b                                              1

 Obs        x         y

  1      12345678    123E5
```

The output from PROC PRINT shows that the value of x was converted into an E5. format, which best represents the x value in a field width of 5. The value 123E5 (= 123×10^5 = 12300000) was then stored in y as a character string.

```
                        Exercise 7-10b                           2

                      The CONTENTS Procedure

[Part of the PROC CONTENTS output is not shown here]

                Alphabetic List of Variables and Attributes

                #    Variable    Type    Len

                1    x           Num      8
                2    y           Char     5
```

c.

```
2            TITLE 'Exercise 7-10c';
3            DATA temp;
4              INPUT x y $ 5.;
5              z=x+y;
6            DATALINES;

NOTE: Character values have been converted to numeric values at the places given by:
      (Line):(Column).
      5:7
NOTE: The data set WORK.TEMP has 1 observations and 3 variables.
NOTE: DATA statement used (Total process time):
      real time           0.10 seconds
      cpu time            0.08 seconds
```

The Log file indicates that the character value has been converted to a numeric value. The output is shown below:

```
          Exercise 7-10c                                          1

Obs        x        y         z

 1      12345678    1      12345679
```

The PROC PRINT output indicates that the value of z is the sum of the x value and the converted y value.

d.

```
2              TITLE 'Exercise 7-10d';
3              DATA temp;
4                INPUT x y $;
5                IF x <= y THEN z = 1;
6                  ELSE z = 0;
7              DATALINES;

NOTE: Character values have been converted to numeric values at the places given by:
      (Line):(Column).
      5:11
NOTE: The data set WORK.TEMP has 2 observations and 3 variables.
NOTE: DATA statement used (Total process time):
      real time               0.09 seconds
      cpu time                0.08 seconds
```

The Log file indicates that the character value has been converted to a numeric value. The output is shown below:

```
          Exercise 7-10d                                          1

Obs        x          y          z

 1      12345678   12345678      1
 2      12345678   1             0
```

The comparisons were done on the basis of the values of x and the converted values of y as indicated in the PROC PRINT output.

e.

```
2              TITLE 'Exercise 7-10e';
3              DATA temp;
4                INPUT x y;
5                z=x||y;
6              DATALINES;

NOTE: Numeric values have been converted to character values at the places given by:
      (Line):(Column).
      5:5    5:8
NOTE: The data set WORK.TEMP has 1 observations and 3 variables.
NOTE: DATA statement used (Total process time):
      real time               0.09 seconds
      cpu time                0.04 seconds
```

The Log file indicates that the numeric value has been converted to a character value. The output is shown below:

```
                    Exercise 7-10e                                            1

 Obs        x        y                z

  1     12345678     1     12345678            1
```

The length for z (i.e., 24) shown in the PROC CONTENTS output indicates that both x and y were transformed to BEST12. format before the two variables were concatenated. The PROC PRINT output also indicates that blank spaces were used to fill up the field width of z.

```
                          Exercise 7-10e                                      2

                        The CONTENTS Procedure

[Part of the PROC CONTENTS output is not shown here]


                 Alphabetic List of Variables and Attributes

                    #     Variable     Type     Len

                    1     x            Num        8
                    2     y            Num        8
                    3     z            Char      24
```

PART II

Statistical Procedures

8

Quick Descriptive Analysis

OBJECTIVE

This chapter covers standard descriptive data analysis such as mean, median, quartiles, percentiles, standard deviation, variance, skewness, kurtosis, and range of scores. In addition, descriptive analysis of subgroup data and differential weighting are demonstrated, along with the one-sample t test of a zero population mean and its 95% confidence limits.

8.1 How to Conduct Quick Descriptive Analysis in SAS

Quick descriptive data analysis can be carried out by the MEANS procedure in SAS. This procedure is applicable only to numeric variables such as grade point average, income, years of education, dosage of a medicine, and so on. In addition to the mean, you may obtain other descriptive information from the MEANS procedure, such as the mode, median, first and third quartiles, various percentiles, variance, standard deviation, range, minimum, maximum, standard error of the sample mean, number of valid and missing data values, skewness, and kurtosis. The primary goals here are to quickly summarize the distribution of a numeric variable in the data and to detect coding errors, if there are any (Example 8.1).

Second, you can apply the MEANS procedure to subsets of the data and describe characteristics of numerical variables based on subsets of observations. This is accomplished by the CLASS or the BY statement or both in PROC MEANS (Example 8.2).

Finally, this chapter demonstrates handy tricks in descriptive data analysis, such as preserving analysis results in an output data set (Examples 8.3, 8.4, and 8.5), using an output data set for subsequent analysis (Example 8.6), and tracking observations with missing values on one or more variables (Example 8.7).

8.2 Examples

There are five examples presented in this section. In all five examples, the raw data file achieve.dat is used. Details about this data file are given in Appendix B. The data file is downloadable from the Web site at www .sagepub.com/pengstudy.

Example 8.1 Describing Data Characteristics With PROC MEANS

In this example, you will learn how to compute simple descriptive statistics for the two variables reading and punc. The first statement is PROC MEANS, followed by two options, **DATA=** and **MAXDEC=**, and 14 statistical keywords. Option **DATA=** invokes the SAS data set achieve to be analyzed by the MEANS procedure. **MAXDEC=** specifies the decimal places to be 4 for the 14 statistics. The meaning of each statistical keyword will be explained in terms of results and is defined in **Section 8.3: How to Write the PROC MEANS Codes**. The second statement, VAR, lists reading and punc to be analyzed by the MEANS procedure.

```
/* The following bolded SAS statements establish the SAS data set 'achieve' */

DATA achieve;
    INFILE 'd:\data\achieve.dat';
    INPUT iv1 1 grade 2 iv2 3 sex $ 4 id $ 6-8 vocab 25-26 reading 27-28
          spelling 29-30 capital 31-32 punc 33-34 usage 35-36
          total1 37-38 maps 39-40 graphs 41-42 refer 43-44
          total2 45-46 concepts 47-48 problem 49-50 total3 51-52
          composite 53-54;
RUN;

TITLE 'Example 8.1 Describing data characteristics with PROC MEANS';

PROC MEANS DATA=achieve MAXDEC=4
          N MIN MAX MEAN MEDIAN Q1 Q3 VAR STD SKEWNESS KURTOSIS T PROBT CLM;
    VAR reading punc;
RUN;
```

Output 8.1 Describing Data Characteristics With PROC MEANS

Example 8.1 Describing data characteristics with PROC MEANS   1

The MEANS Procedure

Part (A)

Variable	N	Minimum	Maximum	Mean	Median	Lower Quartile
reading	120	21.0000	74.0000	49.6000	49.5000	44.0000
punc	120	20.0000	79.0000	49.4000	50.0000	40.0000

Part (B)

Variable	Upper Quartile	Variance	Std Dev	Skewness	Kurtosis
reading	57.0000	113.9227	10.6735	-0.3005	0.0484
punc	59.0000	194.6790	13.9527	-0.1375	-0.4765

Part (C)

Variable	t Value	Pr > |t|	Lower 95% CL for Mean	Upper 95% CL for Mean
reading	50.91	<.0001	47.6707	51.5293
punc	38.78	<.0001	46.8779	51.9221

For purposes of explanation, the output is divided into three parts: (A), (B), and (C). According to **Part (A)** output, the number of nonmissing observations (**N**) on both variables is 120. The minimum of <u>reading</u> score is 21.0000, whereas <u>punc</u>'s lowest score is 20.0000. The maximum for <u>reading</u> is 74.0000, whereas for <u>punc</u>, the highest score is 79.0000. The arithmetic averages (**MEAN**) of <u>reading</u> and <u>punc</u> are 49.6000 and 49.4000, respectively. The median is also the 50th percentile; it equals 49.5000 for <u>reading</u>

and 50.0000 for <u>punc</u>. The Lower Quartile is also the 25th percentile or the first quartile (**Q1** as the keyword); it equals 44.0000 for <u>reading</u> and 40.0000 for <u>punc</u>.

Under **Part (B)**, five additional statistics are printed: upper quartile, variance, standard deviation, skewness, and kurtosis. The upper quartile is also the 75th percentile or the third quartile (**Q3** as the keyword). It equals 57.0000 for <u>reading</u> and 59.0000 for <u>punc</u>. Variance (**VAR** as the keyword) is calculated using degrees of freedom (= sample size minus 1) as the denominator. Standard deviation (**Std Dev** on the SAS output, or **STD** as a keyword in the SAS program) equals the square root of the variance. Thus, the standard deviation for <u>reading</u> is the square root of 113.9227, or 10.6735. For <u>punc</u>, the standard deviation is 13.9527, or the square root of 194.6790. **Skewness** calculates the lack of symmetry in sample data. A positive skewness indicates that the distribution is positively skewed, or skewed to the right. A negative value therefore indicates a negatively skewed distribution; the distribution is said to be skewed to the left. Based on these interpretations, both <u>reading</u> and <u>punc</u> skewnesses suggest a slightly negatively skewed distribution. Since both skewnesses are close to zero, it is necessary to graph both distributions and conduct a statistical test before making a claim that either or both curves are skewed to the left. **Kurtosis** measures the peakedness of a distribution. If a distribution is more peaked than the normal distribution, then this index is positive; in this case, the distribution is described as *leptokurtic*. If a distribution is less peaked, or flatter than the normal distribution, this index is negative. In this case, the distribution is said to be *platykurtic*. By these terms, we can conclude that <u>reading</u>'s distribution is mildly leptokurtic, whereas the <u>punc</u> distribution is platykurtic. The normal distribution is described as *mesokurtic*.

Part (C) presents results of the one-sample t test of a zero population mean for both <u>reading</u> and <u>punc</u>, as well as probability levels associated with the t-test results. The t values for <u>reading</u> and <u>punc</u> are 50.91 and 38.78, respectively. Both t values reached a probability level (p) of less than 0.0001. Based on these results, the null hypotheses of a zero population mean can be rejected at $\alpha = 0.05$ or even 0.01. The 95% confidence intervals of <u>reading</u> and <u>punc</u> population means, constructed from the corresponding sample means using the t distribution, support the hypothesis testing conclusion. The confidence interval for the <u>reading</u> population mean ranges from 47.6707 to 51.5293; it does not include the null hypothetical mean of 0. A similar confidence interval was obtained for <u>punc</u>, with lower and upper limits equal to 46.8779 and 51.9221, respectively. The t test of a zero population mean is requested by the keyword **T**, its p value is requested by **PROBT**, and the confidence interval is requested by **CLM**.

- By default, five descriptive indices are calculated by the MEANS procedure without specifying any keyword: **N**, **MEAN**, **STD**, **MIN**, and **MAX**. Additional statistical indices computed by the MEANS procedure are found in **Section 8.3**.

Example 8.2 Describing Subsets of Data

In this example, data are described by subgroups. Specifically, the data set achieve is divided into subsets by grade levels and sex groups. For each subset, summary information is described for reading and punc.

To define subgroups, CLASS and BY statements are specified. The CLASS statement specifies grade as an independent variable or classification variable. The BY statement specifies sex as a sorting variable. This specification requires data to be presorted by the sex variable. Hence, PROC SORT; and BY sex; statements are inserted immediately before the PROC MEANS statement. Five descriptive indices (i.e., N, MEAN, STD, MIN, and MAX) are computed as the default. Consequently, five descriptive values are printed for reading and punc separately, for each grade level and each sex group.

```
/* See Example 8.1 for the DATA step in creating the SAS data set 'achieve' */

PROC SORT DATA=achieve; BY sex;
RUN;

TITLE 'Example 8.2 Describing subsets of data';

PROC MEANS DATA=achieve MAXDEC=4;
    VAR reading punc;
    CLASS grade;
    BY sex;
RUN;
```

Output 8.2 Describing Subsets of Data

```
                     Example 8.2 Describing subsets of data                           1
---------------------------------------- sex=1 ------------------------------ ------------

          N
  grade  Obs  Variable    N        Mean       Std Dev      Minimum      Maximum
  ------------------------------------------------------------------------------------
      4   21  reading     21     43.0476      10.4378      21.0000      63.0000
              punc        21     40.4000      13.3313      22.0000      65.0000

      5   20  reading     20     51.0000       6.8977      36.0000      62.0000
              punc        20     51.7500      14.2566      23.0000      72.0000

      6   15  reading     15     56.0000       9.7027      34.0000      69.0000
              punc        15     55.2000      14.3437      30.0000      79.0000
  ------------------------------------------------------------------------------------


---------------------------------------- sex=2 ------------------------------ ------------

          N
  grade  Obs  Variable    N        Mean       Std Dev      Minimum      Maximum
  ------------------------------------------------------------------------------------
      4   19  reading     19     41.7368       9.3324      22.0000      55.0000
              punc        19     43.4211      11.9039      20.0000      63.0000
```

5	20	reading	20	50.7000	7.2627	36.0000	60.0000
		punc	20	46.0000	11.9781	21.0000	65.0000
6	25	reading	25	55.2400	11.2483	37.0000	74.0000
		punc	25	52.1200	15.6160	24.0000	77.0000

Because of the CLASS grade; statement, data are analyzed for the 4th, 5th, and 6th grades separately. In addition, the BY sex; statement requires that two gender groups be analyzed separately. Consequently, six combinations of subsets (i.e., 3 grade levels by 2 gender groups) and their corresponding reading and punc descriptive statistics are calculated. The five statistics shown in Output 8.2 are self-explanatory since they have been explained in Output 8.1.

You may wonder what happens if only the CLASS statement is used without the BY statement. Output 8.2a gives away the answer:

Output 8.2a Describing Subsets of Data With One CLASS Statement

Example 8.2a Describing subsets of data with one CLASS statement   1

The MEANS Procedure

grade	N Obs	Variable	N	Mean	Std Dev	Minimum	Maximum
4	40	reading	40	42.4250	9.8238	21.0000	63.0000
		punc	40	46.0500	12.7761	20.0000	65.0000
5	40	reading	40	50.8500	6.9929	36.0000	62.0000
		punc	40	48.8750	13.3189	21.0000	72.0000
6	40	reading	40	55.5250	10.5733	34.0000	74.0000
		punc	40	53.2750	15.0401	24.0000	79.0000

Notice how the sex differences disappear from Output 8.2a. What remains are descriptive statistics of reading and punc by each grade level. If the BY statement is used alone without the CLASS statement, you get Output 8.2b.

Output 8.2b Describing Subsets of Data With One BY Statement

Example 8.2b Describing subsets of data with one BY statement   1

------------------------------------ sex=1 ------------------------------------

Variable	N	Mean	Std Dev	Minimum	Maximum
reading	56	49.3571	10.4035	21.0000	69.0000
punc	56	51.4286	13.9556	22.0000	79.0000

```
------------------------------------------ sex=2 ------------------------------------------------

    Variable      N          Mean         Std Dev        Minimum        Maximum
    ------------------------------------------------------------------------------
    reading       64        49.8125        10.9818        22.0000        74.0000
    punc          64        47.6250        13.8145        20.0000        77.0000
    ------------------------------------------------------------------------------
```

Although appearances are different, both outputs illustrate that either the CLASS or the BY statement can be used alone to carry out the subgroup analysis. Both statements can be included in the same SAS program, but you must specify different variables in each statement. With large data sets, the CLASS statement may require more computing resources than the BY statement, yet both statements yield the same result. If the BY statement is used in the MEANS procedure, data must be presorted according to the ascending values of the BY variable(s). Sorting can be accomplished with the SORT procedure.

Example 8.3 Creating an Output Data Set in PROC MEANS

It is possible to save descriptive results in a SAS data set for further analysis or examination. The **OUTPUT** statement is well suited for this purpose. The OUTPUT statement is followed by an output data set name (OUT=) and statistical indices to be included in the output data set.

How do you name the indices? It is easy; simply create a name that links the statistic to the variable. For instance, two variables, reading and punc, are analyzed for their valid data points, means, standard deviations, minimums, and maximums. Hence, the mean of reading is named meanread (= 49.6, on pages 1 and 2 of Output 8.3), the mean of punc is named meanpunc (= 49.4), the standard deviation for reading is stdread (= 10.6735), and the standard deviation for punc is stdpunc (= 13.9527).

Once the output data set is created, you may display the content of this data set by PROC PRINT. As a good data analyst, you should always read the content of any data set at least once, preferably immediately after the data set is created. By taking this extra step, you can ensure that you did not make mistakes in naming variables or in specifying statistical indices for inclusion in the output data set.

```
/* See Example 8.1 for the DATA step in creating the SAS data set 'achieve' */

TITLE 'Example 8.3 Creating an output data set in PROC MEANS';

PROC MEANS DATA=achieve MAXDEC=4;
    VAR reading punc;
    OUTPUT OUT=aout MEAN=meanread meanpunc STD=stdread stdpunc;
RUN;

TITLE 'Example 8.3 Printing an output data set from PROC MEANS';

PROC PRINT DATA=aout;
RUN;
```

Output 8.3 Creating an Output Data Set in PROC MEANS

```
            Example 8.3 Creating an output data set in PROC MEANS                    1

                              The MEANS Procedure

Variable      N            Mean          Std Dev         Minimum         Maximum
---------------------------------------------------------------------------------
reading      120        49.6000        10.6735         21.0000         74.0000
punc         120        49.4000        13.9527         20.0000         79.0000
---------------------------------------------------------------------------------
```

```
        Example 8.3 Printing an output data set from PROC MEANS                      2

Obs      _TYPE_      _FREQ_      meanread     meanpunc     stdread     stdpunc

 1          0          120         49.6          49.4       10.6735     13.9527
```

The **_TYPE_** variable from page 2 of Output 8.3 indicates that the output is based on the entire sample, because _TYPE_ = 0. Examples 8.4 and 8.5 will further explain and illustrate how other values of the _TYPE_ variable, such as 1, 2, and so on, are constructed and referenced.

The **_FREQ_** variable indicates the number of observations (120) in the data set. Yet the calculation of <u>meanread</u>, <u>meanpunc</u>, <u>stdread</u>, and <u>stdpunc</u> is based on the number of valid observations, excluding missing data.

Both _TYPE_ and _FREQ_ variables are internal variables that are created by SAS. You can refer to these internal variables in the same way as you do to variables defined by yourself.

Example 8.4 One Classification Variable Used in an Output Data Set

If one classification variable (say, <u>sex</u>) is specified in a CLASS statement along with the OUTPUT statement, the CLASS variable will result in an additional _TYPE_ = 1 in the output data set. As shown in Output 8.3, _TYPE_ = 0 means that the corresponding data line is based on the entire data set. Therefore, _TYPE_ = 1 means that the corresponding result is based on a subgroup, defined by a value of <u>sex</u>. In this example, <u>reading</u> scores are analyzed for the entire sample and for the two subgroups formed from the sex variable.

```
/* See Example 8.1 for the DATA step in creating the SAS data set 'achieve' */

TITLE 'Example 8.4 One classification variable used in an output data set';

PROC MEANS DATA=achieve MAXDEC=4;
     VAR reading;
     CLASS sex;
     OUTPUT OUT=aout MEAN=meanread STD=stdread;
RUN;

TITLE '_TYPE_ = 1 based on *sex* CLASS variable';

PROC PRINT DATA=aout;
RUN;
```

Output 8.4 One Classification Variable Used in an Output Data Set

```
        Example 8.4 One classification variable used in an output data set          1

                              The MEANS Procedure

                           Analysis Variable : reading

          N
sex     Obs       N          Mean        Std Dev       Minimum       Maximum
--------------------------------------------------------------------------------
1        56       56       49.3571       10.4035       21.0000       69.0000

2        64       64       49.8125       10.9818       22.0000       74.0000
--------------------------------------------------------------------------------
```

```
         _TYPE_ = 1 based on *sex* CLASS variable                                   2

Obs      sex      _TYPE_     _FREQ_     meanread     stdread

  1                 0         120       49.6000      10.6735
  2        1        1          56       49.3571      10.4035
  3        2        1          64       49.8125      10.9818
```

Note that the _TYPE_ variable takes on two values: 0 and 1. The value
of 0 indicates that the first data line (or Obs = 1) is based on the entire sample (of 120 observations). The value of 1 indicates that the next two data
lines (or Obs = 2 and 3) are based on two subgroups of <u>sex</u>. Because <u>sex</u> was
coded as 1 for females and 2 for males, we know that Obs = 2 is the result
based on 56 girls. The third, and also the last, data line (or Obs = 3) is the
result based on 64 boys.

In the next example, a second CLASS variable, <u>grade</u>, is added to
Example 8.4; let's see what happens.

Example 8.5 Two Classification Variables Used in an Output Data Set

```
/* See Example 8.1 for the DATA step in creating the SAS data set 'achieve' */

TITLE 'Example 8.5 Two classification variables used in an output data set';

PROC MEANS DATA=achieve MAXDEC=4;
    VAR reading;
    CLASS sex grade;
    OUTPUT OUT=aout MEAN=meanread STD=stdread;
RUN;

TITLE '_TYPE_ = 1,2,3 based on *sex* and *grade* CLASS variables';

PROC PRINT DATA=aout;
RUN;
```

Output 8.5 Two Classification Variables Used in an Output Data Set

```
              Example 8.5 Two classification variables used in an output data set        1

                                   The MEANS Procedure

                               Analysis Variable : reading

                          N
  sex        grade      Obs      N         Mean       Std Dev      Minimum       Maximum
  --------------------------------------------------------------------------------------
  1              4       21      21       43.0476      10.4378      21.0000       63.0000

                 5       20      20       51.0000       6.8977      36.0000       62.0000

                 6       15      15       56.0000       9.7027      34.0000       69.0000

  2              4       19      19       41.7368       9.3324      22.0000       55.0000

                 5       20      20       50.7000       7.2627      36.0000       60.0000

                 6       25      25       55.2400      11.2483      37.0000       74.0000
  --------------------------------------------------------------------------------------
```

```
     _TYPE_ = 1,2,3 based on *sex* and *grade* CLASS variables                          2

   Obs    sex    grade    _TYPE_    _FREQ_    meanread    stdread

    1              .          0       120      49.6000    10.6735
    2      4                  1        40      42.4250     9.8238
    3      5                  1        40      50.8500     6.9929
    4      6                  1        40      55.5250    10.5733
    5      1      .           2        56      49.3571    10.4035
    6      2      .           2        64      49.8125    10.9818
    7      1      4           3        21      43.0476    10.4378
    8      1      5           3        20      51.0000     6.8977
    9      1      6           3        15      56.0000     9.7027
   10      2      4           3        19      41.7368     9.3324
   11      2      5           3        20      50.7000     7.2627
   12      2      6           3        25      55.2400    11.2483
```

When there are two CLASS variables specified, such as sex and grade, the _TYPE_ variable takes on four values: 0, 1, 2, and 3. The 0 value continues to refer to the entire sample [_FREQ_ = 120 (= the total sample size), sex= . (missing), and grade=. (missing)]. When _TYPE_= 1, it refers to the three groups of grade, _TYPE_= 2 refers to the two groups of sex, and _TYPE_= 3 refers to the six groups jointly defined by sex and grade.

You may ask, "How many different values of _TYPE_ are there, if three variables are specified in the CLASS statement?" The answer is eight. The first four are identical to the four already shown in Output 8.5; the last four correspond to new subgroups. The new subgroups include (a) subgroups based on the third variable for which _TYPE_ = 4, (b) subgroups based on the first and the third variables jointly (_TYPE_ = 5), (c) subgroups based on the second and the third variables combined (_TYPE_ = 6), and

(d) subgroups based on all three classification variables (_TYPE_ = 7). Can you now figure out all the possible values of _TYPE_ and what they represent, if there are four classification variables?

_____ ## 8.3 How to Write the PROC MEANS Codes

The following PROC MEANS statements were used in one or more of the five examples above. Let's summarize their syntax:

PROC	MEANS	DATA= *sas_dataset_name* *<options>* *<keywords for statistic>*;
	VAR	*variable(s)*;
	CLASS	*classification_variable(s)*;
	BY	*classification_variable(s)*;
	WEIGHT	*weight_variable*;
	FREQ	*frequency_variable*;
	OUTPUT	*<OUT= output_dataset_name>* *<keywords for output statistic>*;

The **PROC MEANS** statement initiates the procedure and specifies a data set to be analyzed. Three helpful options are the following:

MAXDEC= an integer (such as 4)	This option mandates that four (say) decimal places be printed for each output value. In Example 8.1, we specified MAXDEC= 4; hence, all results kept decimal places up to 4. The smallest value you may specify is 0 (no decimals) and the largest is 8 (eight decimal places).
VARDEF=DF	This option specifies the degrees of freedom to be the denominator of variance or standard deviation. Other choices include the total sample size (VARDEF=N), sum of weights (VARDEF=WGT), or sum of weights minus one (VARDEF=WDF). The default is degrees of freedom (DF), which equals sample size minus 1.
NOPRINT	This option suppresses all the output. It is very useful if the main purpose is to create a data set containing the descriptive statistics for further analysis.

The following keywords for statistics can also be included in the PROC MEANS statement; these will be computed for each variable listed in the VAR statement.

N	the number of valid observations on which the analysis is based, excluding the missing values
NMISS	the number of missing scores
MIN	the minimum score
MAX	the maximum score
RANGE	the range (= MAX − MIN) score
MEAN	the arithmetic average
MEDIAN	the median or the 50th percentile
MODE	the modal value
VAR	the sample variance, which is computed using a denominator specified by the VARDEF= option. The default denominator of VAR is the degrees of freedom.
STD	the square root of the variance, as defined above
STDERR	the standard error of sample means, which is defined as the ratio of the standard deviation over the square root of the sample size
SKEWNESS	the skewness of the sample distribution. A positive value indicates the distribution is positively skewed, or skewed to the right. A negative value indicates the distribution is negatively skewed, or skewed to the left. A zero value indicates that the distribution is not skewed.
KURTOSIS	the kurtosis, or the peakedness, index of the sample distribution. If a distribution is more peaked than the normal distribution, then its kurtosis is positive and the distribution is described as *leptokurtic*. On the other hand, if a distribution is less peaked (or flatter) than the normal distribution, then its kurtosis is negative and the distribution is *platykurtic*. When the kurtosis is about zero, the distribution is as peaked as a normal curve and is said to be *mesokurtic*.
P1	the first percentile
P5	the 5th percentile
P10	the 10th percentile
Q1 (also P25)	the first quartile, also the 25th percentile
Q3 (also P75)	the third quartile, also the 75th percentile
P90	the 90th percentile
P95	the 95th percentile
P99	the 99th percentile
QRANGE	the interquartile range, also equals (Q3 − Q1)
SUM	the total score

SUMWGT	the total weight for the entire data set or a subset
CV	the coefficient of variation
CSS	the sum of squared difference between individual scores and their sample mean
USS	the sum of squared scores
T	performs the two-tailed t test of a zero population mean.
PROBT	calculates the significance level (or p value) of the above two-tailed t test. If a one-tailed t-test result is desired, you divide this two-tailed p value by 2.
ALPHA =	(a small probability) specifies a probability for constructing the $(1 - \text{ALPHA}) \times 100\%$ confidence interval of the population mean based on the sample mean. The default is 0.05.
CLM	computes the two-sided $(1 - \text{ALPHA}) \times 100\%$ confidence limits of the population mean based on the sample mean and the t distribution. The default is a 95% confidence interval.
UCLM	computes the one-sided upper limit of the $(1 - \text{ALPHA}) \times 100\%$ confidence interval of the population mean based on the sample mean and the t distribution. If LCLM is also specified, the two-sided confidence limits will be reported. The default is a 95% confidence interval.
LCLM	computes the one-sided lower limit of the $(1 - \text{ALPHA}) \times 100\%$ confidence interval of the population mean based on the sample mean and the t distribution. If UCLM is also specified, the two-sided confidence limits will be reported. The default is a 95% confidence interval.

The second statement, **VAR,** is used to specify one or more numeric variables in the data set for which descriptive analyses are performed. The third statement, **CLASS,** and the fourth statement, **BY,** both are used to specify one or more classification variables. These classification variables are used to divide up the data set into subsets. Within each subset, descriptive analyses are performed. Both CLASS and BY statements serve the same purpose, even though the output appears to be different. Example 8.2 illustrates such a difference. Furthermore, the BY statement requires the data set to be sorted in the ascending order of the BY variables while the CLASS statement does not have such a requirement.

The fifth statement, **WEIGHT,** is used to apply differential weights to data values. All weights must be nonnegative. Zero or fractional numbers are allowed. Negative or missing values are substituted by a zero. When the zero weight is applied to a variable, the variable's summary statistics, such as mean, variance, and standard deviation, will be missing in the output; yet the minimum and the maximum will continue to be data values identified to be the smallest and the largest, respectively.

The sixth statement, **FREQ,** is used when data are grouped. By grouped data, we mean that data have been grouped by distinct data values and frequencies of occurrences, or organized into intervals, represented by a midpoint and the frequency of data values in that interval. To describe a grouped data set, two pieces of information are needed: (1) the distinct data value or midpoint of an interval and (2) its frequency count. In SAS terminology, the frequency count is the value of the FREQ variable.

The last statement, **OUTPUT,** is used to create an output data set so that results from PROC MEANS can be saved for subsequent analysis by another procedure. Immediately after the option **OUT=***output_dataset _name*, one or more statistics may be requested by their keywords. For example, if you'd like to correlate the average of reading with the average of punc for six subgroups defined by sex and grade, you can slightly modify Example 8.5 as follows:

Example 8.6 Output Results of PROC MEANS for Additional Analysis

```
/* See Example 8.1 for the DATA step in creating the SAS data set 'achieve' */

TITLE 'Example 8.6 Output results of PROC MEANS for additional analysis';

PROC MEANS DATA=achieve MAXDEC=4 NOPRINT;
    VAR reading punc;
    CLASS sex grade;
    OUTPUT OUT=aout MEAN= meanread meanpunc;
RUN;

DATA aout2;
    SET aout;
    IF _TYPE_=3;

TITLE2 'Correlating reading and punctuation averages for six subgroups';

PROC CORR DATA=aout2;                        /* This procedure is explained in Ch. 16 */
    VAR meanread meanpunc;
RUN;
```

Output 8.6 Output Results of PROC MEANS for Additional Analysis

```
            Example 8.6 Output results of PROC MEANS for additional analysis         1
              Correlating reading and punctuation averages for six subgroups

                                The CORR Procedure

                          2  Variables:    meanread meanpunc
```

Part (A)

```
                              Simple Statistics

Variable          N         Mean      Std Dev          Sum      Minimum      Maximum

meanread          6     49.62074      6.01165     297.72446     41.73684     56.00000
meanpunc          6     49.48660      4.35356     296.91962     43.42105     55.20000
```

```
Part (B)
                        Pearson Correlation Coefficients, N = 6
                               Prob > |r| under H0: Rho=0

                                    meanread        meanpunc

                    meanread         1.00000          0.80527
                                                      0.0532

                    meanpunc         0.80527          1.00000
                                     0.0532
```

The output does not contain any result from the MEANS procedure because of the NOPRINT option in the PROC MEANS statement. The output is the result of only PROC CORR. There are two parts: **Part (A)** is basically descriptive, including the mean, standard deviation, sum, minimum, and maximum of six subgroups' average reading (meanread) and average punctuation (meanpunc) scores. **Part (B)** presents the correlation (0.80527) between meanread and meanpunc. This correlation is called the Pearson correlation coefficient. Its magnitude reaches the statistical significance level of 0.0532 for $N = 6$. Why only 6 observations? Because the correlation is based on average reading and average punc scores of six subgroups; these six subgroups are formed from two sex groups and three grade levels. Details about PROC CORR and the Pearson correlation coefficient are given in Chapter 16.

8.4 Tip

• How to handle missing or invalid data

Missing data occur because there is insufficient information about a particular observation on a particular variable. Missing data should be treated differently than 0 because in the latter case you do have information about the observation; that information happens to be 0, whereas missing data means you have no information.

If an observation has missing information on one or more variables, the observation is excluded from the computation of descriptive statistics. Yet such an observation is not removed from the SAS data set. So you should not worry about losing that observation permanently. The count of missing observations on each variable is provided by the option **NMISS** in the PROC MEANS statement; below is an illustration of the NMISS option. Try executing this program and not being surprised by its result!

Example 8.7 Illustration of the NMISS Option

```
/* See Example 8.1 for the DATA step in creating the SAS data set 'achieve' */

TITLE 'Example 8.7 Illustration of the NMISS option';

PROC MEANS DATA=achieve NMISS;
    VAR reading;
RUN;
```

8.5 Summary

In this chapter, you learned how to conduct descriptive analysis quickly with PROC MEANS. Specifically, the MEANS procedure was demonstrated to summarize data in their entirety, or in parts.

Various descriptive summary indices can be calculated by the MEANS procedure. The results, based on the entire data set or its subsets, may be saved into an output SAS data analysis for a follow-up analysis or further examination. PROC MEANS may also be used to conduct the one-sample t test of a zero population mean and to construct 95% confidence limits of a population mean. Additional explanation of the MEANS procedure can be found in *Base SAS 9.1.3 Procedures Guide* by SAS Institute Inc. (2006a), or its online documentation at www.sas.com.

8.6 Exercises

1. To compute descriptive statistics for the <u>income</u> variable for each <u>gender</u> and <u>district</u> in her state, Jane decided to write the following program:

```
PROC MEANS VARDEF=DF;
    VAR income;
    BY gender district;
```

Immediately before this procedure, Jane needs to add

a. nothing; the procedure she has written is sufficient.

b. PROC SORT; BY gender district;

c. PROC SORT; BY income;

d. PROC SORT; BY gender; BY district;

2. Given the following program, identify the statement that immediately precedes the PROC MEANS.

```
PROC MEANS;
     BY age;
     VAR height weight;
PROC PRINT; RUN;
```

   a. DATA= ht_wt;
   b. OUTPUT OUT=ht_wt;
   c. DATA; INPUT age height weight;
   d. PROC SORT; BY age;
   e. PROC SORT; BY height weight;

3. Which one of the following two programs will give you the highest and lowest <u>sale</u> in May?

   a.

```
DATA may;
     INPUT name $ sex $ sale dept $;
DATALINES;
[data lines]
;
PROC PRINT DATA=may; RUN;
TITLE 'MAY sales figures';
PROC SORT; BY name; RUN;
PROC MEANS; BY name;
     VAR sale;
     OUTPUT OUT=slsfig MAX=max_sale MIN=min_sale;
PROC PRINT DATA=slsfig; RUN;
```

   b.

```
DATA may;
     INPUT name $ sex $ sale dept $;
DATALINES;
[data lines]
;
PROC PRINT DATA=may; RUN;
TITLE 'MAY sales figures';
PROC MEANS;
     VAR sale;
     OUTPUT OUT=slsfig MAX=max_sale MIN=min_sale;
PROC PRINT DATA=slsfig; RUN;
```

4. The MEANS procedure provides many details on the distribution of a variable. Which of the following is <u>not</u> a result of PROC MEANS?
   a. Range of scores
   b. Degrees of freedom
   c. A test to determine whether data are normally distributed
   d. Correlation coefficient between variables

5. Modify Example 8.2 by adding both <u>grade</u> and <u>sex</u> variables to the CLASS statement and rerun the program. Compare your output with Output 8.2.

6. Modify Example 8.2 by using both <u>grade</u> and <u>sex</u> as BY variables and rerun the program. Compare your results with those obtained from Exercise 5 above.

7. The following are the results of a biology examination taken by 20 ninth graders. Describe the data in terms of its (a) highest score, (b) lowest score, (c) range, (d) mean, (e) standard deviation, and (f) number of missing data.

> 87, 65, 92, 66, 58, 73, ., 82, 86, .,
> 77, 96, 60, 81, ., 69, 76, 80, 90, 71

8. Given the data in Exercise 7 above, conduct a two-tailed t test of a population mean = 80. What is the p value associated with the t test and what are the 95% confidence limits of the population mean based on the sample mean?

8.7 Answers to Exercises

1. b

2. d

3. a

4. b, c, d

5. Compared with Output 8.2, the output below gives information on <u>reading</u> and <u>punc</u> scores for subgroups broken down by <u>grade</u> and <u>sex,</u> which were both defined in the CLASS statement.

```
                                      Exercise 8-5                                          1

                                   The MEANS Procedure

                    N
  grade  sex  Obs  Variable    N         Mean       Std Dev      Minimum        Maximum
  -------------------------------------------------------------------------------------
      4   1    21  reading    21      43.0476       10.4378      21.0000        63.0000
                   punc       21      48.4286       13.3513      22.0000        65.0000

          2    19  reading    19      41.7368        9.3324      22.0000        55.0000
                   punc       19      43.4211       11.9039      20.0000        63.0000

      5   1    20  reading    20      51.0000        6.8977      36.0000        62.0000
                   punc       20      51.7500       14.2566      23.0000        72.0000

          2    20  reading    20      50.7000        7.2627      36.0000        60.0000
                   punc       20      46.0000       11.9781      21.0000        65.0000

      6   1    15  reading    15      56.0000        9.7027      34.0000        69.0000
                   punc       15      55.2000       14.3437      30.0000        79.0000

          2    25  reading    25      55.2400       11.2483      37.0000        74.0000
                   punc       25      52.1200       15.6160      24.0000        77.0000
  -------------------------------------------------------------------------------------
```

6. This output contains information identical to that obtained from Exercise 5 above, except that the reporting format is different. It is up to you to decide if you like this format better or the one above.

```
                                Exercise 8-6                              1
------------------------------- grade=4 sex=1 --------------------------------

    Variable      N          Mean        Std Dev       Minimum       Maximum
    -----------------------------------------------------------------------
    reading      21       43.0476        10.4378       21.0000       63.0000
    punc         21       48.4286        13.3513       22.0000       65.0000
    -----------------------------------------------------------------------


------------------------------- grade=4 sex=2 --------------------------------

    Variable      N          Mean        Std Dev       Minimum       Maximum
    -----------------------------------------------------------------------
    reading      19       41.7368         9.3324       22.0000       55.0000
    punc         19       43.4211        11.9039       20.0000       63.0000
    -----------------------------------------------------------------------


------------------------------- grade=5 sex=1 --------------------------------

    Variable      N          Mean        Std Dev       Minimum       Maximum
    -----------------------------------------------------------------------
    reading      20       51.0000         6.8977       36.0000       62.0000
    punc         20       51.7500        14.2566       23.0000       72.0000
    -----------------------------------------------------------------------


------------------------------- grade=5 sex=2 --------------------------------

    Variable      N          Mean        Std Dev       Minimum       Maximum
    -----------------------------------------------------------------------
    reading      20       50.7000         7.2627       36.0000       60.0000
    punc         20       46.0000        11.9781       21.0000       65.0000
    -----------------------------------------------------------------------


------------------------------- grade=6 sex=1 --------------------------------

    Variable      N          Mean        Std Dev       Minimum       Maximum
    -----------------------------------------------------------------------
    reading      15       56.0000         9.7027       34.0000       69.0000
    punc         15       55.2000        14.3437       30.0000       79.0000
    -----------------------------------------------------------------------


------------------------------- grade=6 sex=2 --------------------------------

    Variable      N          Mean        Std Dev       Minimum       Maximum
    -----------------------------------------------------------------------
    reading      25       55.2400        11.2483       37.0000       74.0000
    punc         25       52.1200        15.6160       24.0000       77.0000
    -----------------------------------------------------------------------
```

7. The data show that (a) the highest score is 96.0000, (b) the lowest score is 58.0000, (c) range = 38.0000, (d) mean = 77.0000, (e) standard deviation = 11.2305, and (f) the number of missing data = 3.

```
                                Exercise 8-7                              1

                             The MEANS Procedure

                          Analysis Variable : score

                                                                      N
    Maximum        Minimum         Range          Mean      Std Dev  Miss
    -----------------------------------------------------------------------
    96.0000        58.0000        38.0000        77.0000     11.2305    3
    -----------------------------------------------------------------------
```

8. To solve this problem with the MEANS procedure, you need to first create a new variable <u>diff,</u> which equals <u>score</u> minus 80. Then include options **T** and **PROBT** in your SAS program. The *t* test, therefore, will be performed on the null hypothesis of a population mean of <u>diff</u> equaling 0.

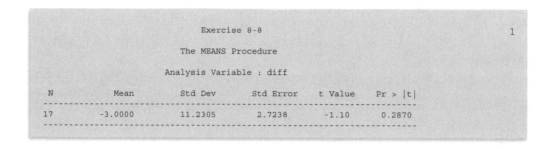

```
                              Exercise 8-8                                      1

                            The MEANS Procedure

                        Analysis Variable : diff

     N         Mean        Std Dev      Std Error     t Value      Pr > |t|
---------------------------------------------------------------------------------
    17       -3.0000       11.2305       2.7238        -1.10        0.2870
---------------------------------------------------------------------------------
```

The output shows that the sample mean of <u>score</u> is 3 points below the hypothesized population mean of 80. The *t* test statistic (*t* = −1.1) is associated with df = 16 and *p* = 0.2870. Therefore, it is not statistically significant at α = 0.05. This *t*-test result indicates that we cannot reject the null hypothesis that the population mean of <u>diff</u> equals 0; hence, we cannot reject the null hypothesis that the population mean of <u>score</u> equals 80.

```
                              Exercise 8-8                                      2

                            The MEANS Procedure

                        Analysis Variable : score

                                                 Lower 95%      Upper 95%
     N         Mean        Std Dev      Std Error  CL for Mean   CL for Mean
---------------------------------------------------------------------------------
    17       77.0000       11.2305       2.7238      71.2258       82.7742
---------------------------------------------------------------------------------
```

Page 2 of the output reports the 95% confidence limits of the population mean based on the sample mean. The lower limit is 71.2258, whereas the upper limit equals 82.7742. This 95% confidence limits include 80. Thus, it supports the retention of the null hypothesis of a population mean equaling 80.

9

Comprehensive Descriptive Analysis and Normality Test

OBJECTIVE

This chapter covers the most comprehensive descriptive analysis of data using the UNIVARIATE procedure. Included in this comprehensive analysis are typical indices of central tendencies, spread, skewness, kurtosis, percentiles, quartiles, missing data, valid data, and so on. Furthermore, the distribution of data is displayed in three different graphs: (1) the stem-and-leaf plot, (2) the box plot, and (3) the normal probability plot. The shape of the data distribution can also be tested against the theoretical normal distribution or examined for extreme values or outliers.

9.1 Comprehensive Descriptive Analysis and the Test of Normality

A comprehensive descriptive data analysis is best carried out by the UNIVARIATE procedure in SAS. This procedure is capable of in-depth examination of quantitative data, variable by variable, including (a) three indices of central tendency (mean, median, mode); (b) six indices of variability (range, standard deviation, variance, coefficient of variation, interquartile range, standard error of the mean); (c) indices of skewness and kurtosis; (d) various percentiles and quartiles; (e) miscellaneous descriptive values such as the total, sample size, sum of weights, and so forth; (f) identification of extreme values in a frequency distribution; (g) three visual displays of data (stem-and-leaf plot, box plot, and normal probability plot); and (h) three tests of central tendency (the t test, the sign test, and the signed rank test) plus four tests of normality (the Shapiro-Wilk test, the Kolmogorov-Smirnov test, the Cramér-von Mises test, and the Anderson-Darling test). This list of features reads like Who's Who in descriptive data analysis, doesn't it? Obviously, you recognize the similarity between the MEANS and the UNIVARIATE procedures. So you ask, "Why bother with the UNIVARIATE procedure?" The extra features listed in (f) through (h) are the reasons why you need this procedure at times when the MEANS procedure can't quite cover all bases, though the MEANS procedure is still handy for quickly summarizing data for multiple variables. These unique features about PROC UNIVARIATE are demonstrated in Examples 9.1 through 9.5.

Four statistical tests of normality are particularly useful for examining the degree to which a data distribution is approximately normal (Example 9.4). Because many parametric statistical procedures require that the underlying population be normally distributed, these tests can help you verify the normality assumption based on a sample.

In addition to the parametric t test, PROC UNIVARIATE performs the sign test based on positive or negative signs of data, deviating positively or negatively from the hypothesized population median. This test allows you to make inferences about the population median with 20 or fewer observations or when data are measured at the ordinal level or higher.

Another test available from PROC UNIVARIATE, but not from PROC MEANS, is the signed rank test. This test is also used to make inferences about a population median (and mean, if the distribution is symmetric). The signed rank test improves over the sign test by using both signs (+ or −) and ranks of data, after adjusting for the sample median. Thus, it is a more powerful test than the sign test when the underlying population is unimodal and symmetric. Both the sign test and the signed rank test are particularly useful for small data sets or with crude measurements, such as ordinal-level data (Example 9.5). In addition to making inferences about a population median, both tests are also applicable to testing the difference between two paired as well as two independent population medians.

With PROC UNIVARIATE, you may also (a) stratify the sample into strata (or subgroups), analyze each stratum separately (Example 9.6), and (b) create an output data set for subsequent analysis (Example 9.7)—these features are available in PROC MEANS as well.

9.2 Examples

There are seven examples demonstrated in this chapter. All examples use either achieve.dat or mydata.dat for demonstration. Details about these data files are given in Appendix B.

Example 9.1 Describing Data Characteristics With PROC UNIVARIATE

This example shows how to compute simple descriptive statistics for the variable reading. The first statement is PROC UNIVARIATE, followed by an option ROUND= 0.01. This option rounds off variable values at the second decimal place prior to computing statistics. The second statement is VAR, which specifies reading to be analyzed.

```
/* The following bolded SAS statements establish the SAS data set 'achieve' */

DATA achieve;
    INFILE 'd:\data\achieve.dat';
    INPUT iv1 1 grade 2 iv2 3 sex $ 4 id $ 6-8 vocab 25-26 reading 27-28
          spelling 29-30 capital 31-32 punc 33-34 usage 35-36
          total1 37-38 maps 39-40 graphs 41-42 refer 43-44
          total2 45-46 concepts 47-48 problem 49-50 total3 51-52
          composite 53-54;
RUN;

TITLE 'Example 9.1 Describing data characteristics with PROC UNIVARIATE';

PROC UNIVARIATE DATA=achieve ROUND=0.01;
    VAR reading;
RUN;
```

Output 9.1 Describing Data Characteristics With PROC UNIVARIATE

```
                    Example 9.1 Describing data characteristics with PROC UNIVARIATE          1

                              The UNIVARIATE Procedure
                                 Variable:  reading
                         Values Rounded to the Nearest Multiple of 0.01

Part (A)
                                        Moments

             N                        120      Sum Weights              120
             Mean                     49.6      Sum Observations        5952
             Std Deviation      10.6734572      Variance          113.922689
             Skewness           -0.3004658      Kurtosis            0.0484073
             Uncorrected SS        308776      Corrected SS          13556.8
             Coeff Variation    21.519067      Std Error Mean      0.97434888
```

Part (B)

```
                         Basic Statistical Measures

            Location                        Variability

     Mean       49.60000      Std Deviation              10.67346
     Median     49.50000      Variance                  113.92269
     Mode       54.00000      Range                      53.00000
                              Interquartile Range        13.00000
```

Part (C)

```
                    Tests for Location: Mu0=0

        Test              -Statistic-      -----p Value------

        Student's t    t   50.90579    Pr > |t|      <.0001
        Sign           M        60     Pr >= |M|     <.0001
        Signed Rank    S      3630     Pr >= |S|     <.0001
```

Part (D)

```
                    Quantiles (Definition 5)

                    Quantile      Estimate

                    100% Max        74.0
                     99%            73.0
                     95%            65.0
                     90%            63.0
                     75% Q3         57.0
                     50% Median     49.5
                     25% Q1         44.0
                     10%            36.0
                      5%            30.0
                      1%            22.0
                      0% Min        21.0
```

Part (E)

```
                    Extreme Observations

        ----Lowest----              ----Highest---

        Value       Obs             Value       Obs

          21          1               68          88
          22         13               69         105
          24         31               70          85
          25          2               73         113
          30         12               74          91
```

For purposes of explanation, the output is divided into five parts: (A) Moments, (B) Basic Statistical Measures, (C) Tests for Location: Mu0=0, (D) Quantiles, and (E) Extreme Observations.

Part (A) <u>Moments:</u> This seemingly nonstatistical term refers to four moments (or characteristics) of the <u>reading</u> distribution and other descriptive indices. The first moment is the mean, the second moment is variance, the third moment is skewness, and the fourth moment is kurtosis. Table 9.1 provides a line-by-line interpretation of the results.

• By default, PROC UNIVARIATE always computes these descriptive results. These statistics can also be obtained from PROC MEANS. Because the SAS data set <u>achieve</u> and the variable <u>reading</u> were previously analyzed

Table 9.1   Line-by-Line Interpretation of Part (A) of Output 9.1

Output			Interpretation
N	120	Sum Weights	120	N is the number of valid observations; **Sum Weights** refers to the total of weights assigned. In the current example, each individual received 1 as the weight. In other words, all are treated equally.
Mean	49.6	Sum Observations	5952	**Mean** is the average; **Sum Observations** is the total of scores.
Std Deviation	10.6734572	Variance	113.922689	**Std Deviation** and **Variance** are indices of dispersion of scores. Both used the degrees of freedom (**df** or N − 1) as denominator because **df** is the default setting of the option **VARDEF=**.
Skewness	−0.3004658	Kurtosis	0.0484073	**Skewness** and **Kurtosis** measure skewness and peakedness of a distribution. Based on the results, we can describe the <u>reading</u> distribution as slightly negatively skewed and more peaked than a normal curve; hence, a leptokurtic curve. These descriptive measures should be tested statistically against 0 before a definitive conclusion is drawn.
Uncorrected SS	308776	Corrected SS	13556.8	**Uncorrected SS** means uncorrected sum of squares; **Corrected SS** means corrected sum of squares.
Coeff Variation	21.519067	Std Error Mean	0.97434888	**Coeff Variation** is coefficient of variation; **Std Error Mean** refers to the standard deviation (or standard error) of means.

167

in Chapter 8, it is not surprising that similar results are obtained. Check this out; compare Output 9.1 with Output 8.1.

- In PROC UNIVARIATE, the standard deviation of the sampling distribution of means, also called the standard error of means, is displayed as **Std Error Mean**. In PROC MEANS, however, the same concept and its value is labeled as **Std Error**. If you compare these values for <u>reading</u> obtained from these two procedures, you should find that they are identical.

Part (B) <u>Basic Statistical Measures:</u> This portion of the output presents two kinds of basic statistics: **Location** and **Variability**. The three location measures are mean (= 49.6), median (= 49.5), and mode (= 54.0). The four variability measures are standard deviation (= 10.6734572), variance (= 113.922689), range (= 53 = 74 − 21), and interquartile range (= 13 = 57 − 44).

Part (C) <u>Tests for Location: Mu0=0:</u> This portion of the output reports three two-tailed statistical tests of the location measures: Student's t test, the sign test, and the signed rank test. The null hypothesis for these tests is the same, namely, the population central location equals 0. The null hypothesis of a zero population value is the default setting for the **Mu0=** option. The Student's t test (t) of a zero population mean is 50.90579. The sign test (M) of a zero population median is 60 and the signed rank test (S) is 3630. All three tests are associated with a two-tailed p value less than 0.0001. Thus, three results indicate that the null hypotheses of a zero population central location can be rejected at $\alpha = 0.0001$.

Part (D) <u>Quantiles:</u> This part of the output prints quartiles and selected percentiles. The heading Quantiles (Definition 5) indicates that the 5th definition for quantiles, also the default, is used to compute these quantiles. Quantiles computed from the 5th definition are derived from the empirical distribution. Specifically, this default takes the average of two adjacent ranked scores to be the pth percentile, if the corresponding cumulative frequency (or $N \times p\%$) equals the rank of the smaller score. The percentile score is the larger score of the two when the corresponding cumulative frequency falls between these two ranked scores. The other four definitions for percentiles are discussed in the *Base SAS 9.1.3 Procedures Guide* (SAS Institute Inc., 2006a) or the online documentation at www.sas.com.

The remaining quantities are explained by the accompanied percentages. Therefore, 74 is the 100th percentile, also the maximal score; 57 is the 75th percentile or Q3; 49.5 is the 50th percentile or median (**Med**); and so on.

The **Range** of the score distribution is 53, which equals 74 − 21. The interquartile range equals 13 (= **Q3** − **Q1** = 57 − 44). The **Mode,** or the most frequently occurring score, is 54.

Part (E) <u>Extreme Observations:</u> This section prints the five lowest scores and the five highest scores. All 10 scores are identified by their corresponding observation number, which is listed under **Obs**. You can use this information to judge if any of these scores are outliers. An outlier needs to be examined carefully before a decision is made about its exclusion from the data set.

Example 9.2 Frequency Tabulation via PROC UNIVARIATE

This example illustrates how to compile a frequency distribution for <u>reading</u>. A frequency distribution is a tabulation of raw scores and the frequency of their occurrences. The tabulation sometimes can be more useful than the summary statistics presented in Output 9.1. To request a frequency distribution, simply type in the option **FREQ;** see the program below:

```
/* See Example 9.1 for the DATA step in creating the SAS data set 'achieve' */

TITLE 'Example 9.2 Frequency tabulation via PROC UNIVARIATE';

PROC UNIVARIATE DATA=achieve FREQ;
     VAR reading;
RUN;
```

Output 9.2 Frequency Tabulation via PROC UNIVARIATE

```
             Example 9.2 Frequency tabulation via PROC UNIVARIATE                    1

                          The UNIVARIATE Procedure
                            Variable:  reading
Part (A)
                                Moments

      N                     120     Sum Weights              120
      Mean                 49.6     Sum Observations        5952
      Std Deviation   10.6734572    Variance          113.922689
      Skewness        -0.3004658    Kurtosis           0.0484073
      Uncorrected SS     308776     Corrected SS         13556.8
      Coeff Variation  21.519067    Std Error Mean    0.97434888

Part (B)

                        Basic Statistical Measures

             Location                     Variability

        Mean      49.60000     Std Deviation         10.67346
        Median    49.50000     Variance             113.92269
        Mode      54.00000     Range                 53.00000
                               Interquartile Range   13.00000
```

Part (C)

Tests for Location: Mu0=0

Test	-Statistic-	-----p Value------
Student's t	t 50.90579	Pr > |t| <.0001
Sign	M 60	Pr >= |M| <.0001
Signed Rank	S 3630	Pr >= |S| <.0001

Part (D)

Quantiles (Definition 5)

Quantile	Estimate
100% Max	74.0
99%	73.0
95%	65.0
90%	63.0
75% Q3	57.0
50% Median	49.5
25% Q1	44.0
10%	36.0
5%	30.0
1%	22.0
0% Min	21.0

Part (E)

Extreme Observations

----Lowest----		----Highest---	
Value	Obs	Value	Obs
21	1	68	88
22	13	69	105
24	31	70	85
25	2	73	113
30	12	74	91

Example 9.2 Frequency tabulation via PROC UNIVARIATE   2

The UNIVARIATE Procedure
Variable: reading

Part (F)

Frequency Counts

Value	Count	Percents Cell	Percents Cum	Value	Count	Percents Cell	Percents Cum	Value	Count	Percents Cell	Percents Cum
21	1	0.8	0.8	45	5	4.2	34.2	58	1	0.8	78.3
22	1	0.8	1.7	46	5	4.2	38.3	59	4	3.3	81.7
24	1	0.8	2.5	47	3	2.5	40.8	60	5	4.2	85.8
25	1	0.8	3.3	48	8	6.7	47.5	61	1	0.8	86.7
30	3	2.5	5.8	49	3	2.5	50.0	62	3	2.5	89.2
33	1	0.8	6.7	50	3	2.5	52.5	63	4	3.3	92.5
34	1	0.8	7.5	51	3	2.5	55.0	64	2	1.7	94.2
36	4	3.3	10.8	52	3	2.5	57.5	65	2	1.7	95.8
37	5	4.2	15.0	53	1	0.8	58.3	68	1	0.8	96.7
39	1	0.8	15.8	54	10	8.3	66.7	69	1	0.8	97.5
40	5	4.2	20.0	55	3	2.5	69.2	70	1	0.8	98.3
42	3	2.5	22.5	56	4	3.3	72.5	73	1	0.8	99.2
43	2	1.7	24.2	57	6	5.0	77.5	74	1	0.8	100.0
44	7	5.8	30.0								

The five parts on page 1 of the output are identical to those in Output 9.1. The new result is **Part (F)** under the heading **Frequency Counts** on page 2. Included in this table are four kinds of information. The first column, under the heading **Value**, presents the raw score value. The second column, under **Count**, gives the frequency of each score's occurrence. The last two columns display the percentages (frequency divided by *N*) and cumulative percentages, respectively. Thus, the last number in the last column is 100.0, or 100%.

Technically, the frequency distribution shown in **Part (F)** is an ungrouped frequency distribution because every raw score is displayed and counted. This presentation format is thorough because it includes every nuance of information in the data set. It can also be tedious, if your data are voluminous.

Example 9.3 Three Visual Displays of Data: Stem-and-Leaf, Box Plot, and Normal Probability Plot

Option **PLOT** in the PROC UNIVARIATE statement produces three visual displays of data: the stem-and-leaf plot, the box plot, and the normal probability plot. The stem-and-leaf plot and the box plot are simple, yet effective, techniques for exploring data. They were pioneered by John W. Tukey in the late 1970s. The normal probability plot provides a way to evaluate sample data against a normal curve. This plot is useful for checking if data meet the normal assumption, which is assumed by many inferential statistical procedures.

```
/* See Example 9.1 for the DATA step in creating the SAS data set 'achieve' */

TITLE 'Example 9.3 Three visual displays';

PROC UNIVARIATE DATA=achieve PLOT;
    VAR reading;
RUN;
```

Output 9.3 Three Visual Displays of Data: Stem-and-Leaf, Box Plot, and Normal Probability Plot

```
                          Example 9.3 Three visual displays                    1

                            The UNIVARIATE Procedure
                              Variable:  reading

Part (A)
                                    Moments

            N                      120    Sum Weights              120
            Mean                  49.6    Sum Observations        5952
            Std Deviation    10.6734572   Variance          113.922689
            Skewness         -0.3004658   Kurtosis            0.0484073
            Uncorrected SS        308776  Corrected SS         13556.8
            Coeff Variation   21.519067   Std Error Mean    0.97434888
```

Part (B)

                              Basic Statistical Measures

              Location   Variability

     Mean   49.60000   Std Deviation   10.67346
     Median   49.50000   Variance   113.92269
     Mode   54.00000   Range   53.00000
                              Interquartile Range   13.00000

Part (C)

                          Tests for Location: Mu0=0

        Test   -Statistic-   -----p Value------

        Student's t   t 50.90579   Pr > |t| <.0001
        Sign   M   60   Pr >= |M| <.0001
        Signed Rank   S   3630   Pr >= |S| <.0001

Part (D)

                          Quantiles (Definition 5)

                    Quantile   Estimate

                    100% Max   74.0
                    99%   73.0
                    95%   65.0
                    90%   63.0
                    75% Q3   57.0
                    50% Median   49.5
                    25% Q1   44.0
                    10%   36.0
                    5%   30.0
                    1%   22.0
                    0% Min   21.0

Part (E)

                          Extreme Observations

            ----Lowest----   ----Highest---

          Value   Obs   Value   Obs

             21   1   68   88
             22   13   69   105
             24   31   70   85
             25   2   73   113
             30   12   74   91

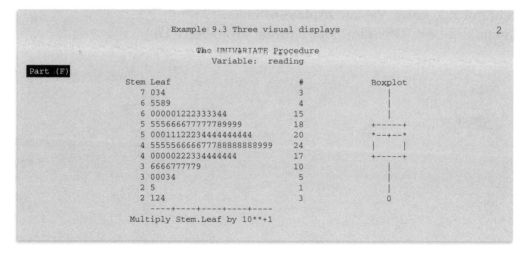

                     Example 9.3 Three visual displays   2

                          The UNIVARIATE Procedure
                             Variable: reading

Part (F)

      Stem Leaf   #   Boxplot
        7 034   3 |
        6 5589   4 |
        6 000001222333344   15 |
        5 555666677777789999   18   +------+
        5 00011122234444444444   20   *--+--*
        4 5555566666677788888888999   24 | |
        4 00000222334444444   17   +------+
        3 6666777779   10 |
        3 00034   5 |
        2 5   1 |
        2 124   3   0
          ----+----+----+----+----
      Multiply Stem.Leaf by 10**+1

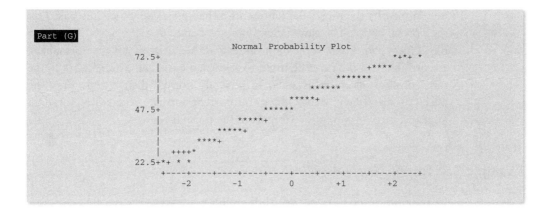

Parts (A) to (E) on page 1 should look familiar to you by now since they are identical to their counterparts in Output 9.1. **Parts (F)** and **(G)** on page 2 are new; they result from the option **PLOT**. The first plot is the stem-and-leaf plot. As the name implies, it consists of stems and several leaves. The stems are "tens" digits; thus, 7 = 70, 6 = 60, and so on. The leaves are the "units" digits. Hence, the first line shows three <u>reading</u> scores: 70, 73, and 74. The second line displays four more scores: 65, 65, 68, and 69. The bottom line shows the three lowest scores: 21, 22, and 24. The frequency of scores in each interval is indicated by the integers, in this case 3, 4, . . . , 3, under the "#" sign.

You may ask, "How about central tendency scores, such as mean or median? Where can I find those?" The answers are found in the plot next to the stem-and-leaf plot, namely, the **Boxplot.** Inside the square box in the **Boxplot,** the symbol "+" refers to the mean. Thus, we know that the mean is in the interval of 50 to 54. The precise value for the mean is **49.6,** reported under **Moments.** The dashed line (---) drawn inside the box corresponds to the median. It too lies in the interval from 50 to 54. The precise value for the median is **49.5,** found under **Quantiles.**

The top and bottom borders of the square box in Boxplot are defined by the 75th and 25th percentiles, respectively. The 75th percentile is located in the score interval of 55 to 59; the 25th percentile is located in the score interval of 40 to 44. Unfortunately, you cannot be more precise about these percentiles in a Boxplot. The precise information is available from **Part (D)** under **Q3** and **Q1.** The vertical lines extended from the borders out in both directions (north and south) are *whiskers.* Whiskers convey range information, because they are drawn as far as the largest or smallest data, but no more than 1.5 times the value of interquartile (= Q3 − Q1). If extreme scores are present, they are indicated by "0", if they exceed 1.5 times the interquartile, or by "*" for extreme scores beyond three interquartiles.

Now let's turn to the Normal Probability Plot—**Part (G).** The plot shows a match between the sample distribution and the standard normal curve. The horizontal axis is the *z* score with a mean of 0 and a standard deviation of 1. The vertical axis is based on the sample data. Two symbols are used to draw the normal probability plot: pluses (**+**) and asterisks (∗). The straight line formed by the pluses (+) represents a theoretical reference line based on the normal curve. The raw data values are drawn as asterisks (*) for which the vertical coordinate is the data value, and the horizontal is the normalized *z* score. Thus, if data can be fitted to a normal curve, all asterisks are in the same position as the pluses. For a perfectly normal distribution, only the pluses (+) are shown. According to the current normal probability plot, data appear not to deviate noticeably from the normal curve.

Example 9.4 Test of Normality

In addition to the normal probability plot, you may carry out a test of normality in the UNIVARIATE procedure. The test helps us to determine if the underlying population of scores is normally distributed. If the normality assumption holds, the sample data should preserve the normal distribution to a certain degree. For this reason, it is a good idea to carry out a test of normality before conducting a parametric procedure. The test is invoked by the option **NORMAL**. The following program tests both <u>reading</u> and <u>punc</u> score distributions to determine if they are normally distributed.

```
/* See Example 9.1 for the DATA step in creating the SAS data set 'achieve' */
TITLE 'Example 9.4 Test of normality';

PROC UNIVARIATE DATA=achieve NORMAL;
    VAR reading punc;
RUN;
```

Output 9.4 Test of Normality

```
                        Example 9.4 Test of normality                              1

                            The UNIVARIATE Procedure
                               Variable:  reading
Part (A)
                                    Moments

           N                         120    Sum Weights                 120
           Mean                      49.6   Sum Observations           5952
           Std Deviation       10.6734572   Variance             113.922689
           Skewness            -0.3004658   Kurtosis              0.0484073
           Uncorrected SS          308776   Corrected SS             13556.8
           Coeff Variation     21.519067    Std Error Mean       0.97434888

Part (B)
                            Basic Statistical Measures

                 Location                        Variability

           Mean      49.60000    Std Deviation         10.67346
           Median    49.50000    Variance             113.92269
           Mode      54.00000    Range                 53.00000
                                 Interquartile Range   13.00000
```

Part (C)

```
                    Tests for Location: Mu0=0

        Test              -Statistic-      -----p Value------

        Student's t     t  50.90579     Pr > |t|    <.0001
        Sign            M        60     Pr >= |M|   <.0001
        Signed Rank     S      3630     Pr >= |S|   <.0001
```

Part (D)

```
                      Tests for Normality

        Test                --Statistic---     -----p Value------

        Shapiro-Wilk        W   0.988186     Pr < W      0.3869
        Kolmogorov-Smirnov  D   0.076584     Pr > D      0.0835
        Cramer-von Mises    W-Sq 0.055213    Pr > W-Sq  >0.2500
        Anderson-Darling    A-Sq 0.371159    Pr > A-Sq  >0.2500
```

Part (E)

```
                   Quantiles (Definition 5)

                   Quantile      Estimate

                   100% Max        74.0
                   99%             73.0
                   95%             65.0
                   90%             63.0
                   75% Q3          57.0
                   50% Median      49.5
                   25% Q1          44.0
                   10%             36.0
                   5%              30.0
                   1%              22.0
                   0% Min          21.0
```

Part (F)

```
                     Extreme Observations

        ----Lowest----          ----Highest---

        Value     Obs           Value     Obs

           21       1              68       88
           22      13              69      105
           24      31              70       85
           25       2              73      113
           30      12              74       91
```

```
                  Example 9.4 Test of normality                    2

                   The UNIVARIATE Procedure
                       Variable:  punc
```

Part (G)

```
                            Moments

        N                      120    Sum Weights           120
        Mean                  49.4    Sum Observations     5928
        Std Deviation   13.9527414    Variance       194.678992
        Skewness        -0.1375285    Kurtosis        -0.4765254
        Uncorrected SS      316010    Corrected SS      23166.8
        Coeff Variation 28.2444157    Std Error Mean  1.2737052
```

Part (H)

```
                   Basic Statistical Measures

             Location                    Variability

        Mean     49.40000     Std Deviation       13.95274
        Median   50.00000     Variance           194.67899
```

```
        Mode     61.00000    Range                   59.00000
                             Interquartile Range     19.00000
```

Part (I)

```
                     Tests for Location: Mu0=0

         Test              -Statistic-      -----p Value------

         Student's t    t   38.78448    Pr > |t|     <.0001
         Sign           M         60    Pr >= |M|    <.0001
         Signed Rank    S       3630    Pr >= |S|    <.0001
```

Part (J)

```
                         Tests for Normality

       Test                   --Statistic---      -----p Value------

       Shapiro-Wilk           W    0.983545    Pr < W      0.1516
       Kolmogorov-Smirnov     D    0.065236    Pr > D      >0.1500
       Cramer-von Mises       W-Sq 0.065033    Pr > W-Sq   >0.2500
       Anderson-Darling       A-Sq 0.452532    Pr > A-Sq   >0.2500
```

Part (K)

```
                    Quantiles (Definition 5)

                    Quantile        Estimate

                    100% Max          79.0
                    99%               79.0
                    95%               72.0
                    90%               65.0
                    75% Q3            59.0
                    50% Median        50.0
                    25% Q1            40.0
                    10%               30.0
                    5%                23.5
                    1%                20.0
                    0% Min            20.0
```

Part (L)

```
                     Extreme Observations

           ----Lowest----          ----Highest---

           Value      Obs          Value      Obs

              20       22             74        90
              20       18             74        91
              21       41             77       117
              22       32             79       119
              22       13             79       120
```

For purpose of explanation, Output 9.4 is divided into 12 parts: Parts (A) to (F) pertain to variable <u>reading,</u> whereas Parts (G) to (L) pertain to <u>punc.</u> In **Part (D)**, the **Tests for Normality** section contains four tests for normality. The highlighted value (W = 0.988186) and its significance level (Pr < W = 0.3869) are the Shapiro-Wilk test of normality for <u>reading.</u> The large p level indicates that the null hypothesis of normally distributed <u>reading</u> scores cannot be rejected at $\alpha = 0.05$. Is this good news or bad news? The answer depends on your reason for conducting the test. Recall that the null hypothesis states that sample data conform to a normal curve. Thus, if you are interested in verifying a normal assumption for the <u>reading</u> distribution, you should be delighted in such a large *p* level as it leads to the retention of the null hypothesis.

Similarly, the normality test of the <u>punc</u> distribution, in **Part (J)**, yields a W statistic of 0.983545, significant at 0.1516. Again, you can conclude that the null hypothesis cannot be rejected at $\alpha = 0.05$ and that the <u>punc</u> distribution is approximately normal.

If, in the future, this test is statistically significant at, say, $\alpha = 0.05$ and the null hypothesis of normality is rejected, you may wish to examine the three plots introduced in Example 9.3 to understand how and where the distribution deviates from the normal curve. For Output 9.4, we focus on the Shapiro-Wilk test because the sample size is less than 2,001. For samples larger than 2,001, we recommend the Kolmogorov-Smirnov test. Details about these four tests of normality are found in **Section 9.4: Tips**.

Example 9.5 The Sign Test and the Signed Rank Test for Small Samples

Sometimes you may wish to draw inferences about an underlying population average based on a small sample that may not be normally distributed. How do you draw conclusions based on small samples? In this example, we demonstrate solutions for this challenge. Let's suppose that we are interested in finding out if students' median grade point average (GPA) in the population is 2.5 on a 4-point scale. Seventeen students provided their GPA information in the raw data file <u>mydata.dat</u>. The null hypothesis of a 2.5 population median is specified by the option MU0= 2.5 in the PROC UNIVARIATE statement. If the null hypothesis is rejected, we know that these 17 students' <u>gpa</u> median is either significantly *higher* or *lower* than 2.5. Failing to reject the null hypothesis indicates that data might come from a population of students whose median GPA is 2.5.

```
/* The following bolded SAS statements establish the SAS data set 'mydata' */

DATA mydata;
    INFILE 'd:\data\mydata.dat';
    INPUT id $ sex $ age gpa critical polpref $ satv;
RUN;

TITLE 'Example 9.5 The sign and the signed rank tests';

PROC UNIVARIATE DATA=mydata MU0=2.5;
    VAR gpa;
RUN;
```

Output 9.5 The Sign Test and the Signed Rank Test for Small Samples

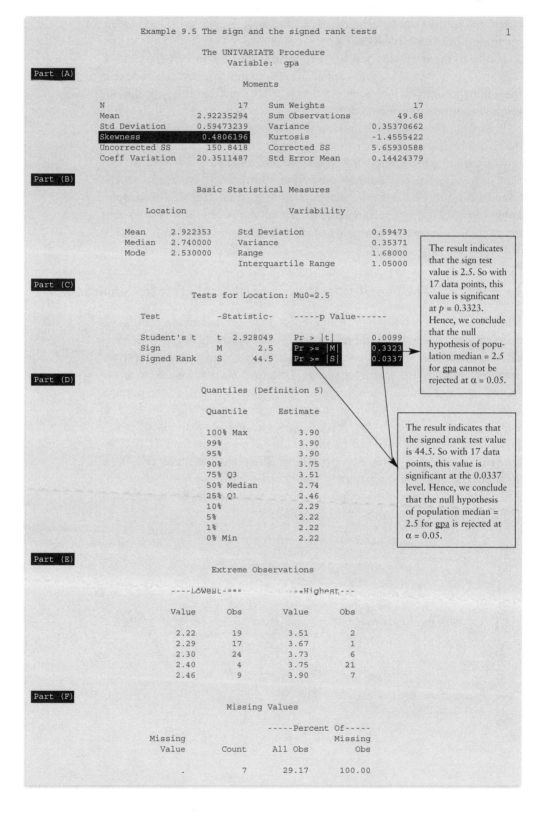

Example 9.5 The sign and the signed rank tests   1

The UNIVARIATE Procedure
Variable: gpa

Part (A)

Moments

N	17	Sum Weights	17
Mean	2.92235294	Sum Observations	49.68
Std Deviation	0.59473239	Variance	0.35370662
Skewness	0.4806196	Kurtosis	-1.4555422
Uncorrected SS	150.8418	Corrected SS	5.65930588
Coeff Variation	20.3511487	Std Error Mean	0.14424379

Part (B)

Basic Statistical Measures

Location		Variability	
Mean	2.922353	Std Deviation	0.59473
Median	2.740000	Variance	0.35371
Mode	2.530000	Range	1.68000
		Interquartile Range	1.05000

The result indicates that the sign test value is 2.5. So with 17 data points, this value is significant at $p = 0.3323$. Hence, we conclude that the null hypothesis of population median = 2.5 for gpa cannot be rejected at $\alpha = 0.05$.

Part (C)

Tests for Location: Mu0=2.5

Test		-Statistic-	-----p Value------	
Student's t	t	2.928049	Pr > |t|	0.0099
Sign	M	2.5	Pr >= |M|	0.3323
Signed Rank	S	44.5	Pr >= |S|	0.0337

Part (D)

Quantiles (Definition 5)

Quantile	Estimate
100% Max	3.90
99%	3.90
95%	3.90
90%	3.75
75% Q3	3.51
50% Median	2.74
25% Q1	2.46
10%	2.29
5%	2.22
1%	2.22
0% Min	2.22

The result indicates that the signed rank test value is 44.5. So with 17 data points, this value is significant at the 0.0337 level. Hence, we conclude that the null hypothesis of population median = 2.5 for gpa is rejected at $\alpha = 0.05$.

Part (E)

Extreme Observations

----Lowest----		----Highest---	
Value	Obs	Value	Obs
2.22	19	3.51	2
2.29	17	3.67	1
2.30	24	3.73	6
2.40	4	3.75	21
2.46	9	3.90	7

Part (F)

Missing Values

		-----Percent Of-----	
Missing Value	Count	All Obs	Missing Obs
.	7	29.17	100.00

The sign test of gpa leads to the conclusion that this particular sample of students represented a population with a 2.5 median GPA because the null hypothesis of the population median = 2.5 cannot be rejected. The sign test carried out by the UNIVARIATE procedure is always a two-tailed test. If you are interested in a one-tailed test, simply half the output probability, printed next to (Pr >= |M|). For this example, a one-tailed probability would be 0.3323/2, or 0.16615.

According to the signed rank test, however, the same null hypothesis about the population median can be rejected at a significance level of 0.0337. This conclusion is inconsistent with that reached by the sign test. How can the inconsistency be resolved? Before you accept either test result, you should realize that there is an assumption associated with the signed rank test. It assumes that the underlying population is symmetric around its median. Failing to meet this assumption weakens the validity of the test. The symmetry of the gpa distribution can be inferred from the plot of its distribution and its skewness, which equals 0.4806196. This value suggests that the sample distribution is skewed to the right with a heavier density of low scores than high scores. It is therefore likely that the assumption of symmetry, required by the signed rank test, is violated. Thus, it is better to rely on the sign test result, rather than the signed rank result. In other words, the median gpa of this group of students is probably around 2.5.

A population median is the value above and below which 50% of all cases lie. In a skewed distribution, median and mean are two different values; this is the case with the gpa distribution. They are, however, identical in a symmetric distribution. Therefore, the test of the population median is the same as the test for the population mean for symmetric distributions.

- If the sample size is more than 10, say, 25, and the underlying population is normal or approximately normal (symmetric and bell-shaped), the test of population mean can be carried out by the one-sample t test. Because the assumption of an underlying normal population is questionable for these data, the t-test result need not be trusted.

Example 9.6 Comprehensive Descriptive Analysis of Subgroups

Examples 9.1 to 9.5 demonstrate the nuts and bolts of PROC UNIVARIATE for an entire data set. In this example, you will learn to replicate these helpful features for subsets of a sample. Specifically, the program below requests separate descriptions of men's and women's performance on satv (SAT-Verbal score) from the file mydata.dat. As this program illustrates, data need to be first sorted into two groups: "F" and "M", or females and males. Afterward, separate analyses for each subgroup are specified by the BY sex; statement.

```
/* See Example 9.5 for the DATA step in creating the SAS data set 'mydata' */

PROC SORT DATA=mydata;
    BY sex;
RUN;

TITLE 'Example 9.6 Comprehensive descriptive analysis of subgroups';

PROC UNIVARIATE DATA=mydata;
    VAR satv;
    BY sex;
RUN;
```

Output 9.6 Comprehensive Descriptive Analysis of Subgroups

```
              Example 9.6 Comprehensive descriptive analysis of subgroups                    1
-------------------------------------------- sex=F --------------------------------------------
                               The UNIVARIATE Procedure
                                   Variable:  satv

                                        Moments

             N                        8      Sum Weights                 8
             Mean                 533.75     Sum Observations         4270
             Std Deviation     146.866071    Variance            21569.6429
             Skewness          -0.6997707    Kurtosis            -0.2403955
             Uncorrected SS       2430100    Corrected SS          150987.5
             Coeff Variation   27.5158916    Std Error Mean       51.9249974

                               Basic Statistical Measures

                   Location                          Variability

               Mean      533.7500      Std Deviation        146.86607
               Median    550.0000      Variance                 21570
               Mode            .       Range              430.00000
                                       Interquartile Range 200.00000

                            Tests for Location: Mu0=0

               Test              -Statistic-      -----p Value------

               Student's t      t   10.27925      Pr > |t|      <.0001
               Sign             M          4      Pr >= |M|     0.0078
               Signed Rank      S         18      Pr >= |S|     0.0078


                             Quantiles (Definition 5)

                             Quantile      Estimate

                             100% Max         710
                             99%              710
                             95%              710
                             90%              710
                             75% Q3           645
                             50% Median       550
```

```
                          25% Q1              445
                          10%                 280
                          5%                  280
                          1%                  280
                          0% Min              280

                      Extreme Observations

              ----Lowest----          ----Highest---

              Value       Obs         Value       Obs

                280         7           530         6
                370         3           570         2
                520         8           610         1
                530         6           680         9
                570         2           710         4

                      Missing Values

                               -----Percent Of-----
              Missing                          Missing
              Value       Count     All Obs        Obs

                 .            1       11.11      100.00
```

```
      Example 9.6 Comprehensive descriptive analysis of subgroups        2

------------------------------------------ sex=M ------------------------------------------

                      The UNIVARIATE Procedure
                          Variable:  satv

                              Moments

      N                      14      Sum Weights                  14
      Mean             518.571429    Sum Observations           7260
      Std Deviation    110.930133    Variance              12305.4945
      Skewness         0.06545668    Kurtosis              -0.1511423
      Uncorrected SS      3924800    Corrected SS          159971.429
      Coeff Variation  21.3914858    Std Error Mean        29.6473252


                      Basic Statistical Measures

            Location                        Variability

        Mean        518.5714    Std Deviation          110.93013
        Median      500.0000    Variance                   12305
        Mode        450.0000    Range                  390.00000
                                Interquartile Range    180.00000

      NOTE: The mode displayed is the smallest of 3 modes with a count of 2.


                      Tests for Location: Mu0=0

            Test            -Statistic-      -----p Value------

        Student's t      t   17.49134      Pr > |t|      <.0001
        Sign             M          7      Pr >= |M|     0.0001
        Signed Rank      S       52.5      Pr >= |S|     0.0001
```

```
                    Quantiles (Definition 5)

                    Quantile        Estimate

                    100% Max             690
                    99%                  690
                    95%                  690
                    90%                  680
                    75% Q3               630
                    50% Median           500
                    25% Q1               450
                    10%                  410
                    5%                   300
                    1%                   300
                    0% Min               300

                    Extreme Observations

        ----Lowest----              ----Highest---

        Value        Obs            Value        Obs

          300         20              510         13
          410         23              630         21
          450         24              660         12
          450         14              680         15
          480         10              690         18

                    Missing Values

                               -----Percent Of-----
        Missing                              Missing
        Value        Count     All Obs          Obs

          .             1         6.67       100.00
```

This output shows that women and men are similar in average <u>satv</u> scores. For women, the average is 533.75, based on 8 women. For men, the average is 518.571429, based on 14 men. As for variance (or standard deviation), the women's group seemed to have greater variability than the men's group. The women's verbal scores are more skewed than the men's. Both curves are about equally flat. These indices are within the ballpark of national SAT-Verbal scores. Other descriptive statistics, such as the median, the mode, and the interquartile range, also confirm that the sample data are similar to the national norm.

It is important to point out that the Mode value (missing expressed as a period, ".") is misleading for the women's group because all raw scores for women appear only once in the data. None of these scores qualifies to be a mode. Therefore, PROC UNIVARIATE cannot compute the mode for women and reports the mode to be a missing score. When the sample distribution is multimodal, namely, having more than one mode, SAS reports only the lowest modal value. To compute all modal values, you must specify the MODES option in the PROC UNIVARIATE statement.

Example 9.7 Creating an Output Data Set in PROC UNIVARIATE

This example demonstrates how to save analysis results from PROC UNIVARIATE into a SAS data set for subsequent use. Specifically, the **OUTPUT** statement is illustrated for its versatile utility and syntax. The leading word OUTPUT is followed by an output data set name (**OUT=myout**) and several statistical indices, to be included in this output data set. Thus, **MEAN=meanage meansatv** names the mean of age and satv, respectively, and includes them in myout. Likewise, **STD=stdage stdsatv** names the standard deviation of age and satv, respectively, and saves them into myout as well. The keyword **PCTLPTS=20 80** requests the 20th and 80th percentiles for both age and satv. The next and final keyword **PCTLPRE=age satv** defines a prefix name for the percentiles requested. The use of this keyword will become clearer when you read the explanation of Output 9.7. Once the output data set, myout, is established, the PRINT procedure displays its content.

```
/* See Example 9.5 for the DATA step in creating the SAS data set 'mydata' */

TITLE 'Example 9.7 Creating an output data set in PROC UNIVARIATE';

PROC UNIVARIATE DATA=mydata NOPRINT;
    VAR age satv;
    OUTPUT OUT=myout MEAN=meanage meansatv STD=stdage stdsatv PCTLPTS= 20 80 PCTLPRE= age satv;
RUN;

PROC PRINT DATA=myout;
RUN;
```

Output 9.7 Creating an Output Data Set in PROC UNIVARIATE

```
              Example 9.7 Creating an output data set in PROC UNIVARIATE              1
                                                                                          1
 Obs    meanage    meansatv    stdage    stdsatv    age20    age80    satv20

  1     24.1176    524.091    2.86972    121.916      22       27       450     660
```

The information displayed in Output 9.7 is precisely what was asked for in the program. Thus, meanage (24.1176) is the mean of the age variable and meansatv (524.091) is the mean of satv; stdage and stdsatv are standard deviations of age and satv, respectively. The next pair of values (age20 and age80) corresponds to the 20th and 80th percentiles of the age variable. Similarly, satv20 and satv80 represent the 20th and 80th percentiles of the satv variable, respectively. These percentiles reveal that neither distribution is symmetric around its mean. The satv distribution is skewed more to the right than the age distribution because satv80 (= 660) is further away than satv20 (= 450) from their mean (= 524.091), compared with age80 (= 27) and age20 (= 22) relative to their mean (= 24.1176).

Other descriptive indices, besides mean, standard deviation, and percentiles, can be named and saved into an output data set as well. For details, read the next section on general syntax of the OUTPUT statement.

- If you include a BY statement in the program, the statistical values for each subgroup will be automatically computed and included. Each subgroup is identified by a distinct value of the BY variable(s).

9.3 How to Write the PROC UNIVARIATE Codes

The following PROC UNIVARIATE statements were illustrated in one or more of the seven examples in **Section 9.2**. Their syntax is summarized as follows:

PROC	UNIVARIATE	DATA= *sas_dataset_name* *<options>*;
	VAR	*variable(s)*;
	BY	*classification_variable(s)*;
	WEIGHT	*weighting_variable*;
	FREQ	*frequency_variable*;
	OUTPUT	*<OUT= sas_dataset_name>*
		<keywords for outputted statistic>
		<PCTLPTS= percentiles PCTLPRE *= prefix for percentiles*
		PCTLNAMES *= suffix for percentiles>*;

The **PROC UNIVARIATE** statement initiates the procedure and specifies a data set to be analyzed. Five useful options may be specified:

ROUND= a round-off unit (such as 0.01) This option saves memory space while processing the SAS program because it truncates, or rounds off, variable values according to the round-off unit (say, the second decimal place) prior to computing statistics.

VARDEF=DF This option specifies that degrees of freedom is to be used in calculating the sample variance and standard deviation. Other choices besides degrees of freedom are possible: sample size (VARDEF=N), sum of weights (VARDEF=WGT), or sum of weights minus one (VARDEF=WDF). The default is degrees of freedom (DF=N − 1).

PLOT (or PLOTS) This option produces three visual displays of data: the stem-and-leaf plot, the box plot, and the normal probability plot. For illustration, refer back to Example 9.3.

NORMAL **(or NORMALTEST)**	This option requests a statistical test of the normal population hypothesis. For illustration, refer back to Example 9.4.
MU0= a list of **numerical values** **(such as 0 2.5 4)**	This option specifies the hypothetical population parameter for the t test, the sign test, and the signed rank test.
FREQ	This option requests a frequency table to be compiled; in the frequency table, variable values, frequencies, percentages, and cumulative percentages are tabulated.
MODES	This option requests a list of all modes when the sample distribution is multimodal.
NOPRINT	This option suppresses the display of the output.

The second statement, **VAR,** is used to list one or more variables in the data set for which analyses are sought. The third statement, **BY,** is used to perform subgroup analyses. It divides the data set into subgroups according to diverse values of the BY variable. Within each subgroup, the same advanced descriptive analyses and the test of normality are conducted. If more than one BY variable is listed, all possible combinations of the BY variables' values are used in dividing up the data set. Be sure to presort the data set in the ascending order of all BY variables, if the BY statement is included in the UNIVARIATE procedure. Presorting a data set can be accomplished with the SORT procedure.

The fourth statement, **WEIGHT,** is used to apply differential weights to data values. All weights must be nonnegative. Zero or positive fractional numbers are allowed; negative or missing values are substituted by a zero. When a zero weight is applied to a variable, the variable's summary statistics, such as mean, variance, standard deviation, and so on, will be missing in the output; yet the minimum and the maximum will continue to be the smallest and the largest actual data values, respectively.

The fifth statement, **FREQ,** is needed for grouped data. By grouped data, we mean data that have been grouped together by identical data values or into intervals, represented by a midpoint and frequency of occurrences in that interval. To describe a grouped data set, two pieces of information are needed: (1) the data value or the midpoint of an interval and (2) its frequency count. In SAS terminology, the frequency count is the value of the FREQ variable.

The last statement, **OUTPUT,** is used to create an output data set so that results from PROC UNIVARIATE can be saved for subsequent analysis by another procedure. Immediately after the OUT=*sas_dataset_name*, one or more statistics may be requested by their keywords. The list below presents keywords you may specify for inclusion in an output data set:

N=	no. of valid data points
SKEWNESS=	the skewness index
KURTOSIS=	the kurtosis index
MEAN=	the arithmetic average
MEDIAN=	the median or the 50th percentile or Q2
MODE=	the modal value
STD=	the standard deviation
VAR=	the variance
STDMEAN=	the standard error of the mean
MAX=	the maximum
MIN=	the minimum
RANGE=	the range
Q1=	the first quartile
Q3=	the third quartile
P1=	the 1st percentile
P5=	the 5th percentile
P10=	the 10th percentile
P90=	the 90th percentile
P95=	the 95th percentile
P99=	the 99th percentile
T=	the t test value
PROBT=	the significance level of the above t test
MSIGN=	the sign test value
PROBM=	the significance level of the above sign test
SIGNRANK=	the signed rank test value
PROBS=	the significance level of the above signed rank test
NORMALTEST=	the statistic for the normality test. If the sample size is less than or equal to 2,000, this statistic is the Shapiro-Wilk test statistic. Otherwise, PROC UNIVARIATE calculates the Kolmogorov-Smirnov statistic.
PROBN=	the significance level of the above normal test

How do you name the statistic? It is easy; simply create a name that jointly represents the statistic and the variable. For instance, combine mean with age or mean with satv and list both after the keyword, such as **MEAN=meanage meansatv**.

As for percentiles, they are requested via the option **PCTLPTS=**. This option is followed by the percentage point(s) corresponding to the specific percentile. If more than one variable's percentiles are requested, you should use the option **PCTLPRE=** to define a prefix name for two or more variables' percentiles. For an illustration of these two options, refer back to Example 9.7. Sometimes there may be a need to request an unusual percentile, such as 58.9. This percentile is acceptable to PROC UNIVARIATE. It will be included in the output under the name of, say, **age58_9** or **satv58_9**, for <u>age</u> and <u>satv</u>, respectively.

Once an output data set is created, it is recommended that its content be displayed by PROC PRINT, preferably right after the data set is created. A responsible data analyst should examine the content of each data set at least once to ensure that no mistake is made in naming variables or choosing the kind of statistic for the output data set.

9.4 Tips

- How to handle missing or invalid data

Missing data means that you do not have any information about an observation on a particular variable. Missing data should be treated differently than 0. A score of 0 means that the information is available, and the score happens to be exactly 0, whereas missing data means you have no information.

The count of missing observations on each variable is automatically printed under headings such as **Missing Value, Count, Percent of All Obs,** and **Percent of Missing Obs**. If an observation has missing information on one or more variables, the observation is excluded from the calculation of descriptive statistics and also from any statistical test performed on these variables. The observation itself is not removed from the SAS data set though; it is simply discounted from analyses.

- The question of which test of normality to use

As Example 9.4 demonstrates, the test of normality is carried out by four statistical tests in the UNIVARIATE procedure: the Shapiro-Wilk test, the Kolmogorov-Smirnov test, the Anderson-Darling test, and the Cramér-von Mises test. Each test has its own special features and sensitivity. The default is the Shapiro-Wilk test, if the sample size is 2,000 or less. The test statistic is denoted by W and ranges from 0 to 1. Small values of W lead to the rejection of the null hypothesis of normality. The sampling distribution of W is highly skewed to the left. Hence, values above 0.90 may still lead to the rejection of the null hypothesis.

The Kolmogorov-Smirnov test D is calculated on the basis of the largest vertical differences between the sample distribution (also called the empirical distribution) and the normal distribution. If the sample size is larger than 2,000, the UNIVARIATE procedure defaults to this test statistic.

Both the Anderson-Darling test and the Cramér-von Mises test are computed on the basis of squared difference between the sample distribution and the normal distribution. The Anderson-Darling test weighs the squared differences by the reciprocal of the product of the cumulative probability multiplied by (1 – the cumulative probability), over the entire range of the score scale. The Cramér-von Mises test does not apply any weight to the squared differences.

When conducting the test of normality, you need to be aware of the power of such a test, and power is directly related to the sample size. If the sample size is large, in hundreds or thousands, the statistical test is so powerful that a minor departure from normality can lead to the rejection of the null hypothesis. Conversely, if the sample size is small, in the 10s or below 10, the test may not be powerful enough to detect serious departure from normality. In both cases, it is recommended that you rely on additional information such as the skewness, kurtosis, normal probability plot, frequency distribution, and so on, to make an informed judgment about the violation of the normality assumption. For small samples, you may wish to raise the level of significance (i.e., α) in order to compensate for the reduced power associated with small sample tests.

- How to use ODS with the UNIVARIATE procedure

The Output Delivery System (ODS) in SAS allows you to (a) select part(s) of the output to be displayed, (b) export part(s) of the output into data set(s), and (c) save the output in formats other than the standard SAS output. To use the ODS, you need to know ODS table names corresponding to various portions of the output. Table 9.2 presents selected ODS table names for the UNIVARIATE procedure and their descriptions.

Table 9.2   Selected ODS Table Names and Descriptions for the UNIVARIATE Procedure

ODS Table Name	Description	Option in the PROC UNIVARIATE Statement
Moments	Sample moments	(default)
BasicMeasures	Basic statistical measures of location and variability	(default)
TestsForLocation	Tests for location	(default)
Quantiles	Quantiles	(default)
ExtremeObs	Extreme observations	(default)
TestsForNormality	Tests for normality	NORMAL
Frequencies	Frequency table	FREQ
Plots	The stem-and-leaf plot, the box plot, and the normal probability plot	PLOT
Modes	Modes	MODES

These ODS table names and related details are tracked in the Log window if you ask for them with the ODS TRACE ON statement in the SAS program. You may turn off this tracking feature with the ODS TRACE OFF statement, also in the SAS program.

```
ODS TRACE ON;
PROC UNIVARIATE DATA=achieve;
    VAR reading;
RUN;
ODS TRACE OFF;
RUN;
```

After executing the program, the following will appear in the Log window listing all ODS table names for the PROC UNIVARIATE output:

```
Output Added:
------------
Name:       Moments
Label:      Moments
Template:   base.univariate.Moments
Path:       Univariate.reading.Moments
------------

Output Added:
------------
Name:       BasicMeasures
Label:      Basic Measures of Location and Variability
Template:   base.univariate.Measures
Path:       Univariate.reading.BasicMeasures
------------

Output Added:
------------
Name:       TestsForLocation
Label:      Tests For Location
Template:   base.univariate.Location
Path:       Univariate.reading.TestsForLocation
------------

Output Added:
------------
Name:       Quantiles
Label:      Quantiles
Template:   base.univariate.Quantiles
Path:       Univariate.reading.Quantiles
------------

Output Added:
------------
Name:       ExtremeObs
Label:      Extreme Observations
Template:   base.univariate.ExtObs
Path:       Univariate.reading.ExtremeObs
------------
```

Based on the list of ODS table names, you may select certain results to be displayed in the Output window. For example, the following program selects **Part (A)** of Example 9.1 to be included in the output:

```
ODS SELECT Univariate.reading.Moments;
PROC UNIVARIATE DATA=achieve ROUND=0.01;
    VAR reading;
RUN;
```

Likewise, you may select certain result(s) to be exported as a SAS data set. For example, the following program exports **Part (A)** of Example 9.1 to the SAS data set <u>descriptive</u>:

```
ODS OUTPUT Moments = descriptive;
PROC UNIVARIATE DATA=achieve ROUND=0.01;
    VAR reading;
RUN;
```

Furthermore, you may select certain results to be stored in file formats other than the SAS standard output. For example, the following program saves the output of Example 9.1 in HTML format in its default style:

```
ODS HTML BODY = 'd:\result\Example9_1Body.html'
         CONTENTS = 'd:\result\Example9_1TOC.html'
         PAGE = 'd:\result\Example9_1Page.html'
         FRAME = 'd:\result\Example9_1Frame.html';
PROC UNIVARIATE DATA=achieve ROUND=0.01;
    VAR reading;
RUN;
ODS HTML CLOSE;
RUN;
```

For additional information about the ODS feature, consult with *SAS Output Delivery System: User's Guide* (SAS Institute Inc., 2006c) and *Base SAS 9.1.3 Procedures Guide* (SAS Institute Inc., 2006a) or the online documentation at www.sas.com.

9.5 Summary

This chapter covers the most comprehensive descriptive analysis procedure in SAS, that is, PROC UNIVARIATE. The UNIVARIATE procedure may be applied for descriptive as well as inferential analyses of the data. For descriptive analyses, PROC UNIVARIATE computes indices for central tendency, variability, skewness, kurtosis, extreme scores, quartiles, and selected percentiles.

For inferential analyses, PROC UNIVARIATE performs the one-sample *t* test, tests of normality, the sign test, and the signed rank test. Each is conducted as a two-tailed test. In addition to the test of normality, PROC UNIVARIATE also draws the normal probability plot, which can serve as a visual device for making inferences about the approximation of the sample distribution to normal.

Two other graphical representations of data include the stem-and-leaf plot and the box plot. Both can be examined to determine if outliers exist, or the shape implies a particular trend or pattern in data. Most of these handy features are not available in PROC MEANS, which is simpler to program and its output less complicated. If you need to learn more about the UNIVARIATE procedure, consult with *Base SAS 9.1.3 Procedures Guide* (SAS Institute Inc., 2006a) or the online documentation available from www.sas.com. Now let's see how much material you have mastered from this chapter.

9.6 Exercises

1. Modify Example 9.4 by inserting the option **PLOT** into the PROC UNIVARIATE statement and deleting reading from the VAR statement. Execute this modified program and interpret the output.

2. Randomly generate 30 data points from the RANNOR function and carry out a test of normality on the sample data.

3. Jeanie has a die that is biased. She wants to know how biased it is, so she rolls the die and records the following results:

2, 1, 4, 3, 6,	5, 1, 4, 3, 5,	2, 5, 4, 1, 3,
4, 1, 2, 1, 5,	5, 3, 5, 1, 5,	1, 2, 4, 6, 2,
1, 6, 4, 3, 3,	3, 2, 4, 1, 2	

a. According to the data, which number is most likely to turn up on the die, if you rolled it?

b. Consider the numbers on Jeanie's die to range from 1 to 6 on a discrete scale, and describe the distribution of numbers she has accumulated thus far.

c. To correct the bias, Jeanie decided to give each number a weight so that the expected value, namely, the probability multiplied by the weight, of each number is the same. What weight should she assign to each number? Write a SAS program to prove the weights are correctly assigned.

4. Larry has two regular dice and he rolls the two dice together 40 times. Consider the total points on his dice to range from 2 to 12; what distribution of total points will he generate?

5. If, on Larry's dice, the Number 2 face was misprinted as 3, what distribution of total points will he generate after he rolls these two dice together 40 times?

6. Given the data below, describe the extreme values of the <u>income</u> variable. Draw plots and discuss whether or not the <u>income</u> distribution is normally distributed.

```
VARIABLES: name      sex   age   room   s.e.s   income (in $1000)
--------------------------------------------------------------------
           ANDY      M     28    122    H        9.6
           SOPHIA    F     42    412    M        7.4
           LOUIS     M     34    213    L        2.3
           LANDERS   M     40    216    M        5.8
           TED       M     68    101    H        8.8
           DICKENS   M     37    135    M        6.3
           RUTH      F     39    430    L        1.3
           CHARLIE   M     54    222    M        4.7
           MICHAEL   M     25    118    M        6.0
           WOLF      M     51    104    H        8.4
           ANNE      F     58    404    H       10.2
           REBECCA   F     43    423    M        7.1
           DAVID     M     47    117    M        5.2
           RICHARD   M     28    240    H        9.2
           SAM       M     36    231    M        6.4
           TINA      F     31    302    M        4.3
           PETER     M     65    108    L        3.3
           SHEILA    F     24    336    M        5.7
           TIM       M     27    115    H        8.2
           LINDA     F     20    425    M        5.5
```

9.7 Answers to Exercises

1.

```
                           Exercise 9-1                                  1

                      The UNIVARIATE Procedure
                           Variable:  punc

                              Moments

N                        120      Sum Weights                  120
Mean                    49.4      Sum Observations            5928
Std Deviation      13.9527414     Variance              194.678992
Skewness           -0.1375285     Kurtosis               -0.4765254
Uncorrected SS        316010      Corrected SS             23166.8
Coeff Variation    28.2444157     Std Error Mean         1.2737052
```

```
                   Basic Statistical Measures

         Location                    Variability

   Mean     49.40000    Std Deviation           13.95274
   Median   50.00000    Variance               194.67899
   Mode     61.00000    Range                   59.00000
                        Interquartile Range     19.00000


                Tests for Location: Mu0=0

      Test            -Statistic-      -----p Value------

      Student's t    t  38.78448    Pr > |t|    <.0001
      Sign           M        60    Pr >= |M|   <.0001
      Signed Rank    S      3630    Pr >= |S|   <.0001


                   Tests for Normality

   Test                   --Statistic---     -----p Value------

   Shapiro-Wilk          W   0.983545    Pr < W       0.1516
   Kolmogorov-Smirnov    D   0.065236    Pr > D      >0.1500
   Cramer-von Mises      W-Sq 0.065033   Pr > W-Sq   >0.2500
   Anderson-Darling      A-Sq 0.452532   Pr > A-Sq   >0.2500


                   Quantiles (Definition 5)

                   Quantile      Estimate

                   100% Max       79.0
                   99%            79.0
                   95%            72.0
                   90%            65.0
                   75% Q3         59.0
                   50% Median     50.0
                   25% Q1         40.0
                   10%            30.0
                   5%             23.5
                   1%             20.0
                   0% Min         20.0


                   Extreme Observations

        ----Lowest----          ----Highest---

        Value      Obs          Value      Obs

          20       22             74        90
          20       18             74        91
          21       41             77       117
          22       32             79       119
          22       13             79       120
```

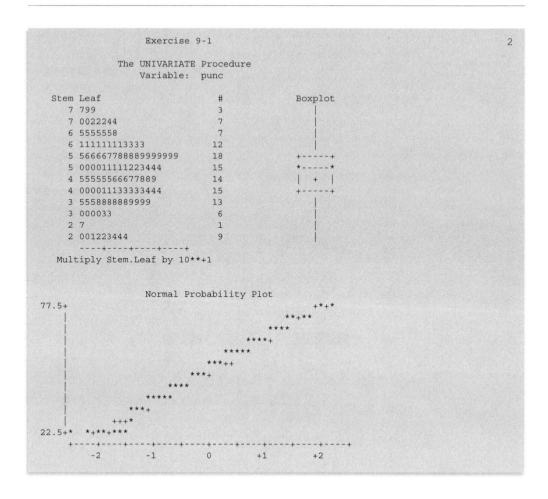

```
                            Exercise 9-1                                              2

                        The UNIVARIATE Procedure
                        Variable:  punc

      Stem Leaf                     #              Boxplot
          7 799                      3                 |
          7 0022244                  7                 |
          6 5555558                  7                 |
          6 111111113333            12                 |
          5 566667788889999999      18              +-----+
          5 000011111223444         15              *-----*
          4 55555566677889          14              |  +  |
          4 000011133333444         15              +-----+
          3 5558888889999           13                 |
          3 000033                   6                 |
          2 7                        1                 |
          2 001223444                9                 |
            ----+----+----+----+
      Multiply Stem.Leaf by 10**+1


                        Normal Probability Plot
       77.5+                                          +*+*
           |                                       **+**
           |                                      ****
           |                                  ****+
           |                                *****
           |                             ***++
           |                           ***+
           |                        ****
           |                      *****
           |                    ***+
           |                ++++*
       22.5+*   *+**+***
           +----+----+----+----+----+----+----+----+----+----+
              -2        -1         0        +1        +2
```

Conclusion: The punc distribution has a mean of 49.4, and a standard deviation of 13.9527414. The curve is slightly negatively skewed (Skewness = –0.1375285) and slightly platykurtic (Kurtosis = –0.4765254). The result of the normality test (W = 0.983545, two-tailed p = 0.1516) is nonsignificant at the 0.05 level. Therefore, the null hypothesis of a normally distributed punc distribution cannot be rejected. This conclusion is also supported by the three plots given above.

2.

```
                            Exercise 9-2                                              1

                        The UNIVARIATE Procedure
                        Variable:  x


                                Moments

      N                      30      Sum Weights                30
      Mean            0.14743989     Sum Observations    4.42319663
      Std Deviation   1.14930043     Variance            1.32089148
      Skewness        0.50501934     Kurtosis            0.56304358
      Uncorrected SS  38.9580086     Corrected SS         38.305853
      Coeff Variation 779.504414     Std Error Mean      0.20983259
```

```
                    Basic Statistical Measures

        Location                        Variability

   Mean      0.147440     Std Deviation           1.14930
   Median    0.096669     Variance                1.32089
   Mode         .         Range                   4.97821
                          Interquartile Range     1.14543


                 Tests for Location: Mu0=0

      Test             -Statistic-      -----p Value------

      Student's t    t  0.702655     Pr > |t|     0.4879
      Sign           M       1        Pr >= |M|     0.8555
      Signed Rank    S     29.5       Pr >= |S|     0.5530


                    Tests for Normality

   Test                  --Statistic---      -----p Value------

   Shapiro-Wilk           W   0.970159     Pr < W       0.5435
   Kolmogorov-Smirnov     D   0.086524     Pr > D      >0.1500
   Cramer-von Mises       W-Sq 0.037784    Pr > W-Sq   >0.2500
   Anderson-Darling       A-Sq 0.267793    Pr > A-Sq   >0.2500


                   Quantiles (Definition 5)

                   Quantile         Estimate

                   100% Max         3.1990312
                   99%              3.1990312
                   95%              2.0950652
                   90%              1.7358459
                   75% Q3           0.7015485
                   50% Median       0.0966693
                   25% Q1          -0.4438817
                   10%             -1.5135356
                   5%              -1.6491491
                   1%              -1.7791766
                   0% Min          -1.7791766


                  Extreme Observations

      ------Lowest-----          -----Highest-----

         Value      Obs          Value      Obs

      -1.77918       28        1.26224       20
      -1.64915       27        1.54728       17
      -1.52579       18        1.92441        6
      -1.50128       13        2.09507       19
      -1.08082       24        3.19903       14
```

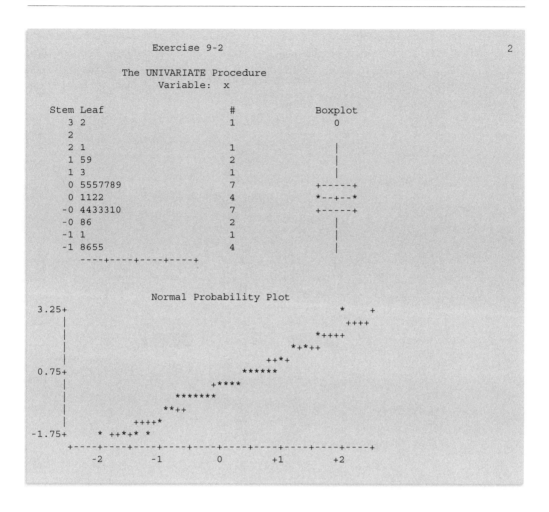

```
                        Exercise 9-2                                    2

                 The UNIVARIATE Procedure
                    Variable:  x

     Stem Leaf                     #              Boxplot
        3 2                        1                 0
        2
        2 1                        1
        1 59                       2                 |
        1 3                        1                 |
        0 5557789                  7              +-----+
        0 1122                     4              *--+--*
       -0 4433310                  7              +-----+
       -0 86                       2                 |
       -1 1                        1                 |
       -1 8655                     4                 |
          ----+----+----+----+

                      Normal Probability Plot
      3.25+                                          *      +
          |                                         ++++
          |                                     *++++
          |                                  *+*++
          |                               ++*+
      0.75+                            ******
          |                         +****
          |                    *******
          |                  **++
          |            ++++*
     -1.75+       *  ++*+* *
          +----+----+----+----+----+----+----+----+----+----+
              -2        -1        0        +1        +2
```

The values of the variable x were generated by the RANNOR function with 2,468 as the seed. The normality test result (W = 0.970159, two-tailed p = 0.5435) is not statistically significant at the 0.05 level. We can conclude that variable x is normally distributed. The three plots given above also support this conclusion.

3.

```
                        Exercise 9-3                                    1

                 The UNIVARIATE Procedure
                    Variable:  number

                          Moments

N                      40      Sum Weights              40
Mean                3.125      Sum Observations        125
Std Deviation  1.63593461      Variance          2.67628205
Skewness       0.15893441      Kurtosis          -1.1979668
Uncorrected SS        495      Corrected SS         104.375
Coeff Variation 52.3499076     Std Error Mean    0.25866397
```

```
                    Basic Statistical Measures

          Location                    Variability

     Mean      3.125000    Std Deviation          1.63593
     Median    3.000000    Variance               2.67628
     Mode      1.000000    Range                  5.00000
                           Interquartile Range    2.50000


                   Tests for Location: Mu0=0

      Test            -Statistic-      -----p Value------

      Student's t    t 12.08131     Pr > |t|    <.0001
      Sign           M       20     Pr >= |M|   <.0001
      Signed Rank    S      410     Pr >= |S|   <.0001


                   Quantiles (Definition 5)

                   Quantile      Estimate

                   100% Max         6.0
                   99%              6.0
                   95%              6.0
                   90%              5.0
                   75% Q3           4.5
                   50% Median       3.0
                   25% Q1           2.0
                   10%              1.0
                   5%               1.0
                   1%               1.0
                   0% Min           1.0


                   Extreme Observations

          ----Lowest----            ----Highest---

          Value      Obs           Value      Obs

            1         39             5         23
            1         31             5         25
            1         26             6          5
            1         24             6         29
            1         19             6         32


                    Frequency Counts
```

	Percents				Percents				Percents	
Count	Cell	Cum	Value	Count	Cell	Cum	Value	Count	Cell	Cum
9	22.5	22.5	3	7	17.5	57.5	5	7	17.5	92.5
7	17.5	40.0	4	7	17.5	75.0	6	3	7.5	100.0

a. Any number from 2 to 5 is equally likely to turn up on the die. Number 1 is most likely to turn up, Number 6 is least likely.

b. From the **Frequency Counts** table, we can see that the distribution of numbers is similar to a uniform distribution, but with a slightly higher frequency for Number 1 and a lower frequency for Number 6.

c. A weight of 0.7407 for Number 1, 0.9524 for Numbers 2 to 5, and 2.2222 for Number 6. The SAS program below can be used to correct the bias associated with Jeanie's die.

```
DATA data1;
  SET ex3;
  c=1;
RUN;

PROC UNIVARIATE DATA=data1 NOPRINT;
  CLASS point;
  VAR c;
  OUTPUT OUT=data2 N=f;
RUN;

DATA data3;
  SET data2;
  IF point=1 THEN weight=40/54;
    ELSE IF 2 <= point <= 5 THEN weight=40/42;
    ELSE IF point=6 THEN weight=40/18;
  prob=f/40;
  exp_v=prob*weight;
RUN;

PROC PRINT DATA=data3;
RUN;
```

4. The following SAS program simulates what Larry might have generated by rolling dice 40 times and each time adding up the points facing up on both dice:

```
DATA ex4;
    DO i=1 TO 40;
    x=FLOOR(RANUNI(123)*6+1);
    y=FLOOR(RANUNI(456)*6+1);
    point=x+y; OUTPUT;
    END;
PROC PRINT DATA=ex4; RUN;
PROC UNIVARIATE DATA=ex4 NORMAL PLOT;
    VAR point;
RUN;
```

```
Exercise 9-4                                                         1

 i    x    y    point

 1    5    2     7
 2    2    6     8
 3    3    2     5
 4    5    3     8
 5    1    2     3
 6    5    3     8
 7    6    2     8
 8    5    4     9
 9    4    6    10
10    1    6     7
11    4    5     9
12    5    2     7
13    4    6    10
14    1    4     5
15    4    3     7
16    4    2     6
17    4    2     6
18    4    4     8
19    1    1     2
20    4    5     9
21    3    1     4
22    5    6    11
23    5    6    11
24    1    5     6
25    6    2     8
26    4    5     9
27    5    2     7
28    5    4     9
29    5    5    10
30    1    1     2
31    2    2     4
32    5    5    10
33    2    6     8
34    3    5     8
35    5    4     9
36    1    4     5
37    5    5    10
38    1    4     5
39    3    2     5
40    1    2     3
```

```
                       Exercise 9-4                                  2

                    The UNIVARIATE Procedure
                       Variable:  point

                            Moments

N                        40    Sum Weights              40
Mean                   7.15    Sum Observations        286
Std Deviation    2.43426396    Variance         5.92564103
Skewness         -0.4867424    Kurtosis         -0.5598604
Uncorrected SS         2276    Corrected SS          231.1
Coeff Variation  34.0456498    Std Error Mean   0.38489093
```

```
                    Basic Statistical Measures

         Location                      Variability

     Mean      7.150000    Std Deviation           2.43426
     Median    8.000000    Variance                5.92564
     Mode      8.000000    Range                   9.00000
                           Interquartile Range     4.00000


                 Tests for Location: Mu0=0

         Test           -Statistic-     -----p Value------

         Student's t    t  18.57669     Pr > |t|    <.0001
         Sign           M      20       Pr >= |M|   <.0001
         Signed Rank    S     410       Pr >= |S|   <.0001


                     Tests for Normality

     Test                --Statistic---     -----p Value------

     Shapiro-Wilk        W   0.947469    Pr < W       0.0621
     Kolmogorov-Smirnov  D   0.161523    Pr > D      <0.0100
     Cramer-von Mises    W-Sq 0.12363    Pr > W-Sq    0.0519
     Anderson-Darling    A-Sq 0.719695   Pr > A-Sq    0.0574


                  Quantiles (Definition 5)

                  Quantile      Estimate

                  100% Max        11.0
                  99%             11.0
                  95%             10.5
                  90%             10.0
                  75% Q3           9.0
                  50% Median       8.0
                  25% Q1           5.0
                  10%              3.5
                  5%               2.5
                  1%               2.0
                  0% Min           2.0


                   Extreme Observations

          ----Lowest----         ----Highest---

          Value     Obs          Value     Obs

              2      30             10       29
              2      19             10       32
              3      40             10       37
              3       5             11       22
              4      31             11       23
```

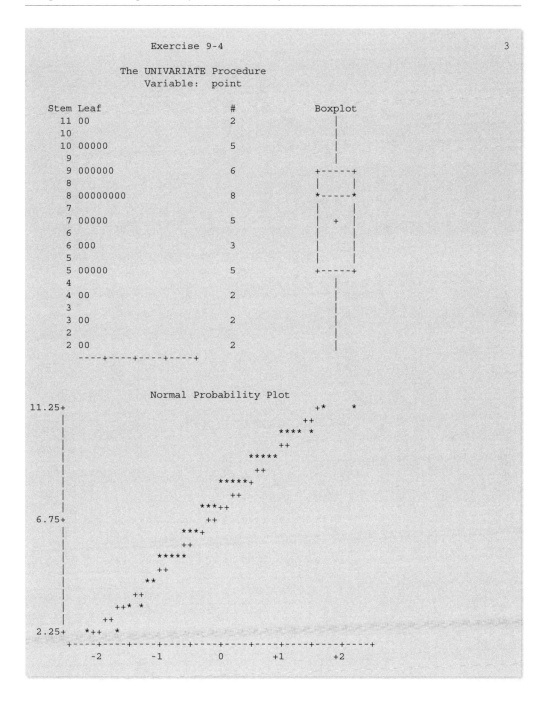

```
                         Exercise 9-4                                       3

                      The UNIVARIATE Procedure
                      Variable:  point

      Stem Leaf                        #              Boxplot
        11 00                          2                 |
        10                                               |
        10 00000                       5                 |
         9                                                |
         9 000000                      6              +------+
         8                                            |      |
         8 00000000                    8              *------*
         7                                            |      |
         7 00000                       5              |   +  |
         6                                            |      |
         6 000                         3              |      |
         5                                            |      |
         5 00000                       5              +------+
         4                                                |
         4 00                          2                  |
         3                                                |
         3 00                          2                  |
         2                                                |
         2 00                          2                  |
           ----+----+----+----+
```

```
                      Normal Probability Plot
      11.25+                                        +*      *
           |                                      ++
           |                                   **** *
           |                                  ++
           |                               *****
           |                             ++
           |                         *****+
           |                       ++
           |                    ***++
       6.75+                    ++
           |                 ***+
           |               ++
           |             *****
           |           ++
           |          **
           |       ++
           |     ++* *
           |   ++
       2.25+  *++   *
           +----+----+----+----+----+----+----+----+----+
               -2        -1        0        +1        +2
```

Conclusion: The Shapiro-Wilk test of normality result ($W = 0.947469$, $p = 0.0621$) is significant at the 0.10 level, which indicates that the population distribution is probably not normal. The stem-and-leaf plot suggests a slightly bimodal distribution. Yet according to the central limit theorem, if this experiment is repeated numerous times with $n = 2$ (dice), the aggregated distribution of all results is approximately normal.

5. SAS program and output:

```
DATA ex5;
    DO i=1 TO 40;
    x=FLOOR(RANUNI(321)*6+1);
    y=FLOOR(RANUNI(654)*6+1);
    IF x=2 THEN x=3; IF y=2 THEN y=3;
    point=x+y; OUTPUT;
    END;
RUN;
PROC PRINT DATA=ex5; RUN;
PROC UNIVARIATE DATA=ex5 NORMAL PLOT;
    VAR point;
RUN;
```

```
        Exercise 9-5                                                           1

 Obs      i     x     y      point

   1      1     3     3        6
   2      2     3     3        6
   3      3     6     1        7
   4      4     3     5        8
   5      5     6     3        9
   6      6     1     1        2
   7      7     6     4       10
   8      8     3     3        6
   9      9     4     3        7
  10     10     4     5        9
  11     11     6     3        9
  12     12     3     3        6
  13     13     5     3        8
  14     14     5     4        9
  15     15     1     1        2
  16     16     5     4        9
  17     17     6     3        9
  18     18     3     3        6
  19     19     4     4        8
  20     20     1     6        7
  21     21     3     4        7
  22     22     6     1        7
  23     23     1     4        5
  24     24     6     4       10
  25     25     1     1        2
  26     26     4     3        7
  27     27     6     6       12
  28     28     4     1        5
  29     29     4     1        5
  30     30     3     6        9
  31     31     5     3        8
  32     32     3     6        9
  33     33     5     1        6
  34     34     6     6       12
  35     35     1     3        4
  36     36     3     3        6
  37     37     1     1        2
  38     38     1     3        4
  39     39     6     3        9
  40     40     3     5        8
```

```
                        Exercise 9-5                                    2

                     The UNIVARIATE Procedure
                       Variable:  point

                           Moments

N                          40    Sum Weights                40
Mean                        7    Sum Observations          280
Std Deviation      2.51151196    Variance            6.30769231
Skewness          -0.3475651     Kurtosis            -0.0295424
Uncorrected SS           2206    Corrected SS              246
Coeff Variation    35.8787422    Std Error Mean      0.39710491


                  Basic Statistical Measures

         Location                      Variability

    Mean      7.000000     Std Deviation          2.51151
    Median    7.000000     Variance               6.30769
    Mode      9.000000     Range                 10.00000
                           Interquartile Range    3.00000


               Tests for Location: Mu0=0

      Test              -Statistic-      -----p Value------

      Student's t    t  17.62758    Pr > |t|     <.0001
      Sign           M        20    Pr >= |M|    <.0001
      Signed Rank    S       410    Pr >= |S|    <.0001


                  Tests for Normality

   Test                 --Statistic---      -----p Value------

   Shapiro-Wilk         W    0.947329    Pr < W        0.0614
   Kolmogorov-Smirnov   D    0.120254    Pr > D        0.1494
   Cramer-von Mises     W-Sq 0.108117    Pr > W-Sq     0.0876
   Anderson-Darling     A-Sq 0.742105    Pr > A-Sq     0.0490


                  Quantiles (Definition 5)

                  Quantile      Estimate

                  100% Max        12.0
                  99%             12.0
                  95%             11.0
                  90%              9.5
                  75% Q3           9.0
                  50% Median       7.0
                  25% Q1           6.0
                  10%              3.0
                  5%               2.0
                  1%               2.0
                  0% Min           2.0
```

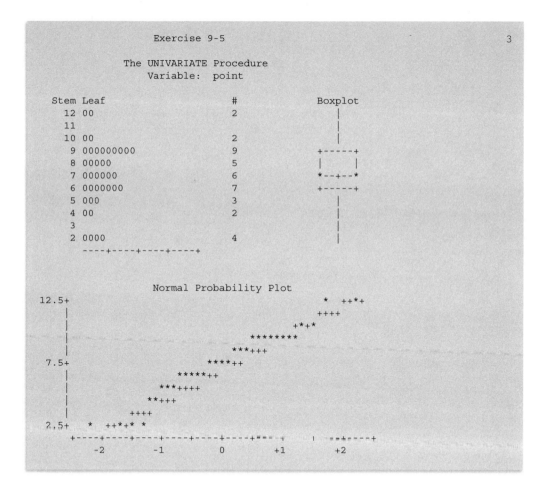

```
                          Extreme Observations

                   ----Lowest----          ----Highest---

                   Value      Obs          Value      Obs

                     2        37              9        39
                     2        25             10         7
                     2        15             10        24
                     2         6             12        27
                     4        38             12        34
```

```
                      Exercise 9-5                                    3

                  The UNIVARIATE Procedure
                  Variable:  point

    Stem Leaf                      #          Boxplot
     12  00                        2             |
     11                                          |
     10  00                        2             |
      9  000000000                 9          +------+
      8  00000                     5          |      |
      7  000000                    6          *--+--*
      6  0000000                   7          +------+
      5  000                       3             |
      4  00                        2             |
      3                                          |
      2  0000                      4             |
         ----+----+----+----+
```

```
                  Normal Probability Plot
    12.5+                                    *   ++*+
        |                                       ++++
        |                                    +*+*
        |                               ********
        |                            ***+++
     7.5+                         ****++
        |                      *****++
        |                   ***+++++
        |                  **+++
        |              ++++
     2.5+    *    ++*+*  *
         +----+----+----+----+----+----+----+    |   ++*+----+
             -2        -1         0        +1         +2
```

Conclusion: The Shapiro-Wilk test of normality result ($W = 0.947329$, $p = 0.0614$) is significant at the 0.10 level, which indicates that the population distribution is probably not normal. The stem-and-leaf plot suggests a slightly bimodal distribution. Yet according to the central limit theorem, if this experiment is repeated numerous times with $n = 2$ (dice), the aggregated distribution of all results is approximately normal.

6.

```
                        Exercise 9-6                                 1

                      The UNIVARIATE Procedure
                        Variable:  income

                             Moments

N                        20    Sum Weights                  20
Mean                  6.285    Sum Observations          125.7
Std Deviation    2.40334745    Variance             5.77607895
Skewness         -0.3038761    Kurtosis             -0.3428044
Uncorrected SS       899.77    Corrected SS          109.7455
Coeff Variation  38.2394184    Std Error Mean       0.53740483


                   Basic Statistical Measures

         Location                       Variability

    Mean      6.285000     Std Deviation           2.40335
    Median    6.150000     Variance                5.77608
    Mode         .         Range                   8.90000
                           Interquartile Range     3.35000


                 Tests for Location: Mu0=0

       Test              -Statistic-     -----p Value------

       Student's t    t  11.69509     Pr > |t|      <.0001
       Sign           M        10     Pr >= |M|     <.0001
       Signed Rank    S       105     Pr >= |S|     <.0001


                   Tests for Normality

     Test                  --Statistic---     -----p Value------

     Shapiro-Wilk       W   0.976927     Pr < W        0.8886
     Kolmogorov-Smirnov D   0.087218     Pr > D       >0.1500
     Cramer-von Mises   W-Sq 0.023643    Pr > W-Sq    >0.2500
     Anderson-Darling   A-Sq 0.170104    Pr > A-Sq    >0.2500


                  Quantiles (Definition 5)

                   Quantile      Estimate

                   100% Max        10.20
                   99%             10.20
                   95%              9.90
                   90%              9.40
                   75% Q3           8.30
                   50% Median       6.15
                   25% Q1           4.95
                   10%              2.80
                   5%               1.80
                   1%               1.30
                   0% Min           1.30
```

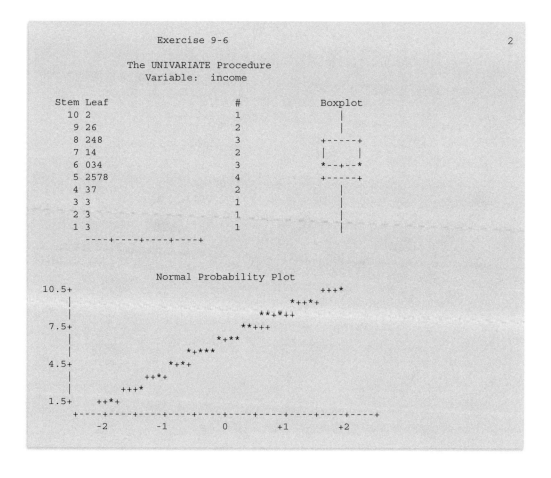

```
                        Extreme Observations

              ----Lowest----              ----Highest---

              Value        Obs            Value        Obs

                1.3          7              8.4          10
                2.3          3              8.8           5
                3.3         17              9.2          14
                4.3         16              9.6           1
                4.7          8             10.2          11
```

Conclusion: The <u>income</u> distribution has a mean of 6.285 (in thousands of dollars) and a standard deviation of 2.40334745. The curve is slightly negatively skewed (Skewness = −0.3038761), more flat than the normal distribution (Kurtosis = −0.3128044); but it is still considered normally distributed because the normality test is not statistically significant at $\alpha = 0.05$. This conclusion is supported by the three plots given below.

```
                Exercise 9-6                                    2

             The UNIVARIATE Procedure
             Variable:   income

 Stem Leaf                         #              Boxplot
   10 2                            1                 |
    9 26                           2                 |
    8 248                          3              +------+
    7 14                           2              |      |
    6 034                          3              *--+--*
    5 2578                         4              +------+
    4 37                           2                 |
    3 3                            1                 |
    2 3                            1                 |
    1 3                            1                 |
      ----+----+----+----+

                Normal Probability Plot
 10.5+                                         +++*
     |                                      *++*+
     |                                    **+*++
  7.5+                                 **+++
     |                               *+**
     |                          *+***
  4.5+                      *+*+
     |                 ++*+
     |            +++*
  1.5+        ++*+
     +----+----+----+----+----+----+----+----+----+----+
        -2        -1         0        +1        +2
```

10

Graphing Data

OBJECTIVE

In this chapter, you will learn how to present data graphically in formats such as vertical bars, horizontal bars, pie charts, star patterns, and 3-D displays. The CHART procedure is particularly well suited for these displays in terms of frequencies or cumulative frequencies, percentages or cumulative percentages, and sums or means for continuous variables. The GCHART procedure is introduced as a handy tool for high-density colored graphs.

10.1 Graphical Data Displays With CHART and GCHART Procedures

This chapter illustrates how to display data graphically with CHART and GCHART procedures. The graphical format includes vertical bars, horizontal bars, pie charts, circular patterns, star patterns, and three-dimensional (3-D) plots. Each of these formats is visual. Thus, they enhance your ability to extract structural information from the display and formulate interpretations based on the information.

Examples primarily showcase charts produced from PROC CHART, although the programs are shown to be easily modified to generate high-density colored charts with the GCHART procedure. You are encouraged to master the nitty-gritty of the CHART procedure first before moving on to the next level—the GCHART procedure—for high-density graphical displays.

10.2 Examples

Raw data file achieve.dat is used in all the 13 examples given in this section. Read Appendix B to learn more details about this data set.

Example 10.1 Frequency Counts by Vertical and Horizontal Bar Charts

This example demonstrates how vertical and horizontal displays of frequencies can be obtained. To create a vertical bar chart, the **VBAR** statement is invoked in the PROC CHART statement. Likewise, the **HBAR** statement generates a horizontal bar chart. Both the statements are followed by a variable name (method in this case) and an option DISCRETE. The **DISCRETE** option is specified to treat values (1 and 2) of the teaching method as discrete values. These two discrete values define the intervals of the X-axis. Immediately after the DATA step of the program, optional output controls such as **LS=90** and **PS=25** are specified. LS=90 restricts the width of the output page to 90 columns per line. PS, on the other hand, defines the page size that approximately equals the length of each output page. Hence, **PS = 25** sets each output page to be 25 lines long. The specification of **PS** directly affects the appearance of each chart.

```
/* The following bolded SAS statements establish the SAS data set 'achieve' */

PROC FORMAT;
    VALUE m 1='phonic' 2='look-say';
    VALUE S 1='exp.' 2='control';
    VALUE sex 1='female' 2='male';
    VALUE g 4='4th grade' 5='5th grade' 6='6th grade';
RUN;


DATA achieve;
    INFILE 'd:\data\achieve.dat';
    INPUT school 1 grade 2 method 3 sex 4 id $ 6-8 vocab 25-26 reading 27-28
          spelling 29-30 capital 31-32 punc 33-34 usage 35-36
          total1 37-38 maps 39-40 graphs 41-42 refer 43-44
          total2 45-46 concepts 47-48 problem 49-50
          total3 51-52 composite 53-54;
    FORMAT school s.  sex sex.  grade g.  method m.;
RUN;


OPTIONS LS=90 PS=25 NODATE PAGENO=1;

TITLE 'Example 10.1 Frequency counts by vertical and horizontal bar charts';

TITLE2 'Vertical bar chart based on two methods of readings';
PROC CHART DATA=achieve;
    VBAR method / DISCRETE;
RUN;

TITLE2 'Horizontal bar chart based on two methods of readings';
PROC CHART DATA=achieve;
    HBAR method / DISCRETE;
RUN;
```

Output 10.1 Frequency Counts by Vertical and Horizontal Bar Charts

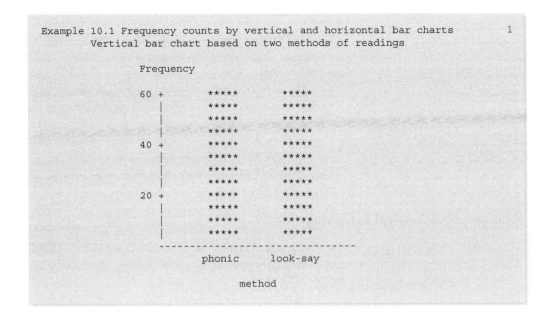

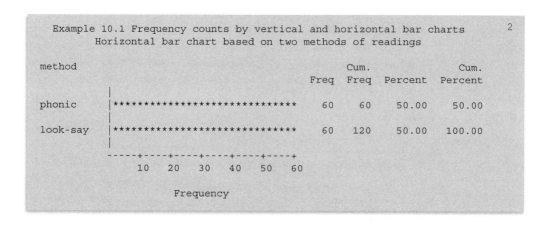

From the output, it is easy to infer that each teaching method was assigned to an equal number (60) of students. This frequency was purposely planned by the researcher so that there was an equal representation of the two teaching methods in this study.

When inspecting both charts, you may like one chart better than the other. That's fine because both charts contain the same information, namely, 60 students learned from the phonic method and the other 60 from the look-say method. There are advantages associated with a horizontal bar chart compared with a vertical chart. These advantages include the following: (a) The frequency is converted to a percentage (50.00%) and (b) both the cumulative percentage and the cumulative frequency are provided for each horizontal bar. If a frequency chart is too long to fit into a output page, PROC CHART automatically displays the results in a horizontal bar chart.

For practice with the GCHART procedure, we modified the SAS program as follows. Try executing this program and compare its output with Output 10.1.

```
TITLE2 'Vertical bar chart based on two methods of readings';
PROC GCHART DATA=achieve;
    VBAR method / DISCRETE;
RUN;

TITLE2 'Horizontal bar chart based on two methods of readings';
PROC GCHART DATA=achieve;
    HBAR method / DISCRETE;
RUN; QUIT;
```

Example 10.2 Vertical Percentage Chart

The vertical bar chart, by default, provides frequency counts only. To obtain percentages, you need an option **TYPE=PERCENT** after the slash (/) on the VBAR statement.

```
/* See Example 10.1 for the DATA step and FORMAT statement */
/* in creating the SAS data set 'achieve'                  */

OPTIONS LS=90 PS=25 NODATE PAGENO=1;

TITLE 'Example 10.2 Vertical percentage chart';

PROC CHART DATA=achieve;
    VBAR method / DISCRETE TYPE=PERCENT;
RUN;
```

Output 10.2 Vertical Percentage Chart

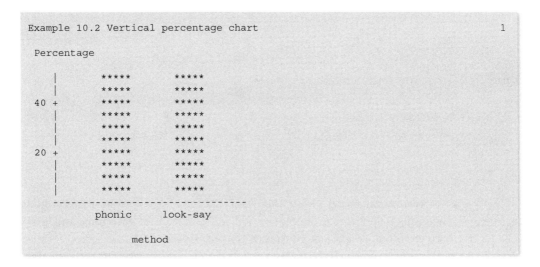

Example 10.3 Vertical Chart for Cumulative Frequency

If you want to include cumulative frequency in a vertical bar chart, you need to specify the option **TYPE=CFREQ** after the slash (/) on the VBAR statement.

```
/* See Example 10.1 for the DATA step and FORMAT statement */
/* in creating the SAS data set 'achieve'                  */

OPTIONS LS=90 PS=25 NODATE PAGENO=1;

TITLE 'Example 10.3 Vertical chart for cumulative frequency';

PROC CHART DATA=achieve;
    VBAR method / DISCRETE TYPE=CFREQ;
RUN;
```

Output 10.3 Vertical Chart for Cumulative Frequency

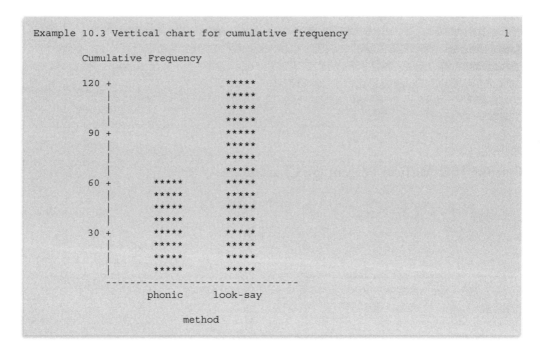

The output shows the cumulative frequency of each teaching method: 60 students taught by the phonic method and 120 students by phonic and look-say methods combined. By subtraction, it is clear that there were another 60 students under the look-say method. For a high-density vertical bar chart, you may try this program instead:

```
PATTERN1 COLOR=blue;        /* Defines the color of the bar to be blue */
PROC GCHART DATA=achieve;
    VBAR method / DISCRETE TYPE=CFREQ;
RUN; QUIT;
```

Example 10.4 Vertical Chart for Cumulative Percentage

If you are interested in obtaining a cumulative percentage bar chart, replace the option TYPE=CFREQ with another option TYPE=CPER-CENT. Applying the CPERCENT option to Example 10.3 results in Output 10.4.

Output 10.4 Vertical Chart for Cumulative Percentage

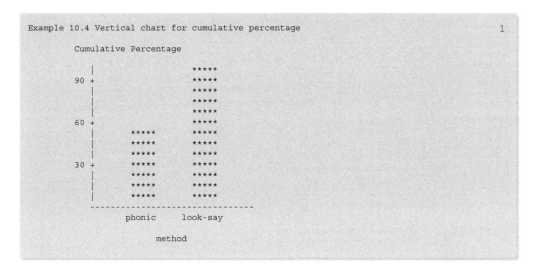

```
Example 10.4 Vertical chart for cumulative percentage                              1

        Cumulative Percentage

          |                      *****
       90 +                      *****
          |                      *****
          |                      *****
          |                      *****
       60 +                      *****
          |          *****       *****
          |          *****       *****
          |          *****       *****
       30 +          *****       *****
          |          *****       *****
          |          *****       *****
          |          *****       *****
          --------------------------------
                    phonic     look-say

                      method
```

This output converts all cumulative frequencies into cumulative percentages. Consequently, the size of the sample is no longer an issue.

Example 10.5 Vertical Bar Chart Based on Averages

So far, Examples 10.1 to 10.4 have been dealing with frequency or percentage of a discrete variable. PROC CHART is capable of displaying the average or total of a continuous variable as well. For example, what is the average income of residents living in the 10 largest cities in the United States? How often do battered women visit a counseling center or middle-way house before they decide to terminate an abusive relationship? These and other similar types of questions call for the description of a continuous variable. For these purposes, PROC CHART has another option, **SUMVAR=**, which summarizes continuous data.

Let's return to the <u>achieve</u> data set and examine the average <u>graphs</u> score obtained from School 1 (the experimental school) and School 2 (the control school). Note that **SUMVAR=graphs** is placed after the slash. Furthermore, another option, **TYPE=MEAN**, is specified to display the average <u>graphs</u> score from each school. Also note that the **PS=** option is now changed to 30 so that the output gives a more detailed calibration of the *Y*-axis.

```
/* See Example 10.1 for the DATA step and FORMAT statement */
/* in creating the SAS data set 'achieve'                  */

OPTIONS LS=90 PS=30 NODATE PAGENO=1;

TITLE 'Example 10.5 Vertical bar chart based on averages';

PROC CHART DATA=achieve;
    VBAR school / DISCRETE TYPE=MEAN SUMVAR=graphs;
RUN;
```

Output 10.5 Vertical Bar Chart Based on Averages

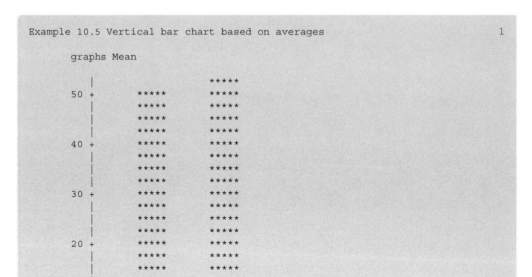

According to the output, the control school students had a higher average <u>graphs</u> test score than the experimental school children, although the difference may not be statistically significant.

In the future, you may wish to report totals, instead of averages, of a continuous variable for groups of different sizes. For example, if you were to investigate the amount of alcohol consumed by teenagers, the total amount would perhaps make more sense than the average. In this case, there is no need to specify the option **TYPE=MEAN**. The absence of the TYPE=MEAN option will be interpreted by PROC CHART as totals.

Example 10.6 A Frequency Bar Chart With Symbols

Previously, Output 10.1 displayed frequency counts by "*". This can be changed; the plotting symbols can be the value of another variable. Suppose you would like to know the count of students by grades in both experimental and control schools. The option **SUBGROUP=grade** can be specified to fill each bar with the values of the variable <u>grade</u>, that is, "4", "5", and "6".

```
/* See Example 10.1 for the DATA step and FORMAT statement */
/* in creating the SAS data set 'achieve'                  */

OPTIONS LS=90 PS=30 NODATE PAGENO=1;

TITLE  'Example 10.6 A frequency bar chart with symbols';

PROC CHART DATA=achieve;
    VBAR school / DISCRETE SUBGROUP=grade;
RUN;
```

Output 10.6 A Frequency Bar Chart With Symbols

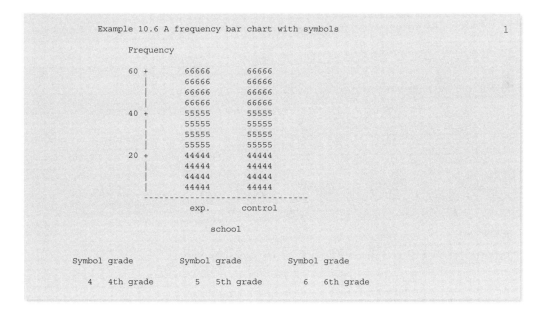

The output demonstrates the advantage of using the option SUB-GROUP=. With this option, it is easier to detect any difference in student enrollments between the two schools for the 4th, 5th, and 6th grades. According to the result, there appear to be no enrollment differences. This research was planned in such a way that an equal number of pupils were recruited from each school at each grade.

The following program, written in the GCHART codes, produces the same output as Output 10.6, with grade levels shown in different colors:

```
PATTERN1 COLOR=red;
PATTERN2 COLOR=blue;
PATTERN3 COLOR=green;
PROC GCHART DATA=achieve;
    VBAR school / DISCRETE SUBGROUP=grade;
RUN; QUIT;
```

The option SUBGROUP= is not limited to frequency counts. It can be used jointly with a continuous variable whose values are expressed along the Y-axis, as in Example 10.7. The SUBGROUP= option can also be used with HBAR or BLOCK chart.

Example 10.7 A Bar Chart With Colors and Averages

This example is carried out by the GCHART procedure to display average <u>graphs</u> scores for the 4th, 5th, and 6th graders enrolled in the experimental and the control schools. The option **SUBGROUP=grade** is specified to fill each bar with three different colors, each corresponding to one grade, as in Example 10.6. Furthermore, **SUMVAR=graphs** and **TYPE=MEAN** are specified to plot average <u>graphs</u> scores on the Y-axis, as in Example 10.5.

```
/* See Example 10.1 for the DATA step and FORMAT statement */
/* in creating the SAS data set 'achieve'                  */

TITLE 'Example 10.7 A bar chart with colors and averages';

PATTERN1 COLOR=yellow;
PATTERN2 COLOR=red;
PATTERN3 COLOR=blue;
PROC GCHART DATA=achieve;
    VBAR school / DISCRETE SUBGROUP=grade SUMVAR=graphs TYPE=MEAN;
RUN; QUIT;
```

Output 10.7 A Bar Chart With Colors and Averages

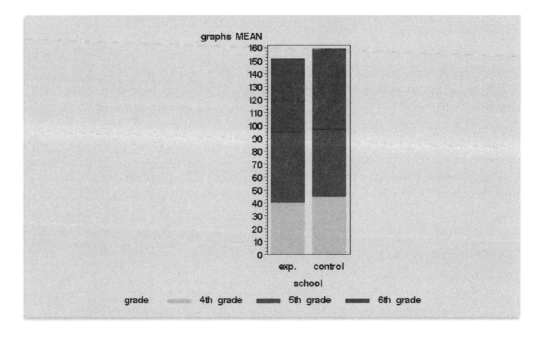

The *Y*-axis should be read as the stacked means of three grades, that is, the mean of the 4th grade in the experimental school is about 40, the mean of the 5th grade in the same school is about 95 – 40 = 55, the mean of the 6th grade is 150 – 95 = 55, and so on. Note how the 6th graders in the control school achieved a higher average than their counterparts in the experimental school. Students in Grades 4 and 5 seemed to perform similarly in both schools. Hence, the overall result favors the control school. To support this interpretation, PROC MEANS is further applied to the data, and its program and results are illustrated in Example 10.8.

If you elected to display the mean <u>graphs</u> scores by the CHART procedure, you can try the following program.

Example 10.7a A Bar Chart With Symbols and Averages

```
OPTIONS LS=90 PS=40 NODATE PAGENO=1;

TITLE 'Example 10.7a A bar chart with symbols and averages';

PROC CHART DATA=achieve;
    VBAR school / DISCRETE SUBGROUP=grade SUMVAR=graphs TYPE=MEAN;
RUN;
```

The output will look similar to Output 10.7, except for the *Y*-axis. The height of the bar chart will represent the overall mean in each school, namely, 50.38 for the experimental school and 53.17 for the control school, shown also in Output 10.5. Within each bar chart, the height of each section, marked by 4 for 4th graders, 5 for 5th graders, and 6 for 6th graders, represents the relative contribution made by each <u>grade</u> level to the overall mean.

For the CHART procedure, the choice of page size (or **PS=** option) is crucial. For Example 10.7a, if **PS** was set at 30, the output would actually show that experimental school pupils did better overall than the control students. That impression would not be correct because it could not be confirmed by the PROC MEANS result. In your own analysis, you should always try various **PS=** options, and then verify the visual appearance with PROC MEANS (or PROC UNIVARIATE), as the next example illustrates.

Example 10.8 Verifying the GCHART Results by PROC MEANS

This example illustrates how to apply the MEANS procedure to help verify the results from PROC GCHART or CHART. Specifically, the MEANS procedure is used to compute means for each school for each grade. The CLASS statement specifies <u>school</u> and <u>grade</u> as two classification variables to compute means for three grades in both the schools.

```
/* See Example 10.1 for the DATA step and FORMAT statement */
/* in creating the SAS data set 'achieve'                  */

TITLE 'Example 10.8 Verifying the GCHART results by PROC MEANS';

PROC MEANS DATA=achieve MEAN;
    CLASS school grade; VAR graphs;
RUN;
```

Output 10.8 Verifying the GCHART Results by PROC MEANS

```
Example 10.8 Verifying the GCHART results by PROC MEANS                         1

                    The MEANS Procedure

                 Analysis Variable : graphs

                               N
        school      grade     Obs              Mean
        -----------------------------------------------
        exp.        4th grade  20         39.7500000

                    5th grade  20         54.6000000

                    6th grade  20         56.8000000

        control     4th grade  20         44.5000000

                    5th grade  20         51.8500000

                    6th grade  20         63.1500000
        -----------------------------------------------
```

The output illuminates what is unclear from Output 10.7, that is, the comparison of two schools at the 4th, 5th, and 6th grade levels. Grade level means show that the control school did better than the experimental school at the 4th and the 6th grades but worse at the 5th grade. These detailed descriptive analyses were not immediately available from the GCHART or CHART results.

Example 10.9 Vertical Charts Side by Side

Previously in Example 10.7, three types of information were bundled into one chart: the average <u>graphs</u> score by <u>school</u> and by <u>grade</u>. The downside of such a stacked-up bar chart is that one cannot usually infer the precise average <u>graphs</u> score for any grade at any school by just eyeballing the chart. There is a need to express six averages (three grades at two schools) separately. This need can be met with a side-by-side chart specified in the following program:

```
/* See Example 10.1 for the DATA step and FORMAT statement */
/* in creating the SAS data set 'achieve'                  */

OPTIONS LS=90 PS=40 NODATE PAGENO=1;

TITLE 'Example 10.9 Vertical charts side by side';

PROC CHART DATA=achieve;
    VBAR school / DISCRETE GROUP=grade SUMVAR=graphs TYPE=MEAN;
RUN;
```

The option **GROUP = grade** is used here to create a side-by-side chart. Other options, such as **SUMVAR = graphs** and **TYPE = MEAN**, yield the same effect as before, namely, the graphs averages are to be plotted as intervals on the *Y*-axis.

Output 10.9 Vertical Charts Side by Side

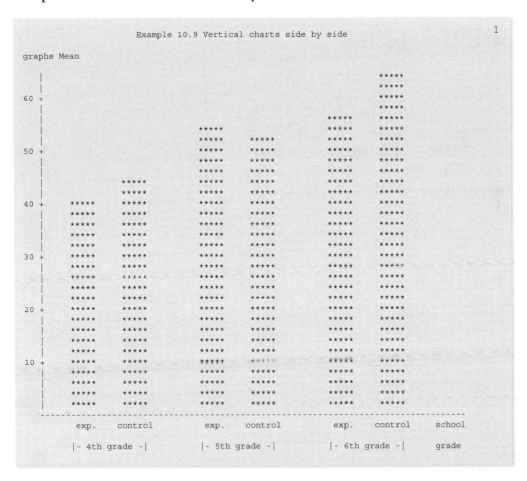

According to the output, the 4th and 6th graders from the control school did better than their counterparts at the experimental school while the reverse is true among the 5th graders. Identical conclusions were previously reached in Output 10.8 by the MEANS procedure.

For a high-density chart, you may wish to modify Example 10.9 into the following with PROC GCHART:

```
PATTERN1 COLOR=red;
PROC GCHART DATA=achieve;
    VBAR school / DISCRETE GROUP=grade SUMVAR=graphs TYPE=MEAN;
RUN; QUIT;
```

Example 10.10 3-D Block Chart

There is yet another way to present multidimensional data in a truly multi-dimensional format, that is, through the block chart. The goal here is the same as in Example 10.9, which is to express average <u>graphs</u> scores for each <u>grade</u> in each <u>school</u> as intervals on the Y-axis. The only difference lies in the **BLOCK** statement that produces a 3-D picture.

```
/* See Example 10.1 for the DATA step and FORMAT statement */
/* in creating the SAS data set 'achieve'                  */

OPTIONS LS=90 PS=60 NODATE PAGENO=1;

TITLE 'Example 10.10 3-D block chart';

PROC CHART DATA=achieve;
    BLOCK school / DISCRETE GROUP=grade SUMVAR=graphs TYPE=MEAN;
RUN;
```

Output 10.10 3-D Block Chart

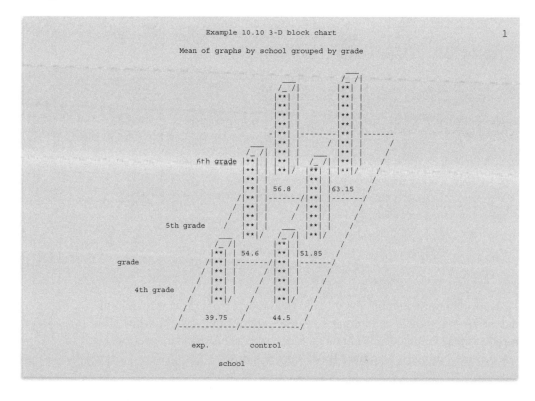

In the 3-D block chart, the floor, or the base, is defined by <u>school</u> (specified on the **BLOCK** statement) and <u>grade</u> (specified by the **GROUP=** option after the slash). The height is proportional to average <u>graphs</u> scores for each <u>grade</u> in each <u>school</u>, as they are presented in Output 10.9 or in Output 10.8. You'd probably agree that the present display is the best of the three presented thus far, because it is 3-D and informative!

Example 10.11 A Star Chart

Yet another representation of the data that reveals and appeals is a starlike chart. In the following program, the **STAR** statement is used to produce a chart that will present average <u>graphs</u> scores across the 4th, 5th, and 6th grades in both schools.

```
/* See Example 10.1 for the DATA step and FORMAT statement */
/* in creating the SAS data set 'achieve'                  */

OPTIONS LS=90 PS=60 NODATE PAGENO=1;

TITLE 'Example 10.11 A star chart';

PROC CHART DATA=achieve;
    STAR grade / DISCRETE SUMVAR=graphs TYPE=MEAN;
RUN;
```

Output 10.11 A Star Chart

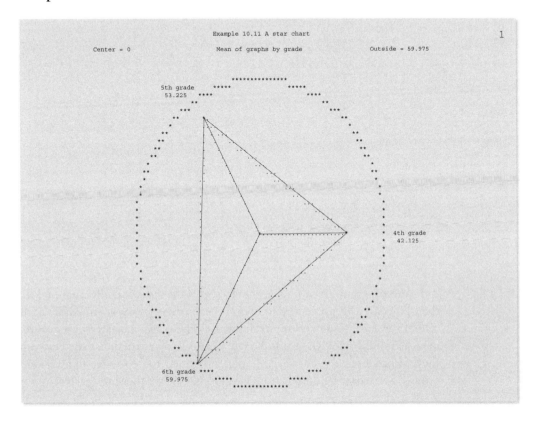

The straight line handdrawn on the star chart connects the center (+) with each star (*) end point. The length of these lines is the average <u>graphs</u> score, which is printed along the circumference of the outer circle. For example, the average <u>graphs</u> score for the 4th grade is 42.125. Can you modify the codes to generate a high-density star chart? (*Hint*: Simply replace PROC CHART with PROC GCHART.)

This output may not fully convince you of the utility of the star chart because there are only three end points. In Example 10.12, a star chart is generated based on 12 end points or 12 group means. When you compare the output of these two examples, you gain a better insight as to when and how to make best use of the star representation.

Example 10.12 Another Star Chart

This example redisplays the <u>achieve</u> data set in such a way that average <u>graphs</u> scores are shown systematically for boys and girls for the three grades in the two schools. As a result, there are 12 subgroups' averages plotted on the star chart.

```
/* See Example 10.1 for the DATA step and FORMAT statement */
/* in creating the SAS data set 'achieve'                  */

OPTIONS LS=90 PS=60 NODATE PAGENO=1;

TITLE 'Example 10.12 Another star chart';

PROC SORT DATA=achieve;
    BY school grade sex;
RUN;

PROC UNIVARIATE DATA=achieve NOPRINT;
    BY school grade sex;
    VAR graphs;
    OUTPUT OUT=summary N=number MEAN=m_graphs;
RUN;

PROC PRINT DATA=summary;  RUN;

DATA new;
    SET summary;
    obs=_N_;

PROC CHART DATA=new;
    STAR obs / DISCRETE SUMVAR=m_graphs;
RUN;
```

In the program given above, the <u>achieve</u> data set is initially analyzed by the UNIVARIATE procedure to obtain the average <u>graphs</u> score within each school for each grade and for each gender. These averages are subsequently exported to PROC PRINT and PROC CHART for a visual display. Between these procedures, a new variable <u>obs</u> is defined to represent the 12 sub-groups. See what the output brings—more spikes on the star chart!

Output 10.12 Another Star Chart

```
                    Example 10.12 Another star chart                            1

  Obs     school       grade       sex       number      m_graphs

    1     exp.        4th grade   female        8        45.0000
    2     exp.        4th grade   male         12        36.2500
    3     exp.        5th grade   female        8        56.3750
    4     exp.        5th grade   male         12        53.4167
    5     exp.        6th grade   female        4        46.7500
    6     exp.        6th grade   male         16        59.3125
    7     control     4th grade   female       13        42.6154
    8     control     4th grade   male          7        48.0000
    9     control     5th grade   female       12        51.1667
   10     control     5th grade   male          8        52.8750
   11     control     6th grade   female       11        62.9091
   12     control     6th grade   male          9        63.4444
```

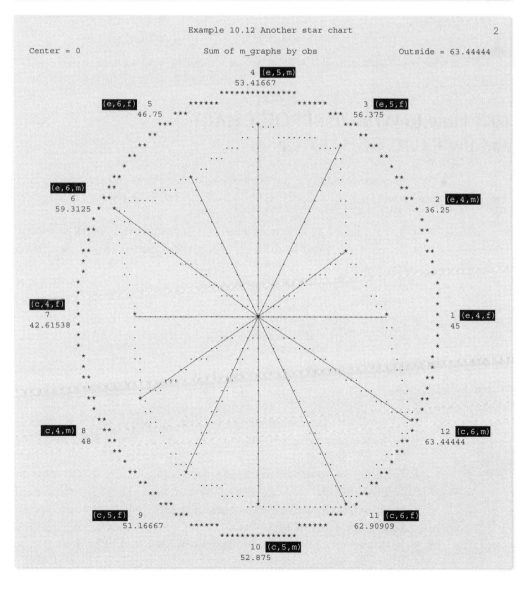

According to the results from the experimental school, girls outperform boys at younger grades, that is, the 4th and 5th, while the reverse is true for older kids from the 6th grade. Among the control school children, the trend is different—girls and boys perform equally well at the 5th and the 6th grades, yet girls score lower than boys at the 4th grade. Exact average <u>graphs</u> scores are printed along the circumference under the subgroup numbers 1 to 12. These numbers are identified under <u>Obs</u> by the PROC PRINT result on page 1. On the star chart on page 2, these are elaborated in parentheses by hand, such as (c, 5, m) for control 5th grade male. Straight lines drawn by hand connect the center (+) with each end point (*), and thus also with the average <u>graphs</u> scores. The length of these lines is proportional to the average <u>graphs</u> scores.

We encourage you to try executing the program below using PROC GCHART and compare its output with Output 10.12:

```
PROC GCHART DATA=new;
     STAR obs / DISCRETE SUMVAR=m_graphs;
RUN; QUIT;
```

10.3 How to Write the PROC CHART and the PROC GCHART Codes

Examples presented so far are illustrations of five charts and six statistics that are possible with PROC CHART or PROC GCHART. Here is a quick review.

- If one is interested in drawing a vertical bar chart, use the **VBAR** statement.
- If one is interested in drawing a horizontal bar chart, use the **HBAR** statement.
- If one is interested in drawing a 3-D block design, use the **BLOCK** statement.
- If one is interested in drawing a pie chart, use the **PIE** statement.
- If one is interested in drawing a star display, use the **STAR** statement.

Likewise, the kind of information displayed is controlled by the option **TYPE=**:

- To display frequencies of a categorical variable, type in **TYPE=FREQ**.
- To display percentages of a categorical variable, type in **TYPE=PCT (or PERCENT)**.
- To display cumulative frequencies of a categorical variable, type in **TYPE=CFREQ**.
- To display cumulative percentages of a categorical variable, type in **TYPE=CPCT (or CPERCENT)**.
- To display totals of a continuous variable, type in **TYPE=SUM**.
- To display averages of a continuous variable, type in **TYPE=MEAN**.

PROC CHART and PROC GCHART codes are similar, consisting of the following statements:

PROC	CHART or GCHART	DATA = *sas_dataset_name;*
	VBAR	*<variables> / <options>;*
	HBAR	*<variables> / <options>;*
	BLOCK	*<variables> / <options>;*
	PIE	*<variables> / <options>;*
	STAR	*<variables> / <options>;*
	BY	*classification_variable(s);*

These statements have been illustrated in Examples 10.1 through 10.12, except for the BY statement. The **BY** statement serves the same purpose as in other procedures, namely, repeating all other statements for each subgroup defined by the BY variable(s). Thus, if a program reads as

```
PROC CHART DATA=achieve;
    BY school;
    VBAR sex / TYPE=PCT;
```

a vertical bar chart will be plotted twice, first for the experimental school children and second for the control school children. If more than one BY variable is listed, all possible combinations of the BY variables' values are used in dividing up the entire data set. Be sure to presort the data set in the ascending order of all BY variables, if the BY statement is included in the CHART or GCHART procedure. Presorting a data set can be accomplished with the SORT procedure.

Variables that appear on any of the **VBAR** through **STAR** statements will each result in a separate plot. For example, if a program is written as

```
PROC CHART;
    VBAR a b c;
```

there will be three vertical bar charts plotted, based on a, b, and c, respectively.

Other options that can appear after the slash (/) include the following:

DISCRETE   This option treats a numeric variable as a categorical or character variable. In other words, even if a variable's values are coded as numeric in the DATA step, such as 1 and 2 on the sex variable, they will be treated as characters by the **DISCRETE** option. As a result, PROC CHART ignores the numeric nature of the variable and prints its values as intervals on the *X*- or *Y*-axis. This option is unnecessary if you are dealing with character variables.

TYPE=FREQ **(PCT or CFREQ or** **CPERCENT/CPCT or** **SUM or MEAN)**	This option is used to specify the type of information to be displayed on the chart. See the explanations previously given.
SUMVAR= **(a variable name)**	This option requests that the mean, the sum, or the frequency of the named variable be presented on the chart. For example, the following program will, on the Y-axis, depict average gpa's of students on various campuses of a university:

```
PROC CHART;
    VBAR campus/TYPE=MEAN SUMVAR=gpa;
```

MIDPOINTS= **(midpoints of intervals)**	This option allows you to set midpoints of all intervals, instead of letting PROC CHART determine them. You may set the midpoints in one of the four ways described below:

1. List midpoints from the smallest to the largest with equal width in between; for example,

```
PROC CHART;
    VBAR campus / TYPE=MEAN SUMVAR=gpa MIDPOINTS=0.5 1.0 1.5 2.0 2.5 3.0 3.5 4.0;
```

2. List the smallest and the largest midpoints, plus the width of intervals:

```
PROC CHART;
    VBAR campus / TYPE=MEAN SUMVAR=gpa MIDPOINTS=0.5 TO 4.0 BY 0.5;
```

3. List the smallest to the largest midpoints and varying interval width:

```
PROC CHART;
    VBAR state / TYPE=MEAN SUMVAR=income MIDPOINTS=10 100 1000 10000;
    /* This specification will produce a log (base 10) scale*/
```

4. List character midpoints in single quotes:

```
PROC CHART;
    VBAR state / TYPE=MEAN SUMVAR=income MIDPOINTS='CA' 'IN' 'NY';
    /* The midpoints for three states are: CA, IN, and NY */
```

If no MIDPOINTS option is specified, PROC CHART will define midpoints according to a logical division of the range of numeric variables or the ascending order of the first letter of character variable values.

GROUP=
(a variable name)

This option requests that a side-by-side chart be presented; for example, the following program

```
PROC CHART;
    VBAR sex / GROUP=major;
```

results in a side-by-side chart on which frequencies of two genders are presented within each <u>major</u>. In other words, the X-axis of the chart is first divided according to various majors. Then for each major, two genders are defined. The vertical dimension is still the frequency (of both sexes).

SUBGROUP=
(a variable name)

This option requests that the values of the SUBGROUP variable be inserted in each bar. For example, if a program reads as

```
PROC CHART;
    VBAR major / SUBGROUP=sex;
```

In this example, the values of <u>sex</u> (such as M, F or 1, 2) are inserted in each bar graph showing the frequency of males and females in each major. Note that only the first letter of each variable value is shown. If two letters are the same, such as "physics" and "psychology", then they will be represented by A, B, and so on, in each bar. The substitute labels are explained on top of the graph in the legend. In addition, observations with missing values are grouped together and shown as a separate group.

LEVELS=
(number of intervals)

This option defines the number of intervals drawn for a continuous numeric variable.

SYMBOL=

"a plotting symbol"

This option defines a symbol that is drawn in the graph. The default is "*". If a printer has the capability of printing overlapping symbols, you may specify this option as, for example, **SYMBOLS= "MWI"**. This option should not be used concurrently with the SUBGROUP= option.

G100

This option causes the frequency count or the percentage of each group (or interval) to be summed to 100 or 100%; it is used with the GROUP= option.

The following three options are used with VBAR or HBAR only.

ASCENDING

This option rearranges intervals of a bar graph from left to right according to their increasing frequencies.

DESCENDING   This option rearranges intervals of a bar graph accord-
                    ing to their decreasing frequencies; its result is the
                    opposite of the option **ASCENDING**.

REF=   This option requests that a reference line be drawn
(a numeric value)   at the value specified. The particular value chosen
                    should be compatible with the specification of
                    TYPE=. For example, if TYPE=PERCENT, then
                    REF= should be specified with a value between 0
                    and 100.

10.4 Tips

- How to handle missing or invalid data

In data analysis, it is important to distinguish missing data from invalid
data and also from zero. Missing data means that you do not have information about an observation on a particular variable, such as age. In this
case, missing values are coded as periods (.) in SAS. On the other hand, if
an individual did give his or her age during data collection, yet such information was miscoded or not usable, such as a value of "810". In the second case, the value is referred to as invalid. Both missing and invalid data
are treated differently than 0 unless 0 happens to be a miscoded data
point for age, say. Otherwise, 0 should be regarded valid as it conveys
meaningful and truthful information.

Missing data, by default, are not included in any CHART or GCHART
output. You can change this, however, by specifying the option MISSING on
the chart statement (such as HBAR, VBAR, and so on) after the slash (/). For
example,

```
PROC CHART;
    VBAR major / MISSING;
```

yields a vertical bar chart in which students with a missing major are
grouped into a separate category and their frequency count is denoted on the
Y-axis. If a program already includes the option SUBGROUP=, then missing
data will be included automatically as part of subgroups shown in a VBAR,
HBAR, or BLOCK graph.

When looking for invalid data, you should pay special attention to the
range of data, the shape of the score distribution, the mean, the standard
deviation, and other descriptive indices to see if any peculiarity shows up;
locate mistake(s) and correct them immediately.

- What is the difference between the GROUP= option and the SUBGROUP= Option?

Both options are used to create an additional dimension on the graph. The use of option GROUP= results in a side-by-side graph, as in Example 10.9. The option SUBGROUP= yields graphs in which each bar is further divided according to the variable specified in the SUBGROUP= option. Two illustrations of the SUBGROUP= option are found in Examples 10.6 and 10.7.

The GROUP= and SUBGROUP= options are used only on HBAR, VBAR, and BLOCK statements.

- When is the option DISCRETE used?

The purpose of DISCRETE is to retain the numeric values of a numeric variable as intervals. The use of this option prevents PROC CHART from automatically or arbitrarily determining intervals for an axis. It is essential that this option be used whenever you want PROC CHART to treat a numeric variable as a character variable. Refer back to Examples 10.1 and 10.11 for an illustration.

- How to use ODS with the CHART procedure

To use the ODS, you need to know ODS table names corresponding to the various portions of the output. Table 10.1 presents selected ODS table names for the CHART procedure and their descriptions.

Table 10.1   Selected ODS Table Names and Descriptions for the CHART Procedure

ODS Table Name	Description	CHART Procedure Statement
HBAR	A horizontal bar chart	HBAR
VBAR	A vertical bar chart	VBAR
BLOCK	A block chart	BLOCK
PIE	A pie chart	PIE
STAR	A star chart	STAR

You may select certain results to be saved in file formats other than the SAS standard output. For example, the following program saves the HBAR portion of the output of Example 10.1 in HTML format in the default style.

```
ODS HTML BODY = 'd:\result\Example10_1Body.html'
        CONTENTS = 'd:\result\Example10_1TOC.html'
        PAGE = 'd:\result\Example10_1Page.html'
        FRAME = 'd:\result\Example10_1Frame.html';

ODS SELECT HBAR;

TITLE 'Example 10.1 Frequency counts by vertical and horizontal bar charts';

TITLE2 'Vertical bar chart based on two methods of readings';
PROC CHART DATA=achieve;
    VBAR method / DISCRETE;
RUN;

TITLE2 'Horizontal bar chart based on two methods of readings';
PROC CHART DATA=achieve;
    HBAR method / DISCRETE;
RUN;

ODS HTML CLOSE;
RUN;
```

For additional information about the ODS feature, consult with *SAS 9.1.3 Output Delivery System: User's Guide* (SAS Institute Inc., 2006c) and *Base SAS 9.1.3 Procedures Guide* (SAS Institute Inc., 2006a) or the online documentation at www.sas.com.

10.5 Summary

In this chapter, you have learned four different ways of summarizing and displaying data: the vertical bar chart, the horizontal bar chart, the block chart, and the star chart. All four chart types can display frequency as well as percentage of counts in each category of a categorical variable, or in each interval of a numeric variable. Furthermore, cumulative frequency as well as cumulative percentage can be presented. If you are interested in discovering the relationship between a categorical variable and a continuous variable, you can consider plotting the mean or the sum of the continuous variable for each category of the categorical variable.

The block chart and the side-by-side vertical chart can convey 3-D information. The star chart uses a circular pattern to display information on percentages, means, or sums of a continuous variable. Now let's turn to exercises to find out how much of this material you have mastered.

10.6 Exercises

1. The manufacturing manager of an automobile company wanted to know what kind of car was most popular on the market. He was particularly interested in three attributes: color (red, black, white), size (subcompact, compact, midsize), and type (2-door, 4-door, 5-door). He conducted a marketing survey with 30 typical buyers; the following are their choices:

Subject		Color			Size			Type		
No.	Age	Red	Black	White	Subcompact	Compact	Midsize	2-door	4-door	5-door
1	55		V			V				V
2	20			V			V	V		
3	35		V				V		V	
4	36	V			V					V
5	19	V				V		V		
6	44			V			V			V
7	59		V			V				V
8	31			V	V			V		
9	29	V				V		V		
10	27		V				V	V		
11	42		V		V					V
12	36		V				V			V
13	18		V			V		V		
14	44			V		V			V	
15	24	V				V		V		
16	20	V			V			V		
17	38		V				V			V
18	42			V	V					V
19	29			V		V				V
20	23			V			V			V
21	52		V		V			V		
22	47		V			V				V
23	34	V					V	V		
24	25	V			V			V		
25	36		V			V		V		
26	41		V			V			V	
27	32		V		V					V
28	24	V			V					V
29	29		V				V	V		
30	38			V	V					V
TOTAL		8	14	8	10	11	9	13	3	14

Answer the following questions by drawing appropriate charts:

    a. What color was the buyers' most favorite choice? How many buyers liked it?

    b. What was the percentage of buyers who did not like a 5-door car?

    c. If buyers were grouped by their ages into three age-groups—those below 30 years, between 30 and 40 years, and above 40 years—what is the percentage of buyers in each age-group? What is the mean <u>age</u> of each group?

2. A teacher wanted to know if computerized instruction was better than the traditional method for teaching elementary students. After administering the two methods for three months, tests were given to the students to assess their achievement. Below are their test results. Use 3-D block charts to display the average performance of each subgroup that is defined by subject, instructional method, and sex.

| | Instructional Method | | | |
| | Computerized | | Traditional | |
Subject	Boys	Girls	Boys	Girls
Arithmetic	85, 70, 90, 82, 63, 84	88, 72, 65, 82, 79, 90	95, 89, 92, 66, 75, 60	85, 82, 88, 79, 80, 75
Arts	77, 89, 69, 82, 70, 87	92, 65, 75, 83, 82, 78	92, 88, 86, 70, 96, 60	77, 82, 79, 85, 72, 80
Reading	68, 75, 85, 92, 66, 90	74, 82, 76, 93, 82, 87	72, 74, 89, 85, 60, 83	82, 86, 77, 72, 74, 88

3. Modify the SAS program in Example 10.7a with PS = 19, 30, and 45 and find out what happens to the output.

4. Modify the SAS program in Example 10.11 with PS = 30 and 45 and find out what happens to the output.

10.7 Answers to Exercises

1. a. Black was the most favorite color, liked by 14 "typical" buyers out of 30.

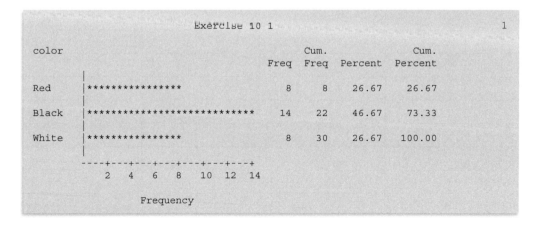

b. 53.33% out of 30 buyers did not like a 5-door car.

```
                        Exercise 10-1                                    2

type                                       Cum.            Cum.
                                   Freq    Freq  Percent   Percent
          |
 2-door   |**************************   13      13    43.33     43.33
          |
 4-door   |******                       3      16    10.00     53.33
          |
 5-door   |**************************** 14      30    46.67    100.00
          |
          ----+---+---+---+---+---+---+
              2   4   6   8  10  12  14

                   Frequency
```

c. 40% of participants were below 30 years of age, with a mean age of 23.91667 years;
    30% of participants were between 30 and 40 years, with a mean age of 35.11111
    years. The remaining 30% were above 40 years, with a mean age of 47.33333 years.

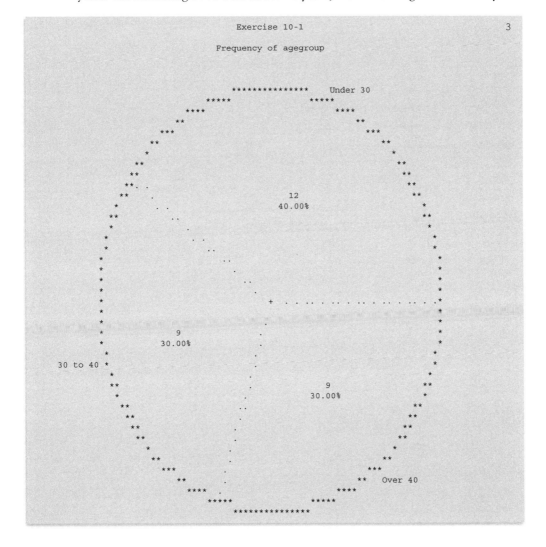

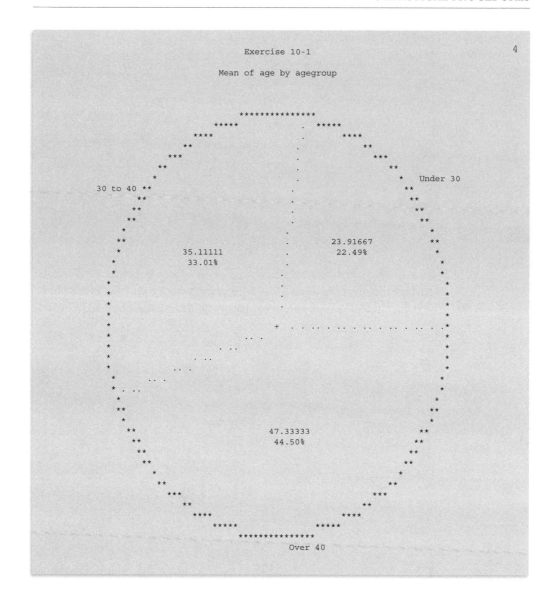

2.

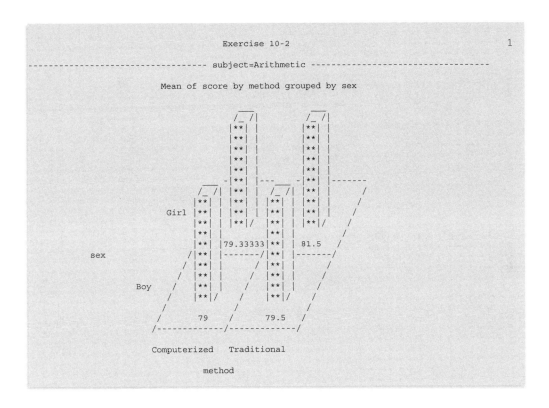

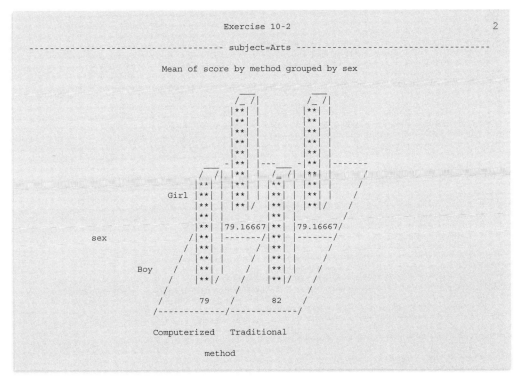

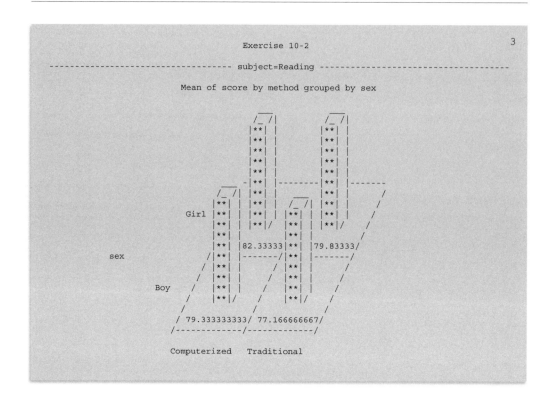

3. a. When PS = 19, a horizontal bar chart is generated displaying the correct frequencies and means, which can be confirmed by the PROC MEANS result.

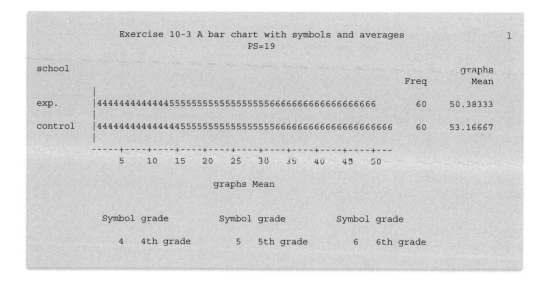

b. When PS = 30, the output shows that experimental school pupils did better over-all than the control school students—this is an incorrect display of the data.

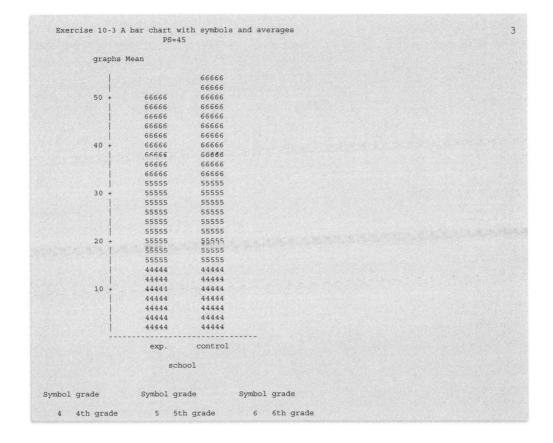

```
Exercise 10-3 A bar chart with symbols and averages                    2
                    PS=30

        graphs Mean

            |       66666
            |       66666       66666
            |       66666       66666
        40 +        66666       66666
            |       55555       66666
            |       55555       55555
            |       55555       55555
        20 +        55555       55555
            |       44444       44444
            |       44444       44444
            |       44444       44444
            -------------------------------
                    exp.        control

                        school


Symbol grade          Symbol grade          Symbol grade

   4   4th grade         5   5th grade         6   6th grade
```

c. When PS = 45, the chart displays the correct means, which can be confirmed by the PROC MEANS result.

```
Exercise 10-3 A bar chart with symbols and averages                    3
                    PS=45

        graphs Mean

            |                   66666
            |                   66666
        50 +        66666       66666
            |       66666       66666
            |       66666       66666
            |       66666       66666
            |       66666       66666
        40 +        66666       66666
            |       66666       66666
            |       66666       66666
            |       66666       66666
            |       55555       55555
        30 +        55555       55555
            |       55555       55555
            |       55555       55555
            |       55555       55555
            |       55555       55555
        20 +        55555       55555
            |       55555       55555
            |       55555       55555
            |       44444       44444
            |       44444       44444
        10 +        44444       44444
            |       44444       44444
            |       44444       44444
            |       44444       44444
            |       44444       44444
            -------------------------------
                    exp.        control

                        school


Symbol grade          Symbol grade          Symbol grade

   4   4th grade         5   5th grade         6   6th grade
```

4. a. When PS = 30, there is a warning message in the log file:

   b. WARNING: A STAR chart for grade cannot be produced;

   c. pagesize, linesize, or proportions do not permit a sufficient radius.

   d. An HBAR chart will be produced instead.

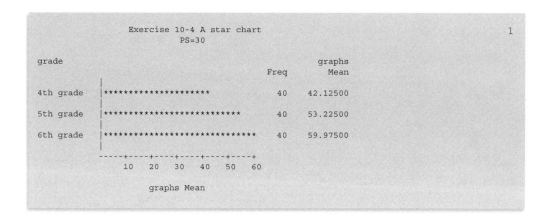

   e. When PS = 45, the star chart generated is smaller than the one generated from PS = 60.

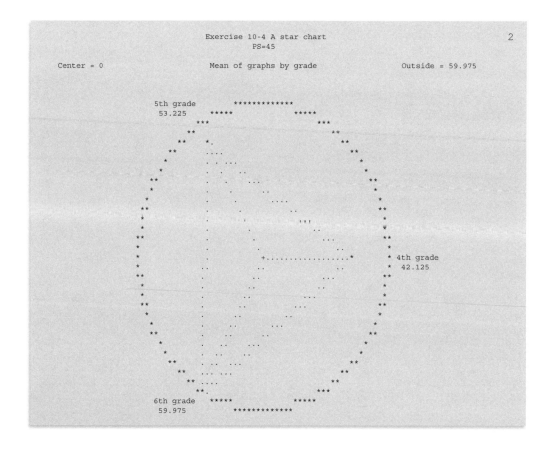

11

Categorical Data Analysis

OBJECTIVE

In this chapter, you will learn how to present and analyze frequency data in a one-way table (based on one categorical variable), two-way table (based on two categorical variables), or three-way table (based on three categorical variables). For two-way and three-way tables, the relationship between the variables can also be described and tested in an inferential framework.

11.1 An Overview of Categorical Data Analysis in the FREQ Procedure

The FREQ procedure is most useful for tabulating frequencies of a categorical variable and for describing and testing the relationship between two, or more, categorical variables. Before proceeding with further details, three terms need to be explained: categorical variable, categories, and categorical data. Suppose that there are 120 male and 80 female members in a country club. In this case, sex (or gender) is a **categorical variable**. There are **two categories** under the sex variable: male and female. The frequencies associated with each category, that is, 120 for males and 80 for females, are **categorical data**. Examples of categorical data or categorical variables abound around you: the enrollment figure of students in an art class over several semesters, tabulation of students' academic standings, the proportion of calories you consume daily in each food category, the presence or absence of HIV in teenagers of various ethnic backgrounds, and so on.

In general, categorical data convey frequency information, proportion information, or the presence or absence of a particular outcome in an observation. According to Stevens' (1946) theory of measurement, categorical variables are measured primarily at the nominal level. Occasionally, variables measured at the ordinal level can also be regarded as categorical variables. For example, in a statistics class, students' grades are assigned according to the normal curve. Hence, approximately 2% of students receive an A, 14% a B, 68% a C, 14% a D, and the remaining 2% an F (those who are to flunk the class). The grading scale, from A (highest) to F (lowest), definitely conveys an ordinal type of information. It can also be treated as a nominal-level categorical variable for which the frequency of students receiving one of these five grades is tabulated and analyzed.

PROC FREQ is well suited to dealing with nominal or ordinal data. It is useful for tabulating frequencies of occurrences in each category, while simultaneously converting frequencies into proportions. To this end, PROC FREQ and PROC CHART are equally useful. There is, however, one major difference between these two procedures: PROC FREQ tabulates frequencies for a one-way, two-way, three-way, or multi-way table, whereas PROC CHART presents tables up to three-way only. A **one-way table** refers to a display of frequencies based on a single categorical variable (Example 11.1). A **two-way table** is a tabulation of joint frequencies of two variables (Example 11.2). Usually, a two-way table uses one dimension, such as columns, to represent one variable and another dimension, such as rows, to represent the second variable. Likewise, a **multi-way table** involves three or more categorical variables (Examples 11.3 and 11.4). A multi-way table is presented on the output as a two-way table for which columns and rows are categories of the last two variables, while the first variable (or the second, . . . , and so on) is fixed at a level or a category.

In addition to summarizing information for categorical variables, PROC FREQ can also be used to test whether frequencies in all categories are equal (Example 11.1). For two-way and multi-way tables, it can be specified to compute the degree of association between two or more categorical variables in a series of indices (Example 11.5). It can test these indices to determine if the null hypothesis of no association is tenable (Examples 11.5 and 11.6). The problem of small samples is dealt with in 2 × 2 tables (Example 11.7). The kappa index of agreement and McNemar's test are demonstrated also for 2 × 2 tables in Example 11.8.

11.2 Examples

Example 11.1 analyzes the raw data file <u>grade.dat</u> that contains grade distributions of several required courses offered in a professional school of a state university. The information was retrieved for the period of 1993 to 1998. There are altogether 248 records in the data set. Students' grades were recorded in one of six categories: A, B, C, D, F, and W, where W stands for "withdrawal". Ethnic background of students was also included. Raw data were grouped data; hence, each record is a summary of information on a course by semester, year, grade, ethnic group, and its frequency. A series of analyses will be performed on the data to reveal facets of the grade distributions that had caused concern—more will be said about this concern later.

Example 11.1 One-Way Frequency Table and Goodness-of-Fit Test

The first attempt in understanding this data set is to tabulate the grade distribution across all courses over the period of 1993 to 1998. To do so, three lines of PROC FREQ statements are needed:

```
/* The following bolded SAS statements establish the SAS data set 'g' */

DATA g;
    INFILE 'd:\data\grade.dat';
    INPUT semester year school $ course $ grade $ race $ 26-42 freq;
    IF grade='R' OR grade='W' OR grade='WX' THEN grade='W';
RUN;


TITLE  'Example 11.1 One-way frequency table and goodness-of-fit test';
TITLE2 'DATA CAME FROM AFFIRMATIVE ACTION OFFICE';


PROC FREQ DATA=g;
    TABLES grade / CHISQ;
    WEIGHT freq;
RUN;
```

The first statement, **PROC FREQ**, initializes the FREQ procedure. The second statement, **TABLES**, tabulates frequencies for the variable <u>grade</u> and carries out a goodness-of-fit test. The goodness-of-fit test of equal proportion is requested by the option **CHISQ** and is defined as

$$\chi^2 = \sum_{\text{all cells}} \frac{(\text{Expected frequency} - \text{Observed frequency})^2}{\text{Expected frequency}},$$

where expected frequency is the total sample size divided by the number of categories. This statistic is called Pearson chi-square. Its sampling distribution is approximately chi-square with the degrees of freedom = the number of categories − 1. The approximation is reasonably good if the expected frequency in each category is at least 10, if the degrees of freedom = 1, or at least 5 if the degrees of freedom exceeds 1.

The third statement, **WEIGHT**, instructs the FREQ procedure to consider the data as *grouped data* in which each data record contains frequency information in the variable <u>freq</u>. Values of the <u>freq</u> variable are the frequency of occurrences of each data record. These frequencies act as weights in determining the total sample size and the size of each category (refer to **Section 11.3** for detailed explanation of this statement).

Output 11.1 One-Way Frequency Table and Goodness-of-Fit Test

```
Example 11.1 One-way frequency table and goodness-of-fit test          1
            DATA CAME FROM AFFIRMATIVE ACTION OFFICE

                        The FREQ Procedure

                                    Cumulative    Cumulative
    grade    Frequency    Percent    Frequency      Percent
    ---------------------------------------------------------------
    A           2025       29.67        2025         29.67
    B           3129       45.85        5154         75.52
    C            940       13.77        6094         89.29
    D            126        1.85        6220         91.14
    F             17        0.25        6237         91.38
    W            588        8.62        6825        100.00


                     Chi-Square Test
                   for Equal Proportions
                   ---------------------
                   Chi-Square    6482.0549
                   DF                    5
                   Pr > ChiSq      <.0001

                   Sample Size = 6825
```

The resulting output reveals six categories of grades, as expected. The majority of students received a B. The next most popular grade was A, followed by C, W, D, and F. The chi-square test of equal proportions is statistically significant ($\chi^2 = 6482.0549$, df = 5, $p < 0.0001$). Therefore, the null hypothesis of equal proportions of students in each of the grade categories is rejected at $\alpha = 0.05$.

- Let's suppose that, in addition to grade, you are also interested in the distribution of race and enrollments in different courses. You may modify Example 11.1 by listing all three variables on the **TABLES** statement, with a space between adjacent variables as follows:

```
PROC FREQ DATA=g;
    TABLES grade race course;
    WEIGHT freq;
RUN;
```

Example 11.2 Two-Way Frequency Tables

Do you want to know the reason for analyzing these data? The Affirmative Action Office of this state university was concerned with grades awarded to students of various racial backgrounds, especially minorities. To shed light on this concern, it was decided that a joint distribution based on both grade and race needed to be examined carefully. This two-way table could be constructed by specifying both variables on the TABLES statement, with an asterisk connecting both:

```
PROC FREQ DATA=g;
    TABLES grade*race;
    WEIGHT freq;
RUN;
```

What if grade distributions were also needed across different courses? This calls for a second two-way table of grade by course. Because the variable grade is specified in both two-way tables, you may combine two TABLES statements into one as follows. The FORMAT= option changes the default format of displaying the cell's information to a numeric format with 13 columns or 13 spaces. In so doing, column headings of the frequency table, such as "AFRICAN AMER." or "ASIAN AMER.", can be on one line.

```
/* See Example 11.1 for the DATA step in creating the SAS data set 'g' */

TITLE  'Example 11.2 Two-way frequency tables';
TITLE2 'DATA CAME FROM AFFIRMATIVE ACTION OFFICE';

PROC FREQ DATA=g;
    TABLES grade*(race course) / FORMAT=13.;
    WEIGHT freq;
RUN;
```

Output 11.2 Two-Way Frequency Tables

```
                    Example 11.2 Two-way frequency tables                    1
                    DATA CAME FROM AFFIRMATIVE ACTION OFFICE

                            The FREQ Procedure

                           Table of grade by race

grade      race

Frequency|
Percent  |
Row Pct  |
Col Pct  |AFRICAN AMER. |ASIAN AMER.  |HISPANIC    |WHITE        |       Total
---------+-------------+-------------+------------+-------------+
A        |          15 |          59 |         23 |        1928 |        2025
         |        0.22 |        0.86 |       0.34 |       28.25 |       29.67
         |        0.74 |        2.91 |       1.14 |       95.21 |
         |        6.44 |       22.96 |      22.77 |       30.93 |
---------+-------------+-------------+------------+-------------+
B        |          80 |         120 |         43 |        2886 |        3129
         |        1.17 |        1.76 |       0.63 |       42.29 |       45.85
         |        2.56 |        3.84 |       1.37 |       92.23 |
         |       34.33 |       46.69 |      42.57 |       46.29 |
---------+-------------+-------------+------------+-------------+
C        |          70 |          50 |         17 |         803 |         940
         |        1.03 |        0.73 |       0.25 |       11.77 |       13.77
         |        7.45 |        5.32 |       1.81 |       85.43 |
         |       30.04 |       19.46 |      16.83 |       12.88 |
---------+-------------+-------------+------------+-------------+
D        |          20 |           9 |          5 |          92 |         126
         |        0.29 |        0.13 |       0.07 |        1.35 |        1.85
         |       15.87 |        7.14 |       3.97 |       73.02 |
         |        8.58 |        3.30 |       4.95 |        1.48 |
---------+-------------+-------------+------------+-------------+
F        |           7 |           0 |          1 |           9 |          17
         |        0.10 |        0.00 |       0.01 |        0.13 |        0.25
         |       41.18 |        0.00 |       5.88 |       52.94 |
         |        3.00 |        0.00 |       0.99 |        0.14 |
---------+-------------+-------------+------------+-------------+
W        |          41 |          19 |         12 |         516 |         588
         |        0.60 |        0.28 |       0.18 |        7.56 |        8.62
         |        6.97 |        3.23 |       2.04 |       87.76 |
         |       17.60 |        7.39 |      11.88 |        8.28 |
---------+-------------+-------------+------------+-------------+
Total              233           257          101          6234          6825
                  3.41          3.77         1.48         91.34        100.00
```

```
                    Example 11.2 Two-way frequency tables              2
                    DATA CAME FROM AFFIRMATIVE ACTION OFFICE

                           The FREQ Procedure

                       Table of grade by course

grade        course

Frequency|
Percent  |
Row Pct  |
Col Pct  |OTHER        |X101         |X202         |      Total
---------+-------------+-------------+-------------+
A        |     1792    |      103    |      130    |     2025
         |    26.26    |     1.51    |     1.90    |    29.67
         |    88.49    |     5.09    |     6.42    |
         |    30.67    |    30.29    |    20.22    |
---------+-------------+-------------+-------------+
B        |     2760    |      139    |      230    |     3129
         |    40.44    |     2.04    |     3.37    |    45.85
         |    88.21    |     4.44    |     7.35    |
         |    47.24    |    40.88    |    35.77    |
---------+-------------+-------------+-------------+
C        |      702    |       68    |      170    |      940
         |    10.29    |     1.00    |     2.49    |    13.77
         |    74.68    |     7.23    |    18.09    |
         |    12.02    |    20.00    |    26.44    |
---------+-------------+-------------+-------------+
D        |       43    |        9    |       74    |      126
         |     0.63    |     0.13    |     1.08    |     1.85
         |    34.13    |     7.14    |    58.73    |
         |     0.74    |     2.65    |    11.51    |
---------+-------------+-------------+-------------+
F        |        5    |        1    |       11    |       17
         |     0.07    |     0.01    |     0.16    |     0.25
         |    29.41    |     5.88    |    64.71    |
         |     0.09    |     0.29    |     1.71    |
---------+-------------+-------------+-------------+
W        |      540    |       20    |       28    |      588
         |     7.91    |     0.29    |     0.41    |     8.62
         |    91.84    |     3.40    |     4.76    |
         |     9.24    |     5.88    |     4.35    |
---------+-------------+-------------+-------------+
Total           5842          340          643        6825
               85.60         4.98         9.42      100.00
```

This output spreads across two pages, each corresponding to one two-way table. The first two-way table is based on the <u>grade</u> distribution by <u>race</u> categories. In this table, six categories of <u>grade</u> are rows, whereas four categories of <u>race</u> are columns. The second two-way table is based on <u>grade</u> by <u>course</u>. Again, six <u>grade</u> categories are rows and two courses (X101, X202), plus all others combined (OTHER), are listed as three columns.

Inside each cell, four numbers are shown. For example, on page 1, the first number listed in the leading upper left corner (the "AFRICAN AMER." by "A" cell) is 15. This number means that 15 African Americans in the entire data set received an "A". However, this number (15) does not necessarily represent 15 distinct individuals because some students took more than one course during the period of this study and could be awarded an A more than once. The second number (0.22 in the same cell) is the percentage of 15 students out of a total sample of 6,825 students. The total sample size is printed at the lower right corner of the table. The third number (0.74) is the row percentage, that is, the percentage of African Americans receiving A out of all A students. So $0.74 = (15/2025) \times 100$, where 2,025 is the row total printed outside the table under the heading "Total" in the first row. The fourth number (6.44) represents the column percentage. The column percentage describes the proportion of African Americans receiving an A out of a total of 233 African Americans. Hence, $6.44 = (15/233) \times 100$.

Can you interpret and verify all cell entries for the group labeled "HISPANIC" and "A"? How about the cell marked "WHITE" and "W"?

The numbers printed outside the table are totals. For example, 2,025, 3,129, and so on are row totals. Likewise, 233, 257, and so on are column totals. The second number directly beneath these numbers is the percentage. Hence, 29.67 is the percentage of 2,025 divided by 6,825 (the total), then multiplied by 100. Can you verify 3.41 and 3.77 under the column headings "AFRICAN AMER." and "ASIAN AMER.," respectively?

Example 11.3 A Three-Way Frequency Table

Now let's get into the nitty-gritty of the data in light of the concern expressed by the Affirmation Action Office. To what extent is the grade distribution of each racial group the same across different courses? To answer this question, we need to further investigate the breakdown of grade distributions based on the variables grade, race, and course, that is, a three-way frequency table. The syntax of a two-way table is easily extended to a three-way table by inserting one more asterisk to link these three variables together.

```
/* See Example 11.1 for the DATA step in creating the SAS data set 'g' */

TITLE  'Example 11.3 A three-way frequency table';
TITLE2 'DATA CAME FROM AFFIRMATIVE ACTION OFFICE';

PROC FREQ DATA=g;
     TABLES course*grade*race / FORMAT=13.;
     WEIGHT freq;
RUN;
```

Since only two-dimensional tables are printed on each page, PROC FREQ prepares the three-way table by a series of two-way tables, each corresponding to one category of the first variable (i.e., <u>course</u>) listed on the **TABLES** statement. According to the output, there are three courses, identified as OTHER, X101, and X202. For each course, a two-way table based on <u>grade</u> and <u>race</u> is presented. Consequently, a total of 3 two-way tables are displayed, one on each page.

Output 11.3 A Three-Way Frequency Table

```
                      Example 11.3 A three-way frequency table                    1
                      DATA CAME FROM AFFIRMATIVE ACTION OFFICE

                             The FREQ Procedure

                           Table 1 of grade by race
                         Controlling for course=OTHER

grade      race

Frequency|
Percent  |
Row Pct  |
Col Pct  |AFRICAN AMER. |ASIAN AMER.   |HISPANIC      |WHITE         |      Total
---------+--------------+--------------+--------------+--------------+
A        |           15 |           51 |           21 |         1705 |       1792
         |         0.26 |         0.87 |         0.36 |        29.19 |      30.67
         |         0.84 |         2.85 |         1.17 |        95.15 |
         |         7.69 |        23.50 |        23.60 |        31.92 |
---------+--------------+--------------+--------------+--------------+
B        |           74 |          103 |           42 |         2541 |       2760
         |         1.27 |         1.76 |         0.72 |        43.50 |      47.24
         |         2.68 |         3.73 |         1.52 |        92.07 |
         |        37.95 |        47.47 |        47.19 |        47.58 |
---------+--------------+--------------+--------------+--------------+
C        |           61 |           45 |           14 |          582 |        703
         |         1.04 |         0.77 |         0.24 |         9.96 |      12.02
         |         8.69 |         6.41 |         1.99 |        82.91 |
         |        31.28 |        20.74 |        15.73 |        10.90 |
---------+--------------+--------------+--------------+--------------+
D        |           12 |            1 |            1 |           29 |         43
         |         0.21 |         0.02 |         0.02 |         0.50 |       0.74
         |        27.91 |         2.33 |         2.33 |        67.44 |
         |         6.15 |         0.46 |         1.12 |         0.54 |
---------+--------------+--------------+--------------+--------------+
F        |            3 |            0 |            0 |            2 |          5
         |         0.05 |         0.00 |         0.00 |         0.03 |       0.09
         |        60.00 |         0.00 |         0.00 |        40.00 |
         |         1.54 |         0.00 |         0.00 |         0.04 |
---------+--------------+--------------+--------------+--------------+
W        |           30 |           17 |           11 |          482 |        540
         |         0.51 |         0.29 |         0.19 |         8.25 |       9.24
         |         5.56 |         3.15 |         2.04 |        89.26 |
         |        15.38 |         7.83 |        12.36 |         9.02 |
---------+--------------+--------------+--------------+--------------+
Total               195            217             89           5341         5842
                   3.34           3.71           1.52          91.42       100.00
```

```
                    Example 11.3 A three-way frequency table              2
                    DATA CAME FROM AFFIRMATIVE ACTION OFFICE

                              The FREQ Procedure

                          Table 2 of grade by race
                        Controlling for course=X101

  grade      race

  Frequency|
  Percent  |
  Row Pct  |
  Col Pct  |AFRICAN AMER. |ASIAN AMER.  |HISPANIC    |WHITE         |    Total
  ---------+--------------+-------------+------------+--------------+
  A        |           0  |          4  |         0  |          99  |    103
           |        0.00  |       1.18  |      0.00  |       29.12  |   30.29
           |        0.00  |       3.88  |      0.00  |       96.12  |
           |        0.00  |      26.67  |      0.00  |       32.04  |
  ---------+--------------+-------------+------------+--------------+
  B        |           3  |          7  |         0  |         129  |    139
           |        0.88  |       2.06  |      0.00  |       37.94  |   40.88
           |        2.16  |       5.04  |      0.00  |       92.81  |
           |       21.43  |      46.67  |      0.00  |       41.75  |
  ---------+--------------+-------------+------------+--------------+
  C        |           4  |          3  |         2  |          59  |     68
           |        1.18  |       0.88  |      0.59  |       17.35  |   20.00
           |        5.88  |       4.41  |      2.94  |       86.76  |
           |       28.57  |      20.00  |    100.00  |       19.09  |
  ---------+--------------+-------------+------------+--------------+
  D        |           1  |          1  |         0  |           7  |      9
           |        0.29  |       0.29  |      0.00  |        2.06  |    2.65
           |       11.11  |      11.11  |      0.00  |       77.78  |
           |        7.14  |       6.67  |      0.00  |        2.27  |
  ---------+--------------+-------------+------------+--------------+
  F        |           0  |          0  |         0  |           1  |      1
           |        0.00  |       0.00  |      0.00  |        0.29  |    0.29
           |        0.00  |       0.00  |      0.00  |      100.00  |
           |        0.00  |       0.00  |      0.00  |        0.32  |
  ---------+--------------+-------------+------------+--------------+
  W        |           6  |          0  |         0  |          14  |     20
           |        1.76  |       0.00  |      0.00  |        4.12  |    5.88
           |       30.00  |       0.00  |      0.00  |       70.00  |
           |       42.86  |       0.00  |      0.00  |        4.53  |
  ---------+--------------+-------------+------------+--------------+
  Total                14            15            2            309         340
                     4.12          4.41         0.59          90.88      100.00
```

Let's now turn our attention to the second two-way table based on the course X101. You would probably have noticed that the layout is strikingly similar to the first two-way table obtained in Output 11.2. Both two-way tables display grade profiles for four ethnic groups of students. The only difference is that the current two-way table draws data from students enrolled in X101 between 1993 and 1998, whereas Output 11.2 is based

```
                   Example 11.3 A three-way frequency table                    3
                   DATA CAME FROM AFFIRMATIVE ACTION OFFICE

                            The FREQ Procedure

                          Table 3 of grade by race
                          Controlling for course=X202

grade      race

Frequency|
Percent  |
Row Pct  |
Col Pct  |AFRICAN AMER. |ASIAN AMER.  |HISPANIC     |WHITE        |     Total
---------+-------------+-------------+-------------+-------------+
A        |           0 |           4 |           2 |         124 |       130
         |        0.00 |        0.62 |        0.31 |       19.28 |     20.22
         |        0.00 |        3.08 |        1.54 |       95.38 |
         |        0.00 |       16.00 |       20.00 |       21.23 |
---------+-------------+-------------+-------------+-------------+
B        |           3 |          10 |           1 |         216 |       230
         |        0.47 |        1.56 |        0.16 |       33.59 |     35.77
         |        1.30 |        4.35 |        0.43 |       93.91 |
         |       12.50 |       40.00 |       10.00 |       36.99 |
---------+-------------+-------------+-------------+-------------+
C        |           5 |           2 |           1 |         162 |       170
         |        0.78 |        0.31 |        0.16 |       25.19 |     26.44
         |        2.94 |        1.18 |        0.59 |       95.29 |
         |       20.83 |        8.00 |       10.00 |       27.74 |
---------+-------------+-------------+-------------+-------------+
D        |           7 |           7 |           4 |          56 |        74
         |        1.09 |        1.09 |        0.62 |        8.71 |     11.51
         |        9.46 |        9.46 |        5.41 |       75.68 |
         |       29.17 |       28.00 |       40.00 |        9.59 |
---------+-------------+-------------+-------------+-------------+
F        |           4 |           0 |           1 |           6 |        11
         |        0.62 |        0.00 |        0.16 |        0.93 |      1.71
         |       36.36 |        0.00 |        9.09 |       54.55 |
         |       16.67 |        0.00 |       10.00 |        1.03 |
---------+-------------+-------------+-------------+-------------+
W        |           5 |           2 |           1 |          20 |        28
         |        0.78 |        0.31 |        0.16 |        3.11 |      4.35
         |       17.86 |        7.14 |        3.57 |       71.43 |
         |       20.83 |        8.00 |       10.00 |        3.42 |
---------+-------------+-------------+-------------+-------------+
Total                24            25            10           584           643
                   3.73          3.89          1.56         90.82        100.00
```

on data from students in all courses. You can apply what you already know about the two-way table to this one and the other two also. Remember, each two-way table on this output is associated with a particular course; thus, it constitutes a subset of the original data.

Presenting one two-way table at a time is the only way PROC FREQ can deal with a display of three-dimensional (3-D) or multidimensional data. This presentation format does not reveal the complex relationship among variables. Instead, you may fall back on PROC CHART (Chapter 10) to expose the intricate structures hidden in the data of higher dimensions; read on. . . .

Example 11.4 Verifying a Three-Way Frequency Table With PROC CHART

To succinctly reveal the relationship among grade, race, and course in a 3-D display, we simplify the original data set. In this simplified data set, (1) students who withdrew from courses, namely, those with the grade "W", are excluded and (2) students' racial backgrounds and grades are both dichotomously coded. Students' racial backgrounds are dichotomously coded either as "Af/H" or "NON_Af/H" in a new variable called race2. "Af/H" means that the student was either an African American or a Hispanic and "NON_Af/H" means an Asian or White student. Likewise, students' grades are simplified to either "ACCEPT" (namely, A, B, or C), or "UNACCEPT" (namely, D or F) in a new variable grade2.

The dichotomous coding of these variables made sense to the Affirmative Action Office because it was concerned with a seemingly higher rate of failing X101 and X202 courses by African American and Hispanic students, but not by Asian American or White students.

Once the data are simplified, percentages of students receiving an acceptable ("ACCEPT") or unacceptable ("UNACCEPT") grade are tabulated by the FREQ procedure for the new race2 variable, year by year for X101, X202, and other courses combined. The result is saved into a SAS data set called percent; it is not shown in the output because of the NOPRINT option. The specification of the **SPARSE** option is to request that all possible combinations of year, course, race2, and grade2 be presented even if a combination does not correspond to an occurrence. Finally, the CHART procedure displays the percentage of students receiving an acceptable grade ("ACCEPT") from each race2 category in each course by each year in a 3-D block format.

```
/* See Example 11.1 for the DATA step in creating the SAS data set 'g' */

DATA pf;
    SET g;
    year=year+1900;
    IF grade ^= 'W';              /* Copies 'g' into 'pf' if student's grade is not 'W' */
    IF race='WHITE' OR race='ASIAN AMER.' THEN race2='NON_Af/H';
      ELSE race2='Af/H';
    IF grade='A' OR grade='B' OR grade='C' THEN grade2='ACCEPT  ';
      ELSE grade2='UNACCEPT';
RUN;
```

```
PROC FREQ DATA=pf;
    TABLES year*course*race2*grade2/OUT=percent SPARSE OUTPCT NOPRINT;
    WEIGHT freq;
RUN;

DATA percent;
    SET percent;
    IF grade2='ACCEPT   ';        /* Copies 'percent' into itself only if the grade is 'ACCEPT' */
RUN;

TITLE  'Example 11.4 Verifying a three-way table with PROC CHART';
TITLE2 'PERCENT of African Americans and Hispanics vs. Asians and Whites with ACCEPT grades';

PROC CHART DATA=percent;
    BLOCK course / GROUP=race2 DISCRETE SUMVAR=pct_row;
    BY year;
RUN;
```

Output 11.4 Verifying a Three-Way Frequency Table With PROC CHART

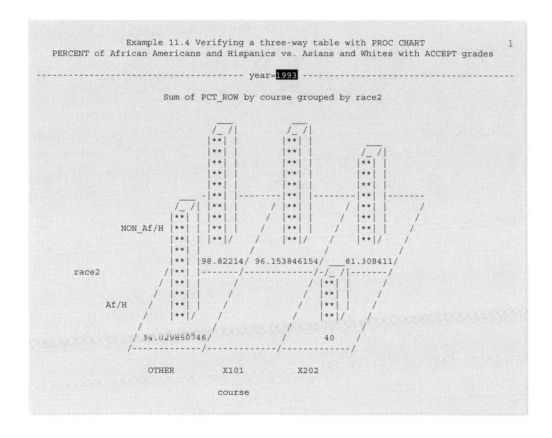

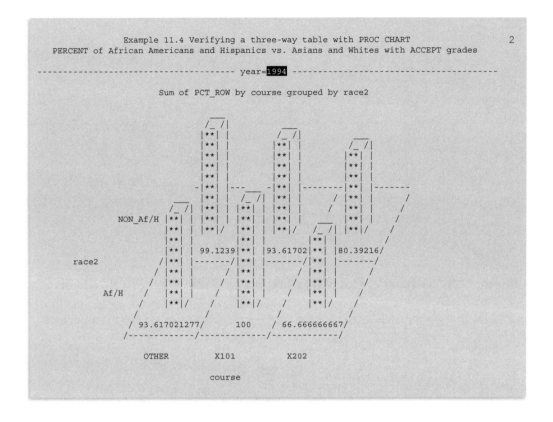

Example 11.4 Verifying a three-way table with PROC CHART
PERCENT of African Americans and Hispanics vs. Asians and Whites with ACCEPT grades

------------------------------------ year=1994 ------------------------------------

Sum of PCT_ROW by course grouped by race2

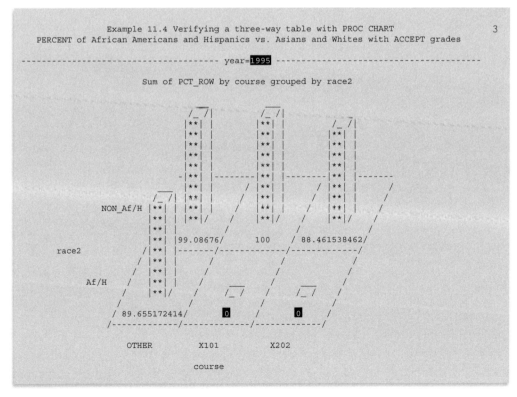

Example 11.4 Verifying a three-way table with PROC CHART
PERCENT of African Americans and Hispanics vs. Asians and Whites with ACCEPT grades

------------------------------------ year=1995 ------------------------------------

Sum of PCT_ROW by course grouped by race2

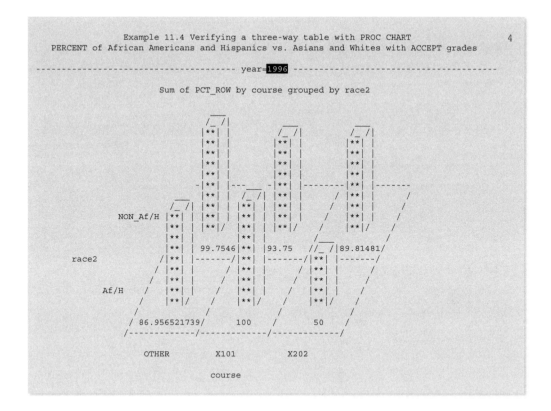

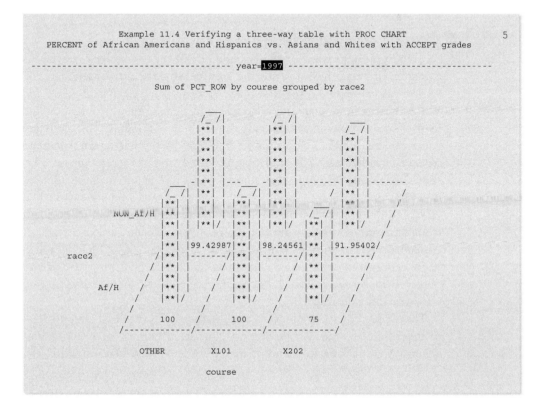

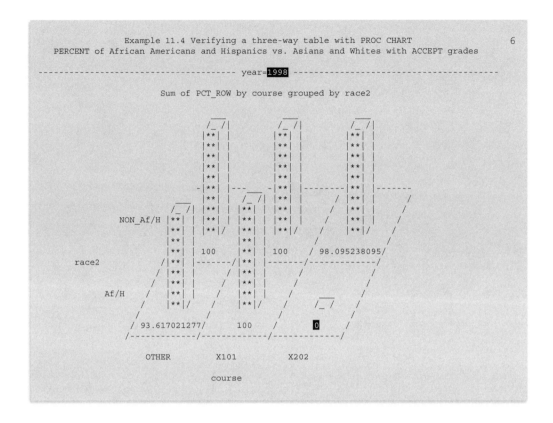

Example 11.4 Verifying a three-way table with PROC CHART

PERCENT of African Americans and Hispanics vs. Asians and Whites with ACCEPT grades

Aren't you impressed by the visual effect of these six block charts? As a matter of fact, they portray the reason why the Affirmative Action Office was contacted in the first place. It was suspected that in X101 and X202, African American and Hispanic students were unfairly graded and their chances of passing these courses were not as good as those of Asian Americans or Whites. According to the pf data set, one African American student enrolled in X101 and two in X202 in 1995. Yet Output 11.4 shows that none of them received an "ACCEPT" grade in these courses. In 1998, one African American and one Hispanic student enrolled in X202 but did not receive an "ACCEPT" grade in this course. It is evident from this output that during the six-year period, a lower percentage of African American and Hispanic students received an "ACCEPT" grade in X202, compared with Asian Americans and Whites. This trend is not observed in X101, contrary to the suspicion of the Affirmative Action Office of this university.

These phenomena are investigated further in Examples 11.5 and 11.6 to determine if indeed there was a consistent pattern of grading bias against African American and Hispanic students in X101 and X202.

Example 11.5 Is There a Relationship Between Two Categorical Variables?

This important question takes the previous six block charts to a higher ground—the data will be subject to statistical tests to determine if the grade distribution is similar across racial groups. To carry out the tests, data are simplified as in Example 11.4, in which the racial identity was recoded either as "Af/H" or "NON_Af/H" in the variable race2. Likewise, students' grades were simplified to either "ACCEPT" (i.e., A, B, or C) or "UNACCEPT" (i.e., D or F) in the variable grade2.

The statistical analyses performed on the two new variables include (1) a chi-square test of independent relationship between these two variables and (2) descriptions of any relationship between them. The chi-square test is particularly suitable for examining whether the grades assigned to the students were dependent on their race. This test is requested by the option **CHISQ** and is defined identically as the chi-square test of goodness-of-fit discussed in Example 11.1:

$$\chi^2 = \sum_{\text{all cells}} \frac{(\text{Expected frequency} - \text{Observed frequency})^2}{\text{Expected frequency}},$$

where expected frequency is requested from the option **EXPECTED**; it is the number of occurrences that would have been expected under the null hypothesis of independence. Numerically, expected frequencies = (row total) × (column total)/(total sample size). When the sample size and the cell size are large enough, the statistic is distributed approximately as a chi-square with degrees of freedom = (the number of columns − 1) × (the number of rows − 1). The approximation gets better with increasing sample sizes. Exactly how large is large enough remains a debatable issue. We will deal with the issue of small samples and small cell sizes in Example 11.7.

The description of any relationship, if it exists, is given by the option **MEASURES** which, as the name implies, provides multiple indices of the strength of the relationship between race2 and grade2.

```
/* See Example 11.1 for the DATA step in creating the SAS data set 'g' */
/* See Example 11.4 for the DATA step in creating the SAS data set 'pf'*/

TITLE  'Example 11.5 Is there a relationship between two categorical variables?';
TITLE2 'DATA CAME FROM AFFIRMATIVE ACTION OFFICE';
TITLE3 'CROSSTABULATION OF grade BY racial status';

PROC FREQ DATA=pf;
    TABLES race2*grade2 / EXPECTED CHISQ MEASURES;
    WEIGHT freq;
RUN;
```

Output 11.5 Is There a Relationship Between Two Categorical Variables?

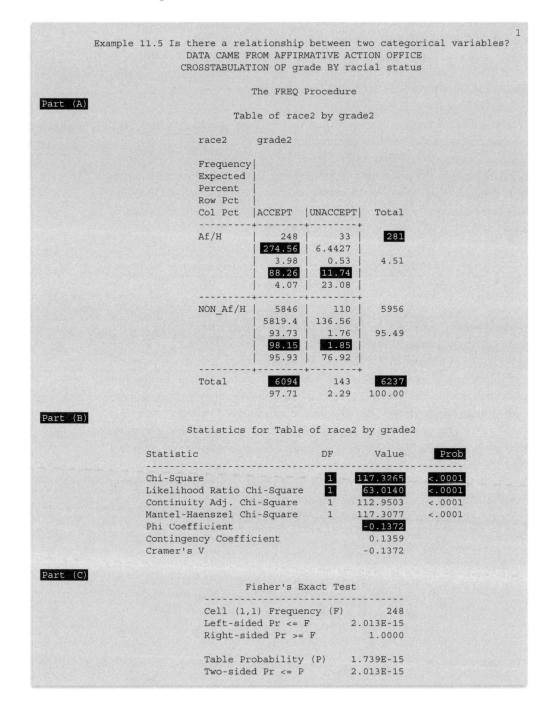

```
                                                                              1
         Example 11.5 Is there a relationship between two categorical variables?
                        DATA CAME FROM AFFIRMATIVE ACTION OFFICE
                       CROSSTABULATION OF grade BY racial status

                                 The FREQ Procedure

Part (A)
                                Table of race2 by grade2

                         race2      grade2

                         Frequency|
                         Expected |
                         Percent  |
                         Row Pct  |
                         Col Pct  |ACCEPT  |UNACCEPT|  Total
                         ---------+--------+--------+
                         Af/H     |    248 |     33 |    281
                                  | 274.56 | 6.4427 |
                                  |   3.98 |   0.53 |   4.51
                                  |  88.26 |  11.74 |
                                  |   4.07 |  23.08 |
                         ---------+--------+--------+
                         NON_Af/H |   5846 |    110 |   5956
                                  | 5819.4 | 136.56 |
                                  |  93.73 |   1.76 |  95.49
                                  |  98.15 |   1.85 |
                                  |  95.93 |  76.92 |
                         ---------+--------+--------+
                         Total         6094     143    6237
                                      97.71    2.29  100.00

Part (B)

                      Statistics for Table of race2 by grade2

             Statistic                       DF       Value      Prob
             ------------------------------------------------------------
             Chi-Square                       1     117.3265    <.0001
             Likelihood Ratio Chi-Square      1      63.0140    <.0001
             Continuity Adj. Chi-Square       1     112.9503    <.0001
             Mantel-Haenszel Chi-Square       1     117.3077    <.0001
             Phi Coefficient                          -0.1372
             Contingency Coefficient                   0.1359
             Cramer's V                               -0.1372

Part (C)
                              Fisher's Exact Test
                      ------------------------------------
                      Cell (1,1) Frequency (F)       248
                      Left-sided Pr <= F        2.013E-15
                      Right-sided Pr >= F          1.0000

                      Table Probability (P)     1.739E-15
                      Two-sided Pr <= P         2.013E-15
```

```
                                                                              2
        Example 11.5 Is there a relationship between two categorical variables?
                   DATA CAME FROM AFFIRMATIVE ACTION OFFICE
                   CROSSTABULATION OF grade BY racial status

                            The FREQ Procedure
Part (D)
                   Statistics for Table of race2 by grade2

            Statistic                              Value      ASE
            ----------------------------------------------------------
            Gamma                                 -0.7522    0.0453
            Kendall's Tau-b                       -0.1372    0.0253
            Stuart's Tau-c                        -0.0170    0.0035

            Somers' D C|R                         -0.0990    0.0193
            Somers' D R|C                         -0.1901    0.0353

            Pearson Correlation                   -0.1372    0.0253
            Spearman Correlation                  -0.1372    0.0253

            Lambda Asymmetric C|R                  0.0000    0.0000
            Lambda Asymmetric R|C                  0.0000    0.0000
            Lambda Symmetric                       0.0000    0.0000

            Uncertainty Coefficient C|R            0.0463    0.0139
            Uncertainty Coefficient R|C            0.0275    0.0084
            Uncertainty Coefficient Symmetric      0.0345    0.0104

Part (E)
                 Estimates of the Relative Risk (Row1/Row2)

          Type of Study                Value       95% Confidence Limits
          --------------------------------------------------------------
          Case-Control (Odds Ratio)    0.1414      0.0939        0.2129
          Cohort (Col1 Risk)           0.8992      0.8615        0.9385
          Cohort (Col2 Risk)           6.3587      4.3915        9.2072

                         Sample Size = 6237
```

Part (A) of Output 11.5 is an ordinary two-way table showing the observed frequency, the expected frequency, the percentage, the row percentage, and the column percentage of each cell's occurrence. For the cell jointly defined by "ACCEPT" and "Af/H", for example, the expected frequency (= 274.56), is calculated from $281 \times 6094/6237 = 274.56$.

Part (B) presents statistical test results to help you determine if there is sufficient evidence to refute the null hypothesis of statistical independence between race2 and grade2. As it turns out, there are more results than you bargained for. The first result is called **Chi-Square**, which stands for Pearson chi-square test with 1 degree of freedom, or $(2 - 1) \times (2 - 1)$. This statistic equals 117.3265, statistically significant at the p level of < 0.0001. The heading **Prob** means p level or **significance level**, as they are often referred to in statistics textbooks.

The second test provided in **Part (B)** is called **Likelihood Ratio Chi-Square**, and it also has 1 degree of freedom and a significant p level of less than 0.0001. Note, however, that this second chi-square value (= 63.0140) and the Pearson chi-square statistic are not identical. The likelihood ratio chi-square test is based on the natural logarithm of observed frequency over expected frequency. The small p level of this test once again provides evidence to reject the null hypothesis of an independent relationship. The alternative hypothesis asserts that there is an association between grades assigned and students' racial background.

You can ignore the fourth chi-square, or the Mantel-Haenszel statistic, because this test requires that both column and row variables be on the ordinal scale. And as the dichotomized race2 in these data is a nominal-level measure, you can discard this result.

The rest of the information in **Part (B)** describes the strength of the relationship between race2 and grade2. The Phi, Contingency, and Cramer's V coefficients are all derived from the Pearson chi-square statistic. The **phi coefficient** would equal zero if there were complete independence between the row and column variables in a 2×2 table. When most data points are classified into the diagonal cells, the phi coefficient is positive. When most data points are in the off-diagonal cells, the phi coefficient is negative. Hence, the current phi coefficient indicates a negative, but moderate, degree of association between race2 and grade2. **Cramer's V** coefficient is also called a rescaled phi coefficient because it is intended to correct for the theoretical upper limit of the squared phi coefficient. Because the upper limit of the squared phi coefficient equals 1 in this case, these two values should be equal. In general, the upper limit of the squared phi coefficient = (the smaller value of rows or of columns) − 1. Thus, for a 2×3 table, the upper limit of the phi coefficient is 1. This upper limit increases to 2 for a 3×3 table or tables with 3 by higher than 3 dimensions.

The second index of association is the **Contingency Coefficient**. This index may be discarded because it could not achieve a maximum value of 1.00 unless there were infinite numbers of rows and columns. So who needs this?

Part (C) presents **Fisher's exact test**, which is part of the default output with the option **CHISQ** for a 2×2 table. Fisher's exact test is suitable for small samples and small cell sizes. A detailed discussion of this exact test is provided in Example 11.7.

Part (D) can be ignored because these indices are suitable only for ordered categories or ordinal variables. It would be far-fetched to assume that the current row and column variables were measured on an ordinal scale.

Part (E) results are unique to 2×2 tables and heath-related studies for which the two rows represent two groups and two columns represent two possible outcomes or traits. In this example, the two groups are "Af/H" (African Americans and Hispanics) students and "NON_Af/H" (Asian Americans and Whites) students and the two outcomes are "ACCEPT" and "UNACCEPT" grades. Thus, the odds ratio is the ratio of 248/33 over

5846/110, which equals 0.14140723, or 0.1414 in Output 11.5. An odds ratio of this magnitude indicates a strong association between the row variable (race2) and the column variable (grade2) because it deviates noticeably from 1, which indicates no association between these two variables. The Cohort (Col1 Risk) = the ratio of 248/281 over 5846/5956, which equals 0.89916882, or 0.8992 in Output 11.5. The Cohort (Col2 Risk) = the ratio of 33/281 over 110/5956, which equals 6.358718861, or 6.3587 in Output 11.5. These two risk measures are suitable for cohort studies in which the two groups are identified on the basis of an explanatory variable (presence or absence of a defect gene, for example). The binary outcome (color blindness or normal vision) is observed for both groups, and their relative risks, as conditioned on both group sizes, are computed for each outcome. Obviously, all three measures in Part (E) are relevant and appropriate for epidemiological or public health studies. Thus, no further explanation is given here.

So what exactly is the relationship? We can say that the association is beyond chance alone, yet it is not strong. The weak association is derived from a comparison of "ACCEPT" and "UNACCEPT" grades earned by African Americans and Hispanics (Af/H) with those earned by Asian Americans and Whites (NON_Af/H). Part (A) results show that 88.26% of African American and Hispanic students earned "ACCEPT" grades, whereas 98.15% of Asian American and White students did so. The differences in these percentages contributed to Pearson and Likelihood ratio chi-square tests being statistically significant at an α level less than 0.0001, and a moderate degree of association between race2 and grade2 (Phi coefficient = −0.1372).

Example 11.6 A Three-Way Frequency Table and Tests

In Example 11.3, we discussed and illustrated the analysis of a three-way frequency table using the grade.dat file. The emphasis in that example was on the description of a three-way relationship between the race of students and the students' grades in several courses taken from 1993 to 1998. We now revisit this three-way table with the purpose of testing if a three-way relationship exists among these three variables.

The statistical test suitable for this purpose is the Cochran-Mantel-Haenszel test. The test is requested by the keyword **CMH**; it is an abbreviation of the names of the three statisticians who invented this test. The **CMH** option is specified on the **TABLES** statement after the slash (/). The data are simplified as in Example 11.4, for which racial identity was recoded either as "Af/H" or "NON_Af/H" into the variable race2. Likewise, students' grades were simplified to either "ACCEPT" (i.e., A, B, or C) or "UNACCEPT" (i.e., D or F) in the variable grade2. The rest of the program is self-explanatory (I hope!).

```
/* See Example 11.1 for the DATA step in creating the SAS data set 'g'  */
/* See Example 11.4 for the DATA step in creating the SAS data set 'pf' */

TITLE  'Example 11.6 A three-way frequency table and tests';
TITLE2 'DATA CAME FROM AFFIRMATIVE ACTION OFFICE';

PROC FREQ DATA=pf;
    TABLES course*race2*grade2 / CMH;
    WEIGHT freq;
RUN;
```

Output 11.6 A Three-Way Frequency Table and Tests

This output is divided into three parts. **Part (A)** presents 3 two-way tables. Each two-way table is a <u>grade2</u> distribution of students classified by <u>race2</u> in a particular course. There were three courses in the data set in total: OTHER, X101, and X202. Therefore, 3 two-way tables are constructed.

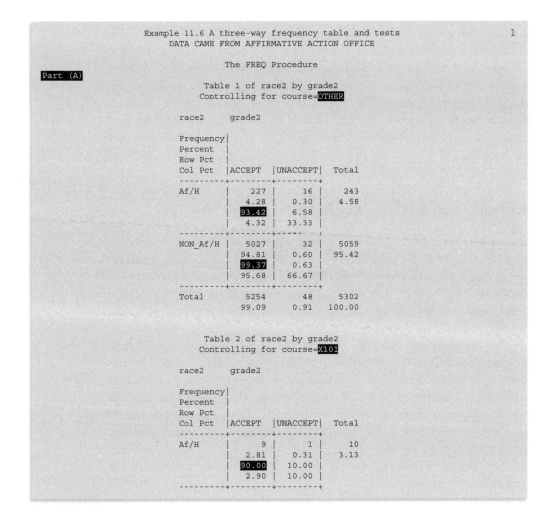

```
              Example 11.6 A three-way frequency table and tests            1
                  DATA CAME FROM AFFIRMATIVE ACTION OFFICE

                          The FREQ Procedure

Part (A)
                       Table 1 of race2 by grade2
                       Controlling for course=OTHER

             race2       grade2

             Frequency|
             Percent  |
             Row Pct  |
             Col Pct  |ACCEPT  |UNACCEPT|  Total
             ---------+--------+--------+
             Af/H     |    227 |     16 |    243
                      |   4.28 |   0.30 |   4.58
                      |  93.42 |   6.58 |
                      |   4.32 |  33.33 |
             ---------+--------+--------+
             NON_Af/H |   5027 |     32 |   5059
                      |  94.81 |   0.60 |  95.42
                      |  99.37 |   0.63 |
                      |  95.68 |  66.67 |
             ---------+--------+--------+
             Total        5254       48     5302
                         99.09     0.91   100.00


                       Table 2 of race2 by grade2
                       Controlling for course=X101

             race2       grade2

             Frequency|
             Percent  |
             Row Pct  |
             Col Pct  |ACCEPT  |UNACCEPT|  Total
             ---------+--------+--------+
             Af/H     |      9 |      1 |     10
                      |   2.81 |   0.31 |   3.13
                      |  90.00 |  10.00 |
                      |   2.90 |  10.00 |
             ---------+--------+--------+
```

```
NON_Af/H |    301 |      9 |    310
         |  94.06 |   2.81 |  96.88
         |  97.10 |   2.90 |
         |  97.10 |  90.00 |
---------+--------+--------+
Total         310       10     320
            96.88     3.13  100.00
```

```
         Table 3 of race2 by grade2
         Controlling for course=X202

race2      grade2

Frequency|
Percent  |
Row Pct  |
Col Pct  |ACCEPT  |UNACCEPT|  Total
---------+--------+--------+
Af/H     |     12 |     16 |     28
         |   1.95 |   2.60 |   4.55
         |  42.86 |  57.14 |
         |   2.26 |  18.82 |
---------+--------+--------+
NON_Af/H |    518 |     69 |    587
         |  84.23 |  11.22 |  95.45
         |  88.25 |  11.75 |
         |  97.74 |  81.18 |
---------+--------+--------+
Total         530       85     615
            86.18    13.82  100.00
```

```
      Example 11.6 A three-way frequency table and tests        2
          DATA CAME FROM AFFIRMATIVE ACTION OFFICE

                  The FREQ Procedure
```

Part (B)

```
           Summary Statistics for race2 by grade2
                  Controlling for course

       Cochran-Mantel-Haenszel Statistics (Based on Table Scores)

     Statistic   Alternative Hypothesis    DF     Value     Prob
     ------------------------------------------------------------------
         1       Nonzero Correlation        1    127.3575   <.0001
         2       Row Mean Scores Differ     1    127.3575   <.0001
         3       General Association        1    127.3575   <.0001
```

Part (C)

```
           Estimates of the Common Relative Risk (Row1/Row2)

  Type of Study   Method            Value     95% Confidence Limits
  ----------------------------------------------------------------------
  Case-Control    Mantel-Haenszel   0.1004    0.0621      0.1623
    (Odds Ratio)  Logit             0.0986    0.0614      0.1584

  Cohort          Mantel-Haenszel   0.8989    0.8621      0.9373
    (Col1 Risk)   Logit             0.9361    0.9058      0.9675

  Cohort          Mantel-Haenszel   6.4440    4.6668      8.8982
    (Col2 Risk)   Logit             6.0469    4.3896      8.3300
```

```
              Breslow-Day Test for
          Homogeneity of the Odds Ratios
          -----------------------------
          Chi-Square                0.9628
          DF                             2
          Pr > ChiSq                0.6179

             Total Sample Size = 6237
```

Part (B) presents a series of tests designed to uncover any relationship among race2, grade2, and course. The first CMH statistic (under the heading "**Statistic 1**") tests the null hypothesis of no linear relationship between race2 and grade2 in any of the three courses against the alternative hypothesis that there is a nonzero correlation in at least one course. This particular test requires both race2 and grade2 to be measured at the ordinal level or higher. Because it is difficult to justify either race2 or grade2 to be an ordinal-level variable, such a test is waived from further interpretation.

The second CMH statistic tests whether the average grade2 score is the same across all race2 categories in all courses. The alternative hypothesis states that at least for one course, the mean score of grade2 is different for diverse race2 categories. Because averaging "ACCEPT" with "UNACCEPT" is an issue here, we assume that an "ACCEPT" grade is a better grade than an "UNACCEPT" grade. Hence, the significant result of the second CMH is worth paying attention to. The significance level (**Prob** on the printout) is less than 0.0001. This means that at least in one course, the means of grade2 are not the same for "NON_Af/H" students as for "Af/H" students. To better understand this rather general conclusion, let's go back to the data and investigate further. In both X101 and X202, the row percentage for "NON Af/H" students receiving an "ACCEPT" grade is much higher than the percentage for "Af/H" students. For X101, the percentage is 97.1% for "NON_Af/H" students receiving an acceptable grade and 90% for "Af/H" students. For X202, the disparity is even greater: 88.25% for "NON_Af/H" and 42.86% for "Af/H" students. In all other courses combined, under "OTHER", the percentages are much closer—99.37% versus 93.42%.

The third CMH statistic is the most generic of all three—it tests the null hypothesis of independence against an alternative hypothesis that a general association between grade2 and race2 exists in at least one course. This test does not require either grade2 or race2 to be measured at the ordinal level or above. Hence, this statistical test is applicable for any three-way table. According to the third statistic (127.3575 with df = 1), the null hypothesis can be rejected at a significance level less than 0.0001. Once again, it is concluded that the data reveal a certain degree of association between the type of grades students received and their race.

The rest of the statistics in **Part (C)**, that is, estimates of relative risks and the **Breslow-Day** test, and so on are primarily related to clinical or epidemiological studies. In those studies, information about a possible cause, such as exposure to disease, is collected either before or after the symptoms have emerged. Subsequently, these statistics are applied to data to establish or refute a link between the cause and the outcome. Because questions addressed by the present data do not lend themselves to these analyses, **Part (C)** is not interpreted.

Example 11.7 What to Do With Small Samples in a 2 × 2 Table

As stated earlier, the chi-square test applied to contingency tables calls for reasonably large expected cell frequencies. In the 2 × 2 case, "large" means 10 or more expected frequencies in each cell. When data fall short of this criterion, there are two alternatives that you can consider: One is to apply the Yates' correction for continuity and the other is to perform an exact test, that is, Fisher's exact test. Both are available in PROC FREQ.

To illustrate these two options, let's turn to the file mydata.dat, which is a small data set, and examine the relation between sex and polpref (political preference). The initial coding of polpref yielded five categories ranging from SD (or Strongly Democrat) to SR (Strongly Republican) with D, I (Independent), and R in between. From these five categories, we first combine SD with D and call the combined category a "NEWD". Likewise, SR and R are clustered into "NEWR". The independents and individuals with missing information on this variable are excluded from the data analysis. The new dichotomous variable is called newpp. With newpp and sex in a 2 × 2 layout, let's investigate any possible link between them via an exact test. Because the mydata.dat data set is based on individual observations, there is no need to include the WEIGHT statement in the SAS program.

The option **EXACT** requests Fisher's exact test to be carried out. The next option, **CHISQ,** computes the Pearson chi-square statistic. Because

```
DATA pp;
    INFILE 'd:\data\mydata.dat';
    INPUT id sex $ age gpa critical polpref $ satv;
    IF polpref='I' or polpref=' ' THEN DELETE;
    IF polpref='SD' or polpref='D' THEN newpp='NEWD';
    IF polpref='SR' or polpref='R' THEN newpp='NEWR';
RUN;

TITLE 'Example 11.7 What to do with small samples in a 2 x 2 table';

PROC FREQ DATA=pp;
    TABLES newpp*sex / EXACT CHISQ EXPECTED;
RUN;
```

some of the expected cell frequencies will be less than 10, the **CHISQ** option automatically calculates a **Continuity Adj. Chi-Square**, which is the chi-square test with Yates' correction. The third option, **EXPECTED**, lists the expected frequency in each cell. Expected frequencies help ensure that either the exact test or the adjusted chi-square is used properly. The 2 × 2 table will display <u>newpp</u> as a row variable and <u>sex</u> as a column variable.

Output 11.7 What to Do With Small Samples in a 2 × 2 Table

```
Example 11.7 What to do with small samples in a 2 × 2 table              1

                    The FREQ Procedure

                 Table of newpp by sex

        newpp        sex

        Frequency|
        Expected |
        Percent  |
        Row Pct  |
        Col Pct  |F        |M        | Total
        ---------+--------+--------+
        NEWD     |      4 |      4 |     8
                 |    3.2 |    4.8 |
                 |  26.67 |  26.67 | 53.33
                 |  50.00 |  50.00 |
                 |  66.67 |  44.44 |
        ---------+--------+--------+
        NEWR     |      2 |      5 |     7
                 |    2.8 |    4.2 |
                 |  13.33 |  33.33 | 46.67
                 |  28.57 |  71.43 |
                 |  33.33 |  55.56 |
        ---------+--------+--------+
        Total           6        9        15
                     40.00    60.00   100.00


        Statistics for Table of newpp by sex

    Statistic                      DF     Value     Prob
    ------------------------------------------------------------
    Chi-Square                      1    0.7143    0.3980
    Likelihood Ratio Chi-Square     1    0.7242    0.3948
    Continuity Adj. Chi-Square      1    0.1004    0.7513
    Mantel-Haenszel Chi-Square      1    0.6667    0.4142
    Phi Coefficient                      0.2182
    Contingency Coefficient              0.2132
    Cramer's V                           0.2182

     WARNING: 100% of the cells have expected counts less
              than 5. Chi-Square may not be a valid test.
```

```
                    Fisher's Exact Test
          -----------------------------------
          Cell (1,1) Frequency (F)             4
          Left-sided Pr <= F              0.9161
          Right-sided Pr >= F             0.3776

          Table Probability (P)           0.2937
          Two-sided Pr <= P               0.6084

                    Sample Size = 15
```

As shown on the output, none of the expected cell frequencies reaches the minimum of 10. Thus, you need to focus on the "**Continuity Adj. Chi-Square**" statistic with Yates' correction. According to its value (0.1004), the probability of obtaining this large or an even larger value is very likely (0.7513). Likewise, the two-tailed Fisher's exact test yields a probability of 0.6084, printed under the heading of **Two-sided Pr <= P**, signaling a strong possibility of obtaining these results under the null hypothesis. Thus, you may conclude that the current data do not render sufficient evidence to reject the null hypothesis of independence between <u>gender</u> and <u>newpp</u>.

• Fisher's exact test is a statistical test of association between two categorical variables when sample sizes are small or the contingency table is sparse. It can be carried out as either a one-tailed or two-tailed test. The two-tailed test is used when you wish to entertain an alternative hypothesis that states that the proportion of female Democrats is either *higher* or *lower* than that of female Republicans. Because there are only two genders being considered in this 2 × 2 table, it is sufficient to concentrate on only one gender group. The one-tailed test marked by **Left-sided** should be reported when the alternative hypothesis implies that the obtained frequency in the leading upper left corner of the table, that is, **4** in the (1,1) cell, is the maximal value. In other words, the proportion of female Democrats in the population is *lower* than that of female Republicans. Likewise, the one-tailed test marked **Right-sided** should be reported when the alternative hypothesis implies that the current value (4) is the minimal value. In other words, the proportion of female Democrats is *higher* than that of female Republicans. Both one-tailed and two-tailed probabilities are derived from permutations of 2 × 2 tables with the same marginals as those observed, namely, 8, 7, 9, and 6 in this case. The sampling distribution of Fisher's exact test is a hypergeometric distribution.

• Fisher's exact test can also be performed for tables with more than two rows or two columns, as long as the percentage of cells with 5 or fewer expected frequencies is no more than 20%. Whenever the Fisher's exact test is performed on tables larger than 2 × 2, the significance level (**Pr** on the printout) is given for two-tailed tests only. Because it is both difficult and time-consuming to generate all possible cell frequencies that indicate a linearly increasing (or decreasing) pattern among multiple groups in order to calculate a one-tailed p level, only two-tailed p levels are given.

- The **Continuity Adj. Chi-Square** statistic is a chi-square approximation to the binomial test statistic in the squared form. It is based on Yates' correction for continuity because it uses a continuous distribution (chi-square) to approximate a discrete distribution (binomial). This test is recommended for contingency tables with df = 1 and with one or more expected cell frequencies less than 5. Because the correction can result in a conservative test, its use sparks debates among statisticians.

Example 11.8 Agreement in a 2 × 2 Table

This example addresses the consistency of classification in a 2 × 2 table. The question entertained is whether students who scored high on the SAT-Verbal test also tend to accumulate a high GPA, and vice versa. High SAT-Verbal is defined as 500 points or higher. High GPA is 3.00 or higher. From the mydata.dat file, the original gpa and satv are converted to dichotomous variables using, respectively, 3.00 and 500 as cutoffs. The new, dichotomized variables are called grade and verbal, respectively.

To explore the relationship between these two variables, the option **AGREE** is invoked on the **TABLES** statement. This option does two things: (1) It computes the **kappa** index of agreement and (2) it performs the McNemar's test to examine if row and column variables are correlated. The option **PLCORR** requests the calculation of a tetrachoric correlation for the 2 × 2 table. Tetrachoric correlations are suitable for ordered dichotomous variables, such as grade and verbal, whose underlying distributions are continuous and assumed to be normal. SAS calculates the maximum likelihood estimate of this correlation based on the Pearson product-moment correlation coefficient. The **MAXITER=** option sets the maximum number of iterations allowed for obtaining the maximum likelihood estimate.

```
DATA agree;
    INFILE 'd:\data\mydata.dat';
    INPUT id sex $ age gpa critical polpref $ satv;
    IF gpa=. or satv=. THEN DELETE;
    IF gpa >= 3.00 THEN grade='high';
    IF gpa < 3.00 THEN grade='low';
    IF satv >= 500 THEN verbal='high';
    IF satv < 500 THEN verbal='low';
RUN;

TITLE 'Example 11.8 Agreement in a 2 x 2 table';
PROC FREQ DATA=agree;
    TABLES grade*verbal / AGREE PLCORR MAXITER=25;
RUN;
```

Output 11.8 Agreement in a 2 × 2 Table

```
          Example 11.8 Agreement in a 2 x 2 table                    1
                    The FREQ Procedure
                  Table of grade by verbal

          grade      verbal

          Frequency|
          Percent  |
          Row Pct  |
          Col Pct  |high    |low     | Total
          ---------+--------+--------+
          high     |      6 |      0 |      6
                   |  35.29 |   0.00 |  35.29
                   | 100.00 |   0.00 |
                   |  54.55 |   0.00 |
          ---------+--------+--------+
          low      |      5 |      6 |     11
                   |  29.41 |  35.29 |  64.71
                   |  45.45 |  54.55 |
                   |  45.45 | 100.00 |
          ---------+--------+--------+
          Total          11        6       17
                      64.71    35.29   100.00


          Statistics for Table of grade by verbal

    Statistic                            Value        ASE
    -----------------------------------------------------
    Gamma                               1.0000     0.0000
    Kendall's Tau-b                     0.5455     0.1320
    Stuart's Tau-c                      0.4983     0.1560

    Somers' D C|R                       0.5455     0.1501
    Somers' D R|C                       0.5455     0.1501

    Pearson Correlation                 0.5455     0.1320
    Spearman Correlation                0.5455     0.1320
    Tetrachoric Correlation             0.9997     0.0000

    Lambda Asymmetric C|R               0.1667     0.5046
    Lambda Asymmetric R|C               0.1667     0.5046
    Lambda Symmetric                    0.1667     0.4436

    Uncertainty Coefficient C|R         0.3133     0.1217
    Uncertainty Coefficient R|C         0.3133     0.1217
    Uncertainty Coefficient Symmetric   0.3133     0.1180


          Estimates of the Relative Risk (Row1/Row2)

    Type of Study            Value      95% Confidence Limits
    ------------------------------------------------------------
    Cohort (Col1 Risk)       2.2000       1.1515       4.2031

       One or more risk estimates not computed --- zero cell.
```

```
Example 11.7 Agreement in a 2 × 2 table                          2

        The FREQ Procedure

Statistics for Table of grade by verbal

        McNemar's Test
------------------------------
Statistic (S)    5.0000
DF                    1
Pr > S           0.0253


        Simple Kappa Coefficient
-------------------------------------------
Kappa                      0.4586
ASE                        0.1710
95% Lower Conf Limit       0.1234
95% Upper Conf Limit       0.7938

        Sample Size = 17
```

According to page 2 of the output, McNemar's test of consistent classifications is 5.0000 and is significant at the 0.0253 level. Thus, you may conclude that it is not by chance alone that 12 individuals (or 70.58% out of 17 observations) scored either "HIGH, HIGH" or "LOW, LOW" on both grade and verbal and only 5 (or 29.41%) scored otherwise.

In terms of degree of consistent classifications, the **kappa** index equals 0.4586, and its 95% confidence limits range from 0.1234 to 0.7938. The kappa index is a simple way of showing how both grade and verbal consistently classify individuals into either (HIGH, HIGH) or (LOW, LOW) cells in the table, compared with what could have resulted from chance, given the fixed marginals. If there is 100% agreement, kappa equals +1. If the observed cell frequencies along the (HIGH, HIGH) and (LOW, LOW) diagonals are equal to or less than what could be expected from the marginals, kappa may take on a value from 0 to −1. So a kappa less than 0 indicates a lack of agreement. For the current data set, both kappa and McNemar's test statistic lead to the rejection of the null hypothesis of no association between grade and verbal. Furthermore, the tetrachoric correlation ($=$ 0.9997) also indicates a strong relationship between the dichotomized and ordered SAT-Verbal scores and GPA.

• McNemar's test is approximately distributed as a chi-square under large samples. As long as each expected cell frequency is at least 10, it is appropriate to rely on the chi-square approximation. Otherwise, the descriptive kappa index and Fisher's exact test should be reported instead.

• The kappa index has other variations available from the FREQ procedure. These include weighted kappa, overall weighted kappa, and test of equal kappas. For details on how to request and interpret these, consult the *SAS/STAT 9.1 User's Guide* (SAS Institute Inc., 2004d), available online from www.sas.com.

- If a frequency table is square and larger than 2 × 2, a test of consistent classifications can still be performed with the **AGREE** option. In this case, PROC FREQ computes the Bowker test for the printout. The Bowker test is an extension of McNemar's test; it examines the same type of symmetry as was demonstrated in Example 11.7. Under large samples, the Bowker test has a sampling distribution of chi-square. Again, large samples can be defended as long as each expected cell frequency is at least 5.

11.3 How to Write the PROC FREQ Codes

Several PROC FREQ statements have been demonstrated in the previous eight examples. These and other useful statements are summarized below:

PROC	FREQ	DATA= *sas_dataset_name*;
	TABLES	*table_specifications < / options>*;
	WEIGHT	*weighting_variable*;
	BY	*classification_variable(s)*;
	OUTPUT	OUT= *sas_dataset_name statistic_list*;

The **PROC FREQ** statement initializes the procedure and specifies the data set to be analyzed. The **TABLES** statement is the core of this procedure. It is divided into two parts: The first is necessary and appears before the slash (/); the second is optional and appears after the slash. What is specified before the slash defines the complexity and appearance of a contingency table. Let's illustrate these specifications:

One-way tables   `TABLES x y z; or TABLES a  z,`

Two-way tables   `TABLES x*y;`
                    `TABLES x*(y z);      [ same as TABLES x*y x*z;]`
                    `TABLES (x--z)*a;     [ same as TABLES x*a y*a z*a;]`
                    `TABLES (a b c)*x;    [ same as TABLES a*x b*x c*x;]`
                    `TABLES (a b)*(x y); [ same as TABLES a*x a*y b*x b*y;]`

- Note that the first variable appearing on the TABLES specification specifies the row variable and the second variable specifies the column variable.

Three-way tables   `TABLES x* y* z;`

- The first variable listed in a three-way table is the variable controlled or fixed, whereas the remaining two variables define rows and columns of a two-way table. Thus, a three-way table specification yields a series of two-way tables. The number of two-way tables equals the levels (or categories) of the first variable.

Options that appear after the slash include AGREE, CHISQUARE (or CHISQ), CMH, EXACT, EXPECTED, MEASURES, PLCORR, MAX-ITER=, FORMAT=, OUT=, SPARSE, NOPRINT, plus ALL, OUTEXPECT, and OUTPCT. All have been demonstrated in Examples 11.1 through 11.8. The last seven options are explained below:

FORMAT=   This option changes the default format of displaying the cell's information. For example, `FORMAT=13.` specifies a numeric format with 13 columns or 13 spaces; refer back to Example 11.2 for an illustration.

OUT=   This option specifies an output data set that contains variable values and frequency, or frequency counts and percentages of cross-tabulations in two-way or higher-dimensional tables.

SPARSE   This option requests that all possible combinations of variable categories be listed even if a combination does not occur in data.

NOPRINT   This option suppresses the display of tables.

ALL   This option generates all tests and measures given separately by **CHISQ, CMH,** and **MEASURES.** So it is a three-in-one, highly efficient option.

OUTEXPECT   This option requests that expected cell frequencies be included in an output data set. It results in a new variable called **EXPECTED.** The output data set is specified by the **OUT=** option.

OUTPCT   Similar to the option **OUTEXPECT,** this option requests that three percentages be included in the output data set. These three are **PCT_COL, PCT_ROW,** and **PCT_TABL,** which refer to, respectively, column percentage, row percentage, and table percentage from a two-way layout. The output data set is specified by the **OUT=** option.

The **WEIGHT** statement is necessary in analyzing grouped data. This statement lists the name of a variable that represents the frequency of occurrence of each data value. As a result, PROC FREQ adjusts the counting of the total sample size and of cell sizes. See Example 11.1 for an illustration of the WEIGHT statement.

The **BY** statement is used to carry out subgroup analyses. Based on the levels (or categories) of the BY variable, PROC FREQ divides the data set into subgroups. Then it constructs contingency tables or tests null hypotheses within each subgroup. If more than one BY variable is specified, all possible combinations of the BY variables' values are used in dividing up the entire data set. Be sure to presort the data set in the ascending order of all BY variables, if the BY statement is included in the FREQ procedure. Presorting a data set can be accomplished with the SORT procedure.

The **OUTPUT** statement exports the results of PROC FREQ to an output SAS data set. The output data set is specified by the OUT= option. You may select all or a portion of results to be included in this output data set. Results generated by those options specified on the TABLES statement are those you can save into this output data set. So **CHISQ, CMH, EXACT,** and **MEASURES** are keywords that appear after the specification of OUT=. Furthermore, you can specify **KAPPA** (simple unweighted kappa), **PCORR** (the Pearson correlation coefficient), **PHI** (the phi coefficient), **N** (the number of nonmissing observations per table), or **NMISS** (the number of missing observations per table), to be part of the output data set. These options plus **EXPECTED, PCT_COL, PCT_ROW,** and **PCT_TABL** provide a comprehensive list of statistics to be saved into a SAS output data set.

11.4 Tips

- How to handle missing or invalid data

Missing data, by default, are not included in any of the PROC FREQ tables or the computation of any statistic. The count of missing observations is not printed beneath each table by default. This default can be overridden with the option **MISSPRINT**. Likewise, missing observations can be incorporated into computation of statistics by the option **MISSING**. Both appear after the slash (/) on the TABLES statement as shown below:

```
PROC FREQ;
     TABLES variables / MISSPRINT MISSING;
```

- What to do with small sample sizes or low cell frequencies

The issue of small sample size is of a secondary concern if you are only interested in reporting or describing patterns of frequencies or degrees of association among categorical variables. This becomes an issue when the frequency table is subject to a statistical test against the null hypothesis of a certain form. All statistical tests performed by PROC FREQ are approximate tests, except for Fisher's exact test. These approximate tests call for reasonably large *expected* cell frequencies. By SAS standards, reasonably large expected cell frequencies mean that each expected cell frequency is at least 1 and at least 80% of cells have 5 or larger expected frequencies. A more conservative criterion is this: For df = 1, the minimal expected frequency is 10; for df $\geq$ 2, the minimal expected cell frequency is 5. If data do not meet these recommendations, you should consider the following alternatives:

1. Switch to Fisher's exact test (also called the Freeman-Halton test for the general R × C tables). The exact test is exact, and PROC FREQ performs the tedious task of determining the p value for one-tailed tests as well as for two-tailed tests. The only drawback with Fisher's exact test is that its computation can be laborious for tables larger than 2 × 2 or sample sizes in hundreds or more.

2. Collapse a few columns or rows together. If, for example, under race on a questionnaire, the "White" category was checked by the majority of respondents, and all other categories were checked by very few. Before data analysis begins, you may combine the low-count categories into one and label it as "Non-White".

3. Continue to collect data until the recommended minimum expected cell frequency is satisfied.

Regardless of which approach you ultimately take, remember that the minimum is applied to the *expected* cell frequencies, not the observed.

- How to use ODS with the FREQ procedure

Table 11.1 presents selected ODS table names for the FREQ procedure and their descriptions.

These ODS table names and corresponding details are tracked in the Log window if you ask for them with the ODS TRACE ON statement in the SAS program. You may turn off this tracking feature with the ODS TRACE OFF statement, also in the SAS program.

Table 11.1   Selected ODS Table Names and Descriptions for the FREQ Procedure

ODS Table Name	Description	Option on the TABLES Statement
OneWayFreqs	One-way table	(default for One-way)
CrossTabFreqs	Cross-tabulation table	(default for n-way)
OneWayChiSq	One-way chi-square test	CHISQ
ChiSq	Chi-square tests	CHISQ (n-way)
Measures	Measures of association	MEASURES

ODS Table Name	Description	Option on the TABLES Statement
FishersExact	Fisher's exact test	EXACT or CHISQ (2×2 table)
CMH	Cochran-Mantel-Haenszel statistics	CMH
CommonRelRisks	Common relative risks	CMH ($k \times 2 \times 2$ table)
BreslowDayTest	Breslow-Day test	CMH ($k \times 2 \times 2$ table)
RelativeRisks	Relative risk estimates	AGREE (2×2 table)
McNemarsTest	McNemar's test of consistent classifications	AGREE (2×2 table)
SimpleKappa	Simple kappa coefficient	AGREE (2×2 table)

```
ODS TRACE ON;
PROC FREQ DATA=g;
    TABLES grade / CHISQ;
    WEIGHT freq;
RUN;
ODS TRACE OFF;
RUN;
```

After executing the program, the following will appear in the Log window listing all ODS table names for the PROC FREQ output:

```
Output Added:
- - - - - - - - - - - -
Name:      OneWayFreqs
Label:     One-Way Frequencies
Template:  Base.Freq.OneWayFreqs
Path:      Freq.grade.OneWayFreqs
- - - - - - - - - - - -

Output Added:
- - - - - - - - - - - -
Name:      OneWayChiSq
Label:     One-Way Chi-Square Test
Template:  Base.Freq.StatFactoid
Path:      Freq.grade.OneWayChiSq
- - - - - - - - - - - -
```

Based on the list of ODS table names, you may select certain results to be displayed in the Output window. For example, the following program selects the chi-square test result of Example 11.1 to be included in the output:

```
ODS SELECT Freq.grade.OneWayChiSq;
PROC FREQ DATA=g;
     TABLES grade / CHISQ;
     WEIGHT freq;
RUN;
```

Likewise, you may select certain result(s) to be exported as a SAS data set. For example, the following program exports the one-way table of Example 11.1 to the SAS data set <u>freqtable</u>:

```
ODS OUTPUT  OneWayFreqs = freqtable;
PROC FREQ DATA=g;
     TABLES grade / CHISQ;
     WEIGHT freq;
RUN;
```

Furthermore, you may select certain results to be saved in file formats other than the SAS standard output. For example, the following program saves the output of Example 11.1 in HTML format in its default style:

```
ODS HTML BODY = 'd:\result\Example11_1Body.html'
         CONTENTS = 'd:\result\Example11_1TOC.html'
         PAGE = 'd:\result\Example11_1Page.html'
         FRAME = 'd:\result\Example11_1Frame.html';
PROC FREQ DATA=g;
     TABLES grade / CHISQ;
     WEIGHT freq;
RUN;
ODS HTML CLOSE;
RUN;
```

For additional information about ODS features, refer to *SAS 9.1.3 Output Delivery System. User's Guide* (SAS Institute Inc., 2006c) and *Base SAS 9.1.3 Procedures Guide* (SAS Institute Inc., 2006a) or the online documentation at www.sas.com.

11.5 Summary

This chapter demonstrates several strategies for describing categorical data and examining implications derived from them. Specifically, you have learned how to organize data by frequencies of observations according to a single categorical variable (one-way tables), two categorical variables (two-way tables), or three categorical variables (three-way tables). These frequencies can also be expressed as percentages, based on totals of each row (row percentage), or totals of each column (column percentage), or totals of the entire table (table percentage or simply percentage).

For two-way and three-way tables, descriptive indices are introduced to quantify the degree of association between row and column variables. These indices measure either a linear correlation or the degree of a general association (or agreement) between two variables.

When samples are sufficiently large, data can be subjected to statistical tests of various null hypotheses. This chapter illustrated at least four tests: The Pearson chi-square test of a general association between row and column variables in a two-way table, Fisher's exact test for 2 × 2 tables, McNemar's test of change in proportions in 2 × 2 tables, and the Cochran-Mantel-Haenszel test of a general association.

If data meet the recommended minimum for expected cell frequencies, the chi-square distribution is an acceptable approximation to the sampling distribution of the Pearson chi-square test statistic, McNemar's test statistic, and the Cochran-Mantel-Haenszel test statistic. Otherwise, Fisher's exact test or the adjusted chi-square test should be reported and interpreted.

Of particular interest is the treatment of 2 × 2 tables. For data that can fit into a simple 2 × 2 table, a series of analyses are available, including the phi coefficient, the kappa index, Fisher's exact test, McNemar's test, the Pearson chi-square test, and so on. All these can be extended to square tables of higher dimensions, such as 3 × 3, 4 × 4, and so on, provided that you exchange the name of McNemar's test for the Bowker test.

11.6 Exercises

1. Given data from Exercise 1 of Chapter 10,

   a. produce one-way frequency tables to explain how potential buyers are different in their preferences for the three attributes of a car.

   b. describe the relationship between age-groups based on the three categories defined in Exercise 1(c) of Chapter 10 and three attributes of a car.

2. At the end of a semester, an instructor needed to summarize course evaluations provided by his 10 students. There were 10 items, each answered by one of five ratings: 1 = strongly disagree, 2 = disagree, 3 = no idea, 4 = agree, and 5 = strongly agree. Data set <u>eval</u> was typed by a secretary. It contains students' responses, where a period (.) means a missing response:

	Data set eval
student	(q1-q10) responses
1	4435534443
2	2344235424
3	5454443554
4	3244431324
5	4323489435
6	3412343..4
7	5455335434
8	2322438123
9	.4.3452332
10	4544347345

Think of a way to help the instructor prepare an evaluation report that includes frequency counts of 1 to 5 responses, missing responses, and invalid responses for all items. In addition, the report should also contain the average, the lowest, the highest, variance, and standard deviation of ratings for each item.

3. A group of residents at the Betty Ford Center were recently surveyed and their demographic information is as follows:

Data set a						
NAME	Sex	AGE	ROOM	S.E.S	INCOME	(in $1000)
Allen	M	28	122	H	9.6	
Joyce	F	42	412	M	7.4	
Chuck	M	34	213	L	2.3	
Kurt	M	40	216	M	5.8	
Dan	M	68	101	H	8.8	
Bob	M	37	135	M	6.3	
Fran	F	39	430	L	1.3	
Tom	M	54	222	M	4.7	
Don	M	25	118	M	6.0	
Clark	M	51	104	H	8.4	
Evelyn	F	58	404	H	10.2	
Rebecca	F	43	423	M	7.1	
Jack	M	47	117	M	5.2	
Doug	M	28	240	H	9.2	
Tim	M	36	231	M	6.4	
Susan	F	31	302	M	4.3	
Sam	M	65	108	L	3.3	
Myrtle	F	24	336	M	5.7	
Rex	M	27	115	H	8.2	
Nancy	F	20	425	M	5.5	

a. Assume that the first digit of a room number represents the floor level. For instance, Room 122 is a room on the first floor and Room 412 is on the fourth floor. Sort the data set first by the floor level of rooms, then by sex of residents. Use the chi-square statistic to test the relationship between residents' sex and the floor level of their rooms.

    b. Use the chi-square statistic to test the relationship between SES and sex of residents.

    c. Use the chi-square statistic to test the relationship between SES of residents and the floor level of their rooms.

    d. Can you infer the three-way relationship from answers to (a), (b), and (c) above? If so, can this inference be supported by a statistical test available from PROC FREQ?

4. Suppose that you are interested in how female and male voters supported either Republican or Democratic presidents in the last presidential election. Data based on 200 cases show the following pattern:

	Republican	Democrat
Female voters	20	80
Male voters	50	50

Write a program to reveal the relationship, if there is any, between the <u>gender</u> of voters and <u>party</u> affiliations of presidential candidates.

5. Given the following two-way classification based on <u>educational levels</u> (1 to 6) of nine job applicants and their <u>job</u> performance (high, medium, low), what conclusion can be made in terms of educational level and job performance, in light of the data and PROC FREQ results?

Data:

job	educ = 1	2	3	4	5	6
high	2	0	0	0	0	0
medium	0	1	2	0	0	0
low	0	0	0	1	2	1

6. As stated earlier, Fisher's exact test statistic follows a hypergeometric distribution. Thus, given a 2 × 2 table with cell frequencies denoted as a, b, c, and d below, the probability of obtaining this exact result is p, according to the hypergeometric distribution, where C stands for the number of combinations of selecting a out of $(a + b)$, for example.

	F	M	Total
NEWD	a	b	a + b
NEWR	c	d	c + d
	a + c	b + d	n

$$p = \frac{C_a^{a+b} \times C_c^{c+d}}{C_{a+c}^n}$$

Given this formula, verify the Left-sided probability (0.9161) and the Right-sided probability (0.3776) for the 2 × 2 table result in Output 11.7.

11.7 Answers to Exercises

1. a.

```
                          Exercise 11-1                                      1

                       The FREQ Procedure

                                      Cumulative    Cumulative
        color    Frequency    Percent    Frequency     Percent
        ------------------------------------------------------------
        Red            8      26.67            8       26.67
        Black         14      46.67           22       73.33
        White          8      26.67           30      100.00

                                      Cumulative    Cumulative
         size    Frequency    Percent    Frequency     Percent
        ------------------------------------------------------------
        Subcompact    10      33.33           10       33.33
        Compact       11      36.67           21       70.00
        Mid-size       9      30.00           30      100.00

                                      Cumulative    Cumulative
         type    Frequency    Percent    Frequency     Percent
        ------------------------------------------------------------
        2-doors       13      43.33           13       43.33
        4-doors        3      10.00           16       53.33
        5-doors       14      46.67           30      100.00
```

b.

```
                     Exercise 11-1                                      2

                  The FREQ Procedure

                Table of age by color

     age        color

     Frequency|
     Percent  |
     Row Pct  |
     Col Pct  |Red      |Black    |White    |   Total
     ---------+--------+--------+--------+
     Under 30 |      6 |      3 |      3 |     12
              |  20.00 |  10.00 |  10.00 |  40.00
              |  50.00 |  25.00 |  25.00 |
              |  75.00 |  21.43 |  37.50 |
     ---------+--------+--------+--------+
```

```
 30 to 40 |      2 |      5 |      2 |      9
          |   6.67 |  16.67 |   6.67 |  30.00
          |  22.22 |  55.56 |  22.22 |
          |  25.00 |  35.71 |  25.00 |
 ---------+--------+--------+--------+
  Over 40 |      0 |      6 |      3 |      9
          |   0.00 |  20.00 |  10.00 |  30.00
          |   0.00 |  66.67 |  33.33 |
          |   0.00 |  42.86 |  37.50 |
 ---------+--------+--------+--------+
    Total        8       14        8       30
               26.67    46.67    26.67   100.00


      Statistics for Table of age by color

 Statistic                    DF      Value      Prob
 ---------------------------------------------------------
 Chi-Square                    4      7.2768    0.1220
 Likelihood Ratio Chi-Square   4      9.3151    0.0537
 Mantel-Haenszel Chi-Square    1      3.1522    0.0758
 Phi Coefficient                      0.4925
 Contingency Coefficient              0.4418
 Cramer's V                           0.3483


 WARNING: 89% of the cells have expected counts less
          than 5. Chi-Square may not be a valid test.

              Sample Size = 30
```

From the two-way table above, it can be concluded that the potential buyers below 30 years of age prefer the color "red," and those above 30 years prefer the color "black." However, the chi-square value (7.2768) is not statistically significant at the 0.05 level.

```
                Exercise 11-1                                    3

            The FREQ Procedure

         Table of age by size

 age       size

 Frequency|
 Percent  |
 Row Pct  |
 Col Pct  |Subcompa|Compact |Mid-size|  Total
          |ct      |        |        |
 ---------+--------+--------+--------+
 Under 30 |      3 |      5 |      4 |     12
          |  10.00 |  16.67 |  13.33 |  40.00
          |  25.00 |  41.67 |  33.33 |
          |  30.00 |  45.45 |  44.44 |
 ---------+--------+--------+--------+
```

```
     30 to 40 |      4 |      1 |      4 |      9
              |  13.33 |   3.33 |  13.33 |  30.00
              |  44.44 |  11.11 |  44.44 |
              |  40.00 |   9.09 |  44.44 |
     ---------+--------+--------+--------+
      Over 40 |      3 |      5 |      1 |      9
              |  10.00 |  16.67 |   3.33 |  30.00
              |  33.33 |  55.56 |  11.11 |
              |  30.00 |  45.45 |  11.11 |
     ---------+--------+--------+--------+
      Total        10       11        9       30
                33.33    36.67    30.00   100.00


         Statistics for Table of age by size

Statistic                        DF      Value      Prob
----------------------------------------------------------
Chi-Square                        4      4.8847     0.2993
Likelihood Ratio Chi-Square       4      5.6217     0.2292
Mantel-Haenszel Chi-Square        1      0.7098     0.3995
Phi Coefficient                          0.4035
Contingency Coefficient                  0.3742
Cramer's V                               0.2853
  WARNING: 100% of the cells have expected counts less
          than 5. Chi-Square may not be a valid test.

             Sample Size = 30
```

From the two-way table above, no conclusive relationship between age of car buyers and the size of cars is observed. This conclusion is further supported by a nonsignificant chi-square value of 4.8847.

```
              Exercise 11-1                                    4

              The FREQ Procedure

            Table of age by type

 age         type

 Frequency|
 Percent  |
 Row Pct  |
 Col Pct  |2-doors |4-doors |5-doors |  Total
 ---------+--------+--------+--------+
 Under 30 |      9 |      0 |      3 |     12
          |  30.00 |   0.00 |  10.00 |  40.00
          |  75.00 |   0.00 |  25.00 |
          |  69.23 |   0.00 |  21.43 |
 ---------+--------+--------+--------+
 30 to 40 |      3 |      1 |      5 |      9
          |  10.00 |   3.33 |  16.67 |  30.00
          |  33.33 |  11.11 |  55.56 |
          |  23.08 |  33.33 |  35.71 |
 ---------+--------+--------+--------+
```

```
      Over 40 |     1 |      2 |      6 |      9
              |  3.33 |   6.67 |  20.00 |  30.00
              | 11.11 |  22.22 |  66.67 |
              |  7.69 |  66.67 |  42.86 |
      --------+-------+--------+--------+--------+
      Total          13       3       14       30
                  43.33   10.00    46.67   100.00


          Statistics for Table of age by type

 Statistic                        DF       Value      Prob
 -----------------------------------------------------------

 Chi-Square                        4      9.8275     0.0434
 Likelihood Ratio Chi-Square       4     11.2615     0.0238
 Mantel-Haenszel Chi-Square        1      6.4010     0.0114
 Phi Coefficient                          0.5723
 Contingency Coefficient                  0.4967
 Cramer's V                               0.4047


 WARNING: 78% of the cells have expected counts less
          than 5. Chi-Square may not be a valid test.


               Sample Size = 30
```

Based on the two-way table above, it can be said that potential buyers below 30 years of age prefer 2-door cars, whereas those above 40 years prefer 5-door cars. This relationship is tested to be statistically significant at $p = 0.0434$ with chi-square = 9.8275.

2.

```
                        Exercise 11-2                              1

                      The FREQ Procedure

                                       Cumulative   Cumulative
             q1     Frequency   Percent  Frequency    Percent
         ------------------------------------------------------------
         DISAGREE          2      22.22          2      22.22
         NO IDEA           2      22.22          4      44.44
         AGREE             3      33.33          7      77.78
         STRONGLY AGREE    2      22.22          9     100.00

                     Frequency Missing = 1


                                       Cumulative   Cumulative
             q2     Frequency   Percent  Frequency    Percent
         ------------------------------------------------------------
         DISAGREE          1      10.00          1      10.00
         NO IDEA           3      30.00          4      40.00
         AGREE             5      50.00          9      90.00
         STRONGLY AGREE    1      10.00         10     100.00
```

q3	Frequency	Percent	Cumulative Frequency	Cumulative Percent
STRONGLY DISAGREE	1	11.11	1	11.11
DISAGREE	2	22.22	3	33.33
NO IDEA	1	11.11	4	44.44
AGREE	3	33.33	7	77.78
STRONGLY AGREE	2	22.22	9	100.00

Frequency Missing = 1

q4	Frequency	Percent	Cumulative Frequency	Cumulative Percent
DISAGREE	2	20.00	2	20.00
NO IDEA	2	20.00	4	40.00
AGREE	4	40.00	8	80.00
STRONGLY AGREE	2	20.00	10	100.00

q5	Frequency	Percent	Cumulative Frequency	Cumulative Percent
DISAGREE	1	10.00	1	10.00
NO IDEA	3	30.00	4	40.00
AGREE	5	50.00	9	90.00
STRONGLY AGREE	1	10.00	10	100.00

q6	Frequency	Percent	Cumulative Frequency	Cumulative Percent
NO IDEA	5	50.00	5	50.00
AGREE	3	30.00	8	80.00
STRONGLY AGREE	1	10.00	9	90.00
INVALID	1	10.00	10	100.00

q7	Frequency	Percent	Cumulative Frequency	Cumulative Percent
STRONGLY DISAGREE	1	10.00	1	10.00
DISAGREE	1	10.00	2	20.00
NO IDEA	2	20.00	4	40.00
AGREE	1	10.00	5	50.00
STRONGLY AGREE	2	20.00	7	70.00
INVALID	3	30.00	10	100.00

q8	Frequency	Percent	Cumulative Frequency	Cumulative Percent
STRONGLY DISAGREE	1	11.11	1	11.11
NO IDEA	3	33.33	4	44.44
AGREE	4	44.44	8	88.89
STRONGLY AGREE	1	11.11	9	100.00

Frequency Missing = 1

q9	Frequency	Percent	Cumulative Frequency	Cumulative Percent
DISAGREE	3	33.33	3	33.33
NO IDEA	3	33.33	6	66.67
AGREE	2	22.22	8	88.89
STRONGLY AGREE	1	11.11	9	100.00

Frequency Missing = 1

```
                                                    Cumulative   Cumulative
                   q10      Frequency    Percent    Frequency     Percent
        ------------------------------------------------------------------
        DISAGREE                  1       10.00          1         10.00
        NO IDEA                   2       20.00          3         30.00
        AGREE                     5       50.00          8         80.00
        STRONGLY AGREE            2       20.00         10        100.00
```

```
                             Exercise 11-2                                     2

                           The MEANS Procedure

      Variable    N          Mean        Std Dev      Minimum       Maximum
      --------------------------------------------------------------------
      q1          9       3.5555556      1.1303883    2.0000000     5.0000000
      q2         10       3.6000000      0.8432740    2.0000000     5.0000000
      q3          9       3.3333333      1.4142136    1.0000000     5.0000000
      q4         10       3.6000000      1.0749677    2.0000000     5.0000000
      q5         10       3.6000000      0.8432740    2.0000000     5.0000000
      q6          9       3.5555556      0.7264832    3.0000000     5.0000000
      q7          7       3.2857143      1.4960265    1.0000000     5.0000000
      q8          9       3.4444444      1.1303883    1.0000000     5.0000000
      q9          9       3.1111111      1.0540926    2.0000000     5.0000000
      q10        10       3.8000000      0.9189366    2.0000000     5.0000000
      --------------------------------------------------------------------
```

3. a.

```
                         Exercise 11-3                                   1
                          Part (a)

                     The FREQ Procedure

                  Table of sex by level

sex          level

Frequency|
Expected |
Percent  |
Row Pct  |
Col Pct  |       1|       2|       3|       4|  Total
---------+--------+--------+--------+--------+
F        |      0 |      0 |      2 |      5 |      7
         |    2.8 |   1.75 |    0.7 |   1.75 |
         |   0.00 |   0.00 |  10.00 |  25.00 |  35.00
         |   0.00 |   0.00 |  28.57 |  71.43 |
         |   0.00 |   0.00 | 100.00 | 100.00 |
---------+--------+--------+--------+--------+
```

```
M           |      8 |      5 |      0 |      0 |     13
            |   5.2  |  3.25  |   1.3  |  3.25  |
            |  40.00 |  25.00 |   0.00 |   0.00 |  65.00
            |  61.54 |  38.46 |   0.00 |   0.00 |
            | 100.00 | 100.00 |   0.00 |   0.00 |
------------+--------+--------+--------+--------+
Total             8        5        2        5       20
               40.00    25.00    10.00    25.00   100.00


          Statistics for Table of sex by level

Statistic                      DF       Value       Prob
--------------------------------------------------------
Chi-Square                      3      20.0000      0.0002
Likelihood Ratio Chi-Square     3      25.8979      <.0001
Mantel-Haenszel Chi-Square      1      16.0683      <.0001
Phi Coefficient                         1.0000
Contingency Coefficient                 0.7071
Cramer's V                              1.0000

WARNING: 88% of the cells have expected counts less
         than 5. Chi-Square may not be a valid test.
```

Because the chi-square statistic (= 20.0000) is significant at the 0.0002 level, there is a statistically significant relationship between the floor level and gender of residents at the Betty Ford Center. The data showed that all women lived on the third or the fourth floor while men lived on the first or the second floor.

Because a warning that 88% of the cells have expected counts less than 5 is issued, you may alternatively consider invoking the **EXACT** option on the TABLES statement and interpreting the probability and significance level of such an exact test.

```
        Fisher's Exact Test
-----------------------------------
Table Probability (P)    1.290E-05
Pr <= P                  2.580E-05

        Sample Size = 20
```

b.

```
                           Exercise 11-3                                 2
                             Part (b)

                        The FREQ Procedure

                     Table of ses2 by sex

      ses2        sex

      Frequency|
      Percent  |
      Row Pct  |
      Col Pct  |F       |M       | Total
      ---------+--------+--------+
      H        |     1  |     5  |     6
               |  5.00  | 25.00  | 30.00
               | 16.67  | 83.33  |
               | 14.29  | 38.46  |
      ---------+--------+--------+
      M        |     5  |     6  |    11
               | 25.00  | 30.00  | 55.00
               | 45.45  | 54.55  |
               | 71.43  | 46.15  |
      ---------+--------+--------+
      L        |     1  |     2  |     3
               |  5.00  | 10.00  | 15.00
               | 33.33  | 66.67  |
               | 14.29  | 15.38  |
      ---------+--------+--------+
      Total          7       13       20
                 35.00    65.00   100.00


      Statistics for Table of ses2 by sex

Statistic                      DF       Value       Prob
-------------------------------------------------------------
Chi-Square                      2      1.4186      0.4920
Likelihood Ratio Chi-Square     2      1.5138      0.4691
Mantel-Haenszel Chi-Square      1      0.5385      0.4631
Phi Coefficient                        0.2663
Contingency Coefficient                0.2574
Cramer's V                             0.2663

WARNING: 83% of the cells have expected counts less
         than 5. Chi-Square may not be a valid test.


              Fisher's Exact Test
         -------------------------------
         Table Probability (P)     0.1073
         Pr <= P                   0.6807

             Sample Size = 20
```

The chi-square statistic (= 1.4186, $p = 0.4920$) is not statistically significant at $\alpha = 0.05$; it can be concluded that there is no relationship between gender and SES of residents at the Betty Ford Center. The result from Fisher's exact test ($p = 0.6807$) supports the same conclusion.

c.

```
                        Exercise 11-3                                3
                          Part (c)

                      The FREQ Procedure

                   Table of ses2 by level

 ses2       level

 Frequency|
 Percent  |
 Row Pct  |
 Col Pct  |      1|      2|      3|      4|  Total
 ---------+--------+--------+--------+--------+
 H        |     4 |     1 |     0 |     1 |     6
          | 20.00 |  5.00 |  0.00 |  5.00 | 30.00
          | 66.67 | 16.67 |  0.00 | 16.67 |
          | 50.00 | 20.00 |  0.00 | 20.00 |
 ---------+--------+--------+--------+--------+
 M        |     3 |     3 |     2 |     3 |    11
          | 15.00 | 15.00 | 10.00 | 15.00 | 55.00
          | 27.27 | 27.27 | 18.18 | 27.27 |
          | 37.50 | 60.00 |100.00 | 60.00 |
 ---------+--------+--------+--------+--------+
 L        |     1 |     1 |     0 |     1 |     3
          |  5.00 |  5.00 |  0.00 |  5.00 | 15.00
          | 33.33 | 33.33 |  0.00 | 33.33 |
          | 12.50 | 20.00 |  0.00 | 20.00 |
 ---------+--------+--------+--------+--------+
 Total         8       5       2       5      20
            40.00   25.00   10.00   25.00  100.00


        Statistics for Table of ses2 by level

 Statistic                      DF      Value      Prob
 ------------------------------------------------------
 Chi-Square                      6      3.7273     0.7135
 Likelihood Ratio Chi-Square     6      4.3884     0.6243
 Mantel-Haenszel Chi-Square      1      0.9863     0.3206
 Phi Coefficient                        0.4317
 Contingency Coefficient                0.3963
 Cramer's V                             0.3053

 WARNING: 100% of the cells have expected counts less
          than 5. Chi-Square may not be a valid test.


                  Fisher's Exact Test
           ----------------------------------
           Table Probability (P)      0.0079
           Pr <= P                    0.8615

                 Sample Size = 20
```

Because the chi-square statistic (= 3.7273, p = 0.7135) is not statistically significant at α = 0.05, there is no relationship between SES of residents and the floor level at the Betty Ford Center. The result from Fisher's exact test (p = 0.8615) supports the same conclusion.

d.

```
                         Exercise 11-3                           4
                          Part (d)

                    The FREQ Procedure

               Table 1 of ses2 by level
               Controlling for sex=F

ses2       level

Frequency|
Percent  |
Row Pct  |
Col Pct  |       1|       2|       3|       4| Total
---------+--------+--------+--------+--------+
H        |      0 |      0 |      0 |      1 |     1
         |   0.00 |   0.00 |   0.00 |  14.29 | 14.29
         |   0.00 |   0.00 |   0.00 | 100.00 |
         |      . |      . |   0.00 |  20.00 |
---------+--------+--------+--------+--------+
M        |      0 |      0 |      2 |      3 |     5
         |   0.00 |   0.00 |  28.57 |  42.86 | 71.43
         |   0.00 |   0.00 |  40.00 |  60.00 |
         |      . |      . | 100.00 |  60.00 |
---------+--------+--------+--------+--------+
L        |      0 |      0 |      0 |      1 |     1
         |   0.00 |   0.00 |   0.00 |  14.29 | 14.29
         |   0.00 |   0.00 |   0.00 | 100.00 |
         |      . |      . |   0.00 |  20.00 |
---------+--------+--------+--------+--------+
Total           0        0        2        5        7
             0.00     0.00    28.57    71.43   100.00


                         Exercise 11-3                           5
                          Part (d)

                    The FREQ Procedure

               Table 2 of ses2 by level
               Controlling for sex=M

ses2       level

Frequency|
Percent  |
Row Pct  |
Col Pct  |       1|       2|       3|       4| Total
---------+--------+--------+--------+--------+
H        |      4 |      1 |      0 |      0 |     5
         |  30.77 |   7.69 |   0.00 |   0.00 | 38.46
         |  80.00 |  20.00 |   0.00 |   0.00 |
         |  50.00 |  20.00 |      . |      . |
---------+--------+--------+--------+--------+
M        |      3 |      3 |      0 |      0 |     6
         |  23.08 |  23.08 |   0.00 |   0.00 | 46.15
         |  50.00 |  50.00 |   0.00 |   0.00 |
         |  37.50 |  60.00 |      . |      . |
---------+--------+--------+--------+--------+
```

```
    L          |     1 |     1 |     0 |     0 |     2
               |  7.69 |  7.69 |  0.00 |  0.00 | 15.38
               | 50.00 | 50.00 |  0.00 |  0.00 |
               | 12.50 | 20.00 |     . |     . |
    ---------+--------+--------+--------+--------+
    Total           8       5       0       0      13
                61.54   38.46    0.00    0.00  100.00
```

Exercise 11-3
Part (d)

The FREQ Procedure

Summary Statistics for ses2 by level
Controlling for sex

Cochran-Mantel-Haenszel Statistics (Based on Table Scores)

Statistic	Alternative Hypothesis	DF	Value	Prob
1	Nonzero Correlation	1	0.6359	0.4252
2	Row Mean Scores Differ	2	0.6410	0.7258
3	General Association	6	.	.

At least 1 statistic not computed--singular covariance matrix.

Total Sample Size = 20

The Cochran-Mantel-Haenszel statistics are not statistically significant. We can conclude that there is no association between SES and floor level for either gender of the residents. Please note that the Cochran-Mantel-Haenszel tests are applicable to ordered levels of SES and floor levels. You may have to recode the SES levels as 1, 2, and 3; then recode them back to "H", "M", and "L" using the FORMAT statement.

4.

Exercise 11-4

The FREQ Procedure

Table of sex by party

```
sex       party

Frequency|
Expected |
Percent  |
Row Pct  |
Col Pct  |Democrat|Republic|  Total
         |        |an      |
---------+--------+--------+
Female   |     80 |     20 |    100
         |     65 |     35 |
         |  40.00 |  10.00 |  50.00
         |  80.00 |  20.00 |
         |  61.54 |  28.57 |
---------+--------+--------+
```

```
       Male    |      50 |      50 |     100
               |      65 |      35 |
               |   25.00 |   25.00 |   50.00
               |   50.00 |   50.00 |
               |   38.46 |   71.43 |
               ---------+--------+--------+
       Total           130       70      200
                     65.00    35.00   100.00


          Statistics for Table of sex by party

Statistic                      DF       Value      Prob
-----------------------------------------------------------
Chi-Square                      1     19.7802    <.0001
Likelihood Ratio Chi-Square     1     20.2687    <.0001
Continuity Adj. Chi-Square      1     18.4835    <.0001
Mantel-Haenszel Chi-Square      1     19.6813    <.0001
Phi Coefficient                        0.3145
Contingency Coefficient                0.3000
Cramer's V                             0.3145


               Fisher's Exact Test
          ----------------------------------
          Cell (1,1) Frequency (F)         80
          Left-sided Pr <= F          1.0000
          Right-sided Pr >= F       6.945E-06

          Table Probability (P)     5.311E-06
          Two-sided Pr <= P         1.389E-05

               Sample Size = 200
```

From the two-way table above, it can be concluded that females are more likely to vote for a Democrat for president, whereas males are evenly split between supporting Republican and Democratic presidential candidates. The statistically significant chi-square value (= 19.7802, $p < 0.0001$) indicates an association between gender and party affiliation of presidential candidates.

5.

```
         Statistics for Table of job by educ

Statistic                      DF       Value      Prob
-----------------------------------------------------------
Chi-Square                     10     18.0000    0.0550
Likelihood Ratio Chi-Square    10     19.0954    0.0391
Mantel-Haenszel Chi-Square      1      7.1138    0.0076
Phi Coefficient                        1.4142
Contingency Coefficient                0.8165
Cramer's V                             1.0000

 WARNING: 100% of the cells have expected counts less
          than 5. Chi-Square may not be a valid test.
```

```
        Fisher's Exact Test
-----------------------------------
Table Probability (P)    7.937E-04
Pr <= P                     0.0238

        Sample Size = 9
```

There is a statistically significant relationship between a worker's educational level and his or her job performance, based on Fisher's exact test's significance level of .0238.

6. The 2 × 2 result obtained in Output 11.7 is as follows:

	F	M	Total
NEWD	4	4	8
NEWR	2	5	7
	6	9	15

Its exact probability is $p = \dfrac{C_4^8 \times C_2^7}{C_6^{15}}$, or 0.2937 according to Output 11.7

Thus, the Left-sided probability of obtaining a leading cell frequency equal to or less than the current cell frequency (= 4) is

$$p_{\text{Left-sided}} = \frac{C_4^8 \times C_2^7 + C_3^8 \times C_3^7 + C_2^8 \times C_4^7 + C_1^8 \times C_5^7 + C_0^8 \times C_6^7}{C_6^{15}} = 0.91608,$$

or 0.9161 in Output 11.7.

The Right-sided probability of obtained a leading cell frequency equal to or more than the current cell frequency (= 4) is

$$p_{\text{Right-sided}} = 1 - 0.9161 + 0.2937 = 0.3776.$$

12

t Test of Population Means

┌─ **O B J E C T I V E** ─────────────────────────────────

This chapter teaches you how to make inferences about one or two population means. Specifically, you learn to perform a *t* test on two independent sample means and draw an appropriate conclusion about the corresponding difference in the underlying populations. Furthermore, the one-sample *t* test and the paired-samples *t* test are also demonstrated. For each of these *t* tests, you will also learn how to calculate their statistical power and estimate a desirable sample size. Three assumptions, namely, normality, equal variance, and random sampling and random assignments, are discussed. Ways to compensate for the violation of these assumptions are also presented.

12.1 An Overview of Three *t* Tests

This chapter is focused on making inferences about one or two population means. Specifically, three *t* tests are demonstrated in this chapter. They are (1) the independent-samples *t* test, (2) the one-sample *t* test, and (3) the paired-sample *t* test. All are carried out by the TTEST procedure. The independent-samples *t* test is used to test the equality between two population means. For example, suppose you'd like to find out if students in the College of Arts and Sciences spend more time studying than students in the School of Music. You'd draw a random sample from these majors at a university and ask the students to honestly record their study time each day for a week. The average amount of study time, in hours, is the basis for comparing the arts and sciences students with the music students. This comparison helps you answer the question, "Are students of arts and sciences more industrious than students of music?" The appropriate statistical test for making such a comparison is the independent-samples *t* test. The formula is as follows:

$$t = \frac{(\overline{X}_1 - \overline{X}_2) - (\mu_1 - \mu_2)}{\sqrt{S_p^2 \left(\frac{1}{n_1} + \frac{1}{n_2}\right)}},$$

where $S_p^2 = \dfrac{(n_1 - 1)S_1^2 + (n_2 - 1)S_2^2}{n_1 + n_2 - 2}$ is the weighted average of the two sample variances.

The numerator of this *t* test is a comparison of the sample mean difference with the corresponding hypothesized population mean difference, though in general, the mean difference between two populations under the null hypothesis is zero. The denominator is the standard error of the difference in two sample means. Furthermore, the standard error is derived from the two sample variances. These two sample variances are pooled, or weighted, by their respective degrees of freedom, in order to yield the S_p^2. The weighted variance is necessary for this *t* test because such a test assumes that both samples are drawn from normal populations with equal but unknown variances. In **Section 12.5: Tips,** suggestions are given as to what to do if data do not satisfy this assumption or two other assumptions, namely, normality and independence, required by this *t* test.

The one-sample *t* test is used to examine a sample mean against a hypothetical population mean when the population variance is unknown, the population distribution is assumed to be normal, and the degrees of freedom are no more than 30 (or sample size is no more than 31). If the sample size is larger than this recommended value, a normal *z* test can be used. The formula for a one-sample *t* test is as follows:

$$t = \frac{\overline{X} - \mu_0}{\hat{\sigma}/\sqrt{n}},$$

where μ_0 = the population mean under the null hypothesis, and

$$\hat{\sigma} = \sqrt{\frac{\sum\limits_{i=1}^{n}(X_i - \overline{X})^2}{n - 1}}.$$

The paired-samples *t* test is suited for comparing means based on matched samples. IQ scores of twins or weights of cancer patients before and after a course of chemotherapy fit into the concept of paired samples. Either these scores are matched because individuals in both samples are related or the scores are correlated because they are gathered from the same persons. The paired-samples *t* test can be viewed as a special case of the one-sample *t* test for which matched scores (e.g., IQ scores of twins, patient's weight before and after chemotherapy) are converted into difference scores. And the one-sample *t* formula is modified to

$$t = \frac{\overline{d} - \mu_d}{\hat{\sigma}_d/\sqrt{n}},$$

where μ_d = the population mean difference under the null hypothesis, usually is 0 (no difference), and

$$\hat{\sigma}_d = \sqrt{\frac{\sum\limits_{i=1}^{n}(d_i - \overline{d})^2}{n - 1}}.$$

Example 12.1 illustrates the independent-samples *t* test. Example 12.2 illustrates the one-sample *t* test, and Example 12.3 the paired-samples *t* test. Each *t*-test example is followed by the demonstration of power calculation (Examples 12.1a, 12.2a, and 12.3a) and the estimation of a desirable sample size (Examples 12.1b, 12.2b, and 12.3b). The power calculation and the sample size estimation are carried out by the POWER procedure.

12.2 Examples

Example 12.1 Independent-Samples *t* Test

In this example, we seek to answer the question, "Are men and women equal in their verbal abilities as measured by the SAT-Verbal test?" In other words, we are testing the following null and alternative hypotheses:

$$H_0 : \mu_{satv_{female}} = \mu_{satv_{male}}$$
$$H_1 : \mu_{satv_{female}} \neq \mu_{satv_{male}}$$

Data came from mydata.dat. This data file contains information about 24 students in terms of their gender (the variable sex), age (age), grade point average (gpa), critical thinking score (critical), political preference (polpref), and SAT-Verbal score (satv). Because of missing data, only 8 females' and 14 males' SAT-Verbal scores are compared. The TTEST procedure is invoked to perform the independent-samples *t* test:

```
/* The following bolded SAS statements establish the SAS data set 'mydata' */

DATA mydata;
    INFILE 'd:\data\mydata.dat';
    INPUT id sex $ age gpa critical polpref $ satv;
RUN;

TITLE 'Example 12.1 Independent-samples t test';

PROC TTEST DATA=mydata ALPHA=0.1;     /* Alpha level is 0.1; hence, confidence level is '
    CLASS sex;                        /* The two samples are defined by 'sex' */
    VAR satv;                         /* The dependent variable is 'satv' */
RUN;
```

Output 12.1 Independent-Samples *t* Test

```
              Example 12.1 Independent-samples t test                        1

                        The TTEST Procedure
Part (A)
                            Statistics

                        Lower CL           Upper CL  Lower CL          Upper CL
  Variable  sex      N     Mean    Mean       Mean   Std Dev  Std Dev  Std Dev

  satv      F        8   435.37  533.75     632.13    103.6   146.87   263.94
  satv      M       14   466.07  518.57     571.07    84.58   110.93   164.78
  satv      Diff (1-2)   -80.14   15.179    110.49    99.498  124.69   169.29
```

```
                                   Statistics

              Variable   sex           Std Err    Minimum    Maximum

                satv     F             51.925       280        710
                satv     M             29.647       300        690
                satv     Diff (1-2)    55.264
```

Part (B)
```
                                   T-Tests

         Variable     Method          Variances    DF     t Value    Pr > |t|

          satv        Pooled          Equal        20       0.27       0.7864
          satv        Satterthwaite   Unequal      11.6     0.25       0.8040
```

Part (C)
```
                              Equality of Variances

         Variable     Method      Num DF    Den DF    F Value    Pr > F

           satv       Folded F       7         13       1.75      0.3627
```

For purposes of explanation, the output is divided into three parts: (A), (B), and (C). Under **Part (A)**, the average performance of 8 women (F) and 14 men (M) on <u>satv</u> is 533.75 and 518.57, respectively. The lower limits of the 90% confidence limits of these means (i.e., **Lower CL Mean**) are 435.37 and 466.07 for women and men, respectively. The upper limits (i.e., **Upper CL Mean**) are 632.13 and 571.07, respectively. The standard deviation for women is 146.87 (**Std Dev**) with the 90% confidence limits = 103.6 (lower under **Lower CL Std Dev**) and 263.94 (upper under **Upper CL Std Dev**). For men, these values are 110.93, 84.58, and 164.78, respectively. The standard error of means for women is 51.925 with minimum at 280 and maximum at 710. For men, these figures are 29.647, 300, and 690, respectively.

Part (A) also contains the mean difference between these two groups. It is expressed as **Diff (1–2)** and equals 15.179. This indicates that the women's average is slightly higher than the men's. So let us find out if such a difference is tested statistically significant at the α level of 0.10.

There are two *t*-test results in **Part (B)**, presented under the **Variances Equal** and **Unequal** headings. These two headings correspond to the equal population variances (the equal variance assumption assumed by the independent-sample *t* test) and the unequal population variances (the equal variance assumption being violated). Because we do not know whether the two population variances are equal and the <u>F</u> and <u>M</u> groups in the current data set do not have equal sample sizes, we should look at the **Unequal** result, that is, *t* = 0.25 with df = 11.6 and significance level = 0.8040. This *t* test is based on the Satterthwaite (1946) modification of the *t* formula given in **Section 12.1** and an adjusted df given below:

$$\text{Satterthwaite adjusted df} = \frac{\left(\dfrac{\hat{\sigma}_1^2}{n_1} + \dfrac{\hat{\sigma}_2^2}{n_2}\right)^2}{\dfrac{1}{(n_1-1)}\left(\dfrac{\hat{\sigma}_1^2}{n_1}\right)^2 + \dfrac{1}{(n_2-1)}\left(\dfrac{\hat{\sigma}_2^2}{n_2}\right)^2},$$

where $n_1 = 8$, $n_2 = 14$, $\hat{\sigma}_1^2 = (146.87)^2$, and $\hat{\sigma}_2^2 = (110.93)^2$.

On the basis of this result, we can conclude that the null hypothesis of no difference on SAT-Verbal scores between females and males cannot be rejected. In other words, it is quite probable to observe a mean difference of 15.179 points under the null hypothesis of equal population means. **Part (C)** presents an *F* test of the equality of two population variances. The *F* test result is not statistically significant at $\alpha = 0.05$. According to Moser and Stevens (1992), when two samples do not have equal sample sizes or equal sample variances, such as is the case with this example, it is better to use Satterthwaite's *t* test than to rely on the result of the *F* test of the equality of variances. Thus, Part (C) is ignored for this example. More details about Moser and Stevens' recommendations are given in **Section 12.5** under the heading of What to Do If Data Do Not Satisfy the Statistical Assumptions.

The TTEST procedure can analyze several dependent variables simultaneously, while using the same independent variable to define groups. For example, for the <u>mydata</u> data file, we could simultaneously compare men and women on <u>age</u>, <u>gpa</u>, and <u>critical</u> scores without having to repeat this procedure three times. You simply add these variables to the VAR statement. Try executing the program below and find out the *t*-test results of gender differences on <u>age</u>, <u>gpa</u>, and <u>critical</u> scores:

```
PROC TTEST DATA=mydata ALPHA=0.1;
    CLASS sex;
    VAR age gpa critical;
RUN;
```

Example 12.1a Power of the Independent-Samples *t* Test

Perhaps the statistically insignificant result obtained in Output 12.1 is due to the low statistical power of the *t* test. The power of a statistical test is its probability of rejecting an incorrect null hypothesis. To calculate the statistical power, we can invoke the POWER procedure. The program first specifies the type of test (two independent-samples test), two group means, two samples sizes, the total sample size, two sample standard deviations, and α levels (0.01, 0.05, and 0.10 in this example). After these specifications, the PLOT statement is specified to generate three power curves, one for each of the α levels specified in the ALPHA= option, based on the total sample size of two groups ranging from 22 to 3,300. All power curves will be plotted using the total sample size as the *X*-axis; therefore, the *Y*-axis is the statistical power.

```
TITLE 'Example 12.1a Power of the independent-samples t test';
PROC POWER;
      TWOSAMPLEMEANS TEST=DIFF              /* The power calculation is for indep. sample t test */
        GROUPMEANS=(533.75 518.57)          /* Two sample means based on F and M are specified   */
        STDDEV=124.69                       /* STDDEV refers to the pooled standard deviation     */
        GROUPWEIGHTS=8 | 14                 /* GROUPWEIGHTS refer to F and M sample sizes         */
        NTOTAL=22                           /* NOTATAL refers to the total (F + M) sample size    */
        ALPHA=0.01, 0.05, 0.10              /* ALPHA refers to the Type I error rate              */
        POWER=.;                            /* POWER is missing because it is to be calculated    */
      PLOT X=n MIN=22 MAX=3300;             /* Plots power curves for n=22 to 3300 for 3 alphas   */
RUN;
```

Output 12.1a Power of the Independent-Samples *t* Test

```
Example 12.1a Power of the independent-samples t test                        1

                    The POWER Procedure
        Two-sample t Test for Mean Difference

              Fixed Scenario Elements

          Distribution                  Normal
          Method                        Exact
          Group 1 Mean                  533.75
          Group 2 Mean                  518.57
          Standard Deviation            124.69
          Group 1 Weight                     8
          Group 2 Weight                    14
          Total Sample Size                 22
          Number of Sides                    2
          Null Difference                    0


              Computed Power

          Index    Alpha    Power

              1     0.01    0.012
              2     0.05    0.058
              3     0.10    0.112
```

The statistical power of the *t* test performed in Example 12.1 is 0.112 at the α level of 0.10. This means that the *t* test performed has a mere probability of 0.112 of rejecting the null hypothesis even if it is incorrect. The output also includes the statistical power of the *t* test at the α level of 0.01 or 0.05. The monotonic increasing relationship between the statistical power, α levels, and sample sizes is shown in Figure 12.1.

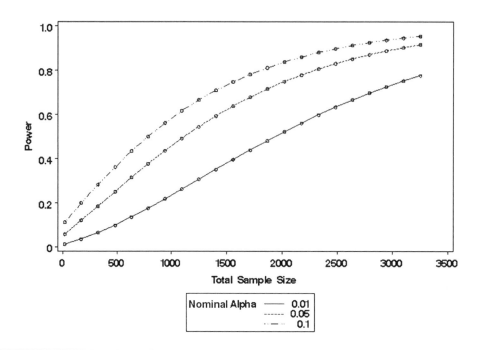

Figure 12.1   Power of Independent-Samples *t* Test

From Figure 12.1, we can conclude that (1) given a fixed sample size, there is a monotonic increasing relationship between the statistical power and the α level and (2) given a fixed α level, there is also a monotonic increasing relationship between the statistical power and the sample size. For the *t* test to achieve a power of 0.8 at the α level of 0.10, we need to increase the total sample size to approximately 1,800. The exact sample-size increase is calculated in Example 12.1b, again using the POWER procedure.

To calculate the power of Satterthwaite's approximate *t* test, we need to replace the TEST=DIFF option in Example 12.1a with the TEST=DIFF_SATT option and to replace STDDEV=124.69 with GROUPSTDDEVS=(146.85 110.93). Try modifying Example 12.1a with these changes and find out the statistical power for Satterthwaite's approximate *t* test performed in Example 12.1, the total sample size needed to achieve a power of 0.80 at an α level of 0.10, and three power curves corresponding to α of 0.01, 0.05, and 0.10 for a range of the total sample size extending from 22 to 3,300.

Example 12.1b Sample Size Estimation for Independent-Samples *t* Tests

Although the statistical power is usually calculated after performing a statistical test, a desirable sample size is estimated before the test. To estimate a sample size, we again invoke the POWER procedure. The program is written similarly as Example 12.1a except for the power specification, now set at 0.8, and the total sample size, now set as missing (.) because this is the number to be estimated.

```
TITLE 'Example 12.1b Sample size estimation for independent-samples t tests';
PROC POWER;
    TWOSAMPLEMEANS TEST=DIFF
        GROUPMEANS=(533.75 518.57)    /* Two sample means based on F and M are specified  */
        STDDEV=124.69                 /* STDDEV refers to the pooled standard deviation   */
        GROUPWEIGHTS=8 | 14           /* GROUPWEIGHTS refer to F and M sample sizes       */
        ALPHA=0.1                     /* ALPHA refers to the Type I error rate            */
        POWER=0.8                     /* POWER refers to the statistical power            */
        NTOTAL=.;                     /* NTOTAL is missing because it is to be calculated */
RUN;
```

Output 12.1b Sample Size Estimation for Independent-Samples *t* Tests

```
Example 12.1b Sample size estimation for independent-samples t tests            1

                        The POWER Procedure
                  Two-sample t Test for Mean Difference

                        Fixed Scenario Elements

              Distribution                    Normal
              Method                           Exact
              Alpha                              0.1
              Group 1 Mean                    533.75
              Group 2 Mean                    518.57
              Standard Deviation             124.69
              Group 1 Weight                       8
              Group 2 Weight                      14
              Nominal Power                      0.8
              Number of Sides                      2
              Null Difference                      0


                        Computed N Total

                   Actual         N
                   Power       Total

                   0.800        1804
```

The output indicates that given the observed mean difference in SAT-Verbal scores, a total of 1,804 subjects (656 men and 1,148 women) are needed for the *t* test to achieve a power of 0.8.

Example 12.2 One-Sample *t* Test

In this example, we are interested in testing whether the population mean of satv (SAT-Verbal) is 500 and whether the population mean critical thinking score is 10. Two sets of null and alternative hypotheses are tested:

$$H_0 : \mu_{satv} = 500 \qquad H_0 : \mu_{critical} = 10$$
$$\text{and}$$
$$H_1 : \mu_{satv} \neq 500 \qquad H_1 : \mu_{critical} \neq 10$$

Data from mydata are used to examine these two sets of hypotheses using two one-sample *t* tests, one for satv and the other for critical. The default α level of 0.05 is applied in both population mean inferences.

```
/* See Example 12.1 for the DATA step in creating the SAS data set 'mydata' */

TITLE 'Example 12.2 One-sample t test';

PROC TTEST DATA=mydata H0=500;     /* The null hypothesis sets the population mean to 500  */
     VAR satv;                     /* The dependent variable is 'satv'                     */
RUN;

PROC TTEST DATA=mydata H0=10;      /* The null hypothesis sets the population mean to 10   */
     VAR critical;                 /* The dependent variable is 'critical'                 */
RUN;
```

Output 12.2 One-Sample *t* Test

```
                         Example 12.2 One-sample t test                           1

                             The TTEST Procedure
 Part (A)
                                 Statistics

               Lower CL          Upper CL  Lower CL          Upper CL
   Variable    N    Mean   Mean     Mean   Std Dev  Std Dev  Std Dev  Std Err

   satv       22  470.04  524.09  578.15   93.796   121.92   174.23   25.992


                                 T-Tests

                   Variable      DF    t Value    Pr > |t|

                    satv         21      0.93      0.3645
```

```
                        Example 12.2 One-sample t test                          2

                            The TTEST Procedure
Part (B)
                                Statistics

                 Lower CL           Upper CL  Lower CL         Upper CL
     Variable    N    Mean    Mean      Mean   Std Dev  Std Dev  Std Dev  Std Err

     critical   22  28.141  30.545     32.95    4.1717   5.4224    7.749   1.1561


                                  T-Tests

                    Variable      DF    t Value    Pr > |t|

                    critical      21      17.77      <.0001
```

Part (A) presents the *t*-test result of the null hypothesis that the population mean satv = 500. A *t* value of 0.93 (df = 21, *p* = 0.3645) indicates that our sample mean of satv (= 524.09) is a possible mean for a sample taken from a population with an SAT-Verbal mean of 500. In other words, we cannot reject the null hypothesis at the α level of 0.05.

Part (B) presents the *t*-test result of the population mean critical = 10. The result indicates that we can reject the null hypothesis with a *t* value = 17.77 (df = 21, *p* < 0.0001). The sample mean of critical (= 30.545) is statistically significantly different from the null value of 10.

Example 12.2a Power of One-Sample *t* Tests

In this example, we demonstrate how to use the POWER procedure to calculate the power of one-sample *t* tests.

```
TITLE  'Example 12.2a  Power of one-sample t tests';
TITLE2 'Variable SATV';
PROC POWER;
     ONESAMPLEMEANS TEST=T         /* The power calculation is for one-sample t test    */
        MEAN=524.09                /* The sample mean for the variable 'satv'           */
        STDDEV=121.92              /* The sample standard deviation for 'satv'          */
        NULLMEAN=500               /* The null hypothesis value for the population mean */
        NTOTAL=22                  /* NTOTAL refers to the sample size                  */
        ALPHA=0.05                 /* ALPHA refers to the Type I error rate             */
        POWER=.;                   /* POWER is missing because it is to be calculated   */
RUN;

TITLE2 'Variable CRITICAL';
PROC POWER;
     ONESAMPLEMEANS TEST=T
        MEAN=30.545
        STDDEV=5.4224
        NULLMEAN=10
        NTOTAL=22
        ALPHA=0.05
        POWER=.;
RUN;
```

Output 12.2a Power of One-Sample *t* Tests

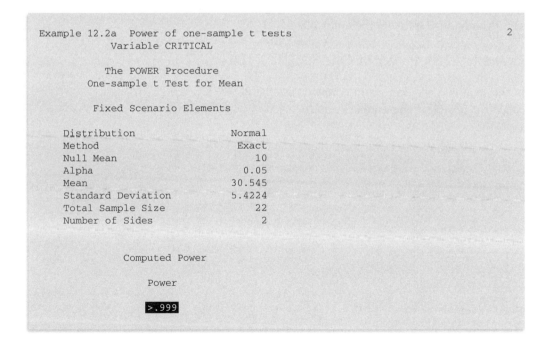

```
Example 12.2a  Power of one-sample t tests                        1
              Variable SATV

           The POWER Procedure
      One-sample t Test for Mean

      Fixed Scenario Elements

   Distribution              Normal
   Method                     Exact
   Null Mean                    500
   Alpha                       0.05
   Mean                      524.09
   Standard Deviation        121.92
   Total Sample Size             22
   Number of Sides                2


        Computed Power

          Power

        0.143
```

```
Example 12.2a  Power of one-sample t tests                        2
              Variable CRITICAL

           The POWER Procedure
      One-sample t Test for Mean

      Fixed Scenario Elements

   Distribution              Normal
   Method                     Exact
   Null Mean                     10
   Alpha                       0.05
   Mean                      30.545
   Standard Deviation        5.4224
   Total Sample Size             22
   Number of Sides                2


        Computed Power

          Power

        >.999
```

Page 1 of the output calculates the power of the one-sample *t* test of the satv mean to be 0.143. Page 2 reports the power of the *t* test of the critical mean to be greater than 0.999. These power calculations are consistent with the statistically insignificant *t*-test result for <u>satv</u> and the significant result for <u>critical</u> shown in Output 12.2.

Example 12.2b Sample Size Estimation for One-Sample *t* Tests

You may ask how large the sample size must be in order for the one-sample *t* test of <u>satv</u> to achieve a power of 0.8. The question is answered by the program below:

```
TITLE   'Example 12.2b  Sample size estimation for one-sample t tests';
TITLE2 'Variable SATV';
PROC POWER;
     ONESAMPLEMEANS TEST=T          /* One-sample t test is specified          */
        MEAN=524.09                 /* Sample mean is specified                */
        STDDEV=121.92               /* Sample standard deviation is specified  */
        NULLMEAN=500                /* MULLMEAN specifies the null mean to be 500 */
        POWER=0.8                   /* POWER specifies the power               */
        ALPHA=0.05                  /* ALPHA specifies the Type I error rate   */
        NTOTAL=.;                   /* NTOTAL is missing because it is to be calculated */
RUN;
```

Output 12.2b Sample Size Estimation for One-Sample *t* Tests

```
Example 12.2b  Sample size estimation for one-sample t tests          1
                    Variable SATV

                   The POWER Procedure
              One-sample t Test for Mean

                   Fixed Scenario Elements

            Distribution              Normal
            Method                     Exact
            Null Mean                    500
            Alpha                       0.05
            Mean                      524.09
            Standard Deviation        121.92
            Nominal Power                0.8
            Number of Sides                2


                    Computed N Total

                 Actual         N
                 Power       Total

                 0.800        203
```

Output 12.2b shows that in order for the one-sample *t* test of <u>satv</u> to achieve a power of 0.8, 203 subjects are needed, approximately 10 times the 22 subjects on whom the one-sample *t* test was based in Output 12.2.

Example 12.3 Paired-Samples *t* Test

As the title implies, the goal here is to conduct a paired-samples *t* test. In other words, we are testing the following null and alternative hypotheses:

$$H_0 : \mu_d = 0$$

$$H_1 : \mu_d \neq 0$$

The raw data file <u>mydata</u> is again used to help infer whether the ability to think critically is different from or about the same as the verbal ability. Because these two tests have different scales, the program specifies the STANDARD procedure to standardize <u>critical</u> and <u>satv</u> scores so that both have a mean of 0 and standard deviation of 1. The <u>pairout</u> data set from the STANDARD procedure contains standardized <u>critical</u> and <u>satv</u> scores. This data set subsequently becomes the input data set for the TTEST procedure. The PAIRED statement is essential for performing the paired-samples *t* test because it specifies which two variables are paired.

```
/* See Example 12.1 for the DATA step in creating the SAS data set 'mydata' */

TITLE 'Example 12.3 Paired-samples t test';

TITLE2 'Standardizing critical and verbal scores';
PROC STANDARD DATA=mydata MEAN=0 STD=1 PRINT OUT=pairout;
    VAR critical satv;
RUN;

TITLE2 'Comparison of standardized critical and verbal scores';
PROC TTEST DATA=pairout;
    PAIRED critical*satv;
RUN;
```

Output 12.3 Paired-Samples *t* Test

```
                    Example 12.3 Paired-samples t test                    1
                    Standardizing critical and verbal scores
Part (A)
                         The STANDARD Procedure

                                      Standard
            Name            Mean      Deviation          N

            critical    30.545455     5.422416          22
            satv       524.090909   121.915626          22
```

```
                    Example 12.3 Paired-samples t test                  2
              Comparison of standardized critical and verbal scores

                           The TTEST Procedure
Part (B)
                               Statistics

                   Lower CL            Upper CL   Lower CL            Upper CL
Difference      N      Mean     Mean       Mean    Std Dev  Std Dev   Std Dev

critical - satv   20   -0.528   -0.026     0.4761   0.8161   1.0731    1.5674

                               Statistics

          Difference          Std Err   Minimum    Maximum

          critical - satv        0.24    -1.769     1.5729
Part (C)
                               T-Tests

          Difference             DF   t Value   Pr > |t|

          critical - satv        19     -0.11     0.9145
```

Part (A) shows that the average performance of 22 students with valid (or nonmissing) data on the critical thinking test (or <u>critical</u>) is 30.545455 and 524.090909 on the SAT-Verbal test (or <u>satv</u>), with standard deviations of 5.422416 and 121.915626, respectively.

Part (B) results are in standardized *z*-score scale. First, the table lists 20 students with complete information on both tests. The mean standardized difference (of <u>critical</u> – <u>satv</u>) is –0.026 with the lower bound of the 95% confidence limit = –0.528 and the upper bound = 0.4761. The standard deviation and its lower and upper bounds of 95% confidence limits are 1.0731, 0.8161, and 1.5674, respectively. The standard error of means is 0.24; the minimum difference is –1.769 and the maximum is 1.5729.

Part (C) presents the paired-samples *t*-test result: the *t* value is –0.11 with 19 degrees of freedom, significant at 0.9145 for a two-tailed test. The *t* value is quite close to its theoretical mean (0); its *p* value implies a quite probable result under the null hypothesis. Both lead to the retention of the null hypothesis of no difference. Therefore, we conclude that the data do not support the alternative hypothesis that the average standardized <u>critical</u> thinking score is different from the average standardized <u>satv</u> score.

Example 12.3a Power of the Paired-Samples *t* Test

This example demonstrates how to use the POWER procedure to calculate the statistical power of a paired-samples *t* test.

```
TITLE 'Example 12.3a Power of the paired-samples t test';
PROC POWER;
    PAIREDMEANS TEST=DIFF    /* The power calculation is for the paired-samples t test    */
      MEANDIFF=-0.026        /* MEANDIFF refers to the observed mean difference           */
      STDDEV=1.0731          /* STDDEV refers to the observed standard deviation          */
      NULLDIFF=0             /* NULLDIFF specifies the null hypothesis value              */
      CORR=0.47367           /* CORR specifies the correlation between the paired variables */
      NPAIRS=22              /* NPAIRS specifies the number of pairs                      */
      ALPHA=0.05             /* ALPHA specifies the Type I error rate                     */
      POWER=.;               /* POWER is missing because it is to be calculated           */
RUN;
```

Output 12.3a Power of the Paired-Samples *t* Test

```
Example 12.3a Power of the paired-samples t test                          1

              The POWER Procedure
        Paired t Test for Mean Difference

          Fixed Scenario Elements

      Distribution                 Normal
      Method                        Exact
      Null Difference                   0
      Alpha                          0.05
      Mean Difference              -0.026
      Standard Deviation           1.0731
      Correlation                 0.47367
      Number of Pairs                  22
      Number of Sides                   2

            Computed Power

            Power

          0.051
```

The statistical power of the paired samples *t* test performed in Example 12.3 is 0.051. This means that the *t* test performed has a mere probability of 0.051 of rejecting the null hypothesis even if it is incorrect.

Example 12.3b Sample Size Estimation for Paired-Samples *t* Tests

This example seeks to answer the question of how large the sample size should be in order to achieve a power of 0.8 for the paired-samples *t* test conducted in Example 12.3. Again, the POWER procedure is invoked to estimate a desirable sample size.

```
TITLE 'Example 12.3b Sample size estimation for paired-samples t tests';
PROC POWER;
     PAIREDMEANS TEST=DIFF      /* The power calculation is for the paired-samples t test     */
        MEANDIFF=-0.026         /* MEANDIFF refers to the observed mean difference            */
        STDDEV=1.0731           /* STDDEV refers to the observed standard deviation           */
        NULLDIFF=0              /* NULLDIFF specifies the null hypothesis value               */
        CORR=0.47367            /* CORR specifies the correlation between the paired variables */
        POWER=0.8               /* POWER specifies the desirable power                        */
        ALPHA=0.05              /* ALPHA specifies the Type I error rate                      */
        NPAIRS=.;               /* NPAIRS is missing because it is to be estimated            */
RUN;
```

Output 12.3b Sample Size Estimation for Paired-Samples *t* Tests

```
Example 12.3b Sample size estimation for paired-samples t tests          1

                    The POWER Procedure
               Paired t Test for Mean Difference

                  Fixed Scenario Elements

          Distribution                Normal
          Method                       Exact
          Null Difference                  0
          Alpha                         0.05
          Mean Difference             -0.026
          Standard Deviation          1.0731
          Correlation                0.47367
          Nominal Power                  0.8
          Number of Sides                  2


              Computed N Pairs

             Actual         N
             Power       Pairs

             0.800       14077
```

We need 14,077 subjects in order for this paired-samples *t* test to achieve a power of 0.8. Note that the sample size of 14,077 is also the number of pairs of <u>critical</u> thinking and <u>satv</u> scores, as each subject took both tests.

12.3 How to Write the PROC TTEST Codes

Based on the examples presented in the previous section, it is obvious that the TTEST procedure is not complex. Most often you only need to know five statements:

PROC	TTEST	DATA= sas_*dataset_name* ALPHA= (*p*)
		H0= *mean_value* COCHRAN;
	CLASS	*independent_variable*;
	VAR	*dependent_variable(s)*;
	PAIRED	*paired_variables*;
	BY	*classification_variable(s)*;

The first statement, **PROC TTEST**, invokes the procedure and specifies a data set to be analyzed. The option **ALPHA=** allows you to specify the $(1 - \text{ALPHA}) \times 100\%$ confidence level. The default is 0.05. The option **H0=** defines the mean under the null hypothesis. The option **COCHRAN** will apply Cochran and Cox's approximation of the p value based on the approximate t statistic when the samples' variances are unequal. According to the literature, Cochran and Cox's approximation leads to conservative test results (Lee & Gurland, 1975). For more information on the approximation, you can refer to the book titled *Experimental Designs* by Cochran and Cox (1957).

The next statement, **CLASS**, identifies a variable that serves as an independent variable to separate observations into two groups. The third statement, **VAR**, specifies one or more dependent variables to be tested against a hypothesized null mean, or compared between the two groups defined by the CLASS variable.

The fourth statement, **PAIRED**, defines set(s) of paired variables to be included in the paired-samples t test. When more than one set of paired variables is specified, you can use the following abbreviations:

PAIRED A*B C*D;	(equals A–B and C–D)
PAIRED (A D) * (C D);	(equals A–C, A–D, B–C, and B–D)
PAIRED (A1-A3):(B1-B3);	(equals A1–B1, A2–B2, and A3–B3)

The last statement, **BY**, serves the same purpose as in all other procedures. It divides the data set into subgroups according to diverse values of the BY variable(s). Within each subgroup, the requested t test is performed. If more than one BY variable is specified, all possible combinations of the BY variables' values are used in dividing up the entire data set. Be sure to presort the data set into the ascending order of all BY variables, if the BY statement is included in the TTEST procedure. Presorting a data set can be accomplished using the SORT procedure.

12.4 How to Write the PROC POWER Codes

The POWER procedure performs power analyses and sample size estimations for various statistical techniques. This section summaries selected statements and specifications relevant to the three types of *t* tests discussed in this chapter.

PROC	POWER;	
	TWOSAMPLEMEANS	*options*;
	ONESAMPLEMEANS	*options*;
	PAIREDMEANS	*options*;
	PLOT	*options*;

The **PROC POWER** statement initiates the procedure. This statement is followed by one of the three statements depending on the type of *t* test requested: TWOSAMPLEMEANS, or ONESAMPLEMEANS, or PAIRED-MEANS. Each statement can have only one option set to missing (.), and therefore, only one value to be estimated. Options common to these three statements include the following:

POWER=   specifies the desired power of the *t* test. If the statistical power is to be estimated, a missing value (.) is specified.

SIDES=   specifies the number of tails, and therefore, the direction of the alternative hypothesis. One of the following four values needs to be specified:

1 – one-sided alternative hypothesis in the same direction as the effect observed in data

2 – two-sided

U – upper one-sided with the alternative mean greater than the null hypothesized mean

L – lower one-sided with the alternative mean less than the null hypothesized mean.

ALPHA=   the Type I error rate(s) specified.

NFRACTIONAL   allows fractional sample sizes to be specified and estimated.

The **TWOSAMPLEMEANS** statement estimates sample sizes and performs power analysis of an independent-samples *t* test. The options associated with this statement include the following:

TEST=   DIFF   specifies the *t* test of the mean difference with a pooled variance. It is the default of this option.

DIFF_SATT   specifies the *t* test of the mean difference with Satterthwaite's unpooled variance and the adjusted degrees of freedom.

GROUPMEANS=	specifies the two group means. You must specify this option or MEANDIFF=, but not both. In Examples 12.1a and 12.1b, these group means are specified to equal the observed group means. They can also be specified to equal hypothesized population means. Alternatively, the mean of one group can be estimated by setting it to missing (.), such as GROUP-MEANS=(5.6,.).
MEANDIFF=	specifies the mean difference between two groups. You must specify this option or GROUPMEANS=, but not both. This value can be based on the observed or a hypothesized mean difference. Alternatively, this mean difference can be estimated by setting it to missing (.).
NULLDIFF=	specifies the mean difference under the null hypothesis. The default value is 0.
GROUPSTDDEVS=	specifies the standard deviation of each group. This specification is valid only when TEST=DIFF_SATT is specified.
STDDEV=	specifies the standard deviation that is assumed to be equal in both groups. In Examples 12.1a and 12.1b, this option is specified to equal the observed pooled standard deviation under Diff (1–2). This option can also be specified to equal a hypothesized standard deviation. Alternatively, this standard deviation can be estimated by setting it to missing (.).
GROUPNS=	specifies the sample size for each group. One sample size can be estimated by setting it to missing (.), while the other is specified. For example, GROUPNS=(9,.).
NPERGROUP=	specifies the common sample size for both groups. This common sample size can be estimated by setting it to missing (.).
GROUPWEIGHTS=	specifies the allocation of weight for each group. In Examples 12.1a and 12.1b, these weights are specified according to each group size. Weight of one group can be estimated by setting it to missing (.). For example, GROUPWEIGHTS=(1,.).
NTOTAL=	specifies the total sample size. This total sample size can be estimated by setting it to missing (.).

The **ONESAMPLEMEANS** statement estimates the sample size and performs power analysis for a one-sample t test. The options associated with this statement include the following:

TEST=T	specifies a t test of the mean.
MEAN=	specifies the single group mean. In Examples 12.2a and 12.2b, this one group mean is specified to equal the

observed mean. It can also be specified to equal a hypothesized mean. Alternatively, this mean value can be estimated by setting it to missing (.).

NULLMEAN= specifies the mean under the null hypothesis. The default value is 0.

STDDEV= specifies the standard deviation. In Examples 12.2a and 12.2b, this standard deviation is specified to equal the observed standard deviation. It can also be specified to equal a hypothesized standard deviation. Alternatively, this standard deviation can be estimated by setting it to missing (.).

NTOTAL= specifies the sample size. This number can be estimated by setting it to missing (.).

The **PAIREDMEANS** statement estimates the sample size and performs power analysis for a paired-samples *t* test. The options associated with this statement include the following:

TEST=DIFF specifies a *t* test of the paired mean difference.

PAIREDMEANS= specifies the two paired means. These two paired means can be specified to equal the observed paired means or hypothetical paired means. You must specify this option or MEANDIFF=, but not both.

MEANDIFF= specifies the paired mean difference. In Examples 12.3a and 12.3b, this option is specified to equal the observed paired mean difference. This option can also be specified to equal a hypothesized paired mean difference. You must specify this option or PAIRED-MEANS=, but not both.

PAIREDSTDDEVS= specifies the standard deviation of each variable used in the paired-samples *t* test. This option can also be specified to equal two hypothesized standard deviations. You must specify this option or STDDEV=, but not both.

STDDEV= specifies the common standard deviation. In Examples 12.3a and 12.3b, this option is specified to equal the observed standard deviation of the difference between critical and satv scores. It can also be specified to equal a hypothesized standard deviation of the difference scores. You must specify this option or PAIREDSTDDEVS=, but not both.

CORR= specifies the correlation between the two variables used in the paired-samples *t* test. In Examples 12.3a and 12.3b, this option is specified to equal the observed correlation. It can also be specified to equal a hypothesized correlation. This correlation must be specified.

NPAIRS= specifies the number of pairs. This number can be estimated by setting it to missing (.).

The **PLOT** statement generates graphs for power analysis or sample size estimations. The options available on the PLOT statement include the following:

INTERPOL=	**NONE**	does not connect estimated values.
	JOIN	connects estimated values with a straight line.
X=	**N**	assigns the X-axis of the plot to represent sample size.
	POWER	assigns the X-axis of the plot to represent statistical power.
Y=	**N**	assigns the Y-axis of the plot to represent sample size.
	POWER	assigns the Y-axis of the plot to represent statistical power.
		[**Note:** X= and Y= options cannot be specified simultaneously.]
MAX=		specifies the maximum of the range of values for the axis specified.
MIN=		specifies the minimum of the range of values for the axis specified.

12.5 Tips

- How to handle missing or invalid data

By default, the TTEST procedure does not include observations that have missing information on either the CLASS variable or the VAR variable. If multiple dependent variables are listed on the VAR statement, PROC TTEST applies the pairwise deletion method to observations, namely, it omits observations only from the dependent variable for which the observations have missing values.

- What are the statistical assumptions associated with the *t* test?

The three *t* tests covered in this chapter assume that (1) the population distribution from which data were drawn is normally distributed and (2) samples are random. For the independent-samples *t* test, a third assumption is that variances of the two normal populations are equal. These assumptions are referred to in the literature as the normality assumption, the independence assumption, and the equal variance assumption.

- What to do if data do not satisfy the statistical assumptions

Statisticians in general agree that violations of the normality assumption can be compensated by using large samples. As a general rule of thumb, large samples refer to 30 or more observations in each sample. In the case of the independent-samples *t* test, it is recommended that you have 30 or more in each group or 60 or more for the total sample.

The consequences of violating the independence assumption can be quite detrimental. Because, in this case, the sampling errors are correlated, the statistic computed according to the *t* formula no longer follows a *t* distribution.

Consequently, the *t*-test result and its associated *p* value are not valid. Obviously, this can be a serious problem. There are several strategies that you can employ to avoid the knotty problem of correlated sampling errors. First, you can assign a random number to each observation in your population and then select a certain number (say, 30) of observations based on the random number. Two random number functions, RANNOR and RANUNI, are helpful in this regard and are illustrated in Chapter 7 (see also Exercise 1 of this chapter). Second, you may use the last two digits of a person's identification number to achieve the randomness in selecting participants; say, you select those with the last two digits from the range of 20 to 39, 50 to 59, or above 70. Third, you may rely on birthdays to randomly select and randomly assign individuals into either a treatment or a control group. For example, select those with birth months in March, June, September, and December. Then assign those with even birthdays to the treatment group and those with odd birthdays to the control group. Remember, the goal in random selection and random assignment is to ensure that each individual in the population has an equal opportunity to be chosen, and in the case of an independent-samples *t* test, that each individual is equally likely to be assigned to either one of the two groups.

The third assumption, that is, the equal population variance assumption, applies to the independent-samples *t* test only. In light of several Monte Carlo studies, this assumption is robust with regard to equal sample sizes. So if possible, you should maintain both sample sizes equal, or at least, very close to each other. According to Moser and Stevens (1992), the *t* test defined in **Section 12.1** is appropriate under the condition of equal sample sizes. If sample sizes are unequal or the two population variances are different, they recommend the Satterthwaite approximate test—namely, the *t* test printed under **Variance Unequal** (refer back to Example 12.1). These recommendations were made in the interest of achieving an optimal statistical power and adequate control of the Type I error rate.

In the worst possible scenario in which sample sizes are unequal and terribly small, and the populations are far from normal, you can still fall back on nonparametric versions of the *t* test. These procedures are explained in Chapter 14.

For a detailed review of statistical assumptions and their robustness, you are encouraged to read an article by Glass, Peckham, and Sanders (1972).

- What is the difference between a one-tailed and a two-tailed *p* value?

A one-tailed *p* value is associated with a one-tailed *t* test, whereas the two-tailed *p* value is associated with a two-tailed *t* test. The choice between a one-tailed and a two-tailed *t* test depends on the purpose of the *t* test. In an exploratory study, a researcher usually does not know beforehand which of the two means is higher. Consequently, he or she states the alternative hypothesis in a nondirectional form; it implies that one mean can be higher or lower (or better or worse) than the other mean. This can be the case in medical studies. For this type of research, a two-tailed *p* value is recommended. A two-tailed *p* value is displayed under the heading "Pr > |t|". A two-tailed test result is the default output for all *t* tests conducted by the TTEST procedure.

If, however, you prefer to carry out a one-tailed t test, the alternative hypothesis is therefore stated as a directional proposition. In this case, a one-tailed p value should be reported. The one-tailed p value is half of the two-tailed p value. Hence, it is obtained by dividing the "Pr > |t|" value by 2. One-tailed p values and directional alternative hypotheses are often desired in confirmatory studies for which a particular outcome (e.g., the treatment group mean is higher than the control group mean) is anticipated, and therefore, needs to be confirmed.

Because a one-tailed p value is always smaller than a two-tailed p value, a one-tailed t test is more powerful than a two-tailed t test, given that the sample size, observed difference in means, and α level are kept as constants. This is a canon law with all statistical tests, not just the t test. You should not, however, report a one-tailed p value merely because it reaches the 0.05 significance level while the two-tailed p value does not. Nor should you look at the data first before deciding whether a one-tailed or two-tailed test should be performed. The decision should always be guided by the purpose of your study.

In power analysis and sample size estimations, the directionality of a t test is specified by the option **SIDES=**. Refer back to **Section 12.4** for a detailed explanation of this option.

- How to use ODS with the TTEST procedure

To use the ODS, you need to know ODS table names corresponding with various portions of the output. Table 12.1 presents ODS table names for the TTEST procedure and their descriptions.

Table 12.1   ODS Table Names and Descriptions for the TTEST Procedure

ODS Table Name	Description	TTEST Procedure Statement
Statistics	Univariate summary statistics	PROC TTEST
TTests	Result of t tests	PROC TTEST
Equality	Tests of equality of variances	CLASS

Based on the list of ODS table names, you may select certain results to be displayed in the Output window. For example, the following program selects the test of equality of variance result of Example 12.1 to be included in the output:

```
ODS SELECT Ttest.Equality;
PROC TTEST DATA=mydata ALPHA=0.1;
    CLASS sex;
    VAR satv;
RUN;
```

Likewise, you may select certain result(s) to be exported as a SAS data set. For example, the following program exports the test of equality of variance result of Example 12.1 to the SAS data set <u>equalvar</u>:

```
ODS OUTPUT  Equality = equalvar;
PROC TTEST DATA=mydata ALPHA=0.1;
     CLASS sex;
     VAR satv;
RUN;
```

Furthermore, you may select certain results to be saved in file formats other than the SAS standard output. For example, the following program saves the output of Example 12.1 in HTML format in its default style:

```
ODS HTML BODY = 'd:\result\Example12_1Body.html'
         CONTENTS = 'd:\result\Example12_1TOC.html'
         PAGE = 'd:\result\Example12_1Page.html'
         FRAME = 'd:\result\Example12_1Frame.html';

PROC TTEST DATA=mydata ALPHA=0.1;
     CLASS sex;
     VAR satv;
RUN;

ODS HTML CLOSE;
RUN;
```

For additional information about the ODS feature, consult with *SAS 9.1.3 Output Delivery System: User's Guide* (SAS Institute Inc., 2006c) and *SAS/STAT User's Guide* (SAS Institute Inc., 2004d) or the online documentation at www.sas.com.

12.6 Summary

Three *t* tests are differentiated and illustrated in this chapter. The independent-samples *t* test is suitable for comparing two means obtained from two unrelated samples. The other two *t* tests, namely, the paired-samples *t* test and the one-sample *t* test, can also be performed by the TTEST procedure. The paired-samples *t* test is applicable to data collected from (1) the same individuals on two different occasions or under two conditions or (2) two groups of individuals who are related. The paired-samples *t* test is a special case of the one-sample *t* test. The one-sample *t* test tests a sample mean against a hypothetical population mean.

For each of these three t tests, power calculation and sample size estimation are also demonstrated using the POWER procedure. You are encouraged to always estimate an adequate sample size before conducting a t-test analysis of data, in order to achieve a desirable statistical power at a given α level. After the data are analyzed by a t test, you should calculate the statistical power to ensure that it is sufficient to test the null hypothesis against the alternative hypothesis.

All three t tests assume that the population distribution(s) possesses certain characteristics. These characteristics are statistical assumptions. These assumptions are discussed under **Section 12.5: Tips**, along with discussions of what to do if one or more assumptions are violated by the data.

12.7 Exercises

1. Randomly generate 30 data points from a standard normal distribution for each of two groups and compare their mean difference. (*Hint*: Use the RANNOR function and the TTEST procedure.)

2. The following are results of an English test for Classes A and B. Is there any significant difference between the two classes on this test?

   A: 72, 66, 89, 87, 78, 92, 69, 76, 80, 77

   B: 74, 86, 76, 92, 84, 79, 86, 89, 90, 82

3. The following are survey results of 16 randomly interviewed adults on the amount of time spent, in hours, on three sports in a typical week. Is there any significant gender difference in the amount of time spent on each sport? What is the statistical power for the t test performed? What does the power mean?

Gender	Age	Swimming	Jogging	Ball Games
Male	27	1.2	0.2	3.3
	42	0.7	1.5	2.1
	37	0	1.2	2.0
	26	1.2	0.6	3.4
	53	2.4	0	0
	24	1.8	0	3.6
	33	0	0.3	2.7
	48	2	0	2.5

(Continued)

(Continued)

Gender	Age	Swimming	Jogging	Ball Games
Female	44	1.2	0.8	0.4
	28	1.6	1.1	2.1
	36	2.0	0.6	1.9
	46	2.2	0.3	0
	24	1.4	0	1.7
	32	0.5	0	2.1
	25	0	1.0	2.6
	30	0	0.5	1.8

4. According to the data in Exercise 3, can you conclude that adults in general spend more time swimming than jogging? What is the statistical power for the *t* test performed? What does the power mean?

5. On the eve of the NCAA championship game, fans were curious about which team would win the 2007 championship: Kentucky or Syracuse. Here are average scores of each team's top 10 players during the NCAA tournament.

Players	1	2	3	4	5	6	7	8	9	10
Kentucky	22.2	12.6	16.1	8.2	19	9.5	22.3	11.5	19.7	14.3
Syracuse	11.4	13.2	12	16.6	20.1	14.3	16.8	15.4	14.2	16.1

Analyze the data to answer the following questions:

a. Which team has a higher average score?
b. Is the difference between mean scores of two teams significant?
c. Which team's coach would have an easier time replacing players on the court? In other words, which team's players have a more homogeneous scoring ability?

6. As stated in the discussion of Example 12.1a, in order to calculate the power of Satterthwaite's approximate *t* test, you need to replace the TEST=DIFF option in Example 12.1a with the TEST=DIFF_SATT option, and replace STDDEV=124.69 with GROUPSTDDEVS=(146.85 110.93). Modify Example 12.1a with these changes and find out the statistical power for the Satterthwaite's approximate *t* test performed in Example 12.1, the total sample size needed to achieve a power of 0.80 at an α level of 0.10 and three power curves corresponding to αs of 0.01, 0.05, and 0.10 for a range of the total sample size extending from 22 to 3,300.

12.8   Answers to Exercises

1. The following data were generated from the RANNOR function using seed= 123456, and subsequently tested by the TTEST procedure.

```
        Exercise 12-1                                                    1

Obs      n     group      value

  1      1       1       -0.10948
  2      1       2       -0.34878
  3      2       1        1.12025
  4      2       2       -2.51377
  5      3       1        1.36300
  6      3       2        0.65790
  7      4       1       -0.49471
  8      4       2       -1.06210
  9      5       1        1.02766
 10      5       2       -0.28383
 11      6       1        0.16910
 12      6       2       -0.08707
 13      7       1       -0.58665
 14      7       2        0.60344
 15      8       1       -1.69741
 16      8       2        0.02942
 17      9       1       -0.41919
 18      9       2        1.98470
 19     10       1        0.23515
 20     10       2       -1.12024
 21     11       1        0.66080
 22     11       2        0.95414
 23     12       1       -0.12908
 24     12       2        0.33244
 25     13       1       -0.48131
 26     13       2       -0.61804
 27     14       1       -0.41520
 28     14       2        0.89147
 29     15       1        2.08281
 30     15       2       -0.68353
 31     16       1       -1.75711
 32     16       2       -0.05267
 33     17       1       -1.65693
 34     17       2       -1.63120
 35     18       1        0.91470
 36     18       2       -0.37230
 37     19       1       -0.37718
 38     19       2        1.44819
 39     20       1       -1.05801
 40     20       2       -0.25334
 41     21       1       -0.69800
 42     21       2        0.45578
 43     22       1       -0.25481
 44     22       2       -0.43200
 45     23       1       -0.65860
 46     23       2        1.00784
 47     24       1       -0.15749
 48     24       2        2.23923
 49     25       1       -0.22921
 50     25       2       -0.38275
 51     26       1       -0.54120
 52     26       2        0.54793
 53     27       1        1.04788
 54     27       2        0.02259
 55     28       1        1.23261
 56     28       2       -0.33605
 57     29       1        2.15686
 58     29       2       -0.08925
 59     30       1        0.57182
 60     30       2       -0.69824
```

```
                              Exercise 12-1                            2

                           The TTEST Procedure

                               Statistics

                         Lower CL              Upper CL  Lower CL            Upper CL
Variable   group        N    Mean     Mean        Mean   Std Dev  Std Dev   Std Dev

value          1       30   -0.351   0.0287     0.4083    0.8095   1.0165    1.3665
value          2       30   -0.365   0.007      0.3788    0.793    0.9958    1.3386
value      Diff (1-2)       -0.498   0.0217     0.5417    0.8518   1.0062    1.2295

                               Statistics

            Variable  group        Std Err   Minimum    Maximum

            value         1        0.1856    -1.757     2.1569
            value         2        0.1818    -2.514     2.2392
            value     Diff (1-2)   0.2598


                               T-Tests

        Variable   Method        Variances    DF    t Value    Pr > |t|

        value      Pooled        Equal        58       0.08      0.9337
        value      Satterthwaite Unequal      58       0.08      0.9337


                        Equality of Variances

        Variable    Method    Num DF   Den DF   F Value   Pr > F

        value      Folded F     29       29      1.04     0.9124
```

Conclusion: The *F* test of the equal variance assumption is not significant at the conventional 0.05 level and both samples have the same size; hence, you need to examine the *t* value (= 0.08) with 58 degrees of freedom (DF). This *t* test is not statistically significant at the α level of 0.05. Hence, we conclude that these random data have equal means.

2.

```
                              Exercise 12-2                            1

                           The TTEST Procedure

                               Statistics

                         Lower CL              Upper CL  Lower CL            Upper CL
Variable   class        N    Mean     Mean        Mean   Std Dev  Std Dev   Std Dev

score      Class A     10   72.454   78.6       84.746    5.9099   8.592    15.686
score      Class B     10   79.497   83.8       88.103    4.1372   6.0148   10.981
score      Diff (1-2)       -12.17   -5.2        1.768    5.6038   7.4162   10.967

                               Statistics

            Variable  class        Std Err   Minimum    Maximum

            score     Class A       2.717       66         92
            score     Class B       1.902       74         92
            score     Diff (1-2)    3.3166
```

```
                              T-Tests

      Variable    Method          Variances     DF    t Value    Pr > |t|

      score       Pooled          Equal         18      -1.57      0.1343
      score       Satterthwaite   Unequal      16.1     -1.57      0.1363


                        Equality of Variances

          Variable    Method      Num DF   Den DF   F Value   Pr > F

          score       Folded F      9        9       2.04     0.3029
```

Conclusion: The *F* test of the equal variance assumption is not significant at the conventional level of 0.05 and both samples have the same size; hence, you examine the *t* value (= −1.57) with 18 degrees of freedom (DF). This *t* test does not reach the α level of 0.05. Hence, we conclude that there is no significant difference between the two classes on this test.

3.

```
                              Exercise 12-3                                   1

                            The TTEST Procedure

                                Statistics

                       Lower CL              Upper CL   Lower CL            Upper CL
Variable   group      N    Mean     Mean        Mean    Std Dev   Std Dev   Std Dev

swim       Male       8   0.4175   1.1625     1.9075    0.5892    0.8911    1.8137
swim       Female     8   0.5453   1.2375     1.9297    0.5474    0.828     1.6851
swim       Diff (1-2)     -0.997   -0.075     0.8474    0.6297    0.8601    1.3565
jog        Male       8   -0.012   0.475      0.962     0.3851    0.5825    1.1855
jog        Female     8   0.1858   0.5375     0.8892    0.2781    0.4207    0.8562
jog        Diff (1-2)     -0.607   -0.063     0.4823    0.372     0.5081    0.8013
ball       Male       8   1.4843   2.45       3.4157    0.7637    1.1551    2.351
ball       Female     8   0.8249   1.575      2.3251    0.5932    0.8972    1.8261
ball       Diff (1-2)     -0.234   0.875      1.9841    0.7572    1.0342    1.6311

                                Statistics

              Variable   group       Std Err   Minimum   Maximum

              swim       Male         0.3151       0        2.4
              swim       Female       0.2927       0        2.2
              swim       Diff (1-2)   0.4301
              jog        Male         0.2059       0        1.5
              jog        Female       0.1487       0        1.1
              jog        Diff (1-2)   0.254
              ball       Male         0.4084       0        3.6
              ball       Female       0.3172       0        2.6
              ball       Diff (1-2)   0.5171
```

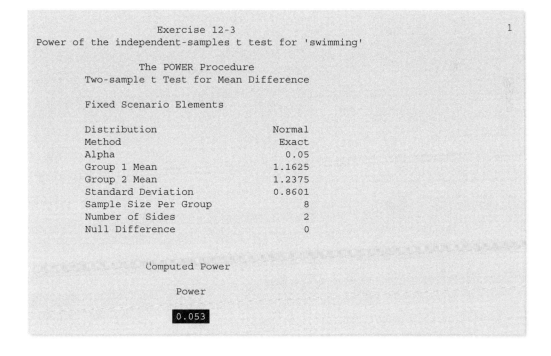

```
                              T-Tests

       Variable    Method          Variances    DF   t Value   Pr > |t|

       swim        Pooled          Equal        14    -0.17     0.8641
       swim        Satterthwaite   Unequal      13.9  -0.17     0.8641
       jog         Pooled          Equal        14    -0.25     0.8092
       jog         Satterthwaite   Unequal      12.7  -0.25     0.8096
       ball        Pooled          Equal        14     1.69     0.1128
       ball        Satterthwaite   Unequal      13.2   1.69     0.1141


                        Equality of Variances

         Variable    Method      Num DF   Den DF   F Value   Pr > F

           swim      Folded F       7        7      1.16     0.8512
           jog       Folded F       7        7      1.92     0.4099
           ball      Folded F       7        7      1.66     0.5210
```

Conclusion: The three *t*-test results are not statistically significant at the α level of 0.05. We can conclude that there is no significant gender difference in the amount of time spent on each sport.

```
                        Exercise 12-3                               1
        Power of the independent-samples t test for 'swimming'

                        The POWER Procedure
                  Two-sample t Test for Mean Difference


                Fixed Scenario Elements

                Distribution              Normal
                Method                    Exact
                Alpha                     0.05
                Group 1 Mean              1.1625
                Group 2 Mean              1.2375
                Standard Deviation        0.8601
                Sample Size Per Group     8
                Number of Sides           2
                Null Difference           0



                      Computed Power

                      Power

                      0.053
```

Conclusion: At the α level of 0.05, the power of the independent-samples *t* test of swimming is 0.053. In other words, the *t* test performed has a mere probability of 0.053 of rejecting the null hypothesis even if it is incorrect.

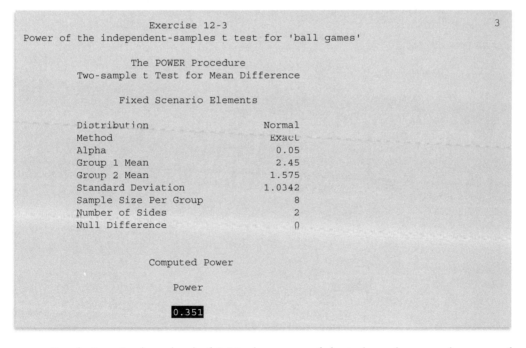

```
                       Exercise 12-3                                    2
    Power of the independent-samples t test for 'jogging'

                     The POWER Procedure
              Two-sample t Test for Mean Difference

                   Fixed Scenario Elements

           Distribution                    Normal
           Method                          Exact
           Alpha                            0.05
           Group 1 Mean                    0.475
           Group 2 Mean                   0.5375
           Standard Deviation             0.5081
           Sample Size Per Group               8
           Number of Sides                     2
           Null Difference                     0


                     Computed Power

                        Power

                       0.056
```

Conclusion: At the α level of 0.05, the power of the independent-samples t test of jogging is 0.056. In other words, the t test performed has a mere probability of 0.056 of rejecting the null hypothesis even if it is incorrect.

```
                       Exercise 12-3                                    3
    Power of the independent-samples t test for 'ball games'

                     The POWER Procedure
              Two-sample t Test for Mean Difference

                   Fixed Scenario Elements

           Distribution                    Normal
           Method                          Exact
           Alpha                            0.05
           Group 1 Mean                     2.45
           Group 2 Mean                    1.575
           Standard Deviation             1.0342
           Sample Size Per Group               8
           Number of Sides                     2
           Null Difference                     0


                     Computed Power

                        Power

                       0.351
```

Conclusion: At the α level of 0.05, the power of the independent-samples t test of ball games is 0.351. In other words, the t test performed has a probability of 0.351 of rejecting the null hypothesis if it is incorrect.

4.

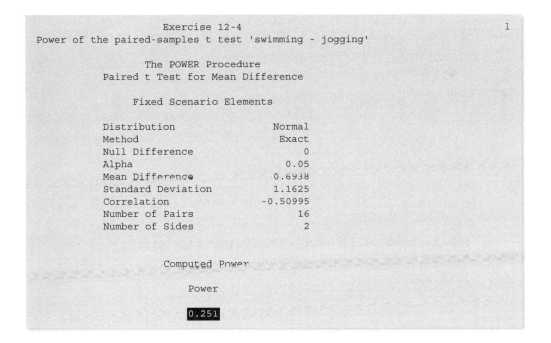

Conclusion: The paired-samples *t*-test result (= 2.39) is statistically significant at the 0.05 level. We can conclude that adults in the sample spent more time swimming than jogging.

Conclusion: At the α level of 0.05, the power of the paired-samples *t* test is 0.251. In other words, the *t* test performed has a probability of 0.251 of rejecting the null hypothesis if it is incorrect.

5.

```
                              Exercise 12-5                                    1

                           The TTEST Procedure

                               Statistics

                   Lower CL              Upper CL  Lower CL          Upper CL
Variable  school       N    Mean    Mean    Mean   Std Dev  Std Dev  Std Dev

score     Kentucky    10  11.873   15.54  19.207    3.526   5.1262   9.3585
score     Syracuse    10  13.171   15.01  16.849   1.7687   2.5714   4.6944
score     Diff (1-2)       -3.28    0.53   4.3402   3.0642   4.0553    5.997

                               Statistics

             Variable  school      Std Err   Minimum   Maximum

             score     Kentucky     1.6211       8.2      22.3
             score     Syracuse     0.8131      11.4      20.1
             score     Diff (1-2)   1.8136


                                 T-Tests

        Variable   Method          Variances    DF   t Value   Pr > |t|

        score      Pooled          Equal        18     0.29     0.7734
        score      Satterthwaite   Unequal    13.3     0.29     0.7746


                        Equality of Variances

           Variable    Method      Num DF   Den DF   F Value   Pr > F

           score       Folded F        9        9      3.97    0.0520
```

a. The Kentucky team had a slightly higher average score.

b. The Syracuse team's coach would have an easier time replacing players on the court. The team had a smaller standard deviation in scores than the Kentucky team.

c. The t-test result (= 0.29) is not significant at the α level of 0.05. We can conclude that there is no statistically significant difference between mean scores of these two teams.

6. The statistical power for the Satterthwaite approximate t test performed in Example 12.1 is 0.110 at an α level of 0.1.

```
                        Exercise 12-6                          1
                        Power Analysis


                      The POWER Procedure
     Two-sample t Test for Mean Difference with Unequal Variances

                     Fixed Scenario Elements

         Distribution                        Normal
         Method                               Exact
         Group 1 Mean                        533.75
         Group 2 Mean                        518.57
         Group 1 Standard Deviation          146.85
         Group 2 Standard Deviation          110.93
         Group 1 Weight                           8
         Group 2 Weight                          14
         Total Sample Size                       22
         Number of Sides                          2
         Null Difference                          0



                       Computed Power

                    Nominal    Actual
          Index      Alpha      Alpha      Power

            1        0.01       0.011      0.013
            2        0.05       0.051      0.057
            3        0.10       0.101      0.110
```

The total sample needed to achieve a power of 0.80 at an α level of 0.10 is 2,134 (776 men and 1,358 women).

```
                        Exercise 12-6                          2
                     Sample Size Estimation


                      The POWER Procedure
     Two-sample t Test for Mean Difference with Unequal Variances

                     Fixed Scenario Elements

         Distribution                        Normal
         Method                               Exact
         Nominal Alpha                          0.1
         Group 1 Mean                        533.75
         Group 2 Mean                        518.57
         Group 1 Standard Deviation          146.85
         Group 2 Standard Deviation          110.93
         Group 1 Weight                           8
         Group 2 Weight                          14
         Nominal Power                          0.8
         Number of Sides                          2
         Null Difference                          0



                      Computed N Total

          Actual     Actual       N
          Alpha      Power      Total

           0.1       0.804       2134
```

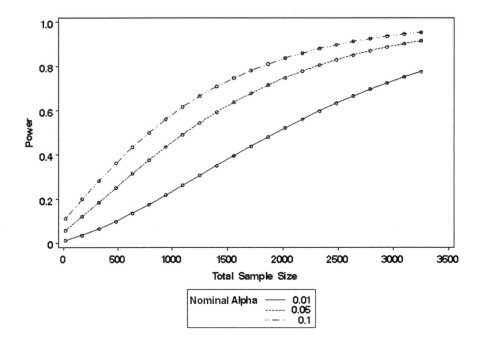

13

Analysis of Variance

┌─ **O B J E C T I V E** ─────────────────────────────────────┐

In this chapter, useful analysis of variance (ANOVA) techniques for comparing group means are presented. Specifically, the one-way ANOVA, two-way ANOVA, randomized block, Latin-square, repeated measures, and analysis of covariance techniques are treated in depth. Statistical assumptions and their robustness are likewise discussed. Tests of planned or complex comparisons of means are also illustrated.

└──┘

13.1 Basic Concepts in Analysis of Variance

13.2 An Overview of the GLM Procedure for ANOVA

13.3 Examples

13.4 How to Write the PROC GLM Codes

Main Effect Design

Completely Factorial Design

Nested Design

Randomized Block Design

13.5 Tips

How to Handle Missing or Invalid Data

What Are the Statistical Assumptions Associated With the F Test Conducted in One-Way Fixed-Effects ANOVA?

What to Do If Data Do Not Satisfy the Statistical Assumptions in One-Way Fixed-Effects ANOVA

What If the Research Design Is Unbalanced?

13.1 Basic Concepts in Analysis of Variance _____

The term *analysis of variance* probably sounds familiar to you, especially if you have been schooled in at least one quantitative methodology course or have been working in the field of social sciences for some time. Analysis of variance (ANOVA), as the name implies, is a statistical technique that is intended to analyze variability in data in order to infer the inequality among population means. This may sound illogical, but there is more to this idea than just what the name implies.

The ANOVA technique extends what an independent-samples t test can do to multiple means. The null hypothesis examined by the independent-samples t test is that two population means are equal. If more than two means are compared, repeated use of the independent-samples t test will lead to a higher Type I error rate (the experiment-wise α level) than the α level set for each t test. A better approach than the t test is to consider all means in one null hypothesis—that is, examining the plausibility of the null hypothesis with a single statistical test. In doing so, researchers not only save time and energy, but more important, they can exercise a better control of the probability of falsely declaring significant differences among means. Such an idea was conceived by Sir R. A. Fisher more than 50 years ago. In his honor, the statistic used in ANOVA is called an F statistic.

The F statistic is a ratio. Its numerator and denominator are both estimates. When the null hypothesis of equal population means holds up, both estimates should be similar because they are estimates of the same quantity, that is, the variance of sampling errors. Under the alternative hypothesis, though, the numerator estimates not only the variance of sampling errors but also the squared treatment effect. And the denominator still estimates the error variance. Thus, the F ratio under the alternative hypothesis is noticeably larger than 1. The extent to which the observed F ratio is larger than 1 provides the basis for rejecting the null hypothesis in ANOVA.

Suppose that data were obtained from a typical state university on students' drinking behavior. The university had a policy banning hard liquors and beer from university properties, including dorms and Greek houses. But everybody knew somebody who drank while living on campus at this university. Students living off campus were even more likely to drink, perhaps. Let's look at weekly average drinks consumed by four groups of students and their variability:

```
                    Example 13.0 Average drinks and variability                  1

                              The MEANS Procedure

                 Analysis Variable : score1 no. of drinks in spring break

Four housing        N
conditions         Obs            Mean         Std Dev        Maximum        Minimum
------------------------------------------------------------------------------------
Dorm                8       3.0000000       1.5118579      6.0000000      1.0000000

Greek               8       3.5000000       0.9258201      5.0000000      2.0000000

Off-campus apt      8       4.2500000       1.0350983      6.0000000      3.0000000

Rented house        8       6.2500000       1.2817399      8.0000000      5.0000000
------------------------------------------------------------------------------------
```

Notice from the printout that all sample means are different; so are sample standard deviations. To what extent can one know that the variation among these four means is not merely the variation that already existed among individuals, even in the same housing condition? The answer lies in an *F* test. The *F* test is formed from the mean square between groups or conditions divided by the mean square within groups. Both mean squares estimate the variance of sampling errors under the null hypothesis, as alluded to before. Under the alternative hypothesis, though, the mean square between groups will be larger than the mean square within groups. This is so because the mean square between groups, in this case, reflects not only sampling errors but also the varying numbers of drinks consumed by students living in four conditions. Thus, a significant *F* is indicated by a magnitude that is larger than 1 and statistically significant (see Example 13.1 for the *F* result and its *p* level).

The *F* test introduced in this chapter is associated with three statistical assumptions. The first assumption is that observations are randomly or independently selected from their respective populations. The second is that the shape of population distributions is normal. And the third is that these normal populations have identical variances. The consequences of violating any or all of these assumptions are discussed in **Section 13.5: Tips.** Suggestions on how to compensate for violating the assumptions are also included in the same section.

___ 13.2 An Overview of the GLM Procedure for ANOVA

The GLM procedure is particularly well suited for analyzing data collected in any ANOVA design. The procedure name, GLM, stands for general linear models, which is the type of statistical models imposed on data in all ANOVA designs. A general linear model accounts for data in terms of main effects, interaction effects, nested effects, time-related effects, or merely sampling errors (or random errors). Correspondingly, types of ANOVA designs specified in the GLM procedure include completely randomized (Example 13.1), randomized factorial (Examples 13.2 and 13.3), randomized block (Example 13.4), Latin-square (Examples 13.5 and 13.6), repeated measures (Example 13.7), analysis of covariance (ANCOVA) (Examples 13.8 and 13.9), and any combination of these designs. Designs can be balanced (or orthogonal) or unbalanced. A balanced design is a design in which groups or cells have an equal number or a proportional number of data points in them. An unbalanced design does not have this property. Whenever possible, you should strive for a balanced design. Reasons for this suggestion are given in **Section 13.5: Tips.**

Two approaches, the univariate and the multivariate tests, for data collected from repeated measures designs are available in PROC GLM. Both are illustrated in Example 13.7.

Besides testing various null hypotheses with an *F* test, the GLM procedure offers a variety of multiple comparison procedures for the means. These include Dunn's (or the Bonferroni *t*) test, the Dunn-Šidák test, the one- and two-tailed Dunnett tests, the Scheffé test, the Newman-Keuls test, and Tukey's Honestly Significant Difference (or HSD) test. All are illustrated in this chapter. Other comparison procedures are presented in the online documentation at www.sas.com under the GLM procedure. Each test can be performed with a user-specified α level (see **Section 13.4**). Alternatively, you may request that a confidence interval be constructed for each pair of means. Tests of cell means for interactions or planned orthogonal contrasts are also available in PROC GLM. These are demonstrated in **Section 13.5**.

13.3 Examples

Data used in the following nine examples are from the raw data file design.dat. They are analyzed according to various ANOVA designs so as to illustrate certain data analysis techniques. All examples assume that the effects are fixed. Because of this, the interpretations of results presented in this chapter are for illustrative purposes only.

Example 13.1 One-Way Analysis of Variance

Do college students drink on campus, even against university policy? You bet, speaking from personal observations and the literature! But just how much do they drink? Let's investigate this issue by interviewing 32 students from a state university. These 32 students were randomly selected in equal numbers from (a) university dorms, (b) Greek houses, (c) off-campus apartments, and (d) rented houses. These students were asked to keep an honest record of drinks consumed during the spring-break week. To encourage these students to be honest, they were told that their data would remain confidential and be part of a national survey of college students' life on campus.

One intriguing question regarding college students' drinking is whether students in different housing arrangements exercised varying degrees of constraints on their drinking behavior and, hence, they drank varying amounts during the spring break. This question can be answered by a one-way ANOVA.

The program below addresses the question of how housing arrangements are related to weekly consumption of beer and hard liquor by college students during the spring break (score1). It consists of four statements. The first statement, **PROC GLM**, identifies a SAS data set design to be analyzed. The second statement, **CLASS**, lists one independent variable, indep1. The third statement, **MODEL**, specifies the design to be a one-way ANOVA design. Following the MODEL statement, the **MEANS** statement is used to carry out comparisons of group means. The two comparison procedures listed after slash (/) are **BON** and **TUKEY**. BON stands for Bonferroni t test, or the Dunn procedure, whereas TUKEY stands for Tukey's Honestly Significant Difference (or HSD) test.

```
/* The following bolded SAS statements establish the SAS data set 'design' */

PROC FORMAT;
    VALUE resident 1='Dorm' 2='Greek' 3='Off-campus apt' 4='Rented house';
RUN;

DATA design;
    INFILE 'd:\data\design.dat';
    INPUT indep1 id score1 score2 score3 sex $ major;
    LABEL indep1='four housing conditions'
          id='student id no.'
          score1='no. of drinks during the spring break'
          score2='no. of drinks during the final week'
          score3='no. of drinks after the final week'
          major='student academic major';
    FORMAT indep1 resident.;
RUN;

TITLE 'Example 13.1 One-way analysis of variance';

PROC GLM DATA=design;
    CLASS indep1;
    MODEL score1=indep1;
    MEANS indep1 / BON TUKEY;
RUN; QUIT;
```

Output 13.1 One-Way Analysis of Variance

```
          Example 13.1 One-way analysis of variance                    1

                    The GLM Procedure

                 Class Level Information

  Class      Levels    Values

  indep1        4      Dorm Greek Off-campus apt Rented house


          Number of Observations Read        32
          Number of Observations Used        32
```

```
                    Example 13.1 One-way analysis of variance                    2

                            The GLM Procedure
Part (A)

Dependent Variable: score1   no. of drinks in spring break

                                    Sum of
    Source                 DF       Squares    Mean Square   F Value   Pr > F

    Model                   3      49.00000000  16.33333333    11.15   <.0001

    Error                  28      41.00000000   1.46428571

    Corrected Total        31      90.00000000
Part (B)
              R-Square     Coeff Var      Root MSE     score1 Mean

              0.544444      28.47239       1.210077      4.250000
Part (C)

    Source                 DF      Type I SS    Mean Square   F Value   Pr > F

    indep1                  3     49.00000000  16.33333333    11.15   <.0001


    Source                 DF      Type III SS  Mean Square   F Value   Pr > F

    indep1                  3     49.00000000  16.33333333    11.15   <.0001
```

```
                    Example 13.1 One-way analysis of variance                    3

                            The GLM Procedure

                 Tukey's Studentized Range (HSD) Test for score1

NOTE: This test controls the Type I experimentwise error rate, but it generally has a
                    higher Type II error rate than REGWQ.


              Alpha                                     0.05
              Error Degrees of Freedom                    28
              Error Mean Square                       1.464286
              Critical Value of Studentized Range     3.86125
              Minimum Significant Difference           1.6519


         Means with the same letter are not significantly different.


           Tukey Grouping          Mean      N    indep1

                        A        6.2500      8    Rented house

                        B        4.2500      8    Off-campus apt
                        B
                        B        3.5000      8    Greek
                        B
                        B        3.0000      8    Dorm
```

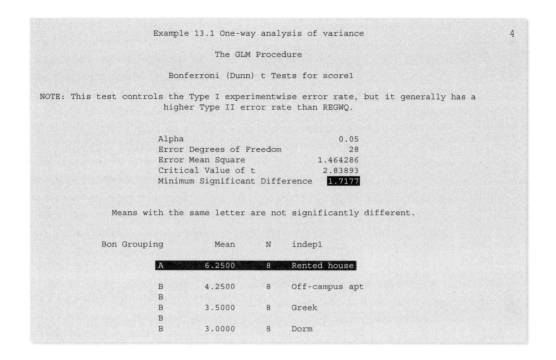

```
                    Example 13.1 One-way analysis of variance                    4

                              The GLM Procedure

                        Bonferroni (Dunn) t Tests for score1

    NOTE: This test controls the Type I experimentwise error rate, but it generally has a
                     higher Type II error rate than REGWQ.


                 Alpha                                     0.05
                 Error Degrees of Freedom                    28
                 Error Mean Square                      1.464286
                 Critical Value of t                     2.83893
                 Minimum Significant Difference           1.7177


         Means with the same letter are not significantly different.


       Bon Grouping          Mean     N    indep1

              A             6.2500     8    Rented house

              B             4.2500     8    Off-campus apt
              B
              B             3.5000     8    Greek
              B
              B             3.0000     8    Dorm
```

Page 1 of the output summarizes the ANOVA design: four levels (or groups) of the <u>indep1</u> factor and 32 data points. According to page 2 of the output, the F test of average drinks reaches a significance level of 0.0001. This means that students living in various environments did drink unequal amounts of beer and hard liquor during the spring break. This conclusion is confirmed by Tukey's HSD test (page 3) and the Bonferroni t test (page 4). Both tests reveal that "Rented house" is the hardest drinking group, which is followed, to a lesser degree, by "Off-campus apt", "Greek", and "Dorm", in that order. The average drink in the "Off-campus apt" group was found to be statistically significantly different from "Rented house" but not significantly different from the other two groups. Likewise, the "Greek" group was not statistically significantly different from the "Dorm" group. These differences are identified by different letters, such as A and B, printed under **Tukey Grouping** and **Bon Grouping**. Groups with the same letter are considered to be not statistically significantly different from each other.

Is it necessary to apply two comparison procedures, such as Tukey and Bonferroni t? For exploration of data and for illustration of these procedures in SAS, the answer is yes. For confirming a theory or cross-validating other findings, no. Because this chapter is intended to expose you to various comparison procedures available in the GLM procedure, two procedures were specified in the program. Tukey's HSD test was specifically developed to examine all possible simple (or pairwise) differences. It controls the Type I error rate at the family-wise level, namely, for the set of all pairwise comparisons. The Bonferroni t test (the Dunn procedure) is more flexible. It can be used to test differences between two means as well as among three or more means. Both procedures can handle equal as well as unequal group sizes. Perhaps you'd ask, "If the Bonferroni *t* test is more flexible than Tukey's test, why will anyone need Tukey's procedure at all?" The answer lies in the statistical power. The statistical power of each test is best understood by the heading **Minimum Significant Difference**. This value sets the criterion by which an observed mean difference is judged to be statistically significant. So the smaller this number, the greater is the power. For the current data, Tukey's test is more powerful because its Minimum Significant Difference (or MSD) of 1.6519 is smaller than 1.7177 for the Bonferroni test. The latter procedure is definitely more flexible; but its flexibility comes at a price. In general, Tukey's test is the most powerful test for all pairwise comparisons, and it controls the experiment-wise Type I error rate at or below the α level specified by the researcher. The Bonferroni test is well suited to a mixture of simple and complex comparisons, especially when the total number of comparisons is neither too few nor too many, say, between 10 and 15. It is important to note that all comparison procedures programmed into GLM examine pairwise differences only. If complex comparisons of means are desired, alternative specifications are needed (see **Section 13.5: Tips**).

Let's now return to page 2 of the output and pick up the rest of the information. **Part (A)** assesses the overall significance with an *F* test (= 11.15) and its *p* level (< 0.0001). Both **Type I** and **Type III SS** in **Part (C)** offer identical information as **Part (A)**. These two parts are identical only in a one-way ANOVA design, because there is only one effect to be tested. Therefore, **Part (C)** can be ignored for a one-way design. **Part (B)** presents four descriptive statistics. The first is **R-Square** (= 0.544444), which is the ratio of SS_{model} to SS_{total}, or 49/90. The R-Square value indicates that 54.4444% of the variability of the number of drinks consumed by students is explained by this one-way ANOVA model. The second is **Coeff Var (C.V.)**, which stands for coefficient of variation or the ratio of standard deviation divided by the overall mean times 100 (= 1.210077 ÷ 4.25 × 100 = 28.47239). The third is **Root MSE** or the square root of Mean Square Error $(=\sqrt{1.46428571} = 1.210077)$. The root MSE is the sample estimate for the population standard deviation. It is used to calculate the MSD reported on pages 3 and 4 of the output. The fourth statistic, **score1 Mean** (= 4.25), is the grand average of the dependent variable, that is, the average number of drinks consumed by 32 college students in this study.

Example 13.2 Two-Way Analysis of Variance

Because there is a common perception that men drink more than women, let's see if gender is a factor in the student survey described above. Let's suppose that out of eight students randomly selected from each of the four housing conditions, half were women and half were men. Hence, it is possible to study the gender effect, the housing condition, and the joint effect of both factors on college students' drinking behavior. The SAS program written below is much like the one presented in Example 13.1 except for the CLASS and the MODEL statements. The CLASS statement now lists indep1 and sex as independent variables. The MODEL statement has three terms listed on the right side of the equal sign (=): <u>indep1</u>, <u>sex</u>, and <u>indep1*sex</u>, which represent two main effects and one interaction, respectively. Thus, the corresponding design is a two-way ANOVA.

```
/* See Example 13.1 for the DATA step in creating the SAS data set 'design' */

TITLE 'Example 13.2 Two-way analysis of variance';

PROC GLM DATA=design;
    CLASS indep1 sex;
    MODEL score1=indep1 sex indep1*sex;
    MEANS sex indep1 / BON;
RUN; QUIT;
```

Output 13.2 Two-Way Analysis of Variance

```
Example 13.2 Two-way analysis of variance                                    1

          The GLM Procedure

        Class Level Information

  Class          Levels    Values

  indep1              4    1 2 3 4

  sex                 2    Female Male


Number of Observations Read         32
Number of Observations Used         32
```

```
                    Example 13.2 Two-way analysis of variance                2

                          The GLM Procedure
```

Part (A)

Dependent Variable: score1   no. of drinks in spring break

Source	DF	Sum of Squares	Mean Square	F Value	Pr > F
Model	7	60.00000000	8.57142857	6.86	0.0002
Error	24	30.00000000	1.25000000		
Corrected Total	31	90.00000000			

Part (B)

R-Square	Coeff Var	Root MSE	score1 Mean
0.666667	26.30668	1.118034	4.250000

Part (C)

Source	DF	Type I SS	Mean Square	F Value	Pr > F
indep1	3	49.00000000	16.33333333	13.07	<.0001
sex	1	8.00000000	8.00000000	6.40	0.0184
indep1*sex	3	3.00000000	1.00000000	0.80	0.5061

Source	DF	Type III SS	Mean Square	F Value	Pr > F
indep1	3	49.00000000	16.33333333	13.07	<.0001
sex	1	8.00000000	8.00000000	6.40	0.0184
indep1*sex	3	3.00000000	1.00000000	0.80	0.5061

```
                    Example 13.2 Two-way analysis of variance                    3

                            The GLM Procedure
Part (D)
                      Bonferroni (Dunn) t Tests for score1

NOTE: This test controls the Type I experimentwise error rate, but it generally has a
              higher Type II error rate than REGWQ.


                  Alpha                            0.05
                  Error Degrees of Freedom           24
                  Error Mean Square                1.25
                  Critical Value of t           2.06390
                  Minimum Significant Difference  0.8158


         Means with the same letter are not significantly different.


            Bon Grouping        Mean      N    sex

                   A          4.7500     16    Male

                   B          3.7500     16    Female
```

```
                    Example 13.2 Two-way analysis of variance                    4

                            The GLM Procedure
Part (E)
                      Bonferroni (Dunn) t Tests for score1

NOTE: This test controls the Type I experimentwise error rate, but it generally has a
              higher Type II error rate than REGWQ.


                  Alpha                            0.05
                  Error Degrees of Freedom           24
                  Error Mean Square                1.25
                  Critical Value of t           2.87509
                  Minimum Significant Difference  1.6072


         Means with the same letter are not significantly different.


            Bon Grouping        Mean      N    indep1

                   A          6.2500      8    Rented house

                   B          4.2500      8    Off-campus apt
                   B
                   B          3.5000      8    Greek
                   B
                   B          3.0000      8    Dorm
```

Output 13.2 has the same appearance as Output 13.1. Therefore, there is no need to explain many of the concepts again; only new terms are discussed here. Page 2 of the output is divided into three parts. **Part (A)** presents the F test for the overall design, its value (= 6.86), and the p level (= 0.0002); all are indicative of some effect being statistically significant in the data. Hence, **Part (C)** becomes relevant at this point. It shows that both main effects are significant at the $p < 0.0001$ and 0.0184 levels, respectively, yet the interaction is not. Look for these results under the heading **Type I SS** and **Pr > F**.

Out of the two significant main effects, the <u>sex</u> effect is new and is followed up by the Bonferroni t test—**Part (D)** on page 3—that shows males (mean = 4.75) indeed drank significantly more than females (mean = 3.75). One question for you to think over is this: Is it necessary to perform the Bonferroni t test on the <u>sex</u> difference, if the F test of the same variable is already statistically significant at $\alpha = 0.05$, based on $p = 0.0184$?

The other statistically significant effect due to <u>indep1</u> has a larger F ratio (= 13.07) in **Part (C)**, compared with 11.15 from **Output 13.1**, though the significance level is identical ($p < 0.0001$). The Bonferroni t-test result reaches the same conclusion as that shown in **Output 13.1**, namely, the 4th group, living in rented houses, drank significantly more than the other three groups [**Part (E)** on page 4].

Example 13.3 Confirming No Interaction With a Plot of Cell Means

How can you cross-validate the lack of significant interactions in data? There is an easy way: Calculate eight cell means and plot these means using the symbols of the <u>sex</u> variable. Here is a program written for this purpose:

```
/* See Example 13.1 for the DATA step in creating the SAS data set 'design' */

TITLE 'Example 13.3 Confirming no interaction with a plot of cell means';

PROC MEANS DATA=design NOPRINT;
    VAR score1;
    OUTPUT OUT=out MEAN=meandrnk;
    CLASS sex indep1;
RUN;

PROC PRINT DATA=out;
RUN;

PROC PLOT DATA=out;
    PLOT meandrnk*indep1=sex / HPOS=50 VPOS=20;
RUN;
```

The program uses three SAS procedures: MEANS, PRINT, and PLOT. The purpose of PROC MEANS is to compute cell means and save them in a SAS data set called <u>out</u>. Note that no printout is requested by the MEANS procedure. Instead, PROC PRINT is used to list the grand mean, eight cell means plus four group means of <u>indep1</u> and two means of <u>sex</u>. This output (page 1 below) is much simpler than what would have been generated by PROC MEANS. The last procedure, PLOT, is used to graphically display eight cell means under four housing conditions using symbols "F" or "M" of the <u>sex</u> variable. Two options, HPOS= and VPOS=, are specified primarily to control the frame of the plot.

Output 13.3 Confirming No Interaction With a Plot of Cell Means

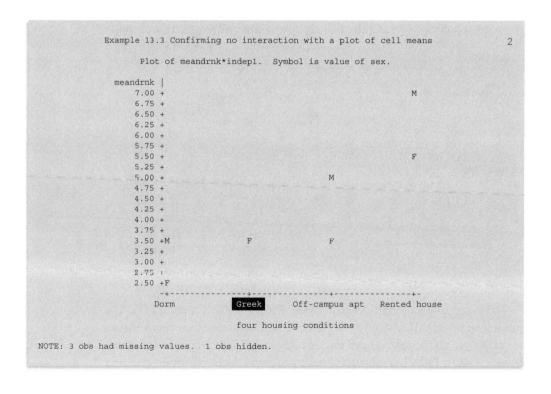

```
Example 13.3 Confirming no interaction with a plot of cell means                 1

   Obs     sex      indep1     _TYPE_      _FREQ_      meandrnk

    1                   .          0          32          4.25
    2                   1          1           8          3.00
    3                   2          1           8          3.50
    4                   3          1           8          4.25
    5                   4          1           8          6.25
    6    Female         .          2          16          3.75
    7    Male           .          2          16          4.75
    8    Female         1          3           4          2.50
    9    Female         2          3           4          3.50
   10    Female         3          3           4          3.50
   11    Female         4          3           4          5.50
   12    Male           1          3           4          3.50
   13    Male           2          3           4          3.50
   14    Male           3          3           4          5.00
   15    Male           4          3           4          7.00
```

```
            Example 13.3 Confirming no interaction with a plot of cell means        2

                 Plot of meandrnk*indep1.  Symbol is value of sex.

         meandrnk |
            7.00 +                                                M
            6.75 +
            6.50 +
            6.25 +
            6.00 +
            5.75 +
            5.50 +                                                F
            5.25 +
            5.00 +                             M
            4.75 +
            4.50 +
            4.25 +
            4.00 +
            3.75 +
            3.50 +M           F               F
            3.25 +
            3.00 +
            2.75 +
            2.50 +F
                 -+---------------+---------------+---------------+-
                  Dorm          Greek       Off-campus apt   Rented house

                        four housing conditions
NOTE: 3 obs had missing values.  1 obs hidden.
```

Notice how, on the page 2 plot, the letter M always lies above F, except for Greek houses where F and M collide because their corresponding means are identical. As long as one gender group (males in this case) constantly drank more than, or at least as much as, the other gender group (females) across the four housing conditions, there is likely to be no statistically significant interaction. Graphing cell means is a good way to infer the presence or the absence of an interaction effect. Of course, if there is no interaction in the population, these two groups will differ by the same magnitude across the four housing conditions. As a general observation, if both main effects are statistically significant, the interaction is unlikely to be also significant. If the interaction is statistically significant, one or both main effects are unlikely to be significant.

Example 13.4 Randomized Block Design

One tactic in conducting experimental or quasi-experimental studies is to control for the impact of extraneous variables that are not the researcher's main interest. One way to handle an extraneous variable is to match subjects on such a variable so that its presence is well represented in all groups of the independent variable. This type of design is called a randomized block design.

Suppose that the amount of drinks consumed by students could be a function of their academic majors. We, therefore, need to control for the variation of majors in each housing condition. Let's factor students' major (major) into the analysis while keeping the housing arrangements (indep1) as the sole independent variable in the study. Both variables are listed on the CLASS statement as sources of effects.

The MODEL statement specifies indep1 and major as the two effects that account for the variation in the dependent variable. There is no interaction of indep1 by major listed on the MODEL statement because, in a block design, the interaction between the independent variable and the matching (or the blocking) variable is assumed nonexistent.

The MEANS statement specifies indep1 to test the mean differences due to housing arrangements, and SIDAK requests the Dunn-Šidák comparison procedure to test the mean differences.

```
/* See Example 13.1 for the DATA step in creating the SAS data set 'design' */

TITLE 'Example 13.4 Randomized block design';

PROC GLM DATA=design;
    CLASS indep1 major;
    MODEL score1=indep1 major;
    MEANS indep1 / SIDAK;
RUN; QUIT;
```

Output 13.4 Randomized Block Design

```
    Example 13.4 Randomized block design                                        1

            The GLM Procedure

          Class Level Information

    Class          Levels    Values

    indep1              4     1 2 3 4

    major               8     1 2 3 4 5 6 7 8


    Number of Observations Read           32
    Number of Observations Used           32
```

```
                        Example 13.4 Randomized block design                    2

                            The GLM Procedure
    Part (A)

    Dependent Variable: score1    no. of drinks in spring break

                                    Sum of
        Source              DF      Squares      Mean Square    F Value    Pr > F

        Model               10    70.50000000     7.05000000     7.59     <.0001

        Error               21    19.50000000     0.92857143

        Corrected Total     31    90.00000000

    Part (B)
                        R-Square    Coeff Var    Root MSE     score1 Mean
                        0.783333    22.67351     0.963624      4.250000

    Part (C)

        Source              DF     Type I SS     Mean Square    F Value    Pr > F

        indep1               3    49.00000000    16.33333333    17.59     <.0001
        major                7    21.50000000     3.07142857     3.31     0.0156


        Source              DF    Type III SS    Mean Square    F Value    Pr > F

        indep1               3    49.00000000    16.33333333    17.59     <.0001
        major                7    21.50000000     3.07142857     3.31     0.0156
```

```
                        Example 13.4 Randomized block design                    3

                            The GLM Procedure

                          Sidak t Tests for score1

    NOTE: This test controls the Type I experimentwise error rate, but it generally has a
                    higher Type II error rate than REGWQ.
```

```
              Alpha                              0.05
              Error Degrees of Freedom             21
              Error Mean Square              0.928571
              Critical Value of t            2.90270
              Minimum Significant Difference  1.3986


     Means with the same letter are not significantly different.


  Sidak Grouping           Mean    N    indep1

                  A       6.2500    8    Rented house

                  B       4.2500    8    Off-campus apt
                  B
                  B       3.5000    8    Greek
                  B
                  B       3.0000    8    Dorm
```

Page 2 of the output is divided into three parts for easy explanation. **Part (A)** shows the overall significance ($F = 7.59$, $p < 0.0001$) of the design model to account for variance in score1. **Part (B)** supports the significant finding with a high **R-Square** (= 0.783333) and a small **Root MSE** (= 0.963624). **Part (C)** presents the F test of indep1 (= 17.59) and its p level (< 0.0001). This F value is larger than the one reported in **Output 13.1**. It is so because the denominator of the present F is slightly smaller than the one before, due to model differences. In other words, by matching students on their majors, we have effectively reduced the sum of squares of errors to such an extent that its mean square (or the reduced SS divided by its reduced degrees of freedom) is still smaller than the value derived from the one-way ANOVA model. Thus, the effort to match subjects was fruitful.

The question, "How effective is the matching?" can also be answered by the F test of the major effect. In **Part (C)**, under **Type I SS**, it shows that such an F test is statistically significant at $\alpha = 0.05$ ($p = 0.0156$). Thus, we conclude that matching students on majors effectively reduced the **Mean Square Error** from 1.46428571 (from Output 13.1) to 0.92857143, reported in Output 13.4.

On page 3 of the output, the SIDAK procedure follows up on the significant F of indep1 by examining all pairwise differences in means. This test result reaches the same conclusion as Output 13.1 or Output 13.2, namely, the 4th group, living in rented houses, drank significantly more than the other three groups. The Dunn-Šidák test is an improvement over the Bonferroni t test (also called the Dunn procedure) because it requires a smaller critical value in computing the MSD than the Bonferroni t test.

Example 13.5 Latin-Square Design

Have you heard of the phrase, "Statistics is Greek to me!"? Well, add Latin on top of the Greek! In ANOVA, there is actually a design called the Latin-square (or LS) design. The LS design is an extension of the randomized block design. In a randomized block design, only one extraneous variable is being controlled, whereas in a LS design, two are controlled. Here is the layout of a LS design—suppose that in the data file design.dat, variable a is the old indep1 variable, that is, the four housing arrangements. Two other variables, b and c, denote two extraneous variables, academic standing and majors, respectively. Let's further suppose that the 32 data items were collected according to the 4 × 4 LS design depicted below:

	c1	c2	c3	c4
	a1	a2	a3	a4
b1	3	4	4	5
	2	4	4	5
	a2	a3	a4	a1
b2	3	3	6	2
	3	3	6	3
	a3	a4	a1	a2
b3	4	7	1	2
	6	8	3	3
	a4	a1	a2	a3
b4	5	4	4	5
	8	6	5	5

As you probably recall from a statistics textbook, a LS design is one in which the number of levels (or groups) of the treatment variable, as well as that of the two extraneous variables, ought to be identical. For this reason, variables b and c were artificially created to also contain four groups, like the four housing conditions under variable a.

In the SAS program, the rearranged data are first read into a SAS data set called ls, and then analyzed by the GLM procedure. On the MODEL statement, three main effects plus one three-way interaction are specified. These are followed by a MEANS statement with the **SCHEFFE** post hoc procedure specified after the slash (/). You should be forewarned that the three-way interaction is not supposed to reach significance because LS designs assume that no interaction exists between the treatment factor and one or all of the extraneous variables.

```
/* The following bolded statements establish the SAS data set 'ls' */

DATA ls;
    INPUT a b c score @@;
    LABEL a='Four housing conditions'
          b='academic standing'
          c='major'
          score='no. of drinks in spring break';
DATALINES;
1 1 1 3   1 1 1 2   2 2 1 3   2 2 1 3   3 3 1 4   3 3 1 6   4 4 1 5   4 4 1 8
2 1 2 4   2 1 2 4   3 2 2 3   3 2 2 3   4 3 2 7   4 3 2 8   1 4 2 4   1 4 2 6
3 1 3 4   3 1 3 4   4 2 3 6   4 2 3 6   1 3 3 1   1 3 3 3   2 4 3 4   2 4 3 5
4 1 4 5   4 1 4 5   1 2 4 2   1 2 4 3   2 3 4 2   2 3 4 3   3 4 4 5   3 4 4 5
RUN;

TITLE 'Example 13.5 Latin-square design';

PROC GLM DATA=ls;
    CLASS a b c;
    MODEL score=a b c a*b*c;
    MEANS b c / SCHEFFE;
RUN; QUIT;
```

Output 13.5 Latin-Square Design

```
    Example 13.5 Latin-square design                              1

        The GLM Procedure

       Class Level Information

    Class        Levels    Values

    a               4      1 2 3 4

    b               4      1 2 3 4

    c               4      1 2 3 4


Number of Observations Read          32
Number of Observations Used          32
```

```
                            Example 13.5 Latin-square design                  2

                                The GLM Procedure
Part (A)

Dependent Variable: score   no. of drinks in spring break

                                        Sum of
         Source              DF         Squares      Mean Square   F Value   Pr > F

         Model               15      77.00000000      5.13333333     6.32    0.0003

         Error               16      13.00000000      0.81250000

         Corrected Total     31      90.00000000

Part (B)
                   R-Square     Coeff Var     Root MSE     score Mean

                   0.855556     21.20913      0.901388     4.250000

Part (C)

         Source              DF       Type I SS      Mean Square   F Value   Pr > F

         a                    3     49.00000000     16.33333333    20.10    <.0001
         b                    3     12.25000000      4.08333333     5.03    0.0121
         c                    3      5.25000000      1.75000000     2.15    0.1335
         a*b*c                6     10.50000000      1.75000000     2.15    0.1031


         Source              DF      Type III SS     Mean Square   F Value   Pr > F

         a                    3     49.00000000     16.33333333    20.10    <.0001
         b                    3     12.25000000      4.08333333     5.03    0.0121
         c                    3      5.25000000      1.75000000     2.15    0.1335
         a*b*c                6     10.50000000      1.75000000     2.15    0.1031
```

```
Part (D)                    Example 13.5 Latin-square design                  3

                                The GLM Procedure

                               Scheffe's Test for score

         NOTE: This test controls the Type I experimentwise error rate.


                      Alpha                              0.05
                      Error Degrees of Freedom             16
                      Error Mean Square                 0.8125
                      Critical Value of F              3.23887
                      Minimum Significant Difference    1.4049


         Means with the same letter are not significantly different.


                   Scheffe Grouping          Mean      N    b

                              A             5.2500      8    4
                              A
                       B      A             4.2500      8    3
                       B      A
                       B      A             3.8750      8    1
                       B
                       B                    3.6250      8    2
```

```
Part (E)                    Example 13.5 Latin-square design                              4

                                 The GLM Procedure

                               Scheffe's Test for score

              NOTE: This test controls the Type I experimentwise error rate.


                        Alpha                               0.05
                        Error Degrees of Freedom              16
                        Error Mean Square                  0.8125
                        Critical Value of F               3.23887
                        Minimum Significant Difference     1.4049


              Means with the same letter are not significantly different.


              Scheffe Grouping             Mean        N     c

                               A         4.8750        8     2
                               A
                               A         4.2500        8     1
                               A
                               A         4.1250        8     3
                               A
                               A         3.7500        8     4
```

Page 1 and **Parts (A)** and **(B)** of page 2 should be familiar to you by now; therefore, there is no need to explain them again. Beginning with **Part (C)**, **Type I SS**, four F tests of main effects and the interaction effect are presented. The main effect of a (the four housing conditions) on drinking behavior is statistically significant as before. The F value is larger than before due to a smaller mean square error. The effect of b is also statistically significant at 0.0121, but the effect of c is not significant ($p = 0.1335$). This means that factor b, but not factor c, was an effective matching variable that accounted for a substantial portion of variance in the number of drinks. The significant F test for factor b is followed up by the Scheffé post hoc test. **Part (D)** on page 3 reveals that the Scheffé test found that the fourth level (seniors) of factor b (academic standing) yielded a significantly higher average number of drinks than the second level (sophomores). So it would be interesting to trace back to data and figure out who were these seniors and sophomores that contributed to this significant difference. In **Part (E)** on page 4, analysis of factor c did not detect any pair of means to be significantly different, as the overall F test of the same effect is not significant.

Earlier in this example, it was pointed out that any LS design assumes that no interaction exists. Fortunately, the interaction was not significant for the present data ($p = 0.1031$). Therefore, the assumption is met.

Example 13.6 Collapsing the Interaction With Residuals in a Latin-Square Design

Because the three-way interaction is tested to be nonsignificant, it becomes another estimate for the variance of sampling errors. One estimate already exists; it is the mean square error, printed in **Part (A)**. Some statistics textbooks suggest that these two be combined in order to increase the degrees of freedom. This recommendation can be easily implemented in a SAS program. Note here that the three-way interaction is removed from the MODEL statement. The removal implies that the three-way interaction is pooled with the error term. The combined mean square may be called the *residual mean square* or *mean square residual*.

```
/* See Example 13.5 for the DATA step in creating the SAS data set 'ls' */

TITLE 'Example 13.6 Collapsing the interaction with residuals in a Latin-square design';

PROC GLM DATA=ls;
    CLASS a b c;
    MODEL score=a b c;
    MEANS b c / SCHEFFE;
RUN; QUIT;
```

Output 13.6 Collapsing the Interaction With Residuals in a Latin-Square Design

[Page 1 output is omitted]

Example 13.6 Collapsing the interaction with residuals in a Latin-square design   2

The GLM Procedure

Dependent Variable: score   no. of drinks in spring break

Source	DF	Sum of Squares	Mean Square	F Value	Pr > F
Model	9	66.50000000	7.38888889	6.92	0.0001
Error	22	23.50000000	1.06818182		
Corrected Total	31	90.00000000			

R-Square	Coeff Var	Root MSE	score Mean
0.738889	21.31977	1.033529	4.250000

Source	DF	Type I SS	Mean Square	F Value	Pr > F
a	3	49.00000000	16.33333333	15.29	<.0001
b	3	12.25000000	4.08333333	3.82	0.0241
c	3	5.25000000	1.75000000	1.64	0.2093

Source	DF	Type III SS	Mean Square	F Value	Pr > F
a	3	49.00000000	16.33333333	15.29	<.0001
b	3	12.25000000	4.08333333	3.82	0.0241
c	3	5.25000000	1.75000000	1.64	0.2093

```
Example 13.6 Collapsing the interaction with residuals in a Latin-square design     3

                          The GLM Procedure

                        Scheffe's Test for score

         NOTE: This test controls the Type I experimentwise error rate.


                    Alpha                            0.05
                    Error Degrees of Freedom           22
                    Error Mean Square            1.068182
                    Critical Value of F          3.04912
                    Minimum Significant Difference 1.5629


             Means with the same letter are not significantly different.


             Scheffe Grouping        Mean      N    b

                          A        5.2500      8    4
                          A
                   B      A        4.2500      8    3
                   B      A
                   B      A        3.8750      8    1
                   B
                   B              3.6250      8    2
```

```
Example 13.6 Collapsing the interaction with residuals in a Latin-square design     4

                          The GLM Procedure

                        Scheffe's Test for score

         NOTE: This test controls the Type I experimentwise error rate.


                    Alpha                            0.05
                    Error Degrees of Freedom           22
                    Error Mean Square            1.068182
                    Critical Value of F          3.04912
                    Minimum Significant Difference 1.5629


             Means with the same letter are not significantly different.


             Scheffe Grouping        Mean      N    c

                          A        4.8750      8    2
                          A
                          A        4.2500      8    1
                          A
                          A        4.1250      8    3
                          A
                          A        3.7500      8    4
```

The output conveys identical messages, as in Output 13.5, in terms of significant results of $\underline{a}$ and $\underline{b}$ main effects. One thing is different, though; the Model F value increases from 6.32 to 6.92, yet the F values of $\underline{a}$, $\underline{b}$, and $\underline{c}$ decrease in magnitude. The reduction in these F values is due to an increase in MS for the error term, which is not offset by an increase in degrees of freedom.

Example 13.7 Repeated Measures Design (SPF$_{p.q}$)

This example illustrates analytical approaches for a repeated measures design. Let's suppose that three data points were collected from each student: one during the spring break (score1), one during the final week (score2), and another after the final week (score3). With these additional measures, it is possible to determine whether college students' drinking habits were related to their stress, assuming greater stress was felt at the end of a semester than during the spring break or after the finals. A repeated measures design is a type of split plot factorial design for which between-block and within-block differences and their interactions are investigated. **Plot** is an agricultural term that refers to a parcel of land, divided into sub-plots that are called **blocks**. Within a block, the soil condition, irrigation, plants, and so on are homogeneous. By the same token, a repeated measures design regards observations in the same treatment level (or group) to be homogeneous. Differences observed within blocks are explained by the repeated factor (time in this example). Differences observed between blocks are explained by the between-block factor, or the four housing arrangements coded as indep1. A repeated measures design with one between-block factor and one within-block factor is denoted as SPF$_{p.q}$, where p is the number of levels for the between-block factor ($p = 4$ in this example) and q is the number of levels for the within-block factor ($q = 3$ in this example). An SPF$_{p.q}$ design yields three effects to be examined: two main effects of the between-block factor and the within-block factor and one interaction effect of these two factors.

In the program below, the CLASS statement lists indep1 as the sole independent variable. The MODEL statement lists score1, score2, and score3 as dependent variables on the left and indep1 on the right-hand side of the equal sign (=). This statement will cause PROC GLM to apply multivariate analyses to the three dependent variables. The next statement, REPEATED, applies univariate analyses to the data. The repeated factor, time, is the overarching variable under which score1, score2, and score3 are its three levels.

```
/* See Example 13.1 for the DATA step in creating the SAS data set 'design' */

TITLE 'Example 13.7 Repeated measures design (SPF p.q)';

PROC GLM DATA=design;
     CLASS indep1;
     MODEL score1-score3=indep1;
     REPEATED time;
RUN; QUIT;
```

Output 13.7 Repeated Measures Design (SPF$_{p.q}$)

```
Example 13.7 Repeated measures design (SPF p.q)                              1

                The GLM Procedure

             Class Level Information

        Class          Levels    Values

        indep1              4    1 2 3 4


   Number of Observations Read         32
   Number of Observations Used         32
```

```
            Example 13.7 Repeated measures design (SPF p.q)                 2

                      The GLM Procedure

Dependent Variable: score1   no. of drinks in spring break

                                 Sum of
    Source               DF      Squares      Mean Square   F Value   Pr > F

    Model                 3    49.00000000    16.33333333    11.15    <.0001

    Error                28    41.00000000     1.46428571

    Corrected Total      31    90.00000000


                R-Square    Coeff Var    Root MSE    score1 Mean

                0.544444    28.47239     1.210077     4.250000


    Source               DF     Type I SS     Mean Square   F Value   Pr > F

    indep1                3    49.00000000    16.33333333    11.15    <.0001


    Source               DF    Type III SS    Mean Square   F Value   Pr > F

    indep1                3    49.00000000    16.33333333    11.15    <.0001
```

```
                Example 13.7 Repeated measures design (SPF p.q)                    3

                            The GLM Procedure

Dependent Variable: score2   no. of drinks in final week

                                    Sum of
        Source              DF      Squares     Mean Square   F Value   Pr > F

        Model                3    52.7500000    17.5833333     7.11     0.0011

        Error               28    69.2500000     2.4732143

        Corrected Total     31   122.0000000


                  R-Square    Coeff Var    Root MSE    score2 Mean

                  0.432377    44.93273     1.572646     3.500000


        Source              DF    Type I SS     Mean Square   F Value   Pr > F

        indep1               3   52.75000000   17.58333333     7.11     0.0011


        Source              DF    Type III SS   Mean Square   F Value   Pr > F

        indep1               3   52.75000000   17.58333333     7.11     0.0011
```

```
                Example 13.7 Repeated measures design (SPF p.q)                    4

                            The GLM Procedure

Dependent Variable: score3   no. of drinks after final week

                                    Sum of
        Source              DF      Squares     Mean Square   F Value   Pr > F

        Model                3    29.6250000     9.8750000     2.11     0.1219

        Error               28   131.2500000     4.6875000

        Corrected Total     31   160.8750000


                  R-Square    Coeff Var    Root MSE    score3 Mean

                  0.184149    46.18802     2.165064     4.687500


        Source              DF    Type I SS     Mean Square   F Value   Pr > F

        indep1               3   29.62500000    9.87500000     2.11     0.1219


        Source              DF    Type III SS   Mean Square   F Value   Pr > F

        indep1               3   29.62500000    9.87500000     2.11     0.1219
```

```
                Example 13.7 Repeated measures design (SPF p.q)              5

                          The GLM Procedure
                  Repeated Measures Analysis of Variance

                  Repeated Measures Level Information

          Dependent Variable       score1    score2    score3

                 Level of time         1         2         3
```

Part (A)

```
     MANOVA Test Criteria and Exact F Statistics for the Hypothesis of no time Effect
                    H = Type III SSCP Matrix for time
                          E = Error SSCP Matrix

                    S=1      M=0      N=12.5

     Statistic                 Value    F Value    Num DF   Den DF   Pr > F

     Wilks' Lambda          0.23666320    43.54       2        27     <.0001
     Pillai's Trace         0.76333680    43.54       2        27     <.0001
     Hotelling-Lawley Trace 3.22541397    43.54       2        27     <.0001
     Roy's Greatest Root    3.22541397    43.54       2        27     <.0001
```

Part (B)

```
     MANOVA Test Criteria and F Approximations for the Hypothesis of no time*indep1 Effect
                    H = Type III SSCP Matrix for time*indep1
                          E = Error SSCP Matrix

                    S=2      M=0      N=12.5

     Statistic                 Value    F Value    Num DF   Den DF   Pr > F

     Wilks' Lambda          0.79355122    1.10        6        54     0.3727
     Pillai's Trace         0.21628459    1.13        6        56     0.3561
     Hotelling-Lawley Trace 0.24776343    1.10        6    34.278     0.3844
     Roy's Greatest Root    0.17821404    1.66        3        28     0.1975

         NOTE: F Statistic for Roy's Greatest Root is an upper bound.
         NOTE: F Statistic for Wilks' Lambda is exact.
```

```
                Example 13.7 Repeated measures design (SPF p.q)              6

                          The CLM Procedure
                  Repeated Measures Analysis of Variance
               Tests of Hypotheses for Between Subjects Effects

     Source            DF    Type III SS    Mean Square   F Value   Pr > F

     indep1             3    128.2083333    42.7361111      5.74     0.0034
     Error             28    208.4166667     7.4434524
```

```
                    Example 13.7 Repeated measures design (SPF p.q)                    7

                               The GLM Procedure
                        Repeated Measures Analysis of Variance
                    Univariate Tests of Hypotheses for Within Subject Effects
Part (C)
                                                                        Adj Pr > F
Source                    DF    Type III SS   Mean Square   F Value   Pr > F   G - G    H - F

time                       2    23.08333333   11.54166667     19.54   <.0001   <.0001   <.0001
time*indep1                6     3.16666667    0.52777778      0.89   0.5062   0.4817   0.4916
Error(time)               56    33.08333333    0.59077381


               Greenhouse-Geisser Epsilon        0.7068
               Huynh-Feldt Epsilon               0.8131
```

This output probably causes your eyes to cross! Let's begin with page 2. This page is identical to page 2 of Output 13.1, based on a one-way ANOVA design. Thus, you can conclude that during the spring break, students drank more or less liquor depending on where they lived.

Pages 3 and 4 display the second and third one-way ANOVA result based on score2 and score3, respectively. Like score1, the F test of students' drinking during the final week is statistically significant at $\alpha = 0.05$ ($F = 7.11$, $p = 0.0011$). The **R-Square** is lower and **MSE** is higher in score2, compared with score1. However, the F test of score3 (i.e., the number of drinks after the final week) is not statistically significant ($p = 0.1219$).

Page 5 is devoted entirely to the multivariate analysis of score1, score2, and score3. **Part (A)** presents four multivariate tests of the main effect, time. **Part (B)** presents tests of the interaction between time and indep1. Each of the four multivariate tests is based on a slightly different alternative hypothesis. The time factor was tested to be statistically significant at $\alpha = 0.05$ by all four multivariate tests. However, none uncovers statistically significant differences in the number of drinks due to the interaction between time and indep1.

The univariate tests are presented on pages 6 and 7. Page 6 displays test results of the between-block factor (indep1). According to the magnitude of the F value (= 5.74) and its p level (= 0.0034), the four housing conditions had an impact on the students' drinking behaviors. This finding has been shown in previous examples.

Page 7 of the output contains univariate analyses of the repeated factor, time, and its interaction with the between-block factor, indep1. Both are tested using the denominator called **Error (time)**. This term is usually referred to in statistics textbooks as the interaction of the repeated factor, time, with the error term of the between-block factor. This error term is smaller than the between-block error term. Verify this by comparing 0.59077381 (page 7) with 7.4434524 (page 6). Using this smaller error term as the denominator, the F test for the time factor in **Part (C)** is significant ($F = 19.54$, $p < 0.0001$). However, the F test for the time*indep1 interaction is not significant ($F = 0.89$, $p = 0.5062$).

You may have noticed that there are three p values listed after the F value in **Part (C)** on page 7. Besides the one you are familiar with (i.e., **Pr > F**), there are two additional column headings that read as "**Adj. Pr > F**" according to the "**G-G**" and "**H-F**" correction formulae, respectively. The **G - G** correction formula refers to the conservative approach proposed by Geisser-Greenhouse, whereas **H - F** refers to the Huynh-Feldt approach. Both approaches seek to correct the p levels of univariate F tests performed on the repeated factor and its interaction with the between-block factor. The corrections are needed because both F tests assume that the variance-covariance matrix of repeated measures is of a certain type. Violation of this assumption results in a positive bias in the F statistic; hence, it is inflated. These correction formulae adjust the significance level downward, by multiplying the degrees of freedom with the **Epsilon** coefficient (Epsilon = 0.7068 for the G-G correction formula, and Epsilon = 0.8131 for the H-F formula), when data do not satisfy this assumption. And data almost always violate this structural requirement assumed for the variance-covariance matrix. In our example, the corrections do not change the significant conclusion reached for the time factor or the nonsignificant conclusion for the time*indep1 interaction.

Example 13.8 Analysis of Covariance (ANCOVA)

Given the purpose of Example 13.7 and its null hypotheses, there exists an alternative way of examining the data to determine if, in fact, time makes a difference in students' drinking behavior. This example demonstrates this alternative analysis strategy, namely, the analysis of covariance, or ANCOVA. To demonstrate this strategy, the first measure, score1, is treated as a covariate. The second measure, score2, is treated as the dependent variable, and indep1 is the independent variable or the treatment factor.

The idea behind ANCOVA is simple. If a variable, namely, the covariate, is linearly related to the dependent variable, yet it is not the main focus of a study, its effect can be partialled out from the dependent variable through the least-squares regression equation. The remaining, or the adjusted, portion of the dependent variable is subsequently analyzed according to the usual ANOVA designs. In this example, students' drinking during the final week is adjusted for their spring break drinking. The adjusted number of drinks is subsequently analyzed by four housing arrangements in a one-way ANOVA.

In programming an ANCOVA design into PROC GLM, it is better to write score1 (the covariate) before indep1 (the independent variable) on the MODEL statement. In doing so, you will only need to interpret the **TYPE I** sum of squares result from page 2 of the output. Furthermore, the **LSMEANS** statement replaces the MEANS statement. LSMEANS stands for the least-squares means. The least-squares means are average number of drinks during the final week after they are adjusted for average number of drinks consumed during the spring break (the covariate). Two options, **PDIFF** and

STDERR, are specified to make a comparison between each pair of adjusted means. PDIFF requests significance levels for tests of all pairs of adjusted means. STDERR requests the *t* test of each adjusted mean against 0 and prints the significance level of the *t* test.

```
/* See Example 13.1 for the DATA step in creating the SAS data set 'design' */

TITLE 'Example 13.8 Analysis of covariance (ANCOVA)';

PROC GLM DATA=design;
    CLASS indep1;
    MODEL score2=score1 indep1;
    LSMEANS indep1 / PDIFF STDERR;
RUN; QUIT;
```

Output 13.8 Analysis of Covariance (ANCOVA)

```
Example 13.8 Analysis of covariance (ANCOVA)                              1

              The GLM Procedure

           Class Level Information

      Class         Levels   Values

      indep1             4    1 2 3 4


   Number of Observations Read           32
   Number of Observations Used           32
```

```
                 Example 13.8 Analysis of covariance (ANCOVA)             2

                       The GLM Procedure
```
Part (A)
```
Dependent Variable: score2   no. of drinks in final week

                                  Sum of
   Source                DF      Squares     Mean Square   F Value   Pr > F

   Model                  4   104.3597561    26.0899390     39.93   <.0001

   Error                 27    17.6402439     0.6533424

   Corrected Total       31   122.0000000
```
Part (B)
```
              R-Square     Coeff Var     Root MSE     score2 Mean

              0.855408      23.09417     0.808296        3.500000
```

Part (C)

Source	DF	Type I SS	Mean Square	F Value	Pr > F
score1	1	102.4000000	102.4000000	156.73	<.0001
indep1	3	1.9597561	0.6532520	1.00	0.4080

Part (D)

Source	DF	Type III SS	Mean Square	F Value	Pr > F
score1	1	51.60975610	51.60975610	78.99	<.0001
indep1	3	1.95975610	0.65325203	1.00	0.4080

Example 13.8 Analysis of covariance (ANCOVA)   3

The GLM Procedure
Least Squares Means

Part (E)

indep1	score2 LSMEAN	Standard Error	Pr > |t|	LSMEAN Number
1	3.77743902	0.32644527	<.0001	1
2	3.21646341	0.30105039	<.0001	2
3	3.75000000	0.28577578	<.0001	3
4	3.25609756	0.38132468	<.0001	4

Part (F)

Least Squares Means for effect indep1
Pr > |t| for H0: LSMean(i)=LSMean(j)

Dependent Variable: score2

i/j	1	2	3	4
1		0.1815	0.9500	0.3733
2	0.1815		0.2096	0.9412
3	0.9500	0.2096		0.3092
4	0.3733	0.9412	0.3092	

NOTE: To ensure overall protection level, only probabilities associated with pre-planned comparisons should be used.

Pages 2 and 3 of Output 13.8 are part and parcel of ANCOVA, although not all results are equally relevant. The MS error (= 0.6533424) and its df (= 27) in **Part (A)** are relevant; they will be referred to later. **Part (B)** depicts four descriptive statistics. The first (**R-Square=0.855408**) describes a strong linear relationship between the dependent variable (score2) and the independent variable (indep1) and the covariate (score1) jointly.

Part (C) tells us that the covariate, score1, is an effective covariate because it accounts for a substantial portion of the sum of squares (**Type I**) in the dependent measure, score2. The substantial sum of squares translates into a large F value (=156.73), significant at $p < 0.0001$. The remaining variance in score2 that is explained by indep1 is, therefore, negligible ($F = 1.00$, $p = 0.4080$).

The nonsignificant effect of <u>indep1</u> on <u>score2</u> is confirmed by comparisons of least squares means (**Part (F)** of page 3). None of these comparisons reaches the α level of 0.05 or even 0.10. **Part (E)** displays the least squares means (or adjusted means) of <u>score2</u>. All are above 3 (ounces or bottles?). Each is further tested against a null hypothesis of zero adjusted mean in the underlying population. All tests yield a highly significant result at $p < 0.0001$. These results indicate that students' drinking during the final week was definitely prevailing in all four housing conditions. The drinking recorded at the end of the semester was evident even after it was adjusted for the amount consumed during the spring break. Too much stress, maybe?

- On the LSMEANS statement, there can be other options besides PDIFF and STDERR. Specifically, the option **ALPHA=** (a small probability, such as 0.10) can be used to specify the confidence level (which equals $1 - p$) of each adjusted mean or difference in a pair of adjusted means. The default is 0.05. The ALPHA= option is specified simultaneously with the PDIFF or the **CL** option. The CL option is similar to the PDIFF option in that the CL option computes a confidence interval for each adjusted mean, whereas the PDIFF option computes the confidence interval for the difference in each pair of adjusted means.

- If you wish to control the Type I error rate in simultaneous tests of adjusted means, you may specify the **ADJUST=** option on the LSMEANS statement, after the slash (/). If ADJUST= **SIDAK**, then the adjusted means are tested by the Dunn-Šidák procedure with a family-wise Type I error controlled at 0.05 (the default) or the level specified by the ALPHA= option. If ADJUST=DUNNETT, adjusted means are tested by the Dunnett procedure, which compares each adjusted mean with a reference mean (the default is the adjusted mean of the last group), at a family-wise α level of 0.05 or the level specified by the ALPHA= option.

Example 13.9 Examining ANCOVA Assumptions

The ANCOVA approach comes with a price. It requires (a) that a linear relationship exist between the covariate and the dependent measure and (b) that there be no interaction between the covariate and the independent variable. The first assumption can be checked by drawing a scatter plot based on <u>score1</u> and <u>score2</u> and computing a Pearson correlation to determine if the relationship is indeed linear and substantial. The second assumption needs to be examined by a statistical test. This example demonstrates how both assumptions can be examined. Note that the interaction of <u>score1</u> with <u>indep1</u> is added to the MODEL statement and the option **SOLUTION** is inserted after the slash (/).

```
/* See Example 13.1 for the DATA step in creating the SAS data set 'design' */

TITLE 'Example 13.9 Examining ANCOVA assumptions';

PROC GLM DATA=design;
    CLASS indep1;
    MODEL score2=score1 indep1 score1*indep1 / SOLUTION;
RUN; QUIT;
```

Output 13.9 Examining ANCOVA Assumptions

```
[Page 1 output is not shown])
                    Example 13.9 Examining ANCOVA assumptions                    2

                           The GLM Procedure

Dependent Variable: score2   no. of drinks in final week

                                    Sum of
    Source                DF        Squares      Mean Square    F Value    Pr > F

    Model                  7      105.2498188     15.0356884     21.54     <.0001

    Error                 24       16.7501812      0.6979242

    Corrected Total       31      122.0000000


                R-Square     Coeff Var     Root MSE     score2 Mean

                0.862703     23.86910      0.835419      3.500000


    Source                DF       Type I SS     Mean Square    F Value    Pr > F

    score1                 1     102.4000000    102.4000000     146.72     <.0001
    indep1                 3       1.9597561      0.6532520       0.94     0.4386
    score1*indep1          3       0.8900627      0.2966876       0.43     0.7368  - NS


    Source                DF     Type III SS     Mean Square    F Value    Pr > F

    score1                 1      45.24687984    45.24687984     64.83     <.0001
    indep1                 3       0.69189216     0.23063072      0.33     0.8034
    score1*indep1          3       0.89006274     0.29668758      0.43     0.7368

                                          Standard
    Parameter          Estimate            Error      t Value    Pr > |t|

    Intercept        -1.565217391 B      1.56777135    -1.00      0.3281
    score1 (β weight) 1.130434783 B      0.24635150     4.59      0.0001
    indep1      1     0.752717391 B      1.71398072     0.44      0.6645
    indep1      2     0.731884058 B      1.99250499     0.37      0.7166
    indep1      3    -0.634782609 B      2.05571926    -0.31      0.7601
    indep1      4     0.000000000 B         .            .         .
    score1*indep1 1  -0.067934783 B      0.32296954    -0.21      0.8352
    score1*indep1 2  -0.213768116 B      0.42072528    -0.51      0.6160
    score1*indep1 3   0.269565217 B      0.39210410     0.69      0.4984
    score1*indep1 4   0.000000000 B         .            .         .

NOTE: The X'X matrix has been found to be singular, and a generalized inverse was used to
      solve the normal equations.  Terms whose estimates are followed by the letter 'B'
      are not uniquely estimable.
```

The *F* test of the interaction effect is, fortunately, not statistically signifi-cant. This implies that there is no sufficient evidence in the present data to support an interaction between the covariate (score1) and the independent variable (indep1). In the section where you find "**Parameter**" and "**Estimate**", the label (β weight) is inserted next to score1. This label is meant to draw your attention to the estimate (1.130434783), which is the regression weight of score2 (the dependent variable) regressing on score1. Technically speaking, this regression weight is β_w, which stands for the regression weight that is assumed equal in all treatment conditions. Suffice it to say, the magnitude of β_w suggests a strong and linear relationship between the covariate and the dependent variable.

13.4 How to Write the PROC GLM Codes

Based on the examples presented so far, you probably have recognized that the GLM procedure is more complex than the TTEST procedure, even though both are used to compare means. The GLM procedure is versatile for a variety of experimental designs and linear models. It provides diverse com-parison procedures to examine pairwise as well as complex contrasts among means. The GLM procedure consists of eight essential statements. Seven are explained here; the eighth statement, CONTRAST, is explained in **Section 13.5: Tips**. Statements not introduced here can be found from the online docu-mentation at www.sas.com.

PROC	GLM	DATA= *sas_dataset_name* *<options>*;
	CLASS	*independent_* or *blocking_variable(s)*;
	MODEL	*dependent_variable(s)* = *effects*;
	MEANS	*main_effects* / *comparison_procedures* *<options>*;
	LSMEANS	*main_effects* / *<options>*;
	REPEATED	*repeated_factor(s)*;
	TEST	H= *effects* E= *error_term*;
	BY	*classification_variable(s)*;

The first statement, **PROC GLM**, initializes the procedure and specifies the data set to be analyzed. In addition, you may specify the option **MANOVA**. This option requests that the GLM procedure rely on a multi-variate method of removing observations from the analysis, namely, the list-wise deletion method. In other words, if an observation has a missing value on one or more independent or dependent variables, the SAS system removes such an observation from the analysis. This option is applied in multivariate analyses, such as Example 13.7, or in the interactive mode of data analysis.

The second statement, **CLASS**, is to identify independent or blocking variables in a design. This statement is required; it must precede the MODEL statement.

The third statement, **MODEL**, is to specify an ANOVA design, also a linear model, for the data. On the left side of the equal sign (=), dependent variable(s) are listed. On the right side, effects such as main effects, interactions, blocking effects, nested effects, and covariates are listed. These effects decompose the total sum of squares of the dependent variable. Below are examples of the MODEL syntax for several commonly used designs:

Main-Effect Design

```
MODEL score=a b;    (two-way ANOVA)    or
MODEL score=a b c; (three-way ANOVA)
```

Completely Factorial Design

```
MODEL score=a b a*b;   same as MODEL score=a | b;
(both are two-way)
MODEL score=a | b | c; same as MODEL score=a b c a*b a*c b*c a*b*c;
(both are three-way)
```

Nested Design

```
MODEL score=a c(b) a*c(b)       same as MODEL score=a | c(b);
MODEL score=a c a*c b(a) c*b(a) same as MODEL score=a | b(a) | c;
MODEL score=a(b) c(b) a*c(b)    same as MODEL score=a(b) | c(b);
```

Randomized Block Design

```
MODEL score=a block;
```

It is sometimes necessary to examine differences among group means. This is accomplished by the **MEANS** statement. A variety of comparison procedures are available; each is sensitive to mean differences under a particular circumstance. These procedures are listed after a slash (/). A few other options are likewise listed after the slash. Interaction effects listed on the MEANS statement, before the slash, will not be tested, however; they are described instead in terms of cell means.

Below is a list of comparison procedures and options for the MEANS statement, listed after the slash (/):

BON   performs a two-tailed Dunn's procedure based on the Bonferroni inequality.

DUNNETT   performs a two-tailed Dunnett's procedure that compares a control group with any other group. The control group is defaulted to the first group. If you wish to change the control group from the first to another, you specify the control group in parentheses as follows:

```
MEANS  drug / DUNNETT (2);
```

According to the statement above, the second group is specified to be the control group of the <u>drug</u> factor. For character factors, single quotes are needed around the group name. For example, the statement below identifies the placebo group as the control group.

```
MEANS  drug / DUNNETT ('placebo');
```

A one-tailed Dunnett's test is also possible with a minor modification of the keyword to **DUNNETTL** or **DUNNETTU**.

DUNNETTL   executes a one-tailed Dunnett's test with the alternative hypothesis stating that the experimental group mean is less than the control mean.

DUNNETTU   executes a one-tailed Dunnett's test with the alternative hypothesis stating that the experimental group mean is greater than the control mean.

SCHEFFE   performs a two-tailed Scheffé procedure. The Scheffé procedure is based on the same F distribution as the overall F test. So if the overall F test is significant at, say, $\alpha = 0.05$, the Scheffé test will surely find either a pair of means or three or more means to be different at the same α level.

SIDAK   performs a two-tailed Dunn-Šidák procedure, based on the t distribution.

SNK	performs a two-tailed Newman-Keuls' modified t test of ordered mean differences.
TUKEY	performs a two-tailed Tukey's HSD test.
HOVTEST	performs the Levene test of homogeneity of variance.
CLDIFF	builds a 95% confidence interval for each pair of means for all comparison procedures, except for the **SNK** procedure. The 95% confidence can be changed using the next option, **ALPHA=**.
ALPHA=	a small probability that specifies the α level for carrying out all comparison procedures listed above. The specification also changes the confidence level for the **CLDIFF** option since confidence level = $(1 - \text{ALPHA}) \times 100\%$.
E=	specifies the denominator for all comparison procedures listed above. If omitted, the default is the mean square residual ($MS_{Residual}$).

The fifth statement, **LSMEANS**, tests single or pairs of least-squares means. This statement is relevant to ANCOVA designs and comparisons of adjusted means (i.e., least-squares means) between groups. Two options are illustrated in Example 13.8: **PDIFF** and **STDERR**. The other three options are the following:

ALPHA=	a small probability that specifies the α level for the test of least-squares means; the default is 0.05.
CL	requests the $(1 - \text{ALPHA}) \times 100\%$ confidence level to be constructed for each least-squares mean.
ADJUST=T or BON or SIDAK or TUKEY or DUNNETT	requests that a t test (specified by **T**), or Bonferroni t test (**BON**), or the Dunn-Šidák test (**SIDAK**), or Tukey's HSD test (**TUKEY**), or the DUNNETT test (**DUNNETT**) be applied to pairs of least-squares means.

The sixth statement, **REPEATED**, names a factor for which repeated measures are analyzed by either a univariate or a multivariate approach (see Example 13.7 for an illustration).

The seventh statement, **TEST**, is used to specify effects to form the numerator and the denominator of an F ratio. In Example 13.5, it was mentioned that for the $4 \times 4 \times 4$ LS design, two estimates for the variance of sampling errors could be considered. One is the mean square of the three-way interaction and the other is the mean square residuals. The latter was used as a denominator for all F tests carried out in Example 13.5. Had we been interested in using the second estimate as the denominator, we would have specified the TEST statement as follows on the next page.

```
TEST  H=a  b  c    E=a*b*c;
```

Finally the last statement, **BY**, serves the same purpose as in all other SAS procedures. It divides the data set into subgroups according to diverse values of the BY variable. Within each subgroup, the same ANOVA design is applied and the same analysis follows accordingly. If more than one BY variable is listed, all possible combinations of the BY variables' values are used in dividing up the entire data set. Be sure to presort the data set in the ascending order of all the BY variables, if the BY statement is included in the GLM procedure. Presorting a data set can be accomplished using the SORT procedure.

13.5 Tips

- How to handle missing or invalid data

By default, PROC GLM does not include observations that have missing information on either the dependent variable(s) or any of the CLASS variables.

When the REPEATED statement is specified to analyze data from a repeated measures design, you are advised to also specify the MANOVA option in the PROC GLM statement.

- What are the statistical assumptions associated with the F test conducted in one-way fixed-effects ANOVA?

The F test carried out in a one-way fixed-effects ANOVA is closely related to the independent-samples t test introduced in Chapter 12. If the one-way linear model presumed for data captures all sources of variations in the dependent variable, the F test assumes, first of all, that subjects are randomly selected from their respective populations, or that they are randomly assigned to conditions of the independent variable. Second, the underlying populations are normally distributed. Third, variances of normal populations are assumed to be equal. These assumptions are referred to in the literature as the independence assumption, the normality assumption, and the equal variance assumption.

Beyond the one-way fixed-effects ANOVA, factorial ANOVA designs, randomized block ANOVA designs, LS designs, repeated measure designs, and ANCOVA make additional statistical assumptions. For a detailed discussion of these assumptions and their robustness, refer to Box (1954), Clinch and Keselman (1982), Glass, Peckham, and Sanders (1972), Kirk (1995), Rogan and Keselman (1977), Tan (1982), and Tomarken and Serlin (1986).

- What to do if data do not satisfy the statistical assumptions in one-way fixed-effects ANOVA

For one-way fixed-effects ANOVAs, statisticians in general agree that the independence assumption is not robust to its violation. It is an important assumption because its violation renders the interpretation of the F test inexact and biased.

The normality assumption is quite robust, especially when the underlying populations are symmetric and sample sizes are equal and greater than 12 in all conditions. Even if population distributions are asymmetric and/or more peaked or flatter than the normal curve, the normality assumption is still robust as long as the population distributions are shaped the same and sample sizes are equal. One way to check the normality assumption is demonstrated in Chapter 9, Example 9.4.

The equal variance assumption is robust in balanced designs if samples are taken from underlying normal populations in which the ratio of the largest variance to the smallest variance is no more than 3. Unfortunately, this assumption is not robust when the ratio of the largest to the smallest variances exceeds 3, even if equal sample sizes are maintained. Under these conditions, alternative parametric tests, such as the Brown-Forsyth test, exist to compensate for the violation of the equal variance assumption. These alternative parametric tests are discussed and illustrated in Clinch and Keselman (1982).

In the worst possible scenario, in which sample sizes are unequal and terribly small and the populations are far from normal, you can still fall back on nonparametric tests. These are explained in Chapter 14.

- What if the research design is unbalanced?

An unbalanced design is a design in which cell sizes are unequal, or some cells have missing observations. For the unbalanced designs, tests of main effects and of interactions are nonorthogonal or statistically dependent. For discussions of these designs and their treatments in SAS, refer to the Four Types of Estimable Functions and the GLM chapters in *SAS/STAT 9.1 User's Guide* (SAS Institute Inc., 2004d) or the online documentation at www.sas.com.

- How to test planned contrasts in PROC GLM

As stated before, PROC GLM is capable of carrying out planned contrasts of main effects and interactions. These planned contrasts are specified by the CONTRAST statement. Suppose a 2 × 3 factorial design includes IQ as the row factor and the method of learning a foreign language as the column factor. The row factor, iq, has two levels, (high and average), and the column factor method, has three levels: the aural method, the translation method, and the combined method. The dependent score is students' comprehension of a passage written in the foreign language they studied. The diagram below may help you grasp the 2 × 3 design and six hypothetical cell means:

	Language Learning		
	Aural	Translation	Combined
High IQ	27	12	39
Average IQ	20	5	4

The graph below depicts hypothetical means of the six cells:

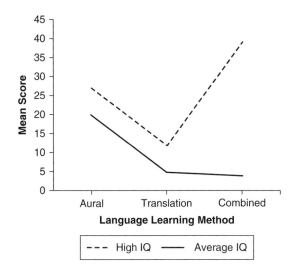

Based on the design and means graphed above, let's suppose that five orthogonal contrasts are of interest:

$$\psi_1 = \overline{Y}_{\text{High IQ}} - \overline{Y}_{\text{Average IQ}}$$

$$\psi_2 = \overline{Y}_{\text{Aural}} - \overline{Y}_{\text{Translation}}$$

$$\psi_3 = \overline{Y}_{\text{Aural}} + \overline{Y}_{\text{Translation}} - 2 \times \overline{Y}_{\text{Combined}}$$

$$\psi_4 = (\overline{Y}_{\text{Aural}} - \overline{Y}_{\text{Translation}})_{\text{High IQ}} - (\overline{Y}_{\text{Aural}} - \overline{Y}_{\text{Translation}})_{\text{Average IQ}}$$

$$\psi_5 = (\overline{Y}_{\text{Aural}} + \overline{Y}_{\text{Translation}} - 2 \times \overline{Y}_{\text{Combined}})_{\text{High IQ}} -$$
$$(\overline{Y}_{\text{Aural}} + \overline{Y}_{\text{Translation}} - 2 \times \overline{Y}_{\text{Combined}})_{\text{Average IQ}}$$

The first contrast is a test of the main effect of <u>iq</u>, the second and the third are tests of main effects of <u>method</u>, and the last two are tests of interactions. To implement these planned orthogonal contrasts into PROC GLM, five CONTRAST statements are written as follows:

```
PROC GLM DATA=ortho ORDER=DATA;
    CLASS iq method;
    MODEL score=iq method iq*method;
    CONTRAST  'psy1'   iq          1   -1;
    CONTRAST  'psy2'   method      1   -1    0;
    CONTRAST  'psy3'   method      1    1   -2;
    CONTRAST  'psy4'   iq*method   1   -1    0   -1    1    0;
    CONTRAST  'psy5'   iq*method   1    1   -2   -1   -1    2;
```

Note that each CONTRAST statement is independent of all others; thus, each ends with a semi-colon (;). Each statement is written according to the following syntax:

CONTRAST 'title of the contrast' effect_name coefficients_to_be_applied_to_group_means;

For a main effect, it is easy to figure out how coefficients are applied to each group (level) under that main effect. Simply multiply successive coefficients, from left to right, with group means that are ordered according to the way data were read. This is the reason why, in the PROC GLM statement, the option ORDER=DATA is included.

It is tricky, however, with interaction effects. Take the <u>iq</u>*<u>method</u> interaction, for example. How does SAS know to multiply −2 in ψ_5 with the mean of the <u>High IQ</u> students in the <u>combined</u> condition? The key lies in the order in which the two variables (or factors) are listed. In the program above, <u>iq</u> precedes <u>method</u>. Therefore, the first three coefficients, namely, 1, 1, and −2, are applied to the high <u>iq</u> group, whereas the last three, −1, −1, and 2, are applied to the average <u>iq</u> group. Within the high <u>iq</u> group, coefficients 1 and 1 are further applied to the first two conditions of <u>method</u>, whereas −2 is applied to the last condition, that is, the <u>combined method</u>. Try using this logic to interpret the coefficients in ψ_4 to make sure that you can write CONTRAST statements for interactions on your own.

After executing the five contrasts, the output shows the following results. Each contrast is tested with 1 and 24 degrees of freedom—the degrees of freedom for the MS error. Four contrasts are statistically significant at $\alpha = 0.01$, but ψ_4 is not. This nonsignificant result is confirmed by the graph and by the cell mean difference (27 − 12 = 20 − 5).

```
Contrast                      DF    Contrast SS    Mean Square   F Value  Pr > F

psy1-on iq                     1    2000.833333    2000.833333    800.33  <.0001
psy2-on method                 1    1125.000000    1125.000000    450.00  <.0001
psy3-on method                 1     201.666667     201.666667     80.67  <.0001
psy4-on iq by method           1       0.000000       0.000000      0.00  1.0000
psy5-on iq by method           1    1306.666667    1306.666667    522.67  <.0001
```

The CONTRAST statement is applicable to (a) orthogonal contrasts, such as the five tested here, (b) nonorthogonal contrasts, (c) simple or pairwise contrasts, and (d) complex contrasts of means.

- How to use ODS with the GLM procedure

To use the ODS, you need to know ODS table names corresponding with various portions of the output. Table 13.1 presents selected ODS table names for the GLM procedure and their descriptions.

Table 13.1   Selected ODS Table Names and Descriptions for the GLM Procedure

ODS Table Name	Description	GLM Procedure Statement
OverallANOVA	Overall ANOVA	(default)
Fitstatistics	R-square, C.V., Root MSE, and dependent variable's mean	(default)
ModelANOVA	ANOVA for model terms	(default)
Means	Group means	MEANS
MCLinesInfo	Multiple comparison information	MEANS / comparison procedure options
MCLines	Multiple comparison output	MEANS / comparison procedure options
MultStat	Multivariate statistics	REPEATED or MANOVA
Epsilons	Greenhouse-Geisser and Huynh-Feldt epsilons	REPEATED
LSMeans	Least-squares means	LSMEANS
Diff	Significance levels for tests of all pairs of least-squares means	LSMEANS / PDIFF

Based on the list of ODS table names, you may select certain results to be displayed in the Output window. For example, the following program selects the BON procedure's result of Example 13.1 to be included in the output:

```
ODS   SELECT Bon.MCLinesInfo Bon.MCLines;
PROC GLM DATA=design;
    CLASS indep1;
    MODEL score1=indep1;
    MEANS indep1 / BON TUKEY;
RUN;
```

Likewise, you may select certain result(s) to be exported as a SAS data set. For example, the following program exports R-square, C.V., Root MSE, and dependent variable's mean of Example 13.1 to the SAS data set fit:

```
ODS   OUTPUT FitStatistics = fit;
PROC GLM DATA=design;
    CLASS indep1;
    MODEL score1=indep1;
    MEANS indep1 / BON TUKEY;
RUN;
```

Furthermore, you may select certain results to be saved in file formats other than the SAS standard output. For example, the following program saves the output of Example 12.1 in HTML format in its default style:

```
ODS HTML BODY = 'd:\result\Example13_1Body.html'
        CONTENTS = 'd:\result\Example13_1TOC.html'
        PAGE - 'd:\result\Example13_1Page.html'
        FRAME = 'd:\result\Example13_1Frame.html';

PROC GLM DATA=design;
    CLASS indep1;
    MODEL score1=indep1;
    MEANS indep1 / BON TUKEY;
RUN;

ODS HTML CLOSE;
RUN;
```

For additional information about the ODS feature, consult with *SAS 9.1.3 Output Delivery System: User's Guide* (SAS Institute Inc., 2006c) and *SAS/STAT 9.1 User's Guide* (SAS Institute Inc., 2004d) or the online documentation at www.sas.com.

13.6 Summary

Haven't you felt like you have had enough of ANOVA? Almost! The ANOVA technique is versatile for testing population mean differences, and so is the GLM procedure—a comprehensive tool for handling a variety of ANOVA designs. The null hypothesis tested in these designs is always the same: that population means are equal. In other words, there is no effect of any kind. The alternative hypothesis states that some means are unequal. The statistic conceptualized by Sir R. A. Fisher to test the null hypothesis is an F value. The F value is a ratio of two estimates. These two estimates should give the same variance of sampling errors under the null hypothesis. Under the alternative hypothesis, though, the numerator should be larger than the denominator because it contains a portion that reflects the effect being tested under the null hypothesis.

Once the null hypothesis is rejected by an F test at a preset α level, one concludes that some means are most likely different from each other. At this point, it is necessary to apply a comparison procedure to pinpoint the specific source of differences among means. PROC GLM provides many such procedures for testing pairs of means. All are performed as a two-tailed test, except for the DUNNETT procedure, which can be performed as a one-tailed test.

If an ANOVA design is balanced, PROC ANOVA can also be specified to test null hypotheses and compare mean differences. And the syntax illustrated in this chapter is equally valid for the ANOVA procedure. There are, however, differences between ANOVA and GLM procedures. In the case of ANCOVA, the GLM procedure can treat a continuous variable as an independent variable, whereas the ANOVA procedure cannot. The GLM procedure provides the CONTRAST statement for testing planned comparisons of main effects and of interactions. These planned comparisons can be complex, based on three or more means. They can be orthogonal as well as nonorthogonal. Yet the CONTRAST statement is not available in the ANOVA procedure, although PROC ANOVA is efficient and versatile for analyzing data collected from a balanced ANOVA design.

13.7 Exercises

1. Four department stores, Macy's, J. C. Penney, Sears, and Target, were selected for a marketing research study of their advertising success. Advertising success was operationally defined as the number of items purchased by four typical customers randomly selected at each store on the second Saturday in July. The following data represent their purchasing behavior:

Subject	Macy's	J. C. Penney	Sears	Target
1	3	0	1	4
2	7	2	3	6
3	5	0	4	2
4	5	10	8	8

a. What is the average number of items purchased by all customers?
b. What are the values of $MS_{between}$ and MS_{within}?
c. Is there any significant difference in the number of items purchased by customers at these four stores?
d. Use the Tukey's method to assess the significance in the number of items bought at Macy's versus J. C. Penney. Write a sentence to help your grandma understand this statistical result.

2. A curious and bright graduate student carried out an investigation of a possible link between the size and wall colors of professors' offices and professors' research productivity. She constructed a reliable and valid measure to quantify the productivity and used it to gather the following data; the higher the number, the greater was the professor's productivity:

Room Color

		Peach	Cream	Gray	Blue
	Small	71	50	104	110
		80	63	112	105
Room	Medium	175	159	133	154
Size		164	152	128	141
	Large	105	109	79	66
		103	113	83	58

a. What is the average productivity by professors located in gray offices?
b. If the president of the unnamed university wished to standardize all professors' offices, what size of offices should this graduate student recommend?
c. Overall, which office wall color is most helpful to professors' productivity?
d. Does size of offices interact with room color in affecting the professors' research productivity? If so, how strong is the interaction?
e. If your answer to (d) above is <u>yes</u>, which combination of room color and size is most conducive to professors' productivity and which combination is the least?

3. A teacher wants to know if computerized instruction is better than the traditional method for teaching elementary school students. After applying these two methods in two different classes for one semester, the teacher administered tests in three subjects, arithmetic, arts, and reading, and obtained the following scores:

	Computerized		Traditional	
	Boys	Girls	Boys	Girls
Arithmetic	85, 70, 90, 82, 63, 84	68, 72, 65, 72, 79, 80	95, 89, 92, 66, 75, 60	75, 82, 78, 69, 70, 75
Arts	77, 89, 69, 82, 70, 87	92, 65, 75, 83, 82, 78	92, 88, 86, 70, 96, 60	77, 82, 79, 85, 72, 80
Reading	68, 75, 85, 92, 66, 80	74, 82, 76, 93, 82, 87	72, 74, 69, 85, 60, 83	82, 86, 77, 72, 74, 88

Answer the following questions based on these data:

a. Do students score differently in the three subjects? (*Hint*: One-way ANOVA)
b. Apply Tukey's procedure to examine differences in three subjects.
c. Do students score differently under two teaching methods? (*Hint*: One-way ANOVA)
d. Do boys and girls score differently?
e. Is there an interaction between and among teaching methods, subject matters, and gender? (*Hint*: Three-way ANOVA)

4. A group of young children has recently been diagnosed as severely depressed beyond the normal acceptable level. A study is therefore proposed and funded by the First Lady's Pocket Grant to investigate whether three antidepression drugs can improve children's depression. Three hospitals are randomly selected (a_1, a_2, a_3) to administer these drugs (t_1, t_2, t_3) to depressed children who come from either single-parent homes (b_1), divorced-then-remarried homes (b_2), or intact families (b_3). Data show the following trend (the higher the score, the better is the drug's effect):

	b_3	b_2	b_1
a_2	6 (t_1)	7 (t_2)	8 (t_3)
a_1	2 (t_2)	1 (t_3)	5 (t_1)
a_3	0 (t_3)	4 (t_1)	1 (t_2)

Perform a suitable statistical analysis on these data and summarize your results in an ANOVA table with $\alpha = 0.05$. Write a sentence to interpret the results.

5. Eight graduate students living on midwestern university campus were surveyed with regard to the government policy on phone wiretapping as a mechanism against terrorism. The survey was carried out at two times: on September 11, 2007, and shortly after Thanksgiving, also in 2007. The instrument used to collect data asked students about their attitude toward the necessity of such a government policy to fight against terrorism. The higher the score, the more supportive was the attitude. In addition, the researcher also collected information from each student regarding his or her stand on a national gun control law. Data exhibit the following trend:

Subject ID	Group	On September 11, 2007	After Thanksgiving, 2007
1	For gun control	4	7
2	For gun control	7	8
3	For gun control	3	5
4	For gun control	2	5
5	Against gun control	10	11
6	Against gun control	8	10
7	Against gun control	9	9
8	Against gun control	7	5

What are different analysis strategies that a data analyst can employ to find out if differences in students' attitudes could be explained by their stands on the national gun control law, time of the survey, and an interaction of these two?

6. In a computer literacy class, the instructor wished to determine if students' learning was different due to different teaching methods. Three methods (encouragement, practice and drill, and self-directed learning) were used in three classes. To better account for the teaching method effect, the instructor decided to measure students' IQ as a covariate. He administered an IQ test at the beginning of the study and a computer literacy test after the study was concluded. Is there any difference in students' computer literacy from three classes after IQ is taken into consideration?

Encouragement		Practice and Drill		Self-Directed Learning	
Test Score	IQ	Test Score	IQ	Test Score	IQ
16	124	17	137	13	112
15	123	15	116	11	104
14	115	18	148	14	111
15	120	17	135	11	105
17	136	19	147	12	103
13	104	18	135	14	113

13.8   Answers to Exercises

1. a. The average number of items purchased by all subjects (also customers) = 4.25.

    b. $MS_{between}$ = 3.66666667 and MS_{within} = 10.16666667.

    c. No, because the F test, $F(3, 12)$ = 0.36, p = 0.7825 is not statistically significant at the α level of 0.05.

    d. Tukey's test is used to examine if pairs of means are statistically significantly different from each other. In this case, the difference between these two means must be at least 6.6935 (= HSD = MSD) in order to be considered statistically significant. Since the mean difference between Macy's (= 5) and J. C. Penney (= 3) is 2, they are not considered significantly different from each other. Therefore, grandma, customers at Macy's and J. C. Penney bought approximately the same amount of stuff on a Saturday in July. Where do you want me to take you to shop?

2. a. 106.50

    b. The medium-sized offices should be recommended because these offices yielded the highest mean level of productivity (= 150.75).

    c. The color "peach" should be recommended for office walls because professors in peach-colored offices produced the most research (mean = 116.333), compared with professors in offices painted in cream, gray, or blue.

    d. Yes, the room size did interact statistically significantly with room colors in affecting professors' research productivity, $F(6, 12)$ = 39.86, p < 0.0001. ω^2 for the interaction effect = 0.9067, effect size = 3.117. Statistical power for detecting the significant interaction effect is nearly 100%. Both ω^2 and the statistical power were obtained by hand calculation, not from SAS directly.

    e. The most conducive combination is a peach-colored and medium-sized office (mean productivity = 169.5); the least is a cream-colored and small office (mean productivity = 56.5).

3. a. No, because the F test of the subject factor, $F(2, 69) = 0.83$, $p = 0.4404$ is not statistically significant at the α level of 0.05.

   b. Tukey's test is used to examine if pairs of means are statistically significantly different from each other. To be considered statistically significant, the observed difference between any two group means should be at least as large as 6.2211 (= HSD = MSD). Results from Tukey's test indicate that none of the pairwise comparisons is statistically significant. These results are consistent with the overall F test.

   c. No, because the F test of the method factor, $F(1, 70) < 0.01$, $p = 0.9586$ is not statistically significant at the α level of 0.05.

   d. No, because the F test of the sex factor, $F(1, 70) = 0.06$, $p = 0.3313$ is not statistically significant at the α level of 0.05.

   e. No, because the result of the F test of the three-way interaction among subject, method, and sex, $F(2, 60) = 0.12$, $p = 0.8878$ is not statistically significant at the α level of 0.05. Furthermore, none of the two-way interactions is statistically significant at $\alpha = 0.05$: (i) subject*method, $F(2, 60) = 0.49$, $p = 0.6132$; (ii) subject*sex, $F(2, 60) = 2.10$, $p = 0.1313$; and (iii) method*sex, $F(1, 60) = 0.00$, $p = 1.0$.

4. This research project calls for the application of the Latin-square (LS) design for which factors <u>a</u> and <u>b</u> are nuisance variables and factor <u>t</u> is the treatment factor. According to this LS design, the SS total is decomposed as follows:

Source	SS	df	MS	F	p
a	48.222	2	24.111	7.75	.1143
b	6.222	2	3.111	1.00	.5000
t	6.889	2	3.444	1.11	.4746
Error	6.222	2	3.111		
Total	67.556	8			

Because the F test of the <u>t</u> main effect is not statistically significant, it is concluded that three antidepression drugs did not produce noticeable differences in improving children's depression after controlling for differences in hospitals and family backgrounds.

5. Strategy A: Apply an SPF$_{p.q}$ design for which the <u>Group</u> variable is the between-block factor and the two measures as levels of the within-block factor.

   Strategy B: Perform a one-way ANOVA using the <u>Group</u> variable as the independent variable and the difference between the two measures as the dependent variable.

Strategy C: Perform two one-way ANOVAs using the <u>Group</u> variable as the independent variable and each of the two measures as the dependent variable. Discuss any discrepancy in findings due to the time of the measures.

Strategy D: Perform a one-way ANCOVA for which the first measure, taken on September 11, 2007, is the covariate and the second measure, taken after Thanksgiving 2007, is the dependent variable. The <u>Group</u> variable is the independent variable.

Strategy E: Apply the nonparametric test of Strategy B.

Strategy F: Apply the nonparametric test of Strategy C.

6. The ANCOVA result is summarized as follows:

Source	SS	df	MS	F	p
IQ	48.2862	1	48.2862	89.48	<0.0001
Method	2.0633	2	1.0317	1.91	0.2096
Error	4.3172	8	0.5396		
Total	54.6667	11			

From the ANCOVA result, we can conclude that <u>IQ</u> is an effective covariate, $F(1, 8)$ = 89.48, $p < 0.0001$. After adjusting for <u>IQ</u>, the effect of <u>method</u>s is not statistically significant, $F(2, 8) = 1.91$, $p = 0.2096$. However, the appropriateness of using ANCOVA to analyze data for this study is questionable because <u>IQ</u> is found to interact with the method, $F(2, 6) = 6.59$, $p = 0.0306$.

14

Inferences About Two or More Population Typical Scores by Ranks

OBJECTIVE

In this chapter, you will learn how to infer the equality between two or more population typical scores by nonparametric tests. These nonparametric tests are alternatives to the independent-samples *t* test and the *F* test of one-way analysis of variance when sample sizes are small and data do not satisfy the assumptions of the *t* or *F* test.

14.1 An Overview of Statistical Tests of Typical Scores by Ranks

Oftentimes, when data are measured at the ordinal level, or the sample size is small, it is difficult to justify the use of a t test or an F test for making inferences about two or more population means. Therefore, alternative statistical tests have to be used. These tests are referred to as distribution-free or nonparametric tests because they do not assume a specific shape (such as normal) for the underlying population distribution, and the parameter of interest is not necessarily the arithmetic mean. Data required by nonparametric tests are measured usually at the ordinal level. This is an advantage of nonparametric tests over parametric tests, such as the t test.

In this chapter, you will learn how to conduct nonparametric tests of two or more populations' typical scores with the NPAR1WAY procedure and how to interpret the results. Within the nonparametric framework, a typical score is comparable to a central location (or location parameter) in the population; yet it need not be the mean of the distribution. In other words, the NPAR1WAY procedure provides a nonparametric version of the independent-samples t test (Example 14.1) and of the F test used in one-way analysis of variance (Example 14.2). The nonparametric test of one population typical score is the sign test or the signed rank test. These two tests are carried out by the UNIVARIATE procedure (refer back to Chapter 9, Example 9.5).

To compare two or more population typical scores, PROC NPAR1WAY offers several nonparametric tests. The Wilcoxon test and the median test are demonstrated in this chapter; the Van der Waerden test and the Savage test are shown at www.sagepub.com/pengstudy. Each test is suitable for a particular type of data (refer to **Section 14.4: Tips**). These tests are performed either as an exact test or as an approximate test. The exact tests are appropriate for all situations, especially when sample sizes are very small and data are sparse or skewed or contain lots of ties. The approximate tests are well suited for large samples. Exact tests begin by rearranging observations from the smallest to the largest and assigning ranks accordingly. Next, these ranks are transformed into scaled scores, depending on the specific test statistic being computed. These scaled scores are linearly combined in the two-sample case to form the test statistic. In the multiple sample case, scaled scores are not linearly combined, but the final statistic still reflects location differences among multiple samples.

Various names have been given to the nonparametric version of the independent-samples t test, such as the Wilcoxon test, the Wilcoxon rank sum test, or the Mann-Whitney U test. Likewise, the multiple-sample Wilcoxon test is actually the Kruskal-Wallis test, the median test is the Brown-Mood test, and so on. Table 14.1 summarizes various names of the tests provided by PROC NPAR1WAY.

Table 14.1   Nonparametric Tests From PROC NPAR1WAY for Testing Location Differences

	Nonparametric Tests		
SAS Keywords	Exact *for* Two Samples	Exact *for* Multiple Samples	Approximate *for* Two and Multiple Samples
WILCOXON	Wilcoxon rank sum or Mann-Whitney *U*	Kruskal-Wallis	chi-square (or *Z* or *t* test)
MEDIAN	Median	Brown-Mood	chi-square (or *Z* or *t* test)
VW	Van der Waerden	Multiple-samples Van der Waerden	chi-square (or *Z* or *t* test)
SAVAGE	Savage	Multiple-samples Savage	chi-square (or *Z* or *t* test)

14.2 Examples

Example 14.1 Nonparametric Tests of Two Sample Means

Do children learn better from pictures or from words? To answer this question, an investigation was conducted on 19 children in the second and third grades in Wisconsin. Children were randomly assigned to one of two conditions: picture (9 children) or verbal (10 children). In the picture condition, children were instructed to listen to tape-recorded stories while looking at pictures corresponding to story schemes. In the verbal condition, children also listened to stories from a tape recorder but simultaneously read stories that were typed on index cards placed in front of them.

Two stories were presented and all children finished listening to both. Following each story, the experimenter administered a 10-item test to measure children's level of comprehension and memory. A total of 20 items were given and the mean percentage of correct responses by each student was the dependent variable. Data were recorded in the file learn.dat. Based on these data, we will try to answer the question, "Do children learn better from pictures or from words?" Two variables are analyzed by the NPAR1WAY procedure: group and score. Variable group identifies the condition to which each child was assigned, and score is each child's percentage of correct answers. The program below requests an exact test as well as the chi-square approximate test based on ranks. Furthermore, the median test is performed to test the null hypothesis that the two samples are from populations with the same median.

```
DATA learn;
    INFILE 'd:\data\learn.dat';
    INPUT group $ score;
RUN;


TITLE 'Example 14.1 Nonparametric tests of two sample means';

PROC NPAR1WAY DATA=learn WILCOXON MEDIAN;
    CLASS group;
    VAR score;
    EXACT;
RUN;
```

Output 14.1 Nonparametric Tests of Two Sample Means

```
            Example 14.1 Nonparametric tests of two sample means          1

                     The NPAR1WAY Procedure

              Wilcoxon Scores (Rank Sums) for Variable score
                     Classified by Variable group
Part (A)
                        Sum of      Expected      Std Dev        Mean
         group    N     Scores      Under H0      Under H0       Score
        -----------------------------------------------------------------
         picture  9     135.0       90.0          12.242076      15.00
         verbal   10    55.0        100.0         12.242076      5.50

                 Average scores were used for ties.


                     Wilcoxon Two-Sample Test
Part (B)
                 Statistic (S)              135.0000
Part (C)
                 Normal Approximation
                 Z                          3.6350
                 One-Sided Pr >  Z          0.0001
                 Two-Sided Pr > |Z|         0.0003

                 t Approximation
                 One-Sided Pr >  Z          0.0009
                 Two-Sided Pr > |Z|         0.0019
Part (D)
                 Exact Test
                 One-Sided Pr >=  S            1.083E-05
                 Two-Sided Pr >= |S - Mean|    2.165E-05

             Z includes a continuity correction of 0.5.

Part (E)
                        Kruskal-Wallis Test

                     Chi-Square       13.5119
                     DF               1
                     Pr > Chi-Square  0.0002
```

Page 1 of the output is the results of the keyword WILCOXON. According to **Part (A)**, the mean rank (= 15) for the picture condition is much higher than the mean rank (= 5.50) for the verbal condition. The Wilcoxon statistic (**S**) of 135.0000 in **Part (B)** represents the sum of ranks assigned to the picture condition (the smaller sample). The S statistic is statistically significant according to its exact sampling distribution. The p level for a one-tailed test is 1.083E–05, or 0.00001083 see **Part (D)**; the p level for a two-tailed test is 2.165E–05, or 0.00002165; also see **Part (D)**. Both are statistically significant at the α level of 0.05 or even 0.01. Based on the exact test result, we can conclude that there is a significant difference between the two learning conditions; the picture condition helped children retain story schemes better than the verbal condition. The difference between a one-tailed and a two-tailed p level is explained in Chapter 12, **Section 12.5**.

Three approximate tests of the Wilcoxon two-sample test are offered: the **normal Z test** and **Student's t test**, both listed in **Part (C)**, and the **chi-square** test, also the Kruskal-Wallis Test under **Part (E)**. The normal Z test is formed from the ratio of the Wilcoxon S divided by its standard error. The Student's t test uses the same ratio as Z, but compares the ratio to a Student's t distribution to determine its significance level. The chi-square approximation is based on the chi-square distribution with degrees of freedom = 1 (or the number of samples – 1). The chi-square test is always a two-tailed test. It is the test cited most often by textbook authors, among the three approximate tests. The approximation is good as long as each sample size is at least 6 or more. Although there are slight differences in the p level reported by each approximate test, all three approximate test results nevertheless support the rejection of the null hypothesis of no difference—a conclusion already arrived at by the exact test.

```
              Example 14.1 Nonparametric tests of two sample means            2

                        The NPAR1WAY Procedure

Part (F)
         Median Scores (Number of Points Above Median) for Variable score
                        Classified by Variable group

                          Sum of      Expected       Std Dev         Mean
         group      N     Scores      Under H0       Under H0        Score
         --------------------------------------------------------------------
         picture    9       9.0       4.263158       1.116484         1.0
         verbal    10       0.0       4.736842       1.116484         0.0

                   Average scores were used for ties.


                        Median Two-Sample Test
Part (G)
                   Statistic (S)                     9.0000
Part (H)
                   Normal Approximation
                   Z                                 4.2426
                   One-Sided Pr >  Z                 <.0001
                   Two-Sided Pr > |Z|                <.0001
Part (I)
                   Exact Test
                   One-Sided Pr >=  S               1.083E-05
                   Two-Sided Pr >= |S - Mean|       1.083E-05
```

Part (J)

```
                           Median One-Way Analysis

                      Chi-Square          18.0000
                      DF                        1
                      Pr > Chi-Square      <.0001
```

Page 2 of the output shows the results of using the keyword MEDIAN. According to **Part (F)**, the mean score (= 1.0) for the picture condition is higher than the mean score (= 0.0) for the verbal condition. This information indicates that all the scores from the picture condition are higher than the combined median score, whereas all the scores from the verbal condition are lower than or equal to the combined median score. The median test statistic (**S**) of 9.0000 in **Part (G)** represents the sum of scores assigned to the picture condition. The *S* statistic is statistically significant according to its exact sampling distribution. The *p* levels for both one-tailed and two-tailed tests are 1.083E–05, or 0.00001083; see **Part (I)**. Both are statistically significant at the α level of 0.05 or even 0.01. Based on the exact test result, we can conclude that there is a significant difference in the median score between the two learning conditions; the picture condition helped children retain story schemes better than the verbal condition.

Two approximate tests of the median test are offered: the **normal Z test**, in **Part (H)**, and the **chi-square** test, also the Median One-Way Analysis, under **Part (J)**. The normal Z test is formed from the ratio of the median test statistic divided by its standard error. The chi-square approximation is based on the chi-square distribution with degrees of freedom = 1 (or the number of samples – 1). The approximation is good as long as the total sample size is more than 20. Like the chi-square approximate test to the Wilcoxon test, this chi-square test is always a two-tailed test. Both approximate tests support the rejection of the null hypothesis of two equal population medians—a conclusion already supported by the exact test.

• The NPAR1WAY procedure, like its counterpart, the TTEST procedure, is able to analyze several dependent variables while using the same independent variable to define samples. Below is an illustration of how both income and expense are compared between samples defined by jobs.

```
PROC NPAR1WAY DATA=economy;
    CLASS jobs;
    VAR income expense;
RUN;
```

Example 14.2 Nonparametric One-Way Analysis of Variance by Ranks

As mentioned earlier, PROC NPAR1WAY can provide nonparametric tests of multiple samples. These nonparametric tests are comparable to their parametric counterpart, namely, the F test. The aim of these nonparametric tests is to determine if multiple samples yield similar "average" scores on a dependent variable. The concept of "average" refers to either an average rank or the average of transformed ranks. The following program invokes the Kruskal-Wallis test of average ranks with the keyword **WILCOXON**.

The file learn.dat provides the data base. For this example, four samples are created, two from each condition. The original two samples were split into approximately equal sized subgroups. The new grouping variable is called grp.

```
DATA non1way;
    INFILE 'd:\data\learn.dat';
    INPUT group $ score;
    IF group='picture' AND _N_ < 5 THEN grp=1;
      ELSE IF group='picture' AND _N_ < 10 THEN grp=2;
      ELSE IF group='verbal'  AND _N_ < 15 THEN grp=3;
      ELSE grp=4;
RUN;

TITLE 'Example 14.2 Nonparametric one-way analysis of variance by ranks';

PROC NPAR1WAY DATA=non1way WILCOXON;
    CLASS grp;
    VAR score;
    EXACT;
RUN;
```

Output 14.2 Nonparametric One-Way Analysis of Variance by Ranks

```
        Example 14.2 Nonparametric one-way analysis of variance by ranks         1

                          The NPAR1WAY Procedure

                 Wilcoxon Scores (Rank Sums) for Variable score
                          Classified by Variable grp
Part (A)
                           Sum of      Expected      Std Dev        Mean
          grp     N        Scores      Under H0      Under H0       Score
          ------------------------------------------------------------------
           1      4         66.0         40.0        9.995613       16.50
           2      5         69.0         50.0       10.796496       13.80
           3      5         35.0         50.0       10.796496        7.00
           4      5         20.0         50.0       10.796496        4.00
```

```
                       Average scores were used for ties.


                               Kruskal-Wallis Test

Part (B)         Chi-Square                              14.7350
                 DF                                            3
Part (C)         Asymptotic Pr >  Chi-Square             0.0021
Part (D)         Exact      Pr >= Chi-Square           1.410E-05
```

The last column in **Part (A)** shows the mean ranks for the four samples. These mean ranks suggest that these four groups did not perform similarly. The Kruskal-Wallis chi-square test statistic = 14.7350 with 3 degrees of freedom; see **Part (B)**. This statistic is significant at 0.0021, based on the chi-square approximate sampling distribution; see **Part (C)**. It is significant at 1.410E–5, or 0.0000141, according to the exact sampling distribution; see **Part (D)**. Both p values are very small, indicating that the null hypothesis of no difference in average ranks can be rejected at an α level of 0.01. Thus, at least two mean ranks are different from each other. Stated alternatively, the four samples scored differently on the 20-item test. Data reveal that the best-performing group is the first group, followed by the second, the third, and the fourth group. Whether or not these mean ranks are statistically significantly different from each other is a question that can only be answered by further tests that are designed for this purpose. Unfortunately, the NPAR1WAY procedure in SAS 9.1 does not perform these tests.

14.3 How to Write the PROC NPAR1WAY Codes

Based on the examples presented so far, you might have found the NPAR1WAY procedure to be user-friendly and simple. Here are its five statements:

```
PROC    NPAR1WAY            DATA= sas_dataset_name <options>
                            <statistic_names>;

        CLASS               independent_variable;

        VAR                 dependent_variable(s);

        EXACT               <statistic_names>;

        BY                  classification_variable(s);
```

The first statement, **PROC NPAR1WAY**, initiates the procedure and specifies the data set to be analyzed. In addition, you may specify any of the four nonparametric statistical tests: the Wilcoxon (**WILCOXON**), the median

(**MEDIAN**), the Van der Waerden (**VW**), and the Savage (**SAVAGE**) test. Along with these four nonparametric tests, the parametric one-way analysis of variance can also be specified by the **ANOVA** option. The **ANOVA** results can be used as a basis for comparison between parametric and nonparametric analyses.

The second statement, **CLASS**, identifies an independent variable that separates observations into two or more groups. The third statement, **VAR**, specifies one or more dependent (or outcome) variables whose transformed scores are to be compared among groups defined by the CLASS variable.

The fourth statement, **EXACT**, is used whenever you wish to perform an exact test on the transformed scores of one or more dependent variables. Exact tests are well suited for data sets that are small, skewed, sparse, or heavily tied. If data sets are large, considerable computing time and memory are required to perform the exact test. To cap the computing time, you may specify the option **MAXTIME=** (in seconds). Alternatively, you may conduct approximate tests (i.e., chi-square, normal Z) or compute the exact p value using the Monte Carlo estimation method. The Monte Carlo estimation method is invoked by the **MC** option on this statement.

Finally, the last statement, **BY**, serves the same purpose as in all other procedures. It divides the data set into subgroups according to diverse values of the BY variable. Within each subgroup, the nonparametric test is performed according to the CLASS and VAR specifications. If more than one BY variable is listed, all possible combinations of the BY variables' values are used in dividing up the entire data set. Be sure to presort the data set in the ascending order of all the BY variables, if the BY statement is included in the NPAR1WAY procedure. Presorting a data set can be accomplished using the SORT procedure.

14.4 Tips

- How to handle missing or invalid data

By default, PROC NPAR1WAY does not consider observations that have missing information on either the CLASS variable or the VAR variable.

- How does PROC NPAR1WAY treat ties?

Ties in data refer to identical scores from different individuals. Because they are identical, PROC NPAR1WAY assigns an average rank to all of them. For example, the following scores show two sets of ties. The ultimate ranks are based on the mean of consecutive ranks. Hence, Rank 3 is the average of 2, 3, and 4; Rank 8.5 is the average of 8 and 9.

Original Scores	Ranked Scores	Ranks Assigned
19	11	1
19	14	3
17	14	3
16	14	3
15	15	5
14	16	6
14	17	7
14	19	8.5
11	19	8.5

- For what type of data should you choose the Wilcoxon test?

The Wilcoxon test is the most versatile of all nonparametric tests because it does not make any assumption about the shape of the underlying population. It merely assumes that the underlying populations have identical shape or form. It is more powerful than the median test because the Wilcoxon score preserves ranking information, whereas the median test does not. For multiple groups, this test is equivalent to the Kruskal-Wallis test.

- For what type of data should you choose the median test?

The median test assigns a score of 1 to observations whose values are higher than the median and 0 to those below or equal to the median. The test is most suitable for data drawn from a double exponential distribution. The double exponential distribution is symmetric around the midpoint and spiky at the central region. The shape is not bell-like but, instead, triangular. For a double exponential curve, the sample median is the most efficient estimator of the location parameter. It is sometimes called the Type I extreme value curve. The median test is identical to the Brown-Mood test for multiple-sample comparisons.

- For what type of data should you choose the exact test, and therefore, the EXACT; statement?

Exact tests are precise statistical tests based on permutations of ranks or transformed scores of data. As indicated earlier, exact tests are well suited for data sets that are small, skewed, sparse, or heavily tied. When data sets are large, considerable computing time and memory are required in generating the exact sampling distribution. For these data sets, approximate tests based on asymptotic theories, or the Monte Carlo estimation method for estimating the exact p value, are suitable.

- How to use ODS to save the NPAR1WAY result as data sets

To use the ODS, you need to know ODS table names corresponding to various portions of the output. Table 14.2 presents selected ODS table names for the NPAR1WAY procedure and their descriptions.

Table 14.2   Selected ODS Table Names and Descriptions for the NPAR1WAY Procedure

ODS Table Name	Description	PROC NPAR1WAY Option
WilcoxonScores	Wilcoxon scores	WILCOXON
WilcoxonTest	Wilcoxon two-samples test	WILCOXON
KruskalWallisTest	Kruskal-Wallis test	WILCOXON
MedianScores	Median scores	MEDIAN
MedianTest	Median two-samples test	MEDIAN
MedianAnalysis	Median one-way analysis	MEDIAN

Based on the list of ODS table names, you may select certain results to be exported as a SAS data set. For example, the following program exports the results of the Wilcoxon test of Output 14.1 to a SAS data set, <u>outnpar,</u> and prints out the content using the PRINT procedure:

```
ODS OUTPUT WilcoxonTest = outnpar;
PROC NPAR1WAY DATA=learn WILCOXON;
     CLASS group;
     VAR score;
     EXACT;
RUN;
PROC PRINT DATA=outnpar;
RUN;
```

```
See Output 14.1 for page 1 results

                              The SAS System                              2

     Obs    Name1    Label1                cValue1           nValue1

      1    _WIL_    Statistic (S)          135.0000        135.000000
      2
      3             Normal Approximation                       .
```

4	Z_WIL	Z	3.6350	3.635004
5	PR_WIL	One-Sided Pr > Z	0.0001	0.000139
6	P2_WIL	Two-Sided Pr > |Z|	0.0003	0.000278
7				.
8		t Approximation		
9	PTR_WIL	One-Sided Pr > Z	0.0009	0.000947
10	PT2_WIL	Two-Sided Pr > |Z|	0.0019	0.001894
11				.
12		Exact Test		.
13	XPR_WIL	One-Sided Pr >= S	1.083E-05	0.000010825
14	XP2_WIL	Two-Sided Pr >= |S - Mean|	2.165E-05	0.000021650

14.5 Summary

A series of statistical inferential methods were presented in this chapter that help researchers make inferences about the equality between or among population typical scores. They are referred to in textbooks as distribution-free or nonparametric methods. These methods are most useful when data or underlying population distributions do not meet the assumptions required by parametric tests such as t or F. Two types of nonparametric tests are introduced: the exact test and the approximate test. The exact test is preferred when samples are small or when data are skewed or irregular or contain several ties. The approximate test is suitable for large samples for which the asymptotic approximation is fairly good. Both types can be carried out as a one-tailed or two-tailed test in the NPAR1WAY procedure.

Data required by PROC NPAR1WAY are ordinal-level or ranked data. Even if data are more precise than ordinal, such as height and weight measurements, they are always converted to ranks first by the NPAR1WAY procedure before conducting nonparametric tests. These ranks are subsequently analyzed to determine if the null hypothesis of no difference in population locations should be rejected.

In general, statisticians agree that nonparametric tests of population locations are preferred over parametric tests of means in any of the following situations:

a. Sample sizes are small.

b. Data are measured by ordinal or nominal scales.

c. Medians or average ranks of the populations are the primary goal of inference making from the sample data.

d. Medians or average ranks are more representative of the locations of the populations than the arithmetic mean.

e. The population distributions are unknown, or cannot be assumed to follow a known probability distribution, such as the normal curve.

f. It is highly unlikely that population variances are equal.

14.6 Exercises

1. A human resource firm conducted a survey about people's satisfaction with their modern lives. Ten customers at a discount store were asked to report their contentment with modern life on a 7-point Likert-type scale, where 1 meant "strongly dissatisfied" and 7 meant "strongly satisfied." Results are as follows, with the first 5 customers being well dressed and the last 5 casually outfitted. What conclusion can you draw from the data with regard to these two groups' level of contentment?

Subject	1	2	3	4	5	6	7	8	9	10
Rating	2	1	1	2	4	5	3	4	7	6

2. The following data are collected from 20 ninth graders on a geology test. Is there any difference in average performance between boys and girls?

Boys	87	64	89	83	96	78	68	78	69	74
Girls	78	75	86	72	82	85	81	77	71	80

3. If grades were assigned to the previous geology scores according to the criteria below, is there any difference in boys' and girls' grades?

A+ 90 and above

A 85 to 89

B+ 80 to 84

B 75 to 79

B– 70 to 74

C+ 65 to 69

C 60 to 64

F 59 and below

4. A completely randomized experiment was conducted to determine if various reading strategies helped students comprehend reading materials differently. Four college students were randomly assigned to each of five treatment conditions that taught students to employ a distinct reading strategy in reading John Updike's work titled *A Hotel in New Hampshire*. The level of students' comprehension was later measured by a reading test. Scores show the following trend:

Group 1	Group 2	Group 3	Group 4	Group 5
19	17	17	20	14
21	18	16	25	10
28	13	11	30	9
30	12	15	33	11

a. Carry out a one-way analysis of variance of the data with an overall *F* test.
b. Conduct a Kruskal-Wallis test on the same data.
c. What is your conclusion based on findings from (a) and (b)?

5. Write a SAS program to compare <u>income</u> averages of four groups, based on two <u>regions</u> and two <u>educational</u> levels; incomes are in thousands of dollars.

<u>Region</u>

		Urban	Rural
	High	90	50
		70	20
		60	10
			40
<u>Educ</u>			
	Low	70	50
		60	30
		40	10
		50	10
		40	

14.7 Answers to Exercises

1. The Wilcoxon statistic ($S = 16.5000$) is statistically significant at the α level of 0.05, for both the one-tailed and the two-tailed tests. We can conclude that the well-dressed customers are less satisfied with their modern lives than casually dressed customers.

```
                            Exercise 14-1                              1

                        The NPAR1WAY Procedure

              Wilcoxon Scores (Rank Sums) for Variable score
                    Classified by Variable group

                            Sum of     Expected      Std Dev      Mean
group                 N     Scores     Under H0      Under H0     Score
-----------------------------------------------------------------------
Well dressed          5     16.50       27.50       4.743416      3.30
Causally outfitted    5     38.50       27.50       4.743416      7.70

                 Average scores were used for ties.


                      Wilcoxon Two-Sample Test

                 Statistic (S)              16.5000

                 Normal Approximation
                 Z                          -2.2136
                 One-Sided Pr <  Z           0.0134
                 Two-Sided Pr > |Z|          0.0269
```

```
                    t Approximation
                    One-Sided Pr <  Z              0.0271
                    Two-Sided Pr > |Z|             0.0541

                    Exact Test
                    One-Sided Pr <=  S             0.0119
                    Two-Sided Pr >= |S - Mean|     0.0238

             Z includes a continuity correction of 0.5.


                        Kruskal-Wallis Test

                   Chi-Square          5.3778
                   DF                       1
                   Pr > Chi-Square     0.0204
```

2. The Wilcoxon statistic ($S = 104.0000$) is not statistically significant at the $\alpha = 0.05$ level. We can conclude that there is no significant difference in average performance between boys and girls on the geology test.

```
                    Exercise 14-2                                    1

                    The NPAR1WAY Procedure

          Wilcoxon Scores (Rank Sums) for Variable score
                   Classified by Variable sex

                     Sum of    Expected      Std Dev       Mean
   sex       N       Scores    Under H0      Under H0      Score
   ------------------------------------------------------------------
   Boy      10       104.0       105.0      13.208849      10.40
   Girl     10       106.0       105.0      13.208849      10.60

          Average scores were used for ties.


                    Wilcoxon Two-Sample Test

             Statistic (S)              104.0000

             Normal Approximation
             Z                           -0.0379
             One-Sided Pr <  Z            0.4849
             Two-Sided Pr > |Z|           0.9698

             t Approximation
             One-Sided Pr <  Z            0.4851
             Two-Sided Pr > |Z|           0.9702

             Exact Test
             One-Sided Pr <=  S           0.4853
             Two-Sided Pr >= |S - Mean|   0.9706

          Z includes a continuity correction of 0.5.


                        Kruskal-Wallis Test

                   Chi-Square          0.0057
                   DF                       1
                   Pr > Chi-Square     0.9397
```

3. The Wilcoxon statistic (S = 97.5000) based on grades is not statistically significant at the α level of 0.05. We can conclude that there is no significant difference in the grades between boys and girls on the geology test.

```
                            Exercise 14-3                              1

                        The NPAR1WAY Procedure


                Wilcoxon Scores (Rank Sums) for Variable grade
                        Classified by Variable sex

                        Sum of      Expected       Std Dev         Mean
   sex         N        Scores      Under H0       Under H0        Score
   ---------------------------------------------------------------------
   Boy        10         97.50        105.0       13.003036        9.750
   Girl       10        112.50        105.0       13.003036       11.250

               Average scores were used for ties.


                        Wilcoxon Two-Sample Test

                Statistic (S)                   97.5000

                Normal Approximation
                Z                               -0.5383
                One-Sided Pr <   Z               0.2952
                Two-Sided Pr >  |Z|              0.5903

                t Approximation
                One-Sided Pr <   Z               0.2983
                Two-Sided Pr >  |Z|              0.5966

                Exact Test
                One-Sided Pr <-  S               0.3055
                Two-Sided Pr >= |S - Mean|       0.6110

            Z includes a continuity correction of 0.5.


                        Kruskal-Wallis Test

                Chi-Square            0.3327
                DF                         1
                Pr > Chi-Square       0.5641
```

4. a. The parametric F test (= 11.7415, df = 4 and 15, p = 0.0002) of group differences shows that different reading strategies resulted in significantly different degrees of comprehension of Updike's work.

```
                         Exercise 14-4                              1

                      The NPAR1WAY Procedure

                 Analysis of Variance for Variable score
                      Classified by Variable group

              group                N                 Mean
              ------------------------------------------------
                1                   4               24.500
                2                   4               15.000
                3                   4               14.750
                4                   4               27.000
                5                   4               11.000


Source     DF     Sum of Squares    Mean Square    F Value    Pr > F
--------------------------------------------------------------------
Among       4         763.200          190.800      11.7415    0.0002
Within     15         243.750           16.250

            Average scores were used for ties.
```

b. The Kruskal-Wallis test once again shows a significant diference (chi-square = 15.5350, df = 4, p = 0.0037), just as the F test in (a) did.

```
                         Exercise 14-4                              2

                      The NPAR1WAY Procedure

            Wilcoxon Scores (Rank Sums) for Variable score
                   Classified by Variable group

                     Sum of      Expected    Std Dev       Mean
group      N         Scores      Under H0    Under H0      Score
--------------------------------------------------------------------
1          4         63.50        42.0      10.571063     15.8750
2          4         33.50        42.0      10.571063      8.3750
3          4         31.00        42.0      10.571063      7.7500
4          4         68.50        42.0      10.571063     17.1250
5          4         13.50        42.0      10.571063      3.3750

            Average scores were used for ties.


                     Kruskal-Wallis Test

             Chi-Square           15.5350
             DF                         4
             Pr > Chi-Square       0.0037
```

c. Based on the parametric test result in (a) and the nonparametric test result in (b), it can be concluded that reading strategies did result in differential levels of comprehension by students when reading literary works, such as *A Hotel in New Hampshire*.

5. The parametric *F* test (= 4.4882, df = 3 and 12, *p* = 0.0248) of group differences reveals that the average incomes of the four groups formed by two educational levels and two regions are significantly different. People from the urban area with a high educational level have the highest average income (= 65.000000 thousands). The lowest average (= 25.000000) belonged to people from the rural area with a low educational level. The result of the Kruskal-Wallis test (chi-square = 7.4227, df = 3, *p* = 0.0423) is similar to results derived from the *F* test.

```
                          Exercise 14-5                                    1

                     The NPAR1WAY Procedure

           Analysis of Variance for Variable income
                 Classified by Variable group

              group                  N                Mean
              ----------------------------------------------
              High-Urban             4            65.000000
              High-Rural             3            26.666667
              Low-Urban              5            52.000000
              Low-Rural              4            25.000000


Source     DF    Sum of Squares    Mean Square     F Value    Pr > F
----------------------------------------------------------------------
Among      3       4428.333333     1476.111111       4.4882    0.0248
Within    12       3946.666667      328.888889

           Average scores were used for ties.
```

```
                          Exercise 14-5                                    2

                     The NPAR1WAY Procedure

        Wilcoxon Scores (Rank Sums) for Variable income
                 Classified by Variable group

                        Sum of      Expected      Std Dev         Mean
group            N      Scores      Under H0      Under H0        Score
-----------------------------------------------------------------------
High-Urban       4        50.0        34.00       8.160882    12.500000
High-Rural       3        16.0        25.50       7.356120     5.333333
Low-Urban        5        51.0        42.50       8.735703    10.200000
Low-Rural        4        19.0        34.00       8.160882     4.750000

           Average scores were used for ties.


                     Kruskal-Wallis Test

           Chi-Square                      7.4227
           DF                                   3
           Asymptotic Pr >  Chi-Square     0.0596
           Exact        Pr >= Chi-Square   0.0423
```

15

Examining Trends in Data

OBJECTIVE

In this chapter, you will learn how to display, and subsequently examine, data that are derived from two or more variables. Specifically, you will learn how to effectively show trends or hidden structures in data by displaying data points in 2-D plots, by indicating the membership in subgroups such as male and female in a plot, by adjusting the origin of axes or the plotting symbol, by imposing reference lines, and by labeling axes with character values. Tactics such as overlaying several plots on a graph or showing graphs side by side are also included.

15.1 Why and How to Examine Trends in Data _____

As a Chinese proverb proclaims, "A picture is worth a thousand words!" True, a visual display of data often reveals the intricate trends and structures hidden in a data set. The subtle richness of data sometimes cannot be detected by statistical tests aimed at means, variances, or other summative indices. Hence, it is highly recommended that data be shown visually in a plot, especially when the goal of data analysis is to examine relationships between or among variables.

The PLOT procedure is particularly well suited for projecting data points onto a two-dimensional (2-D) graph so that you can study the relationship among variables. You can also investigate the reasons why certain regions of the graph are sparse while others are filled with data points. The graphic output may be used to assess the fit of a regression model to actual data. High-density plots can be drawn using the GPLOT procedure. Because of the complexity of the GPLOT procedure, only a handful of its useful and unique features are illustrated in this chapter.

There are many different techniques to manipulate the appearance of a plot. Yet these manipulations should not be used to distort trends in data or to lead a reader to misinterpretations. The types of techniques you may apply to graphs in the PLOT procedure include

(a) lengthening or shortening the vertical or the horizontal axis (Examples 15.1, 15.4, and 15.4a),

(b) choosing the starting and the ending value for each axis (Example 15.2),

(c) imposing a reference line parallel to the vertical or the horizontal axis (Example 15.2),

(d) reversing the Y-axis scale so that the smallest value is on the top and the largest value is at the origin (Example 15.2),

(e) choosing the plotting symbol (Example 15.3),

(f) using the same scales for X- and Y-axes to present several plots (Examples 15.5 and 15.5a),

(g) incorporating several plots on the same print page (Examples 15.5 and 15.5a), and

(h) using a character variable to define the X-axis (Example 15.6).

15.2 Examples

Example 15.1 Plotting the Relationship Between Two Continuous Variables

What is the relationship between students' grade point average (GPA) and their SAT-Verbal scores? To answer this question, you may choose a graphical representation. This example illustrates how to present a relationship between two continuous variables via a 2-D graph, also called a scatter plot. The file mydata.dat provides the data from which two variables, gpa and satv, are plotted as X- and Y-axes, respectively.

```
/* The following bolded SAS statements establish the SAS data set 'mydata' */

DATA mydata;
    INFILE 'd:\data\mydata.dat';
    INPUT id $ sex $ age gpa critical polpref $ satv;
    LABEL polpref='political preference';
RUN;

OPTIONS NODATE PAGENO=1 LS=90;       /* These options are for output appearances   */
                                     /* NODATE is to prohibit the printing of dates */
                                     /* PAGENO= is to number the first page of this output */
                                     /* LS= is to control the width of the output page */

TITLE 'Example 15.1 Plotting the relationship between gpa and satv';

PROC PLOT DATA=mydata NOMISS;        /* NOMISS excludes those missing on 'satv' or 'gpa' */
    PLOT satv*gpa;
RUN; QUIT;
```

The SAS program is straightforward. It first invokes the PLOT procedure; then it defines a 2-D graph using satv as the Y-axis and gpa as the X-axis. The option **NOMISS** means that any observation with a missing value on either of these two variables is ignored in defining the two axes. By default, the PLOT procedure includes all observations in the defining scales of X- and Y-axes, as long as they contain valid values on at least one of the variables.

Output 15.1 Plotting the Relationship Between Two Continuous Variables

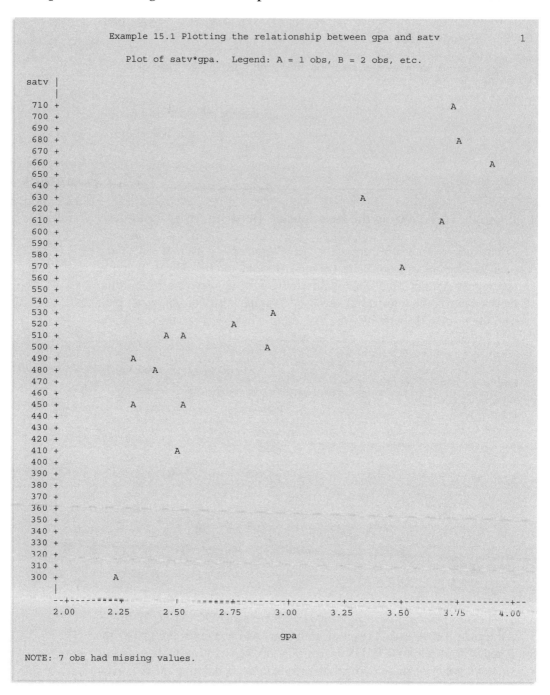

```
            Example 15.1 Plotting the relationship between gpa and satv                1

               Plot of satv*gpa.   Legend: A = 1 obs, B = 2 obs, etc.

satv |
     |
 710 +                                                                    A
 700 +
 690 +
 680 +                                                                    A
 670 +
 660 +                                                                           A
 650 +
 640 +
 630 +                                                    A
 620 +
 610 +                                                            A
 600 +
 590 +
 580 +
 570 +                                                     A
 560 +
 550 +
 540 +
 530 +                              A
 520 +                           A
 510 +           A  A
 500 +                           A
 490 +     A
 480 +        A
 470 +
 460 +
 450 +     A        A
 440 +
 430 +
 420 +
 410 +        A
 400 +
 390 +
 380 +
 370 +
 360 +
 350 +
 340 +
 330 +
 320 +
 310 +
 300 +  A
     |
   --+---------+---------+---------+---------+---------+---------+---------+---------+--
     2.00      2.25      2.50      2.75      3.00      3.25      3.50      3.75      4.00

                                          gpa

NOTE: 7 obs had missing values.
```

According to the plot, there appears to be a positive relationship between gpa and satv scores. The plotting symbol "A" represents a single observation, "B" represents 2 observations, "C" represents 3 observations, and so on. These interpretations are given on top of the graph under "Legend". Because the satv scale is more spread out than the gpa scale, using 10-point increments on satv seems to have created too many intervals for only 17 (= 24 − 7) data points. We may need to redefine the Y-axis so that it starts, say, at 275 and ends at 725 with an increment of 50. Furthermore, a reference line may be imposed at 500 for satv scores so that the relationship between GPA and SAT-Verbal may be examined, for example, among those who scored above the national average (= 500) on satv versus those who scored below the national average. These features are illustrated in Example 15.2.

- To generate a high-density plot using the GPLOT procedure, try the following program:

```
GOPTIONS CTITLE=black HTITLE=2 FTITLE=swiss HTEXT=1 FTEXT=swissb BORDER;
SYMBOL1 VALUE=dot COLOR=black;
PROC GPLOT DATA=mydata;
    PLOT satv*gpa;
RUN; QUIT;
```

Example 15.2 Defining an Axis and Imposing Reference Lines

This example illustrates how to define an axis for SAT-Verbal scores (satv) in terms of its starting point (= 275), ending point (= 725), and increment (= 50) with the **VAXIS=** option. It also demonstrates how to impose a reference line at 500 points (**VREF=500**) for SAT-Verbal scores.

```
/* See Example 15.1 for the DATA step in creating the SAS data set 'mydata' */

OPTIONS NODATE PAGENO=1 LS=90;

TITLE 'Example 15.2 Defining an axis and imposing reference lines';

PROC PLOT DATA=mydata NOMISS;
    PLOT satv*gpa / VAXIS=275 TO 725 BY 50 VREF=500;
RUN; QUIT;
```

Output 15.2 Defining an Axis and Imposing Reference Lines

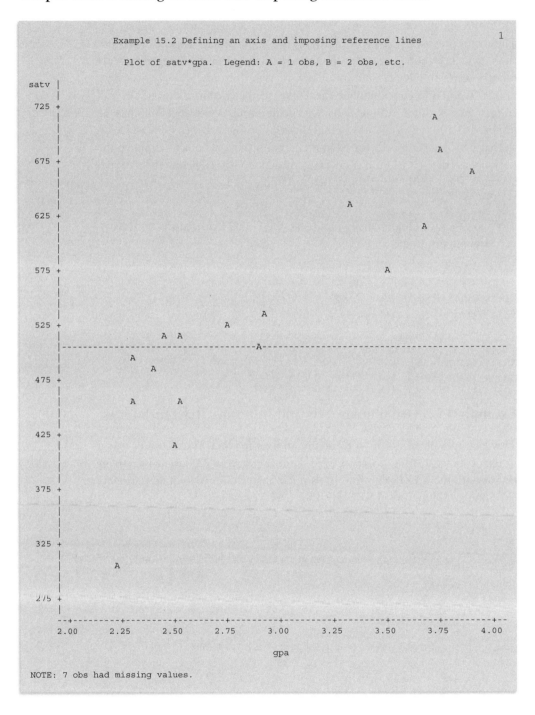

```
                    Example 15.2 Defining an axis and imposing reference lines        1

                       Plot of satv*gpa.   Legend: A = 1 obs, B = 2 obs, etc.

  satv |
       |
   725 +
       |                                                                   A
       |
       |
       |                                                                   A
   675 +
       |
       |                                                                        A
       |
       |                                              A
   625 +
       |                                                      A
       |
       |
       |
   575 +                                                 A
       |
       |
       |
   525 +                              A
       |                    A  A
       |- - - - - - - - - - - - - - - - - - -A- - - - - - - - - - - - - - - - - - - - - - -
       |              A
       |                 A
   475 +
       |
       |              A       A
       |
   425 +
       |                 A
       |
       |
   375 +
       |
       |
       |
   325 +
       |        A
       |
   275 +
       |
        --+---------+---------+---------+---------+---------+---------+---------+---------+--
         2.00      2.25      2.50      2.75      3.00      3.25      3.50      3.75      4.00

                                          gpa

 NOTE: 7 obs had missing values.
```

The output shows that options were appropriately specified to make the satv scale look less cluttered than before. From the graph, you can see that among those who scored above 500 on satv, the relationship between gpa and satv appears to be more linear than the relationship suggested by the entire plot. This is an intuitive impression that needs further statistical testing.

- If you would like to manipulate the X-axis, simply replace the word **VAXIS** with **HAXIS**, which stands for horizontal axis.
- To impose a reference line on the horizontal axis, use the option **HREF=**. This will result in a reference line drawn parallel to the Y-axis at a particular value on the X-axis.
- Reference lines can be drawn with any symbol you select from the standard keyboard. To redefine the symbol for the vertical reference line, use the option **VREFCHAR='symbol'**. For the horizontal reference line, use the option **HREFCHAR='symbol'**. Both are specified on the PLOT statement after the slash (/).
- To reverse the Y-axis so that it will be drawn from high to low, you can specify the keyword **VREVERSE**, after the slash (/). This keyword may be useful when the Y-axis is defined negatively, as is the monthly balance on a credit card or the number of credit hours needed before graduation. Similarly, you may reverse the X-axis using the keyword **HREVERSE**.
- To generate a high-density plot using the GPLOT procedure, try the following program:

```
GOPTIONS CTITLE=red HTITLE=2 FTITLE=swiss HTEXT=1 FTEXT=swissb BORDER;
SYMBOL1 VALUE=circle COLOR=blue;
PROC GPLOT DATA=mydata;
    PLOT satv*gpa / VAXIS=275 to 725 BY 50 VREF=500 CVREF=BLACK;
RUN; QUIT;
```

Example 15.3 Changing the Plotting Symbol

A plot can display a three-way relationship between two continuous variables (i.e., gpa and satv) and one discrete variable (i.e., sex). One way to show this relationship is to present the plot of gpa and satv with sex symbols (No pun intended here!). This is done by adding the sex variable to the PLOT statement after an equal sign (=):

```
/* See Example 15.1 for the DATA step in creating the SAS data set 'mydata' */

OPTIONS NODATE PAGENO=1 LS=90;

TITLE 'Example 15.3 Changing the plotting symbol';

PROC PLOT DATA=mydata NOMISS;
    PLOT satv*gpa=sex / VAXIS=275 TO 725 BY 50;
RUN; QUIT;
```

Output 15.3 Changing the Plotting Symbol

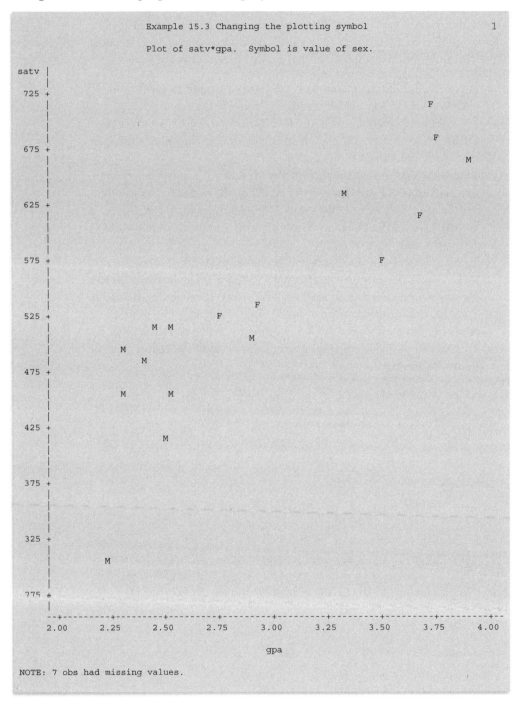

Example 15.3 Changing the plotting symbol 1

Plot of satv*gpa. Symbol is value of sex.

NOTE: 7 obs had missing values.

In place of using default symbols, such as A for 1 observation, B for 2, and so on, the output here is enriched with additional information about the genders of the 17 students. With this additional information, you can now recognize a few low-performing male students who scored low on SAT-Verbal and also had average-to-low GPAs. The performance of the female students appears to be more uniform than that of the males for both variables. To obtain a high-density plot, try this program:

```
GOPTIONS CTITLE=black HTITLE=2 FTITLE=swiss HTEXT=1 FTEXT=swissb BORDER;
SYMBOL1 VALUE=triangle COLOR=red;
SYMBOL2 VALUE=square   COLOR=green;

PROC GPLOT DATA=mydata;
    PLOT satv*gpa=sex / VAXIS=275 TO 725 BY 50;
RUN; QUIT;
```

Example 15.4 Manipulating the Length of Each Axis

In the previous examples, graphs occupied lots of space on each page, even for very simple graphs, such as Output 15.3. This problem can be solved with two options: **VPOS=** and **HPOS=**. Not surprisingly, VPOS= controls the length of a print page, and HPOS= controls the width. Execute the program and see for yourself, if you like, the graph rescaled by these new specifications:

```
/* See Example 15.1 for the DATA step in creating the SAS data set 'mydata' */

OPTIONS NODATE PAGENO=1 LS=90;

TITLE 'Example 15.4 Manipulating the length of each axis';

PROC PLOT DATA=mydata NOMISS;
    PLOT satv*gpa=sex / VAXIS=275 TO 725 BY 50 VPOS=30 HPOS=60;
RUN; QUIT;
```

Output 15.4 Manipulating the Length of Each Axis

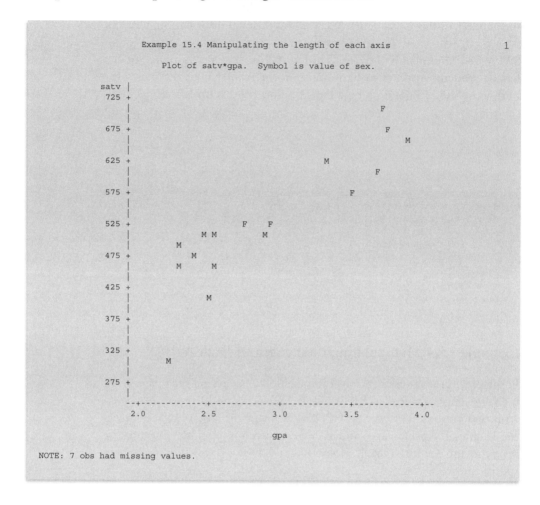

Example 15.4 Manipulating the length of each axis   1

Plot of satv*gpa. Symbol is value of sex.

Notice how the output looks more informative than all the previous graphs, because it is smaller, thus displaying information in a succinct way. The specifications of 30 for the vertical axis and 60 for the horizontal axis refer to print positions. Most statistics books recommend 3:4 or 2:3 as the ratio of the vertical length to the horizontal width. In the future, you may try different specifications of VPOS= and HPOS= before selecting the one that makes the most sense to you.

- On smaller plots such as the one illustrated in this example, you may wish to frame the plot with a border, separating the plot from its title and legend. This wish is granted by adding the option **BOX** to the PLOT statement after the slash (/).

Example 15.4a Manipulating the Length of Each Axis With BOX

```
/* See Example 15.1 for the DATA step in creating the SAS data set 'mydata' */

OPTIONS NODATE PAGENO=1 LS=90;

TITLE 'Example 15.4a Manipulating the length of each axis with BOX';

PROC PLOT DATA=mydata NOMISS;
    PLOT satv*gpa=sex / VAXIS=275 TO 725 BY 50 VPOS=30 HPOS=60 BOX;
RUN; QUIT;
```

Output 15.4a Manipulating the Length of Each Axis With BOX

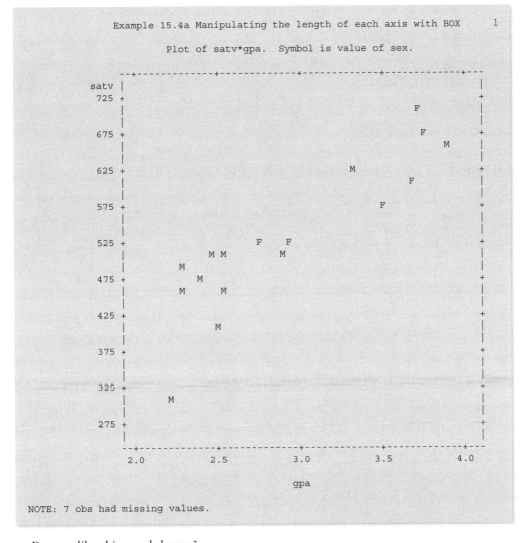

```
              Example 15.4a Manipulating the length of each axis with BOX      1

                    Plot of satv*gpa.   Symbol is value of sex.

           --+--------------+--------------+--------------+--------------+---
     satv  |                                                              |
      725 +                                                             +
           |                                                   F          |
           |                                                              |
      675 +                                                   F         +
           |                                                     M        |
           |                                                              |
      625 +                                        M                    +
           |                                            F                 |
           |                                                              |
      575 +                                     F                       +
           |                                                              |
           |                                                              |
      525 +                        F    F                              +
           |                  M M       M                                 |
           |              M                                               |
      475 +            M                                                +
           |          M       M                                           |
           |                                                              |
      425 +              M                                              +
           |                                                              |
           |                                                              |
      375 +                                                             +
           |                                                              |
           |                                                              |
      325 +                                                             +
           |        M                                                     |
           |                                                              |
      275 +                                                             +
           |                                                              |
           --+--------------+--------------+--------------+--------------+---
             2.0            2.5            3.0            3.5            4.0

                                       gpa

NOTE: 7 obs had missing values.
```

Do you like this graph better?

Example 15.5 Presenting Several Plots on the Same Page

Sometimes, it is convenient to superimpose one or more graphs on a reference plot. The purpose is to make comparisons and judgments about three or more variables simultaneously. In the program below, the **PLOT** statement is used once but it defines two plots. The first plot is <u>age</u> by <u>gpa</u> and the second is <u>critical</u> (thinking) by <u>gpa</u>. The first plot serves as a reference plot, whereas the second plot is superimposed on the first. While the first plot is drawn by the default symbol, the second plot is drawn by another symbol (*) in order to be distinguished from the first. The choice of the length and width of the overlaid plot was made after a few experiments with the **VPOS=** and **HPOS=** options.

```
/* See Example 15.1 for the DATA step in creating the SAS data set 'mydata' */

OPTIONS NODATE PAGENO=1 LS=90;

TITLE 'Example 15.5 Presenting several plots on the same page';

PROC PLOT DATA=mydata NOMISS;
    PLOT age*gpa critical*gpa='*' / VPOS=20 HPOS=60 OVERLAY;
RUN; QUIT;
```

Output 15.5 Presenting Several Plots on the Same Page

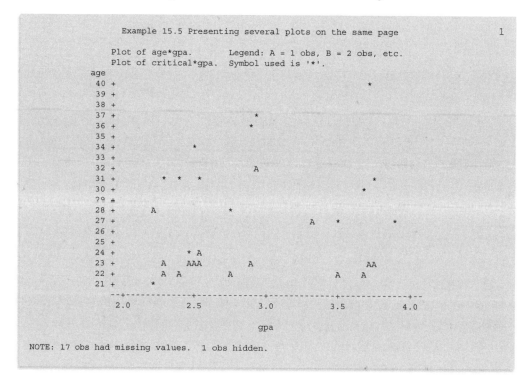

The overlaid plot suggests that there is no relationship between gpa and age; but there appears to be a slight positive relationship between critical thinking and gpa, which we sort of expected.

- The overlaid format should be used with caution. First, it is used most often on plots for which there is commonality. In this example, gpa is shared by both plots. Second, the scales of age and critical thinking are comparable: values of age span from 22 to 28 years, whereas critical scores range from 21 to 40. Therefore, the age scale, plotted on the Y-axis, makes sense for critical scores as well. For these reasons, the **OVERLAY** option is a good choice for these two plots.
- If the **PLOT** statement and the **OVERLAY** option had been written differently, as in Example 15.5a, the output would show both graphs side by side (Output 15.5a), instead of one on top of the other. To fit both graphs to the output page width of 90 characters, Example 15.5a has to specify **HPERCENT**=50 and **VPERCENT**=33. These specifications result in each graph drawn in 50% of the width and 33% of length of the print page. A print page is defined by the **PAGESIZE** (or **PS**)= and **LINESIZE** (or **LS**)= options on the **OPTIONS** statement. For details on these print controls, refer back to Chapter 5, **Section 5.5**. These choices were finalized after a few experiments with these two options. Alternatively, you may set both options to a value larger than 100%. In this case, the graph is drawn over two print pages.
- For a high-density plot, try the program below:

```
GOPTIONS CTITLE=black HTITLE=2 FTITLE=swiss HTEXT=1 FTEXT=swissb;
SYMBOL1 VALUE=square   COLOR=red;
SYMBOL2 VALUE=triangle COLOR=blue;

PROC GPLOT DATA=mydata;
    PLOT age*gpa critical*gpa / OVERLAY;
RUN; QUIT;
```

Example 15.5a Presenting Several Plots on the Same Page Side by Side

```
/* See Example 15.1 for the DATA step in creating the SAS data set 'mydata' */

OPTIONS NODATE PAGENO=1 LS=90;

TITLE 'Example 15.5a Presenting several plots on the same page side by side';

PROC PLOT DATA=mydata NOMISS HPERCENT=50 VPERCENT=33;
    PLOT age*gpa;
    PLOT critical*gpa='*' / OVERLAY;
RUN; QUIT;
```

Output 15.5a Presenting Several Plots on the Same Page Side by Side

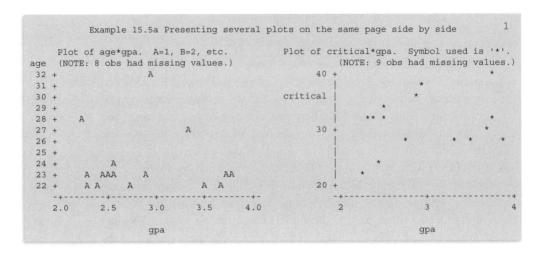

Example 15.6 Using Characters as Tick Points on an Axis

What if you'd like to use character values, instead of numeric values, to define the X-axis? The PLOT procedure provides a way for character values to be shown as tick points on either the Y- or the X-axis. Character values are specified in single quotes next to the options **HAXIS=** or **VAXIS=**. In this program, a plot is defined by SAT-Verbal scores (satv) and political preferences (polpref) using the five categories of polpref as tick points on the X-axis. The five categories of polpref are **SD** for Strongly Democrat, **D** for Democrat, **I** for independent, **R** for Republican, and **SR** for Strongly Republican.

```
/* See Example 15.1 for the DATA step in creating the SAS data set 'mydata' */

OPTIONS NODATE PAGENO=1 LS=90;

TITLE 'Example 15.6 Using characters as tick points on an axis';

PROC PLOT DATA=mydata NOMISS;
    PLOT satv*polpref / HAXIS='SD' 'D' 'I' 'R' 'SR'
                        VAXIS=275 TO 725 BY 50 VPOS=30 HPOS=50;
RUN; QUIT;
```

Output 15.6 Using Characters as Tick Points on an Axis

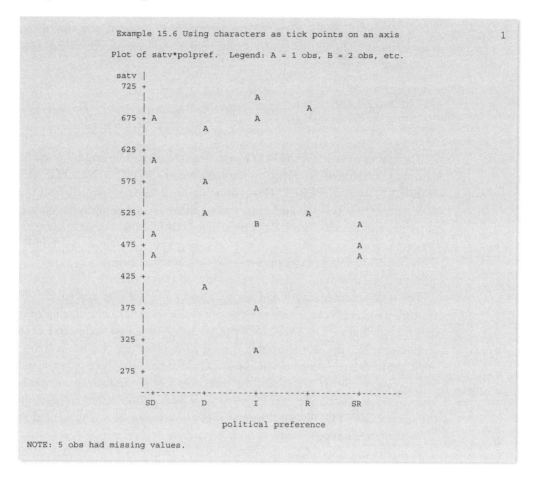

```
            Example 15.6 Using characters as tick points on an axis          1

            Plot of satv*polpref.  Legend: A = 1 obs, B = 2 obs, etc.

        satv |
         725 +
             |                              A
             |                                      A
         675 + A                            A
             |              A
             |
         625 +
             |    A
             |
         575 +                    A
             |
             |
         525 +                    A                 A
             |                        B                      A
             |  A
         475 +                                               A
             |  A                                            A
             |
         425 +
             |              A
             |
         375 +                        A
             |
             |
         325 +                        A
             |
             |
         275 +
             |
             --+---------+---------+---------+---------+--------
               SD        D         I         R         SR

                          political preference
```

NOTE: 5 obs had missing values.

The output shows that a wide range of SAT-Verbal scores were obtained within each group of political preferences, except for the **R** and **SR** categories. The average of these scores, however diverse, is similar for all five groups.

- For a high-density plot, try the program below:

```
GOPTIONS CTITLE=black HTITLE=2 FTITLE=swiss HTEXT=1 FTEXT=swissb;
SYMBOL1 VALUE=star COLOR=red;

PROC GPLOT DATA=mydata;
    PLOT satv*polpref / HAXIS='SD' 'D' 'I' 'R' 'SR' VAXIS=275 TO 725 BY 50;
RUN; QUIT;
```

15.3 How to Write the PROC PLOT Codes

Based on the examples presented in the previous section, you may have found that the PLOT procedure is unthreatening. It's easy, if you can first master these three statements:

PROC	PLOT	DATA= *sas_dataset_name* <options>;
	PLOT	*plot_definitions* < / options>;
	BY	*classification_variable(s)*;

The first statement, **PROC PLOT,** initializes the procedure and specifies the data set to be plotted. You may additionally specify **NOMISS, NOLEGEND, HPERCENT=,** and **VPERCENT=** as options. The **NOMISS** option defines the scales of the two axes without observations that have a missing value on one or more variables specified for the plot. The **NOLEGEND** option suppresses the printing of the legend, which explains the plotting symbols. The HPER-CENT= and VPERCENT= options specify the plot to be drawn in a percentage of the width and the length, respectively, of a print page.

The second statement, **PLOT,** is part and parcel of this procedure. All controls and specifications for the plot appear in this statement. Each plot is defined minimally by two variables: the Y-axis variable first, followed by the X-axis variable. If a third variable is used as the plotting symbol, its name appears after an equal sign (=) on the PLOT definition. If a three-dimensional (3-D) contour plot is requested, the third (or depth) variable also appears after an equal sign on the PLOT statement, which is followed by a slash and the option **CONTOUR.** An illustration of the contour plot is presented at www.sagepub.com/pengstudy.

A variety of options have been illustrated in Examples 15.2 through 15.6; they will not be repeated here. One thing that is worth noting is that the PLOT statement follows the distributive law. What is meant by this is that

```
PLOT (y1 y2)* (x1 x2);
```

is equivalent to `PLOT y1*x1 y1*x2 y2*x1 y2*x2;`

and

`PLOT y* (a–d);`   is equivalent to `PLOT y*a y*b y*c y*d;`

On the PLOT statement, you may define a log (base 10) scale by the **HAXIS** (or **VAXIS**)= option. Below is an example:

```
PROC PLOT;
    PLOT yrs_edu*salary / HAXIS=10 100 1000;
RUN;
```

Finally, the last statement, BY, serves the same purpose as in all other SAS procedures. It divides the data set into subgroups according to the diverse values of the BY variable. Within each subgroup, the same plot(s) are drawn based on the PLOT definitions. If more than one BY variable is listed, all possible combinations of the BY variables' values are used in dividing up the entire data set. Be sure to presort the data set in the ascending order of all the BY variables, if the BY statement is included in the PLOT procedure. Presorting a data set can be accomplished using the SORT procedure.

15.4 Tips

- How to handle missing or invalid data

By default, PROC PLOT does not, and cannot, display observations that have missing information on one or more variable(s) specified for the plot. Yet if an observation has information on at least one variable, its value will be used to define the axes for the plot, by default. If you wish to get around this default, you can invoke the **NOMISS** option in the PROC PLOT statement so that only observations with complete information are used to define the axes.

- What to do with hidden observations on the plot

Hidden observations are a result of an undersized graph or crude scales. You can reveal these hidden observations by enlarging the plot or changing the scales. Below is a list of tactics you may try:

1. Enlarge the print page size by specifying **OPTIONS PS=66 LS=132;** at the beginning of the program. When you choose this tactic and print the output on regular-sized paper, make sure you decrease the font size to accommodate the entire output.
2. Use several print pages for a single plot by specifying, for example, **VPERCENT=120** and/or **HPERCENT=120** in the PROC PLOT statement.
3. Define the vertical and/or the horizontal axis in greater detail. For example, you may choose an increment of 10, instead of 100, for GRE scores so that finer intervals are shown. The increment is specified by the **HAXIS=** (or **VAXIS=**) option.

A combination of these three approaches may be tried before you find a suitable specification that brings out all relevant aspects of data on a graph.

- Plotting several pictures on the same printout page

The option **OVERLAY** will accomplish this goal. There are actually two ways of using this option: one is to superimpose one plot on top of the other; the second is to present two or more plots side by side on the same print page. Both are illustrated in Example 15.5.

- Using data sets created by other procedures as input

PROC PLOT is useful for visually depicting a relationship between two variables, such as the predicted value of an outcome variable versus its prediction error. In this case, both variables are derived from a regression model, say, by PROC REG. Next, they are saved into a SAS data set using the OUTPUT OUT=*sas_dataset_name* statement in PROC REG. This output data set is subsequently specified in PROC PLOT for a depiction of the relationship between the predicted value and its error, also called residual.

- How to use ODS with the PLOT procedure

To use the ODS, you need to know ODS table names corresponding with various portions of the output. Table 15.1 presents selected ODS table names for the PLOT procedure and their descriptions.

Table 15.1   Selected ODS Table Names and Descriptions for the PLOT Procedure

ODS Table Name	Description	PLOT Statement Option
Plot	A single plot (e.g., Example 15.1)	(default)
Overlaid	An overlaid plot (e.g., Example 15.5)	OVERLAY
PercentPlots	A side-by-side plot (e.g., Example 15.5a)	OVERLAY

These ODS table names and the related details are tracked in the Log window if you request them with the ODS TRACE ON statement in the SAS program. You may turn off this tracking feature with the ODS TRACE OFF statement, also in the SAS program:

```
ODS TRACE ON;
PROC PLOT DATA=mydata NOMISS;
    PLOT satv*gpa;
    PLOT age*gpa critical*gpa='*' / VPOS=20 HPOS=60 OVERLAY;
RUN;
ODS TRACE OFF;
RUN;
```

After executing the program, the following will appear in the Log window listing all ODS table names for the PROC PLOT output:

```
Output Added:
-------------
Name:       Plot
Label:      Plot of age*gpa
Data Name:  BatchOutput
Path:       Plot.Plot
-------------

Output Added:
-------------
Name:       Overlaid
Label:      Overlaid Plots
Data Name:  BatchOutput
Path:       Plot.Overlaid
-------------
```

Based on the list of ODS table names, you may select certain results to be displayed in the Output window. For example, the following program selects the overlaid plot to be included in the output:

```
ODS SELECT Plot.Overlaid;
PROC PLOT DATA=mydata NOMISS;
    PLOT satv*gpa;
    PLOT age*gpa critical*gpa='*' / VPOS=20 HPOS=60 OVERLAY;
RUN;
```

Furthermore, you may select certain results to be saved in file formats other than the SAS standard output. For example, the following program saves the overlaid plot in HTML format in its default style:

```
ODS SELECT Plot.Overlaid;
ODS HTML BODY = 'f:\test\Overlaid_Body.html'
        CONTENTS = 'f:\test\Overlaid_TOC.html'
        PAGE = 'f:\test\Overlaid_Page.html'
        FRAME = 'f:\test\Overlaid_Frame.html';

PROC PLOT DATA=mydata NOMISS;
    PLOT satv*gpa;
    PLOT age*gpa critical*gpa='*' / VPOS=20 HPOS=60 OVERLAY;
RUN;
ODS HTML CLOSE;
RUN;
```

For additional information about the ODS feature, refer to *SAS 9.1.3 Output Delivery System: User's Guide* (SAS Institute Inc., 2006c) and *Base SAS 9.1.3 Procedures Guide* (SAS Institute Inc., 2006a), or the online documentation at www.sas.com.

15.5 Summary

Several illustrations of the PLOT procedure were offered in this chapter as ways to reveal the richness in your data. These illustrations highlight features of the PLOT procedure that are applicable to a single graph as well as to multiple graphs presented on the same page. The GPLOT procedure is also introduced to help you produce high-density plots. Although you are free to manipulate the appearance of any plot to achieve certain visual effects, the bottom line is honesty, not to lie with a picture! Patience is also needed when you search for a desirable specification for the plot. Never forget the primary reason why plots are needed: They enhance our ability to discover nuances in data. They are not meant to tell a different story than the one truly implied and supported by the data.

15.6 Exercises

1. A psychologist wanted to examine the relationship between anxiety and age. He administered an anxiety test to 20 veterans and the following data were obtained. Draw a 2-D picture to show the relationship between the veterans' anxiety level and age.

Age	Anxiety	Age	Anxiety
22	14	44	45
25	25	47	39
25	34	51	41
27	38	53	40
31	43	56	35
33	49	58	31
34	51	62	32
37	48	65	29
41	49	66	25
43	46	67	18

2. The same psychologist also wished to determine the relationship between lawyers' age and their marital satisfaction. He administered an instrument that measured marital satisfaction to a second sample of 20 lawyers and obtained these data:

Age	Satisfaction	Age	Satisfaction
28	52	56	24
32	48	58	28
35	44	62	33
39	39	64	38
42	35	67	41
45	36	69	46
47	38	73	45
48	29	77	52
52	27	79	45
53	24	82	46

   a. Use a 2-D picture to show the relationship between lawyers' age and their satisfaction with marriage.

   b. Use the OVERLAY option to superimpose the first graph (from Exercise 1) on the graph from this exercise.

   c. Based on the overlaid graph from (b), what can you conclude?

3. Given the data in Exercise 3 of Chapter 12, use the OVERLAY option to show the relationship between <u>age</u> and the three kinds of sports in a side-by-side format.

15.7 Answers to Exercises

1.

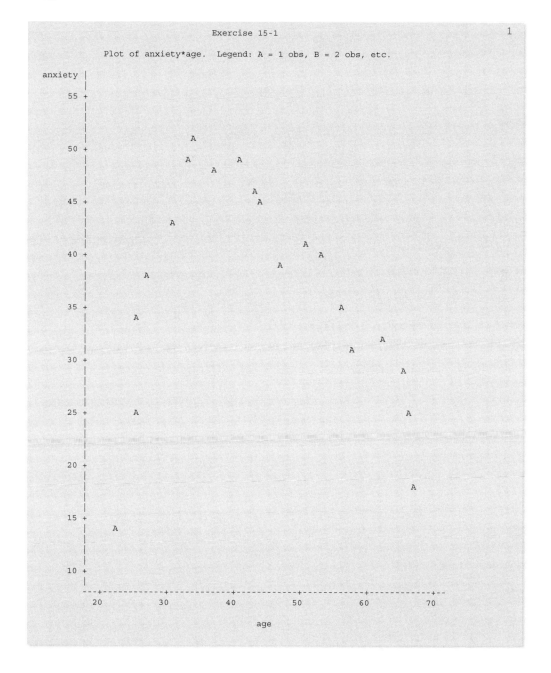

```
                                    Exercise 15-1                                    1

                    Plot of anxiety*age.  Legend: A = 1 obs, B = 2 obs, etc.

 anxiety |
         |
     55 +
         |
         |
         |
         |                            A
     50 +
         |                        A           A
         |                            A
         |
         |                            A
     45 +                                 A
         |
         |                    A
         |
         |                                        A
     40 +                                             A
         |                                        A
         |                 A
         |
     35 +                                                      A
         |                 A
         |
         |                                                 A
         |                                             A
     30 +
         |                                                          A
         |
         |
     25 +             A                                           A
         |
         |
     20 +
         |                                                          A
         |
     15 +
         |         A
         |
         |
     10 +
         |
         ---+-----------+-----------+-----------+-----------+-----------+--
            20          30          40          50          60          70

                                        age
```

2. a.

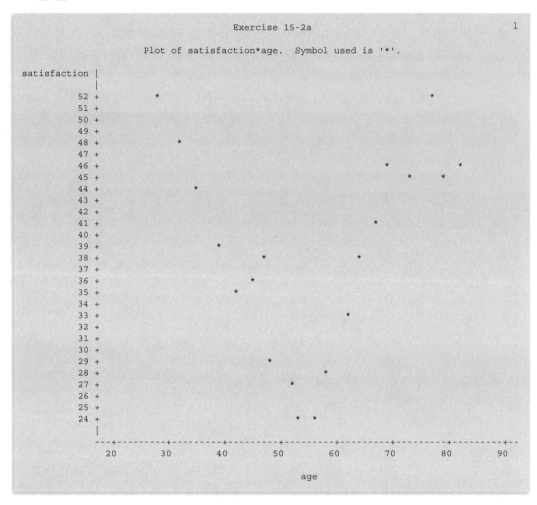

b.

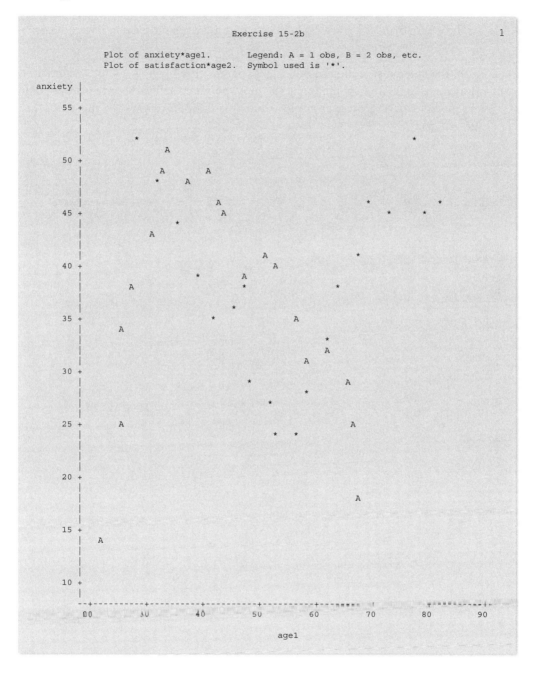

c. The overlay plot shows that age and anxiety have an inverted-U-shaped relationship, whereas age and marriage satisfaction show a V-shaped relationship. For those
between 30 and 55 years, both anxiety and marriage satisfaction have a negative
relationship with age.

3. From the side-by-side plot below, it is apparent that jogging is the least favored
sport for all ages and swimming is the most popular. Ball games are also popular
and more so among younger adults, those less than 32 years, than those in other
age-groups.

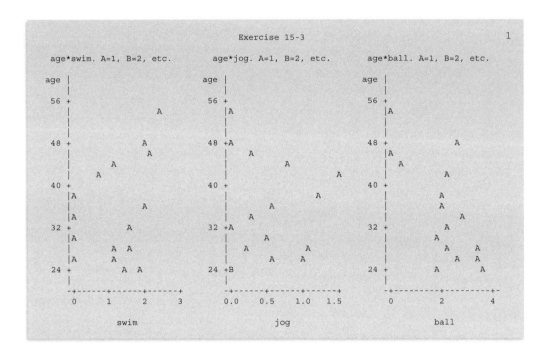

16

Correlation

O B J E C T I V E

Six correlation coefficients, namely, Pearson *r*, point-biserial, Spearman rank correlation, Kendall's tau-b, Hoeffding's *D* coefficient, and Cronbach's alpha, are available from PROC CORR. Each is suitable for use as a measure of association between a pair of variables that possess certain attributes. All six coefficients are defined and demonstrated in this chapter along with their proper applications and interpretations. Other types of correlation coefficients, including biserial, rank-biserial, tetrachoric, and phi, are discussed as special cases of Pearson *r* or projected estimates of Pearson *r* under special circumstances.

16.1 How to Quantify the Strength of an Association _____

In Chapter 15, you learned how to uncover trends or hidden structures in data by examining the visual display of relationships between or among variables. If a relationship is revealed, the next step is to measure this relationship and assess its statistical significance. This chapter shows you how to express the nature and degree of an association between quantitative variables in five indices. These five indices are (1) the Pearson product-moment correlation coefficient, (2) the Spearman rank correlation coefficient, (3) Kendall's tau-b coefficient, (4) Hoeffding's measure of dependence, D, and (5) Cronbach's coefficient alpha. All are computed by the CORR procedure. The following data are used to define the first four indices. The fifth index, the coefficient alpha, is illustrated in Example 16.5.

Suppose I observed five customers at a discount store and recorded the length of time each customer spent in the store (called the X variable) plus the number of items they purchased (called the Y variable). Here is the information I gathered:

Customer	X = Time Spent in Minutes	R_x Rank of X	R_{xy} Bivariate Rank	R_y Rank of Y	Y = Items Purchased
1	11	1	1	1	1
2	15	2	2	2.5	2
3	20	5	5	5	4
4	18	4	4	4	3
5	16	3	2.5	2.5	2
Mean	16				2.4
Sum	80				12.0

The concept of R_{xy}, or bivariate rank, needs explanation:

R_{xy} = 1 + the number of observations that have both X and Y values less than the ith observation.

An observation that is tied on both X and Y values with the ith observation contributes ¼ to R_{xy}.

An observation that is tied on either X or Y and also has the other value less than the ith observation's counterpart contributes ½ to R_{xy}.

The Pearson product-moment correlation coefficient (hereafter referred to as the Pearson correlation coefficient or r) measures the degree to which X and Y simultaneously increase or decrease, relative to their respective means, in units of the X's and Y's standard deviations. The formula is as follows:

$$r = \frac{N \sum(xy) - (\sum x)(\sum y)}{\sqrt{[N\sum(x^2) - (\sum x)^2][N\sum(y^2) - (\sum y)^2]}}$$

$$= \frac{5 \times (11 + 30 + 80 + 54 + 32) - (80)(12)}{\sqrt{[5 \times (121 + 225 + 400 + 324 + 256) - 80^2][5 \times (1 + 4 + 16 + 9 + 4) - 12^2]}}$$

$$= 0.97,$$

a very high positive correlation, indeed, between a customer's time spent in a store and items purchased.

Based on the same data, the next correlation index, the Spearman rank correlation coefficient or r_s, is computed as follows:

$$r_s = 1 - \frac{6 \times \sum D^2}{N(N^2 - 1)} = 1 - \frac{6 \times \sum (R_x - R_y)^2}{5(25 - 1)}$$

$$= 1 - \frac{6 \times [(1-1)^2 + (2-2.5)^2 + (5-5)^2 + (4-4)^2 + (3-2.5)^2]}{5 \times 24} = 0.975.$$

Again, a very high positive association is indicated by the r_s coefficient. Note that the Spearman r_s relies on the customers' ranks in X and Y, instead of original scores. Ranks are assigned within each variable column. So, for X scores, ranks assigned are 1, 2, 5, 4, and 3 for Customers 1 through 5, respectively. For Y scores, the successive ranks are 1, 2.5, 5, 4, and 2.5. Customers 2 and 5 both are assigned the rank of 2.5 because their Y scores were identical. In this case, the average of ranks (= (2 + 3)/2 = 2.5) that would have been given to these two customers is assigned.

The third coefficient, Kendall's tau-b, measures the degree of consistency in X and Y rankings. It is defined as follows:

$$\text{tau-b} = \left(\frac{2(\text{number of inversions})}{\text{number of pairs of cases}}\right),$$

where number of pairs $= \binom{5}{2}$ or 10 in this case, and number of inversions = number of reverse ranks by X and Y, = 0 in this case.

Therefore, tau-b = 1 − 0 = 1.

The fourth, Hoeffding's D coefficient, is also based on ranks. It is defined as

$$D = 30 \frac{(N-2)(N-3)D_1 + D_2 - 2(N-2)D_3}{N(N-1)(N-2)(N-3)(N-4)}$$
$$= 30 \frac{(5-2)(5-3)D_1 + D_2 - 2(5-2)D_3}{5 \times 4 \times 3 \times 2 \times 1}$$
$$= 0.375,$$

where

$$D_1 = \sum (R_{xy} - 1)(R_{xy} - 2) = 0 + 0 + 12 + 6 + 0.75 = 18.75$$
$$D_2 = \sum (R_x - 1)(R_x - 2)(R_y - 1)(R_y - 2) = 0 + 0 + 144 + 36 + 1.5 = 181.5$$
$$D_3 = \sum (R_x - 2)(R_y - 2)(R_{xy} - 1) = 0 + 0 + 36 + 12 + 0.75 = 48.75$$

Hoeffding's D, like the Spearman r_s coefficient, is sensitive to the relative ranks in X and Y, as well as their consistency. Unfortunately, it is also sensitive to ties in data. Under circumstances where there are no ties, D ranges from –0.5 to 1, with 1 implying a complete consistency in X and Y ranks. When there are ties, the maximum can fall below 1 and the minimum below –0.5, especially, with a small data set. Thus, this index should be used with caution.

The fifth index, Cronbach's coefficient alpha, is typically used to express the reliability of a test or an assessment tool. It is not applicable to the data presented above. Its definition, application, and interpretation are presented in Example 16.5.

16.2 Examples

Example 16.1 Four Ways to Quantify the Strength of a Relationship

This example illustrates how to carry out the analysis of the degree of association between two quantitative variables using the CORR procedure. Four correlation indices are specified with options **PEARSON**, **SPEARMAN**, **KENDALL**, and **HOEFFDING**, respectively. The file mydata.dat provides data for correlations between each pair of age, gpa, critical, and satv:

```
/* The following bolded SAS statements establish the SAS data set 'mydata' */

DATA mydata;
    INFILE 'd:\data\mydata.dat';
    INPUT id $ sex $ age gpa critical polpref $ satv;
    LABEL polpref='political preference'
        satv='SAT-Verbal';
RUN;
```

```
TITLE 'Example 16.1 Four ways to quantify the strength of a relationship';

PROC CORR DATA=mydata PEARSON SPEARMAN KENDALL HOEFFDING;
     VAR age gpa critical satv;
RUN;
```

Output 16.1 Four Ways to Quantify the Strength of a Relationship

```
           Example 16.1 Four ways to quantify the strength of a relationship            1

                               The CORR Procedure

                 4  Variables:     age      gpa     critical satv
```

Part (A)

```
                               Simple Statistics

Variable        N        Mean      Std Dev       Median      Minimum      Maximum  Label

age            17    24.11765      2.86972     23.00000     22.00000     32.00000
gpa            17     2.92235      0.59473      2.74000      2.22000      3.90000
critical       22    30.54545      5.42242     30.00000     21.00000     40.00000
satv           22   524.09091    121.91563    510.00000    280.00000    710.00000  SAT-Verbal
```

Part (B)

```
                      Pearson Correlation Coefficients
                       Prob > |r| under H0: Rho=0
                          Number of Observations

                             age           gpa      critical          satv

     age                 1.00000      -0.05812      -0.00285      -0.15821
                                        0.8307        0.9920        0.5584
                              17            16            15            16


     gpa                -0.05812       1.00000       0.20774       0.88857
                          0.8307                      0.4575        <.0001
                              16            17            15            17


     critical           -0.00285       0.20774       1.00000       0.47367
                          0.9920        0.4575                      0.0349
                              15            15            22            20


     satv               -0.15821       0.88857       0.47367       1.00000
     SAT-Verbal           0.5584        <.0001        0.0349
                              16            17            20            22
```

Part (C)

```
                     Spearman Correlation Coefficients
                       Prob > |r| under H0: Rho=0
                          Number of Observations

                             age           gpa      critical          satv

     age                 1.00000      -0.03435       0.05233      -0.06563
                                        0.8995        0.8531        0.8092
                              17            16            15            16


     gpa                -0.03435       1.00000       0.15010       0.89380
                          0.8995                      0.5934        <.0001
                              16            17            15            17


     critical            0.05233       0.15010       1.00000       0.39015
                          0.8531        0.5934                      0.0890
                              15            15            22            20


     satv               -0.06563       0.89380       0.39015       1.00000
     SAT-Verbal           0.8092        <.0001        0.0890
                              16            17            20            22
```

```
          Example 16.1 Four ways to quantify the strength of a relationship       2

                                The CORR Procedure
Part (D)
                            Kendall Tau b Correlation Coefficients
                                Prob > |r| under H0: Rho=0
                                  Number of Observations

                             age            gpa        critical         satv

      age                1.00000        0.00000         0.05712       -0.05855
                                         1.0000          0.7904         0.7725
                              17             16              15             16

      gpa                0.00000        1.00000         0.13944        0.73606
                          1.0000                         0.4817         <.0001
                              16             17              15             17

      critical           0.05712        0.13944         1.00000        0.31425
                          0.7904         0.4817                         0.0613
                              15             15              22             20

      satv              -0.05855        0.73606         0.31425        1.00000
      SAT-Verbal         0.7725         <.0001          0.0613
                              16             17              20             22
```

```
                             Hoeffding Dependence Coefficients
                                 Prob > D under H0: D=0
                                  Number of Observations

                             age            gpa        critical         satv

      age                0.40898       -0.05746        -0.04802       -0.04068
                          <.0001         1.0000          1.0000         0.9998
                              17             16              15             16

      gpa               -0.05746        0.97049        -0.03014        0.47892
                          1.0000         <.0001          0.9056         <.0001
                              16             17              15             17

      critical          -0.04802       -0.03014         0.74821        0.02583
                          1.0000         0.9056          <.0001         0.1195
                              15             15              22             20

      satv              -0.04068        0.47892         0.02583        0.94663
      SAT-Verbal         0.9998         <.0001          0.1195         <.0001
                              16             17              20             22
```

To explain the results in detail, the output is partitioned into five parts:
Parts (A) through **(E)**. In **Part (A)**, simple descriptive statistics, such as the
number of nonmissing data points, mean, standard deviation, median, minimum, and maximum, are provided for each variable specified on the VAR
statement.

The second part, **Part (B)**, contains Pearson correlation coefficients for
each pair of variables specified. You should note that this matrix of correlations is symmetric along its diagonal. Thus, the upper half of the matrix
duplicates what is in the lower half. We, therefore, need to focus only on
the lower triangle (the lower left-hand corner) of the matrix for interpretation. According to the printout, the Pearson r between <u>age</u> and <u>gpa</u> is
−0.05812 (Did you find it yet?). This value is tested against a null hypothesis

of zero linear correlation in the population. It is tested to be nonsignificant because the p level = 0.8307, based on a two-tailed test and 16 observations who had valid values on both variables. Other entries in the **Part (B)** matrix, namely, the three numbers shown at each intersection of the column and row variables, are interpreted likewise, all according to the heading that reads like this:

Pearson Correlation Coefficients
Prob > |r| under H0: Rho=0
Number of Observations

Results in **Parts (C)** through **(E)** are presented in the same format but based on different correlation indices. **Part (C)** is the Spearman rank correlation, **Part (D)** is Kendall's tau-b coefficient, and **Part (E)** is Hoeffding's dependence coefficient, D. Next, let's see if you can answer the following questions:

Question 1:   What is the Pearson r between gpa and critical thinking? How statistically significant is this correlation?

Question 2:   What is the Spearman r_s between critical thinking and satv scores? How statistically significant is this correlation?

Question 3:   Among the four correlation indices computed for gpa and satv, which is the highest and which is the lowest?

Question 4:   Can you give an intuitive explanation to the answers you came up with for Question 3 above? Should your explanation have anything to do with the definitions or formulae presented in the beginning of this chapter?

Question 5:   Why does the number of observations change from 15 to 16, 17, 20, and 22 for different correlation coefficients? *Hint*: Go back to raw data and examine the pattern of missing scores for each variable.

Answers to these five questions are found in **Section 16.4**.

Example 16.2 Compare Women and Men in Terms of Pearson r

In this example, the goal is to compare women and men on only one type of correlation index, namely Pearson r, between each pair of age, gpa, critical, and satv. For this purpose, the PROC CORR statement is simplified to include only the **PEARSON** option, although Pearson r is already the default of PROC CORR. The statement BY is added in order to yield subgroup analyses based on <u>sex</u>. Each subgroup analysis requires that the observations be arranged in the ascending order of <u>sex</u> values, or "F" before "M". Thus, the SORT procedure is invoked prior to the CORR procedure.

```
/* See Example 16.1 for the DATA step in creating the SAS data set 'mydata' */

PROC SORT DATA=mydata;
    BY sex;
RUN;

TITLE 'Example 16.2 Compare women and men in terms of Pearson r';

PROC CORR DATA=mydata PEARSON;
    VAR age gpa critical satv;
    BY sex;
RUN;
```

Output 16.2 Compare Women and Men in Terms of Pearson *r*

```
                       Example 16.2 Compare women and men in terms of Pearson r                            1
 Part (A)
---------------------------------------- sex=F ----------------------------------------

                                    The CORR Procedure

                    4  Variables:     age      gpa      critical satv


                                    Simple Statistics

Variable          N         Mean      Std Dev          Sum      Minimum      Maximum  Label

age               7     24.57143      3.90969    172.00000     22.00000     32.00000
gpa               6      3.38833      0.44093     20.33000      2.74000      3.75000
critical          9     31.11111      4.48454    280.00000     27.00000     40.00000
satv              8    533.75000    146.86607         4270    280.00000    710.00000  SAT-Verbal


                            Pearson Correlation Coefficients
                             Prob > |r| under H0: Rho=0
                               Number of Observations

                               age           gpa      critical          satv

    age                    1.00000      -0.44559       0.42154      -0.35523
                                          0.3759        0.3462        0.4896
                                 7             6             7             6

    gpa                   -0.44559       1.00000       0.13117       0.86571
                            0.3759                       0.8044        0.0258
                                 6             6             6             6

    critical               0.42154       0.13117       1.00000       0.52217
                            0.3462        0.8044                      0.1843
                                 7             6             9             8

    satv                  -0.35523       0.86571       0.52217       1.00000
    SAT-Verbal              0.4896        0.0258        0.1843
                                 6             6             8             8
```

```
                  Example 16.2 Compare women and men in terms of Pearson r                    2
Part (B)
-------------------------------------- sex=M --------------------------------------------
                                  The CORR Procedure

                     4  Variables:    age      gpa     critical  satv


                                  Simple Statistics

Variable        N       Mean      Std Dev        Sum      Minimum      Maximum  Label

age            10    23.80000     2.04396    238.00000    22.00000     28.00000
gpa            11     2.66818     0.51708     29.35000     2.22000      3.90000
critical       13    30.15385     6.13523    392.00000    21.00000     40.00000
satv           14   518.57143   110.93013       7260     300.00000    690.00000  SAT-Verbal


                          Pearson Correlation Coefficients
                          Prob > |r| under H0: Rho=0
                             Number of Observations

                          age          gpa        critical         satv

         age            1.00000      0.30914      -0.67448      -0.14507
                                     0.3848        0.0666        0.6893
                          10           10            8            10


         gpa            0.30914      1.00000      -0.00255       0.83207
                        0.3848                     0.9948        0.0015
                          10           11            9            11


         critical      -0.67448     -0.00255      1.00000        0.46656
                        0.0666       0.9948                      0.1263
                          8            9            13            12


         satv          -0.14507      0.83207      0.46656        1.00000
         SAT-Verbal     0.6893       0.0015       0.1263
                          10           11            12           14
```

As a result of the subgroup analyses, the output yields two sets of findings: **Part (A)** based on all women and **Part (B)** on all men. Each set has a familiar appearance similar to Output 16.1; it begins with a summary of descriptive statistics, followed by a correlation matrix. Because only Pearson r was requested, the output gives only one correlation matrix for each gender group.

Let's see if you can glean any difference between women and men; try answering these questions:

Question 1: What is the correlation between <u>age</u> and <u>gpa</u> for women, and for men? Should you be concerned about the positive and negative signs associated with the same correlation but for two different groups?

Question 2: How about the correlation between <u>age</u> and <u>critical</u> scores for women, and for men? Are you surprised to see that both correlations have opposite signs? Furthermore, while one is not significant, why is the other significant at the 0.07 level?

Question 3: The correlation between <u>gpa</u> and <u>satv</u> scores is significant at
$p = 0.0001$ based on the entire data set; why is the same correlation not so high for either women or men, though still
significant at a small p level?

Answers to these questions are found in **Section 16.4**.

Example 16.3 How to Save a Correlation Matrix and What to Do With It

As you know by now, a correlation matrix is a square block of correlation
coefficients, symmetric along the diagonal. It is different from an ordinary
data matrix (refer back to **Section 4.1**). While an ordinary data matrix is an
observation-by-variable grid, like a spread sheet, a correlation matrix contains relational information between column and row variables. For this reason, a correlation matrix needs to be recognized and saved as such. The
program shows you how to save a correlation matrix into a SAS data set and
subsequently submit it to PROC PRINT.

In the PROC CORR statement, two options are used: **NOPRINT** and
OUTP=. The **NOPRINT** option suppresses the display of any PROC CORR
result, because the purpose is to create an output data matrix. The **OUTP=**
option is used to define a SAS data set that contains Pearson correlation
coefficients. Because **OUTP=** requests Pearson correlation, there is no need
to specify **PEARSON** again. PROC PRINT then takes this SAS data set and
prints it out as a TYPE=CORR data set.

```
/* See Example 16.1 for the DATA step in creating the SAS data set 'mydata' */

TITLE 'Example 16.3 How to save a correlation matrix and what to do with it';

PROC CORR DATA=mydata NOPRINT OUTP=outcorr;
    VAR age gpa critical satv;
RUN;

PROC PRINT DATA=outcorr;
RUN;
```

Output 16.3 How to Save a Correlation Matrix and What to Do With It

```
    Example 16.3 How to save a correlation matrix and what to do with it        1

Obs    _TYPE_    _NAME_        age       gpa     critical      satv

 1     MEAN                 24.1176    2.9224    30.5455    524.091
 2     STD                   2.8697    0.5947     5.4224    121.916
 3     N                    17.0000   17.0000    22.0000     22.000
 4     CORR      age         1.0000   -0.0581    -0.0029     -0.158
 5     CORR      gpa        -0.0581    1.0000     0.2077      0.889
 6     CORR      critical   -0.0029    0.2077     1.0000      0.474
 7     CORR      satv       -0.1582    0.8886     0.4737      1.000
```

   This output looks much different from the ones you have seen in the previous examples. It presents a succinct summary of the correlation matrix plus descriptive statistics of those four variables named in the VAR statement. The first three observations contain the mean (MEAN), the standard deviation (STD), and the number of valid cases (N) on the variables <u>age</u>, <u>gpa</u>, <u>critical</u>, and <u>satv</u>. The correlation matrix itself is saved in Obs 4 through 7. It is ready for further analysis, such as regression or factor analysis, if a researcher deems it necessary. In Chapter 17, you will read an example of regression analysis using a correlation matrix as its input.

Example 16.4 Partial Correlation Coefficient

This example illustrates the calculation of a partial correlation between <u>gpa</u> and <u>satv</u>, while controlling for the <u>critical</u> thinking ability. Two correlation indices are requested by the PEARSON and SPEARMAN keywords. The computation of a partial correlation coefficient is specified by the **PARTIAL** statement.

```
/* See Example 16.1 for the DATA step in creating the SAS data set 'mydata' */

TITLE 'Example 16.4 Partial correlation coefficient';

PROC CORR DATA=mydata PEARSON SPEARMAN;
    VAR gpa satv;
    PARTIAL critical;
RUN;
```

Output 16.4 Partial Correlation Coefficient

```
                    Example 16.4 Partial correlation coefficient                      1

                            The CORR Procedure

                    1 Partial Variables:    critical
                    2         Variables:    gpa       satv
```

Part (A)

```
                            Simple Statistics

Variable        N         Mean       Std Dev      Median      Minimum      Maximum

critical       15      30.33333       5.00951     31.00000     21.00000     40.00000
gpa            15       2.99000       0.60056      2.90000      2.22000      3.90000
satv           15     536.66667     109.65313    520.00000    300.00000    710.00000

                            Simple Statistics

                         Partial      Partial
            Variable     Variance     Std Dev     Label

            critical
            gpa           0.37165      0.60963
            satv            11595    107.67944     SAT-Verbal
```

Part (B)

```
            Pearson Partial Correlation Coefficients, N = 15
                  Prob > |r| under H0: Partial Rho=0

                                    gpa              satv

            gpa                  1.00000          0.89054
                                                  <.0001


            satv                 0.89054          1.00000
            SAT-Verbal           <.0001

            Spearman Partial Correlation Coefficients, N = 15
                  Prob > |r| under H0: Partial Rho=0

                                    gpa              satv

            gpa                  1.00000          0.90169
                                                  <.0001


            satv                 0.90169          1.00000
            SAT-Verbal           <.0001
```

For discussion purposes, the output is divided into two parts. **Part (A)** presents summative information about the three variables analyzed in the program. **Part (B)** presents the partial Pearson correlation (= 0.89054, $p < 0.0001$) and partial Spearman rank correlation (= 0.90169, $p < 0.0001$). Both are statistically significant at $\alpha = 0.05$, or even 0.01. If you compare each partial correlation with its nonpartial counterpart from Output 16.1, you'll discover that both partial correlations are higher. So you may ask, "Is critical thinking ability a suppressor variable in both GPA and SAT-Verbal performance?" or "Does this phenomenon happen by chance?" To answer these questions adequately, you need more subjects and a valid and reliable instrument to measure critical thinking. The current data set is insufficient to shed definitive light on either question.

Example 16.5 Cronbach's Alpha for Internal Consistency

This example illustrates the computation of Cronbach's coefficient alpha and its interpretation. This coefficient is used in psychological and educational assessment as an index of reliability. It reflects the degree to which all test items or subtests contribute to the total score. If all items or subtests are congruent with each other, they naturally correlate highly with the total score, which is defined to be the sum of all item scores or of subtests. Using this idea, Cronbach devised the alpha coefficient as an index of internal consistency. It is computed as

$$\text{Cronbach's alpha} = \left(\frac{n}{n-1}\right)\left(1 - \frac{\text{sum of variances in } n \text{ items}}{\text{variance of the total scores}}\right),$$

where n = the number of items (or subtests) that made up the whole test.

The data file <u>achieve.dat</u> is used to illustrate how coefficient alpha is obtained from PROC CORR. The data contain several subtests that make up a verbal intelligence total score. The subtests are listed on the INPUT statement from <u>vocab</u> to <u>usage</u>. To compute this coefficient, simply specify **ALPHA** in the PROC CORR statement. The next option, **NOSIMPLE**, omits the computation of simple descriptive statistics for these subtests, since this has been done in Chapter 8.

```
DATA achieve;
    INFILE 'd:\data\achieve.dat';
    INPUT iv1 1 grade 2 iv2 3 sex 4 id 6-8 vocab 25-26 reading 27-28
        spelling 29-30 capital 31-32 punc 33-34 usage 35-36;
RUN;

TITLE "Example 16.5 Cronbach's alpha for internal consistency";

PROC CORR DATA=achieve ALPHA NOSIMPLE;
    VAR vocab reading spelling capital punc usage;
RUN;
```

Output 16.5 Cronbach's Alpha for Internal Consistency

```
             Example 16.5 Cronbach's alpha for internal consistency          1

                              The CORR Procedure

      6  Variables:    vocab    reading  spelling capital  punc     usage
```

Part (A)

```
                         Cronbach Coefficient Alpha

                       Variables                 Alpha
                       ---------------------------------
                       Raw                      0.902058
                       Standardized             0.904121
```

Part (B)

```
                 Cronbach Coefficient Alpha with Deleted Variable
```

Deleted Variable	Raw Variables		Standardized Variables	
	Correlation with Total	Alpha	Correlation with Total	Alpha
vocab	0.664365	0.895200	0.670738	0.896729
reading	0.730143	0.886825	0.735028	0.887300
spelling	0.745357	0.882696	0.748075	0.885358
capital	0.769342	0.878980	0.757946	0.883883
punc	0.699374	0.890878	0.688118	0.894203
usage	0.817940	0.871371	0.821113	0.874310

Part (C)

```
                    Pearson Correlation Coefficients, N = 120
                           Prob > |r| under H0: Rho=0

              vocab      reading     spelling     capital       punc       usage

vocab        1.00000     0.64886     0.62265     0.48998     0.39874     0.66100
                         <.0001      <.0001      <.0001      <.0001      <.0001

reading      0.64886     1.00000     0.60310     0.57806     0.53133     0.68984
             <.0001                  <.0001      <.0001      <.0001      <.0001

spelling     0.62265     0.60310     1.00000     0.62978     0.57516     0.66638
             <.0001      <.0001                  <.0001      <.0001      <.0001

capital      0.48998     0.57806     0.62978     1.00000     0.74037     0.69342
             <.0001      <.0001      <.0001                  <.0001      <.0001

punc         0.39874     0.53133     0.57516     0.74037     1.00000     0.63845
             <.0001      <.0001      <.0001      <.0001                  <.0001

usage        0.66100     0.68984     0.66638     0.69342     0.63845     1.00000
             <.0001      <.0001      <.0001      <.0001      <.0001
```

The output is divided into three parts for interpretation. Beginning with **Part (A)**, we read the coefficient alpha computed for the raw scores (0.902058) as well as for the standardized scores (0.904121). Raw scores are values taken directly from the data, whereas the standardized scores are rescaled values so that the rescaled mean = 0 and variance = 1. Because both alphas are quite high, one can conclude that the test is a reliable assessment instrument.

Part (B) presents alpha coefficients for the total test without the subtest listed in the first column. For example, if <u>vocab</u> is removed from the total test, then the reduced test has an alpha reliability of 0.89200 for the raw scores or 0.896729 for the standardized scores. Both are now lower than their corresponding reliabilities for the full test that includes <u>vocab</u>.

If a subtest, or an item, is correlated highly with the total test, the removal of such a subtest, or item, has a noticeable effect on the alpha coefficient reported in this table. Such is the case with the <u>usage</u> subtest. Among the six subtests, this subtest correlates the highest with the total score. Hence, its deletion lowers the test reliability substantially.

Part (C) of the output is, in essence, the same as **Part (B)** of Output 16.1, so you are spared from redundant explanations.

- Cronbach's alpha coefficient achieves the maximum value of 1 when all pairs of variables (subtests or items) are perfectly positively correlated. If some variables are negatively correlated, this coefficient can fall below zero. As a rule of thumb, a reliable test should have an alpha coefficient of at least 0.80.

_____ 16.3 How to Write the PROC CORR Codes

The CORR procedure is easy to program; five statements are often specified:

PROC	CORR	DATA= _sas_dataset_name_ < _options_ >;
	VAR	_variable_list_;
	WITH	_2nd_variable_list_;
	PARTIAL	_variables_to_be_removed_;
	BY	_classification_variable(s)_;

The first statement, **PROC CORR**, initializes the procedure and specifies the data set to be analyzed. In addition, you may specify one or more of the correlation indices: **PEARSON, ALPHA, SPEARMAN, KENDALL,** or **HOEFFDING**. Note that the **PEARSON** option (i.e., Pearson _r_) is the default of PROC CORR. The **ALPHA** option also activates the **PEARSON** option. Other options available in the PROC CORR statement include the following:

RANK   rearranges the correlations from the largest to the smallest on the output.

NOMISS   removes observations from the calculation of any correlation if they contain missing values on one or more variables listed in the VAR or WITH statement.

OUTP=   defines an output data set that contains Pearson correlations, mean, standard deviation, and sample size for variables being correlated. This is a TYPE=CORR data set. This option also implies the **PEARSON** option, so there is no need to specify both (see Example 16.3).

OUTS=   defines an output data set that contains Spearman's rank correlations, mean, standard deviation, and sample size for variables being correlated. This is a TYPE=CORR data set. This option also implies the **SPEARMAN** option, so there is no need to specify both.

OUTK=   defines an output data set that contains Kendall's tau-b correlations, mean, standard deviation, and sample size for variables being correlated. This is a TYPE=CORR data set. This option also implies the **KENDALL** option, so there is no need to specify both.

OUTH=   defines an output data set that contains Hoeffding's _D_ coefficients, mean, standard deviation, and sample size for variables being correlated. This is a TYPE=CORR data set. This option also implies the **HOEFFDING** option, so there is no need to specify both.

NOSIMPLE   excludes simple descriptive statistics such as mean, standard deviation, median, maximum, and minimum from the output (see Example 16.5).

NOPRINT   suppresses the display of any PROC CORR result. This is a useful option to specify, especially when your intent is to create an output data set based on correlations for subsequent data processing. Example 16.3 illustrates its use.

The second statement, **VAR**, lists names of numeric variables for which correlations are calculated for all possible pairs. If this statement is omitted, then all numeric variables in the data set are correlated.

The third statement, **WITH**, is optional. It makes a second list of variables that are to be correlated with each variable from the VAR list. As a result, correlations are not computed among pairs of variables listed on either the VAR or the WITH statement. So if a program reads as follows,

```
PROC CORR;
    VAR a b c;
```

the output will contain a correlation matrix for the a*b, a*c, and b*c pairs. However, if the WITH statement is added to the program, as follows,

```
PROC CORR;
    VAR a b c;
    WITH x y z;
```

the new output will contain correlations for the a*x, a*y, a*z, b*x, b*y, b*z, c*x, c*y, and c*z pairs.

The fourth statement, **PARTIAL**, is specified to compute partial correlation coefficients by controlling for the variables listed on this statement. The computation of partial correlation coefficients is based on observations that have complete information on all variables. This requirement is equivalent to specifying the **NOMISS** option. The PARTIAL statement cannot be used concurrently with the HOEFFDING option.

The last statement, **BY**, serves the same purpose as in all other procedures. It divides the data set into subgroups according to diverse values of the BY variable. The same correlations are computed for each subgroup according to variables specified on the VAR statement or VAR and WITH statements. If more than one BY variable is listed, all possible combinations of the BY variables' values are used in dividing up the data set. Be sure to presort the data set in the ascending order of all BY variables, if the BY statement is included in the CORR procedure. Presorting a data set can be accomplished using the SORT procedure.

16.4 Tips

- How to handle missing or invalid data

When computing correlation coefficient(s) for a pair of variables, PROC CORR, by default, does not include observations that have a missing value on either of the two variables. These observations are not excluded from the calculation of other correlations as long as they contain full information for these other correlations. If multiple dependent variables are listed on the VAR statement, PROC CORR applies the pairwise deletion method to observations, namely, it omits observations only from the pair of variables for which the observations have at least one missing value.

The way PROC CORR handles missing values results in changing sample sizes, for example, from 15 to 16, 17, 20, and 22 in Output 16.1. (This is the hint to Question 5 at the end of Output 16.1.)

- For what type of data should you compute the Pearson correlation coefficient?

Ideally, the Pearson correlation coefficient should be computed for two continuous variables whose underlying joint distribution is a bivariate normal distribution. The bivariate normality assumption is particularly important when interpreting the statistical test of Pearson correlation coefficients. It is not easy to compensate for violations of the bivariate normal assumption when the sample size is small, say less than 10, and the true correlation is high (say, $|\rho| > 0.80$). Without convincing evidence that the bivariate normality assumption is met, statistical tests are not to be trusted for small samples. (This is the hint to Question 2 of Output 16.2.)

- Do you want to boost Pearson correlations? Try these . . .

The Pearson correlation is probably the most widely used and also misused coefficient for reporting associations between two quantitative variables. Not only does Pearson r require a normality assumption (refer to the previous paragraph); its magnitude is easily influenced by factors other than the true underlying population correlation, ρ. These factors are compiled for you to take note of.

First, the magnitude of the coefficient is influenced by measurement errors in the data. Because measurement errors are not easily identified or quantified for each individual, they are usually corrected at the group level. Such a correction can be inferred from the reliability of the measurement instrument. Below is the formula for the correction of attenuation in the Pearson correlation:

$$\text{Corrected Pearson } r_{xy} = \frac{\text{Uncorrected Pearson } r_{xy}}{\sqrt{(\text{reliability of } X)(\text{reliability of } Y)}}.$$

So, whenever possible, X and Y values should be measured reliably so as not to attenuate Pearson r too much.

Second, the magnitude of Pearson r is influenced by the homogeneity (or lack of variability) in X and Y. If, for example, you compute the correlation between height and weight for 10-year-olds as well as for adults and children together, you will find that the first r is much smaller than the second. This is so because 10-year-olds are very similar in their heights and weights. The spread of their heights and weights is too limited to reveal any systematic pattern in a correlation. But we know for a fact that taller persons in general weigh more. Therefore, the second correlation based on a group of adults and children is more likely to show such a positive relationship between height and weight; hence, it is higher. Look at the scatter plot in Figure 16.1; pay special attention to the two reference lines drawn on each axis. Can you predict the value of Pearson r for the region labeled "10-year-olds"? Whatever the correlation really is, it is bound to be smaller than the r based on the entire scatter plot.

So the greater the group diversity (or heterogeneity of variance), the higher the correlation. (This is the hint to Question 3 of Output 16.2.)

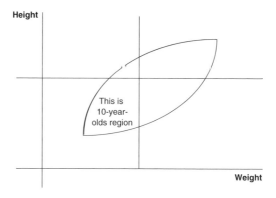

Figure 16.1   Scatter Plot of Weight and Height

- For what type of data should you compute the Spearman rank correlation?

The Spearman rank correlation is an extension of the Pearson correlation coefficient for ranked data. It is well suited for data measured at the ordinal level or ranked data. This correlation index does not make any assumption about the shape of population distributions. It is simple to compute, even by hand. And it is suitable for small data sets.

Although the Spearman rank correlation places few requirements on data, it is sensitive to linear relationships. For this reason, it is not surprising that its value was the highest among the four correlations displayed in Output 16.1. (This is the hint to Questions 3 and 4 of Output 16.1.)

- For what type of data should you compute Kendall's tau-b coefficient?

Kendall's tau-b coefficient is suitable for any type of ranked data, especially for those based on human judgments or those with ties. The interpretation of this coefficient is straightforward. If, for example, tau-b = 0.75 for two judges' rankings of 10 drawings submitted by 10 retirees living in a retirement center, this means that the likelihood for two randomly selected drawings to be ranked consistently by the two judges is 75% more than the likelihood that these drawings would be ranked inconsistently by the same two judges.

Kendall's tau-b has been extended to contexts in which three or more ranks are given to each observation. For instance, in a harp competition, 5 judges rate the performance of 17 harpists. The degree of agreement among these 5 judges can be expressed by a tau-b coefficient. This coefficient is also applicable to data with many ties. Because of these attributes, tau-b is a versatile correlation index; it is often recommended for social science research.

- For what type of data should you compute Hoeffding's D coefficient?

Like Spearman r_s and Kendall's tau-b, Hoeffding's D is suitable for any type of ranked data. The computation can be time-consuming by hand. So it is nice to have it programmed into PROC CORR. The D coefficient is sensitive to differences in X and Y ranks. But, unlike Spearman r_s, it does not square these differences. So equal weights are given to the difference in X and Y ranks. Theoretically, it ranges from –0.5 to 1. When the sample size is small, this D coefficient should not be computed for data with lots of ties. (This is the hint to Questions 3 and 4 in Output 16.1.)

- Does a strong correlation imply causation or importance?

In a word, no. A strong or high correlation usually means that two variables, such as income and expense, increase or decrease their values in a systematic, related way. If you look at a group of adults, you'll find that people with more income also tend to spend more. Conversely, people with meager incomes tend to spend less. Hence, these two variables are positively correlated to a great extent. Such a high correlation does not mean that a person's expense causes his or her income to go up or down. Both variables are influenced by factors such as spending habits, economics, occupations, and so on, just to name a few. The correlation coefficient alone provides an insufficient basis for proving that one variable is the cause of the other.

Other examples of strong correlations in the social sciences include interest and ability in a particular subject, verbal ability, and memory. The existence of strong positive or negative correlations may prompt a curiosity in us to look further into the matter and investigate it scientifically to find out if one variable indeed causes the other variable. A well-documented case along this line is smoking and lung cancer. After years of overwhelming evidence showing a strong link between smoking and lung cancer, scientists have now drawn a conclusion of causation that smoking indeed causes lung cancer, especially in habitual smokers. Even second-hand smoking is now suspected to have caused lung cancer in people who work or live around heavy smokers.

By the same token, a high correlation does not imply a more important finding than a low correlation. The magnitude of a correlation coefficient quantifies the degree of association between two variables; it should not reflect value judgments held by the one who interprets it.

- What does it mean to partial out a variable's variance from other variables?

Partial correlations are derived from the usual correlation between two variables (say, X and Y) while controlling for the third variable (say, Z). Numerically, the partial correlation is a correlation of two residuals. One residual is obtained by regressing X on Z and the other is obtained from regressing Y on Z. A residual is the difference between the actual and the predicted values in regression. In a nutshell, the partial correlation is a correlation of residuals of X with residuals of Y after both are regressed on Z. This concept is used extensively in the social sciences.

- How to obtain point-biserial, biserial, rank-biserial, tetrachoric, or phi correlation coefficients from SAS

Both point-biserial and biserial correlations are used extensively in testing and assessment. The point-biserial correlation is a special case of the Pearson product-moment correlation when one variable is dichotomous, such as gender, whereas the other is continuous, such as critical thinking. The program below demonstrates the point-biserial correlation between gender and critical thinking scores using the CORR procedure:

```
DATA mydata;
    INFILE 'd:\data\mydata.dat';
    INPUT id $ sex $ age gpa critical polpref $ satv;
    IF sex='M' THEN gender=1;
     ELSE gender=0;
RUN;
```

```
PROC CORR DATA=mydata;
    VAR gender critical;
RUN;
```

The result shows that the point-biserial correlation between <u>gender</u> and <u>critical</u> is −0.08884 ($p = 0.6942$). The correlation coefficient is tested to be statistically nonsignificant. The negative sign indicates that men, coded as 1, have lower <u>critical</u> scores on average than women, coded as 0.

```
Pearson Correlation Coefficients
    Prob > |r| under H0: Rho=0
       Number of Observations

                  gender      critical

gender          1.00000      -0.08884
                              0.6942
                    24            22

critical       -0.08884      1.00000
                0.694
                    22            22
```

Biserial correlation is used to measure the association between one artificially dichotomous variable and one continuous variable. The artificially dichotomous variable is assumed to have an underlying normal distribution, such as a test item score recorded as 0 (fail) and 1 (pass), when in fact the cognitive ability underlying the test item is assumed to be normally distributed. Biserial correlation is a projected estimate of Pearson r when one variable is crudely measured on a dichotomous scale. It is calculated by the free %BISERIAL macro program downloadable from www.sas.com. Below is a SAS program that demonstrates how this macro program is used to compute the biserial correlation between the artificially dichotomized GPA (<u>newgpa</u>) and the continuous <u>critical</u> thinking scores.

The %INCLUDE statement links the %BISERIAL macro, located at d:\sas_macro\fusion24991_1_biserial.sas, to the SAS program. The %BISERIAL statement initializes the SAS macro with the four parameters specified within the parentheses. The DATA= parameter identifies the SAS input data set. The BINARY= parameter identifies the artificially dichotomous variable (<u>newgpa</u>), whereas the CONTIN= parameter identifies the continuous variable (<u>critical</u>). Finally, the OUT= parameter names a SAS output data set whose content is subsequently revealed using the PRINT procedure.

```
DATA mydata;
    INFILE 'd:\data\mydata.dat';
    INPUT id $ sex $ age gpa critical polpref $ satv;
    IF gpa < 3 THEN newgpa=0;
        ELSE newgpa=1;
RUN;

%INCLUDE 'd:\sas_macro\fusion24991_1_biserial.sas';

%BISERIAL(DATA=mydata, BINARY=newgpa, CONTIN=critical, OUT=outresult)

PROC PRINT DATA=outresult;
RUN;
```

The output shows that the biserial correlation is −0.032106. Two other correlation coefficients also computed by this macro are the point-biserial correlation = −0.024519 (listed under **pntbisrl**) and the rank-biserial correlation = −0.125 (listed under **rnkbisrl**). The rank-biserial correlation is well suited for measuring the correlation between a ranked variable, measured on an ordinal scale without ties, and an artificially dichotomous variable whose underlying distribution is composed of untied ranks (Cureton, 1956; Glass, 1966).

```
            The SAS System                                              1

 Obs     pntbisrl     biserial     rnkbisrl

  1      -0.024519    -0.032106      -0.125
```

The tetrachoric correlation is used to measure the correlation between two artificially dichotomous variables whose underlying distributions are assumed to be normal. It is a projected estimate of Pearson r when two variables are measured crudely on a dichotomous scale with a normal underlying distribution. This correlation is obtained from the FREQ procedure by specifying the PLCORR option on the TABLES statement (refer back to Example 11.8). Unfortunately, neither PROC FREQ nor any other procedure in SAS provides a test for the bivariate normality assumption that is assumed by the tetrachoric correlation.

The phi coefficient is a special case of Pearson r, when it is computed for two dichotomously coded variables. It is well suited for frequency data arranged in a 2×2 table. It can be obtained from the FREQ procedure also. Refer back to Chapter 11, especially Example 11.5, for the syntax of the FREQ procedure and an interpretation of the phi coefficient.

- How to use ODS to save a correlation matrix

To use the ODS with PROC CORR, you need to know ODS table names corresponding with various portions of the output. Table 16.1 presents selected ODS table names for the CORR procedure and their descriptions.

Table 16.1   Selected ODS Table Names and Descriptions for the CORR Procedure

ODS Table Name	Description	Option in the PROC CORR Statement
SimpleStats	Simple statistics	(default)
PearsonCorr	Pearson correlations	(default) or PEARSON
SpearmanCorr	Spearman rank correlations	SPEARMAN
KendallCorr	Kendall's tau-b correlations	KENDALL
HoeffdingCorr	Hoeffding's D coefficients	HOEFFDING
CronbachAlpha	Cronbach's coefficient alphas	ALPHA
CronbachAlphaDel	Cronbach's coefficient alphas with deleted variable	ALPHA

Based on these ODS table names, you may select certain results to be exported as a SAS data set. For example, the following program exports the Pearson correlation matrix of Example 16.1 to a SAS data set cpearson and prints out the content with the PRINT procedure:

```
ODS OUTPUT PearsonCorr = cpearson;
PROC CORR DATA=mydata PEARSON SPEARMAN KENDALL HOEFFDING;
    VAR age gpa critical satv;
RUN;
PROC PRINT DATA=cpearson;
RUN;
```

See Output 16.1 for pages 1 to 2 results

The SAS System   3

Obs	Variable	Label	age	gpa	critical	satv	Page
1	age		1.00000	0.05812	-0.00285	-0.15821	_
2	gpa		-0.05812	1.00000	0.20774	0.88857	0.8307
3	critical		-0.00285	0.20774	1.00000	0.47367	0.9920
4	satv	SAT-verbal	-0.15821	0.88857	0.47367	1.00000	0.5584

Obs	Pgpa	Pcritical	Psatv	Nage	Ngpa	Ncritical	Nsatv
1	0.8307	0.9920	0.5584	17	16	15	16
2	_	0.4575	<.0001	16	17	15	17
3	0.4575	_	0.0349	15	15	22	20
4	<.0001	0.0349	_	16	17	20	22

Compared with Output 16.3, which resulted from using the OUTP= option, this SAS data set has a different structure and content. It is not suitable to be used as an input data set for other procedures such as PROC REG.

16.5 Summary

A number of correlation coefficients were introduced in this chapter. The first four, namely, the Pearson r, Spearman r_s, Kendall's tau-b, and Hoeffding's D coefficients are used to quantify the association between two quantitative variables, measured at the ordinal level or higher. Their usage, implementation in PROC CORR, interpretation, and limitations were discussed. The fifth coefficient, Cronbach's alpha, is frequently reported as a reliability index in educational and psychological assessment scales. It was illustrated in this chapter for raw as well as standardized data. Other types of correlation coefficients, such as point-biserial, biserial, rank-biserial, tetrachoric, and phi, are either special cases of Pearson r or projected estimates of Pearson r under special circumstances. They are defined and demonstrated in **Section 16.4: Tips**, along with cautions in interpreting these coefficients.

16.6 Exercises

1. A psychologist was interested in studying the relationship between anxiety level, personal income, and age. He administered an anxiety inventory to 20 salespersons, and collected information on their annual income and age. Data are shown below; the higher the anxiety score, the greater was the anxiety.

Age	Anxiety	Annual Income	Age	Anxiety	Annual Income
22	14	100	44	45	318,000
25	25	800	47	39	484,000
25	34	980	51	41	389,000
27	38	1,200	53	40	331,000
31	43	2,300	56	35	289,200
33	49	4,500	58	31	412,000
34	51	126,000	62	32	358,000
37	48	241,000	65	29	617,000
41	49	345,000	66	25	241,000
43	46	268,000	67	18	179,000

a. What is the Pearson correlation coefficient between age and anxiety level?

b. The psychologist believed that the relationship between age and anxiety level was affected by personal income. How do you remove the effect of personal income from the correlation computed in (a) above? Is the new or adjusted correlation higher or lower than the one obtained in (a)?

2. A group of 10 students took the GRE-General recently, and the following are their scores:

Student	Verbal	Quantitative	Analogy	Total
1	430	680	580	1,690
2	460	620	500	1,580
3	370	680	710	1,760
4	590	490	540	1,620
5	480	450	520	1,450
6	460	660	610	1,730
7	520	740	730	1,990
8	610	560	690	1,860
9	380	580	430	1,390
10	630	500	560	1,690

a. Compute the correlation (i) between Verbal and Quantitative and (ii) between Verbal and Analogy.

b. Compute an appropriate correlation of each subtest with the total score.

3. The following data were retrieved from p. 3925 of the *SAS/STAT® 9.1 User's Guide* (SAS Institute Inc., 2004d). The data set was based on 31 adult males and their physical fitness measures defined as follows:

oxygen = The oxygen intake rate (ml per kg body weight per minute)

age = Age in years

weight = Body weight in kilograms

runtime = Time taken to run 1.5 miles in minutes

rstheart = Heart rate while resting

runheart = Heart rate while running (oxygen measure was taken at the same time)

maxheart = Maximum heart rate recorded while running

a. Which pair of variables yield the highest Pearson r?
b. Which pair of variables yield the lowest Spearman r_s?
c. Which pair(s) of variables yield significant ($p < 0.05$) Kendall's tau-b coefficients?
d. Which pair(s) of variables yield nonsignificant ($p > 0.10$) Hoeffding's D?

```
TITLE 'Physical fitness data based on 31 adult males';
DATA fit;
   INPUT age weight oxygen runtime rstheart runheart maxheart @@;   DATALINES;
     44 89.47 44.609 11.37 62 178 182    40 75.07 45.313 10.07 62   185 185
     44 85.84 54.297  8.65 45 156 168    42 68.15 59.571  8.17 40   166 172
     38 89.02 49.874  9.22 55 178 180    47 77.45 44.811 11.63 58   176 176
     40 75.98 45.681 11.95 70 176 180    43 81.19 49.091 10.85 64   162 170
     44 81.42 39.442 13.08 63 174 176    38 81.87 60.055  8.63 48   170 186
     44 73.03 50.541 10.13 45 168 168    45 87.66 37.388 14.03 56   186 192
     45 66.45 44.754 11.12 51 176 176    47 79.15 47.273 10.60 47   162 164
     54 83.12 51.855 10.33 50 166 170    49 81.42 49.156  8.95 44   180 185
     51 69.63 40.836 10.95 57 168 172    51 77.91 46.672 10.00 48   162 168
     48 91.63 46.774 10.25 48 162 164    49 73.37 50.388 10.08 67   168 168
     57 73.37 39.407 12.63 58 174 176    54 79.38 46.080 11.17 62   156 165
     52 76.32 45.441  9.63 48 164 166    50 70.87 54.625  8.92 48   146 155
     51 67.25 45.118 11.08 48 172 172    54 91.63 39.203 12.88 44   168 172
     51 73.71 45.790 10.47 59 186 188    57 59.08 50.545  9.93 49   148 155
     49 76.32 48.673  9.40 56 186 188    48 61.24 47.920 11.50 52   170 176
     52 82.78 47.467 10.50 53 170 172
RUN;
```

4. This chapter has presented a number of correlation coefficients to quantify the association between two variables. Based on what you learned from this chapter, can you complete the table below?

Variable X	Variable Y	Correlation Index	SAS Statements
Continuous	Continuous		
Ordinal or rank-ordered	Ordinal or rank-ordered		
Ordinal or rank-ordered with ties	Ordinal or rank-ordered with ties	Kendall's tau-b for consistency in ranks	
Ordinal or rank-ordered	Ordinal or rank-ordered	Hoeffding's D coefficients, ranging from -0.5 to 1, equal weights are given to differences in ranks.	

Variable X	Variable Y	Correlation Index	SAS Statements
Test scores	Test scores		
Continuous	Dichotomous		
Continuous	Dichotomous (assumed continuous and normally distributed)		
Ordinal or rank-ordered without ties	Dichotomous (assumed ranked without ties)		
Dichotomous (assumed continuous and normally distributed)	Dichotomous (assumed continuous and normally distributed)		
Nominal	Nominal		

16.7 Answers to Exercises

1. a. −0.23454

   b. Use partial correlation that is higher (−0.44253) in absolute values than the original correlation.

2. a. i. $r = -0.48365$ between Verbal and Quantitative.
      ii. $r = 0.16804$ between Verbal and Analogy.

   b. correlation of Total with Verbal = 0.34906 (the lowest)

      correlation of Total with Quantitative = 0.58354

      correlation of Total with Analogy = 0.92531 (the highest)

3. a. The highest Pearson r is between <u>runheart</u> and <u>maxheart</u> (= 0.92975)

   b. The lowest Spearman r_s is between <u>rstheart</u> and <u>weight</u> (= −0.02958)

   c. These variable pairs yield significant ($p < 0.05$) Kendall's tau-b coefficients: <u>age</u> with <u>maxheart</u>; <u>oxygen</u> with <u>runtime</u>; <u>oxygen</u> with <u>runheart</u>; <u>oxygen</u> with <u>rstheart</u>; <u>runtime</u> with <u>rstheart</u>; <u>rstheart</u> with <u>runheart</u>; <u>runheart</u> with <u>maxheart</u>.

   d. The following variable pairs yield nonsignificant ($p > 0.10$) Hoeffding's D coefficients: <u>age</u> with <u>runheart</u>; <u>age</u> with <u>runtime</u>; <u>age</u> with <u>rstheart</u>; <u>age</u> with <u>weight</u>; <u>age</u> with <u>oxygen</u>; <u>weight</u> with <u>rstheart</u>; <u>weight</u> with <u>oxygen</u>; <u>weight</u> with <u>runheart</u>; <u>weight</u> with <u>maxheart</u>; <u>weight</u> with <u>runtime</u>; <u>oxygen</u> with <u>maxheart</u>.

4.

Variable X	Variable Y	Correlation Index	SAS Statements
Continuous	Continuous	Pearson product-moment correlation coefficient	PROC CORR PEARSON;
Ordinal or rank-ordered	Ordinal or rank-ordered	Spearman rank coefficient	PROC CORR SPEARMAN;
Ordinal or rank-ordered with ties	Ordinal or rank-ordered with ties	Kendall's tau-b for consistency in ranks	PROC CORR KENDALL;
Ordinal or rank-ordered	Ordinal or rank-ordered	Hoeffding's D coefficients, ranging from -0.5 to 1, equal weights are given to differences in ranks.	PROC CORR HOEFFDING;
Test scores	Test scores	Cronbach's alpha	PROC CORR ALPHA;
Continuous	Dichotomous	Point-biserial correlation coefficient	PROC CORR PEARSON;
Continuous	Dichotomous (assumed continuous and normally distributed)	Biserial correlation coefficient	MACRO Program %BISERIAL
Ordinal or rank-ordered without ties	Dichotomous (assumed ranked without ties)	Rank-biserial correlation coefficient	MACRO Program %BISERIAL
Dichotomous (assumed continuous and normally distributed)	Dichotomous (assumed continuous and normally distributed)	Tetrachoric correlation coefficient	PROC FREQ; TABLES / PLCORR;
Nominal	Nominal	Phi coefficient	PROC FREQ; TABLES /MEASURES;

17

When Do You Stop Worrying and Start Loving Regression?

OBJECTIVE

This chapter focuses on the construction and assessment of regression models in the social sciences. Features of the versatile REG procedure, including the simple and the multiple regression models, three selection procedures, and residual examinations, are illustrated using 10 examples. These examples demonstrate a progressive strategy for answering a real-world question with real-world data. Regression concepts are explained in layman's terms. Statistical assumptions are emphasized and verified in the regression model building process.

17.1 Basic Concepts in Regression

With a chapter title like this one, I hope that you can finally lower your guard against regression. Regression is a wonderful statistical technique. It is easy to understand and even easier to perform using the REG procedure.

The main goal of regression analysis is to predict an individual's unknown or future measure on an outcome variable with information already gathered from other variables. One application of regression is in the care of cancer patients, where doctors and nurses are interested in predicting how much pain patients will feel following a chemotherapy treatment. To know this, medical researchers first gather information about the cancer patients' profile such as age, gender, length of chemotherapy, and degree of susceptibility to infections. Next, they record the degree of pain reported by cancer patients after, say, 6 months of chemotherapy. Based on these data, researchers construct a regression equation that places degree of pain (the variable of interest) on the left-hand side and predictor variables, such as age, sex, length of therapy, and susceptibility on the right-hand side of the equation. Thus, in the future, doctors and nurses can plug the values of predictor variables into the equation and get a prediction for a patient's propensity to feel pain during chemotherapy.

Before we go any further into regression theories, let us define a few terms:

Predictor or independent variable: the variable whose value is known and can be used to form a prediction equation, expressed as X.

Outcome or dependent variable: the variable whose value is to be predicted from the prediction equation, expressed as Y. The outcome variable value is expressed in lowercase as y. The predicted variable is written as $\hat{Y}$ and its predicted value in lowercase as $\hat{y}$.

Prediction (regression) equation: an algebraic equation linking one or multiple predictors to the outcome variable. The formation of a prediction equation depends on statistical estimation methods. In the next paragraph, specifics about the equation, the estimation method, and related statistical concepts will be explained.

A typical equation used in regression has the following general appearance:

$$\hat{y} = b_0 + b_1 x_1 + b_2 x_2 + \cdots + b_p x_p,$$

where $\hat{y}$ is the predicted outcome variable value for the true Y value, b_0 is the constant of the equation, and $b_1, \ldots, b_p$ are estimated parameters corresponding to predictor values $x_1, \ldots, x_p$. The above equation represents a linear model because it relates the predicted values of Y to the parameters in a linear way.

If the prediction equation is a good one, the predicted value $\hat{y}$ should be similar to the observed value y. Thus, the discrepancy between these two is called a *residual* or *prediction error*. The smaller the residual, the better is the fit of an equation to that data point. For this reason, one estimation method of parameters used by the REG procedure and statisticians is the *least-squares method*. The least-squares method seeks to minimize the sum of squared residuals for a given data set to derive estimated values for the parameters, written as $b_0, b_1, \ldots, b_p$. These estimates obtained under the least-squares method are called the *least-squares estimates*. In other words, the least-squares estimates minimize the sum of squared differences between the observed y and the predicted y; b_0 is alternatively called the Y *intercept* and is needed as long as the outcome variable and some of the predictors are on an interval scale, and $b_1, \ldots, b_p$ are called *regression coefficients* or *regression weights*. When these weights are expressed in a standardized form, they are also called *beta weights*. The unstandardized weights are simply called *b weights*.

Another way to know if a model is good is to correlate the predicted value with its observed value. Such a correlation is typically expressed as a Pearson product-moment correlation coefficient, which is written as R. The squared R (or R^2) indicates the percentage in Y variance that is accounted for by the linear relationship between Y and X, or several Xs. Both $|R|$ and R^2 are between 0 and +1; the larger the value, the better is the model's fit to the data.

Finally, a good model produces small residuals. The standard deviation of residuals is the *standard error of prediction*. The standard error of prediction is also the square root of the mean square error (or MSE on the output). When making a judgment about the goodness of fit of a model or the relative merits of several models, you may use MSE as a criterion, along with R^2, as well as statistical tests of the entire model and of each individual regression weight.

17.2 An Overview of the REG Procedure

The REG procedure is the most versatile procedure in SAS for performing general-purpose regression analyses. It employs the method of least squares to estimate the regression coefficients. Output includes a variety of statistics, such as R^2, its adjusted value, the MSE, the mean of the outcome variable, the predicted Y values, the residuals, a variety of influence statistics, the Durbin-Watson statistic and test for examining if residuals are serially correlated, and the serial correlation among residuals. Individualized results, such as the predicted Y values, the residuals, and so on, can be plotted graphically. On the graph, certain observations can be highlighted with the PAINT statement. With this tool, you may anchor the interpretation of the plot on the painted observations.

Inferential results are diverse and voluminous, including the F test of the model, t or F test of each estimated regression coefficient, confidence interval of individual predicted values, confidence interval of the average predicted value, standardized residuals, and t ratios of the standardized residuals.

Furthermore, the REG procedure provides multiple methods for selecting a best set of predictors for predicting an outcome variable. Each method offers a unique definition for the "best" set. Once the best model is identified, it is subjected to an F test for its overall significance as well as other indicators of the fit of the model to the data.

Most of the PROC REG results can be saved into a SAS data set for further processing. Likewise, a preprocessed data set, such as a correlation matrix or covariance matrix, can also be accepted as legitimate input data for the REG procedure to analyze.

What's more, the fitting of a regression model can be carried out interactively. First, you propose an initial model for the data. The REG procedure applies the model to the data and, afterward, presents the results on the screen. At that point, you may modify the initial model and resubmit the second model to the REG procedure for analysis. After a short while, you are presented with the results on the screen and the process of model fitting continues. This cyclic process goes on until you are satisfied with the model and its residuals meet their statistical assumptions. This type of computing approach is called "interactive"; it is available on a variety of platforms. Consult your local SAS experts about this handy approach.

Having read these comments, it is perhaps apparent that you don't have a thing to worry about when it comes to using PROC REG for regression. Start loving it now!

17.3 Examples

All the examples illustrated in this chapter use the same data file, salary.dat (Turnbull & Williams, 1974). Turnbull and Williams were interested in investigating pay differences between female and male teachers in Great Britain. In addition to gender, other factors that might have contributed to differentials in pay were also examined. These included the type of schools teachers taught in, their academic degrees, the length of their service, whether they took a break from their teaching careers, and so on. The ultimate question we'd like to pose concerning the data is, "Did male and female teachers with comparable experience and academic backgrounds earn comparable salaries in Great Britain in that era?" In search of a credible answer to this question, Examples 17.1 to 17.5 demonstrate a progressive strategy of regression analysis of the salary data. First, a simple regression model based on a single predictor for teachers' pay is considered (Example 17.1). Next, the simple model is expanded to include two predictors (Example 17.2). Third, a categorical variable, that is, private versus public schools, is included and explained in a three-predictor model (Example 17.3). Fourth, all potential predictors are considered in a series of selection processes so that they may be narrowed down to a set that is most sensible and effective (Example 17.4). Fifth, statistical assumptions about residuals are checked for the model selected from the fourth step (Example 17.5). Note that the results and data analysis strategies shown in this chapter are different from those reported in Turnbull and Williams's article. You are encouraged to read the article and compare their results and modeling techniques with ours.

The last example (Example 17.6) is a demonstration of using a correlation matrix as input for the REG procedure. In all analyses, the dependent variable, logs, is teacher's salary expressed in log of base 10 scale, as recommended by Turnbull and Williams in their 1974 article. Furthermore, the predictor variable degree (the class of academic degrees) was in squared form in the file salary.dat. So degree was square rooted; the new variable is called sqrtdg.

Example 17.1 Simple Regression Analysis

For the 90 teachers included in the file salary.dat, a simple regression model is constructed from service as the sole predictor. The service was the length of time, in months, that these teachers were in the teaching profession. It is probably the single most important factor in determining a teacher's salary.

To implement a simple regression model via the REG procedure, you need only two statements: PROC REG and MODEL. On the PROC REG statement, the SAS data set is identified. On the MODEL statement, the label "M1" identifies the regression model as the first model; such a label is optional. "M1" is followed by the regression model for predicting the log of teachers' salary (on the left of the equal sign) with the length of service (on the right of the equal sign). After the slash (/), **P** and **R** are listed. These two options request the computation of, respectively, predicted values and the analysis of residuals to be outputted. Bear in mind that the outcome variable is on the scale of $\log_{10}$ of salaries in British pounds.

```
/* The following bolded SAS statements establish the SAS data set 'salary' */

DATA salary;
    INFILE 'd:\data\salary.dat';
    INPUT salary service sex degree school grad break;
    logs=log10(salary);
    sqrtdg=sqrt(degree);
    LABEL salary='teachers pay in pounds'
          logs='log 10 of salary'
          service='length of teaching in months'
```

```
            sex='1=M, 2=F'
            degree='class of degree, squared'
            sqrtdg='academic degree'
            school='0=private, 1=public'
            grad='1=trained grad, 0=others'
            break='1=break 2 yrs, 0=others';
RUN;

TITLE 'Example 17.1 Simple regression analysis';

PROC REG DATA=salary;
M1:  MODEL logs=service / P R;

RUN; QUIT;
```

Output 17.1 Simple Regression Analysis

```
                      Example 17.1 Simple regression analysis                    1

                              The REG Procedure
                                 Model: M1
                       Dependent Variable: logs log 10 of salary

                        Number of Observations Read        90
                        Number of Observations Used        90
```

Part (A)

```
                          Analysis of Variance

                                    Sum of          Mean
          Source              DF    Squares        Square    F Value    Pr > F

          Model                1    0.85007       0.85007     138.16    <.0001
          Error               88    0.54143       0.00615
          Corrected Total     89    1.39150
```

Part (B)

```
                    Root MSE              0.07844    R-Square     0.6109
                    Dependent Mean        3.22004    Adj R-Sq     0.6065
                    Coeff Var             2.43595
```

Part (C)

```
                          Parameter Estimates

                                           Parameter    Standard
Variable    Label                     DF    Estimate      Error    t Value    Pr > |t|

Intercept   Intercept                  1     3.08703    0.01401    220.27    <.0001
service     length of teaching in months 1  0.00076796 0.00006533  11.75    <.0001
```

```
                      Example 17.1 Simple regression analysis                    2

                              The REG Procedure
                                 Model: M1
                       Dependent Variable: logs log 10 of salary
```

Part (D)

```
                          Output Statistics

       Dependent Predicted  Std Error            Std Error  Student
  Obs  Variable   Value   Mean Predict  Residual  Residual  Residual  -2-1 0 1 2   Cook's D

    1    2.9913    3.0924    0.0136     -0.1011    0.0772    -1.309  |   **|      |   0.027
    2    3.0065    3.0978    0.0133     -0.0913    0.0773    -1.181  |   **|      |   0.021
```

Obs						Student Residual	-2-1 0 1 2		Cook's D
3	3.0120	3.1009	0.0131	-0.0889	0.0773	-1.149	**|	|	0.019
4	3.0969	3.1016	0.0130	-0.004710	0.0773	-0.0609	|	|	0.000
5	3.0120	3.1016	0.0130	-0.0896	0.0773	-1.159	**|	|	0.019
6	3.0120	3.1016	0.0130	-0.0896	0.0773	-1.159	**|	|	0.019
7	3.0077	3.1078	0.0126	-0.1000	0.0774	-1.292	**|	|	0.022
8	3.0302	3.1101	0.0125	-0.0799	0.0774	-1.031	**|	|	0.014
9	3.1106	3.1101	0.0125	0.000522	0.0774	0.00674	|	|	0.000
10	3.0806	3.1101	0.0125	-0.0294	0.0774	-0.380	|	|	0.002
11	3.1310	3.1108	0.0124	0.0201	0.0774	0.260	|	|	0.001
12	3.0806	3.1108	0.0124	-0.0302	0.0774	-0.390	|	|	0.002
13	3.0430	3.1162	0.0121	-0.0732	0.0775	-0.945	*|	|	0.011
14	3.0484	3.1185	0.0120	-0.0701	0.0775	-0.904	*|	|	0.010
15	3.0519	3.1193	0.0119	-0.0674	0.0775	-0.869	*|	|	0.009
16	3.1000	3.1193	0.0119	-0.0193	0.0775	-0.248	|	|	0.001
17	3.0519	3.1193	0.0119	-0.0674	0.0775	-0.869	*|	|	0.009
18	3.0519	3.1193	0.0119	-0.0674	0.0775	-0.869	*|	|	0.009
19	3.0394	3.1231	0.0117	-0.0837	0.0776	-1.079	**|	|	0.013
20	3.0465	3.1270	0.0114	-0.0805	0.0776	-1.037	**|	|	0.012
21	3.1649	3.1270	0.0114	0.0380	0.0776	0.489	|	|	0.003
22	3.0726	3.1285	0.0114	-0.0559	0.0776	-0.720	*|	|	0.006
23	3.1474	3.1285	0.0114	0.0189	0.0776	0.243	|	|	0.001
24	3.0726	3.1285	0.0114	-0.0559	0.0776	-0.720	*|	|	0.006
25	3.2025	3.1293	0.0113	0.0732	0.0776	0.943	|*	|	0.009
26	3.1641	3.1377	0.0108	0.0263	0.0777	0.339	|	|	0.001
27	3.0924	3.1385	0.0108	-0.0461	0.0777	-0.594	*|	|	0.003
28	3.0924	3.1385	0.0108	-0.0461	0.0777	-0.594	*|	|	0.003
29	3.1749	3.1446	0.0105	0.0303	0.0777	0.390	|	|	0.001
30	3.1535	3.1469	0.0103	0.006580	0.0778	0.0846	|	|	0.000
31	3.1535	3.1477	0.0103	0.005812	0.0778	0.0747	|	|	0.000
32	3.1294	3.1569	0.009859	-0.0275	0.0778	-0.354	|	|	0.001
33	3.1281	3.1577	0.009824	-0.0296	0.0778	-0.380	|	|	0.001
34	3.1173	3.1592	0.009754	-0.0419	0.0778	-0.539	*|	|	0.002
35	3.2586	3.1661	0.009455	0.0925	0.0779	1.188	|**	|	0.010
36	3.1858	3.1661	0.009455	0.0197	0.0779	0.253	|	|	0.000
37	3.1553	3.1661	0.009455	-0.0108	0.0779	-0.139	|	|	0.000
38	3.1581	3.1723	0.009213	-0.0142	0.0779	-0.182	|	|	0.000
39	3.2891	3.1976	0.008485	0.0915	0.0780	1.174	|**	|	0.008
40	3.3456	3.1976	0.008485	0.1480	0.0780	1.897	|***	|	0.021
41	3.2634	3.1976	0.008485	0.0658	0.0780	0.844	|*	|	0.004
42	3.1511	3.1769	0.009047	-0.0258	0.0779	-0.331	|	|	0.001
43	3.3122	3.1938	0.008565	0.1184	0.0780	1.519	|***	|	0.014
44	3.3195	3.1945	0.008548	0.1250	0.0780	1.603	|***	|	0.015
45	3.3549	3.2053	0.008363	0.1496	0.0780	1.918	|***	|	0.021
46	3.3426	3.2084	0.008328	0.1343	0.0780	1.721	|***	|	0.017
47	3.4760	3.2091	0.008320	0.2668	0.0780	3.421	|******	|	0.067
48	3.2292	3.2114	0.008300	0.0177	0.0780	0.227	|	|	0.000
49	3.2533	3.2153	0.008278	0.0381	0.0780	0.488	|	|	0.001

Example 17.1 Simple regression analysis   3

The REG Procedure
Model: M1
Dependent Variable: logs log 10 of salary

Output Statistics

Obs	Dependent Variable	Predicted Value	Std Error Mean Predict	Residual	Std Error Residual	Student Residual	-2-1 0 1 2	Cook's D
50	3.2279	3.2199	0.008268	0.008001	0.0780	0.103	|	0.000
51	3.2617	3.2207	0.008268	0.0411	0.0780	0.527	|*	0.002
52	3.4156	3.2214	0.008269	0.1942	0.0780	2.490	|****	0.035
53	3.2355	3.2399	0.008438	-0.004324	0.0780	-0.0554	|	0.000
54	3.2355	3.2475	0.008593	-0.0120	0.0780	-0.154	|	0.000
55	3.3343	3.2475	0.008593	0.0867	0.0780	1.112	|**	0.008
56	3.2676	3.2483	0.008611	0.0193	0.0780	0.248	|	0.000
57	3.3230	3.2506	0.008667	0.0724	0.0780	0.929	|*	0.005
58	3.2676	3.2560	0.008815	0.0117	0.0779	0.150	|	0.000
59	3.2676	3.2575	0.008862	0.0101	0.0779	0.130	|	0.000
60	3.3444	3.2575	0.008862	0.0869	0.0779	1.115	|**	0.008
61	3.3553	3.2583	0.008885	0.0970	0.0779	1.244	|**	0.010

61	3.3553	3.2583	0.008885	0.0970	0.0779	1.244		|** |	0.010
62	3.3069	3.2583	0.008885	0.0486	0.0779	0.623		|* |	0.003
63	3.2676	3.2614	0.008984	0.006286	0.0779	0.0807		| |	0.000
64	3.2676	3.2652	0.009117	0.002446	0.0779	0.0314		| |	0.000
65	3.2999	3.2675	0.009201	0.0324	0.0779	0.416		| |	0.001
66	3.4176	3.2752	0.009506	0.1425	0.0779	1.830		|*** |	0.025
67	3.3662	3.2813	0.009775	0.0849	0.0778	1.091		|** |	0.009
68	3.2676	3.2844	0.009917	-0.0168	0.0778	-0.215		| |	0.000
69	3.3126	3.2867	0.0100	0.0259	0.0778	0.333		| |	0.001
70	3.4178	3.3051	0.0110	0.1127	0.0777	1.451		|** |	0.021
71	3.2896	3.3074	0.0111	-0.0178	0.0776	-0.230		| |	0.001
72	3.2355	3.3097	0.0113	-0.0742	0.0776	-0.956		*| |	0.010
73	3.4156	3.3236	0.0121	0.0921	0.0775	1.188		|** |	0.017
74	3.2676	3.3243	0.0121	-0.0567	0.0775	-0.731		*| |	0.007
75	3.2882	3.3320	0.0126	-0.0438	0.0774	-0.565		*| |	0.004
76	3.3069	3.3366	0.0129	-0.0298	0.0774	-0.385		| |	0.002
77	3.2882	3.3374	0.0130	-0.0491	0.0774	-0.635		*| |	0.006
78	3.2355	3.3397	0.0131	-0.1042	0.0773	-1.347		**| |	0.026
79	3.3113	3.3458	0.0135	-0.0345	0.0773	-0.447		| |	0.003
80	3.3681	3.3527	0.0140	0.0154	0.0772	0.199		| |	0.001
81	3.2355	3.3597	0.0145	-0.1241	0.0771	-1.610		***| |	0.046
82	3.2882	3.3612	0.0146	-0.0729	0.0771	-0.946		*| |	0.016
83	3.3257	3.3789	0.0158	-0.0531	0.0768	-0.692		*| |	0.010
84	3.4381	3.3842	0.0162	0.0538	0.0767	0.702		|* |	0.011
85	3.4378	3.3965	0.0171	0.0412	0.0765	0.539		|* |	0.007
86	3.2882	3.3988	0.0173	-0.1106	0.0765	-1.445		**| |	0.053
87	3.3553	3.4226	0.0191	-0.0674	0.0761	-0.886		*| |	0.025
88	3.3867	3.4349	0.0201	-0.0482	0.0758	-0.636		*| |	0.014
89	3.3153	3.4388	0.0204	-0.1234	0.0757	-1.629		***| |	0.096
90	3.3010	3.4434	0.0207	-0.1423	0.0757	-1.881		***| |	0.133

Part (E)

Sum of Residuals		0
Sum of Squared Residuals		0.54143
Predicted Residual SS (PRESS)		0.56689

On page 1 of the output, results are divided into **Parts (A)**, **(B)**, and **(C)**. **Part (A)** contains the F test of the overall regression fit and its significance level. The F ratio (= 138.16) and its p level (< 0.0001) are convincing evidence that the fit is good. This is confirmed by other indices from **Parts (B)** and **(C)**.

The proportion of variance in <u>logs</u> that is explained by <u>service</u> is 0.6109, reported as **R-Square**. Underneath this value is the adjusted R^2 (**Adj R-Sq**), which, at 0.6065, is credible. For differences between these two, read the paragraph below on R^2 and adjusted R^2. Other results in **Part (B)** include the square root of MSE from **Part (A)** (= 0.07844 = $\sqrt{0.00615}$), which is also called the *standard error of prediction*, the mean of the <u>logs</u> (= 3.22004), and the coefficient of variation (= 2.43595 under **Coeff Var**).

Part (C) presents the regression equation and a detailed examination of the regression coefficient and the Y intercept. The equation is

$$\overset{\wedge}{\text{logs}} = (3.08703) + (0.00076796) \times service.$$

Next to the **Parameter Estimate** is **Standard Error,** which is used to form the t test for each regression coefficient estimate. Therefore, the t test of the Y intercept equals 220.27 (or 3.08703/0.01401). This value reaches a p level of less than 0.0001 for a two-tailed test. (If you divide the p level by 2, you obtain a p level for a one-tailed test.) By the same token, the t test of the regression coefficient for <u>service</u> is a ratio of the estimate divided by its standard error. Based on a two-tailed p level less than .0001, this t statistic indicates that <u>service</u> is a statistically significant predictor.

Beginning with page 2, you will see detailed results presented at the individual level. On **Part (D)**, next to each observation (Obs) is the observed Y value (**Dependent Variable** or <u>logs</u>). This is followed by the predicted value (**Predicted Value**), the standard error of the mean predicted value (**Std Error Mean Predict**), the residual or the difference of $y - \hat{y}$ (**Residual**), the standard error of the residual (**Std Error Residual**), and the studentized residual (**Student Residual** = Residual/Std Error Residual). These values are used to determine if the regression equation fits some observations better than others, and whether the poorly fitted observations were indeed outliers. The effort in identifying outliers is further aided by graphics of residuals and an influence statistic, called Cook's D. On the graphical plot of residuals, expressed as "*", you should look for two things: (1) the magnitude of residuals or the number of "*" next to the reference line at 0 and (2) any systematic pattern in the plot to alert you that there might exist correlations among the residuals.

Regarding the magnitude of residuals, the 47th observation (Obs = 47) is associated with six *s and an unusually large Cook's D. Both indicate that this teacher's salary, in $\log_{10}$ scale, was poorly predicted. At this point, you should examine the raw data to make sure that his or her data were entered correctly. Next, you may choose to keep this data point and the results or to delete this case and reanalyze the remaining 89 cases.

As for the pattern in the residual plot, you look for a systematic rise or fall of *s on either side of the reference line at 0. Any systematic rise or fall of *s indicates that the corresponding residuals are correlated. Because the overall F test of the model requires that residuals be independent, a serious violation of this assumption results in an invalid F result. In Example 17.5, several strategies are demonstrated to help you verify that this and two other assumptions are satisfactorily met. From the current residual plot, it seems that there is a slight correlation among residuals, because they do not appear to be randomly scattered on both sides of the reference line at 0.

Part (E) on page 3 displays the sum of residuals, sum of squared residuals, and predicted residual sum of squares. In my opinion, this part is not important, so it is left alone.

- R^2 and adjusted R^2

R^2 is actually Pearson r squared. The Pearson r is the correlation between the observed Y and the predicted Y. The R^2 indicates the amount in the Y variance that is explained by the predictor(s). The higher the R^2 value, the better is the prediction.

Why do we need adjusted R^2, if R^2 is so straightforward? The adjusted R^2 is needed because the unadjusted R^2 is a positively biased estimator of its population counterpart. The amount of positive bias is proportional to the ratio of k/N, where k is the number of parameters in a regression model including the Y intercept and N is the number of observations. For this reason, the adjusted R^2 came into being. The adjusted R^2 computed from the REG procedure was first proposed by M. Ezekiel in 1929. It is commonly referred to as the Wherry formula-1 (Yin & Fan, 2001). Wherry's adjusted R^2 formula-1 is defined as

$$\text{adjusted } R^2 = 1 - (1 - R^2)\left(\frac{N-1}{N-k}\right).$$

As the sample size increases and the ratio of k/N decreases, the amount of bias lessens. As a responsible researcher and data analyst, you should always report the adjusted R^2 because it is a more accurate estimator for the population R^2 than the unadjusted R^2.

Example 17.1a Displaying the Regression Line and the 95% Confidence Interval of Means

Sometimes you may be interested in displaying the regression equation and the 95% confidence interval of predicted values overlaid with the scatter plot of the data points. You may do so with the help of the GPLOT procedure as it is applied to the salary data set.

```
/* See Example 17.1 for the DATA step in creating the SAS data set 'salary' */

GOPTIONS FTEXT=swissb HTEXT=2 FTITLE=swiss HTITLE=3;

SYMBOL1 V=dot CV=red HEIGHT=1        /* Specifying color and plotting symbol for data points */
        CI=green                     /* Specifying color for Regression line   */
        CO=blue                      /* Specifying color for Confident limits  */
        WIDTH=2                      /* Specifying width of the line */
        INTERPOL=rlclm95;            /* Requesting linear regression with 95% CLM */

TITLE 'Example 17.1a Displaying regression line and 95% CLM';

PROC GPLOT DATA=salary;
     PLOT logs*service / REGEQN;     /* REGEQN requests the display of the regression equation */
RUN; QUIT;
```

Output 17.1a Displaying the Regression Line and the 95% Confidence Interval of Means

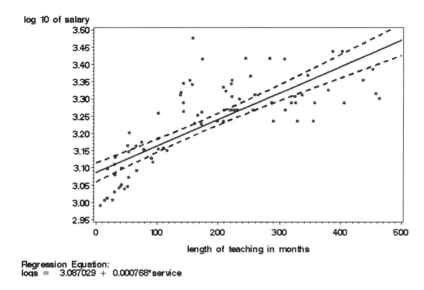

Regression Equation:
logs =   3.087029 + 0.000768*service

Example 17.2 Two-Predictor Regression Model

This example demonstrates how to improve predictions by adding a second predictor to the previous regression model. The second predictor added is the class of academic degrees, coded as sqrtdg in the program below. The model label now reads "M2" to be distinguished from the M1 model.

```
/* See Example 17.1 for the DATA step in creating the SAS data set 'salary' */

TITLE 'Example 17.2 Two-predictor regression model';

PROC REG DATA=salary;
M2:  MODEL logs=service sqrtdg / P R;

RUN; QUIT;
```

Output 17.2 Two-Predictor Regression Model

```
              Example 17.2 Two-predictor regression model                1

                       The REG Procedure
                          Model: M2
               Dependent Variable: logs log 10 of salary

              Number of Observations Read          90
              Number of Observations Used          90
```

Part (A)

Analysis of Variance

Source	DF	Sum of Squares	Mean Square	F Value	Pr > F
Model	2	1.09217	0.54608	158.72	<.0001
Error	87	0.29933	0.00344		
Corrected Total	89	1.39150			

Part (B)

Root MSE	0.05866	R-Square	0.7849
Dependent Mean	3.22004	Adj R-Sq	0.7799
Coeff Var	1.82161		

Part (C)

Parameter Estimates

Variable	Label	DF	Parameter Estimate	Standard Error	t Value	Pr > |t|
Intercept	Intercept	1	3.06800	0.01072	286.11	<.0001
service	length of teaching in months	1	0.00072858	0.00004908	14.84	<.0001
sqrtdg	academic degree	1	0.04309	0.00514	8.39	<.0001

Example 17.2 Two-predictor regression model   2

The REG Procedure
Model: M2
Dependent Variable: logs log 10 of salary

Part (D)

Output Statistics

Obs	Dependent Variable	Predicted Value	Std Error Mean Predict	Residual	Std Error Residual	Student Residual	-2-1 0 1 2	Cook's D
1	2.9913	3.0731	0.0105	-0.0818	0.0577	-1.417	| **| |	0.022
2	3.0065	3.0782	0.0102	-0.0717	0.0578	-1.242	| **| |	0.016
3	3.0120	3.0811	0.0101	-0.0691	0.0578	-1.196	| **| |	0.014
4	3.0969	3.0818	0.0100	0.0151	0.0578	0.261	| | |	0.001
5	3.0120	3.0818	0.0100	-0.0698	0.0578	-1.209	| **| |	0.015

[Obs 6 to 49 are not shown]

Example 17.2 Two-predictor regression model   3

The REG Procedure
Model: M2
Dependent Variable: logs log 10 of salary

Output Statistics

Obs	Dependent Variable	Predicted Value	Std Error Mean Predict	Residual	Std Error Residual	Student Residual	-2-1 0 1 2	Cook's D
50	3.2279	3.1940	0.006908	0.0338	0.0582	0.581	| |* |	0.002
51	3.2617	3.1948	0.006910	0.0670	0.0582	1.150	| |** |	0.006
52	3.4156	3.2817	0.009478	0.1340	0.0579	2.314	| |**** |	0.048
53	3.2355	3.2130	0.007077	0.0225	0.0582	0.387	| | |	0.001
54	3.2355	3.2203	0.007201	0.0153	0.0582	0.262	| | |	0.000
55	3.3343	3.3926	0.0185	-0.0584	0.0557	-1.048	| **| |	0.040

[Obs 56 to 90 are not shown]

Part (E)

Sum of Residuals	0
Sum of Squared Residuals	0.29933
Predicted Residual SS (PRESS)	0.32398

This output has the same appearance as Output 17.1, so there is no need to explain the headings again. Let's get right down to business—compare the results of Model 1 (M1) and Model 2 (M2). To facilitate this comparison, six indices are evaluated; they are listed in Table 17.1.

Table 17.1   Comparison of Model 1 and Model 2

Model	F (p Level)	√MSE	Adjusted R²	t Test of Y Intercept (p Level)	t Test of Estimates (p Level)	Plot of Residuals
M1	138.16 (< 0.0001)	0.07844	0.6065	220.27 (< 0.0001)	11.75 (< 0.0001)-service	Slight correlation
M2	158.72 (< 0.0001)	0.05866	0.7799	286.11 (< 0.0001)	14.84 (< 0.0001)-service 8.39 (< 0.0001)-sqrtdg	More random than M1; smaller residuals in general
Recommendation	Small p	Small	Large	Small p	Small p	Random

The last row of Table 17.1 provides a guideline for each index. For example, if overall F tests and p levels are used to compare M1 and M2, a statistically better model is the one associated with a larger F and smaller p. Other recommendations are likewise interpreted.

Based on all six indices, one can conclude that M2 is better than M1. Maybe an even better model is yet to be discovered. Let's now turn to the third model, which includes a categorical variable, school, as one of the predictors.

Example 17.3 How to Handle a Categorical Predictor in Regression

This example showcases the inclusion of a categorical predictor in a regression model. The categorical predictor is the school type (school), which is either private (coded as 0) or public (coded as 1). The numerical codings of this categorical variable are nominal. These codings do not imply any meaningful, quantitative difference between private and public schools. They are dummy codings, as they are often referred to in textbooks. To incorporate dummy codings into a regression model, you list them on the **MODEL** statement like all other predictors; see the SAS program below:

```
/* See Example 17.1 for the DATA step in creating the SAS data set 'salary' */

TITLE 'Example 17.3 How to handle a categorical predictor in regression';

PROC REG DATA=salary;
M3:  MODEL logs=service sqrtdg school / P R;

RUN; QUIT;
```

Output 17.3 How to Handle a Categorical Predictor in Regression

```
          Example 17.3 How to handle a categorical predictor in regression        1

                              The REG Procedure
                                Model: M3
                    Dependent Variable: logs log 10 of salary

                      Number of Observations Read        90
                      Number of Observations Used        90
```

Part (A)

```
                            Analysis of Variance

                                    Sum of         Mean
            Source           DF     Squares        Square    F Value    Pr > F

            Model             3     1.11786        0.37262   117.11     <.0001
            Error            86     0.27363        0.00318
            Corrected Total  89     1.39150
```

Part (B)

```
                  Root MSE               0.05641    R-Square     0.8034
                  Dependent Mean         3.22004    Adj R-Sq     0.7965
                  Coeff Var              1.75176
```

Part (C)

```
                            Parameter Estimates

                                            Parameter    Standard
   Variable   Label                   DF     Estimate      Error    t Value   Pr > |t|

   Intercept  Intercept                1     3.05444      0.01136   268.84    <.0001
   service    length of teaching in months  1  0.00072246  0.00004725  15.29  <.0001
   sqrtdg     academic degree          1     0.03965      0.00509     7.80    <.0001
   school     0=private, 1=public      1     0.03491      0.01228     2.84    0.0056
```

```
          Example 17.3 How to handle a categorical predictor in regression        2

                              The REG Procedure
                                Model: M3
                    Dependent Variable: logs log 10 of salary
```

Part (D)

```
                            Output Statistics

        Dependent Predicted   Std Error            Std Error Student                    Cook's
   Obs  Variable    Value  Mean Predict  Residual  Residual Residual   -2-1 0 1 2          D

     1   2.9913    3.0595     0.0111     -0.0682    0.0553   -1.233 |     **|      |     0.015
     2   3.0065    3.0995     0.0123     -0.0930    0.0550   -1.690 |    ***|      |     0.036
     3   3.0120    3.1024     0.0122     -0.0904    0.0551   -1.641 |    ***|      |     0.033
     4   3.0969    3.0682     0.0108      0.0287    0.0554    0.519 |       |*     |     0.003
     5   3.0120    3.0682     0.0108     -0.0562    0.0554   -1.015 |     **|      |     0.010
```
[Obs 6 to 49 are not shown]

```
          Example 17.3 How to handle a categorical predictor in regression        3

                              The REG Procedure
                                Model: M3
                    Dependent Variable: logs log 10 of salary

                            Output Statistics

        Dependent Predicted   Std Error            Std Error Student                    Cook's
   Obs  Variable    Value  Mean Predict  Residual  Residual Residual   -2-1 0 1 2          D

    50   3.2279    3.2143    0.009754     0.0136    0.0556    0.244 |       |      |     0.000
    51   3.2617    3.2151    0.009753     0.0467    0.0556    0.840 |       |*     |     0.005
    52   3.4156    3.2951     0.0103      0.1206    0.0555    2.174 |       |****  |     0.040
    53   3.2355    3.1982    0.008563     0.0373    0.0558    0.669 |       |*     |     0.003
    54   3.2355    3.2054    0.008671     0.0301    0.0557    0.540 |       |*     |     0.002
    55   3.3343    3.3989     0.0179     -0.0647    0.0535   -1.209 |     **|      |     0.041
```
[Obs 56 to 90 are not shown]

```
Part (E)
                    Sum of Residuals                           0
                    Sum of Squared Residuals             0.27363
                    Predicted Residual SS (PRESS)        0.30427
```

Based on the results of Model 3 (M3) and the recommendations given in Table 17.2, can you identify the best model among these three? My answer is Model 3, because M3 is a winner in every category it competes in.

Table 17.2 Author's Choice Among Models 1, 2, and 3

Model	F (p Level)	√MSE	Adjusted R²	t Test of Y Intercept (p Level)	t Test of Estimates (p Level)	Plot of Residuals
M1	138.16 (< 0.0001)	0.07844	0.6065	220.27 (< 0.0001)	11.75 (< 0.0001)	Slight correlation (?)
M2	158.72 (< 0.0001)	0.05866	0.7799	286.11 (< 0.0001)	14.84 (< 0.0001)- service 8.39 (< 0.0001)- sqrtdg	More random than M1; smaller residuals in general
M3	117.11 (< 0.0001)	0.05641	0.7965	268.84 (< 0.0001)	15.29 (< 0.0001)- service 7.80 (< 0.0001)- sqrtdg 2.84 (= 0.0056)- school	More random than M1; except for Case #90, residuals are generally small
Recommendation	Small p	Small	Large	Small p	Small p	Random

So the third model predicts the log of teachers' salary better than the other two. "What about the dummy variable <u>school</u>?" you may ask. Good question. The <u>school</u> variable was originally coded as 0 or 1 for private or public school, respectively. These codings were intended to differentiate between two types of schools. So the <u>school</u> coefficient is applied to either 0 or 1. What happens next? The <u>school</u> coefficient is added to the Y intercept for public school teachers (because <u>school</u> = 1) and zero is added to the Y intercept for private school teachers (because <u>school</u> = 0). As a result, there are two regression equations for predicting teachers' salary, in $\log_{10}$ scale:

For private school teachers,

$$\hat{\log s} = 3.05444 + (0.00072246) \times service + (0.03965) \times sqrtdg.$$

For public school teachers,

$$\begin{aligned}\hat{\log s} &= 3.05444 + (0.00072246) \times service + (0.03965) \times sqrtdg + (0.03491) \times 1 \\ &= 3.05444 + 0.03491 + (0.00072246) \times service + (0.03965) \times sqrtdg \\ &= 3.08935 + (0.00072246) \times service + (0.03965) \times sqrtdg.\end{aligned}$$

These two regression equations have identical regression coefficients, based on <u>service</u> and <u>sqrtdg</u>, but different Y intercepts. If, however, you suspected that private and public school teachers might not share the same regression coefficients, then you would need two regression models to explain teachers' salary.

- As a general rule, categorical variables enter into a regression equation as dummy variables. The number of dummy variables needed is always one less than the number of categories. For example, if a categorical variable, such as <u>gender,</u> has two categories, then one dummy variable with a value of 0 or 1 is needed. If a categorical variable, such as <u>ses</u>, has three categories, then you need two dummy variables. In this case, one category is represented by the combination of (0, 1) on the two dummy variables, the second by (1, 0), and the third by (0, 0), which means neither the first category nor the second. The representation of categorical variables by a set of dummy variables is called **indicator coding** or **reference cell coding**. So, do you get the drill?

  Question: If you were to code the marital status of 100 survey respondents into a regression analysis, how would you structure the data so that all five categories—single, married, separated, divorced, and not applicable—might be meaningfully represented in a regression equation? How would you interpret the regression result for people in each of these five categories?

Example 17.4 Selecting the Best Set of Predictors

Recall that the raw data file <u>salary.dat</u> contains information besides teachers' length of teaching career, the type of school he or she taught in, and his or her academic degree. How does one decide if some or all pieces of information are needed for future predictions? This is a practical and legitimate question. Fortunately, there are statistical approaches in place that can assist you in narrowing down potential models. Eight such approaches are available in the REG procedure. They are referred to as *selection methods*. Three are illustrated here: the forward, the backward, and the stepwise selection methods. These methods are specified on the MODEL statement after the slash (/). Each is distinguished by a keyword such as **FORWARD** (or **F**) for the forward method, **BACKWARD** (or **B**) for the backward method, and **STEPWISE** (or **S**) for the stepwise method. Each selection method yields a model, labeled as M4, M5, or M6. In addition, the full model (FULL) is also specified as a baseline model to be compared with M4, M5, and M6.

```
/* See Example 17.1 for the DATA step in creating the SAS data set 'salary' */

TITLE 'Example 17.4 Selecting the best set of predictors';

PROC REG DATA=salary;
M4:     MODEL logs=service sex sqrtdg school grad break / SELECTION=FORWARD;
M5:     MODEL logs=service sex sqrtdg school grad break / SELECTION=BACKWARD;
M6:     MODEL logs=service sex sqrtdg school grad break / SELECTION=STEPWISE;
FULL:   MODEL logs=service sex sqrtdg school grad break;

RUN; QUIT;
```

Output 17.4 Selecting the Best Set of Predictors

```
                    Example 17.4 Selecting the best set of predictors              1
 Part (A)
                                  The REG Procedure
                                     Model: M4
                         Dependent Variable: logs log 10 of salary

                          Number of Observations Read        90
                          Number of Observations Used        90

                             Forward Selection: Step 1

          Variable service Entered: R-Square = 0.6109 and C(p) = 82.7816

                                Analysis of Variance

                                      Sum of          Mean
         Source               DF      Squares        Square     F Value    Pr > F

         Model                 1      0.85007       0.85007      138.16     <.0001
         Error                88      0.54143       0.00615
         Corrected Total      89      1.39150

                           Parameter    Standard
              Variable     Estimate       Error    Type II SS  F Value  Pr > F

              Intercept     3.08703      0.01401    298.52183   48519.5  <.0001
              service       0.00076796   0.00006533   0.85007    138.16  <.0001

                         Bounds on condition number: 1, 1
---------------------------------------------------------------------------------
                             Forward Selection: Step 2

          Variable sqrtdg Entered: R-Square = 0.7849 and C(p) = 9.3113
```

```
                                Analysis of Variance

                                   Sum of            Mean
      Source              DF       Squares          Square    F Value    Pr > F

      Model                2       1.09217         0.54608     158.72    <.0001
      Error               87       0.29933         0.00344
      Corrected Total     89       1.39150

                       Parameter     Standard
          Variable      Estimate       Error    Type II SS  F Value  Pr > F

          Intercept     3.06800       0.01072   281.65008   81861.0  <.0001
          service       0.00072858    0.00004908   0.75813    220.35  <.0001
          sqrtdg        0.04309       0.00514     0.24210     70.37  <.0001

               Bounds on condition number: 1.0092, 4.0369
--------------------------------------------------------------------------------
                          Forward Selection: Step 3

        Variable school Entered: R-Square = 0.8034 and C(p) = 3.3008

                                Analysis of Variance

                                   Sum of            Mean
      Source              DF       Squares          Square    F Value    Pr > F

      Model                3       1.11786         0.37262     117.11    <.0001
      Error               86       0.27363         0.00318
      Corrected Total     89       1.39150

                       Parameter     Standard
          Variable      Estimate       Error    Type II SS  F Value  Pr > F

          Intercept     3.05444       0.01136   229.96708   72275.9  <.0001
          service       0.00072246    0.00004725   0.74391    233.80  <.0001
          sqrtdg        0.03965       0.00509     0.19337     60.77  <.0001
          school        0.03491       0.01228     0.02570      8.08  0.0056

               Bounds on condition number: 1.0698, 9.4381
--------------------------------------------------------------------------------
                          Forward Selection: Step 4

        Variable sex Entered: R-Square = 0.8062 and C(p) = 4.0657

                                Analysis of Variance

                                   Sum of            Mean
      Source              DF       Squares          Square    F Value    Pr > F

      Model                4       1.12183         0.28046      88.40    <.0001
      Error               85       0.26967         0.00317
      Corrected Total     89       1.39150

                       Parameter     Standard
          Variable      Estimate       Error    Type II SS  F Value  Pr > F

          Intercept     3.05023       0.01195   206.54353   65102.0  <.0001
          service       0.00073118    0.00004782   0.74169    233.78  <.0001
          sex           0.01507       0.01348     0.00396      1.25  0.2669
          sqrtdg        0.03930       0.00509     0.18922     59.64  <.0001
          school        0.02979       0.01309     0.01643      5.18  0.0254

               Bounds on condition number: 1.2131, 18.03
--------------------------------------------------------------------------------
                          Forward Selection: Step 5

        Variable grad Entered: R-Square = 0.8082 and C(p) = 5.1894
```

```
                          Analysis of Variance

                             Sum of          Mean
          Source          DF  Squares        Square   F Value   Pr > F

          Model            5   1.12464       0.22493   70.80    <.0001
          Error           84   0.26686       0.00318
          Corrected Total 89   1.39150

                      Parameter    Standard
           Variable    Estimate      Error   Type II SS  F Value  Pr > F

           Intercept    3.05182     0.01208   202.69487  63802.3  <.0001
           service      0.00072763  0.00004800   0.72996   229.77  <.0001
           sex          0.01459     0.01350     0.00371     1.17   0.2828
           sqrtdg       0.04536     0.00821     0.09691    30.50   <.0001
           school       0.03087     0.01315     0.01751     5.51   0.0212
           grad        -0.02233     0.02374     0.00281     0.88   0.3496

          Bounds on condition number: 2.7937, 45.023
---------------------------------------------------------------------------
   No other variable met the 0.5000 significance level for entry into the model.

                      Summary of Forward Selection

          Variable                        Number  Partial  Model
   Step Entered  Label                    Vars In R-Square R-Square  C(p)    F Value

     1  service  length of teaching in months   1   0.6109   0.6109  82.7816  138.16
     2  sqrtdg   academic degree                2   0.1740   0.7849   9.3113   70.37
     3  school   0=private, 1=public            3   0.0185   0.8034   3.3008    8.08
     4  sex      1=M, 2=F                       4   0.0028   0.8062   4.0657    1.25
     5  grad     1=trained grad, 0=others       5   0.0020   0.8082   5.1894    0.88

                      Summary of Forward Selection

                        Step Pr > F

                          1  <.0001
                          2  <.0001
                          3  0.0056
                          4  0.2669
                          5  0.3496
```

```
                  Example 17.4 Selecting the best set of predictors       2
Part (B)
                           The REG Procedure
                             Model: M5
                  Dependent Variable: logs log 10 of salary

                  Number of Observations Read          90
                  Number of Observations Used          90

                      Backward Elimination: Step 0

          All Variables Entered: R-Square = 0.8087 and C(p) = 7.0000

                        Analysis of Variance

                             Sum of          Mean
          Source          DF  Squares        Square   F Value   Pr > F

          Model            6   1.12524       0.18754   58.46    <.0001
          Error           83   0.26625       0.00321
          Corrected Total 89   1.39150
```

Variable	Parameter Estimate	Standard Error	Type II SS	F Value	Pr > F
Intercept	3.05093	0.01231	196.90948	61383.1	<.0001
service	0.00072395	0.00004897	0.70113	218.57	<.0001
sex	0.01554	0.01374	0.00411	1.28	0.2612
sqrtdg	0.04504	0.00828	0.09484	29.56	<.0001
school	0.03077	0.01322	0.01739	5.42	0.0223
grad	-0.02293	0.02390	0.00295	0.92	0.3400
break	0.00640	0.01470	0.00060750	0.19	0.6646

Bounds on condition number: 2.8151, 61.312

Backward Elimination: Step 1

Variable break Removed: R-Square = 0.8082 and C(p) = 5.1894

Analysis of Variance

Source	DF	Sum of Squares	Mean Square	F Value	Pr > F
Model	5	1.12464	0.22493	70.80	<.0001
Error	84	0.26686	0.00318		
Corrected Total	89	1.39150			

Variable	Parameter Estimate	Standard Error	Type II SS	F Value	Pr > F
Intercept	3.05182	0.01208	202.69487	63802.3	<.0001
service	0.00072763	0.00004800	0.72996	229.77	<.0001
sex	0.01459	0.01350	0.00371	1.17	0.2828
sqrtdg	0.04536	0.00821	0.09691	30.50	<.0001
school	0.03087	0.01315	0.01751	5.51	0.0212
grad	-0.02233	0.02374	0.00281	0.88	0.3496

Bounds on condition number: 2.7937, 45.023

Backward Elimination: Step 2

Variable grad Removed: R-Square = 0.8062 and C(p) = 4.0657

Analysis of Variance

Source	DF	Sum of Squares	Mean Square	F Value	Pr > F
Model	4	1.12183	0.28046	88.40	<.0001
Error	85	0.26967	0.00317		
Corrected Total	89	1.39150			

Variable	Parameter Estimate	Standard Error	Type II SS	F Value	Pr > F
Intercept	3.05023	0.01195	206.54353	65102.0	<.0001
service	0.00073118	0.00004782	0.74169	233.78	<.0001
sex	0.01507	0.01348	0.00396	1.25	0.2669
sqrtdg	0.03930	0.00509	0.18922	59.64	<.0001
school	0.02979	0.01309	0.01643	5.18	0.0254

Bounds on condition number: 1.2131, 18.03

Backward Elimination: Step 3

Variable sex Removed: R-Square = 0.8034 and C(p) = 3.3008

Analysis of Variance

Source	DF	Sum of Squares	Mean Square	F Value	Pr > F
Model	3	1.11786	0.37262	117.11	<.0001
Error	86	0.27363	0.00318		
Corrected Total	89	1.39150			

```
                    Parameter     Standard
         Variable   Estimate        Error    Type II SS  F Value  Pr > F

         Intercept    3.05444      0.01136    229.96708   72275.9  <.0001
         service      0.00072246   0.00004725   0.74391    233.80  <.0001
         sqrtdg       0.03965      0.00509      0.19337     60.77  <.0001
         school       0.03491      0.01228      0.02570      8.08  0.0056

             Bounds on condition number: 1.0698, 9.4381
---------------------------------------------------------------------------------
         All variables left in the model are significant at the 0.1000 level.

                    Summary of Backward Elimination

         Variable                          Number Partial   Model
Step  Removed   Label                      Vars In R-Square R-Square  C(p)   F Value

 1    break    1=break 2 yrs, 0=others        5    0.0004   0.8082   5.1894   0.19
 2    grad     1=trained grad, 0=others       4    0.0020   0.8062   4.0657   0.88
 3    sex      1=M, 2=F                        3    0.0028   0.8034   3.3008   1.25

                    Summary of Backward Elimination

                        Step Pr > F

                          1  0.6646
                          2  0.3496
                          3  0.2669
```

```
              Example 17.4 Selecting the best set of predictors            3
Part (C)
                          The REG Procedure
                            Model: M6
               Dependent Variable: logs log 10 of salary

                  Number of Observations Read        90
                  Number of Observations Used        90

                      Stepwise Selection: Step 1

        Variable service Entered: R-Square = 0.6109 and C(p) = 82.7816

                       Analysis of Variance

                               Sum of        Mean
     Source            DF      Squares      Square    F Value   Pr > F

     Model              1      0.85007      0.85007    138.16   <.0001
     Error             88      0.54143      0.00615
     Corrected Total   89      1.39150

                    Parameter     Standard
         Variable   Estimate        Error    Type II SS  F Value  Pr > F

         Intercept    3.08703      0.01401    298.52103   48519.5  <.0001
         service      0.00076796   0.00006533   0.85007    138.16  <.0001

              Bounds on condition number: 1, 1
---------------------------------------------------------------------------------
                      Stepwise Selection: Step 2

        Variable sqrtdg Entered: R-Square = 0.7849 and C(p) = 9.3113

                       Analysis of Variance

                               Sum of        Mean
     Source            DF      Squares      Square    F Value   Pr > F

     Model              2      1.09217      0.54608    158.72   <.0001
     Error             87      0.29933      0.00344
     Corrected Total   89      1.39150
```

Variable	Parameter Estimate	Standard Error	Type II SS	F Value	Pr > F
Intercept	3.06800	0.01072	281.65008	81861.0	<.0001
service	0.00072858	0.00004908	0.75813	220.35	<.0001
sqrtdg	0.04309	0.00514	0.24210	70.37	<.0001

Bounds on condition number: 1.0092, 4.0369

Stepwise Selection: Step 3

Variable school Entered: R-Square = 0.8034 and C(p) = 3.3008

Analysis of Variance

Source	DF	Sum of Squares	Mean Square	F Value	Pr > F
Model	3	1.11786	0.37262	117.11	<.0001
Error	86	0.27363	0.00318		
Corrected Total	89	1.39150			

Variable	Parameter Estimate	Standard Error	Type II SS	F Value	Pr > F
Intercept	3.05444	0.01136	229.96708	72275.9	<.0001
service	0.00072246	0.00004725	0.74391	233.80	<.0001
sqrtdg	0.03965	0.00509	0.19337	60.77	<.0001
school	0.03491	0.01228	0.02570	8.08	0.0056

Bounds on condition number: 1.0698, 9.4381

All variables left in the model are significant at the 0.1500 level.

No other variable met the 0.1500 significance level for entry into the model.

Summary of Stepwise Selection

Step	Variable Entered	Variable Removed	Label	Number Vars In	Partial R-Square	Model R-Square	C(p)
1	service		length of teaching in months	1	0.6109	0.6109	82.7816
2	sqrtdg		academic degree	2	0.1740	0.7849	9.3113
3	school		0=private, 1=public	3	0.0185	0.8034	3.3008

Summary of Stepwise Selection

Step	F Value	Pr > F
1	138.16	<.0001
2	70.37	<.0001
3	8.08	0.0056

Example 17.4 Selecting the best set of predictors   4

Part (D)

The REG Procedure
Model: FULL
Dependent Variable: logs log 10 of salary

Number of Observations Read   90
Number of Observations Used   90

Analysis of Variance

Source	DF	Sum of Squares	Mean Square	F Value	Pr > F
Model	6	1.12524	0.18754	58.46	<.0001
Error	83	0.26625	0.00321		
Corrected Total	89	1.39150			

				Parameter	Standard		
	Root MSE		0.05664	R-Square	0.8087		
	Dependent Mean		3.22004	Adj R-Sq	0.7948		
	Coeff Var		1.75893				

Parameter Estimates

Variable	Label	DF	Parameter Estimate	Standard Error	t Value	Pr > |t|
Intercept	Intercept	1	3.05093	0.01231	247.76	<.0001
service	length of teaching in months	1	0.00072395	0.00004897	14.78	<.0001
sex	1=M, 2=F	1	0.01554	0.01374	1.13	0.2612
sqrtdg	academic degree	1	0.04504	0.00828	5.44	<.0001
school	0=private, 1=public	1	0.03077	0.01322	2.33	0.0223
grad	1=trained grad, 0=others	1	-0.02293	0.02390	-0.96	0.3400
break	1=break 2 yrs, 0=others	1	0.00640	0.01470	0.44	0.6646

The output is divided into four parts, (A) through (D), each corresponding to one selection method's result or the full model's. **Part (A)** contains results from the forward selection method. The forward method selects the most statistically significant predictor (service), that is, the one correlated most highly with the outcome, at the first step. At the second step, sqrtdg is chosen because it yields the highest partial correlation with the outcome, after the first predictor is partialled out. This process continues until no more predictors meet the 0.50 significance level for the partial F statistic. After five steps, the forward selection procedure stopped because of this default criterion for termination. And the regression equation constructed by the forward method consists of five predictors:

Model 4

$$\hat{logs} = 3.05182 + (0.00072763) \times service + (0.01459) \times sex +$$
$$(0.04536) \times sqrtdg + (0.03087) \times school + (-0.02233) \times grad$$

For the sex, school, and grad categorical variables, you should know by now how to substitute simple codings into the equation so that a regression model may be obtained for, say, male teachers who taught in private schools with some graduate training (sex = 1, school = 0, and grad = 1).

Part (B) is the result of the backward selection method that successively removes insignificant predictors from the full model, one at each step. Insignificant predictors are those predictors that, when entered into the regression equation last, would not substantially improve the fit of the model to data. Consequently, they are removed from the model. According to the output, the backward method eliminates three predictors because they did not meet the default significance level of 0.10 for staying in the model. The final model constructed from the backward method is identical to M3 from Output 17.3. Therefore, it is not repeated here.

The stepwise method works like a forward selection method with a backward look. The algorithm constructs the model by adding statistically significant predictors into the equation, one at a time, much like the forward method. Yet at each step after adding a predictor, the stepwise method also examines those predictors already in the model to see if any of those need to be removed, using the rationale of the backward method. So the stepwise method combines the best of both worlds, so to speak. There is one thing you must keep in mind, namely, that the default significance level for selecting and for removing a predictor from the model is 0.15 by the stepwise method. This significance level is different from that set by the forward method (0.50) or by the backward method (0.10).

According to **Part (C)** of the output, the stepwise method decides on the same model as the backward method or M3 from Output 17.3, so it won't be repeated here. Finally, the full model that includes all predictors appears in **Part (D)**. It is made up of these ingredients:

Full Model

$$\hat{\log}s = (3.05093) + (0.00072395) \times service + (0.01554) \times sex + (0.04504) \times sqrtdg + (0.03077) \times school + (-0.02293) \times grad + (0.0064) \times break$$

Categorical variables such as sex, school, grad, and break should be replaced by their respective dummy codings for specific cases, such as female teachers (sex = 0) from public schools (school = 1) with a break in their teaching career (break = 1) and with graduate training (grad = 1).

So, "which model is the most sensible and by what criteria?", you may ask. This is a good question. To begin building a case for the best model, one needs to compile information into a table similar to Table 17.2. This table should include criteria such as an F test of the overall model, the square root of MSE, adjusted R^2, a t test (or F test) of each regression coefficient, and, additionally, three blank columns. The blank columns will be completed with information on residuals from Example 17.5. The models under comparison are M3 (identical to M5 and M6), M4, and the full model; they are identified as three rows in the table.

Using the guidelines given in Tables 17.1 and 17.2, you may, at this moment, pick one or two models as contenders for the best model. Once residuals from each model are examined for their statistical assumptions in Example 17.5, you will be able to complete this comparison table and defend your choice of the best model with confidence.

Example 17.5 Are Residuals Acceptable?
Checking Their Statistical Assumptions

Until now, the emphasis of regression analysis has been on what a regression model is, how to obtain the estimates for regression coefficients, and how to interpret statistical results. What is absent in these discussions are assumptions required by t and F tests. In fact, there are four; all four are concerned with residuals:

1. Residuals are statistically independent.

2. Residuals are equally variable along the predictor's scale.

3. Residuals are normally distributed.

4. Residuals' average is zero.

If a regression model is correct, the residuals should exhibit tendencies to confirm these assumptions, or at least, they should not deny any of the assumptions.

Of these four assumptions, the last, that is, zero mean for residuals, is guaranteed by the least-squares estimation of regression coefficients. Because this method has been programmed into the REG procedure as its default for estimating coefficients, there is no need to worry about this assumption. The remaining three need to be verified, though. In Examples 17.5a through 17.5c, SAS programs and output are shown to help determine if assumptions (a) through (c) are met for M3 (based on the backward and the stepwise methods), M4 (based on the forward method), and the full model.

To verify the independence assumption among residuals, Example 17.5a below specifies the option **DWPROB** on the MODEL statement after the slash (/). This option requests the calculation of the Durbin-Watson statistic (D) and the p values associated with the test of D. The D statistic provides a way to examine if residuals are serially correlated or related to adjacent values in a systematic way. The first-order autocorrelation among residuals is also computed by this option.

Example 17.5a Are Residuals Acceptable?
Checking the Independence Assumption

```
/* See Example 17.1 for the DATA step in creating the SAS data set 'salary' */

TITLE 'Example 17.5a Checking the independence assumption';

PROC REG DATA=salary;
M3:     MODEL logs=service sqrtdg school / DWPROB;
M4:     MODEL logs=service sex sqrtdg school grad / DWPROB;
FULL:   MODEL logs=service sex sqrtdg school grad break / DWPROB;

RUN; QUIT;
```

Output 17.5a Are Residuals Acceptable?
Checking the Independence Assumption

```
[Page 1 output is not shown]
                    Example 17.5a Checking the independence assumption              2

                               The REG Procedure
                                  Model: M3
                     Dependent Variable: logs log 10 of salary

                     Durbin-Watson D                     0.812
                     Pr < DW                             <.0001
                     Pr > DW                             1.0000
                     Number of Observations                 90
                     1st Order Autocorrelation           0.534

NOTE: Pr<DW is the p-value for testing positive autocorrelation, and Pr>DW is the p-value for
      testing negative autocorrelation.
```

```
[Page 3 output is not shown]
                    Example 17.5a Checking the independence assumption              4

                               The REG Procedure
                                  Model: M4
                     Dependent Variable: logs log 10 of salary

                     Durbin-Watson D                     0.847
                     Pr < DW                             <.0001
                     Pr > DW                             1.0000
                     Number of Observations                 90
                     1st Order Autocorrelation           0.522

NOTE: Pr<DW is the p-value for testing positive autocorrelation, and Pr>DW is the p-value for
      testing negative autocorrelation.
```

```
[Page 5 output is not shown]
                    Example 17.5a Checking the independence assumption              6

                               The REG Procedure
                                  Model: FULL
                     Dependent Variable: logs log 10 of salary

                     Durbin-Watson D                     0.880
                     Pr < DW                             <.0001
                     Pr > DW                             1.0000
                     Number of Observations                 90
                     1st Order Autocorrelation           0.508

NOTE: Pr<DW is the p-value for testing positive autocorrelation, and Pr>DW is the p-value for
      testing negative autocorrelation.
```

The null hypothesis tested by the Durbin-Watson statistic states that there is no serial correlation among residuals. The alternative hypothesis states that not only does there exist a serial correlation, but that it is of the form $\rho_s = \rho^s$, where s is the number of steps between residuals.

According to the output, three D statistics are similar: 0.812, 0.847, and 0.880. These values correspond to a positive serial correlation of 0.534, 0.522, and 0.508, respectively. How do you know if these correlations are significantly different from zero? The output for each model includes two p values (Pr < DW and Pr > DW) indicating the statistical significance of the D statistic. The **Pr < DW** is the p value associated with the Durbin-Watson test of a positive serial correlation, whereas the **Pr > DW** is the p value associated with testing a negative serial correlation. Because all three p values under Pr < DW are less than 0.0001, their corresponding Ds are statistically significant at the 0.05 significance level. This is bad news because they suggest that none of these models meet the independence assumption.

Next, let's examine the equal variance assumption among residuals. This assumption is often referred to as the homoscedasticity assumption. But who needs this BIG word, if it simply means "equal variance"? To verify the equal variance assumption, one can plot residuals against $\hat{y}$ values, that is, the predicted $\log_{10}$ of salaries for 90 teachers. The statement for this plot is **PLOT R.*P.;** following the **MODEL** statement. The term **R.** stands for residuals and it is formed from the keyword **R** and a period (.). Likewise, the term **P.** stands for predicted values and it is formed from **P** and a period (.).

Example 17.5b Are Residuals Acceptable?
Checking the Equal Variance Assumption

```
/* See Example 17.1 for the DATA step in creating the SAS data set 'salary' */

TITLE 'Example 17.5b Checking the equal variance assumption';

GOPTIONS FTEXT=swissb HTEXT=2 FTITLE=swiss HTITLE=3;

SYMBOL1 V=dot CV=black HEIGHT=1;

PROC REG DATA=salary NOPRINT;
M3:      MODEL logs=service sqrtdg school; PLOT R.*P.;
M4:      MODEL logs=service sex sqrtdg school grad; PLOT R.*P.;
FULL:    MODEL logs=service sex sqrtdg school grad break; PLOT R.*P.;

RUN; QUIT;
```

Output 17.5b Are Residuals Acceptable?
Checking the Equal Variance Assumption

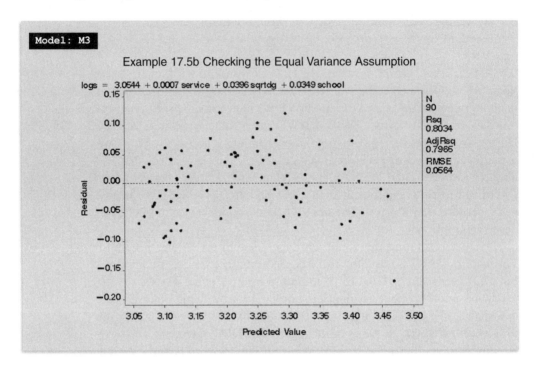

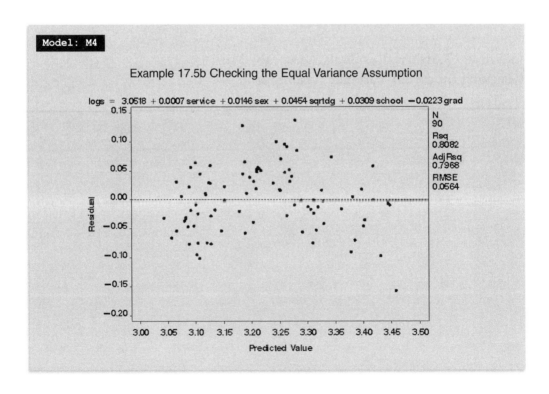

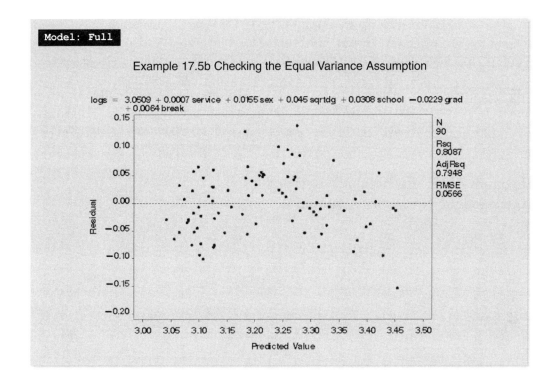

These three plots do not show a violation of the equal variance assumption because the spread of residuals is even over the range of the predicted logs. This profile supports the equal variance assumption. In practice, the plot of residuals needs to be drawn against each continuous predictor using a statement similar to **PLOT R.*SERVICE;**. If the equal variance assumption is upheld, the residual plot displays a horizontal band around zero as in the picture below:

In the next example, the third assumption, that of normality, is tested. To carry out this test, the UNIVARIATE procedure is invoked. Data needed by PROC UNIVARIATE are residuals. So an output data set containing residuals is created by the statement OUTPUT OUT=*sas_dataset_name*, one for each model fitted. Thus, three sets of residuals are formed. Each data set could have been analyzed separately by the UNIVARIATE procedure. Instead, they are merged into one SAS data set called <u>combine</u>. The <u>combine</u> data set is subsequently submitted to the UNIVARIATE procedure for a **NORMAL** test of three sets of residuals. The three sets are named "r_m3", "r_m4", and "r_full", corresponding to the regression models that produced each data set.

Example 17.5c Are Residuals Acceptable?
Checking the Normality Assumption

```
/* See Example 17.1 for the DATA step in creating the SAS data set 'salary' */

TITLE 'Example 17.5c Checking the normality assumption';

PROC REG DATA=salary;
M3:     MODEL logs=service sqrtdg school; OUTPUT OUT=m3 R=r_m3;
M4:     MODEL logs=service sex sqrtdg school grad; OUTPUT OUT=m4 R=r_m4;
FULL:   MODEL logs=service sex sqrtdg school grad break; OUTPUT OUT=full R=r_full;

RUN;

DATA combine; MERGE m3 m4 full; RUN;

PROC UNIVARIATE DATA=combine NORMAL;
    VAR r_m3 r_m4 r_full;
RUN;
```

Output 17.5c Are Residuals Acceptable?
Checking the Normality Assumption

```
[Pages 1-3 are not shown. NS stands for nonsignificant—a commentary inserted by the author.]
                    Example 17.5c Checking the normality assumption                    4

                            The UNIVARIATE Procedure
 Part (A)                    Variable:  r_m3  (Residual)

                                    Moments

        N                         90    Sum Weights              90
        Mean                       0    Sum Observations          0
        Std Deviation     0.05544857    Variance         0.00307454
        Skewness          -0.1253695    Kurtosis         -0.0562824
        Uncorrected SS    0.27363436    Corrected SS     0.27363436
        Coeff Variation            .    Std Error Mean   0.00584479

                        Basic Statistical Measures

              Location                       Variability

         Mean      0.00000     Std Deviation        0.05545
         Median   -0.00249     Variance             0.00307
         Mode     -0.05618     Range                0.29034
                               Interquartile Range  0.08092

     NOTE: The mode displayed is the smallest of 3 modes with a count of 2.
```

```
                    Tests for Location: Mu0=0

        Test              -Statistic-      -----p Value------

        Student's t       t          0    Pr > |t|    1.0000
        Sign              M         -1    Pr >= |M|   0.9161
        Signed Rank       S       13.5    Pr >= |S|   0.9570

                        Tests for Normality

    Test                  --Statistic---    -----p Value------

    Shapiro-Wilk          W    0.991959    Pr < W      0.8636 -- NS
    Kolmogorov-Smirnov    D    0.050192    Pr > D      >0.1500
    Cramer-von Mises      W-Sq 0.023025    Pr > W-Sq   >0.2500
    Anderson-Darling      A-Sq 0.165845    Pr > A-Sq   >0.2500


                    Quantiles (Definition 5)

                    Quantile          Estimate

                    100% Max         0.12240580
                    99%              0.12240580
                    95%              0.09410394
                    90%              0.07037253
                    75% Q3           0.04199411
                    50% Median      -0.00248533
                    25% Q1          -0.03892587
                    10%             -0.06908615
                    5%              -0.09036058
                    1%              -0.16793086
                    0% Min          -0.16793086


                      Extreme Observations

        -------Lowest------        ------Highest------

            Value      Obs            Value      Obs

        -0.1679309      90        0.0941039      67
        -0.1011081       7        0.0946564      60
        -0.0944196      86        0.1048016      61
        -0.0929978       2        0.1205636      52
        -0.0903606       3        0.1224058      43
```

```
                Example 17.5c Checking the normality assumption        5
Part (B)
                    The UNIVARIATE Procedure
                      Variable:  r_m4   (Residual)

                              Moments

    N                       90    Sum Weights               90
    Mean                     0    Sum Observations           0
    Std Deviation     0.05475802  Variance          0.00299844
    Skewness           -0.018214  Kurtosis          0.02367164
    Uncorrected SS    0.26686126  Corrected SS      0.26686126
    Coeff Variation          .    Std Error Mean     0.005772

                    Basic Statistical Measures

            Location                    Variability

        Mean      0.00000    Std Deviation          0.05476
        Median   -0.00063    Variance               0.00300
        Mode     -0.01850    Range                  0.29402
                             Interquartile Range    0.07722
```

```
                    Tests for Location: Mu0=0

          Test              -Statistic-      -----p Value------

          Student's t    t           0    Pr > |t|    1.0000
          Sign           M          -2    Pr >= |M|   0.7520
          Signed Rank    S       -10.5    Pr >= |S|   0.9666

                      Tests for Normality

        Test                  --Statistic---     -----p Value------

        Shapiro-Wilk          W   0.995338   Pr < W      0.9892 -- NS
        Kolmogorov-Smirnov    D   0.038211   Pr > D      >0.1500
        Cramer-von Mises      W-Sq 0.014922  Pr > W-Sq   >0.2500
        Anderson-Darling      A-Sq 0.124622  Pr > A-Sq   >0.2500

                      Quantiles (Definition 5)

                    Quantile            Estimate

                    100% Max         0.13722822
                    99%              0.13722822
                    95%              0.09174385
                    90%              0.06480800
                    75% Q3           0.04072022
                    50% Median      -0.00063334
                    25% Q1          -0.03650423
                    10%             -0.07418473
                    5%              -0.08986466
                    1%              -0.15679371
                    0% Min          -0.15679371

                      Extreme Observations

          -------Lowest------        ------Highest------

              Value      Obs            Value      Obs

          -0.1567937      90         0.0917438      45
          -0.1010108       2         0.0957088      61
          -0.0965387      55         0.1001619      60
          -0.0945951       7         0.1283401      43
          -0.0898647      86         0.1372282      52
```

                    Example 17.5c Checking the normality assumption   6

Part (C)

```
                        The UNIVARIATE Procedure
                       Variable:  r_full  (Residual)

                               Moments

        N                         90    Sum Weights              90
        Mean                       0    Sum Observations          0
        Std Deviation     0.05469566    Variance         0.00299162
        Skewness          0.02333333    Kurtosis         0.01795592
        Uncorrected SS    0.26625376    Corrected SS     0.26625376
        Coeff Variation            .    Std Error Mean   0.00576543

                      Basic Statistical Measures

             Location                        Variability

        Mean       0.00000    Std Deviation          0.05470
        Median    -0.00281    Variance               0.00299
        Mode      -0.01740    Range                  0.29306
                              Interquartile Range    0.07977

                    Tests for Location: Mu0=0

          Test              -Statistic-      -----p Value------

          Student's t    t           0    Pr > |t|    1.0000
          Sign           M           0    Pr >= |M|   1.0000
          Signed Rank    S        -3.5    Pr >= |S|   0.9889
```

```
                        Tests for Normality

        Test                    --Statistic---      -----p Value------

        Shapiro-Wilk            W     0.995663       Pr < W      0.9930  --  NS
        Kolmogorov-Smirnov      D     0.04737        Pr > D      >0.1500
        Cramer-von Mises        W-Sq  0.016939       Pr > W-Sq   >0.2500
        Anderson-Darling        A-Sq  0.127885       Pr > A-Sq   >0.2500

                        Quantiles (Definition 5)

                        Quantile           Estimate

                        100% Max           0.1400970
                        99%                0.1400970
                        95%                0.0881371
                        90%                0.0656564
                        75% Q3             0.0426714
                        50% Median        -0.0028122
                        25% Q1            -0.0370951
                        10%              -0.0742876
                        5%               -0.0873771
                        1%               -0.1529629
                        0% Min           -0.1529629


                        Extreme Observations

        -------Lowest------            ------Highest------

            Value        Obs              Value        Obs

        -0.1529629        90           0.0881371        45
        -0.1009151         2           0.0965723        61
        -0.0944685        55           0.1019735        60
        -0.0934999         7           0.1298468        43
        -0.0873771        86           0.1400970        52
```

Based on the test of the null hypothesis of normally distributed residuals, the probability of obtaining the Shapiro-Wilk's W statistic is high. This means that it is likely that residuals are normally distributed for the three models. Thus, it is concluded that the normality assumption is not violated by M3, M4, or the full model.

Now, the examination of all statistical assumptions is completed. Let's summarize findings in the following table that you were asked to prepare prior to Example 17.5.

Based on the information disclosed in Table 17.3, I'd say the full model is an overkill. Compared with M3 or M4, the full model includes a large number of predictors for little gain in the overall fit of the model. Between M3 and M4, M3 is simpler and its three predictors in the model are statistically significant contributors to the prediction of $\log_{10}$ of salary. Furthermore, M3 is comparable to M4 in terms of the square root of MSE, the adjusted R^2, the overall fit of model to data, and the extent of satisfying statistical assumptions. Thus, it is concluded that M3 is the best model. According to M3, there was no differential between male and female teachers' salaries, expressed on the $\log_{10}$ scale, in Great Britain during that era. Rather, the differentials seem to have stemmed primarily from the private versus the public schools—a finding also confirmed by Turnbull and Williams (1974).

There is only one problem with M3: Its residuals are serially correlated. To correct this problem, additional predictors, such as service squared, the

Table 17.3 Comparison of Models 3, 4, and the Full Model

Model	F (p Level)	$\sqrt{MSE}$	Adjusted R^2	t Test of Y Intercept (p Level)	t Test of Estimates (p Level)	Plot of Residuals	F (p Level)	Normality W (p Level)
M3 (= backward = stepwise)	117.11 (< 0.0001)	0.05641	0.7965	268.84 (< 0.0001)	15.29 (< .0001)-service 7.80 (< 0.0001)-sqrtdg 2.84 (< 0.0001)-school	0.812 (< 0.0001, 0.534) Not OK	OK	0.992 (0.8636)
M4 (= forward)	70.80 (< 0.0001)	0.05639	0.7968	252.59 (< 0.0001)	15.16 (< 0.0001)-service 1.108 (= 0.2628)-sex 5.52 (< 0.0001)-sqrtdg 2.35 (= 0.0201)-school −0.94 (= 0.3496)-grad	0.847 (< 0.0001, 0.522) Not OK	OK	0.995 (0.9892)
Full	58.46 (< 0.0001)	0.05664	0.7948	247.76 (< 0.0001)	14.78 (< 0.0001)-service 1.13 (= 0.2612)-sex 5.44 (< 0.0001)-sqrtdg 2.33 (= 0.0223)-school −0.96 (= 0.3400)-grad 0.44 (= 0.6646)-break	0.880 (< 0.0001, 0.508) Not OK	OK	0.996 (0.9930)
Recommendation	Small p	Small	Large	Small p	Small p	Close to 2 or NS (p small in absolute value)	Horizontal band around 0, random	Large p

log transformation of <u>service</u>, and so on, are needed. You are encouraged to try your hand at finding a still better model!

Example 17.6 Using a Correlation Matrix as Input

This example illustrates how the REG procedure can work with a correlation matrix as well as a raw data matrix. In the SAS program, the raw data file <u>salary.dat</u> is first submitted to the CORR procedure to obtain a Pearson correlation coefficient matrix. This matrix is not printed by the CORR procedure; rather, it becomes the input for the next procedure, REG. Because the Pearson correlation is suitable for continuous variables, it is computed for the variables <u>logs</u>, <u>service</u>, and <u>sqrtdg</u> only. Accordingly, the MODEL statement in the REG procedure specifies only <u>service</u> and <u>sqrtdg</u> as predictors. This model is identical to M2 illustrated in Example 17.2. Because of the absence of individualized information in a correlation matrix, options such as **P**, **R**, and **DWPROB** are no longer applicable.

```
/* See Example 17.1 for the DATA step in creating the SAS data set 'salary' */

PROC CORR DATA=salary OUTP=corr NOPRINT;
     VAR logs service sqrtdg;
RUN;

TITLE 'Example 17.6 Using a correlation matrix as input';

PROC REG DATA=corr;
corr:    MODEL logs=service sqrtdg;

RUN; QUIT;
```

Output 17.6 Using a Correlation Matrix as Input

```
              Example 17.6 Using a correlation matrix as input                1
                          The REG Procedure
                            Model: corr
                  Dependent Variable: logs log 10 of salary

                          Analysis of Variance

                           Sum of        Mean
Source                DF    Squares      Square     F Value    Pr > F

Model                  2    1.09217     0.54608      158.72     <.0001
Error                 87    0.29933     0.00344
Corrected Total       89    1.39150

            Root MSE            0.05866    R-Square     0.7849
            Dependent Mean      3.22004    Adj R-Sq     0.7799
            Coeff Var           1.82161
```

```
                          Parameter Estimates

                                    Parameter      Standard
     Variable   Label               DF    Estimate        Error   t Value   Pr > |t|

     Intercept  Intercept            1    3.06800      0.01072    286.11    <.0001
     service    length of teaching in months  1  0.00072858  0.00004908   14.84    <.0001
     sqrtdg     academic degree      1    0.04309      0.00514      8.39    <.0001
```

The results show an overall significant fit of the model to the data ($F = 158.72$, $p < 0.0001$). The adjusted R^2 is similar to those based on M3 and M4 models from Example 17.5. The t tests of each regression coefficient as well as of the Y intercept are all significant at $p < 0.0001$, and the results are identical to those obtained in Output 17.2.

Many data sets are correlational in nature and are in the form of a correlation matrix. Therefore, it is helpful for the REG procedure to accept a correlation matrix as input data. A correlation matrix is recognized by SAS as a TYPE=CORR data set. Using correlation matrices as input has another advantage: it saves time. Processing time can be an important consideration when data comprise more than a thousand observations with a hundred or more variables.

There are limitations with using a TYPE=CORR data set as input, though. The first limitation is that a number of REG statements are no longer applicable if there are no individual-based data. For example, the PLOT statement cannot be specified without individual residuals or $\hat{y}$ values. Other statements such as FREQ, WEIGHT, REWEIGHT, PAINT, and ID are likewise rendered useless without individual data.

The second limitation is related to the first in that you will not be able to interpret regression results at the individual level. Hence, the P, R, CLM, CLI, DWPROB, INFLUENCE, and PARTIAL options are invalid with the TYPE=CORR data set. Without individual observations, these options cannot be specified on the MODEL statement and, hence, cannot appear in an output data set specified by the OUTPUT OUT= statement.

If a correlation matrix is created in the DATA step, rather than being produced by the CORR procedure, make sure you identify it as a TYPE=CORR data set. An illustration of a TYPE=CORR data set is found in Example 16.3 of Chapter 16.

17.4 How to Write the PROC REG Codes

From the examples presented earlier, you may have mastered several fundamental REG statements already. This section summarizes the syntax of the REG procedure in the following seven statements, of which only the first two are required:

PROC	REG	DATA= *sas_dataset_name <options>*;
	MODEL	*Y_variable = X_variables < / options>*;
	PLOT	*plot_definitions < / options>*;
	PAINT	*<condition	ALLOBS> < / options>*;
	PRINT	*<options>*;
	OUTPUT	*OUT = sas_dataset_name <keywords = names>*;
	BY	*classification_variable(s)*;

The first statement, **PROC REG**, initializes the REG procedure and specifies the data set to be analyzed. If needed, one or more of the following options can be added:

SIMPLE   requests that simple descriptive statistics, such as mean and standard deviation, be computed for each variable included in the regression analysis.

CORR   computes a correlation matrix for all variables used in the regression analysis.

OUTEST=
data_set_name   produces a SAS data set that contains estimates of regression parameters.

NOPRINT   suppresses printing or listing of the regression results.

LINEPRINTER (or LP) requests that plots be outputted in the ASCII format.

ALPHA=   a small probability that defines the confidence level of the parameter estimates to be $(1 - ALPHA) \times 100\%$. The default is 0.05.

The second statement, **MODEL**, is required. The syntax of a MODEL statement mirrors a regression equation. On the left-hand side of the equal sign (=), you type in the name of the outcome or Y variable. On the right-hand side, type in one or more predictors' names, separated by a blank space. Multiple MODEL statements can be written within the same REG procedure. Each may be identified by a label. The label must precede the word MODEL and is followed by a colon (:). Refer back to Example 17.4 or 17.5 for an illustration. After the slash (/), a number of useful options are available:

P   calculates each observation's predicted value of Y.

R   calculates the residual for each observation.

DWPROB calculates the Durbin-Watson statistic (D), the p values associated with the test of the D statistic, and the first-order autocorrelation among residuals.

SELECTION= requests a method for selecting a best set of predictors for predicting Y; choices are

FORWARD (or F)	the forward selection method
BACKWARD (or B)	the backward deletion method
STEPWISE (or S)	the stepwise selection method
MAXR	the maximum R^2 improvement method
MINR	the minimum R^2 improvement method
RSQUARE	the R^2 method
ADJRSQ	the adjusted R^2 method
CP	the most ideal CP selection method

SLENTRY= specifies the significance level for a predictor to enter into a regression model.

SLSTAY= specifies the significance level for a predictor to stay in a regression model.

INCLUDE=2 requests that the first two (say) predictors in the MODEL statement be always included in the regression model.

CLM calculates a $(1 - \text{ALPHA})\, 100\%$ confidence interval for an average y given fixed X values; the upper limit of this interval is called UCLM and the lower limit is LCLM. Both UCLM and LCLM can be outputted to a SAS data set.

CLI calculates a $(1 - \text{ALPHA})\, 100\%$ confidence interval for an individual y given fixed X values; the upper limit of this interval is called UCL and the lower limit is LCL. Both UCL and LCL can be outputted to a SAS data set.

INFLUENCE calculates the influence of each observation on the parameter estimates and on the y.

STB requests the beta weights.

The third statement, **PLOT,** was previously illustrated in Example 17.5b. This statement is most useful for checking if residuals show equal variability along the scale of the predicted Y or a continuous predictor. It can also be used to help determine if residuals are randomly distributed, that is, if they are uncorrelated with the predicted Y or with any of the continuous predictors. Below are examples of the PLOT statement. Please note that x1 and y are variables specified by data analysts. **P., R., UCLM.,** and **LCLM.** are variables created from specifying options P, R, and CLM, respectively.

Purpose	PLOT Examples (Used With the **LINEPRINTER** Option on the **PROC REG** Statement)
(a) Plotting residuals against x1	PLOT R.*x1;
(b) Plotting residuals against predicted y	PLOT R.*P.;
(c) Combining (a) and (b) above	PLOT R.*(x1 P.);
(d) Plotting predicted y against x1 with a special symbol, '#'	PLOT P.*x1='#';
(e) Plotting 4 graphs using the same scale of x1. This PLOT statement must be preceded by a MODEL statement with the option CLM.	PLOT y*x1='A' P.*x1='P' UCLM.*x1='U' LCLM.*x1='L'/OVERLAY;

The next statement, **PAINT**, is used to highlight a subset of observations. Once painted, these observations can be easily identified on a plot or on the output. The PAINT statement is best understood by illustrations. Please note that id and name below are variables defined by data analysts; **OBS.**, **P.**, and **R.** are generated by the REG procedure; and **LE**, **OR**, and **AND** are logical operators:

Purpose	PAINT Examples
(a) Highlighting the individual whose id = 13	PAINT id=13;
(b) Highlighting the individual whose name is 'Joanne'	PAINT name='Joanne';
(c) Combining (a) and (b) above	PAINT name='Joanne' | id=13;
(d) Highlighting the first 25 observations	PAINT OBS. LE 25;
(e) Highlighting those with absolute residuals greater than 2	PAINT R. > 2 OR R. < ?2;
(f) Highlighting those whose predicted y is greater than 99 and whose residual is less than −2	PAINT P. > 99 AND R. < −2;
(g) Changing the highlighting symbol to '$'	PAINT / SYMBOL='$';
(h) Resetting the PAINT function, i.e., annulling the highlighting feature	PAINT ALLOBS / RESET;
(i) Using the default PAINT symbol for highlighting	PAINT ALLOBS;

The **PRINT** statement is used interactively. Once it is issued, the regression result is immediately shown on the screen. With no options specified, the PRINT statement displays all regression results obtained up to that moment. Two examples below illustrate the PRINT statement; note that logs, service, and sqrtdg are variables defined by data analysts:

Purpose	PRINT Examples
(a) Displaying the predicted y and residuals on the screen	`PRINT P. R.;`

(b) Defining a simple regression model
Adding a new variable sqrtdg to the model
Displaying the regression model of predicting
logs from service and sqrtdg on the screen
	`MODEL logs=service;`
	`ADD sqrtdg;`
	`PRINT;`
	`RUN;`

The statement **OUTPUT OUT**=*sas_dataset_name* is used to preserve regression results in a separate data set for subsequent analysis. The OUTPUT statement is applicable only if the input data for PROC REG are individual observations. It cannot be specified if a TYPE=CORR data set is the input data set. Any or all of the statistics requested on the MODEL statement after the slash (/) can be renamed on the OUTPUT statement. For instance, the following program renames the predicted y to pred, the residual to resid, Cook's D influence statistic to d, and the upper limit of a 95% confidence interval of the average $\hat{y}$ to u and the lower limit to l, based on the CLM option:

```
PROC REG DATA=salary ALPHA=0.05;
    MODEL logs=service sqrtdg school / P R CLM;
    OUTPUT OUT=outreg
            P=pred
            R=resid
            COOKD=d
            UCLM=u
            LCLM=l;
RUN; QUIT;
```

Finally, the last statement, **BY**, serves the same purpose as in all other procedures. It divides the data set into subgroups according to diverse values of the BY variable(s). Within each subgroup, the same regression analyses are performed according to the MODEL statement. Regression results are as many as there are subgroups. If more than one BY variable is specified, all possible combinations of the BY variables' values are used in dividing up the entire data set. Be sure to presort the data set in the ascending order of all BY variables, if the BY statement is included in the REG procedure. Presorting a data set can be accomplished using the SORT procedure.

17.5 Tips

- How to handle missing or invalid data

By default, the REG procedure does not consider observations that have missing information on either the outcome variable or the predictors. If a correlation or a covariance matrix is used as the input data set, the calculation of correlations or covariances should be based on the same database. This can be achieved using the NOMISS option on the PROC CORR statement (refer back to **Section 16.3** of Chapter 16).

- How to combine an input data set with the **OUT=** data set

First, both data sets must have distinct names. Second, both data sets must be based on individual observations. To combine them into one data set, you invoke the MERGE statement in the DATA step. An illustration of how this is given in Example 17.5c.

- How to use ODS with the REG procedure

To use ODS, you need to know ODS table names corresponding with various portions of the output. Table 17.4 presents selected ODS table names for the REG procedure and their descriptions.

Table 17.4   Selected ODS Table Names and Descriptions for the REG Procedure

ODS Table Name	Description	Option on the MODEL Statement
ANOVA	Model ANOVA table	(default)
FitStatistics	Model fit statistics	(default)
ParameterEstimates	Model parameter estimates	(default)
OutputStatistics	Output statistics table	P, R, CLM, etc.
ResidualStatistics	Residual statistics	P, R, CLM, etc.
DWStatistic	Durbin-Watson statistic	DW, DWPROB
SelParmEst	Parameter estimates for selection method	SELECTION=
ConditionBounds	Bounds on condition number	SELECTION=
SelectionSummary	Summary for selection method	SELECTION=

These ODS table names and related details can be tracked in the Log window using the ODS TRACE ON statement in the SAS program. You may turn off this tracking feature with the ODS TRACE OFF statement, also in the SAS program:

```
ODS TRACE ON;
PROC REG DATA=salary;
M1:  MODEL logs=service / P R;
RUN; QUIT;
ODS TRACE OFF;
RUN;
```

After executing the program, the following will appear in the Log window listing all ODS table names for the PROC REG output:

```
Output Added:
-------------
Name:       NObs
Label:      Number of Observations
Template:   Stat.Reg.NObs
Path:       Reg.M1.Fit.logs.NObs
-------------

Output Added:
-------------
Name:       ANOVA
Label:      Analysis of Variance
Template:   Stat.REG.ANOVA
Path:       Reg.M1.Fit.logs.ANOVA
-------------

Output Added:
-------------
Name:       FitStatistics
Label:      Fit Statistics
Template:   Stat.REG.FitStatistics
Path:       Reg.M1.Fit.logs.FitStatistics
-------------

Output Added:
-------------
Name:       ParameterEstimates
Label:      Parameter Estimates
Template:   Stat.REG.ParameterEstimates
Path:       Reg.M1.Fit.logs.ParameterEstimates
-------------

Output Added:
-------------
Name:       OutputStatistics
Label:      Output Statistics
Template:   Stat.Reg.OutputStatistics
Path:       Reg.M1.ObswiseStats.logs.OutputStatistics
-------------
```

```
Output Added:
-------------
Name:        ResidualStatistics
Label:       Residual Statistics
Template:    Stat.Reg.ResidualStatistics
Path:        Reg.M1.ObswiseStats.logs.ResidualStatistics
-------------
```

Based on the list of ODS table names, you may select certain results to be displayed in the Output window. For example, the following program selects **Part (D)** of Example 17.1 to be included in the output:

```
ODS SELECT Reg.M1.ObswiseStats.logs.OutputStatistics;
PROC REG DATA=salary;
M1:   MODEL logs=service / P R;
RUN; QUIT;
```

Likewise, you may select certain result(s) to be exported as a SAS data set. For example, the following program exports **Part (D)** of Example 17.1 to the SAS data set <u>outstat:</u>

```
ODS OUTPUT Reg.M1.ObswiseStats.logs.OutputStatistics = outstat;
PROC REG DATA=salary;
M1:   MODEL logs=service / P R;
RUN; QUIT;
```

Furthermore, you may select certain results to be saved in file formats other than the SAS standard output. For example, the following program saves the output of Example 17.1 in HTML format in the default style:

```
ODS HTML BODY = 'd:\result\Example17_1Body.html'
         CONTENTS = 'd:\result\Example17_1TOC.html'
         PAGE = 'd:\result\Example17_1Page.html'
         FRAME = 'd:\result\Example17_1Frame.html';
PROC REG DATA=salary;
M1:   MODEL logs=service / P R;
RUN; QUIT;
ODS HTML CLOSE;
RUN;
```

For additional information about the ODS feature, refer to *SAS 9.1.3 Output Delivery System: User's Guide* (SAS Institute Inc., 2006c) and *SAS/STAT 9.1 User's Guide* (SAS Institute Inc., 2004d) or the online documentation at www.sas.com.

17.6 Summary

Ample examples and tips were presented in this chapter to demonstrate the essential concepts and issues encountered in regression analysis. The concepts discussed include the construction of a regression model, the estimation of regression coefficients by the least-squares method, the F test of the overall fit, the t test of each regression coefficient, standard error of prediction, R^2, adjusted R^2, forward/backward/stepwise selection methods, residuals, influence statistics, the Durbin-Watson statistic, its test, the first-order autocorrelation among residuals, and the confidence interval of average predicted values.

The issues raised in this chapter include the limitation of the least squares method, the statistical assumptions required of residuals, how to verify these assumptions, how to deal with categorical predictors in regression, how to interpret results based on dummy-coded categorical predictors, and the superiority of the adjusted R^2 over the unadjusted R^2.

So you are armed with a wealth of information and skills in regression. Let's see if you missed anything.

17.7 Exercises

1. At the end of the explanation of Output 17.5, you were urged to consider adding new predictors into the regression model, M3, to improve the fit and make the serial correlation go away. Now it is your turn. Try the following steps and see if you can further improve M3:

    a. Transform the <u>salary</u> variable into LOG of <u>salary</u> using the base of 10.

    b. Create new predictors such as the log 10 or natural log transformation of <u>service</u> and a multiplicative term of <u>service</u> multiplied with <u>sqrtdg</u>.

    c. Add these new predictors to the equation and run a regression analysis based on this new full model.

    d. Use a selection procedure (forward, backward, or stepwise) to find the "best" set of predictors that are derived from the new full model; set the selection for entry, or for stay, at 0.05.

    e. Examine residuals generated from Steps (c) and (d) to see if they meet statistical assumptions.

    f. Which model, (c) or (d), is better and why?

2. Is the model you constructed for Exercise 1 better or worse than the best model identified in Example 17.5? Why?

3. A teacher wanted to predict his students' SAT scores by their high school gpa, motivation, iq, and confidence scores. Both motivation and confidence were measured on a 10-point scale; the higher the score, the greater was the student's motivation toward academic success or confidence in himself or herself. The following data are collected from his students who graduated last year.

Student	SAT	gpa	motivation	iq	confidence
A	1,120	3.1	8	125	6
B	730	2.8	5	118	5
C	870	3.5	2	136	7
D	1,360	3.4	7	127	6
E	680	3.2	6	108	5
F	990	3.6	5	112	4
G	1,030	2.9	7	98	3
H	1,210	3.4	8	105	8
I	760	3.5	6	86	3
J	880	3.0	6	112	4

a. What is the regression equation based on gpa, motivation, iq, and confidence to predict students' SAT scores?
b. Find the best model for predicting students' SAT scores.
c. Do residuals violate their statistical assumptions?
d. Use the GPLOT procedure to display the regression line based on motivation as the sole predictor of SAT scores and the 95% confidence interval of predicted SAT scores.

17.8 Answers to Exercises

1. c. Let lservice = log 10 of service; then the new full model is

$$\hat{\text{logs}} = (2.69531) + (0.23682) \times lservice$$
$$+ (0.00178) \times sex + (0.01398) \times sqrtdg + (0.03162) \times school$$
$$+ (-0.01272) \times break + (0.00882) \times (lservice \times sqrtdg)$$

```
                                  Exercise 17-1c                                        1

                                The REG Procedure
                                  Model: EX1c
                      Dependent Variable: logs log 10 of salary

                      Number of Observations Read          90
                      Number of Observations Used          90

                                Analysis of Variance

                                   Sum of          Mean
        Source              DF     Squares         Square     F Value     Pr > F

        Model                6     1.23672        0.20612     110.53      <.0001
        Error               83     0.15478        0.00186
        Corrected Total     89     1.39150

                   Root MSE            0.04318   R-Square     0.8888
                   Dependent Mean      3.22004   Adj R-Sq     0.8807
                   Coeff Var           1.34109

                                Parameter Estimates

                                         Parameter    Standard
    Variable    Label                DF   Estimate      Error    t Value   Pr > |t|

    Intercept   Intercept             1    2.69531     0.02475    108.89    <.0001
    lservice    log 10 of service     1    0.23682     0.01197     19.78    <.0001
    sex         1=M, 2=F              1    0.00178     0.01044      0.17    0.8650
    sqrtdg      academic degree       1    0.01398     0.03654      0.38    0.7029
    school      0=private, 1=public   1    0.03162     0.01003      3.15    0.0023
    break       1=break 2 yrs, 0=others  1  -0.01272   0.01134     -1.12    0.2653
    lservicexsqrtdg                   1    0.00882     0.01639      0.54    0.5921
```

```
                                  Exercise 17-1c                                        2

                                The REG Procedure
                                  Model: EX1c
                      Dependent Variable: logs log 10 of salary

                      Durbin-Watson D                  1.378
                      Pr < DW                          0.0007
                      Pr > DW                          0.9993
                      Number of Observations              90
                      1st Order Autocorrelation        0.249

NOTE: Pr<DW is the p-value for testing positive autocorrelation, and Pr>DW is the p-value
      for testing negative autocorrelation
```

d. The model from the stepwise selection method:

$$\hat{logs} = (2.69542) + (0.23566) \times lservice + (0.03276) \times sqrtdg + (0.03232) \times school$$

```
                          Exercise 17-1d                                    3

                          The REG Procedure
                           Model: EX1d
                 Dependent Variable: logs log 10 of salary

                 Number of Observations Read        90
                 Number of Observations Used        90


                     Stepwise Selection: Step 1


         Variable lservice Entered: R-Square = 0.7528 and C(p) = 98.4609


                          Analysis of Variance

                                  Sum of        Mean
         Source           DF      Squares      Square    F Value   Pr > F

         Model             1      1.04751     1.04751     267.98   <.0001
         Error            88      0.34399     0.00391
         Corrected Total  89      1.39150


                      Parameter    Standard
         Variable      Estimate     Error    Type II SS  F Value  Pr > F

         Intercept     2.68884     0.03311    25.77679   6594.33  <.0001
         lservice      0.25572     0.01562     1.04751    267.98  <.0001

                 Bounds on condition number: 1, 1
---------------------------------------------------------------------------

                     Stepwise Selection: Step 2


         Variable sqrtdg Entered: R-Square = 0.8708 and C(p) = 12.4204


                          Analysis of Variance

                                  Sum of        Mean
         Source           DF      Squares      Square    F Value   Pr > F

         Model             2      1.21169     0.60585     293.14   <.0001
         Error            87      0.17981     0.00207
         Corrected Total  89      1.39150


                      Parameter    Standard
         Variable      Estimate     Error    Type II SS  F Value  Pr > F

         Intercept     2.70468     0.02414    25.94004   12551.2  <.0001
         lservice      0.23774     0.01154     0.87766    424.66  <.0001
         sqrtdg        0.03587     0.00402     0.16418     79.44  <.0001




                          Exercise 17-1d                                    4

                          The REG Procedure
                           Model: EX1d
                 Dependent Variable: logs log 10 of salary

                     Stepwise Selection: Step 2
```

```
                    Bounds on condition number: 1.0316, 4.1262
------------------------------------------------------------------------------------

                            Stepwise Selection: Step 3


               Variable school Entered: R-Square = 0.8866 and C(p) = 2.6167


                                  Analysis of Variance

                                     Sum of          Mean
          Source              DF     Squares         Square      F Value     Pr > F

          Model                3     1.23370         0.41123      224.13     <.0001
          Error               86     0.15779         0.00183
          Corrected Total     89     1.39150


                            Parameter       Standard
           Variable          Estimate         Error     Type II SS  F Value  Pr > F

           Intercept         2.69542         0.02290     25.41218   13849.9  <.0001
           lservice          0.23566         0.01089      0.85975    468.57  <.0001
           sqrtdg            0.03276         0.00390      0.12961     70.64  <.0001
           school            0.03232         0.00933      0.02201     12.00  0.0008

                    Bounds on condition number: 1.0896, 9.5706
------------------------------------------------------------------------------------


          All variables left in the model are significant at the 0.0500 level.

      No other variable met the 0.0500 significance level for entry into the model.



                            Summary of Stepwise Selection

          Variable      Variable                              Number  Partial  Model
  Step    Entered       Removed      Label                   Vars In R-Square R-Square

    1     lservice                   log 10 of service          1     0.7528   0.7528
    2     sqrtdg                     academic degree            2     0.1180   0.8708
    3     school                     0=private, 1=public        3     0.0158   0.8866

                            Summary of Stepwise Selection

                     Step   C(p)       F Value     Pr > F

                       1   98.4609     267.98      <.0001
                       2   12.4204      79.44      <.0001
```


```
                        Exercise 17-1d                                        5

                        The REG Procedure
                         Model: EX1d
              Dependent Variable: logs log 10 of salary

                    Summary of Stepwise Selection

                  Step   C(p)      F Value     Pr > F

                    3   2.6167      12.00       0.0008
```

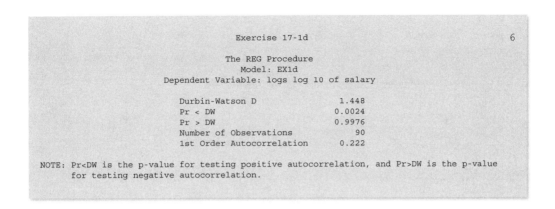

```
                    Exercise 17-1d                              6

                    The REG Procedure
                      Model: EX1d
           Dependent Variable: logs log 10 of salary

           Durbin-Watson D                  1.448
           Pr < DW                          0.0024
           Pr > DW                          0.9976
           Number of Observations              90
           1st Order Autocorrelation        0.222

NOTE: Pr<DW is the p-value for testing positive autocorrelation, and Pr>DW is the p-value
      for testing negative autocorrelation.
```

e. Residuals generated from (c) and (d) meet the statistical assumptions.

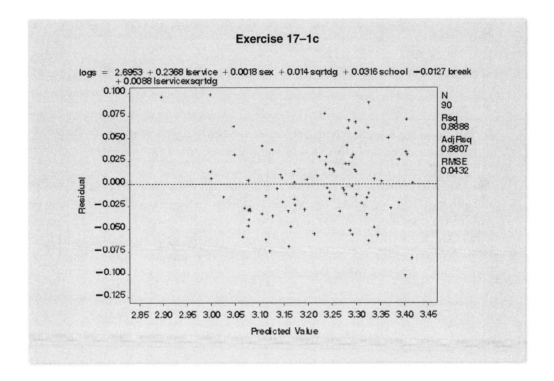

Exercise 17–1c

logs = 2.6953 + 0.2368 lservice + 0.0018 sex + 0.014 sqrtdg + 0.0316 school −0.0127 break + 0.0088 lservicexsqrtdg

N 90
Rsq 0.8888
AdjRsq 0.8807
RMSE 0.0432

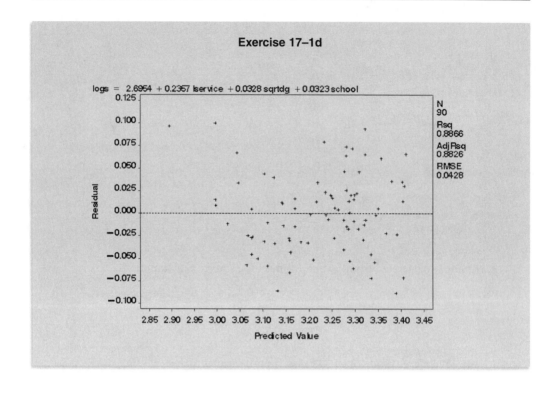

f. The model from (d) has almost the same predictive power as the model from (c), but it uses fewer predictors. As a result, the model from (d) is better.

2. The model from 1(d) above is considered better than the best model (M3) identified in Example 17.5. The adj-R^2 for Model 1(d) from Exercise 1 is higher than that of M3 from Example 17.5. At the same time, the Durbin-Watson D statistic based on Model 1(d) is 1.448 (Pr < DW = 0.0024), which is statistically significant at the 0.05 level—bad news for a regression model. However, the autocorrelation among residuals is lower than that for M3—good news.

3. a. $\hat{SAT} = (-1868.48357) + (347.11987) \times gpa + (110.48677) \times motivation$
$+ (9.68312) \times iq + (-9.29278) \times confidence$

```
              Exercise 17-3a                                    1

              The REG Procedure
                Model: Ex3a
              Dependent Variable: sat

Number of Observations Read          10
Number of Observations Used          10
```

```
                           Analysis of Variance

                              Sum of          Mean
Source                  DF    Squares        Square    F Value    Pr > F

Model                    4    312888         78222      3.09      0.1240
Error                    5    126722         25344
Corrected Total          9    439610


             Root MSE            159.19938    R-Square       0.7117
             Dependent Mean      963.00000    Adj R-Sq       0.4811
             Coeff Var            16.53161


                          Parameter Estimates

                        Parameter      Standard
Variable       DF       Estimate         Error     t Value    Pr > |t|

Intercept       1     -1868.48357     1075.66899    -1.74      0.1429
gpa             1       347.11987      215.24900     1.61       0.1677
motivation      1       110.48677       37.22416     2.97       0.0312
iq              1         9.68312        5.53570     1.75       0.1407
confidence      1        -9.29278       46.64733    -0.20       0.8499
```

b. Applying the stepwise selection method and setting SLENTRY and SLSTAY to 0.15, the following model was obtained:

$$\hat{SAT} = (-1752.20366) + (329.53197) \times gpa + (107.32230) \times motivation + (8.90494) \times iq$$

```
                            Exercise 17-3b                              2

                           The REG Procedure
                            Model: EX3b
                        Dependent Variable: sat

                 Number of Observations Read        10
                 Number of Observations Used        10

                    Stepwise Selection: Step 1


       Variable motivation Entered: R-Square = 0.2780 and C(p) = 6.5226


                           Analysis of Variance

                              Sum of          Mean
Source                  DF    Squares        Square    F Value    Pr > F

Model                    1    122232         122232     3.08      0.1173
Error                    8    317378          39672
Corrected Total          9    439610


                  Parameter      Standard
Variable          Estimate        Error    Type II SS  F Value   Pr > F

Intercept         566.57143     234.46616    231652     5.84     0.0421
motivation         66.07143      37.64127    122232     3.08     0.1173


               Bounds on condition number: 1, 1
```

```
                        Stepwise Selection: Step 2


          Variable iq Entered: R-Square = 0.5470 and C(p) = 3.8575


                           Analysis of Variance

                                    Sum of           Mean
      Source              DF        Squares          Square      F Value      Pr > F

      Model               2         240466           120233         4.23      0.0626
      Error               7         199144           28449
      Corrected Total     9         439610


                         Parameter        Standard
            Variable      Estimate          Error     Type II SS   F Value   Pr > F

            Intercept    -547.12457       581.26016       25206       0.89   0.3779
            motivation     92.93584        34.49190      206538       7.26   0.0309
            iq              8.45173         4.14580      118234       4.16   0.0809
```


```
                             Exercise 17-3b                                    3

                            The REG Procedure
                             Model: EX3b
                         Dependent Variable: sat

                        Stepwise Selection: Step 2

               Bounds on condition number: 1.1709, 4.6836
----------------------------------------------------------------------------------

                        Stepwise Selection: Step 3

          Variable gpa Entered: R-Square = 0.7095 and C(p) = 3.0397


                           Analysis of Variance

                                    Sum of           Mean
      Source              DF        Squares          Square      F Value      Pr > F

      Model               3         311882           103961         4.88      0.0474
      Error               6         127728           21288
      Corrected Total     9         439610


                         Parameter        Standard
            Variable      Estimate          Error     Type II SS   F Value   Pr > F

            Intercept   -1752.20366       828.07194       95316       4.48   0.0787
            gpa           329.53197       179.91544       71416       3.35   0.1167
            motivation    107.32230        30.85323      257581      12.10   0.0132
            iq              8.90494         3.59478      130633       6.14   0.0480

               Bounds on condition number: 1.2521, 10.497
----------------------------------------------------------------------------------


      All variables left in the model are significant at the 0.1500 level.

    No other variable met the 0.1500 significance level for entry into the model.
```

```
                          Summary of Stepwise Selection

          Variable    Variable    Number   Partial    Model
   Step   Entered     Removed     Vars In  R-Square   R-Square    C(p)     F Value  Pr > F

     1    motivation                  1      0.2780     0.2780    6.5226    3.08    0.1173
     2    iq                          2      0.2690     0.5470    3.8575    4.16    0.0809
     3    gpa                         3      0.1625     0.7095    3.0397    3.35    0.1167
```

```
                                                                                    4
                                 Exercise 17-3b

                                The REG Procedure
                                 Model: EX3b
                            Dependent Variable: sat

                      Durbin-Watson D                   2.065
                      Pr < DW                          0.5587
                      Pr > DW                          0.4413
                      Number of Observations               10
                      1st Order Autocorrelation        -0.090

NOTE: Pr<DW is the p-value for testing positive autocorrelation, and Pr>DW is the p-value
      for testing negative autocorrelation.
```

c. The Durbin-Watson D statistic (2.065) is not statistically significant at the 0.05 level. The plots of residuals against the predicted values and each continuous predictor indicate the support for the equal variance assumption and the randomness assumption for residuals.

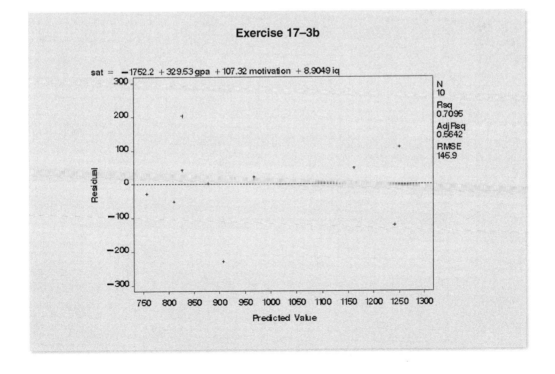

d.

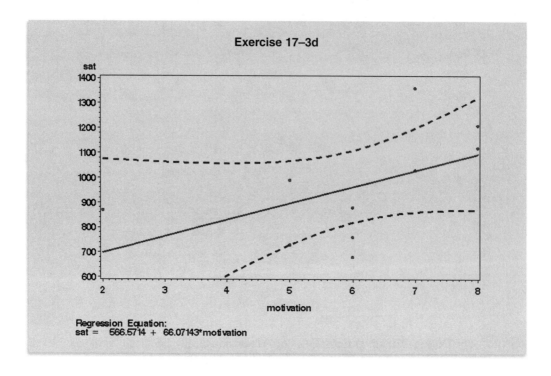

PART III

Advanced Data and File Management

18 Selecting Variables or Observations From a SAS Data Set

OBJECTIVE

When a SAS data set contains more variables or observations than needed, it increases the processing time. This chapter demonstrates how you can be prudent with the number and type of variables or observations you actually need for an analysis. A parsimonious SAS program is analogous to a lean body; it runs efficiently. It also makes it easier to interpret results and diagnose errors.

When a SAS data set contains more variables or observations than necessary, it increases the processing time. One way to speed up the processing of a SAS program is to be prudent with only those variables or observations that are needed for analyses. This chapter presents several strategies to attain this goal. Some strategies are used for variable selection, whereas others are for observation selection.

18.1 Keeping Variables via the KEEP Statement or the KEEP= Option

Both the KEEP statement and the KEEP= option are intended to retain variables in a SAS data set or for analysis in the PROC step. The retention can be either permanent or temporary. The KEEP statement is used as a stand-alone statement in the DATA step. The KEEP= option is specified in parentheses as a data set option in the PROC step, such as DATA= sas_dataset_name(KEEP=x y z). Examples 18.1 to 18.11 use a small raw data file called a.dat with four records of three numbers each.

Data values in a.dat

1	2	3
100	200	300
−1	−2	−3
0	.	−5

For each example shown, you are urged to follow along by executing the program and checking your result.

Example 18.1 KEEP Statement Used in the DATA Step

```
TITLE 'Example 18.1 KEEP statement used in the DATA step';

DATA one;
     INFILE 'd:\data\a.dat';
     INPUT x y z;
     average = MEAN(x,y,z);
     KEEP average;
RUN;

PROC PRINT DATA=one;
RUN;
```

Output 18.1 KEEP Statement Used in the DATA Step

```
Example 18.1 KEEP statement used in the DATA step                    1

                    Obs      average

                     1          2.0
                     2        200.0
                     3         -2.0
                     4         -2.5
```

Example 18.2 Using the KEEP Statement With the SET Statement

```
TITLE 'Example 18.2 Using the KEEP statement with the SET statement';

DATA one;
     INFILE 'd:\data\a.dat';
     INPUT x y z;
RUN;

DATA two;
     SET one;                /* Copies SAS data set 'one' into another SAS data set 'two' */
     KEEP x y;               /* while keeping 'x' and 'y' variables only in 'two'         */
RUN;

PROC PRINT DATA=two;
RUN;
```

Output 18.2 Using the KEEP Statement With the SET Statement

```
Example 18.2 Using the KEEP statement with the SET statement                    1

                    Obs        x        y

                     1         1        2
                     2        100      200
                     3        -1       -2
                     4         0        .
```

Example 18.3 Using the KEEP= Option With a SAS Data Set

```
TITLE 'Example 18.3 Using the KEEP= option with a SAS data set';

DATA one;
     INFILE 'd:\data\a.dat';
     INPUT x y z;
RUN;

DATA three (KEEP= x y);
     SET one;                /* Copies SAS data set 'one' into another SAS data set 'three' */
RUN;                         /* while keeping 'x' and 'y' variables only in 'three'         */

PROC PRINT DATA=three;
RUN;
```

Output 18.3 Using the KEEP= Option With a SAS Data Set

This output is identical to Output 18.2; hence, it is not repeated here.

Example 18.4 Using the KEEP= Option
With a SAS Data Set: An Alternative Approach

```
TITLE 'Example 18.4 Using the KEEP= option with a SAS data set, an alternative approach';

DATA one;
    INFILE 'd:\data\a.dat';
    INPUT x y z;
RUN;

DATA four;
    SET one (KEEP= x y);     /* Copies SAS data set 'one' into another SAS data set 'four' */
RUN;                         /* while keeping 'x' and 'y' variables only in 'four'          */

PROC PRINT DATA=four;
RUN;
```

Output 18.4 Using the KEEP= Option With a SAS Data Set:
An Alternative Approach

This output is identical to Output 18.2.

Example 18.5 Using the KEEP= Option in the PROC Step

```
TITLE 'Example 18.5 Using the KEEP= option in the PROC step';

DATA one;
    INFILE 'd:\data\a.dat';
    INPUT x y z;
RUN;

PROC PRINT DATA=one (KEEP=x y);     /* PROC PRINT prints only 'x' and 'y' variable values */
RUN;
```

Output 18.5 Using the KEEP= Option in the PROC Step

This output is identical to Output 18.2.

18.2 Removing Variables via the
DROP Statement or the DROP= Option

Both the DROP statement and the DROP= option are intended to exclude
variables from a SAS data set or from a PROC step. The DROP statement is
used as a stand-alone statement within the DATA step. The DROP= option
is used in parenthesis as a data set option in the PROC step, such as DATA=
sas_datasetname(DROP= a b c). The exclusion can be permanent or

temporary. It is not difficult to recognize the contrasting purpose of the
KEEP versus the DROP statement or the KEEP= versus the DROP= option.
Their syntaxes are virtually identical—compare Example 18.6 with Example
18.1, 18.7 with 18.2, 18.8 with 18.3, 18.9 with 18.4, and 18.10 with 18.5.
Execute these examples and find out what appears in the output.

Example 18.6 DROP Statement Used in the DATA Step

```
TITLE 'Example 18.6 DROP statement used in the DATA step';

DATA six;
     INFILE 'd:\data\a.dat';
     INPUT x y z;
     Average = MEAN(x,y,z);
     DROP x y z;
RUN;

PROC PRINT DATA=six;
RUN;
```

Output 18.6 DROP Statement Used in the DATA Step

```
Example 18.6 DROP statement used in the DATA step                          1

                    Obs      average

                     1          2.0
                     2        200.0
                     3         -2.0
                     4         -2.5
```

Example 18.7 Using the DROP Statement With the SET Statement

```
TITLE 'Example 18.7 Using the DROP statement with the SET statement';

DATA six;
     INFILE 'd:\data\a.dat';
     INPUT x y z;
RUN;

DATA seven;
     SET six;                 /* Copies SAS data set 'six' into another SAS data set 'seven' */
     DROP z;                  /* while dropping variable 'z'                                 */
RUN;

PROC PRINT DATA=seven;
RUN;
```

Output 18.7 Using the DROP Statement With the SET Statement

```
Example 18.7 Using the DROP statement with the SET statement                    1

                    Obs        x        y

                     1         1        2
                     2        100      200
                     3        -1       -2
                     4         0        .
```

Example 18.8 Using the DROP= Option With a SAS Data Set

```
TITLE 'Example 18.8 Using the DROP= option with a SAS data set';

DATA six;
    INFILE 'd:\data\a.dat';
    INPUT x y z;
RUN;

DATA eight (DROP= z);
    SET six;                /* Copies SAS data set 'six' into another SAS data set 'eight' */
RUN;                        /* while dropping variable 'z'                                 */

PROC PRINT DATA=eight;
RUN;
```

Output 18.8 Using the DROP= Option With a SAS Data Set

This output is identical to Output 18.7.

Example 18.9 Using the DROP= Option
With a SAS Data Set: An Alternative Approach

```
TITLE 'Example 18.9 Using the DROP= option with a SAS data set, an alternative approach';

DATA six;
    INFILE 'd:\data\a.dat';
    INPUT x y z;
RUN;

DATA nine;
    SET six (DROP= z);      /* Copies SAS data set 'six' into another SAS data set 'nine' */
RUN;                        /* while dropping variable 'z'                                */

PROC PRINT DATA=nine;
RUN;
```

Output 18.9 Using the DROP= Option
With a SAS Data Set: An Alternative Approach

This output is identical to Output 18.7.

Example 18.10 Using the DROP= Option in the PROC Step

```
TITLE 'Example 18.10 Using the DROP= option in the PROC step';

DATA six;
    INFILE 'd:\data\a.dat';
    INPUT x y z;
RUN;

PROC PRINT DATA=six (DROP= z);     /* PROC PRINT prints only 'x' and 'y' variable values */
RUN;
```

Output 18.10 Using the DROP= Option in the PROC Step

This output is identical to Output 18.7.

Example 18.11 Using KEEP= and DROP= With Multiple SAS Data Sets

```
TITLE 'Example 18.11 Using KEEP= and DROP= with multiple data sets';
DATA six;
    INFILE 'd:\data\a.dat';
    INPUT x y z;
RUN;

DATA eleven (DROP= z)       /* Copies data set 'six' into 'eleven' while dropping 'z'    */
     twelve (KEEP= x y);    /* Copies data set 'six' into 'twelve' while keeping 'x' & 'y' */
    SET six;
RUN;

TITLE2 'DROP= z';
PROC PRINT DATA=eleven;
RUN;

TITLE2 'KEEP= x y';
PROC PRINT DATA=twelve;
RUN;
```

Output 18.11 Using KEEP= and DROP= With Multiple SAS Data Sets

```
Example 18.11 Using KEEP= and DROP= with multiple data sets          1
                DROP= z

            Obs        x        y

             1         1        2
             2       100      200
             3        -1       -2
             4         0        .
```

```
Example 18.11 Using KEEP= and DROP= with multiple data sets          2
                KEEP= x y

            Obs        x        y

             1         1        2
             2       100      200
             3        -1       -2
             4         0        .
```

18.3 Selecting Observations by the IF Statement

The IF statement targets certain observations to be isolated from the rest of the data so that they can be analyzed or treated differently. The IF conditions are written as shown in Table 18.1.

Table 18.1   IF Conditional Expressions and Their Explanations

IF Conditional Expression	Explanation
IF sex = 'female';	if sex is equal to 'female'
IF age < 65;	if age is less than 65
IF (sex = 'female' AND age < 65);	if sex is equal to 'female' AND if age is less than 65 The parentheses are unnecessary but are recommended
IF name ^= 'Goodwill';	if name is not equal to 'Goodwill'
IF gre >= 750;	if gre is greater than or equal to 750
IF income <= 10000;	if income is less than or equal to 10000
IF (gre >= 750 OR income <= 10000);	if gre is greater than or equal to 750 OR if income is less than or equal to 10000

When a conditional expression is evaluated in an IF statement, the result is either true (coded as 1) or false (coded as 0). The following points should be kept in mind when interpreting the IF conditional expressions:

- In a comparison statement involving operators such as < (less than), > (greater than), = (equal to), <= (less than or equal to), >= (greater than or equal to), or ^= (not equal to), numeric values are compared directly with the condition as in "IF age < 65;", "IF gre >= 750;", or "IF income <= 10000;". When missing values are compared, they are treated as the smallest number (or negative infinity). Thus, a missing income in the example above meets the condition of being less than 10,000.
- The operator < can also be written as **LT**, > as **GT**, = as **EQ**, <= as **LE**, >= as **GE**, and ^= as **NE**.
- Two conditions can be joined through the AND (or &) and OR (or |) operators. In the above example, "IF (gre >= 750 OR income <= 10000);", the two conditions are (a) gre score not less than 750 and (b) income not more than 10,000 dollars. When either condition is met, the entire IF statement is satisfied. When you want both conditions to be met, the statement should be rewritten with the AND operator joining the two conditions:

  IF (gre >= 750 AND income <= 10000);

- Character variable values in equal (=) comparisons are checked character by character and case by case. Hence, "IF sex = 'female';" is different from "IF sex = 'Female';" because the former is written in lowercase, whereas the latter is written in upper- and lowercase. By the same token, the statement "IF name ^= 'Goodwill';" is different from "IF name ^= 'GOODWILL';".
- If you accidentally compare a numeric variable with a character variable, say, by using the equal sign (=), the character variable will be converted to a numeric according to rules outlined in **Section 7.11**, Chapter 7.

Example 18.12 Conditional Selection by IF

```
TITLE 'Example 18.12 Conditional Selection by IF';

DATA correct;
    INPUT name $ 1-10 sex $ ans;
    IF ans = 60;                       /* The correct answer is 60 */

DATALINES;
Joe Doe    m   3
Baby M     f   .
Tammy Fae f  -1
Nancy R.   f  60
Mr. Right m  60
RUN;

PROC PRINT DATA=correct;
RUN;
```

Although five observations are read, there will be only two kept in the data set <u>correct</u> because Nancy R. and Mr. Right gave a correct answer. Output 18.12 confirms this logic.

Output 18.12 Conditional Selection by IF

```
Example 18.12 Choosing those who answered correctly                    1

        Obs       name       sex     ans

         1      Nancy R.      f       60
         2      Mr. Right     m       60
```

In Example 18.13, the IF statement is used to select those observations with an incorrect answer, that is, anything other than 60.

Example 18.13 Conditional Selection by IF and Negation

```
TITLE 'Example 18.13 Conditional selection by IF and negation';

DATA incorrect;
     INPUT name $ 1-10 sex $ ans;
     IF ans ^= 60;

DATALINES;
Joe Doe     m    3
Baby M      f    .
Tammy Fae f  -1
Nancy R.   f   60
Mr. Right m   60
RUN;

PROC PRINT DATA=incorrect;
RUN;
```

The execution of this program should yield three observations in the <u>incorrect</u> data set.

Output 18.13 Conditional Selection by IF and Negation

```
Example 18.13 Choosing those who answered incorrectly                  1

        Obs       name       sex     ans

         1      Joe Doe       m        3
         2      Baby M        f        .
         3      Tammy Fae     f       -1
```

One question about this example deserves further discussion:

Why did Baby M, who had a missing score, end up in the data set?

According to the logic of the IF statement, Baby M's missing score is treated as the smallest number (or negative infinity). Thus, it does not equal 60 (i.e., the correct answer or the criterion). Consequently, she rightfully belonged in the <u>incorrect</u> data set.

18.4 Selecting Observations by IF–THEN/ELSE

The IF–THEN/ELSE statements are just a more elaborate way of specifying the IF statement. The syntax is as follows:

IF *conditional expression* THEN *statement*;
<ELSE *statement*;>

The evaluation of the IF *conditional expression* results in either a true or a false outcome. In a true case, the THEN statement is executed. In a false case, the ELSE statement is executed. The ELSE statement is optional, though; it need not be a part of the IF–THEN statement. Explanations of a conditional expression are given in **Section 18.3: Selecting Observations by the IF Statement.**

Example 18.14 Removing Observations With DELETE

```
TITLE 'Example 18.14 Removing observations with DELETE';

DATA exclude;
    INPUT name $ 1-10 sex $ ans;
    IF ans = . THEN DELETE;      /* Any observation with a missing 'ans' will not be included */

DATALINES;
Joe Doe    m   3
Baby M     f   .
Tammy Fae  f  -1
Nancy R.   f  60
Mr. Right  m  60
RUN;

PROC PRINT DATA=exclude;
RUN;
```

Output 18.14 Removing Observations With DELETE

```
Example 18.14 Removing observations with DELETE                                    1

        Obs      name      sex    ans

         1      Joe Doe      m      3
         2      Tammy Fae    f     -1
         3      Nancy R.     f     60
         4      Mr. Right    m     60
```

Example 18.15 Separating Observations Into Two SAS Data Sets

```
TITLE 'Example 18.15 Separating observations into two SAS data sets';
DATA college hischool;
     INPUT  name $ 1-10 sex $ educ;

     IF educ < 0 THEN DELETE;             /* Deletes observations with missing and */
                                          /* negative response on 'educ'           */

         ELSE IF educ <= 12 THEN OUTPUT hischool; /* If 'educ' is less than or equal to 12, */
                                          /* then the observation is included in    */
                                          /* the 'hischool' SAS data set.           */

         ELSE OUTPUT college;             /* If 'educ' is greater than 12,         */
                                          /* then the observation is included in   */
                                          /* the 'college' SAS data set.           */

DATALINES;
Joe Doe    m   3
Baby M     f   .
Tammy Fae  f   12
Nancy R.   f   16
Mr. Right  m   20
RUN;

TITLE2 'DATA=college';

PROC PRINT DATA=college;
RUN;

TITLE2 'DATA=hischool';

PROC PRINT DATA=hischool;
RUN;
```

Guess who ended up in the <u>hischool</u> data set and who in the <u>college</u> data file? Pay special attention to Baby M. Where is she and why is she not in either SAS data set?

Output 18.15 Separating Observations Into Two SAS Data Sets

```
Example 18.15 Separating observations into two SAS data sets          1
                 DATA=college

         Obs        name        sex      educ

          1      Nancy R.        f        16
          2      Mr. Right       m        20
```

```
Example 18.15 Separating observations into two SAS data sets          2
                 DATA=hischool

         Obs        name        sex      educ

          1      Joe Doe         m         3
          2      Tammy Fae       f        12
```

18.5 Selecting Observations by WHERE

The WHERE statement specifies a condition or conditions under which an observation is evaluated. If an observation meets the condition(s), it is included in a SAS data set or used in a PROC step. Otherwise, it is not included in a SAS data set or used in a PROC step. The WHERE statement is more efficient and elaborate than the IF statement for including observations conditionally in a SAS data set. The syntax of the WHERE statement is simple:

WHERE *where_expression*;

The *where_expression* is a conditional expression or a simple arithmetic operation (namely, +, −, *, /, **). Other SAS functions are not acceptable in a *where_expression*. Below are illustrations of the *where_expression*:

```
WHERE ans = 60;
WHERE ans ^= .;
WHERE zipcode = '60612';
```

The evaluation of a *where_expression* is the same as that of a *conditional expression* in the IF statement. The five examples shown below use a variety of WHERE statements to select observations.

Example 18.16 WHERE Used With
Arithmetic Operations and Logical Operators

```
TITLE 'Example 18.16 WHERE used with + and > operators';

DATA select;
     INPUT name $ 1-10 sex $ weight iq;

DATALINES;
Joe Doe    m    13    75
Baby M     f    .     90
Tammy Fae  f    150   50
Nancy R.   f    100   101
Mr. Right  m    160   120
RUN;

DATA heavy;
     SET select;              /* Copies all observations from 'select' into 'heavy';  */
     WHERE (weight+iq) > 200; /* accepting observations with combined 'weight' & 'iq' */
RUN;                          /* greater than 200                                     */

PROC PRINT DATA=heavy;
RUN;
```

The result consists of only two observations: Nancy R. and Mr. Right. This is so because their combined <u>weight</u> and <u>iq</u> meet the condition, that is, greater than 200.

Output 18.16 WHERE Used With
Arithmetic Operations and Logical Operators

```
Example 18.16 WHERE used with + and > operators                    1

  Obs      name       sex    weight      iq

   1      Nancy R.      f       100      101
   2      Mr. Right     m       160      120
```

Example 18.17 WHERE Used in the PROC Step

```
TITLE 'Example 18.17 WHERE used in the PROC step';

DATA select;
    INPUT name $ 1-10 sex $ weight iq;
DATALINES;
Joe Doe    m    13    75
Baby M     f     .    90
Tammy Fae  f   150    50
Nancy R.   f   100   101
Mr. Right  m   160   120
RUN;

PROC PRINT DATA=select;
    WHERE (weight+iq) > 200;
RUN;
```

Try writing and executing this program on your own. If your program is correct, the output will look familiar to you; compare it with Output 18.16.

Output 18.17 WHERE Used in the PROC Step

```
Example 18.16 WHERE used in the PROC step                          1

  Obs      name       sex    weight      iq

   4      Nancy R.      f       100      101
   5      Mr. Right     m       160      120
```

Example 18.18 WHERE Used With BETWEEN–AND Operator

```
TITLE 'Example 18.18 WHERE used with BETWEEN-AND';

DATA select;
    INPUT name $ 1-10 sex $ weight iq;
```

```
DATALINES;
Joe Doe     m    13    75
Baby M      f     .    90
Tammy Fae f    150    50
Nancy R.    f    100   101
Mr. Right  m    160   120
RUN;

PROC PRINT DATA=select;
     WHERE iq BETWEEN 89 AND 199;
RUN;
```

According to the program's logic, three observations qualify for the condition "`iq BETWEEN 89 AND 199`". Check this out with the output given below.

Output 18.18 WHERE Used With BETWEEN–AND Operator

```
Example 18.18 WHERE used with BETWEEN-AND                                    1

Obs     name          sex     weight     iq

 2      Baby M         f         .        90
 4      Nancy R.       f        100      101
 5      Mr. Right      m        160      120
```

- The BETWEEN–AND operator in the WHERE statement can be specified in negation, such as,

```
WHERE iq NOT BETWEEN 89 AND 199;
```

or in arithmetic operations, such as,

```
WHERE iq BETWEEN weight*0.5 AND weight*0.9;
```

Are you impressed so far? There is more to come.

Example 18.19 WHERE Used With CONTAINS Operator

```
TITLE 'Example 18.19 WHERE used with CONTAINS operator';

DATA select;
     INPUT name $ 1-10 sex $ weight iq;
DATALINES;
Joe Doe     m    13    75
Baby M      f     .    90
```

```
Tammy Fae f  150   50
Nancy R.  f  100  101
Mr. Right m  160  120
RUN;

PROC PRINT DATA=select;
    WHERE name CONTAINS 'a';
RUN;
```

Note that the CONTAINS operator works with character variables only. The condition is specified in single or double quotes. Thus, according to the WHERE statement, those observations whose <u>name</u> contains the lowercase "a" are to be singled out. Sure enough, three observations are pinpointed in Output 18.19.

Output 18.19 WHERE Used With CONTAINS Operator

```
Example 18.19 WHERE used with CONTAINS operator                        1

  Obs    name         sex    weight      iq

   2     Baby M        f        .         90
   3     Tammy Fae     f       150        50
   4     Nancy R.      f       100       101
```

The next example shows how missing values can be quickly spotted with the IS NULL (also IS MISSING) operator that is used within a WHERE statement.

Example 18.20 WHERE Used With IS NULL (or IS MISSING) Operator

```
TITLE 'Example 18.20 WHERE used with IS NULL (or IS MISSING) operator';

DATA select;
    INPUT name $ 1-10 sex $ weight iq;
DATALINES;
Joe Doe   m   13    75
Baby M    f    .    90
Tammy Fae f  150    50
Nancy R.  f  100   101
Mr. Right m  160   120
RUN;

PROC PRINT DATA=select;
    WHERE weight IS NULL;
RUN;
```

Guess who showed up in the output?—it is Baby M by herself!

Output 18.20 WHERE Used With IS NULL (or IS MISSING) Operator

```
Example 18.20 WHERE used with IS NULL (or IS MISSING) operator                    1

        Obs      name      sex      weight      iq

         2      Baby M      f          .        90
```

The IS NULL (or IS MISSING) operator can be used on numeric as well as on character variables. There are still other operators that can be teamed up with the WHERE statement. They are documented in *SAS 9.1.3 Language Reference: Dictionary* (SAS Institute Inc., 2006b).

18.6 Selecting Observations by the WHERE= Option

The WHERE= option is a SAS data set option; it is written like the WHERE statement as

(WHERE= (*where_expression*)).

The option WHERE= (*where_expression*) specifies the condition that is applied to a SAS data set for selecting observations that meet the condition. The *where_expression* has the same syntax as the *where_expression* in a WHERE statement. The WHERE= option appears in parentheses following a SAS data set name in the DATA step or the PROC step. Example 18.21 demonstrates the WHERE= option used with the SET statement. If you take a careful look at it, you'll discover that it is Example 18.16 in disguise.

Example 18.21 WHERE= Option Specified in the DATA Step

```
TITLE 'Example 18.21 WHERE= option specified in the DATA step';

DATA select;
     INPUT name $ 1-10 sex $ weight iq;
DATALINES;
Joe Doe   m   13   75
Baby M    f    .   90
```

```
Tammy Fae f   150    50
Nancy R.  f   100   101
Mr. Right m   160   120
RUN;

DATA heavy;
     SET select (WHERE=((weight+iq) > 200));/* Copies observations from 'select' into 'heavy'; */
                                            /* accepting those with a combined 'weight' & 'iq' */
RUN;                                        /* is greater than 200                             */


PROC PRINT DATA=heavy;
RUN;
```

If the logic used in the current example is the same as that in Example 18.16, what sort of output do you expect?

Output 18.21 WHERE= Option Specified in the DATA Step

```
Example 18.21 WHERE= option specified in the DATA step                              1

        Obs        name        sex     weight       iq

         1       Nancy R.        f        100       101
         2       Mr. Right       m        160       120
```

The WHERE= option can be used in a PROC step as well. Let's rewrite Examples 18.16 and 18.21 into the following:

Example 18.22 WHERE= Option Specified in the PROC Step

```
TITLE 'Example 18.22 WHERE specified in the PROC step';

DATA select;
     INPUT name $ 1-10 sex $ weight iq;
DATALINES;
Joe Doe    m    13    75
Daby M     f     .    90
Tammy Fae f  150    50
Nancy R.   f  100   101
Mr. Right m  160   120
RUN;


PROC PRINT DATA=select (WHERE=((weight+iq) > 200));
RUN;
```

The output is identical to Output 18.16 and Output 18.21 except for the Obs numbers; it is therefore not repeated here. As an exercise, you are encouraged to rewrite Examples 18.17, 18.18, 18.19, and 18.20 with WHERE= as a SAS data set option.

18.7 Block Selection of Observations via FIRSTOBS= and OBS= Options

The two options introduced in this section lead to block selection of observations from an existing SAS data set. The first option, FIRSTOBS=, specifies the starting observation number in a SAS data set. The second option, OBS=, specifies the ending observation number. These two options are often used together to tag a range of observations.

Example 18.23 FIRSTOBS= Used With SET in the DATA Step to Define a Starting Observation

```
TITLE 'Example 18.23 FIRSTOBS= used with SET to define a starting observation';

DATA select;
    INPUT name $ 1-10 sex $ weight iq;
DATALINES;
Joe Doe    m    13    75
Baby M     f    .     90
Tammy Fae  f   150    50
Nancy R.   f   100   101
Mr. Right  m   160   120
RUN;

DATA heavy;
    SET select (FIRSTOBS=3);  /* Copies observations from 'select' into 'heavy' starting with */
                             /* the third observation till the end of the data set         */

PROC PRINT DATA=heavy;
RUN;
```

The output, as expected, includes only the last three observations in the data set heavy. The first observation, Tammy Fae, in heavy is actually the third observation from select.

Output 18.23 FIRSTOBS= Used With SET in the DATA Step to Define a Starting Observation

```
Example 18.23 FIRSTOBS= used with SET to define a starting observation          1

          Obs      name       sex    weight     iq

           1     Tammy Fae     f       150      50
           2     Nancy R.      f       100     101
           3     Mr. Right     m       160     120
```

Example 18.24 Specifying a Range of Observations
With FIRSTOBS= and OBS= in the PROC Step

```
TITLE 'Example 18.24 A range of observations specified in the PROC step';

DATA select;
    INPUT name $ 1-10 sex $ weight iq;
DATALINES;
Joe Doe    m    13    75
Baby M     f    .     90
Tammy Fae  f    150   50
Nancy R.   f    100   101
Mr. Right  m    160   120
RUN;


PROC PRINT DATA=select (FIRSTOBS=2 OBS=4);
RUN;
```

The output shows that only the middle three observations (i.e., the second to the fourth) are listed by the PRINT procedure. The other two observations (the first and the fifth) are still in the select data set, but are not processed by PROC PRINT.

Output 18.24 Specifying a Range of Observations
With FIRSTOBS= and OBS= in the PROC Step

```
Example 18.24 A range of observations specified in the PROC step                      1

        Obs     name        sex     weight      iq

         2      Baby M       f         .        90
         3      Tammy Fae    f        150       50
         4      Nancy R.     f        100       101
```

Example 18.25 Specifying a Range of
Observations With FIRSTOBS= and OBS= in INFILE

```
TITLE 'Example 18.25 A range of observations specified on the INFILE statement';

DATA select;
    INFILE 'd:\data\select.dat' FIRSTOBS=2 OBS=4;
    INPUT name $ 1-10 sex $ weight iq;
RUN;

PROC PRINT DATA=select;
RUN;
```

Output 18.25 Specifying a Range of Observations
With FIRSTOBS= and OBS= in INFILE

The number of observations on the output is exactly three. These observations are identical to those in Output 18.24, so they are not repeated here.

If your raw data are included as part of the SAS program, you can specify the FIRSTOBS= and OBS= options on the INFILE statement to select a range of observations. A modified Example 18.25 is as follows, with raw data included.

Example 18.26 Modifying Example 18.25 With Raw Data Included

```
TITLE 'Example 18.26 Modifying Example 18.25 with raw data included';

DATA select;
     INFILE DATALINES FIRSTOBS=2 OBS=4;
     INPUT name $ 1-10 sex $ weight iq;
DATALINES;
Joe Doe    m    13    75
Baby M     f     .    90
Tammy Fae  f   150    50
Nancy R.   f   100   101
Mr. Right  m   160   120
RUN;


PROC PRINT DATA=select;
RUN;
```

Once again, only the middle three observations, that is, Baby M, Tammy Fae, and Nancy R., are included in the select data set. The output is identical to Output 18.24 and Output 18.25 except for the Obs numbers.

18.8 Designated Selection of
Observations via the POINT= Option

The POINT= option is often used in a SET statement to specifically select observations that are indexed by the POINT= variable values. The variable name assigned to the POINT= option is only temporary; it is not retained or included in the resultant SAS data set. The following example demonstrates how you can select odd-numbered observations from the select data set. Though DO–END statements are explained in Chapter 19, you should be able to trace the logic in the program below with remarks inserted between matching /* and */.

When the POINT= option is used, you must include a STOP statement to stop DATA step processing. Because POINT= directs the SAS compiler to read only those observations that are specified in the DO statement, the compiler cannot locate an end-of-file indicator. If data are read sequentially, the compiler will automatically find the end-of-file indicator, which is located at the end of the data records. And an end-of-file indicator will end a DATA step automatically. Failure to locate an end-of-file indicator or its substitute can cause the DATA step to go into a continuous loop. Thus, the STOP statement is necessary to prevent this continuous loop from occurring.

Example 18.27 POINT= Option Used in the SET Statement

```
TITLE 'Example 18.27 POINT= option used in the SET statement';

DATA select;
      INPUT name $ 1-10 sex $ weight iq;
DATALINES;
Joe Doe    m    13    75
Baby M     f    .     90
Tammy Fae  f   150    50
Nancy R.   f   100   101
Mr. Right  m   160   120
RUN;

DATA odd;
      DO index=1 to 5 by 2;      /* The DO statement is applied to 1st, 3rd, 5th 'index' value  */
          SET select POINT=index; /* Observations are copied to 'odd' according to 'index' value */
          OUTPUT;                /* Forwards the observation picked by POINT= to 'odd' data set */
      END;                       /* A matching END is needed for each DO                        */

      STOP;                      /* STOP statement is needed to prevent an infinite loop        */
RUN;

PROC PRINT DATA=odd;
RUN;
```

Output 18.27 POINT= Option Used in the SET Statement

```
Example 18.27 POINT= option used in the SET statement                                1

     Obs        name       sex     weight      iq

      1       Joe Doe       m         13       75
      2       Tammy Fae     f        150       50
      3       Mr. Right     m        160      120
```

18.9 Summary

This chapter has illustrated strategies that allow you to select certain variables to be included in a SAS data set or for data analysis. Specifically, the application of DROP (or DROP=) and KEEP (or KEEP=) results in either temporary or permanent selection of variables. For large SAS programs and sizable data sets, these strategies help reduce data processing time, which can be important and noticeable.

Additional strategies were also shown to construct a subset of observations from a SAS data set. These strategies are for the purpose of (a) conditional selection, (b) block selection, or (c) designated selection of observations. A variety of examples were given to meet the research needs for selecting observations in a special way.

18.10 Exercises

1. What values and variables are contained in data set <u>b</u> and data set <u>c</u> after executing this SAS program?

```
DATA a;
     INPUT x y;
     z=x+y;
DATALINES;
1 1
2 4
3 6
RUN;

DATA b; SET a (DROP=z);
u=x*y;
PROC PRINT;
RUN;

DATA c (DROP=z); SET a;
     v=x+z;
PROC PRINT;
RUN;
```

a.

	data b				*data c*			
x	y	u		x	y	u	z
1	1	1		1	1	2	2
2	4	8		2	4	12	6
3	6	18		3	6	27	9

b.

x	y	u	z	x	y	v
1	1	1	2	1	1	2
2	4	8	6	2	4	12
3	6	18	9	3	6	27

c.

x	y	u	z	x	y	v	z
1	1	1	2	1	1	2	2
2	4	8	6	2	4	12	6
3	6	18	9	3	6	27	9

d.

x	y	u	x	y	v
1	1	1	1	1	3
2	4	8	2	4	8
3	6	18	3	6	12

2. Identify a statement (or statements) below that will cause an error in execution if they are appended at the end of this DATA step:

```
DATA q;
    INPUT (x1-x4) (2.);
    z= MEAN(of x1-x4);
DATALINES;
12345678
23456789
RUN;
```

    a. DATA a; SET q; KEEP z;
    b. DATA b; SET q; DROP x1-x4;
    c. DATA c; SET q; (KEEP=z);
    d. DATA d; (DROP=x1-x4); SET q;
    e. DATA e; KEEP z; SET q;
    f. KEEP z; DATA f; SET q;

3. What is contained in the data set <u>b</u> after the following SAS program is executed successfully?

```
DATA a;
INPUT x y z;
DATALINES;
 9 11 16
 8 15 16
13 16 20
RUN;
DATA b; SET a; DROP z;
        x = y;
RUN;
```

a.	<u>x</u>	<u>y</u>	b.	<u>x</u>	<u>y</u>	c.	<u>x</u>	<u>y</u>
	9	9		8	8		11	11
	8	8		15	15		15	15
	13	13		12	12		16	16

4. Which of the following IF conditional statements is erroneous?
    a. IF AGE >= 20 | AGE <= 30;
    b. IF (AGE => 20 OR <= 30);
    c. IF 20 <= AGE <= 30;
    d. IF AGE >= 20 & AGE <= 30;

5. When comparison operators are executed,
    a. missing values are evaluated as true.
    b. missing values are evaluated as false.
    c. zeroes are evaluated as true.
    d. zeroes are evaluated as false.

6. What will happen if, in Example 18.3, the DELETE statement is used once immediately after the INPUT statement?

7. Rewrite Example 18.17 in the style of WHERE= as a SAS data set option in PROC PRINT.

8. Rewrite Example 18.18 in the style of WHERE= as a SAS data set option in PROC PRINT.

9. Rewrite Example 18.19 in the style of WHERE= as a SAS data set option in PROC PRINT.

10. Rewrite Example 18.20 in the style of WHERE= as a SAS data set option in PROC PRINT.

11. Rewrite Example 18.12 in the style of a WHERE statement in the DATA step and WHERE= as a SAS data set option in PROC PRINT.

12. Rewrite Example 18.13 in the style of a WHERE statement in the DATA step and WHERE= as a SAS data set option in PROC PRINT.

13. Run the following programs and find out (by the PRINT procedure) what is contained in each SAS data set:

a.

```
DATA a; INPUT x y; IF x+y <= 10;
DATALINES;
10
9
5    6
36   .
RUN;
```

b.

```
DATA b; INPUT x y; IF x > y THEN DELETE;
DATALINES;
10
9
5    6
36   .
RUN;
```

c.

```
DATA c; INPUT x y; IF SQRT (x) < 5 THEN OUTPUT;
DATALINES;
10
9
5    6
36   .
RUN;
```

d.

```
DATA d; INPUT x y; DELETE; z = x-y; OUTPUT;
DATALINES;
10
9
5    6
36   .
RUN;
```

e.

```
DATA e; INPUT x y; z=LAG1(x); sum1=x+z; sum2=0;
    sum2=SUM(sum2,sum1,LAG1(sum1),LAG2(sum1));
DATALINES;
10
9
5    6
36   .
RUN;
```

14. It is easy to form a lagged variable using the LAG function. But how can you form leads (future values of a variable)? Use data set a below to process your logic so that data set b becomes the end result.

DATA SET a

year	gnp	price
2006	200	800
2007	304	900
2008	420	1000

DATA SET b

year	gnp	price	nextgnp
2006	200	800	900
2007	304	900	1000
2008	420	1000	

Hint: Use the PROC SORT and DESCENDING statements.

15. Reshape data set a from Exercise 9(b) in Chapter 7 to form data set b so that there is one observation for each decade for each state with the following variables:

STATE	DECADE	POPGAIN

16. Assuming that data set d has 100 observations, how do you
    a. select the first 10 observations from data set d to form data set a?
    b. select every 10th observations from data set d to form data set b?
    c. randomly select 10 observations from data set d to form data set c?

Hint: To successfully complete this question, you need to first create a data set d that contains 100 observations and a few variables (say x, y, and z) and then proceed to solve parts (a) to (c).

18.11 Answers to Exercises

1. d

2. c, d, e, f

3. c

4. b

5. b, d

6. Data set one will contain 0 observations and 0 variables. No output will be displayed in the Output window.

7.
```
PROC PRINT DATA=select (WHERE=(weight+iq>200));
```

8.
```
PROC PRINT DATA=select (WHERE=(iq BETWEEN 89 AND 199));
```

9.
```
PROC PRINT DATA=select (WHERE=(name CONTAINS 'a'));
```

10.
```
PROC PRINT DATA=select (WHERE=(weight IS NULL));
```

11.
```
/* Example 18.12 rewritten using the WHERE statement */
DATA correct;
  INPUT name $ 1-10 sex $ ans;
  WHERE ans = 60;

/* Example 18.12 rewritten using the WHERE= option */
PROC PRINT DATA= correct (WHERE= (ans = 60)); RUN;
```

12.
```
/* Example 18.13 rewritten using the WHERE statement */
DATA incorrect;
  INPUT name $ 1-10 sex $ ans;
  WHERE ans ^= 60;

/* Example 18.13 rewritten using the WHERE= option */
PROC PRINT DATA = incorrect (WHERE= (ans ^= 60)); RUN;
```

13.

Question	Obs	x	y	z	sum1	sum2
(a)	1	36	.			
(b)	1	5	6			
(c)	1	10	9			
	2	5	6			
(d)			(no output)			
(e)	1	10	9	.	.	0
	2	5	6	10	15	15
	3	36	.	5	41	56

14.

```
DATA data1;
  INPUT year gnp price;
DATALINES;
2006  200   800
2007  304   900
2008  420  1000
;
PROC SORT; BY DESCENDING year;

DATA data2;
  SET data1;
  nextgnp=LAG1(price);
RUN;

PROC SORT; BY year; RUN;

PROC PRINT DATA=data2;
RUN;
```

15. Content of data set <u>b</u>

```
Obs    STATE    DECADE    POPGAIN
 1      NY        40       1360
 2      NY        50       1952
 3      NY        60       1455
 4      NJ        40        675
 5      NJ        50       5152
 6      NJ        60         18
 7      PA        40        533
 8      PA        50       2136
 9      PA        60       2431
10      OH        40       1048
11      OH        50        875
12      OH        60        403
13      IN        40       1111
14      IN        50       1111
15      IN        60       1111
```

16. SAS program to generate 100 observations:

```
DATA d;
  DO i=1 TO 100;
     x=RANNOR(0);
     y=RANNOR(0);
     z=RANNOR(0); OUTPUT;
  END;
RUN;
```

a. Selecting the first 10 observations:

```
DATA a;
  SET d (FIRSTOBS=1 OBS=10); RUN;
PROC PRINT; RUN;
```

b. Selecting every 10th observation:

```
/* Solution #1 */
DATA b;
  SET d;
  IF MOD(_N_, 10)=0; /* _N_ is an internal variable referring to 'Obs' */
RUN;
PROC PRINT; RUN;

/* Solution #2 */

DATA b;
  DO index=10 TO 100 BY 10;
    SET d POINT=index;
    OUTPUT;
  END;
  STOP;
RUN;
PROC PRINT; RUN;
```

c. Randomly selecting 10 observations:

```
DATA temp;
  SET d;
  id=RANUNI(0);
RUN;

PROC SORT; BY id; RUN;

DATA c;
  SET temp (FIRSTOBS=1 OBS=10);
RUN;
PROC PRINT; RUN;
```

19

Repetitive and Conditional Data Processing

OBJECTIVE

This chapter presents techniques that help simplify repetitive and conditional data processing in a SAS program. Repetitive data processing is needed when identical SAS statements are applied to more than one variable in a SAS data set. Conditional data processing refers to the situation in which data transformation takes place only if the conditions specified by users are met. Both types of data processing can be easily accomplished using the techniques demonstrated in this chapter.

As stated before, the instrument that is used most often by pollsters, policymakers, government agencies, market analysts, health researchers, and social scientists to gather information from a targeted population is a survey. Surveys typically consist of positively and negatively worded items. A positively worded item on attitudes toward "Faith-based schools", for example, may read like this:

"I believe our government should support faith-based schools."

Its counterpart, written in the negative tone, may read like this:

"I do not believe our government should support faith-based schools."

Responses to both types of items are usually collected using a Likert-type scale. A Likert-type scale typically ranges from 1 to 5, where 1 can mean "Strongly Disagree" and 5 "Strongly Agree", or the reverse. If a 5-point Likert-type scale is used for these two statements, you know right away that there is a problem with the meaning of each point on the scale—"1" to a positively worded item means the opposite of "1" on a negative item. These differences have to be reconciled before data can be meaningfully analyzed and interpreted. So you need a mechanism that consistently and repeatedly transforms responses from one or more negatively worded item(s) to those based on positive items, or vice versa—only one type of transformation is needed, not both.

One SAS programming tool, namely, the DO–END statement, is particularly well suited for repetitive processing of data. Variables that are repetitively processed are usually arranged in an ARRAY; hence, the syntax of the ARRAY statement is introduced first. Later, you will learn how to carry out repetitive data transformations under conditions specified by the IF statement. In sum, this chapter offers techniques you can readily put to good use.

19.1 What Is ARRAY and How Do You Use It?

ARRAY is a SAS statement written in the DATA step. It is used to group several variables into a set so that identical transformations or manipulations can be applied to these variables. Here are six examples of the ARRAY statement:

Example 19.1 A Numeric Array a With 0 Initial Values

```
ARRAY a {3} pretest midterm final (0 0 0);
```

Example 19.2 A Character Array <u>stores</u> With the Length of Elements Specified at 10 Characters

```
ARRAY stores {4} $ 10 big_lots k_mart target wal_mart;
```

Example 19.3 A Character Array <u>names</u> With Initial Values Specified

```
ARRAY names {*} $ 12 first last ('anybody' 'everybody')
```

Example 19.4 An Array <u>numeral</u> Containing All Numeric Variables From a SAS Data Set

```
ARRAY numeral {*} _NUMERIC_ ;    /* _NUMERIC_ indicates all numeric variables are included */
```

Example 19.5 An Array <u>char</u> Containing All Character Variables From a SAS Data Set

```
ARRAY char {*} _CHARACTER_ ;    /* _CHARACTER_ indicates all character variables are included */
```

Example 19.6 An Array <u>class</u> With Upper and Lower Bounds of Its Size Specified

```
ARRAY class {1:4} freshmen sophomore junior senior;
```

Having seen these six examples, you may have gotten an idea about the ARRAY statement. Specifically, the ARRAY statement follows the syntax below:

ARRAY *arrayname {subscript}* < $ > < length > *array_elements* <(initial_ values)>;

Each part of the ARRAY statement is explained below:

arrayname   is the name of the array. When naming an array, you should follow the same principles as those outlined in **Section 4.1** for naming a SAS data set or a variable. The name should not be a SAS function name or a variable name that is also an array element.

{*subscript*}   specifies the size of the array. The *subscript* can be an asterisk (*), a number, or the lower and the upper bounds of the size of the array. If an asterisk is used, SAS will go ahead and count the number of elements in the array (Examples 19.3, 19.4, and 19.5). If a number is used, SAS will interpret it as the total number of elements in the array (Examples 19.1 and 19.2). If lower and upper bounds are specified, they are separated by a colon (:) (Example 19.6). The lower bound of an array's size is usually 1 and the upper bound is usually the total number of elements in the array. Braces ({ }) can be replaced by brackets ([ ]) or parentheses (( )).

$ is used to declare that the array elements are character variables; hence, the array is also character. Examples 19.2, 19.3, and 19.5 illustrate a character array. If an array's elements are previously declared character, then the "$" is unnecessary, as in Example 19.5.

length   specifies the length of elements in a character array (Examples 19.2 and 19.3).

array elements   are variables grouped in an array. These variables should be from a SAS data set. They should be either all character or all numeric variables. The special SAS internal variable list, _NUMERIC_, can be used to refer to all numeric variables in a SAS data set (Example 19.4). Likewise, _CHARACTER_ refers to all character variables in a SAS data set (Example 19.5).

(initial values)   specify the initial value or values of array elements (Example 19.1 for numeric variables and Example 19.3 for character variables). Initial values are specified in parentheses with at least one space in between. Character initial values should be enclosed by single quotes.

Technically, the ARRAY statements illustrated above are explicit arrays. They always appear as part of a DATA step. Table 19.1 presents selected SAS

Table 19.1   SAS Functions Related to ARRAY

Function	Example	Explanation
DIM	`ARRAY a {*} a1-a10;` `y = DIM(a);`	This function returns the number of elements in an array; namely, the size of the array. Therefore, y equals 10.
LBOUND	`ARRAY a {*} a1-a10;` `y = LBOUND(a);`	This function returns the lower bound of an array's size; therefore, y equals 1.
HBOUND	`ARRAY a {*} a1-a10;` `y = HBOUND(a);`	This function returns the upper bound of an array's size; therefore, y equals 10.

functions that are related to ARRAY statements. These functions allow you to write flexible SAS codes that accommodate the changing size of an array.

19.2 The Use of ARRAY and DO–END Statements for Repetitive Data Processing

Combining an ARRAY statement with DO–END statements is an effective way to process variables repetitively. Pairs of DO–END statements are sometimes referred to as DO loops. Nesting one DO loop within another makes an even more powerful tool for repetitive data processing. The general syntax of the DO–END statement is as follows. Between the DO and END statements are executable SAS statements.

DO *index_variable=specification*;

SAS *statements*;

END;

The specification of the DO *index_variable* is the key in controlling the conditions under which the SAS statements are executed. The *index_variable* is an auxiliary variable that is usually dropped after the DO loop ends. In Examples 19.7 to 19.10, we demonstrate the use and style of the DO loop. Afterward, we summarize three styles of specifying the *index_variable*.

Example 19.7 Reverse Scaled Scores From 1–5 to 5–1

In this example, an array q is created to include five questions from a survey, q1 to q5. These five questions were worded negatively. Therefore, it is desirable to reverse responses to these questions; that is, 1 is reversed to 5, 2 to 4, and so on. The use of an array along with a DO loop allows these transformations to be applied uniformly to all responses to these five questions.

```
DATA reverse;
    INPUT name $ q1-q10;
    ARRAY q {*} q1-q5;
    DO i=1 TO 5;                 /* Sets the values of index variable from 1 to 5 */
        q(i)=6 - q(i);           /* Reverses the scores of first 5 questions */
    END;
    average=MEAN(OF q1-q10);
    DROP i;                      /* Removes the index variable from data set 'reverse' */

DATALINES;
Johnny 5 5 5 5 5 1 1 1 1 1
Ritche 1 1 1 1 1 5 5 5 5 5
RUN;

TITLE 'Example 19.7 Reverse Scales of from 1-5 to 5-1';
PROC PRINT DATA=reverse;
RUN;
```

Apparently, Johnny gave one extreme response to all questions and Ritche did the same with the opposite extreme response. So after the proper transformation, you should expect Johnny's <u>average</u> to be 1 and Ritche's to be 5. Here is the result to prove this expectation to be true:

Output 19.7 Reverse Scaled Scores From 1–5 to 5–1

				Example 19.7 Reverse Scales of from 1-5 to 5-1									1
Obs	name	q1	q2	q3	q4	q5	q6	q7	q8	q9	q10	average	
1	Johnny	1	1	1	1	1	1	1	1	1	1	1	
2	Ritche	5	5	5	5	5	5	5	5	5	5	5	

Without the ARRAY and DO–END statements, you have to transform all negatively worded items one at a time. The following program offers a glimpse of this alternative approach. It can become tedious when the number of questions or items is much greater than 5.

```
DATA reverse;
     INPUT name $ q1-q10;
     q1=6 - q1;
     q2=6 - q2;
     q3=6 - q3;
     q4=6 - q4;
     q5=6 - q5;
     average=MEAN(OF q1-q10);
```

Example 19.8 Reverse Scaled Scores for Selected Questions

This example demonstrates how to reverse scores for selected questions. Try to unpack the logic of the program on your own:

```
DATA reverse;
     INPUT name $ q1-q10;
     ARRAY q {*} q1-q10;
     DO i=1,3,5,7,9;                    /* Sets the values of index variable to 1,3,5,7,9 */
        q(i)=6 - q(i);                  /* Reverses scores of questions 1,3,5,7,9 */
     END;
     average=MEAN(OF q1-q10);
     DROP i;                            /* Removes the index variable from data set 'reverse' */

DATALINES;
Johnny 5 5 5 5 5 1 1 1 1 1
Ritche 1 1 1 1 1 5 5 5 5 5
RUN;

TITLE 'Example 19.8 Reverse scaled scores for selected questions';
PROC PRINT DATA=reverse;
RUN;
```

Output 19.8 Reverse Scaled Scores for Selected Questions

```
                    Example 19.8 Reverse scaled scores for selected questions          1

 Obs     name      q1    q2    q3    q4    q5    q6    q7    q8    q9    q10    average

  1      Johnny     1     5     1     5     1     1     5     1     5     1       2.6
  2      Ritche     5     1     5     1     5     5     1     5     1     5       3.4
```

Example 19.9 Seasonal Change

In this example, two arrays are defined: (1) sale, which includes the sales figures for four quarters, sale1 to sale4, and (2) change, which keeps track of changes in sales for two adjacent quarters. With the help of a DO loop, the seasonal changes in sales can be calculated easily and tracked as elements in the change array. Pay attention to the use of LBOUND(change) and HBOUND(change) as the starting and ending values of the DO *index_variable*.

```
DATA change;
    INPUT company $ sale1-sale4;
    ARRAY sale {*} sale1-sale4;              /* Sales from 4 seasons are in array 'sale' */
    ARRAY change {*} change1-change3;        /* Seasonal changes are in array 'change'   */
    DO i=LBOUND(change) TO HBOUND(change);
        change{i}=sale{i+1} - sale{i};       /* Changes are computed for adjacent seasons */
    END;
    DROP i;

DATALINES;
Nofrill   10   20   30  40
Fancy    100  200  300 400
RUN;

TITLE 'Example 19.9 Seasonal change';
PROC PRINT DATA=change;
RUN;
```

Output 19.9 Seasonal Change

```
                          Example 19.9 Seasonal change                            1

 Obs    company    sale1    sale2    sale3    sale4    change1    change2    change3

  1     Nofrill       10       20       30       40        10         10         10
  2     Fancy        100      200      300      400       100        100        100
```

Example 19.10 Computing Alternating Averages

This example illustrates how to compute alternating averages using the ARRAY and DO–END statements. Suppose each student has completed six vision tests, alternating the use of right and left eyes. Average scores for the right and the left eyes need to be computed separately.

```
DATA eye;
    INPUT name $ test1-test6;
    ARRAY test {*} test1-test6;

    DO i=LBOUND(test) TO HBOUND(test) BY 2;   /* Index value increases by 2 each time   */

        sumright=SUM(sumright, test(i));      /* Totals the score from the right eye    */
        sumleft=SUM(sumleft, test(i+1));      /* Totals the score from the left eye     */

    END;

    meanright=sumright/(DIM(test)/2);         /* Computes the average for the right eye */
    meanleft=sumleft/(DIM(test)/2);           /* Computes the average for the left eye  */

    DROP i;                                   /* Drops the index variable from 'eye' data set */

DATALINES;
Johnny  5 0 5 0 5 0
Ritche  1 2 2 3 3 4
RUN;

TITLE 'Example 19.10 Computing alternating averages';
PROC PRINT DATA=eye;
RUN;
```

Johnny's and Ritche's data are systematic in such a way that Johnny's right eye is consistently 5 points better than his left eye. Ritche's left eye is 1 point better than his right eye on successive tests. And the results confirm these data patterns.

Output 19.10 Computing Alternating Averages

```
                    Example 19.10 Computing alternating averages                    1

Obs   name   test1 test2 test3 test4 test5 test6 sumright sumleft meanright meanleft

 1   Johnny    5     0     5     0     5     0       15       0        5         0
 2   Ritche    1     2     2     3     3     4        6       9        2         3
```

Now you have studied four applications of the DO–END statement; let's go back and reexamine the index variable used in these statements. The index variable guides the execution of the DO–END statements by pointing to a specific element in the ARRAY to be processed. Three styles of the index_variable specification are demonstrated in Examples 19.7 to 19.10:

Style 1 A range of sequential index values, such as the following:

```
DO i=1 TO 5;
```
(from the 1st element to the 5th element; see Example 19.7)

`DO i=LBOUND(arrayname)` `TO HBOUND(arrayname);`	(from the lower bound of the array size to the upper bound of the array size; see Example 19.9)
`DO i=1 TO count-3;`	(from the 1st element to the (count – 3)th element, where count is a variable name specified prior to the DO–END statements)

<u>Style 2</u> A list of distinct index value(s), such as the following:

`DO i=1,3,5,7,9;`	(the 1st, 3rd, 5th, 7th, and 9th elements; see Example 19.8)
`DO i=3;`	(the 3rd element)

<u>Style 3</u> A range of discontinuous, yet cyclic index values, such as the following:

`DO i=1 TO 10 BY 2;`	(from the 1st to the 10th element, skipping every other element in between)

`DO i=LBOUND(arrayname)`
`TO HBOUND(arrayname)`
`BY 2;`
	(from the lower bound of the array size to the upper bound of the array size, skipping every other element in between; see Example 19.10)

`DO i=10 TO 1 BY -2;`	(from the 10th element down to the 1st element, also the lowest value of i, skipping every other element in between)

The index value will remain in the data set after it is created in the DO statement. To remove it from the data set, simply use the DROP statement, shown in Examples 19.7, 19.8, 19.9, and 19.10. The DROP statement is explained in **Section 18.2**.

19.3 The Use of IF and IF–THEN/ELSE Statements for Conditional Data Processing

Technically speaking, the use of DO–END creates a condition for executing SAS statement(s) sandwiched between the DO and END statements. In this sense, these DO statements can be conceived as part of conditional data processing. Another way to carry out the conditional data processing is through the use of IF or IF–THEN/ELSE statements. The IF or IF–THEN/ELSE statements were previously explained in **Sections 18.3** and **18.4**. In Example 19.11, we demonstrate how to transform <u>average</u> into letter <u>grade</u> according to different criteria for "A", "B", "C", and so on.

Example 19.11 Conditional Data Transformation Using IF–THEN/ELSE

```
DATA roster;
    INFILE 'd:\data\roster.dat';
    INPUT name $ sex $ id $ stand pretest first second final;
    LENGTH grade $ 6;                          /* Defines the length of letter grades */
    average = MEAN(OF pretest first second final);
    IF average >= 40 THEN grade = 'A';
        ELSE IF average >= 35 THEN grade = 'B';
            ELSE IF average >= 30 THEN grade = 'C';
                ELSE grade = 'failed';
RUN;

TITLE 'Example 19.11 Conditional data transformation using IF-THEN/ELSE';
PROC PRINT DATA=roster;
    VAR average grade;
RUN;
```

Output 19.11 Conditional Data Transformation Using IF–THEN/ELSE

```
Example 19.11 Conditional data transformation using IF-THEN/ELSE                    1

                    Obs     average      grade

                      1     28.3333      failed
                      2     42.7500      A
                      3     30.2500      C
                      4     32.0000      C
                      5     33.7500      C
                      6     43.2500      A
                      7     36.7500      B
                      8     38.7500      B
                      9     45.2500      A
                     10     31.2500      C
                     11     34.0000      C
                     12     43.5000      A
                     13     40.7500      A
                     14     31.0000      C
```

The output proves that the grades were indeed assigned according to <u>average</u> scores. Thus, the successive IF–THEN/ELSE statements worked according to the grading criteria and the logic of conditional data processing. Sometimes you may wish to combine the use of IF–THEN/ELSE with DO–END statements to transform data repetitively and conditionally. Example 19.12 demonstrates such a use for transforming negatively worded items on two forms of a survey. On Form A, items numbered 1, 3, 5, 7, and 9 were negatively worded, whereas on Form B, items 2, 4, 6, 8, and 10 were negatively worded.

Example 19.12 Conditional Data Transformation
Using IF–THEN/ELSE and DO–END

```
DATA survey;
    INPUT form $ item1-item10;
    ARRAY a {*} item1-item10;

    IF form='A' THEN DO;      /* Reverses responses on items 1, 3, 5, 7, and 9 of Form A */
        DO i=1,3,5,7,9;
            a(i)=6 - a(i);
        END; END;

    ELSE IF form='B' THEN DO; /* Reverses responses on items 2, 4, 6, 8, and 10 of Form B */

        DO i=2,4,6,8,10;
            a(i)=6 - a(i);
        END; END;

    ELSE DELETE;              /* The observation is deleted if Form is neither A or B */

    DROP i;                   /* Drops the index variable 'i' */

DATALINES;
A 1 1 1 1 1 1 1 1 1 1
A 5 5 5 5 5 5 5 5 5 5
B 1 1 1 1 1 1 1 1 1 1
B 5 5 5 5 5 5 5 5 5 5
. 1 2 3 4 5 1 2 3 4 5
RUN;

TITLE 'Example 19.12 Conditional data transformation using IF-THEN/ELSE and DO-END';
PROC PRINT DATA=survey;
RUN;
```

Output 19.12 Conditional Data Transformation
Using IF–THEN/ELSE and DO–END

```
        Example 19.12 Conditional data transformation using IF-THEN/ELSE and DO-END          1

  Obs   form   item1   item2   item3   item4   item5   item6   item7   item8   item9   item10

   1     A       5       1       5       1       5       1       5       1       5       1
   2     A       1       5       1       5       1       5       1       5       1       5
   3     B       1       5       1       5       1       5       1       5       1       5
   4     B       5       1       5       1       5       1       5       1       5       1
```

19.4 Summary

In this chapter, you have learned techniques that simplify repetitive/ conditional data processing in SAS programs. The simplification is achieved via the combined use of the ARRAY statement with the DO–END statements. You may even nest one DO loop within another to increase the efficiency in repetitive data processing. Conditional data processing can be accomplished also by using the ARRAY statement coupled with IF or IF–THEN/ELSE statements.

19.5 Exercises

1. After executing the following SAS program, what will be the values of <u>special</u>?

```
DATA a;
    INPUT day month @@;
    ARRAY date (2) day month;
    special=date(2);    /* The second element in the array 'date' */
DATALINES;
13 12 11
10  9
 .
 8  7  6
RUN;
PROC PRINT DATA=a;
RUN;
```

       a. 12, 9, . (missing), and 7
       b. 12, 10, . (missing), and 7
       c. 12, 9, and 7
       d. 13, 12, 10, 9, 8, and 7

2. Suppose a SAS data set <u>a</u> contains variables <u>x</u>, <u>y</u>, and <u>z</u>. Which ARRAY statement below will include all three variables as its elements?

       a. `ARRAY k(*); x, y, z;`
       b. `ARRAY k(*) x z;`
       c. `ARRAY k(2) x y z;`
       d. `ARRAY k(3) x z;`
       e. `ARRAY k(3) x y z;`

3. Which SAS program will <u>not</u> generate an output like the one below for variables <u>a</u>, <u>b</u>, and <u>u</u>?

a	b	u
5	39	5
5	39	39
25	16	25
25	16	16
.	17	.
.	17	17

       a.

```
DATA example; INPUT a b @@; ARRAY c {*} a b;
    u = c{1}; OUTPUT;
    u = c{2}; OUTPUT;
DATALINES;
5 39 25 16 . 17
RUN;
PROC PRINT DATA=example; RUN;
```

b.

```
DATA example; INPUT a b @@; ARRAY c (2) a b;
    u = c(1); OUTPUT;
    u = c(2); OUTPUT;
DATALINES;
5 39 25 16 . 17
RUN;
PROC PRINT DATA=example; RUN;
```

c.

```
DATA example; INPUT a b; ARRAY c {*} a b;
    u = c{1}; OUTPUT;
    u = c{2}; OUTPUT;
DATALINES;
5 39 25 16 . 17
RUN;
PROC PRINT DATA=example; RUN;
```

4. What will be the values of q after the following SAS program is executed?

```
DATA a;
    INPUT x y;
    ARRAY z (2) x y;
    q = z(2);        /* The second element in the array 'q' */
DATALINES;
99 98 97
04
52 53
54
55
RUN;
```

a. 98	b. 98	c. 99	d. 99
.	52	04	.
53	55	52	53

5. Which description is <u>correct</u> regarding the following SAS program?

```
DATA math;
   DO i=1 TO 2;
   DO n=1 TO 10; q = UNIFORM (0);
   INPUT geometry arithmetic;  OUTPUT;
   END;
 DATALINES;
```

a. The INPUT statement should be placed before the DO statements.
b. Data records should consist of two variables and 20 observations.

c. The UNIFORM (0) function will generate five-, six-, and seven-digit random even numbers.

d. To successfully complete two DO loops, one more END statement is needed.

6. All of the following SAS programs are correct <u>except</u> for

a.

```
DATA a; INPUT x;
DATALINES;
10
12
RUN;
PROC PRINT DATA=a; RUN;
```

b.

```
DATA b; INPUT x y; ARRAY z (*) x y;
     t=x; OUTPUT;
     e=y; OUTPUT;
DATALINES;
10
12
14
15
RUN;
PROC PRINT DATA=b; RUN;
```

c.

```
DATA c;
DO i=1 TO 4;
    INPUT x @@; OUTPUT;
END;
DATALINES;
1 2 3 4
RUN;
```

d.

```
DATA d;
DO i=1 TO 4;
   INPUT s(i) f(i);
END;
DATALINES;
10
12
14
60
RUN;
```

7. Which SAS program will generate an output like the one below for variables a, b, and v?

a	b	v
5	39	5
5		
25		
25		
.	17	.
.	17	17

a.

```
DATA example; INPUT a b @@; ARRAY c {*} a b;
     v = c{1}; OUTPUT;
     v = c{2}; OUTPUT;
DATALINES;
5 39 25 16 . 17
RUN;
PROC PRINT DATA=example; RUN;
```

b.

```
DATA example; INPUT a b @@; ARRAY c (2) a b;
     v = c(1); OUTPUT;
     v = c(2); OUTPUT;
DATALINES;
5 39 25 16 . 17
RUN;
PROC PRINT DATA=example; RUN;
```

c.

```
DATA example; INPUT a b; ARRAY c {*} a b;
     v = c{1}; OUTPUT;
     v = c{2}; OUTPUT;
DATALINES;
5 39 25 16 . 17
RUN;
PROC PRINT DATA=example; RUN;
```

8. Suppose a data file response includes 10 rows and 15 columns. It represents 10 subjects' responses on 15 questions. For example, the first subject responded A in the first question, B in the second, B in the third, and so on. "A", "B", "C", "D", and

"E" represent "Strongly Agree", "Agree", "Undecided", "Disagree", and "Strongly Disagree", respectively. You are asked to complete the following tasks:

a. Read the data file <u>response</u> into a SAS data set and print its content. (*Hint*: Use the INFILE statement.)

b. Transfer original characteristic responses to <u>numeric data,</u> in which A should be changed to 5, and B to 4, C to 3, D to 2, and E to 1, but Questions 5, 6, 8, 10, 11, 12, and 15 must be recoded reversely (i.e., A = 1, B = 2, C = 3, D = 4, and E = 5).

c. Blanks or other symbols unacceptable to the scale should be treated as missing values. Count the number of missing responses by each subject (or observation).

d. Find the mean and standard deviation of each subject's responses.

```
Data file response
ABBADECDAEDDCAE
BCBBEEBDADDDBBD
CBCCDDBDBDDCCBD
AAAA EBEAEEEAAE
BAACEDACBCCDBCD
ABBADDCCCDEDBBB
BBACCCCDADDDBCC
CAB  gqDCDEEBAE
BACD DACBCEEAAD
AABAEEAEAEDDAAE
```

9. There are mistakes in the following SAS program. Can you identify them?

```
DATA a;
     INPUT name $ sex $ dept $ sale code $;
     IF dept='tools' then code='1';
       else IF dept='repairs' then code='2';
       else code=' ';
DATALINES;
CINDY   F   TOOLS    12.45
ANDY    M   REPAIRS  34.50
SIMON   M   TOOLS    2.34
RUN;
```

10. Identify the mistake(s) in the following SAS program:

```
DATA a;
INPUT name $ score;
     IF score<=60 THEN grade=C;
     ELSE IF 60<score<=80 THEN grade=B;
     ELSE IF 80<score<=100 THEN grade=A;
     END;
DATALINES;
Beth  78
Ben   100
David 56
Frances    88
Mike  92
RUN;
```

11. A colleague of yours turns to you for help. He has prepared a 10-item test for 500 students in an introductory psychology course. To discourage students from cheating, he prepared three versions of the test by rearranging the order of items as follows:

Form	Item Order									
A	1	2	3	4	5	6	7	8	9	10
B	10	9	8	7	6	5	4	3	2	1
C	2	1	4	3	6	5	8	7	10	9

His teaching assistant collected the answer sheets and scanned them into a raw data file, including the test form that each student answered. Before the test can be graded, items of Forms B and C must be aligned with those of Form A. Your colleague needs your help in accomplishing this work in SAS. Write a set of SAS statements not only to help this colleague but also for other tests that are longer than 10 items.

12. A researcher was interested in comparing activities of the left and the right sides of people's brains when they are looking at 3D photos. Suppose that eight subjects were presented with five photos in this study, and their brain activities were measured by fMARI. The researcher quantified the results from fMARI into a score between 1 and 10, shown below; the higher the score, the greater was the brain activity. Compute the average left- and right-brain activity for all five photos combined.

	Photo 1		Photo 2		Photo 3		Photo 4		Photo 5	
	Left	Right	Left	Right	Left	Right	Left	Right	Left	Right
Subject 1	2	5	1	7	2	9	2	7	2	10
Subject 2	3	5	1	7	3	10	2	5	2	9
Subject 3	1	6	1	7	3	5	1	6	1	9
Subject 4	2	8	2	5	4	5	1	7	1	8
Subject 5	4	10	2	5	1	9	1	7	1	6
Subject 6	2	7	2	6	1	5	1	3	1	10
Subject 7	1	8	3	8	4	9	4	10	4	8
Subject 8	3	6	3	19	3	8	4	10	3	9

19.6 Answers to Exercises

1. b

2. e

3. c

4. b

5. d

6. d

7. a, b

8. a. The content of the data set <u>response:</u>

```
                              Original Response A-E                                    1

Obs   q1   q2   q3   q4   q5   q6   q7   q8   q9   q10  q11  q12  q13  q14  q15

 1    A    B    B    A    D    E    C    D    A    E    D    D    C    A    E
 2    B    C    B    B    E    E    B    D    A    D    D    D    B    B    D
 3    C    B    C    C    D    D    B    D    B    D    D    C    C    B    D
 4    A    A    A    A         E    B    E    A    E    E    E    A    A    E
 5    B    A    A    C    E    D    A    C    B    C    C    D    B    C    D
 6    A    B    B    A    D    D    C    C    C    D    E    D    B    B    B
 7    B    B    A    C    C    C    C    D    A    D    D    D    B    C    C
 8    C    A    B              g    q    D    C    D    E    E    B    A    E
 9    B    A    C    D         D    A    C    B    C    E    E    A    A    D
10    A    A    B    A    E    E    A    E    A    E    D    D    A    A    E
```

b. Recoded data from the data set <u>response</u> and (c) missing responses:

```
                              Original Response A-E                                    2
                                                                                     m
                                                                                     i
                                               a    a    a    a    a    a            s
        a    a    a    a    a    a    a    a    n    n    n    n    n    n    s
   O    n    n    n    n    n    n    n    n    n    s    s    s    s    s    s    i
   b    s    s    s    s    s    s    s    s    s    1    1    1    1    1    1    n
   s    1    2    3    4    5    6    7    8    9    0    1    2    3    4    5    g

   1    5    4    4    5    4    5    3    4    5    5    4    4    3    5    5    0
   2    4    3    4    4    5    5    4    4    5    4    4    4    4    4    4    0
   3    3    4    3    3    4    4    4    4    4    4    4    3    3    4    4    0
   4    5    5    5    5    .    5    4    5    5    5    5    5    5    5    5    1
   5    4    5    5    3    5    4    5    3    4    3    4    4    3    4    5    0
   6    5    4    4    5    4    4    3    3    3    4    5    4    4    4    2    0
   7    4    4    5    3    3    3    3    4    5    4    4    4    3    3    3    0
   8    3    5    4    .    .    .    .    4    3    4    5    5    4    5    5    4
   9    4    5    3    2    .    4    5    3    4    3    5    5    5    5    4    1
  10    5    5    4    5    5    5    5    5    5    5    4    4    5    5    5    0
                                                                                     =
                                                                                     6
```

d. Mean and standard deviation (**std_dev**) of each subject (**Obs**) on all 15 questions:

```
Mean and Std Dev for each observation                    3

        Obs        mean       std_dev

          1      4.33333      0.72375
          2      4.13333      0.51640
          3      3.66667      0.48795
          4      4.92857      0.26726
          5      3.93333      0.79881
          6      3.86667      0.83381
          7      3.73333      0.70373
          8      4.27273      0.78625
          9      4.07143      0.99725
         10      4.80000      0.41404
```

9. The correct SAS program should be as follows:

```
DATA a;
    INPUT name $ sex $ dept $ sale;
    IF dept='TOOLS' then code='1';
       else IF dept='REPAIRS' then code='2';
       else code=' ';
DATALINES;
CINDY    F    TOOLS    12.45
ANDY     M    REPAIRS 34.50
SIMON    M    TOOLS    2.34
RUN;
```

10. The correct SAS program should be as follows:

```
DATA a;
INPUT name $ score;
    IF score<=60 THEN grade='C';
    ELSE IF 60<score<=80 THEN grade='B';
    ELSE IF 80<score<=100 THEN grade='A';
DATALINES;
Beth  78
Ben   100
David 56
Frances    88
Mike  92
RUN;
```

11. One solution:

```
DATA test;
  INPUT form $ a1-a10;
  ARRAY a {*} a1-a10;
  ARRAY b {*} item1-item10;

  IF form='A' THEN DO;
    DO i=1 TO HBOUND(a);
      b(i)=a(i);
    END; OUTPUT; END;
```

```
   ELSE IF form='B' THEN DO;
     DO i=1 TO HBOUND(a);
       b(i)=a{11-i};
     END; OUTPUT; END;

   ELSE DO;
     DO i=1 TO HBOUND(a) BY 2;
       b(i)=a(i+1);
       b(i+1)=a(i);
     END; OUTPUT; END;

   DROP a1-a10 i;

DATALINES;
A 1 2 3 4 5 6 7 8 9 10
B 10 9 8 7 6 5 4 3 2 1
C 2 1 4 3 6 5 8 7 10 9
RUN;

PROC PRINT DATA=test; RUN;
```

12.

```
DATA brain;
    INPUT id $ test1-test10;
    ARRAY test {*} test1-test10;

    DO i=LBOUND(test) TO HBOUND(test) BY 2;
        sumleft=SUM(sumleft, test(i));
        sumright=SUM(sumright, test(i+1));
    END;

    meanright=sumleft/(DIM(test)/2);
    meanleft=sumright/(DIM(test)/2);
    DROP i;

DATALINES;
Subject1  2  5  1  7  2  9  2  7  2 10
Subject2  3  5  1  7  3 10  2  5  2  9
Subject3  1  6  1  7  3  5  1  6  1  9
Subject4  2  8  2  5  4  5  1  7  1  8
Subject5  4 10  2  5  1  9  1  7  1  6
Subject6  2  7  2  6  1  5  1  3  1 10
Subject7  1  8  3  8  4  9  4 10  4  8
Subject8  3  6  3 19  3  8  4 10  3  9
RUN;

PROC MEANS DATA=brain;
    VAR meanright meanleft;
RUN;
```

```
                            The SAS System                              1

                          The MEANS Procedure

Variable    N         Mean        Std Dev       Minimum        Maximum
-----------------------------------------------------------------------
meanright   8     2.1250000      0.7166390     1.4000000      3.2000000
meanleft    8     7.5750000      1.3625082     6.2000000     10.4000000
-----------------------------------------------------------------------
```

20

Structuring
SAS Data Sets

OBJECTIVE

In this chapter, you will learn how to structure, and restructure, SAS data sets. Specifically, you will learn how to perform the following tasks:

- structuring SAS data sets with the OUTPUT statement,
- creating raw data files from SAS data sets,
- concatenating two or more SAS data sets,
- merging two or more SAS data sets,
- updating SAS data sets, and
- matching observations by variable values.

20.1 Why Do You Structure or Restructure SAS Data Sets?

Until now, most examples and topics covered in this book involve a single SAS data set. In this chapter, you will learn how to manipulate two or more SAS data sets simultaneously. There are at least seven cases in which there is a need to handle multiple data sets:

❶ A subset of observations needs to be selected from two different data sets.

❷ Variables from one data set need to be added to another data set.

❸ Variable values of one data set need to be modified based on the information from another data set.

❹ Observations of one data set need to be added to another data set.

❺ Information from several data sets needs to be combined.

❻ The existing structure (or data layout) of a data set needs to be modified.

❼ Raw data files need to be created.

Six statements are particularly helpful to meet the needs outlined above: OUTPUT, FILE and PUT, SET, MERGE, and UPDATE. Of these six, the OUTPUT statement can be used in both the DATA step and the PROC step. Furthermore, the OUTEST= option can be specified to store estimates of population parameters into a SAS data set. The OUTEST= option is available in most statistical procedures (refer back to Chapter 17 for the specific syntax used in regression analysis).

20.2 Establishing SAS Data Sets With the OUTPUT Statement in the DATA Step

The OUTPUT statement inserted in a DATA step allows you to control when an observation is completely formed and, therefore, written into a SAS data set. Examples 20.1 to 20.3 illustrate the usefulness of the OUTPUT state-ment. As previously explained, comments enclosed by /* and * / are for clarification purposes.

Example 20.1 Creating Several Observations From a Single Data Record

This example first reads three students' scores on three quizzes into the SAS data set, <u>math101</u>. It then rearranges the data set so that each data record has one student's score on one quiz. The rearranged data set is well suited to the analysis of data collected from repeated-measures designs or randomized block designs that are implemented by PROC GLM.

```
TITLE 'Example 20.1 Creating several observations from a single data record';

DATA math101;
    INPUT name $ quiz1-quiz3;
    quiz=1; score=quiz1; OUTPUT;
    quiz=2; score=quiz2; OUTPUT;
    quiz=3; score=quiz3; OUTPUT;
    DROP quiz1-quiz3;      /* Removes the original 'quiz1'-'quiz3' from data set 'math101' */

DATALINES;
jim   70 80 86
john  80 85 76
jane  90 85 83
RUN;

PROC PRINT DATA=math101;
RUN;

PROC GLM DATA=math101;
    CLASS name quiz;       /* Identifies 'name' and 'quiz' as two independent variables */
    MODEL score=name quiz; /* Fits a block design model, also repeated-measure, to data */
RUN; QUIT;
```

Output 20.1 Creating Several Observations From a Single Data Record

```
Example 20.1 Creating several observations from a single data record        1

              Obs     name     quiz     score

               1      jim        1        70
               2      jim        2        80
               3      jim        3        86
               4      john       1        80
               5      john       2        85
               6      john       3        76
               7      jane       1        90
               8      jane       2        85
               9      jane       3        83
```

```
Example 20.1 Creating several observations from a single data record          2

                        The GLM Procedure

                     Class Level Information

          Class          Levels    Values

          name              3       jane jim john

          quiz              3       1 2 3


          Number of Observations Read          9
          Number of Observations Used          9
```

```
         Example 20.1 Creating several observations from a single data record      3

                             The GLM Procedure

Dependent Variable: score

                                   Sum of
   Source                   DF      Squares     Mean Square    F Value    Pr > F

   Model                     4    105.3333333    26.3333333       0.58    0.6930

   Error                     4    180.6666667    45.1666667

   Corrected Total           8    286.0000000


            R-Square     Coeff Var     Root MSE     score Mean

            0.368298     8.229325      6.720615      81.66667


   Source                   DF     Type I SS     Mean Square    F Value    Pr > F

   name                      2    88.66666667    44.33333333       0.98    0.4500
   quiz                      2    16.66666667     8.33333333       0.18    0.8382


   Source                   DF    Type III SS    Mean Square    F Value    Pr > F

   name                      2    88.66666667    44.33333333       0.98    0.4500
   quiz                      2    16.66666667     8.33333333       0.18    0.8382
```

According to page 3 of Output 20.1, three students did not differ statistically significantly from each other on three quizzes combined, $F(2, 4) = 0.98$, $p = 0.4500$. Averages of the three quizzes were also not statistically significantly different from one another, $F(2, 4) = 0.18$, $p = 0.8382$.

Example 20.2 Creating Two Data Sets From a Raw Data Source

In this example we demonstrate how to establish two data sets from one raw data source. Specifically, two variables of each data record are read: type of the record and <u>name</u> of the county. If <u>type</u> = "c", then the record is identi-fied to be about to the county's general profile. Therefore, the next two vari-ables are read as the <u>population</u> of the county and its number of <u>households</u>; and the entire record goes to a SAS data set called <u>county</u>.

If <u>type</u> = "r", then the record is identified to be about the county's rev-enue. Therefore, the next two variables are read as the <u>income</u> and the <u>tax</u> revenue of the county; and the record goes into the SAS data set <u>revenue</u>.

```
TITLE 'Example 20.2 Creating two data sets from a raw data source';

DATA county revenue;
     INPUT type $ 1. name $ @;
     IF type='c' THEN DO;
          INPUT pop COMMA10. household 10.;
          OUTPUT county;          /* Outputs observation to 'county' data set if type='c' */
       END;
     ELSE IF type='r' THEN DO;
          INPUT income 10. tax 10.;
          OUTPUT revenue;         /* Outputs observation to 'revenue' data set if type='r' */
       END;
DATALINES;
c  Monroe      8,000       2567
c  Green      15,340       4032
c  Richland   98,367      57892
r  Monroe     19000        3520
r  Green      65000       20000
r  Richland   75000       35000
RUN;

TITLE2 'DATA=county';
PROC PRINT DATA=county; RUN;

TITLE2 'DATA=revenue';
PROC PRINT DATA=revenue; RUN;
```

Once this program is submitted, you will see that both <u>county</u> and <u>rev-enue</u> data sets have three observations and six variables each. However, the <u>county</u> data set contains valid values only on four variables, <u>type</u>, <u>name</u>, <u>pop</u>, and <u>household</u>, whereas the <u>revenue</u> data set contains valid values on <u>type</u>, <u>name</u>, <u>income</u>, and <u>tax</u>.

Output 20.2 Creating Two Data Sets From a Raw Data Source

```
    Example 20.2 Creating two data sets from a raw data source          1
                          DATA=county

   Obs    type    name        pop     household     income     tax

    1      c      Monroe      8000       2567          .         .
    2      c      Green      15340       4032          .         .
    3      c      Richland   98367      57892          .         .
```

```
    Example 20.2 Creating two data sets from a raw data source              2
                           DATA=revenue

    Obs    type    name       pop    household    income    tax

     1      r      Monroe      .         .         19000     3520
     2      r      Green       .         .         65000    20000
     3      r      Richland    .         .         75000    35000
```

Example 20.3 Generating Test Data for a Regression Model

In this example, 20 observations are generated by a DO loop and the RAN-NOR function. After each observation is created, the OUTPUT statement forwards the observation to an input buffer that acts like a holding place until all 20 observations are created and the data set <u>a</u> is complete.

```
TITLE 'Example 20.3 Generating test data for a regression model';

DATA a;
    DO n=1 to 20;              /* Generates 20 observations within the SAS data set 'a' */

        x = RANNOR(123);    /* Variable 'x' is generated from a normal distribution */

        y = 3 + 8 * x + RANNOR(456);  /* Variable 'y' is a linear combination of 'x' and */
                                      /* random error, normally distributed              */
        OUTPUT;
    END;
RUN;

PROC REG DATA=a;              /* REG is used to uncover the relationship between 'y' & 'x' */
    MODEL y=x;
RUN;
```

Once you submit this program, pay special attention to estimates of the regression model. Should you be surprised to find that the estimated intercept of the regression equation is about 3 and the estimated slope is about 8?

Output 20.3 Generating Test Data for a Regression Model

```
            Example 20.3 Generating test data for a regression model               1

                                The REG Procedure
                                  Model: MODEL1
                              Dependent Variable: y

                                Analysis of Variance

                                    Sum of         Mean
    Source               DF         Squares        Square     F Value    Pr > F

    Model                 1        465.73190      465.73190    382.86    <.0001
    Error                18         21.89592        1.21644
    Corrected Total      19        487.62782
```

```
            Root MSE                1.10292    R-Square      0.9551
            Dependent Mean          5.10587    Adj R-Sq      0.9526
            Coeff Var              21.60108


                         Parameter Estimates

                        Parameter     Standard
    Variable    DF      Estimate       Error     t Value    Pr > |t|

    Intercept    1       2.67697       0.27610      9.70     <.0001
    x            1       8.04575       0.41119     19.57     <.0001
```

20.3 How to Create Raw
Data Files From a SAS Data Set

So far the discussion has been focused on establishing SAS data sets. Sometimes the need is the opposite; a raw data file needs to be created from an existing SAS data set. This can be accomplished by two statements: FILE and PUT.

Example 20.4 Creating an External
Raw Data File With FILE and PUT Statements

The statements FILE and PUT, as a pair, are much like the INFILE and INPUT statements. While INFILE and INPUT are used to create a SAS data set (Chapter 4), FILE and PUT are written to create a raw data file outside a SAS program. In this example, a raw data file, roster.dat, is first read into a SAS data set roster. Afterward, a new variable, average, is formed from the mean of pretest, first, second, and final. This new variable average, along with the original demographic variables, is subsequently written to a raw data file called new.dat. The raw data file new.dat is stored on the d: drive in the folder data.

```
TITLE 'Example 20.4 Creating an external raw data file with FILE and PUT statements';

DATA roster;
    INFILE 'd:\data\roster.dat';
    INPUT name $ sex $ id $ stand pretest first second final;
    average = MEAN(pretest,first,second,final);
    FILE 'd:\data\new.dat';
    PUT name $10. @11 sex $1. @16 id $2. @19 stand 1. +2 average 4.;
RUN;
```

Note how the syntax of the PUT statement is virtually identical to that of the INPUT statement. The only exception is that the PUT statement is best written in a formatted input style (refer back to Chapter 4). By the formatted input style, you may recognize variables instantly by their locations on each data record. After Example 20.4 is executed, you will find the following content in the file located at d:\data\new.dat:

Columns

1	2	3	4	5	6	7	8	9	10	11	12	13	14	15	16	17	18	19	20	21	22	23	24	25
J	O	H	N							m					1			1					2	8
D	A	N								m					2			4					4	3
L	Y	N	N							f					3			1					3	0
C	A	T	H	Y						f					4			2					3	2
J	A	M	E	S						m					5			2					3	4
T	I	M								m					6			4					4	3
H	O	P	E							f					7			4					3	7
T	E	D								m					8			2					3	9
S	A	S	S	Y						f					9			4					4	5
N	A	N	C	Y						f					1	0		3					3	1
P	A	U	L							m					1	1		3					3	4
L	I	N								m					1	2		4					4	4
T	O	M								m					1	3		4					4	1
B	O	B								m					1	4		1					3	1

If you are working in a mainframe environment, you may not be required to enclose filenames roster.dat and new.dat in single quotes. Check out this rule with your local SAS consultant or a system expert.

20.4 The Use of the SET Statement for Data Set (Re)Structuring

The SET statement is used primarily to read observations from one or more sources into one or more data sets. You have seen the application of the SET statement in Chapters 4, 8, and elsewhere. Essentially, there are two uses of the SET statement:

(1) to copy observations from one SAS data set to another SAS data set (Examples 20.5), and

(2) to combine several SAS data sets vertically to form one SAS data set (Example 20.6).

Example 20.5 SET Used to Copy Observations From One SAS Data Set to Another

```
TITLE 'Example 20.5 Copying observations from one SAS data set to another';

DATA roster;
    INFILE 'd:\data\roster.dat';
    INPUT name $ sex $ id $ stand pretest first second final;
    average = MEAN(pretest,first,second,final);

DATA new;
    SET roster;
    IF sex = 'm';    /* Only males' data are selected to be included in the data set 'new' */

PROC PRINT DATA=new;
RUN;
```

The output below shows that only males were copied into the data set new:

Output 20.5 SET Used to Copy Observations From One SAS Data Set to Another

	Example 20.5 Copying observations from one SAS data set to another								1
Obs	name	sex	id	stand	pretest	first	second	final	average
1	JOHN	m	1	1	9	31	45	.	28.3333
2	DAN	m	2	4	18	46	53	54	42.7500
3	JAMES	m	5	2	14	31	47	43	33.7500
4	TIM	m	6	4	20	45	51	57	43.2500
5	TED	m	8	2	12	44	52	47	38.7500
6	PAUL	m	11	3	15	24	48	49	34.0000
7	LIN	m	12	4	18	48	54	54	43.5000
8	TOM	m	13	4	21	48	52	42	40.7500
9	BOB	m	14	1	11	32	41	40	31.0000

Example 20.6 Combining Data Sets Vertically

This example demonstrates how you can read the raw data file <u>roster.dat</u> into two SAS data sets: <u>male</u> and <u>female</u>. These two data sets are subsequently combined vertically into <u>both</u> by the SET statement.

```
TITLE 'Example 20.6 Combining data sets vertically';

DATA male;
    INFILE 'd:\data\roster.dat';
    INPUT name $ sex $ id $ stand pretest first second final;
    average = MEAN(pretest,first,second,final);
    IF sex='m';

DATA female;
    INFILE 'd:\data\roster.dat';
    INPUT name $ sex $ id $ stand pretest first second final;
    average = MEAN(pretest,first,second,final);
    IF sex='f';

DATA both;
    SET male female;     /* Combines the two data sets, 'male' and 'female', */
                         /* into 'both' data set                            */

PROC PRINT DATA=both;
RUN;
```

As shown in Output 20.6, the <u>both</u> data set combines the <u>male</u> data set and the <u>female</u> data set, as expected. Males appear first, followed by females. This is so because the SET statement lists the <u>male</u> data set name first, then <u>female</u> next. The SET statement, therefore, combines two SAS data sets vertically, one data set followed by another.

Output 20.6 Combining Data Sets Vertically

```
                    Example 20.6 Combining data sets vertically                        1

Obs    name     sex    id    stand    pretest    first    second    final    average

  1     JOHN     m      1      1          9        31        45        .      28.3333
  2     DAN      m      2      4         18        46        53       54      42.7500
  3     JAMES    m      5      2         14        31        47       43      33.7500
  4     TIM      m      6      4         20        45        51       57      43.2500
  5     TED      m      8      2         12        44        52       47      38.7500
  6     PAUL     m     11      3         15        24        48       49      34.0000
  7     LIN      m     12      4         18        48        54       54      43.5000
  8     TOM      m     13      4         21        48        52       42      40.7500
  9     BOB      m     14      1         11        32        41       40      31.0000
 10     LYNN     f      3      1          7        38        33       43      30.2500
 11     CATHY    f      4      2         12        34        50       32      32.0000
 12     HOPE     f      7      4         17        34        46       50      36.7500
 13     SASSY    f      9      4         18        50        57       56      45.2500
 14     NANCY    f     10      3         15        29        39       42      31.2500
```

Example 20.6 illustrates one important use of the SET statement, namely, to link two or more SAS data sets vertically. The syntax for this use is as follows:

DATA *data_set_name*;

SET *data_set1 data_set2* ... ;

Vertically combining two or more data sets means that data records are sequentially and linearly stacked up one after the other. For this type of combination, it is important to make sure that data records from different data sets include variables with identical variable name, variable length, and variable format. If this is not the case, missing values will appear under variables that were not common to all the data sets. Missing values are shown on the printout as a period (.).

20.5 The Use of the MERGE Statement for Data Set (Re)Structuring

The MERGE statement is best used to link observations from two or more SAS data sets side by side. In other words, one data set may contain information about individuals' height and weight, whereas the second data set has information about their GRE scores and GPA. Linking these two data sets will result in a more complete profile about all individuals. There is one precaution, however; you need at least one linking variable. The linking variable should identify observations on an individual basis and is shared by both data sets; it could be a name, social security number, or student pin number. The linking variable is specified in the BY statement, as in Example 20.7. Without the linking variable, data records are connected horizontally from the first record to the last, whether they are matched or not. For this reason, it is recommended that you always include a BY variable with a MERGE statement. Before the data sets can be merged, observations in each data set must be presorted in the same order as values of the linking variable. The sorting can be accomplished using the SORT procedure (Chapter 6). The syntax of MERGE and BY statements is as follows:

DATA *data_set_name*;

MERGE *data_set1 data_set2* ... ;

BY *variable(s)*;

Example 20.7 MERGE Two Data Sets With a BY Variable

In Example 20.2, two SAS data sets, <u>county</u> and <u>revenue</u>, were created with the OUTPUT statement. Yet each data set contains only partial information about its observations. Thus, this example illustrates how you can use the MERGE statement to combine these two data sets horizontally. Observations are matched by the <u>name</u> of counties, which also form the unit of analysis. The complete profile of each county is displayed in Output 20.7.

```
/* See Example 20.2 for the DATA step in creating the SAS data sets 'county' and 'revenue' */

TITLE 'Example 20.7 MERGE two data sets with a BY variable';

PROC SORT DATA=county (KEEP= name pop household); BY name; RUN;

PROC SORT DATA=revenue (KEEP= name income tax); BY name; RUN;

DATA combined;
     MERGE county revenue;
     BY name;
RUN;

TITLE2 'DATA=combined';
PROC PRINT DATA=combined; RUN;
```

Output 20.7 MERGE Two Data Sets With a BY Variable

```
     Example 20.7 MERGE two data sets with a BY variable                       1
                   DATA=combined

  Obs    name         pop      household     income      tax

   1     Green       15340        4032        65000      20000
   2     Monroe       8000        2567        19000       3520
   3     Richland    98367       57892        75000      35000
```

20.6 The Use of the UPDATE Statement for Data Set (Re)Structuring

The UPDATE statement is used to update a *master* data set with current information found in another data set, called a *transaction* data set. This statement is well suited for clinical settings or agencies for whom timely information about patients, credit card holders, criminals on parole, and so on needs to be kept current in the database. When specifying the UPDATE statement, you need two data sets. The first is a master data set, whereas the second is a transaction data set, written according to the following syntax:

DATA *data_set_name;*

UPDATE *master_data_set transaction_data_set;*

BY *variable(s);*

In updating a master data set with a transaction data set, it is wise to use at least one BY variable, such as the id number, name, or social security number, in order to update each observation correctly based on the BY variable(s). In Example 20.8, JOHN's <u>final</u> score, recorded in the SAS data set <u>new,</u> is used to update the master data set <u>roster.</u> The result is a data set that is current and complete.

Example 20.8 Updating a Master File With UPDATE

```
TITLE 'Example 20.8 Updating a master file with UPDATE';

DATA roster;
    INFILE 'd:\data\roster.dat';
    INPUT name $ sex $ id $ stand pretest first second final;
RUN;

DATA new;
    INPUT name $ final;
DATALINES;
JOHN   100
DAN     55
RUN;

PROC SORT DATA=roster;  BY name;  RUN;

PROC SORT DATA=new;  BY name;   RUN;

DATA current;
    UPDATE roster new;
    BY name;
RUN;

PROC PRINT DATA=current;
RUN;
```

Here is the output based on complete information of each observation:

Output 20.8 Updating a Master File With UPDATE

Obs	name	sex	id	stand	pretest	first	second	final
1	BOB	m	14	1	11	32	41	40
2	CATHY	f	4	2	12	34	50	32
3	DAN	m	2	4	18	46	53	55
4	HOPE	f	7	4	17	34	46	50
5	JAMES	m	5	2	14	31	47	43
6	JOHN	m	1	1	9	31	45	100
7	LIN	m	12	4	18	48	54	54
8	LYNN	f	3	1	7	38	33	43
9	NANCY	f	10	3	15	29	39	42
10	PAUL	m	11	3	15	24	48	49
11	SASSY	f	9	4	18	50	57	56
12	TED	m	8	2	12	44	52	47
13	TIM	m	6	4	20	45	51	57
14	TOM	m	13	4	21	48	52	42

Example 20.8 Updating a master file with UPDATE   1

20.7 The Use of the IN= Option in a SET, MERGE, or UPDATE Statement

The IN=*variable_name* option is used along with a SET, MERGE, or UPDATE statement to pinpoint the source of a data value during the copying, merging, or updating process. The value of the IN= variable equals 1 for those observations that came from that particular data set. For observations not from that data set, the value of the IN= variable equals 0. The IN= option is specified in parentheses as a data set option, associated with the SET (Example 20.9), MERGE (Example 20.10), or UPDATE (Example 20.11) statement.

Example 20.9 IN= Used in a SET Statement

```
TITLE 'Example 20.9 IN= used in a SET statement';

DATA roster;
    INFILE 'd:\data\roster.dat';
    INPUT name $ sex $ id $ stand pretest first second final;
    average = MEAN(pretest,first,second,final);
RUN;

DATA male;
    SET roster;
    IF sex = 'm';
RUN;

DATA female;
    SET roster;
    IF sex = 'f';
RUN;

DATA new;
    SET female(IN=f) male(IN=m);
    IF f THEN gender='Female';      /* If an observation is from the 'female' data set, */
                                    /* then gender='Female'                             */
    IF m THEN gender='Male';        /* If an observation is from the 'male' data set,   */
                                    /* then gender='Male'                               */
RUN;

PROC PRINT DATA=new;
RUN;
```

Example 20.9 combines data from two data sets, <u>male</u> and <u>female</u>. After each observation is read, a new variable <u>gender</u> is created, depending on the source of each observation. If it came from the <u>female</u> data set, then <u>f</u> =1 and its value on <u>gender</u> is "Female". If it came from the <u>male</u> data set, then <u>m</u> =1 and <u>gender</u>'s value is "Male".

Output 20.9 IN= Used in a SET Statement

```
                    Example 20.9 IN= used in a SET statement                    1

Obs    name    sex   id   stand   pretest   first   second   final   average   gender

  1    LYNN     f     3     1         7        38      33      43     30.2500   Female
  2    CATHY    f     4     2        12        34      50      32     32.0000   Female
  3    HOPE     f     7     4        17        34      46      50     36.7500   Female
  4    SASSY    f     9     4        18        50      57      56     45.2500   Female
  5    NANCY    f    10     3        15        29      39      42     31.2500   Female
  6    JOHN     m     1     1         9        31      45       .     28.3333   Male
  7    DAN      m     2     4        18        46      53      54     42.7500   Male
  8    JAMES    m     5     2        14        31      47      43     33.7500   Male
  9    TIM      m     6     4        20        45      51      57     43.2500   Male
 10    TED      m     8     2        12        44      52      47     38.7500   Male
 11    PAUL     m    11     3        15        24      48      49     34.0000   Male
 12    LIN      m    12     4        18        48      54      54     43.5000   Male
 13    TOM      m    13     4        21        48      52      42     40.7500   Male
 14    BOB      m    14     1        11        32      41      40     31.0000   Male
```

Example 20.10 IN= Used in a MERGE Statement

This example demonstrates how to create a data set, called <u>new2</u>, that includes observations that are part of both the <u>x</u> and <u>y</u> data sets. In other words, if an observation is a part of one data set but not the other, it cannot appear in <u>new2</u>. Consequently, only Tammy Fae met this criterion.

```
TITLE 'Example 20.10 IN= used in a MERGE statement';

DATA x;
     INPUT name $ 1-10 sex $ weight;
DATALINES;
Joe Doe    m  13
Baby M     f   .
Tammy Fae  f 150
RUN;

DATA y;
     INPUT name $ 1-10 iq;
DATALINES;
Tammy Fae    50
Nancy R.    101
Mr. Right   120
RUN;

PROC SORT DATA=x;  BY name;  RUN;

PROC SORT DATA=y;  BY name;  RUN;

DATA new2;
     MERGE x (IN=a) y (IN=b);
     BY name;
     IF a AND b;               /* Selects those observations who have information  */
                               /* in both 'x' and 'y' data sets                    */
RUN;

PROC PRINT DATA=new2;
RUN;
```

Output 20.10 IN= Used in a MERGE Statement

```
Example 20.10 IN= used in a MERGE statement                    1

  Obs       name        sex     weight      iq

   1      Tammy Fae       f        150      50
```

Example 20.11 IN= Used in an UPDATE Statement

This example shows how to identify those observations whose information has been recently updated, namely, those with r = 1, from the recent data set; include those in a new data set called new3 and subsequently display the contents of new3 by the PRINT procedure.

```
TITLE 'Example 20.11 IN= used in an UPDATE statement';

DATA roster;
     INFILE 'd:\data\roster.dat';
     INPUT name $ sex $ id $ stand pretest first second final;
RUN;

DATA recent;
     INPUT name $ final;
DATALINES;
JOHN 100
RUN;

PROC SORT DATA=roster;  BY name;  RUN;

DATA new3;
     UPDATE roster recent(IN=r);     /* Updates 'roster' with information from 'recent', */
     BY name;                        /* only if an observation came from 'recent' and    */
     IF r;                           /* the name matches in both 'roster' and 'recent'   */
RUN;

PROC PRINT DATA=new3;
RUN;
```

Output 20.11 IN= Used in an UPDATE Statement

```
             Example 20.11 IN= used in an UPDATE statement                    1

  Obs    name    sex    id    stand    pretest    first    second    final

   1     JOHN     m      1      1         9         31       45       100
```

- When using the IN= option, you need to specify a variable name in accordance with the naming principles outlined in Chapter 4. Although values and the name of the IN= variable can be used for data set restructuring, they will not be retained in any SAS data set.

20.8 Summary

This chapter was devoted to strategies for structuring, establishing, and managing multiple data sets or data files. Six statements are particularly useful for these purposes: OUTPUT, FILE and PUT, SET, MERGE, and UPDATE. Once these statements are executed, it is recommended that you verify the result using simple procedures such as PRINT or CONTENTS. The useful IN= option was introduced in this chapter to help you keep track of the source of an observation in the SET, MERGE, or UPDATE statement.

20.9 Exercises

1. Given the following two sets of data, p and q, which SAS statements can generate the data set r?

data set p		data set q			data set r	
id	x	id	x		Id	x
1	10	1	.	→	1	.
2	65	3	65		2	65
		4	89		3	65
					4	89

   a. DATA r; SET p q;
   b. DATA r; SET p q; BY id;
   c. DATA r; MERGE p q;
   d. DATA r; MERGE p q; BY id;
   e. DATA r; UPDATE p q; BY id;

2. Assuming that data set one has three variables, x, y, and z, and data set two also has three variables, a, b, and c, which SAS statements below will include all six variables?

   a. DATA both;
          MERGE one two;

   c. DATA both;
          SET one two;

   b. DATA both;
          MERGE one two; BY x;

   d. DATA both;
          SET one two;
          BY x;

3. Which of the following SAS programs does not create two data sets (senior and young) after its execution?

a.

```
DATA subjects;
INPUT name $ age sex $;
IF age >= 65 THEN OUTPUT senior;
IF age < 65 THEN OUTPUT young;
IF age = . THEN DELETE;
```

b.

```
DATA senior young;
INPUT name $ age sex $;
IF age >= 65 THEN OUTPUT senior;
IF age < 65 THEN OUTPUT young;
IF age = . THEN DELETE;
```

c.

```
DATA subjects;
    INPUT name $ age sex $;
DATALINES;
Jones 40 F
Brown 70 M
;
DATA senior; SET subjects;
    IF age < 65 THEN DELETE;
    IF age = . THEN DELETE;
DATA young; SET subjects;
    IF age >= 65 THEN DELETE;
    IF age = . THEN DELETE;
```

4. Which of the following SAS statements will <u>not</u> generate an output in the Output window:
   a. `LIST;`
   b. `OUTPUT;`
   c. `KEEP;`
   d. `SET;`

5. Which of the following statements will merge two SAS data sets vertically?
   a. `DATA tv; SET comedy; drama;`
   b. `DATA cars; SET mustang; SET porsche;`
   c. `DATA music; SET rock SET jazz;`
   d. `DATA icecream; SET vanilla mint;`
   e. `DATA beach; SET sand, water;`

6. Given data sets <u>a</u> and <u>b</u> below, what will be the result after the following SAS statement is executed?

   `UPDATE a b;`

data set a			
id	x	y	z
1	2	.	7
2	6	.	8

data set b			
id	x	y	z
1	2	.	4
2	5	6	.

	id	x	y	z
a.	1	2	.	4
	2	5	6	.
b.	1	2	.	4
	2	5	.	.
c.	1	2	.	4
	2	5	6	8
d.	1	2	.	4
	2	5	.	8

7. Given the following data sets, a and b, what SAS statements will combine these two data sets to form the data set c?

data set a		
name	ht	wt
Bob	80	62
Ray	82	53
Sam	73	59

data set b		
name	ht	wt
Sue	64	58
Sally	92	49
Lisa	85	63

→

data set c		
name	ht	wt
Bob	80	62
Ray	82	53
Sam	73	59
Sue	64	58
Sally	92	49
Lisa	85	63

a. `DATA c; SET a; SET b;`
b. `DATA c; SET a b;`
c. `DATA c; MERGE a b;`
d. `DATA c; UPDATE a b; BY name;`
e. `DATA c; MERGE a b; BY name;`

8. Given data sets <u>a</u> and <u>b</u> from Exercise 7, what SAS statements will form the data set <u>c</u> below, assuming data set <u>a</u> and data set <u>b</u> have been presorted by <u>wt</u>?

   a. DATA c; SET a; SET b; BY name;

data set <u>c</u>		
<u>name</u>	<u>ht</u>	<u>wt</u>
Sally	92	49
Ray	82	53
Sue	64	58
Sam	73	59
Bob	80	62
Lisa	85	63

   b. DATA c; SET a; SET b; BY wt;
   c. DATA c; MERGE a b; BY wt;
   d. DATA c; UPDATE a b; BY wt;
   e. DATA c; SET a b; BY wt;

9. Immediately following SAS Programs #1 and #2, what SAS statement(s) will establish the data set <u>table</u>, as shown below?

```
Program #1

DATA a; INPUT name $ year x ;
DATALINES;
TOM 2 9
MARY 1 5
NANCY 3 7
;
PROC SORT DATA=a; BY name;
```

```
Program #2

DATA b; INPUT name $ year y;
DATALINES;
TOM 2 23
NANCY 3 11
ALICE 4 9
;
PROC SORT DATA=b; BY name;
```

data set <u>table</u>

Obs	name	year	x	y
1	ALICE	4	.	9
2	MARY	1	5	.
3	NANCY	3	7	11
4	TOM	2	9	23

   a. DATA table; UPDATE a b;
   b. DATA table; UPDATE a b; BY name;
   c. DATA table; MERGE a b;
   d. DATA table; MERGE a b; BY name;

10. Which SAS program will produce a data set for <u>males</u> and another for <u>females</u>?

a.

```
DATA males females;
INPUT name $ sex $;
IF sex='m' THEN OUTPUT males;
IF sex='f' THEN OUTPUT females;
```

b.

```
DATA total;
INPUT name $ sex $ ;
IF sex='m'; OUTPUT males;
IF sex='f'; OUTPUT females;
```

c.

```
DATA total;
INPUT name $ male $ female $;
DATA male; SET total; DROP female; PROC PRINT;
DATA female; SET total; KEEP female; PROC PRINT;
```

d.

```
DATA total;
INPUT name $ male $ female $;
IF name=male; OUTPUT=male;
IF name=female; OUTPUT=female;
```

11. Which set of SAS statements below combines data vertically?
    a. DATA both; SET males; SET females;
    b. DATA both; SET males females;
    c. DATA both; SET (males + females);
    d. DATA both; SET males by females;

12. Which statements will combine data sets <u>a</u> and <u>b</u> to form the data set <u>c</u>?

data set <u>a</u>		
<u>yr</u>	<u>x</u>	<u>y</u>
1	x1	y1
2	x2	y2
3	x3	y3
4	x4	y4
5	x5	y5

data set <u>b</u>		
<u>yr</u>	<u>z</u>	<u>y</u>
2	z2	y2
4	z4	y4
5	z5	y5
6	z6	y6
7	z7	y7

data set <u>c</u>			
<u>yr</u>	<u>x</u>	<u>y</u>	<u>z</u>
2	x2	y2	z2
4	x4	y4	z4
5	x5	y5	z5

```
a. DATA c; MERGE a(IN=key) b; BY year; IF key;
b. DATA c; MERGE a(IN=key1) b(IN=key2); BY yr; IF key1 & key2;
c. DATA c; MERGE a(IN=key) b; BY y; IF key;
d. DATA c; MERGE a(IN=key1) b(IN=key2); BY y; IF key1 & key2;
```

13. Given data sets a and b from Exercise 12, which SAS statements will generate the data set d?

data set d			
yr	x	y	z
2	x2	y2	z2
4	x4	y4	z4
5	x5	y5	z5
6	.	y6	z6
7	.	y7	z7

```
a. DATA d; MERGE a(IN=key) b; BY yr; IF key;
b. DATA d; MERGE a b(IN=key); BY yr; IF key;
c. DATA d; MERGE a b(IN=key); BY y; IF key;
d. DATA d; MERGE a(IN=key) b; BY y; IF key;
e. DATA d; MERGE a b(IN=key); BY z; IF key;
```

14. Which description of the following SAS program is incorrect?

```
INPUT school;
    SET red (IN=a) blue; BY college;
    IF a THEN school = 'INDIANA';
    ELSE school= 'DUKE';
PROC PRINT DATA=school;
RUN;;
```

a. The IN=a in the SET statement instructs the SAS system to create an internal temporary variable named a.

b. If an observation is from the SAS data set red, the value of a is 1; otherwise its value is 0.

c. When the DATA step processes the option IN=a, the SAS system creates the variable a within the SAS data set red for good.

15. Given data sets a and b below, apply various SET, MERGE, and UPDATE statements to determine what is contained in the data set c:

data set a		
id	x	y
1	12	13
2	15	.

data set b		
id	x	z
1	.	4
3	17	6
3	18	.

		data set c			
		id	x	y	z
a.	DATA c; SET a b;				
b.	DATA c; SET a; SET b;				
c.	DATA c; SET a b; BY id;				
d.	DATA c; MERGE a b;				
e.	DATA c; MERGE a b; BY id;				
f.	DATA c; UPDATE a b; BY id;				
g.	DATA c; SET b;				
	IF x = . THEN SET a;				
	ELSE y = MEAN(x, z);				

16. Given the two data sets <u>number</u> and <u>time</u> below, can you think of a way to combine them so that a travel agent may generate complete information for your spring vacation travel that consists of the date, flight number, carrier, from (city), to (city), time of departure, and arrival?

data set <u>number</u>

variables:	Date	Flight Number	Carrier
	0304	23	NW
	0312	405	U.S.
	0314	74	American
	0320	328	TWA
	0325	18	NW
	0329	92	TWA
	0330	266	Eastern

data set <u>time</u>

	Date	From	To	Depart	Arrival
variables:	0304	New York	L.A.	9:45am	5:05pm
	0312	Chicago	Miami	3:20pm	9:35pm
	0313	Indianapolis	Twin Cities	8:30am	10:15pm
	0320	Denver	St Louis	1:00pm	6:08pm
	0325	St Louis	Cleveland	4:15pm	7:12pm
	0329	Boston	San Francisco	7.55am	3:16pm
	0330	Madison	Indianapolis	2:18pm	11:43pm

17. Reshape the following list of fathers and sons into a list showing three generations: fathers, sons, and grandsons. In case of two-generation families, show fathers and sons only.

Fathers	Sons
Adam	Cain
Cain	Enoch
Adam	Abel
Adam	Seth
Seth	Enos
Abel	Faithful
Joseph	Emmanuel

20.10 Answers to Exercises

1. d
2. a, c
3. a
4. a
5. d
6. c
7. b
8. e
9. b, d
10. a
11. b

12. b, d

13. c

14. c

15.

Questions	id	x	y	z
(a) DATA C; SET A B;	1	12	13	.
	2	15	.	.
	1	.	.	4
	3	17	.	6
	3	18	.	.
(b) DATA C; SET A; SET B;	1	.	13	4
	3	17	.	6
(c) DATA C; SET A B; BY ID;	1	12	13	.
	1	.	.	4
	2	15	.	.
	3	17	.	6
	3	18	.	.
(d) DATA C; MERGE A B;	1	.	13	4
	3	17	.	6
	3	18	.	.
(e) DATA C; MERGE A B; BY ID;	1	.	13	4
	2	15	.	.
	3	17	.	6
	3	18	.	.
(f) DATA C; UPDATE A B; BY ID;	1	12	13	4
	2	15	.	.
	3	18	.	6
(g) DATA C; SET B;	1	12	4	0
IF x=. THEN SET A;	3	17	6	11.5
ELSE y=MEAN (x,z);	3	18	.	18.0

16. (*Hint*: Use PROC SORT/MERGE with the IN= variable properly defined.)

```
                             The SAS System                                    1

                 Flight_
Obs   Date       number   Carrier     From        To            Depart    Arrival

1     0304          23    NW          New York    L.A.          9:45am    5:05pm
2     0312         405    U.S.        Chicago     Miami         3:20pm    9:35pm
3     0320         328    TWA         Denver      St Louis      1:00pm    6:08pm
4     0325          18    NW          St Louis    Cleveland     4:15pm    7:12pm
5     0329          92    TWA         Boston      San Francisco 7.55am    3:16pm
6     0330         266    Eastern     Madison     Indianapolis  2:18pm    11:43pm
```

17. (The following SAS program is one of several possible solutions.)

```
DATA a;
  INPUT father $ son $;
DATALINES;
Adam       Cain
Cain       Enoch
Adam       Abel
Adam       Seth
Seth       Enos
Abel       Faithful
Joseph     Emmanuel
RUN;

PROC SORT; BY son; RUN;

DATA b;
  SET a;
  RENAME father=son; RENAME son=grandson;
RUN;

PROC SORT; BY son; RUN;

DATA c d;
  MERGE a b;
  BY son;
  IF father=' ' THEN DELETE;
  IF grandson=' ' THEN OUTPUT d;
    ELSE OUTPUT c;
RUN;

DATA e;
  SET d;
  DROP grandson;
  RENAME father=son; RENAME son=grandson;
RUN;

PROC SORT; BY son; RUN;

DATA f;
  MERGE c e; BY son;
RUN;

DATA g;
  SET f; IF father=' ';
  DROP father;
  RENAME son=father; RENAME grandson=son;
RUN;

DATA final;
  SET c g;
RUN;

PROC PRINT DATA=final;
RUN;
```

```
         The SAS System                                    1

Obs     father     son          grandson

 1      Adam       Abel         Faithful
 2      Adam       Cain         Enoch
 3      Adam       Seth         Enos
 4      Joseph     Emmanuel
```

Appendix A _____

What Lies Beyond This Book?

Information on Reference Books, Hotlines, Internet Resources, and SAS Users Groups

Where to go from here? In this appendix, we provide you with information on (1) reference books, (2) hotlines from the SAS Institute, (3) Internet resources, and (4) SAS users groups.

(1) Reference Books

You can start using the following reference books to continually polish up your skills as a data analyst and programmer of SAS:

- SAS Institute Inc. (2006a). *Base SAS® 9.1.3 procedures guide* (2nd ed.), *volumes 1, 2, 3, & 4.* Cary, NC: Author.
- SAS Institute Inc. (2006b). *SAS® 9.1.3 language reference: Dictionary* (5th ed.). Cary, NC: Author.
- SAS Institute Inc. (2006c). *SAS® 9.1.3 output delivery system: User's guide, volumes 1 & 2.* Cary, NC: Author.
- SAS Institute Inc. (2005). *SAS® 9.1.3 language reference: Concepts* (3rd ed.). Cary, NC: Author.
- SAS Institute Inc. (2004a). *SAS® 9.1 companion for Windows.* Cary, NC: Author.
- SAS Institute Inc. (2004b). *SAS/ETS® 9.1 user's guide.* Cary, NC: Author.
- SAS Institute Inc. (2004c). *SAS/GRAPH® 9.1 reference, volumes 1 & 2.* Cary, NC: Author.
- SAS Institute Inc. (2004d). *SAS/STAT® 9.1 user's guide.* Cary, NC: Author.
- Online documentation for SAS version 9.1.3 at http://support.sas.com/documentation/onlinedoc/91pdf/index_913.html

Place book orders with the SAS Institute at http://support.sas.com/publishing/index.html

(2) Hotlines From the SAS Institute

(Retrieved April 9, 2008, from www.sas.com/contact/intro.html)

Technical support phone	919-677-8008
SAS Institute corporate number	919-677-8000
SAS Institute fax number	919-677-4444
Training	800-333-7660

(3) Internet Resources

A Network of SAS Users

When you have a question about SAS output, error messages, or programming techniques, you may wish to discuss these issues with other SAS users or seek their advice. The Internet is a convenient platform for discussing questions and exchanging ideas. For SAS users, the most active users group is SAS-L. Once subscribed, you will automatically receive e-mails exchanged daily among members of this group. Instructions on how to join SAS-L as a subscriber are given below.

To subscribe to the SAS-L users group, send an e-mail to LISTSERV@UGA.CC.UGA.EDU. In the body of the message, type

SUBSCRIBE SAS-L [your name] (for example, SUBSCRIBE SAS-L Joanne Peng)

To unsubscribe from the list, send an e-mail to LISTSERV@UGA.CC.UGA.EDU. In the body of the message, type

UNSUBSCRIBE SAS-L (for example, UNSUBSCRIBE SAS-L)

Archived SAS-L discussions are at www.listserv.uga.edu/archives/sas-l.html

Online Help From the SAS Institute

The SAS Institute has its own home page at www.sas.com. From this home page, the company offers services in the following categories:

- A SAS knowledge base at http://support.sas.com/resources
- Technical support at http://support.sas.com/techsup
- Training at http://support.sas.com/training/index.html
- SAS discussion forums at http://support.sas.com/forums/index.jspa
- Overall customer support at http://support.sas.com

Resources From This Book at www.sagepub.com/pengstudy

This Web site provides electronic materials for the following:

- Data sets used in this book
- SAS programs included in this book
- SAS outputs shown in this book
- Keys to exercises in this book (for teachers only)
- Additional exercises
- Keys to additional exercises (for teachers only)
- Useful Web links to advanced learning of SAS and statistical analysis

(4) SAS Users Groups

There are numerous local, regional, and international SAS users groups throughout the United States and the world. These users groups hold meetings that are both technological and enjoyable. They provide opportunities for novice SAS users to exchange tips with experienced SAS users. They are also the premier source of ideas and news about SAS products and services. For information on a local SAS users group in your region, or the SAS Global Forum Annual Conference, go to http://support.sas.com/user-groups/index.html.

Appendix B _____

Data Sets Used in This Book

Data file: <u>a.dat</u>

Data file: <u>achieve.dat</u>

Data file: <u>design.dat</u>

Data file: <u>grade.dat</u>

Data file: <u>learn.dat</u>

Data file: <u>mydata.dat</u>

Data file: <u>roster.dat</u>

Data file: <u>salary.dat</u>

Data file: <u>select.dat</u>

Data file: <u>y777.dat</u>

All the raw data files can be downloaded from the Web site www.sagepub.com/pengstudy.

Data file: a.dat

This data file contains three records and three variables. The following are the DATA statements for reading this data file and a description of the three variables.

```
DATA a;
    INFILE 'd:\data\a.dat';
    INPUT x y z;
```

Variable Number	Variable Name
1	x
2	y
3	z

Variable Number	1	2	3
	1	2	3
	100	200	300
	−1	−2	−3
	0	.	−5

Data file: achieve.dat

This data file contains 20 variables collected from 120 elementary school children in a midwestern town. Fifteen of the 20 variables are the child's test scores of cognitive abilities and the remaining 5 variables describe the child's background or demographics. Below are the DATA statements for reading this data file and a description of the 20 variables and their locations in the data file.

```
DATA achieve;
    INFILE 'd:\data\achieve.dat';
    INPUT iv1 1 grade 2 iv2 3 sex $ 4 id 6-8 vocab 25-26 reading 27-28
        spelling 29-30 capital 31-32 punc 33-34 usage 35-36 total1 37-38
        maps 39-40 graphs 41-42 refer 43-44 total2 45-46 concepts 47-48
        problem 49-50 total3 51-52 composite 53-54;
```

Column	Variable Name	Description
1	iv1	1 = experimental school, 2 = control school
2	grade	grade level: 4 = fourth grade, 5 = fifth grade, 6 = sixth grade
3	iv2	method of teaching reading: 1 = phonics method, 2 = look-say method
4	sex	1 = female, 2 = male
5	(BLANK)	
6-8	id	identification number
9-24	(BLANK)	
25-26	vocab	vocabulary test score
27-28	reading	reading test score
29-30	spelling	spelling test score
31-32	captial	capitalization test score
33-34	punc	punctuation test score
35-36	usage	usage test score
37-38	total1	total of spelling through usage, standardized score according to the national norm
39-40	maps	maps test score
41-42	graphs	graphs test score
43-44	refer	reference test score
45-46	total2	total of maps through reference, standardized score according to the national norm
47-48	concepts	concepts test score
49-50	problem	problem-solving test score
51-52	total3	total of concepts and problem solving scores
53-54	composite	total of all scores from vocabulary through problem-solving, standardized by the national norm

```
Column no.   00000000011111111112222222222333333333344444444445555555556
             12345678901234567890123456789012345678901234567890123456789 0
            1411 1              28213228442833303147363 5253030
            1412 2              32253448483040403427344232373 4
            1412 3              34363846432037423433363344383 6
            1412 4              34503841514042533449454942464 3
            1411 5              37303746474243534440465045484 1
```

Column no.	0000000001111111111222222222233333333334444444444555555555 6 1234567890123456789012345678901234567890123456789012345 67890
1411 6	3737434650344342402412414744440
1411 7	4146434263424853475251534448 47
1411 8	4344384650494663585157645560 50
1411 9	4453535761535653445751665762 53
1411 10	4643574861485447525752485049 49
1421 11	2630322924302938444041332931 31
1422 12	2830334451233844373940424041 35
1422 13	3022243222232523274732253832 28
1422 14	3233333543423844373739504748 38
1422 15	3437213239252951314542454444 37
1422 16	3643384141384044474445394040 41
1422 17	3944473339464140494044393537 41
1422 18	4345302920302740313937393236 38
1422 19	4636455044284238344439464546 42
1422 20	4646514847494940402414942464 6
2412 61	3947374850364353404546465148 45
2412 62	3946433720303257344345454444 41
2412 63	4455455763605661635259586461 55
2412 64	4449495745444946474947504849 48
2411 65	4448514848384646473434554848 46
2411 66	4740434224343649274239523544 41
2411 67	4850513744494553495445545547 49
2411 68	4854514859575457475252485150 52
2411 69	4848574639324444314339334036 43
2411 70	4963575965535859527060685964 59
2421 71	3424344439253640524245384441 36
2421 72	4039474422253442373638413236 37
2421 73	4154555059345055496456556460 52
2421 74	4340536363555857375750624252 49
2421 75	4448384855484740404943534850 46
2421 76	4650365559464947525451504748 49
2421 77	4642213141363236343134394040 39
2422 78	4654476145575255405851626262 53
2422 79	4647575557625857635458557163 54
2422 80	4648615757555855495252685562 53
1513 21	3651213121332638473139234333 37
1512 22	4945610365526066505457565154 53
1512 23	5149364738484261505054525152 50
1512 24	5351576354706157536458506457 56
1512 25	5654525845465068666466636606 258
1512 26	5660556559606055586961474345 56
1511 27	5754465458465166695664595356 56
1511 28	5757706870686972667471827478 66
1512 29	5758686061606259586962646665 61
1512 30	5857685152585753566558545150 256
1522 31	3237405135233753504951492638 39
1522 32	4046323338483835474442376048 43
1522 33	4252363530413641534948685762 48
1522 34	4436484533464351535352655761 47
1521 35	4457553545564855476054665158 52
1521 36	5156483630303664505556494648 49
1521 37	5151613127253659565055525754 49
1521 38	5345442323212857394346444344 43
1521 39	5354485243524953506556545856 54
1521 40	5459654972626255746666568495 860
2511 81	4437592945394347296246424946 43
2511 82	4945525663434545132544649575 349
2511 83	5146615861525857636963646646 456
2512 84	5149594752394970566636354605 754
2512 85	5154574754655659666563545554 56

```
Column no.   00000000011111111112222222222333333333344444444445555555556
             12345678901234567890123456789012345678901234567890123456789 0

             2512 86        55455849356251536152556046535 2
             2512 87        55573663565853616156597346605 7
             2512 88        55575878595061686162645864616 0
             2511 89        57545754596559517176666680736 2
             2511 90        58545565596060615064584651485 6
             2521 91        28364440413640473553454957534 0
             2522 92        34402127383029293235323735363 4
             2521 93        38626168725664595372616763655 8
             2521 94        50565260545856594353524653505 3
             2521 95        51483658434646555353546051565 1
             2521 96        53485865565458535864586560625 6
             2521 97        56475578584358577171666553595 7
             2521 98        56546560565860595667616663645 9
             2522 99        57593858504648534743484455505 2
             2522 100       57574243454844553967545449525 3
             1612 41        28594757515753495577608277805 6
             1612 42        47445938434947523641434259504 6
             1612 43        54555148404446375955504246445 0
             1612 44        54445245465449635551565656565 2
             1612 45        63705952686260666871685461586 4
             1612 46        64374336244938495937484731394 5
             1612 47        64626575655966736256647875766 6
             1612 48        66688775728179687664696663646 9
             1612 49        66524750615754666244576250565 7
             1612 50        69606561746566636870675950546 3
             1622 51        26747073745468757370738897926 7
             1622 52        44405443404646456235473846424 4
             1622 53        44485148513646667061665859585 2
             1622 54        50424333352334415951505659584 7
             1622 55        50425243307049494550484559524 8
             1622 56        52444748335245554035435838484 5
             1621 57        54486745464450413339385953564 9
             1621 58        56605450535453554565555663605 7
             1621 59        58597363465760705061605646515 8
             1621 60        58605283657368705966655246496 0
             2611 101       28343141403036415063515453544 1
             2611 102       35553543383036686861665656605 0
             2611 103       41525454496556416247505953565 1
             2611 104       52444054614951416260545435444 9
             2611 105       54695468616562736879736563646 4
             2611 106       56635973657067726277707465706 5
             2611 107       63616878657672606584707961706 7
             2611 108       63657071517366730563677869746 7
             2612 109       64636787707675765061627263686 6
             2612 110       68655147386851686572686563646 3
             2622 111       44404348563345493648444250464 4
             2621 112       44444030303935375037414261524 3
             2622 113       59735248405448707364698271766 5
             2622 114       59606464587064586263615442485 8
             2622 115       60635252587058706568685661586 1
             2622 116       61566845384449607667686250565 8
             2622 117       63568371776875586862637273726 6
             2622 118       64645445614652707665706461626 2
             2621 119       64627068797072607068666267646 6
             2621 120       65645454796563727079747171716 7
```

Data file: <u>design.dat</u>

This data file contains 32 records and 7 variables. It is used for the examples on one-way and two-way ANOVAs, randomized block design, repeated-measures design, and ANCOVA. The following are the DATA statements for reading this data file and a description of the 7 variables.

```
DATA design;
    INFILE 'd:\data\design.dat';
    INPUT indep1 id score1 score2 score3 sex $ major;
    LABEL indep1='four living conditions'
          id='student id no.'
          score1='no. of drinks during the spring break'
          score2='no. of drinks during the final week'
          score3='no. of drinks after the final week'
          major='student academic major';
```

Variable Number	Variable Name	Description
1	indep1	the first independent or group variable (4 living conditions)
2	id	subjects' id numbers
3	score1	the first observed dependent score or outcome measure (no. of drinks during the spring break)
4	score2	the second observed dependent score or outcome measure (no. of drinks during the final week)
5	score3	the third observed dependent score or outcome measure (no. of drinks after the final week)
6	sex	gender of students
7	major	subjects' major—a categorical variable

Variable no.	1	2	3	4	5	6	7
	1	1	3	3	4	Female	1
	1	2	2	0	1	Female	2
	1	3	2	2	3	Female	3
	1	4	3	2	2	Female	4
	1	5	1	0	0	Male	5
	1	6	3	3	6	Male	6
	1	7	4	4	6	Male	7
	1	8	6	5	8	Male	8
	2	9	4	3	5	Female	1
	2	10	4	1	2	Female	2

Variable no.	1	2	3 4 5	6	7
	2	11	3 2 3	Female	3
	2	12	3 1 3	Female	4
	2	13	2 1 2	Male	5
	2	14	3 3 4	Male	6
	2	15	4 4 6	Male	7
	2	16	5 4 6	Male	8
	3	17	4 4 5	Female	1
	3	18	4 3 4	Female	2
	3	19	3 2 4	Female	3
	3	20	3 2 2	Female	4
	3	21	4 3 3	Male	5
	3	22	6 6 6	Male	6
	3	23	5 5 8	Male	7
	3	24	5 5 8	Male	8
	4	25	5 4 5	Female	1
	4	26	5 3 3	Female	2
	4	27	6 6 6	Female	3
	4	28	6 6 6	Female	4
	4	29	7 7 9	Male	5
	4	30	8 6 7	Male	6
	4	31	5 4 5	Male	7
	4	32	8 8 8	Male	8

Data file: grade.dat

This data file contains 368 records and 7 variables that pertain to grading profiles of a professional school at a state university for the academic years 1993–1998. Each record represents a particular grade (say, A) given to a racial group (say, HISPANIC) in one semester of an academic year and its frequency. The following are the DATA statements for reading this data file and a description of the 7 variables.

```
DATA g;
    INFILE 'd:\data\grade.dat';
    INPUT semester year school $ course $ grade $ race $ 26-42 freq;
    IF grade='R' OR grade='W' OR grade='WX' THEN grade='W';
```

Variable Number	Variable name	Description
1	semester	first (1) or second (2) semester
2	year	academic year
3	school	school of the enrolled students
4	course	course number
5	grade	grade of students
6	race	racial background
7	freq	frequency of grades

Variable no.	1	2	3	4	5	6	7
	1	93	PROF	X101	A	WHITE	8
	1	93	PROF	X101	B	ASIAN AMER.	2
	1	93	PROF	X101	B	WHITE	22
	1	93	PROF	X101	C	ASIAN AMER.	2
	1	93	PROF	X101	C	WHITE	16
	1	93	PROF	X101	D	WHITE	2
	1	93	PROF	X101	WX	AFRICAN AMER.	1
	1	93	PROF	X101	WX	WHITE	1
	1	93	PROF	X202	A	HISPANIC	2
	1	93	PROF	X202	A	WHITE	13
	1	93	PROF	X202	B	WHITE	32
	1	93	PROF	X202	C	AFRICAN AMER.	3
	1	93	PROF	X202	C	HISPANIC	1
	1	93	PROF	X202	C	WHITE	42
	1	93	PROF	X202	D	AFRICAN AMER.	4
	1	93	PROF	X202	D	HISPANIC	3
	1	93	PROF	X202	D	WHITE	18
	1	93	PROF	X202	F	AFRICAN AMER.	2
	1	93	PROF	X202	F	WHITE	2
	1	93	PROF	X202	WX	AFRICAN AMER.	1
	1	93	PROF	X202	WX	WHITE	2
	1	93	PROF	OTHER	A	ASIAN AMER.	4
	1	93	PROF	OTHER	A	AFRICAN AMER.	8
	1	93	PROF	OTHER	A	HISPANIC	9
	1	93	PROF	OTHER	A	WHITE	256
	1	93	PROF	OTHER	B	ASIAN AMER.	4
	1	93	PROF	OTHER	B	AFRICAN AMER.	12
	1	93	PROF	OTHER	B	HISPANIC	16
	1	93	PROF	OTHER	B	WHITE	449
	1	93	PROF	OTHER	C	ASIAN AMER.	2
	1	93	PROF	OTHER	C	AFRICAN AMER.	14
	1	93	PROF	OTHER	C	HISPANIC	4
	1	93	PROF	OTHER	C	WHITE	124
	1	93	PROF	OTHER	D	AFRICAN AMER.	4
	1	93	PROF	OTHER	D	WHITE	9
	1	93	PROF	OTHER	F	WHITE	1
	1	93	PROF	OTHER	R	AFRICAN AMER.	5
	1	93	PROF	OTHER	R	HISPANIC	3
	1	93	PROF	OTHER	R	WHITE	69
	1	93	PROF	OTHER	W	AFRICAN AMER.	2
	1	93	PROF	OTHER	W	HISPANIC	1
	1	93	PROF	OTHER	W	WHITE	63
	1	93	PROF	OTHER	WX	ASIAN AMER.	1
	1	93	PROF	OTHER	WX	WHITE	7
	1	94	PROF	X101	A	ASIAN AMER.	2
	1	94	PROF	X101	A	WHITE	12
	1	94	PROF	X101	B	WHITE	17
	1	94	PROF	X101	C	ASIAN AMER.	1
	1	94	PROF	X101	C	AFRICAN AMER.	2
	1	94	PROF	X101	C	WHITE	12
	1	94	PROF	X101	D	ASIAN AMER.	1
	1	94	PROF	X101	D	WHITE	1
	1	94	PROF	X101	F	WHITE	1
	1	94	PROF	X101	R	AFRICAN AMER.	1
	1	94	PROF	X101	R	WHITE	1
	1	94	PROF	X101	W	WHITE	1
	1	94	PROF	X202	A	ASIAN AMER.	2
	1	94	PROF	X202	A	WHITE	18
	1	94	PROF	X202	B	ASIAN AMER.	2

Variable no.	1	2	3	4	5	6	7
	1	94	PROF	X202	B	AFRICAN AMER.	1
	1	94	PROF	X202	B	WHITE	33
	1	94	PROF	X202	C	ASIAN AMER.	1
	1	94	PROF	X202	C	AFRICAN AMER.	1
	1	94	PROF	X202	C	WHITE	26
	1	94	PROF	X202	D	ASIAN AMER.	3
	1	94	PROF	X202	D	AFRICAN AMER.	1
	1	94	PROF	X202	D	WHITE	16
	1	94	PROF	X202	F	WHITE	1
	1	94	PROF	X202	WX	ASIAN AMER.	1
	1	94	PROF	X202	WX	WHITE	7
	1	94	PROF	OTHER	A	ASIAN AMER.	7
	1	94	PROF	OTHER	A	AFRICAN AMER.	1
	1	94	PROF	OTHER	A	HISPANIC	2
	1	94	PROF	OTHER	A	WHITE	255
	1	94	PROF	OTHER	B	ASIAN AMER.	17
	1	94	PROF	OTHER	B	AFRICAN AMER.	15
	1	94	PROF	OTHER	B	HISPANIC	9
	1	94	PROF	OTHER	B	WHITE	390
	1	94	PROF	OTHER	C	ASIAN AMER.	7
	1	94	PROF	OTHER	C	AFRICAN AMER.	13
	1	94	PROF	OTHER	C	HISPANIC	4
	1	94	PROF	OTHER	C	WHITE	116
	1	94	PROF	OTHER	D	ASIAN AMER.	1
	1	94	PROF	OTHER	D	AFRICAN AMER.	3
	1	94	PROF	OTHER	D	WHITE	6
	1	94	PROF	OTHER	R	ASIAN AMER.	2
	1	94	PROF	OTHER	R	AFRICAN AMER.	6
	1	94	PROF	OTHER	R	HISPANIC	5
	1	94	PROF	OTHER	R	WHITE	100
	1	94	PROF	OTHER	W	WHITE	3
	1	94	PROF	OTHER	WX	ASIAN AMER.	1
	1	94	PROF	OTHER	WX	AFRICAN AMER.	1
	1	94	PROF	OTHER	WX	WHITE	9
	1	95	PROF	X101	A	WHITE	12
	1	95	PROF	X101	B	ASIAN AMER.	2
	1	95	PROF	X101	B	WHITE	27
	1	95	PROF	X101	C	WHITE	14
	1	95	PROF	X101	D	AFRICAN AMER.	1
	1	95	PROF	X101	W	WHITE	1
	1	95	PROF	X101	WX	WHITE	2
	1	95	PROF	X202	A	ASIAN AMER.	1
	1	95	PROF	X202	A	WHITE	19
	1	95	PROF	X202	B	ASIAN AMER.	3
	1	95	PROF	X202	B	WHITE	27
	1	95	PROF	X202	C	WHITE	19
	1	95	PROF	X202	D	AFRICAN AMER.	2
	1	95	PROF	X202	D	WHITE	9
	1	95	PROF	X202	W	AFRICAN AMER.	1
	1	95	PROF	OTHER	A	ASIAN AMER.	14
	1	95	PROF	OTHER	A	AFRICAN AMER.	1
	1	95	PROF	OTHER	A	HISPANIC	2
	1	95	PROF	OTHER	A	WHITE	284
	1	95	PROF	OTHER	B	ASIAN AMER.	24
	1	95	PROF	OTHER	B	AFRICAN AMER.	10
	1	95	PROF	OTHER	B	HISPANIC	3
	1	95	PROF	OTHER	B	WHITE	446
	1	95	PROF	OTHER	C	ASIAN AMER.	12
	1	95	PROF	OTHER	C	AFRICAN AMER.	9
	1	95	PROF	OTHER	C	HISPANIC	1
	1	95	PROF	OTHER	C	WHITE	88

Variable no.	1	2	3	4	5	6	7
	1	95	PROF	OTHER	D	AFRICAN AMER.	3
	1	95	PROF	OTHER	D	WHITE	8
	1	95	PROF	OTHER	R	HISPANIC	1
	1	95	PROF	OTHER	R	WHITE	15
	1	95	PROF	OTHER	W	WHITE	2
	1	95	PROF	OTHER	WX	WHITE	4
	1	96	PROF	X101	A	WHITE	12
	1	96	PROF	X101	B	AFRICAN AMER.	1
	1	96	PROF	X101	B	WHITE	26
	1	96	PROF	X101	C	HISPANIC	1
	1	96	PROF	X101	C	WHITE	7
	1	96	PROF	X101	D	WHITE	3
	1	96	PROF	X101	W	AFRICAN AMER.	1
	1	96	PROF	X101	W	WHITE	5
	1	96	PROF	X202	A	ASIAN AMER.	1
	1	96	PROF	X202	A	WHITE	21
	1	96	PROF	X202	B	WHITE	42
	1	96	PROF	X202	C	ASIAN AMER.	1
	1	96	PROF	X202	C	AFRICAN AMER.	1
	1	96	PROF	X202	C	WHITE	32
	1	96	PROF	X202	D	ASIAN AMER.	2
	1	96	PROF	X202	D	WHITE	9
	1	96	PROF	X202	F	AFRICAN AMER.	1
	1	96	PROF	X202	W	ASIAN AMER.	1
	1	96	PROF	X202	W	WHITE	1
	1	96	PROF	X202	WX	HISPANIC	1
	1	96	PROF	X202	WX	WHITE	1
	1	96	PROF	OTHER	A	ASIAN AMER.	8
	1	96	PROF	OTHER	A	AFRICAN AMER.	3
	1	96	PROF	OTHER	A	HISPANIC	1
	1	96	PROF	OTHER	A	WHITE	259
	1	96	PROF	OTHER	B	ASIAN AMER.	24
	1	96	PROF	OTHER	B	AFRICAN AMER.	6
	1	96	PROF	OTHER	B	HISPANIC	1
	1	96	PROF	OTHER	B	WHITE	415
	1	96	PROF	OTHER	C	ASIAN AMER.	8
	1	96	PROF	OTHER	C	AFRICAN AMER.	6
	1	96	PROF	OTHER	C	HISPANIC	3
	1	96	PROF	OTHER	C	WHITE	99
	1	96	PROF	OTHER	D	AFRICAN AMER.	1
	1	96	PROF	OTHER	D	HISPANIC	1
	1	96	PROF	OTHER	D	WHITE	2
	1	96	PROF	OTHER	F	AFRICAN AMER.	1
	1	96	PROF	OTHER	R	ASIAN AMER.	3
	1	96	PROF	OTHER	R	AFRICAN AMER.	2
	1	96	PROF	OTHER	R	WHITE	46
	1	96	PROF	OTHER	W	WHITE	4
	1	96	PROF	OTHER	WX	AFRICAN AMER.	10
	1	96	PROF	OTHER	WX	HISPANIC	1
	1	96	PROF	OTHER	WX	WHITE	6
	1	97	PROF	X101	A	WHITE	24
	1	97	PROF	X101	B	ASIAN AMER.	2
	1	97	PROF	X101	B	AFRICAN AMER.	1
	1	97	PROF	X101	B	WHITE	23
	1	97	PROF	X101	C	HISPANIC	1
	1	97	PROF	X101	C	WHITE	7
	1	97	PROF	X101	D	WHITE	1
	1	97	PROF	X101	W	AFRICAN AMER.	2
	1	97	PROF	X101	WX	AFRICAN AMER.	1

Variable no.	1	2	3	4	5	6	7
	1	97	PROF	X101	WX	AFRICAN AMER.	1
	1	97	PROF	X202	A	WHITE	25
	1	97	PROF	X202	B	ASIAN AMER.	2
	1	97	PROF	X202	B	AFRICAN AMER.	2
	1	97	PROF	X202	B	HISPANIC	1
	1	97	PROF	X202	B	WHITE	38
	1	97	PROF	X202	C	WHITE	15
	1	97	PROF	X202	D	ASIAN AMER.	2
	1	97	PROF	X202	D	HISPANIC	1
	1	97	PROF	X202	D	WHITE	2
	1	97	PROF	X202	F	WHITE	3
	1	97	PROF	X202	W	AFRICAN AMER.	1
	1	97	PROF	X202	WX	AFRICAN AMER.	1
	1	97	PROF	X202	WX	WHITE	1
	1	97	PROF	OTHER	A	ASIAN AMER.	9
	1	97	PROF	OTHER	A	HISPANIC	1
	1	97	PROF	OTHER	A	WHITE	312
	1	97	PROF	OTHER	B	ASIAN AMER.	19
	1	97	PROF	OTHER	B	AFRICAN AMER.	13
	1	97	PROF	OTHER	B	HISPANIC	6
	1	97	PROF	OTHER	B	WHITE	416
	1	97	PROF	OTHER	C	ASIAN AMER.	10
	1	97	PROF	OTHER	C	AFRICAN AMER.	10
	1	97	PROF	OTHER	C	WHITE	106
	1	97	PROF	OTHER	D	WHITE	4
	1	97	PROF	OTHER	F	WHITE	1
	1	97	PROF	OTHER	R	ASIAN AMER.	5
	1	97	PROF	OTHER	R	AFRICAN AMER.	3
	1	97	PROF	OTHER	R	WHITE	92
	1	97	PROF	OTHER	W	ASIAN AMER.	1
	1	97	PROF	OTHER	W	AFRICAN AMER.	1
	1	97	PROF	OTHER	W	WHITE	2
	1	97	PROF	OTHER	WX	WHITE	3
	1	98	PROF	X101	A	ASIAN AMER.	2
	1	98	PROF	X101	A	WHITE	31
	1	98	PROF	X101	B	ASIAN AMER.	1
	1	98	PROF	X101	B	AFRICAN AMER.	1
	1	98	PROF	X101	B	WHITE	14
	1	98	PROF	X101	C	AFRICAN AMER.	2
	1	98	PROF	X101	C	WHITE	3
	1	98	PROF	X101	WX	WHITE	3
	1	98	PROF	X202	A	WHITE	28
	1	98	PROF	X202	B	ASIAN AMER.	0
	1	98	PROF	X202	B	WHITE	44
	1	98	PROF	X202	C	WHITE	28
	1	98	PROF	X202	D	WHITE	2
	1	98	PROF	X202	F	AFRICAN AMER.	1
	1	98	PROF	X202	F	HISPANIC	1
	1	98	PROF	X202	W	AFRICAN AMER.	1
	1	98	PROF	X202	W	WHITE	3
	1	98	PROF	X202	WX	WHITE	5
	1	98	PROF	OTHER	A	ASIAN AMER.	9
	1	98	PROF	OTHER	A	AFRICAN AMER.	2
	1	98	PROF	OTHER	A	HISPANIC	6
	1	98	PROF	OTHER	A	WHITE	339
	1	98	PROF	OTHER	B	ASIAN AMER.	15
	1	98	PROF	OTHER	B	AFRICAN AMER.	18
	1	98	PROF	OTHER	B	HISPANIC	7
	1	98	PROF	OTHER	B	WHITE	425
	1	98	PROF	OTHER	C	ASIAN AMER.	6
	1	98	PROF	OTHER	C	AFRICAN AMER.	9
	1	98	PROF	OTHER	C	HISPANIC	2
	1	98	PROF	OTHER	C	WHITE	49

```
Variable no.    1  2     3     4      5      6                    7
                1  98   PROF  OTHER   D      AFRICAN AMER.        1
                1  98   PROF  OTHER   F      AFRICAN AMER.        2
                1  98   PROF  OTHER   R      ASIAN AMER.          2
                1  98   PROF  OTHER   R      WHITE               43
                1  98   PROF  OTHER   W      ASIAN AMER.          1
                1  98   PROF  OTHER   WX     ASIAN AMER.          1
                1  98   PROF  OTHER   WX     WHITE               14
```

Data file: <u>learn.dat</u>

This data file contains 19 records and 2 variables. The following are the DATA
statements for reading this data file and a description of the 2 variables.

```
DATA learn;
    INFILE 'd:\data\learn.dat';
    INPUT group $ score;
```

Variable Number	Variable Name	Description
1	group	condition of learning: picture or verbal
2	score	percentage of correct responses on 20 test items

```
Variable no.        1        2
                picture    79
                picture    80
                picture    81
                picture    82
                picture    83
                picture    78
                picture    77
                picture    76
                picture    75
                verbal     61
                verbal     61
                verbal     62
                verbal     63
                verbal     64
                verbal     65
                verbal     60
                verbal     59
                verbal     58
                verbal     57
```

Data file: <u>mydata.dat</u>

This data file contains 24 records and 7 variables. The following are the DATA statements for reading this data file and a description of the 7 variables.

```
DATA mydata;
    INFILE 'd:\data\mydata.dat';
    INPUT id $ sex $ age gpa critical polpref satv;
```

Variable Number	Variable Name	Description
1	id	student ID number
2	sex	gender of students
3	age	age in years
4	gpa	grade point average
5	critical	critical thinking scores
6	polpref	political preference (SD=Strongly Democratic, D=Democratic, I=Independent, R=Republican, SR=Strongly Republican, . = [missing score])
7	satv	the SAT-Verbal score on a 200–800 scale

Variable no.	1	2	3	4	5	6	7
	1	F	22	3.67	30	SD	610
	2	F	22	3.51	27	D	570
	3	F	.	.	30	I	370
	4	M	22	2.40	31	SR	480
	5	M	24	2.53	.	I	510
	6	F	23	3.73	40	I	710
	7	M	.	3.90	27	D	660
	8	F	28	.	30	R	.
	9	M	23	2.46	24	SR	510
	10	M	23	2.53	31	SD	450
	11	F	32	2.93	37	R	530
	12	M	.	.	39	I	680
	13	F	.	.	27	.	280
	14	M	23	2.90	36	.	500
	15	M	.	.	30	SR	.
	16	M	.	.	40	R	690
	17	M	22	2.29	31	SD	490
	18	F	22	2.74	28	D	520
	19	M	28	2.22	21	I	300
	20	M	27	3.33	27	.	630
	21	F	23	3.75	31	SD	680
	22	M	.	.	21	I	500
	23	M	23	2.49	34	D	410
	24	M	23	2.30	.	SR	450

Data file: <u>roster.dat</u>

This data file contains 14 records and eight variables. The following are the DATA statements for reading this data file and a description of the eight variables.

```
DATA roster;
    INFILE 'd:\data\roster.dat';
    INPUT name $ sex $ id $ stand pretest first second final;
    composite=pretest + first + second + final;
```

Variable Number	Variable Name	Description
1	name	students' names
2	sex	gender of students
3	id	student ID number
4	stand	students' academic standing, 1=freshman, 2=sophomore, 3=junior, 4=senior
5	pretest	students' pretest score
6	first	students' first test score
7	second	students' second test score
8	final	students' final test score

Variable no.	1	2	3	4	5	6	7	8
	JOHN	m	1	1	11	31	45	.
	DAN	m	2	4	18	46	53	54
	LYNN	f	3	1	7	38	33	43
	CATHY	f	4	2	12	34	50	32
	JAMES	m	5	2	14	31	47	43
	TIM	m	6	4	20	45	51	57
	HOPE	f	7	4	17	34	46	50
	TED	m	8	2	12	44	52	47
	SASSY	f	9	4	18	50	57	56
	NANCY	f	10	3	15	29	39	42
	PAUL	m	11	3	15	24	48	49
	LIN	m	12	4	18	48	54	54
	TOM	m	13	4	21	48	52	42
	BOB	m	14	1	11	32	41	40

Data file: <u>salary.dat</u>

This data file contains 90 records and seven variables. It is concerned with sex differentials in teacher's pay in Great Britain (Turnbull & Williams, 1974). Some variables are continuous, some are nominal, and the rest are ordinal. The following are the DATA statements for reading this data file and a description of the seven variables.

```
DATA salary;
    INFILE 'd:\data\salary.dat';
    INPUT salary service sex degree school grad break;
    logs=log10(salary);
    sqrtdg=sqrt(degree);
    LABEL salary='teachers pay in pounds'
        logs='log 10 of salary'
        service='length of teaching in months'
        sex='1=M, 2=F'
        degree='class of degree, squared'
        sqrtdg='academic degree'
        school='0=private, 1=public'
        grad='1=trained grad, 0=others'
        break='1=break 2 yrs, 0=others';
```

Variable Number	Variable Name	Description
1	salary	one year salary in pounds sterling
2	service	service as a teacher in months
3	sex	dummy variable for sex, 1 for men, 0 for women
4	degree	class of degree for graduates, coded 0 to 6 (ordinal variable and squared)
5	school	type of school, 0 for private and 1 for public
6	grad	1 for trained graduates, 0 for untrained graduates or trained non-graduate teachers
7	break	1 for break in service of more than two years, 0 otherwise

Variable no.	1	2	3	4	5	6	7
	980.2	07	0	0	0	0	0
	1015	14	1	0	1	0	0
	1028	18	1	0	1	1	0
	1250	19	0	0	0	0	0

Variable no.	1	2	3	4	5	6	7
	1028	19	0	0	0	1	0
	1028	19	0	0	0	0	0
	1018	27	0	0	1	0	0
	1072	30	0	0	1	0	0
	1290	30	1	0	0	0	0
	1204	30	0	0	1	0	0
	1352	31	1	4	1	1	0
	1204	31	0	0	0	0	0
	1104	38	0	0	0	0	0
	1118	41	0	0	0	0	0
	1127	42	1	0	1	0	0
	1259	42	1	0	1	0	0
	1127	42	0	0	0	0	0
	1127	42	1	0	0	0	0
	1095	47	0	0	0	0	1
	1113	52	0	0	1	0	1
	1462	52	1	4	1	1	0
	1182	54	0	0	0	0	0
	1404	54	0	0	0	0	0
	1182	54	0	0	0	0	0
	1594	55	0	4	1	1	0
	1459	66	0	0	0	0	0
	1237	67	0	0	0	0	0
	1237	67	1	0	1	0	0
	1496	75	1	0	1	0	0
	1424	78	0	0	0	0	0
	1424	79	1	0	0	0	0
	1347	91	0	0	0	0	0
	1343	92	0	0	0	0	1
	1310	94	1	0	0	0	0
	1814	103	1	4	0	1	0
	1534	103	0	0	0	0	0
	1430	103	0	0	0	0	0
	1439	111	1	0	1	0	0
	2216	144	1	16	1	1	0
	1834	144	0	16	0	1	1
	1416	117	1	0	0	0	1
	2052	139	0	0	1	0	0
	2087	140	1	4	1	1	1
	2264	154	0	4	1	1	1
	2201	158	0	16	0	1	1
	2992	159	1	25	1	1	1
	1695	162	1	0	0	0	0
	1792	167	1	0	0	0	0
	1690	173	0	0	1	0	1
	1827	174	0	0	1	0	1
	2604	175	0	4	1	1	0
	1720	199	0	0	0	0	0
	1720	209	0	0	0	0	0
	2159	209	1	16	1	0	0
	1852	210	1	0	1	0	0
	2104	213	1	0	1	0	0
	1852	220	0	0	0	0	1
	1852	222	0	0	0	0	0
	2210	222	0	0	1	0	0
	2266	223	1	0	1	0	0
	2027	223	1	0	1	0	0
	1852	227	0	0	0	0	0
	1852	232	0	0	1	0	1

Variable no.	1	2	3	4	5	6	7
	2616	245	0	9	0	1	0
	2324	253	1	0	1	0	0
	1852	257	0	0	0	0	1
	2054	260	0	0	1	0	0
	2617	284	1	9	1	1	0
	1948	287	1	0	1	0	0
	1720	290	0	0	0	0	1
	2604	308	0	4	1	0	0
	1852	309	0	0	0	0	1
	1942	319	1	0	1	0	0
	2027	325	0	0	1	0	0
	1942	326	0	0	0	0	0
	1720	329	0	0	0	0	0
	2334	346	0	4	1	1	1
	1720	355	0	0	0	0	1
	1942	357	0	0	0	0	0
	2117	380	0	0	0	0	1
	2742	387	1	4	1	1	1
	2740	403	0	4	1	1	1
	1942	406	0	0	1	0	0
	2266	437	0	0	1	0	0
	2436	453	0	0	0	0	0

Data file: select.dat

This data file contains 5 records and 4 variables. The following are the DATA statements for this data file and a description of the 4 variables.

```
DATA select;
    INFILE 'd:\data\select.dat';
    INPUT name $ 1-10 sex $ weight iq;
```

Column Number	Variable Name	Description
1–10	name	subject name stored in columns 1 to 10
11	sex	subject gender
14–16	weight	subject body weight
19–21	iq	subject IQ test score

```
Column no.      00000000011111111112222222223
                12345678901234567890123456789
                Joe Doe    m    13    75
                Baby M     f     .    90
                Tammy Fae  f   150    50
                Nancy R.   f   100   101
                Mr. Right  m   160   120
```

Data file: y777.dat

This data file contains 20 records and 16 variables. Data are collected from an instrument that was designed to evaluate a research design course (Y777). The following are the DATA statements for reading this data file and a description of the 16 variables.

```
DATA y777;
    INFILE 'd:\data\y777.dat';
    INPUT id $ a1-a5 b1-b5 q16 q17 q18 q19 q20a $;
```

Variable Number	Variable Name	Description
1	id	id number assigned to Y777 course evaluation booklet
2	a1	students' self-reported current knowledge of sampling methods and sampling distributions
3	a2	students' self-reported current ability of applying ANOVA–fixed effects model
4	a3	students' self-reported current ability of applying multiple comparison procedures
5	a4	students' self-reported current ability of applying randomized block designs
6	a5	students' self-reported current knowledge of Latin-squares design and its efficiency
7	b1	students' self-reported prior knowledge of sampling methods and sampling distributions
8	b2	students' self-reported prior ability of applying ANOVA–fixed effects model

(Continued)

(Continued)

Variable Number	Variable Name	Description
9	b3	students' self-reported prior ability of applying multiple comparison procedures
10	b4	students' self-reported prior ability of randomized block designs
11	b5	students' self-reported prior knowledge of Latin-squares design and its efficiency
12	q16	hours spent per week in studying the materials for this course
13	q17	aptitude in statistics
14	q18	attitude toward learning statistics
15	q19	anxiety about learning statistics
16	q20a	hope to become a faculty member at a university

Variable no.	1	2	3	4	5	6	7	8	9	10	11	12	13	14	15	16
1	4	5	3	5	3	1	2	3	1	1	24	5	1	3	yes
2	4	5	4	5	2	1	2	2	1	1	5	5	1	3	yes
3	5	5	3	4	3	1	3	2	1	1	10	5	1	3	yes
4	3	5	4	4	3	1	4	2	1	2	20	5	1	3	yes
5	5	4	5	4	4	1	4	2	1	1	.	5	2	3	yes
6	5	5	4	3	5	2	3	3	1	1	30	3	5	3	yes
7	4	5	4	4	4	1	3	3	1	1	17	3	5	3	no
8	3	4	5	4	3	2	3	2	1	1	15	3	5	3	yes
9	4	4	3	5	2	1	3	3	1	1	10	3	5	.	.
10	3	5	4	4	3	1	3	1	2	1	.	3	2	.	yes
11	3	4	5	4	3	1	3	2	1	1	25	4	2	.	no
12	2	5	4	5	4	1	4	2	1	1	20	4	2	.	yes
13	4	3	4	4	4	1	2	1	3	2	8	4	2	1	yes
14	5	4	3	3	3	2	2	2	1	1	60	4	2	1	yes
15	3	5	4	3	4	3	3	3	1	1	23	4	3	1	.
16	3	5	5	4	3	1	3	3	2	2	15	5	1	1	yes
17	4	4	4	4	3	1	3	2	1	1	9	5	1	1	yes
18	4	5	4	5	3	1	4	2	1	1	14	5	1	1	yes
19	3	5	4	3	4	1	3	1	1	1	22	5	1	1	yes
20	2	4	4	3	5	.	.	.	.	.	35	5	1	1	no

Appendix C _____

Converting SPSS, Stata, Excel, Minitab, and SYSTAT Data Set Files to SAS Data Sets or Data Set Files

Data set files created in SPSS, Stata, Excel, Minitab, and SYSTAT can be converted into SAS data sets for further processing in SAS.

Converting SPSS Portable (or Data) Files

Method 1: SPSS Portable Files Converted in SAS Programs

This method is applicable to SPSS portable files. Therefore, an SPSS data set must be first saved as a portable file (say, example.por). Afterward, this SPSS portable file can be read into a SAS data set (say, outexample) using PROC CONVERT as demonstrated in the following SAS program:

```
FILENAME in 'd:\spss\data\example.por';   /* Links 'in' to the location of file 'example.por' */
PROC CONVERT
     SPSS=in                              /* Identifies 'in' to be a SPSS portable file, and  */
     OUT=outexample;                      /* convernts it to a SAS data set 'outexample'      */
RUN;

PROC PRINT DATA=outexample;
RUN;
```

Method 2: SPSS Portable (or Data) Files Converted by dfPower DBMS/Copy for Windows

Steps to follow:

1. Launch **DBMS/Copy** V8 or its latest version

2. Click on the **Interactive tab**

599

3. Where it asks for **Files of type,** select **SPSS Portable** or **SPSS for Windows**

4. Find the SPSS portable or data file at the correct location (for example, d:\spss\data\example.por or d:\spss\data\example.sav), click on **Open,** and then click on **Ok** in a new window

5. You can create extra formatted values in the pop-up dialog box "**Create Extra Formatted Values?**"; afterward, click on **Done**

6. You can now proceed directly to the output database or enhance the transfer in the pop-up dialog box "**Power Panel**"; then click on **OK**

7. Where it asks for **Save as** type, select **SAS for Windows V7/8/9**

8. Locate the path (for example, d:\sas\data\) and name the file (for example, outexample.sas7bdat)

9. Click on **Save**

10. Click on **Do-It!** to complete the conversion

Method 3: SPSS Portable (or Data) Files Converted by Stat/Transfer

Steps to follow:

1. Launch **Stat/Transfer 9** or its latest version

2. Where it asks for **Input File** Type, select **SPSS Portable** or **SPSS for Windows**

3. Enter path and file name (for example, d:\spss\data\example.por or d:\spss\data\example.sav)

4. Where it asks for **Output File Type,** select **SASV7-9**

5. Enter path and name (for example, d:\sas\data\outexample)

6. Click on **Transfer**

Converting Stata Files

The following two methods will convert a Stata file (say, example.dta) to a SAS file (say, outexample.sas7bdat)

Method 1: Stata Files Converted by dfPower DBMS/Copy for Windows

Note: DBMS/Copy for Windows 8.00 does not support Stata 10 data files. If you have a data set in Stata 10 format, you can use the Stata command

". saveold" to save a data file in the Stata 8/Stata 9 format, for example, .saveold "d:\sas\data\example.dta". Afterward, follow the steps below to convert this file to a SAS data set file.

Steps to follow:

1. Launch DBMS/Copy V8 or its latest version

2. Click on the **Interactive** tab

3. Where it asks for **Files of type**, select **Stata SE or V8** (*.dta)

4. Find the Stata file at the correct location (for example, d:\stata\data\example.dta), click on **Open** and then click on **Ok** in a new window

5. You can create extra formatted values in the pop-up dialog box "**Create Extra Formatted Values?**"; afterward click on **Done**

6. You can now proceed directly to the output database or enhance the transfer in the pop-up dialog box "**Power Panel**"; then click on **OK**

7. Where it asks for **Save as type**, select **SAS for Windows V7/8/9**

8. Locate the path (for example, d:\sas\data\) and name the file (for example, outexample.sas7bdat)

9. Click on **Save**

10. Click on **Do-It!** to complete the conversion

Method 2: Stata Files Converted by Stat/Transfer

Steps to follow:

1. Launch **Stat/Transfer 9** or its latest version

2. Where it asks for **Input File Type**, select **Stata**

3. Enter path and file name (for example, d:\stata\data\example.dta)

4. Where it asks for **Output File Type**, select **SAS V7-9**

5. Enter path and name (for example, d:\sas\data\outexample)

6. Click on **Transfer**

Converting Excel Spreadsheet Files

The following methods convert an Excel file to a SAS data file. For the first three methods, Excel 2007 files are required to be saved as Excel Workbook (.xls) files before they can be converted.

Method 1: Excel Files Converted by SAS Import Wizard

Let's assume that you have an Excel file, called <u>example.xls</u>. This file can be converted to a SAS data set (<u>outexample</u>) using SAS Import Wizard as follows:

Steps to follow:

1. In SAS, pull down the File menu and select **Import Data**

2. Select **Microsoft Excel 97, 2000 or 2002 workbook**

3. Click **Next**

4. Find the Excel file (for example, <u>d:\Excel\data\example.xls</u>)

5. Choose the right sheet and name the **Member**

6. Locate the file in the folder preferred; then click on **Finish**

Method 2: Excel Files Converted in SAS Programs

Given an Excel file, for example, <u>example.xls</u>, PROC IMPORT can be used to convert it into a SAS data set (<u>outexample</u>) in a SAS program. PROC IMPORT is a SAS procedure that imports a data file written in a specified format into a SAS program. Below is an illustration of this method:

```
PROC IMPORT
    OUT=outexample                          /* Names the output SAS data set 'outexample'    */
    DATAFILE= "d:\Excel\data\example.xls"   /* Identifies the Excel file name and location   */
    DBMS=EXCEL REPLACE;                      /* Identifies the DBMS format as an Excel sheet  */
RUN;
PROC print data=outexample;
Run;
```

Method 3: Excel Files Converted by dfPower DBMS/Copy for Windows

All the steps are identical to those used for SPSS portable or data files and Stata data files except in the selection of file types, where you should select Excel (*.xls) for **Files of type.**

Method 4: Excel Files Converted by Stat/Transfer

All the steps are identical to those used for SPSS portable or data files and Stata data files except in the selection of file types, where you should select Excel for **Input File Type.**

Converting Minitab Files

Method 1: Minitab Files Converted by dfPower DBMS/Copy for Windows

All the steps are identical to those used for SPSS portable or data files and Stata data files except in the selection of file types, where you should select **Minitab (*.mtw)** for **Files of type.**

Method 2: Minitab Files Converted by Stat/Transfer

All the steps are identical to those used for SPSS portable or data files and Stata data files except in the selection of file types, where you should select **Minitab** for **Input File Type.**

Converting SYSTAT Files

Method 1: SYSTAT Files Converted by dfPower DBMS/Copy for Windows

All the steps are identical to those used for SPSS portable or data files and Stata data files except in the selection of file types, where you should select **SYSTAT (*.syd or *.sys)** for **Files of type.**

Method 2: SYSTAT Files Converted by Stat/Transfer

All the steps are identical to those used for SPSS portable or data files and Stata data files except in the selection of file types, where you should select **SYSTAT** for **Input File Type.**

Converting Data Sets in Different Formats to a SAS Data Set File Using Stat/Transfer for the Unix System

If you are a Unix user, you can accomplish the file conversion using Stat/Transfer for Unix. Version 9 of Stat/Transfer for the Unix system runs on six platforms, namely, HP-9000 (HP-UX), IBM RS/6000 (AIX), Intel/AMD (x86) (Linux), Intel/AMD (x86-64) (Linux), Sun SPARC (32 Bit Solaris), and Sun SPARC (364 Bit Solaris). As of April 2008, Access, Minitab, ODBC®, and STATISTICA are not yet available for Unix.

Let's suppose that you have four data files in different formats called, respectively, example.por, example.xls, example.dta, and example.sys. These files can be converted to a SAS data set file (outexample.sas7bdat) using Stat/Transfer for Unix.

Steps to follow:

1. Invoke **Stat/Transfer**: At the operating system prompt, type: *st*

   Make sure to type *st* in the directory in which the Stat/Transfer was installed or specify the path to Stat/Transfer (for example, ~/bin/st).

2. Run **Stat/Transfer** using the **COPY** command

   Type the following command after the Unix prompt:

COPY	example.por	outexample.sas7bdat	−*x1* −*x2* . . .	\<Enter>
	example.xls	outexample.sas7bdat	−*x1* −*x2* . . .	\<Enter>
	example.dta	outexample.sas7bdat	−*x1* −*x2* . . .	\<Enter>
	example.sys	outexample.sas7bdat	−*x1* −*x2* . . .	\<Enter>

NOTE: Unix is case sensitive; command and file names are typed exactly in upper- and lowercase.

Parameters −xi following the file name allow certain options to be selected, such as automatic optimization of variables or suppression of warning messages.

If file conversions must be carried out on the mainframe and your data files are stored locally on a personal computer, you need to copy your data files from a local site (such as Windows PC) to a remote site (such as the mainframe system) first. This step is accomplished using **SSH Secure Shell** for Windows, or secure **FTP (SFTP)** through **MacSFTP** for **Mac OS** and **Mac OS X**. Once the conversion is successfully completed, as illustrated above, the SAS data set files can be copied from the remote site back to the local site for further analysis. Additional information on converting data files or sharing SAS data set files can be obtained from *Base SAS 9.1.3 Procedures Guide* (SAS Institute Inc., 2006a) and *SAS 9.1 Companion for Windows* (SAS Institute Inc., 2004a).

References _____

Box, G. E. P. (1954). Some theorems on quadratic forms applied in the study of analysis of variance problems, I. Effect of inequality of variance in the one-way classification. *Annals of Mathematical Statistics, 25,* 290–302.

Clinch, J. J., & Keselman, H. J. (1982). Parametric alternatives to the analysis of variance. *Journal of Educational Statistics, 7,* 207–214.

Cochran, W. G., & Cox, G. M. (1957). *Experimental designs* (2nd ed.). New York: Wiley.

Cureton, E. E. (1956). Rank-biserial correlation. *Psychometrika, 21,* 287–290.

Glass, G. V. (1966). Note on rank biserial correlation. *Educational and Psychological Measurement, 26,* 623–631.

Glass, G. V., Peckham, P. D., & Sanders, J. R. (1972). Consequences of failure to meet assumptions underlying the fixed effects analyses of variance and covariance. *Review of Educational Research, 42,* 237–288.

Kirk, R. E. (1995). *Experimental design: Procedures for the behavioral sciences* (3rd ed.). Belmont, CA: Brooks/Cole.

Lee, A. F. S., & Gurland, J. (1975). Size and power of tests for equality of means of two normal populations with unequal variances. *Journal of the American Statistical Association, 70,* 933–941.

Moser, B. K., & Stevens, G. R. (1992). Homogeneity of variance in the two-sample means test. *The American Statistician, 46*(1), 19–21.

Newton, R. R., & Rudestam, K. E. (1999). *Your statistical consultant: Answers to your data analysis questions.* Thousand Oaks, CA: Sage.

Rogan, J. C., & Keselman, H. J. (1977). Is the ANOVA F-test robust to variance heterogeneity when sample sizes are equal? An investigation via a coefficient of variation. *American Educational Research Journal, 14,* 493–498.

SAS Institute Inc. (2004a). *SAS® 9.1 companion for Windows.* Cary, NC: Author.

SAS Institute Inc. (2004b). *SAS/ETS® 9.1 user's guide.* Cary, NC: Author.

SAS Institute Inc. (2004c). *SAS/GRAPH® 9.1 reference, volumes 1 & 2.* Cary, NC: Author.

SAS Institute Inc. (2004d). *SAS/STAT® 9.1 user's guide.* Cary, NC: Author.

SAS Institute Inc. (2005). *SAS® 9.1.3 language reference: Concepts* (3rd ed.). Cary, NC: Author.

SAS Institute Inc. (2006a). *Base SAS® 9.1.3 procedures guide* (2nd ed.), *volumes 1, 2, 3, & 4.* Cary, NC: Author.

SAS Institute Inc. (2006b). *SAS® 9.1.3 language reference: Dictionary* (5th ed.). Cary, NC: Author.

SAS Institute Inc. (2006c). *SAS® 9.1.3 output delivery system: User's guide, volumes 1 & 2.* Cary, NC: Author.

Satterthwaite, F. E. (1946). An approximate distribution of estimates of variance components. *Biometrics Bulletin, 2,* 110–114.

Scheuren, F. (2004). *What is a survey?* Retrieved August 7, 2007, from www .whatisasurvey.info

Stevens, S. S. (1946). On the theory of scales of measurement. *Science, 103,* 677–680.

Tan, W. Y. (1982). Sampling distributions and robustness of *t, F* and variance-ratio in two samples and ANOVA models with respect to departure from normality. *Communications in Statistics—Theory and Methods, 11,* 486–511.

Tomarken, A. J., & Serlin, R. C. (1986). Comparison of ANOVA alternatives under variance heterogeneity and specific noncentrality structures. *Psychological Bulletin, 99,* 90–99.

Turnbull, P., & Williams, G. (1974). Sex differentials in teachers' pay. *Journal of the Royal Statistical Society, A-137,* 245–258.

Yin, P., & Fan, X. (2001). Estimating R^2 shrinkage in multiple regression: A comparison of different analytical methods. *Journal of Experimental Education, 69*(2), 203–224.

Credits _____

The sample programs, logs, and outputs in this book were generated using Version 9.1.3 of the SAS Systems for Windows, Copyright © 2004 by SAS Institute Inc.

SAS® and all other SAS Institute Inc. products or service names are registered trademarks or trademarks of SAS Institute Inc., Campus Drive, Cary, NC 27513, USA.

Access™, Excel®, and Windows® are the trademarks of Microsoft Corporation, One Microsoft Way, Redmond, WA 98052-6399, USA.

dfPower® DBMS/Copy is the registered trademark of DataFlux Corpration, 940 NW Cary Parkway, Suite 201, Cary, NC 27513, USA.

Minitab® is the registered trademark of Minitab Inc., Quality Plaza, 1829 Pine Hall Road, State College, PA 16801-3008, USA.

SPSS® is the registered trademark of SPSS, Inc., 444 North Michigan Avenue, Chicago, IL 60611-3962, USA.

Stata® is the registered trademark of StataCorp LP, 4905 Lakeway Drive, College Station, TX 77845, USA.

Stat/Transfer® is the registered trademark of Circle Systems, 1001 Fourth Avenue, Suite 3200, Seattle, WA 98154, USA.

STATISTICA® is the registered trademark of StatSoft, Inc., 2300 East 14th Street, Tulsa, OK 74104, USA.

SYSTAT® is the registered trademark of Systat Software, Inc., 1735 Technology Drive, Ste 430, San Jose, CA 95110, USA.

Other brands and product names are trademarks of their respective companies.

Index _____

Page numbers followed by *e* (such as 266–269*e*) indicate examples, logs, or output. *t* indicates table and *f* indicates figure.

About the Author _____

Chao Ying Joanne Peng (PhD in Quantitative Educational Psychology with a minor in Statistics from the University of Wisconsin–Madison) is Professor of Educational Inquiry Methodology and Adjunct Professor of Statistics at Indiana University–Bloomington. She has taught applied statistics and data analysis at major Research I universities for the past 30 years, including the University of Wisconsin–Madison, the University of Iowa, the University of North Carolina at Chapel Hill, National Taiwan University, and Indiana University. She is a member of the American Statistical Association, the American Educational Research Association, the American Psychological Association, and the SAS Users Group International. Her research and professional interests include statistical consultation, logistic regression, missing data methods, statistical computing, experimental designs, and survey methodology. She has published extensively on these topics in refereed journals and is the author of *SAS and Statistical Analysis* (13th edition, 2007, in Complex Chinese) and coauthor of *SAS 1-2-3* (6th edition, 2008, also in Complex Chinese).